CCNA®

Certification

Study Guide

Volume 2

Exam 200-301 v1.1

Second Edition

T0293439

CCNA®

Certification

Study Guide

Volume 2

Exam 200-301 v1.1

Second Edition

Todd Lammle

Donald Robb

SYBEX®

A Wiley Brand

Published by John Wiley & Sons, Inc., Hoboken, New Jersey.
Published simultaneously in Canada and the United Kingdom.

ISBNs: 9781394302154 (paperback), 9781394302178 (ePDF), 9781394302161 (ePub)

Library of Congress Control Number: 2024948041

Cover image: © Jeremy Woodhouse/Getty Images
Cover design: Wiley

SKY10087989_101624

Acknowledgments

There were many people who helped us build the new CCNA books in 2024 and 2025. First, Kenyon Brown helped me put together the book direction and managed the internal editing at Wiley, so thank you, Ken, for working diligently for many months to keep these books moving along.

Thanks also to Kim Wimpsett, my most excellent and highly dependable developmental editor at Wiley for well over a decade. She always does an excellent job, and I refuse to work on a book without her now!

We'd also like to thank John Sleeva and Tiffany Tayler for their hard work and edits in books one and two, respectively. They really helped us create fine-tuned books.

In this book, I enjoyed collaborating with Donald Robb from Canada. He played a crucial role in crafting the new table of contents and was instrumental in writing, editing, and thoroughly addressing the latest exam topics across various chapters. His expertise is unparalleled, and he worked tirelessly alongside me daily to bring this book to life. I'm confident you'll appreciate his contributions as much as I do. You can connect with Donald through his well-known blog at `https://the-packet-thrower.com`. He also serves as a leading moderator and contributor on Reddit: `https://www.reddit.com/r/ccna`.

About the Authors

Todd Lammle is widely regarded as one of the foremost authorities on Cisco certification and internetworking, holding certifications across nearly every Cisco certification category. With a career spanning over three decades, Todd has established himself as a globally recognized author, speaker, trainer, and consultant. His expertise extends across a broad range of technologies, including LANs, WANs, and large-scale enterprise wireless networks, both licensed and unlicensed. In recent years, he has specialized in implementing extensive Cisco security networks, particularly utilizing Firepower/FTD and ISE.

What sets Todd apart is his deep, hands-on experience, which is evident in his writing and training materials. He's not just an author; he's a seasoned networking engineer with practical knowledge gained from working on some of the largest and most complex networks in the world. His experience includes significant contributions to companies such as Xerox, Hughes Aircraft, Texaco, AAA, Cisco, and Toshiba, among many others. This real-world experience allows Todd to bring a unique, practical perspective to his work, making his books and training sessions invaluable resources for IT professionals at all levels.

Todd has authored more than 120 books, solidifying his reputation as a leading voice in the industry. Some of his most popular titles include the *CCNA: Cisco Certified Network Associate Study Guide*, *CCNA Wireless Study Guide*, *CCNA Data Center Study Guide*, *CCNP SNCF (Firepower)*, and *CCNP Security*. All of these works are published by Sybex, a respected name in technical publishing.

In addition to his writing and speaking engagements, Todd runs an international consulting and training company based in Idaho. His company provides expert guidance and training to organizations around the world, helping them to navigate the complexities of modern networking technologies. Despite his busy professional life, Todd still finds time to enjoy the natural beauty of Idaho, often spending his free time at the lake in the mountains, where he enjoys the outdoors with his beloved golden retrievers.

For those looking to dive deeper into Todd Lammle's work, you can find his extensive range of books at `https://www.lammle.com/order-our-books`. Additionally, Todd is accessible to his readers and clients through his website at `www.lammle.com`, where you can find more resources, updates, and ways to connect with him directly.

Donald Robb, widely recognized online as the-packet-thrower, brings over two decades of experience in the IT industry. His career has spanned a diverse array of roles, beginning with help desk support and evolving into a position as one of the most respected consultants in the field. Donald has honed expert-level skills across various IT domains, including networking, security, collaboration, data center management, wireless technologies, and service providers. His depth of knowledge and technical expertise have made him a sought-after professional in the industry.

Currently, Donald is a principal network architect for Walt Disney Studios. In this role, he serves as a subject matter expert on various technologies, playing a critical role in shaping the company's network architecture and ensuring its reliability and performance. His work involves leading the design and implementation of complex networks and guiding teams and stakeholders through the technical intricacies of modern IT infrastructures.

Over the years, Donald has collaborated with major industry vendors and smaller, specialized companies, earning many advanced certifications along the way. His achievements include becoming a double JNCIE and obtaining most of Cisco's professional-level certifications, demonstrating his deep technical proficiency and commitment to continuous learning. His expertise has also been recognized through his selection as a Cisco Champion for four consecutive years, an honor awarded to top influencers in the networking community.

In addition to his hands-on work in the field, Donald has made significant contributions to IT education. He has had the privilege of working alongside Todd Lammle, a legendary figure in the IT world, co-authoring several books and developing courses that have helped countless professionals advance their careers. Through his extensive experience, certifications, and educational efforts, Donald Robb has solidified his reputation as a leading authority in the IT industry.

Contents at a Glance

Contents

Introduction

Welcome to the exciting world of Cisco certification! If you've picked up this book because you want to improve yourself and your life with a better, more satisfying, and secure job, you've done the right thing. Whether your plan is to enter the thriving, dynamic IT sector or to enhance your skill set and advance your position within it, being Cisco certified can seriously stack the odds in your favor to help you attain your goals.

Cisco certifications are powerful instruments of success that also just happen to improve your grasp of all things internetworking. As you progress through this book, you'll gain a complete understanding of networking that reaches far beyond Cisco devices. By the end of this book, you'll comprehensively know how disparate network topologies and technologies work together to form the fully operational networks that are vital to today's very way of life in the developed world. The knowledge and expertise you'll gain here are essential for and relevant to every networking job. It's why Cisco certifications are in such high demand—even at companies with few Cisco devices!

NOTE For up-to-the-minute updates covering additions or modifications to the Cisco certification exams, as well as additional study tools, review questions, videos, and bonus materials, be sure to visit the Todd Lammle website and forum at `www.lammle.com/ccna`.

Cisco's Network Certifications

Way back in 1998, obtaining the Cisco Certified Network Associate (CCNA) certification was the first pitch in the Cisco certification climb. It was also the official prerequisite to each of the more advanced levels. But that changed in 2007, when Cisco announced the Cisco Certified Entry Network Technician (CCENT) certification. Then again, in May 2016, Cisco announced new updates to the CCENT and CCNA Routing and Switching (R/S) tests. Today, things have changed dramatically again.

In July 2019, Cisco switched up the certification process more than it has in the last 20 years! Cisco announced all new certifications that started in February 2020, and then again, an update and revision in the summer of 2024, which is probably why you're reading this book!

So what's changed? For starters, the CCENT course and exam (ICND1 and ICND2) no longer exist, nor do the terms Routing & Switching (rebranded to Enterprise). On top of that, the CCNA is no longer a prerequisite for any of the higher certifications at all, meaning that you'll be able to jump straight to CCNP without having to take the new CCNA exam if you have already achieved the CCNA or have enough background to skip the CCNA.

The new Cisco certification process will look like Figure I.1.

FIGURE I.1 The Cisco certification path

Entry	Associate	Professional	Expert
Starting point for individuals interested in starting a career as a networking professional.	Master the essentials needed to launch a rewarding career and expand your job possibilities with the latest technologies.	Select core technology track and a focused concentration exam to customize your professional-level certification.	This certification is accepted worldwide as the most prestigious certification in the technology industry.
Cisco Certified Support Technician (CCST)	CCNA	CCNP Enterprise	CCIE Enterprise Infrastructure

First, the CCST entry-level certification was added, and you can find the Wiley study guide for the CCST Network book authored by Todd Lammle and Donald Robb as well as this study guide at `https://www.lammle.com/order-our-books`.

If you have an entry-level network background, you will want to head directly to CCNA, using this book and the abundant resources on `www.lammle.com/ccna`, of course!

The Todd Lammle CCNA program, starting with this book, is a powerful tool to get you started in your CCNA studies, and it's vital to understand that material found in this book and at `www.lammle.com/ccna` before you go on to conquer any other certifications!

What Does This Book Cover?

This second book in the CCNA series covers everything you need to know to pass the new CCNA 200-301 v1.1 exam and starts right where the first book in the series left off.

But regardless of which Cisco Certification path you choose, as I've said, taking plenty of time to study and practice with routers or a router simulator is the real key to success.

You will learn the following information in this book:

Chapter 1: Enhanced Switched Technologies This chapter will start off with STP protocols and dive into the fundamentals, covering the modes as well as the various flavors of STP. VLANs, trunks, and troubleshooting are covered as well. Finally, PortFast will also be discussed.

Chapter 2: Security with ACLs This chapter covers security and access lists, which are created on routers to filter the network. IP standard, extended, and named access lists are covered in detail. Written and hands-on labs, along with review questions, will help you study for the security and access-list portion of the Cisco exams.

Chapter 3: Internet Protocol Version 6 (IPv6) This is a fun chapter chock-full of some great information. IPv6 is not the big, bad scary creature that most people think it is, and it's a really important objective on the latest exam, so study this chapter carefully—don't just skim it.

Chapter 4: Troubleshooting IP, IPv6, and VLANs This chapter will cover detailed troubleshooting, and because this is such a major focus of the Cisco CCNA objectives I'd be letting you down if I didn't make sure you've got this important topic down. So to ensure that your skills are solid, we're going to begin by diving deep into troubleshooting with IP, IPv6, and virtual LANs (VLANs) now. You absolutely must also have the fundamentals of IP and IPv6 routing and knowledge of VLANs and trunking nailed down tight if you're going to win at this.

Chapter 5: Network Address Translation (NAT) In this chapter, we're going to dig into Network Address Translation (NAT), Dynamic NAT, and Port Address Translation (PAT), also known as NAT Overload. Of course, I'll demonstrate all the NAT commands.

Chapter 6: IP Services This chapter covers how to find neighbor device information using the proprietary Cisco Discovery Protocol (CDP) and the industry-standard Link Layer Discovery Protocol (LLDP). I'll also discuss how to make sure our times are synchronized with our devices using Network Time Protocol (NTP). After that, I'll show you the Simple Network Management Protocol (SNMP) and the type of alerts sent to the network management station (NMS). You'll learn about the oh-so-important syslog logging and configuration, and then, finally, I'll cover how to configure Secure Shell (SSH).

Chapter 7: Security Fundamentals This chapter will help you to define key security concepts (threats, vulnerabilities, exploits, and mitigation techniques) as well as describe security program elements (user awareness, training, and physical access control). We'll also cover authentication, authorization and accounting, and password policies.

Chapter 8: First Hop Redundancy Protocol (HSRP) This chapter will start off by telling you the reasons why we need a layer 3 redundancy protocol and then move into how to build redundancy and load-balancing features into your network elegantly with routers that you might even have already. You really don't need to buy some overpriced load-balancing device when you know how to configure and use Hot Standby Router Protocol (HSRP).

Chapter 9: Quality of Service (QoS) *Quality of service (QoS)* refers to the way resources are controlled so that the quality of services is maintained. In this chapter I'm going to cover how QoS solves problems by using classification and marking tools, policing, shaping and re-marking, providing congestion management and scheduling tools, and finally, link-specific tools.

Chapter 10: Wireless Technologies Because I know you've crushed all of the previous chapters, you're ready to dive into this one! If that's not exactly you, just know that the two chapters on switching provide a really nice review on switching and VLANs. So, let's start this chapter by defining a basic wireless network as well as basic wireless principles. We'll talk about different types of wireless networks, the minimum devices required to create a simple wireless network, and some basic wireless topologies as well. After that, I'll get into basic security by covering WPA, WPA2, and WPA3.

Chapter 11: Configuring Legacy Wireless Controllers After Chapter 10 you now know how wireless works, so now we're going to guide you through configuring a wireless network from beginning to end. We'll start by telling you all about how to get a Cisco Wireless LAN Controller up and running before showing you how to join access points to our new WLC. We'll also dig deep into how to configure the WLC to support wireless networks. By the end of this chapter, you'll triumph by having an actual endpoint join your wireless LAN!

Chapter 12: Configuring Modern Wireless Controllers This chapter walks you through setting up a virtual Cisco 9800 controller and using port channels. Then, we will create a simple WPA2 WLAN using PSK, just as we did with the WLC. Then, we will join our new wireless network with my test PC to confirm everything works as advertised! Finally, we will finish up the chapter by exploring how to work with cloud-managed access points.

Chapter 13: Virtualization, Containers, and VRFs In this chapter, we'll begin to address modern challenges by introducing you to virtualization basics. We'll then walk you through its common components and features to close the topic by comparing some of the virtualization products on the market as of this writing. After that, we'll explore important automation concepts and components to provide you with sure footing to jump into the SDN and configuration management chapters following this one.

Chapter 14: Software-Defined Networking (SDN) Automation has gotten popular enough to be included on the CCNA exam—it even has its own DevNet certification track! Even so, most companies still aren't keen on fully managing their network with a bunch of Python scripts on a shared drive. So a better solution is to go with something called a software-defined networking (SDN) controller to centrally manage and monitor the network instead of doing everything manually, and that is what this chapter is all about!

Chapter 15: Automation and REST APIs When preparing for the CCNA, manually configuring everything while practicing the topics in this book is a great way to gain hands-on experience and become proficient with IOS commands. However, by the time you're nearing the exam, you might find that repeating basic configurations, like adding VLANs over and over, becomes tedious. This is why automation is gaining traction in the workplace—it helps prevent these errors and saves time by reducing the need for repetitive tasks. In this chapter, we'll introduce the concept of automation and explore REST APIs, which are the preferred method for automating network devices today.

Chapter 16: Configuration Management In this chapter we're going to take things to a whole new level, diving deeper into configuration management tools like Ansible, Puppet, and Terraform. These great features make it possible to automate almost everything in your infrastructure!

Appendix A: Answers to the Written Labs This appendix provides the answers to the end-of-chapter written lab.

Appendix B: Answers to the Review Questions This appendix provides the answers to the end-of-chapter review questions.

Interactive Online Learning Environment and Test Bank

The interactive online learning environment that accompanies the *CCNA Certification Study Guide: Exam 200-301 v1.1* provides a test bank with study tools to help you prepare for the certification exams and increase your chances of passing them the first time! The test bank includes the following elements:

Sample tests All of the questions in this book are provided, including the assessment test, which you'll find at the end of this introduction, and the review questions at the end of each chapter. In addition, you'll find a practice exam for each book in the series. Use these questions to test your knowledge of the study guide material. The online test bank runs on multiple devices.

Electronic flashcards The flashcards are included for quick reference and are great tools for learning quick facts. You can even consider these additional simple practice questions, which is essentially what they are.

PDF of glossary of terms There is a glossary included that covers the key terms used in this book.

NOTE The Sybex Interactive Online Test Bank, flashcards, and glossary can be accessed at `http://www.wiley.com/go/Sybextestprep`.

Todd Lammle Bonus Material and Labs Be sure to check `www.lammle.com/ccna` for directions on how to download all the latest bonus materials created specifically to help you study for your CCNA exam.

Todd Lammle Videos I have created a full CCNA series of videos that can be purchased at `www.lammle.com/ccna`.

NOTE Like all exams, the CCNA certification from Cisco is updated periodically and may eventually be retired or replaced. At some point after Cisco is no longer offering this exam, the old editions of our books and online tools will be retired. If you have purchased this book after the exam was retired or are attempting to register in the Sybex online learning environment after the exam was retired, please know that we make no guarantees that this exam's online Sybex tools will be available once the exam is no longer available.

CCNA Exam Overview

Cisco has designed the new CCNA program to prepare you for today's associate-level job roles in IT technologies. The CCNA 200-301 v1.1 exam now includes security and automation and programmability, and there is even a new CCNA DevNet certification. The new CCNA program has one certification that covers a broad range of fundamentals for IT careers.

The new CCNA certification covers a huge amount of topics, including

- Network fundamentals
- Network access
- IP connectivity
- IP services
- Security fundamentals
- Wireless
- Automation and programmability

Are There Any Prerequisites for Taking the CCNA Exam?

Not really, but having experience is really helpful. Cisco has no formal prerequisites for CCNA certification, but you should have an understanding of the exam topics before taking the exam.

CCNA candidates often also have

- One or more years of experience implementing and administering Cisco solutions
- Knowledge of basic IP addressing
- A good understanding of network fundamentals

How to Use This Book

If you want a solid foundation for the serious effort of preparing for the new CCNA exam, then look no further. I've spent hundreds of hours putting together this book with the sole intention of helping you to pass the Cisco exams as well as really learning how to correctly configure Cisco routers and switches!

This book is loaded with valuable information, and you will get the most out of your study time if you understand the way in which this book is organized.

So to maximize your benefit from this book, I recommend the following study method:

1. Take the assessment test that's provided at the end of this introduction. (The answers are at the end of the test.) It's okay if you don't know any of the answers; that's why you bought this book! Carefully read over the explanations for any questions you get wrong and note the chapters in which the relevant material is covered. This information should help you plan your study strategy.

2. Study each chapter carefully, making sure you fully understand the information and the test objectives listed at the beginning of each one. Pay extra-close attention to any chapter that includes material covered in questions you missed.
3. Answer all of the questions related to each chapter. (The answers appear in Appendix A and Appendix B.) Note the questions that confuse you and study the topics they cover again until the concepts are crystal clear. And again—do not just skim these questions! Make sure you fully comprehend the reason for each correct answer. Remember, these will not be the exact questions you will find on the exam, but they're written to help you understand the chapter material and ultimately pass the exam!
4. Try your hand at the practice questions that are exclusive to this book. The questions can be found only at `http://www.wiley.com/go/sybextestprep`. Don't forget to check out `www.lammle.com/ccna` for the most up-to-date Cisco exam prep questions, videos, hands-on labs, and Todd Lammle boot camps.
5. Test yourself using all the flashcards, which are also found on the download link listed in the Sybex downloads. These are brand-new and updated flashcards to help you prepare for the CCNA exam and a wonderful study tool!

To learn every bit of the material covered in this book, you'll have to apply yourself regularly and with discipline. Try to set aside the same time period every day to study, and select a comfortable and quiet place to do so. I'm confident that if you work hard, you'll be surprised at how quickly you learn this material!

If you follow these steps and really study—*doing hands-on labs every single day* in addition to using the review questions, the practice exams, the Todd Lammle video sections, and the electronic flashcards, as well as all the written labs—it would actually be hard to fail the Cisco exams. But understand that studying for the Cisco exams is a lot like getting in shape—if you do not go to the gym every day, it's not going to happen!

Where Do You Take the Exam?

You may take the CCNA Composite or any Cisco exam at any of the Pearson VUE authorized testing centers. For information, check `www.vue.com` or call 877-404-EXAM (3926).

To register for a Cisco exam, follow these steps:

1. Determine the number of the exam you want to take. (The CCNA exam number is 200-301.)
2. Register with the nearest Pearson VUE testing center. At this point, you will be asked to pay for the exam in advance. You can schedule exams up to six weeks in advance or as late as the day you want to take them—but if you fail a Cisco exam, you must wait five days before you will be allowed to retake it. If something comes up and you need to cancel or reschedule your exam appointment, contact Pearson VUE at least 24 hours in advance.
3. When you schedule the exam, you'll get instructions regarding all appointment and cancellation procedures, the ID requirements, and information about the testing center location.

Tips for Taking Your Cisco Exams

The Cisco exams contain about 50 or more questions and must be completed in about 90 minutes or so. It's hard to write this information down today because it changes so often. You must get a score of about 85 percent to pass this exam, but again, each exam can be different.

Many questions on the exam have answer choices that at first glance look identical—especially the syntax questions! So remember to read through the choices carefully because close just doesn't cut it. If you get commands in the wrong order or forget one measly character, you'll get the question wrong. So, to practice, do the hands-on exercises at the end of this book's chapters over and over again until they feel natural to you.

Also, never forget that the right answer is the Cisco answer. In many cases, more than one appropriate answer is presented, but the *correct* answer is the one that Cisco recommends. On the exam, you will always be told to pick one, two, or three options, never "choose all that apply." The Cisco exam may include the following test formats:

- Multiple-choice single answer
- Multiple-choice multiple answer
- Drag-and-drop
- Router simulations

Cisco proctored exams will not show the steps to follow in completing a router interface configuration, but they do allow partial command responses. For example, `show run`, `sho running`, or `sh running-config` would be acceptable.

Here are some general tips for exam success:

- Arrive early at the exam center so you can relax and review your study materials.
- Read the questions *carefully*. Don't jump to conclusions. Make sure you're clear about *exactly* what each question asks. "Read twice, answer once," is what I always tell my students.
- When answering multiple-choice questions that you're not sure about, use the process of elimination to get rid of the obviously incorrect answers first. Doing this greatly improves your odds if you need to make an educated guess.
- You can no longer move forward and backward through the Cisco exams, so double-check your answer before clicking Next because you can't change your mind.

After you complete an exam, you'll get an immediate, online notification of your pass or fail status, a printed examination score report that indicates your pass or fail status, and your exam results by section. (The test administrator will give you the printed score report.)

Test scores are automatically forwarded to Cisco within five working days after you take the test, so you don't need to send your score to the company. If you pass the exam, you'll receive confirmation from Cisco, typically within two to four weeks, sometimes a bit longer.

CCNA Certification Exam 200-301 v1.1 Objectives

The following table shows where each objective is covered in this book series:

Objective	Book, Chapter
1.0 Network Fundamentals	**Volume 1, Chapters 1/3/4/12/14** **Volume 2, Chapters 3/4/10/13/14**
1.1 Explain the role and function of network components	Volume 1, Chapter 1
1.1.a Routers	Volume 1, Chapter 1
1.1.b Layer 2 and Layer 3 switches	Volume 1, Chapter 1
1.1.c Next-generation firewalls and IPS	Volume 1, Chapter 1
1.1.d Access points	Volume 2, Chapter 10
1.1.e Controllers	Volume 2, Chapter 10
1.1.f Endpoints	Volume 1, Chapter 5
1.1.g Servers	Volume 1, Chapter 5
1.1.h PoE	Volume 1, Chapter 2
1.2 Describe characteristics of network topology architectures	Volume 1, Chapter 1
1.2.a Two-tier	Volume 1, Chapter 1
1.2.b Three-tier	Volume 1, Chapter 1 Volume 2, Chapter 14
1.2.c Spine-leaf	Volume 1, Chapter 1
1.2.d WAN	Volume 1, Chapter 1
1.2.e Small office/home office (SOHO)	Volume 1, Chapter 1
1.2.f On-premises and cloud	Volume 1, Chapter 14
1.3 Compare physical interface and cabling types	Volume 1, Chapter 2
1.3.a Single-mode fiber, multimode fiber, copper	Volume 1, Chapter 2
1.3.b Connections (Ethernet shared media and point-to-point)	Volume 1, Chapter 2

Objective	Book, Chapter
1.4 Identify interface and cable issues (collisions, errors, mismatch duplex, and/or speed)	Volume 1, Chapter 2
1.5 Compare TCP to UDP	Volume 1, Chapter 3
1.6 Configure and verify IPv4 addressing and subnetting	Volume 1, Chapter 3/4/5 Volume 2, Chapter 4
1.7 Describe private IPv4 addressing	Volume 1, Chapter 3
1.8 Configure and verify IPv6 addressing and prefix	Volume 2, Chapter 3 Volume 2, Chapter 4
1.9 Describe IPv6 address types	Volume 2, Chapter 3
1.9.a Unicast (global, unique local, and link local)	Volume 2, Chapter 3
1.9.b Anycast	Volume 2, Chapter 3
1.9.c Multicast	Volume 2, Chapter 3
1.9.d Modified EUI 64	Volume 2, Chapter 3
1.10 Verify IP parameters for Client OS (Windows, Mac OS, Linux)	Volume 1, Chapter 5 Volume 2, Chapter 4
1.11 Describe wireless principles	Volume 2, Chapter 10
1.11.a Nonoverlapping Wi-Fi channels	Volume 2, Chapter 10
1.11.b SSID	Volume 2, Chapter 10
1.11.c RF	Volume 2, Chapter 10
1.11.d Encryption	Volume 2, Chapter 10
1.12 Explain virtualization fundamentals (server virtualization, containers, and VRFs)	Volume 2, Chapter 13
1.13 Describe switching concepts	Volume 1, Chapter 12
1.13.a MAC learning and aging	Volume 1, Chapter 12
1.13.b Frame switching	Volume 1, Chapter 12
1.13.c Frame flooding	Volume 1, Chapter 12
1.13.d MAC address table	Volume 1, Chapter 12

Objective	Book, Chapter
2.0 Network Access	**Volume 1, Chapter 1/8** **Volume 2, Chapters 1/6/12**
2.1 Configure and verify VLANs (normal range) spanning multiple switches	Volume 1, Chapter 13
2.1.a Access ports (data and voice)	Volume 1, Chapter 13
2.1.b Default VLAN	Volume 1, Chapter 13
2.1.c InterVLAN connectivity	Volume 1, Chapter 13
2.2 Configure and verify interswitch connectivity	Volume 1, Chapter 13
2.2.a Trunk ports	Volume 1, Chapter 13
2.2.b 802.1Q	Volume 1, Chapter 13
2.2.c Native VLAN	Volume 1, Chapter 13
2.3 Configure and verify Layer 2 discovery protocols (Cisco Discovery Protocol and LLDP)	Volume 1, Chapter 8 Volume 2, Chapter 6
2.4 Configure and verify (Layer 2/Layer 3) EtherChannel (LACP)	Volume 2, Chapter 1
2.5 Interpret basic operations of Rapid PVST+ Spanning Tree Protocol	Volume 2, Chapter 1
2.5.a Root port, root bridge (primary/secondary), and other port names	Volume 2, Chapter 1
2.5.b Port states and roles	Volume 2, Chapter 1
2.5.c PortFast	Volume 2, Chapter 1
2.5.d Root guard, loop guard, BPDU filter, and BPDU guard	Volume 2, Chapter 1
2.6 Describe Cisco Wireless Architectures and AP modes	Volume 2, Chapter 11/12
2.7 Describe physical infrastructure connections of WLAN components (AP, WLC, access/trunk ports, and LAG)	Volume 2, Chapter 11/12
2.8 Describe network device management access (Telnet, SSH, HTTP, HTTPS, console, TACACS+/RADIUS, and cloud managed)	Volume 1, Chapter 8
2.9 Interpret the wireless LAN GUI configuration for client connectivity, such as WLAN creation, security settings, QoS profiles, and advanced settings	Volume 2, Chapter 11/12

Objective	Book, Chapter
3.0 IP Connectivity	**Volume 1, Chapter 9** **Volume 2, Chapters 4/8**
3.1 Interpret the components of routing table	Volume 1, Chapter 9 Volume 2, Chapter 4
3.1.a Routing protocol code	Volume 1, Chapter 9
3.1.b Prefix	Volume 1, Chapter 9
3.1.c Network mask	Volume 1, Chapter 9
3.1.d Next hop	Volume 1, Chapter 9
3.1.e Administrative distance	Volume 1, Chapter 9
3.1.f Metric	Volume 1, Chapter 9
3.1.g Gateway of last resort	Volume 1, Chapter 9
3.2 Determine how a router makes a forwarding decision by default	Volume 1, Chapter 9
3.2.a Longest prefix match	Volume 1, Chapter 9
3.2.b Administrative distance	Volume 1, Chapter 9
3.2.c Routing protocol metric	Volume 1, Chapter 9
3.3 Configure and verify IPv4 and IPv6 static routing	Volume 1, Chapter 9 Volume 2, Chapter 3/4
3.3.a Default route	Volume 1, Chapter 9
3.3.b Network route	Volume 1, Chapter 9
3.3.c Host route	Volume 1, Chapter 9
3.3.d Floating static	Volume 1, Chapter 9
3.4 Configure and verify single area OSPFv2	Volume 1, Chapter 10
3.4.a Neighbor adjacencies	Volume 1, Chapter 10
3.4.b Point-to-point	Volume 1, Chapter 10
3.4.c Broadcast (DR/BDR selection)	Volume 1, Chapter 10
3.4.d Router ID	Volume 1, Chapter 10
3.5 Describe the purpose, functions, and concepts of first hop redundancy protocols	Volume 2, Chapter 8

Objective	Book, Chapter
4.0 IP Services	**Volume 1, Chapter 3/9** **Volume 2, Chapter 5/6/9**
4.1 Configure and verify inside source NAT using static and pools	Volume 2, Chapter 5
4.2 Configure and verify NTP operating in a client and server mode	Volume 2, Chapter 6
4.3 Explain the role of DHCP and DNS within the network	Volume 1, Chapter 3/9
4.4 Explain the function of SNMP in network operations	Volume 1, Chapter 3 Volume 2, Chapter 6
4.5 Describe the use of syslog features, including facilities and severity levels	Volume 2, Chapter 6
4.6 Configure and verify DHCP client and relay	Volume 1, Chapter 9
4.7 Explain the forwarding per-hop behavior (PHB) for QoS such as classification, marking, queuing, congestion, policing, and shaping	Volume 2, Chapter 9
4.8 Configure network devices for remote access using SSH	Volume 2, Chapter 6
4.9 Describe the capabilities and functions of TFTP/FTP in the network	Volume 1, Chapter 3
5.0 Security Fundamentals	**Volume 1, Chapter 15** **Volume 2, Chapter 2/7/10/11/12/14**
5.1 Define key security concepts (threats, vulnerabilities, exploits, and mitigation techniques)	Volume 2, Chapter 7 Volume 2, Chapter 7
5.2 Describe security program elements (user awareness, training, and physical access control)	Volume 2, Chapter 7
5.3 Configure and verify device access control using local passwords	Volume 2, Chapter 7
5.4 Describe security password policy elements, such as management, complexity, and password alternatives (multifactor authentication, certificates, and biometrics)	Volume 2, Chapter 7
5.5 Describe IPsec remote access and site-to-site VPNs	Volume 1, Chapter 14
5.6 Configure and verify access control lists	Volume 2, Chapter 2

Objective	Book, Chapter
5.7 Configure and verify Layer 2 security features (DHCP snooping, dynamic ARP inspection, and port security)	Volume 2, Chapter 7 Volume 2, Chapter 7
5.8 Compare authentication, authorization, and accounting concepts	Volume 2, Chapter 7
5.9 Describe wireless security protocols (WPA, WPA2, and WPA3)	Volume 2, Chapter 10
5.10 Configure and verify WLAN within the GUI using WPA2 PSK	Volume 2, Chapter 11/12
6.0 Automation and Programmability	**Volume 1, Chapter 15** **Volume 2, Chapters 14/15/16**
6.1 Explain how automation impacts network management	Volume 2, Chapter 14
6.2 Compare traditional networks with controller-based networking	Volume 2, Chapter 14
6.3 Describe controller-based, software defined architecture (overlay, underlay, and fabric)	Volume 2, Chapter 14
6.3.a Separation of control plane and data plane	Volume 2, Chapter 14
6.3.b Northbound and Southbound APIs	Volume 2, Chapter 14
6.4 Explain AI (generative and predictive) and machine learning in network operations	Volume 1, Chapter 15
6.5 Describe characteristics of REST-based APIs (authentication types, CRUD, HTTP verbs, and data encoding)	Volume 2, Chapter 15
6.6 Recognize the capabilities of configuration management mechanisms such as Ansible and Terraform	Volume 2, Chapter 16
6.7 Recognize components of JSON-encoded data	Volume 2, Chapter 15

How to Contact the Publisher

If you believe you have found a mistake in this book, please bring it to our attention. At John Wiley & Sons, we understand how important it is to provide our customers with accurate content, but even with our best efforts, an error may occur.

In order to submit your possible errata, please email it to our Customer Service Team at `wileysupport@wiley.com` with the subject line "Possible Book Errata Submission."

Assessment Test

1. What is the sys-id-ext field in a BPDU used for?
   - **A.** It is a 4-bit field inserted into an Ethernet frame to define trunking information between switches.
   - **B.** It is a 12-bit field inserted into an Ethernet frame to define VLANs in an STP instance.
   - **C.** It is a 4-bit field inserted into a non-Ethernet frame to define EtherChannel options.
   - **D.** It is a 12-bit field inserted into an Ethernet frame to define STP root bridges.
2. You have four RSTP PVST+ links between switches and want to aggregate the bandwidth. What solution will you use?
   - **A.** EtherChannel
   - **B.** PortFast
   - **C.** BPDU Channel
   - **D.** VLANs
   - **E.** EtherBundle
3. What configuration parameters must be configured the same between switches for LACP to form a channel? (Choose three.)
   - **A.** Virtual MAC address
   - **B.** Port speeds
   - **C.** Duplex
   - **D.** PortFast enabled
   - **E.** Allowed VLAN information
4. Which router command allows you to view the entire contents of all access lists?
   - **A.** `show all access-lists`
   - **B.** `show access-lists`
   - **C.** `show ip interface`
   - **D.** `show interface`
5. You receive notice that packets on an interface appear to be allowed through an IPv4 ACL. You verify that the ACL is applied to the correct interface. Which misconfigurations cause this behavior? (Choose two.)
   - **A.** The ACL is empty.
   - **B.** A matching permit statement is too broadly defined.
   - **C.** The packets fail to match any permit statement.
   - **D.** A matching deny statement is too high in the access list.
   - **E.** A matching permit statement is too high in the access list.

6. What are the main types of access control lists (ACLs)? (Choose two.)
   - **A.** Standard
   - **B.** IEEE
   - **C.** Extended
   - **D.** Specialize

7. You need to connect to a remote IPv6 server in your virtual server farm. You can connect to the IPv4 servers but not the critical IPv6 server you desperately need. Based on the following output, what could your problem be?

```
C:\>ipconfig
   Connection-specific DNS Suffix  . : localdomain
   IPv6 Address. . . . . . . . . . . : 2001:db8:3c4d:3:ac3b:2ef:1823:8938
   Temporary IPv6 Address. . . . . . : 2001:db8:3c4d:3:2f33:44dd:211:1c3d
   Link-local IPv6 Address . . . . . : fe80::ac3b:2ef:1823:8938%11
   IPv4 Address. . . . . . . . . . . : 10.1.1.10
   Subnet Mask . . . . . . . . . . . : 255.255.255.0
   Default Gateway . . . . . . . . . : 10.1.1.1
```

   - **A.** The global address is in the wrong subnet.
   - **B.** The IPv6 default gateway has not been configured or received from the router.
   - **C.** The link-local address has not been resolved, so the host cannot communicate with the router.
   - **D.** There are two IPv6 global addresses configured. One must be removed from the configuration.

8. What command is used to view the IPv6-to-MAC-address resolution table on a Cisco router?
   - **A.** `show ip arp`
   - **B.** `show ipv6 arp`
   - **C.** `show ip neighbors`
   - **D.** `show ipv6 neighbors`
   - **E.** `show arp`

9. An IPv6 ARP entry is listed with a status of REACH. What can you conclude about the IPv6-to-MAC-address mapping?
   - **A.** The interface has communicated with the neighbor address, and the mapping is current.
   - **B.** The interface has not communicated within the neighbor-reachable time frame.
   - **C.** The ARP entry has timed out.
   - **D.** IPv6 can reach the neighbor address, but the addresses have not yet been resolved.

10. Which protocol is used to send a destination network unknown message back to originating hosts?

A. TCP

B. ARP

C. ICMP

D. BootP

11. Which of the following is considered to be the inside host's address after translation?

A. Inside local

B. Outside local

C. Inside global

D. Outside global

12. You connect to your NGFW, and your inside local addresses are not being translated to the inside global addresses. Which of the following commands will show you if your inside globals are allowed to use the NAT pool?

```
ip nat pool Corp 198.18.41.129 198.18.41.134 netmask 255.255.255.248
ip nat inside source list 100 int pool Corp overload
```

A. `debug ip nat`

B. `show access-list`

C. `show ip nat translation`

D. `show ip nat statistics`

13. You want to send a console message to a syslog server, but you only want to send status messages of 3 and lower. Which of the following commands will you use?

A. `logging trap emergencies`

B. `logging trap errors`

C. `logging trap debugging`

D. `logging trap notifications`

E. `logging trap critical`

F. `logging trap warnings`

G. `logging trap alerts`

14. You want to enable SSH on a switch. Which conditions must be met before SSH can operate normally on a Cisco IOS switch? (Choose two.)

A. IP routing must be enabled on the switch.

B. A console password must be configured on the switch.

C. Telnet must be disabled on the switch.

D. The switch must be running a k9 (crypto) IOS image.

E. The `ip domain-name` command must be configured on the switch.

15. Which of the following defines the differences between AAA authentication and authorization?
    - **A.** Authentication identifies and verifies a user attempting to access a system, and authorization controls the tasks the user can perform.
    - **B.** Authentication controls the system processes a user can access, and authorization logs the activities the user initiates.
    - **C.** Authentication verifies a username and password, and authorization handles the communication between the authentication agent and the user database.
    - **D.** Authentication identifies a user who is attempting to access a system, and authorization validates the user's password.
16. You want to use a password manager application to make administration easier. In which ways does a password manager reduce the chance of a hacker stealing a user's password? (Choose two.)
    - **A.** It automatically provides a second authentication factor that is unknown to the original user.
    - **B.** It uses an internal firewall to protect the password repository from unauthorized access.
    - **C.** It protects against keystroke logging on a compromised device or website.
    - **D.** It stores the password repository on the local workstation with built-in antivirus and anti-malware functionality.
    - **E.** It encourages users to create stronger passwords.
17. You want to use HSRP version 2, but you need to know the multicast address and port number for configuration on the NGFW. What's the multicast and port number?
    - **A.** 224.0.0.2, UDP port 1985
    - **B.** 224.0.0.2. TCP port 1985
    - **C.** 224.0.0.102, UDP port 1985
    - **D.** 224.0.0.102, TCP port 1985
18. Which command displays the status of all HSRP groups on a Cisco router or layer 3 switch?
    - **A.** `show ip hsrp`
    - **B.** `show hsrp`
    - **C.** `show standby hsrp`
    - **D.** `show standby`
    - **E.** `show hsrp groups`
19. Which QoS mechanism will drop traffic if a session uses more than the allotted bandwidth?
    - **A.** Congestion management
    - **B.** Shaping
    - **C.** Policing
    - **D.** Marking

20. Which QoS per-hop behavior changes the value of the ToS field in the IPv4 packet header?
    A. Shaping
    B. Classification
    C. Policing
    D. Marking
21. WPA3 replaced the default open authentication with which of the following enhancements?
    A. AES
    B. OWL
    C. OWE
    D. TKIP
22. What's the maximum data rate for the 802.11a standard?
    A. 6 Mbps
    B. 11 Mbps
    C. 22 Mbps
    D. 54 Mbps
23. What DNS record do you need to create for APs to automatically discover the WLC?
    A. CISCO-WLC-CONTROLLER
    B. WLC-CONTROLLER
    C. CISCO-AP-CONTROLLER
    D. CISCO-DISCOVER-CONTROLLER
    E. CISCO-CAPWAP-CONTROLLER
24. What's the default QoS queue for a WLAN?
    A. Gold
    B. Platinum
    C. Bronze
    D. Silver
    E. Diamond
25. Your boss read about WPA3 and wants you to explain it to them. What replaced the default open authentication with which of the following enhancements?
    A. AES
    B. OWL
    C. OWE
    D. TKIP

26. Which AP modes serve wireless traffic? (Choose two.)
    - A. Local
    - B. Monitor
    - C. FlexConnect
    - D. Sniffer
    - E. SE-Connect
27. What is zero-touch provisioning (ZTP) in the context of Meraki devices?
    - A. Automatic network diagram generation.
    - B. Preconfigured devices automatically download their configurations upon connection.
    - C. Manual setup of each device in the network.
    - D. Automated backup of device configurations to the cloud.
28. Why would you install virtualization in your data center over physical server deployment?
    - A. Reduced need for power and cooling
    - B. Easier physical access to servers
    - C. Faster deployment of applications
    - D. Improved physical security
29. Why is configuring a standard hardware switch harder than a distributed virtual switch?
    - A. Lack of VLAN support
    - B. No trunking capability
    - C. Manual configuration on each hypervisor
    - D. Inability to connect virtual machines to the network
30. Which protocol is commonly used as a southbound interface in SDN environments to communicate between the SDN controller and network devices?
    - A. SNMP
    - B. NETCONF
    - C. HTTP
    - D. SMTP
31. Which protocol is commonly used for REST APIs in Catalyst Center?
    - A. SSH
    - B. SMTP
    - C. SNMP
    - D. HTTP

32. Which of the following is a key constraint of a RESTful API?

- **A.** The server must store the session state.
- **B.** The client initiates requests to the server.
- **C.** Only XML data can be used.
- **D.** All requests must use the GET method.

33. In REST APIs, which of the following best describes HATEOAS?

- **A.** It requires clients to manage the server state.
- **B.** It mandates the use of the JSON data format.
- **C.** It ensures that the API is self-discoverable.
- **D.** It is a method for encrypting API requests.

34. What is a key benefit of using infrastructure as code (IaC) in network management?

- **A.** It allows network devices to be configured manually.
- **B.** It ensures that network configurations are consistently applied across environments.
- **C.** It requires no initial setup for automation.
- **D.** It replaces the need for monitoring tools in network management.

35. Which configuration management tool does not require agents to be installed on target systems and uses SSH for applying configurations?

- **A.** Puppet
- **B.** Chef
- **C.** Ansible
- **D.** Terraform

Answers to Assessment Test

1. B. To allow for the PVST+ to operate, there's a field inserted into the BPDU to accommodate the extended system ID so that PVST+ can have a root bridge configured on a per-STP instance. The extended system ID (VLAN ID) is a 12-bit field, and we can even see what this field is carrying via `show spanning-tree` command output. See Chapter 1 for more information.

2. A. Cisco's EtherChannel can bundle up to eight ports between switches to provide resiliency and more bandwidth between switches. See Chapter 1 for more information.

3. B, C, E. All the ports on both sides of every link must be configured exactly the same between switches or it will not work. Speed, duplex, and allowed VLANs must match. See Chapter 1 for more information.

4. B. To see the contents of all access lists, use the `show access-lists` command. See Chapter 2 for more information.

5. B, E. If all or too much traffic is being allowed, your permit statements are configured too broadly, and/or the statement is too high in the ACL. See Chapter 2 for more information.

6. A, C. Standard and extended access control lists (ACLs) are used to configure security on a router. See Chapter 2 for more information.

7. B. There is no IPv6 default gateway listed in the output, which will be the link-local address of the router interface sent to the host as a router advertisement. Until this host receives the router address, the host will communicate with IPv6 only on the local subnet. See Chapter 3 for more information.

8. D. The command `show ipv6 neighbors` provides the ARP cache on a router. See Chapter 3 for more information.

9. A. If the state is STALE when the interface has not communicated within the neighbor-reachable time frame, the next time the neighbor communicates, the state will be REACH. See Chapter 4 for more information.

10. C. ICMP is the protocol at the Network layer that is used to send messages back to an originating router. See Chapter 4 for more information.

11. C. An inside global address is considered to be the IP address of the host on the private network after translation. See Chapter 5 for more information.

12. B. Once you create your pool, the command `ip nat inside source` must be used to say which inside locals are allowed to use the pool. In this question, we need to see if access list 100 is configured correctly, if at all, so `show access-list` is the best answer. See Chapter 5 for more information.

13. B. There are eight different trap levels. If you choose, for example, level 3, level 0 through level 3 messages will be displayed. See Chapter 6 for more information.

14. D, E. To use SSH in Cisco Router, the IOS image must a k9 (crypto) image, and you must configure the IP DNS domain for the router. See Chapter 6 for more information.

15. A. AAA stands for authentication, authorization, and accounting.

    Authentication: Specify who you are (usually via login username and password). Authorization: Specify what actions you can do and what resources you can access. Accounting: Monitor what you do and how long you do it (can be used for billing and auditing). See Chapter 7 for more information.

16. C, E. It protects against keystroke logging on a compromised device or website and encourages users to create stronger passwords. See Chapter 7 for more information.

17. C. In version 1, HSRP messages are sent to the multicast IP address 224.0.0.2 and UDP port 1985. HSRP version 2 uses the multicast IP address 224.0.0.102 and UDP port 1985. See Chapter 8 for more information.

18. D. `Show standby` is your friend when dealing with HSRP. See Chapter 8 for more information.

19. C. When traffic exceeds the allocated rate, the policer can take one of two actions. It can either drop traffic or re-mark it to another class of service. The new class usually has a higher drop probability. See Chapter 9 for more information.

20. D. QoS marking changes the value of the ToS field in the IPv4 packet header. See Chapter 9 for more information.

21. A. The IEEE 802.11i standard replaced Wired Equivalent Privacy (WEP) with a specific mode of the Advanced Encryption Standard (AES) known as the Counter Mode Cipher Block Chaining-Message Authentication Code (CBC-MAC) protocol. This allows AES-Counter Mode CBC-MAC Protocol (AES-CCMP) to provide both data confidentiality (encryption) and data integrity. See Chapter 10 for more information.

22. C. IEEE 802.11b and IEEE 802.11g both run in the 2.4 GHz RF range. See Chapter 10 for more information.

23. E. For the DNS method, you need to create an A record for CISCO-CAPWAP-CONTROLLER that points to the WLC management IP. See Chapter 11 for more information.

24. D. WLANs default to the Silver queue, which effectively means no QoS is being utilized. See Chapter 11 for more information.

25. C. The 802.11 "open" authentication support has been replaced with Opportunistic Wireless Encryption (OWE) enhancement, which is an enhancement, not a mandatory certified setting. See Chapter 11 for more information.

26. A, C. The two AP modes listed that can serve wireless traffic are local and FlexConnect. See Chapter 11 for more information.

27. B. ZTP allows Meraki devices to automatically download their preconfigured settings from the cloud once connected to the network, simplifying deployment. See Chapter 12 for more information.

28. C. Virtualization allows us to deploy applications much faster than physical deployments. See Chapter 13 for more information.

29. C. Standard switches require each hypervisor to be configured manually. See Chapter 13 for more information.

30. B. NETCONF is a popular protocol used for communication between the SDN controller and network devices. It allows the controller to configure and manage the devices programmatically. See Chapter 14 for more information.

31. D. REST APIs in Catalyst Center typically use HTTP or HTTPS as the transport protocol for managing and interacting with network devices programmatically. See Chapter 14 for more information.

32. B. In RESTful APIs, the communication is client-server based, where the client initiates the requests and the server processes and responds to these requests. See Chapter 15 for more information.

33. C. HATEOAS (Hypermedia as the Engine of Application State) is a constraint of REST APIs that ensures the API can guide the client on how to interact with it by providing links to other related resources dynamically. See Chapter 15 for more information.

34. B. IaC helps to automate network management by defining configurations in code, ensuring that they are applied consistently across environments, and reducing configuration drift and human errors. See Chapter 16 for more information.

35. C. Ansible is an agentless configuration management tool that uses SSH to connect to and configure target systems, making it simple to use and widely supported in network management. See Chapter 16 for more information.

Chapter 1

Enhanced Switched Technologies

THE FOLLOWING CCNA EXAM TOPICS ARE COVERED IN THIS CHAPTER:

✓ **2.0 Network Access**

- 2.4 Configure and verify (Layer 2/Layer 3) EtherChannel (LACP)
- 2.5 Interpret basic operations of Rapid PVST+ Spanning Tree Protocol
  - 2.5.a Root port, root bridge (primary/secondary), and other port names
  - 2.5.b Port states and roles
  - 2.5.c PortFast
  - 2.5.d Root guard, loop guard, BPDU filter, and BPDU guard

Long ago, a company called Digital Equipment Corporation (DEC) created the original version of the *Spanning Tree Protocol (STP)*. The IEEE later created its own version of STP called 802.1d. Cisco has moved toward another industry standard in its newer switches, called 802.1w. We'll explore both the old and new versions of STP in this chapter, but first, I'll define some important STP basics.

Routing protocols like RIP and OSPF have processes for preventing loops from occurring at the Network layer, but if you have redundant physical links between your switches, these protocols won't do a thing to stop loops from occurring at the Data Link layer. That's exactly why STP was developed—to put an end to loop issues in a layer 2 switched network. This is why, in this chapter, we'll be thoroughly exploring the key features of this vital protocol as well as how it works within a switched network.

After covering STP in detail, we'll move on to explore EtherChannel at the end of this chapter.

NOTE To find up-to-the-minute updates for this chapter, please see `www.lammle.com/ccna`.

Spanning Tree Protocol (STP)

STP achieves its primary objective of preventing network loops on layer 2 network bridges or switches by monitoring the network to track all links and shut down the redundant ones. STP uses the spanning-tree algorithm (STA) to first create a topology database and then search out and disable redundant links. With STP running, frames will be forwarded on only premium, STP-chosen links.

The STP is a great protocol to use in networks like the one shown in Figure 1.1.

This is a switched network with a redundant topology that includes switching loops. Without some type of layer 2 mechanism in place to prevent a network loop, this network is vulnerable to nasty issues like broadcast storms, multiple frame copies, and MAC table thrashing! Figure 1.2 shows how this network would work with STP working on the switches.

FIGURE 1.1 A switched network with switching loops

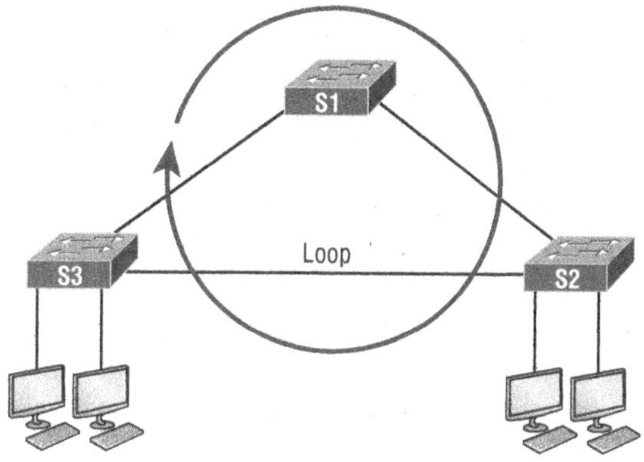

FIGURE 1.2 A switched network with STP

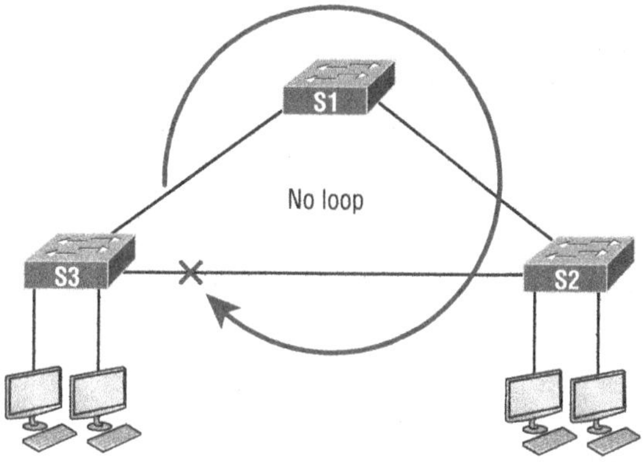

There are a few types of spanning-tree protocols, but I'll start with the IEEE version 802.1d, which happens to be the default on all Cisco IOS switches.

Spanning-Tree Terms

Now, before I get into describing the details of how STP works within a network, it would be good for you to have these basic ideas and terms down first:

Root bridge The *root bridge* is the bridge with the lowest and, therefore, the best bridge ID. The switches within the STP network elect a root bridge, which becomes the focal point in the network. All other decisions in the network, like which ports on the non-root bridges should be blocked or put in forwarding mode, are made from the perspective of the root bridge, and once it has been elected, all other bridges must create a single path to it. The port with the best path to the root bridge is called the root port.

Non-root bridges These are all bridges that aren't the root bridge. Non-root bridges exchange BPDUs with all the other bridges and update the STP topology database on all switches. This prevents loops and helps defend against link failures.

BPDU All switches exchange information to use for the subsequent configuration of the network. Each switch compares the parameters in the *Bridge Protocol Data Unit (BPDU)* that it sends to a neighbor with the parameters in the BPDU that it receives from other neighbors. Inside the BPDU is the bridge ID.

Bridge ID The bridge ID is how STP keeps track of all the switches in the network. It's determined by a combination of the bridge priority, which is 32,768 by default on all Cisco switches, and the base MAC address. The bridge with the lowest bridge ID becomes the root bridge in the network. Once the root bridge is established, every other switch must make a single path to it. Most networks benefit by forcing a specific bridge or switch to be on the root bridge by setting its bridge priority lower than the default value.

Port cost Port cost determines the best path when multiple links are used between two switches. The cost of a link is determined by the bandwidth of a link, and this path cost is the deciding factor used by every bridge to find the most efficient path to the root bridge.

Path cost A switch may encounter one or more switches on its path to the root bridge, and there may be more than one possible path. All unique paths are analyzed individually, and a path cost is calculated for each unique path by adding the individual port costs encountered on the way to the root bridge.

Bridge Port Roles

STP uses roles to determine how a port on a switch will act within the spanning-tree algorithm.

Root port The root port is the link with the lowest path cost to the root bridge. If more than one link connects to the root bridge, then a port cost is found by checking the bandwidth of each link. The lowest-cost port becomes the root port. When multiple links connect to the same device, the port connected to the lowest port number on the upstream switch will be the one that's used. The root bridge can never have a root port designation, whereas every other switch in a network must have one and only one root port.

Designated port A *designated port* is one that's been determined to have the best (lowest) cost to get to on a given network segment, compared to other ports on that segment. A designated port will be marked as a forwarding port, and you can have only one forwarding port per network segment.

Non-designated port A *non-designated port* is one with a higher cost than the designated port. These are basically the ones left over after the root ports and designated ports have been determined. Non-designated ports are put in blocking or discarding mode—they are not forwarding ports!

Forwarding port A forwarding port forwards frames and will be either a root port or a designated port.

Blocked port A blocked port won't forward frames to prevent loops. A blocked port will still always listen to BPDU frames from neighbor switches, but it will drop any and all other frames received and will never transmit a frame.

Alternate port This corresponds to the blocking state of 802.1d and is a term used with the newer 802.1w (Cisco Rapid Spanning Tree Protocol). An alternative port is located on a switch connected to a LAN segment with two or more switches connected, and one of the other switches holds the designated port.

Backup port This corresponds to the blocking state of 802.1d and is a term now used with the newer 802.1w. A backup port is connected to a LAN segment where another port on that switch is acting as the designated port.

Spanning-Tree Port States

So, you plug your host into a switch port, the light turns amber, and your host doesn't get a DHCP address from the server. You wait and wait, and finally the light goes green after almost a full minute—that's an eternity in today's networks! This is the STA transitioning through the different port states verifying that you didn't create a loop with the device you just plugged in. STP would rather time out your new host than allow a loop into the network because that would effectively bring your network to its knees. Let's talk about the transition states; then, later in this chapter, we'll talk about how to speed up this process.

The ports on a bridge or switch running IEEE 802.1d STP can transition through five different states:

Disabled (technically, not a transition state) A port in the administratively disabled state doesn't participate in frame forwarding or STP. A port in the disabled state is virtually nonoperational.

Blocking As I mentioned, a blocked port won't forward frames; it just listens to BPDUs. The purpose of the blocking state is to prevent the use of looped paths. All ports are in blocking state by default when the switch is powered up.

Listening This port listens to BPDUs to make sure no loops occur on the network before passing data frames. A port in listening state prepares to forward data frames without populating the MAC address table.

Learning The switch port listens to BPDUs and learns all the paths in the switched network. A port in learning state populates the MAC address table but still doesn't forward data frames. Forward delay refers to the time it takes to transition a port from listening to learning mode, or from learning to forwarding mode, which is set to 15 seconds by default and can be seen in the `show spanning-tree` output.

Forwarding This port sends and receives all data frames on the bridged port. If the port is still a designated or root port at the end of the learning state, it will enter the forwarding state.

NOTE

Switches populate the MAC address table in learning and forwarding modes only.

Switch ports are most often in either the blocking or forwarding state. A forwarding port is typically the one that's been determined to have the lowest (best) cost to the root bridge. But when and if the network experiences a topology change due to a failed link or because someone has added in a new switch, you'll see the ports on a switch transitioning through listening and learning states.

As I said earlier, blocking ports is a strategy for preventing network loops. Once a switch determines the best path to the root bridge for its root port and any designated ports, all other redundant ports will be in blocking mode. Blocked ports can still receive BPDUs—they just don't send out any frames.

If a switch determines that a blocked port should become the designated or root port because of a topology change, it will go into listening mode and check all BPDUs it receives to make sure it won't create a loop once the port moves into forwarding mode.

Convergence

Convergence occurs when all ports on bridges and switches have transitioned to either forwarding or blocking modes. No data will be forwarded until convergence is complete. Yes—you read that right: when STP is converging, all host data stops transmitting through the switches! So, if you want to remain on speaking terms with your network's users, or remain employed for any length of time, you must make sure that your switched network is physically designed really well so that STP can converge quickly!

Convergence is vital because it ensures that all devices have a coherent database. And making sure this happens efficiently will definitely require your time and attention. The original STP (802.1d) takes 50 seconds to go from blocking to forwarding mode by default, and I don't recommend changing the default STP timers. You can adjust those timers for a large network, but the better solution is simply to opt out of using 802.1d at all! We'll get to the various STP versions in a minute.

Link Costs

Now that you know about the different port roles and states, you need to really understand all about path costs before we put this all together. Port cost is based on the speed of the link, and Table 1.1 breaks down the need-to-know path costs for you. Port cost is the cost of a single link, whereas path cost is the sum of the various port costs to the root bridge.

TABLE 1.1 IEEE STP link costs

Speed	Cost
10 Mb/s	100
100 Mb/s	19
1000 Mb/s	4
10,000 Mb/s	2

These costs will be used in the STP calculations to choose a single root port on each bridge. You absolutely need to memorize this table, but no worries—I'll guide you through lots of examples in this chapter to help you do that quite easily!

Now it's time to take everything we've learned so far and put it all together.

Spanning-Tree Operations

Let's start neatly summarizing what you've learned so far using the simple three-switch network connected together as shown in Figure 1.3.

FIGURE 1.3 STP operations

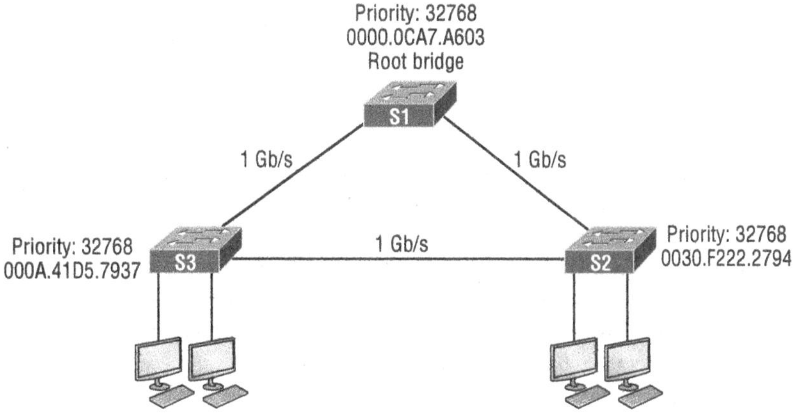

Basically, STP's job is to find all the links in the network and shut down any redundant ones, thereby preventing network loops from occurring. It achieves this by first electing a root bridge that will have all ports forwarding and will also act as a point of reference for all other devices within the STP domain.

In Figure 1.4, S1 has been elected the root bridge based on bridge ID. Because the priorities are all equal to 32,768, we'll compare MAC addresses and find that the MAC address of S1 is lower than that of S2 and S3, meaning that S1 has a better bridge ID.

Once all switches agree on the root bridge, they must then determine their one and only root port—the single path to the root bridge. It's really important to remember that a bridge can go through many other bridges to get to the root, so it's not always the shortest path that will be chosen. That role will be given to the port that happens to offer the fastest, highest bandwidth. Figure 1.4 shows the root ports for both non-root bridges (the RP signifies a root port, and the F signifies a designated forwarding port).

Looking at the cost of each link, it's clear why S2 and S3 are using their directly connected links because a gigabit link has a cost of 4. For example, if S3 chose the path through S2 as its root port, we'd have to add up each port cost along the way to the root, which would be 4 + 4 for a total cost of 8.

FIGURE 1.4 STP operations

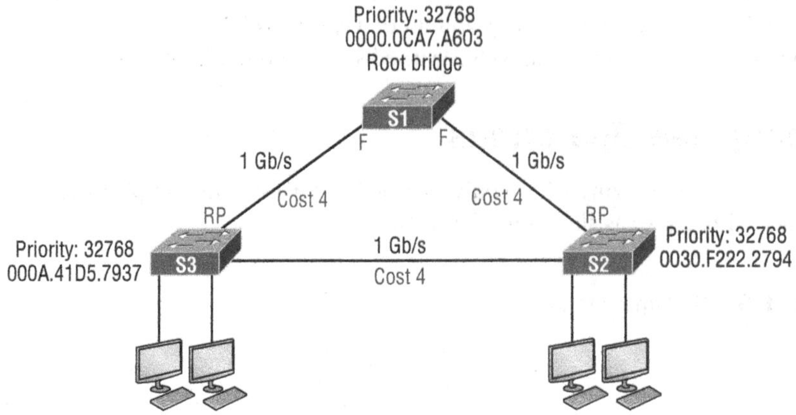

Every port on the root bridge is a designated, or forwarding, port for a segment, and after the dust settles on all other non-root bridges, any port connection between switches that isn't either a root port or a designated port will predictably become a non-designated port. These will again be put into the blocking state to prevent switching loops.

At this point, we have our root bridge with all ports in forwarding state and we've found our root ports for each non-root bridge. Now the only thing left to do is to choose the one forwarding port on the segment between S2 and S3. Both bridges can't be forwarding on a segment because that's exactly how we would end up with loops. So, based on the bridge ID, the port with the best and lowest would become the only bridge forwarding on that segment, with the one having the highest, worst bridge ID put into blocking mode. Figure 1.5 shows the network after STP has converged.

FIGURE 1.5 STP operations

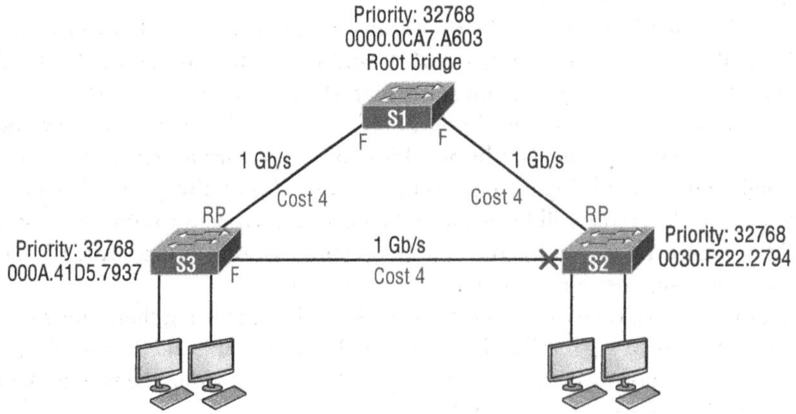

Because S3 had a lower bridge ID (better), S2's port went into blocking mode. Let's discuss the root bridge election process more completely now.

Selecting the Root Bridge

The bridge ID is used to elect the root bridge in the STP domain and to determine the root port for each of the remaining devices when there's more than one potential root port available because they have equal-cost paths. This key bridge ID is 8 bytes long and includes both the priority and the MAC address of the device, as illustrated in Figure 1.6. Remember—the default priority on all devices running the IEEE STP version is 32,768.

FIGURE 1.6 STP operations

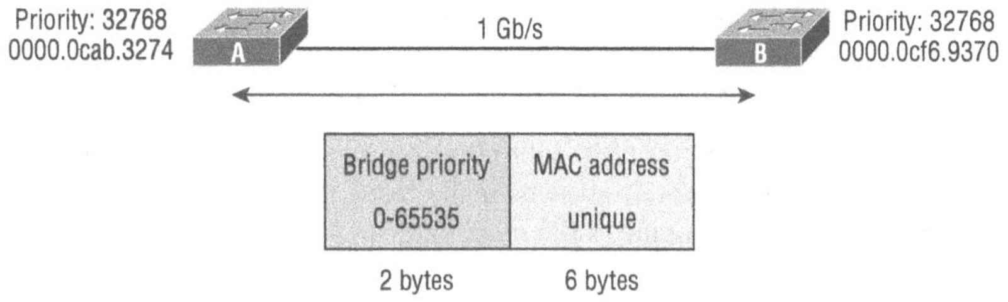

So, to determine the root bridge, you combine the priority of each bridge with its MAC address. If two switches or bridges happen to have the same priority value, the MAC address becomes the tiebreaker for figuring out which one has the lowest and, therefore, best ID. This means that because the two switches in Figure 1.6 are both using the default priority of 32,768, the MAC address will be the determining factor instead. And because Switch A's MAC address is 0000.0cab.3274 and Switch B's MAC address is 0000.0cf6.9370, Switch A wins and will become the root bridge. A really easy way to figure out the lowest MAC address is to just start reading from the left toward the right until you find a lesser value. For Switch A, I only needed to get to 0000.0ca before stopping. Switch A wins because switch B is 0000.0cf. Never forget that the lower value is always the better one when it comes to electing a root bridge!

I want to point out that prior to the election of the root bridge, BPDUs are sent every 2 seconds out all active ports on a bridge/switch by default, and they're received and processed by all bridges. The root bridge is elected based on this information. You can change the bridge's ID by lowering its priority so that it will become a root bridge automatically. Being able to do that is important in a large switched network because it ensures that the best paths will actually be the ones chosen. Efficiency is always awesome in networking!

Types of Spanning-Tree Protocols

There are several varieties of spanning-tree protocols in use today:

IEEE 802.1d The original standard for bridging and STP, which is really slow but requires very few bridge resources. It's also referred to as Common Spanning Tree (CST).

PVST+ The Cisco proprietary enhancement for STP that provides a separate 802.1d spanning-tree instance for each VLAN. Know that this is just as slow as the CST protocol, but with it, we get to have multiple root bridges. This creates more efficiency of the links in the network, but it does use more bridge resources than CST does.

IEEE 802.1w Also called Rapid Spanning Tree Protocol (RSTP), this iteration enhanced the BPDU exchange and paved the way for much faster network convergence, but it still only allows for one root bridge per network like CST. The bridge resources used with RSTP are higher than CST's but less than PVST+.

Rapid PVST+ Cisco's version of RSTP that also uses PVST+ and provides a separate instance of 802.1w per VLAN. It gives us really fast convergence times and optimal traffic flow but predictably requires the most CPU and memory of all.

Common Spanning Tree

If you're running CST in your switched network with redundant links, there will be an election to choose what STP considers to be the best root bridge for your network. That switch will also become the root for all VLANs in your network, and all bridges in your network will create a single path to it. You can manually override this selection and pick whichever bridge you want if it makes sense for your particular network.

Figure 1.7 shows how a typical root bridge would look on your switched network when running CST.

FIGURE 1.7 Common STP example

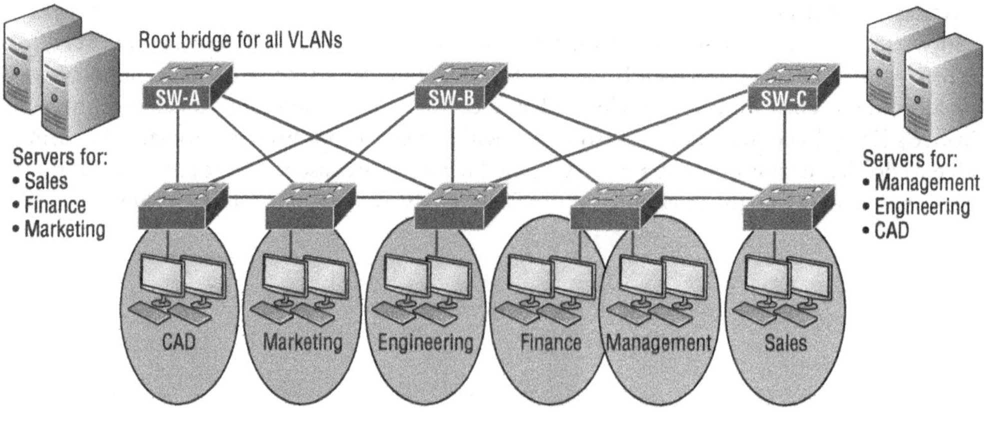

Notice that switch A is the root bridge for all VLANs even though it's really not the best path for some VLANs because all switches must make a single path to it! This is where Per-VLAN Spanning Tree+ (PVST+) comes into play. Because it allows for a separate instance of STP for each VLAN, it frees up the individual selection of the most optimal path.

Per-VLAN Spanning Tree+

PVST+ is a Cisco proprietary extension to 801.2d STP that provides a separate 802.1 spanning-tree instance for each VLAN configured on your switches. All of Cisco's proprietary extensions were created to improve convergence times, which is 50 seconds by default. Cisco IOS switches run 802.1d PVST+ by default, which means you'll have optimal path selection, but the convergence time will still be slow.

Creating a per-VLAN STP instance for each VLAN is worth the increased CPU and memory requirements because it allows for per-VLAN root bridges. This feature allows the STP tree to be optimized for the traffic of each VLAN by allowing you to configure the root bridge in the center of each. Figure 1.8 shows how PVST+ would look in an optimized switched network with multiple redundant links.

FIGURE 1.8 PVST+ provides efficient root bridge selection.

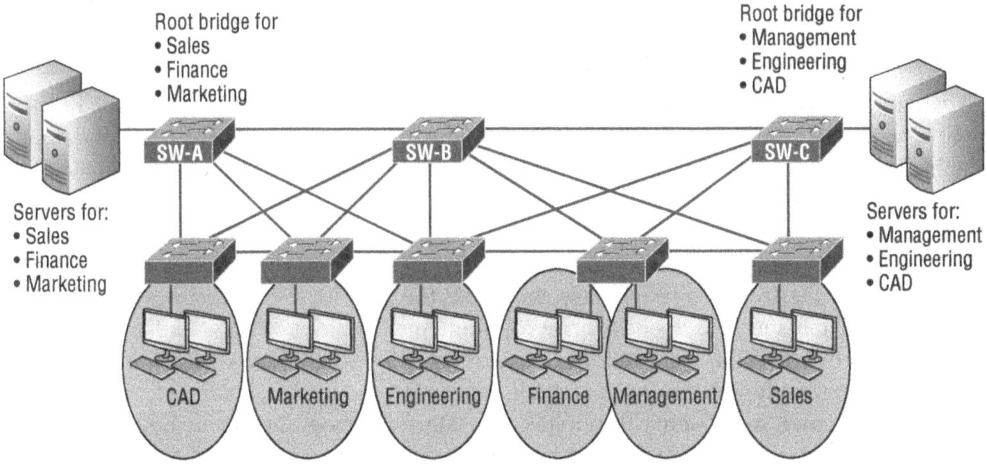

This root bridge placement clearly enables faster convergence as well as optimal path determination. This version's convergence is really similar to 802.1 CST's, which has one instance of STP, no matter how many VLANs you have configured on your network. The difference is that with PVST+, convergence happens on a per-VLAN basis, with each VLAN running its own instance of STP. Figure 1.8 shows us that we now have a nice, efficient root bridge selection for each VLAN.

To allow for the PVST+ to operate, there's a field inserted into the BPDU to accommodate the extended system ID so that PVST+ can have a root bridge configured on a per-STP instance, as shown in Figure 1.9. The bridge ID actually becomes smaller—only 4 bits—which means that we would configure the bridge priority in blocks of 4,096 rather than in increments of 1 as we did with CST. The extended system ID (VLAN ID) is a 12-bit field, and we can even see what this field is carrying via `show spanning-tree` command output, which I'll show you soon.

FIGURE 1.9 PVST+ unique bridge ID

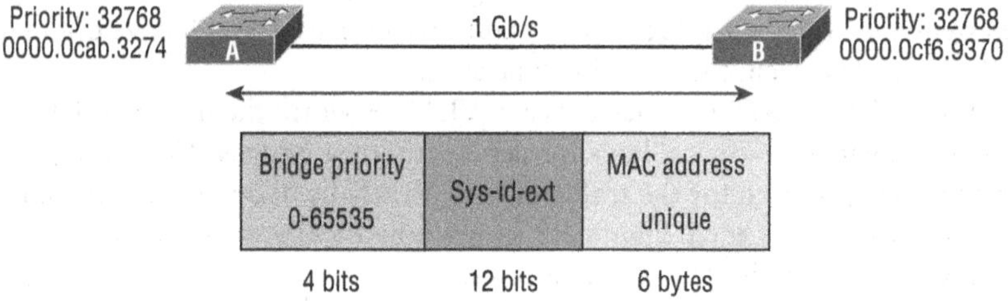

But still, isn't there a way we can do better than a 50-second convergence time? That's a really long time in today's world!

Rapid Spanning Tree Protocol 802.1w

Wouldn't it be wonderful to have a solid STP configuration running on your switched network, regardless of switch type, and still have all the features we just discussed built in and enabled on every one of your switches, too? RSTP serves up exactly this amazing capacity right to our networking table!

Cisco created proprietary extensions to "fix" all the sinkholes and liabilities the IEEE 802.1d standard threw at us, with the main drawback being that they require extra configuration because they're Cisco proprietary. But RSTP, the new 802.1w standard, brings us most of the patches needed in one concise solution. Again, efficiency is golden!

RSTP, or IEEE 802.1w, is essentially an evolution of STP that allows for much faster convergence. But even though it does address all the convergence issues, it still only permits a single STP instance, so it doesn't help to take the edge off suboptimal traffic flow issues. And as I mentioned, to support that faster convergence, the CPU usage and memory demands are slightly higher than CST's. The good news is that Cisco IOS can run the Rapid PVST+ protocol—a Cisco enhancement of RSTP that provides a separate 802.1w spanning-tree instance for each VLAN configured within the network. But all that power needs fuel, and although this version addresses both convergence and traffic flow issues, it also demands the most CPU and memory of all solutions. And it's also good news that Cisco's newest switches don't have a problem with this protocol running on them.

NOTE Keep in mind that Cisco documentation may say STP 802.1d and RSTP 802.1w, but it is referring to the PVST+ enhancement of each version.

Understand that RSTP wasn't meant to be something completely new and different. The protocol is more of an evolution than an innovation of the 802.1d standard, which offers faster convergence whenever a topology change occurs. Backward compatibility was a must when 802.1w was created.

So, RSTP helps with convergence issues that were the bane of traditional STP. Rapid PVST+ is based on the 802.1w standard in the same way that PVST+ is based on 802.1d. The operation of Rapid PVST+ is simply a separate instance of 802.1w for each VLAN. Here's a list to clarify how this all breaks down:

- RSTP speeds the recalculation of the spanning tree when the layer 2 network topology changes.
- It's an IEEE standard that redefines STP port roles, states, and BPDUs.
- RSTP is extremely proactive and very quick, so it doesn't need the 802.1d delay timers.
- RSTP (802.1w) supersedes 802.1d while remaining backward compatible.
- Much of the 802.1d terminology and most parameters remain unchanged.
- 802.1w is capable of reverting to 802.1d to interoperate with traditional switches on a per-port basis.

And to clear up confusion, there are also five terminology adjustments between 802.1d's five port states to 802.1w's, compared here, respectively:

802.1d state	**802.1w state**	
Disabled	=	Discarding
Blocking	=	Discarding
Listening	=	Discarding
Learning	=	Learning
Forwarding	=	Forwarding

Make note of the fact that RSTP basically just goes from discarding to learning to forwarding, whereas 802.1d requires five states to transition.

The task of determining the root bridge, root ports, and designated ports hasn't changed from 802.1d to RSTP, and understanding the cost of each link is still key to making these decisions well. Let's take a look at an example of how to determine ports using the revised IEEE cost specifications in Figure 1.10.

FIGURE 1.10 RSTP example 1

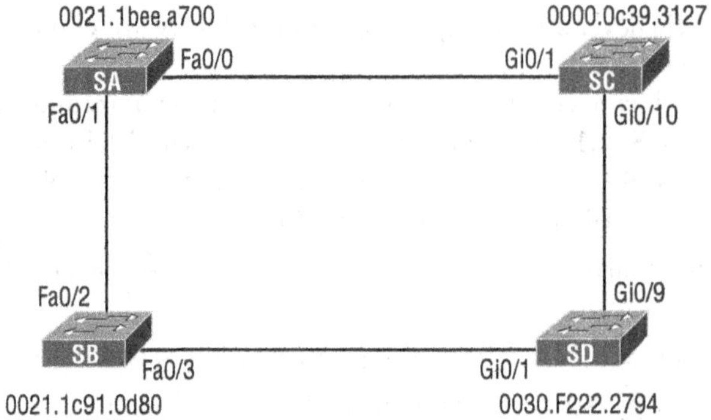

Can you figure out which is the root bridge? How about which port is the root and which ones are designated? Well, because SC has the lowest MAC address, it becomes the root bridge, and because all ports on a root bridge are forwarding designated ports, well, that's easy, right? Ports Gi0/1 and Gi0/10 become designated forwarding ports on SC.

But which one would be the root port for SA? To figure that out, we must first find the port cost for the direct link between SA and SC. Even though the root bridge (SC) has a Gigabit Ethernet port, it's running at 100 Mbps because SA's port is a 100-Mbps port, giving it a cost of 19. If the paths between SA and SC were both Gigabit Ethernet, their costs would only be 4, but because they're running 100 Mbps links instead, the cost jumps to a whopping 19!

Can you find SD's root port? A quick glance at the link between SC and SD tells us that's a Gigabit Ethernet link with a cost of 4, so the root port for SD would be its GI0/9 port.

The cost of the link between SB and SD is also 19 because it's also a Fast Ethernet link, bringing the full cost from SB to SD to the root (SC) to a total cost of 19 + 4 = 23. If SB were to go through SA to get to SC, then the cost would be 19 + 19, or 38, so the root port of SB becomes the Fa0/3 port.

The root port for SA would be the Fa0/0 port because that's a direct link with a cost of 19. Going through SB to SD would be 19 + 19 + 4 = 42, so we'll use that as a backup link for SA to get to the root, just in case we need to.

Now, all we need is a forwarding port on the link between SA and SB. Because SA has the lowest bridge ID, Fa0/1 on SA wins that role. Also, the Gi0/1 port on SD would become a designated forwarding port. This is because the SB Fa0/3 port is a designed root port and you must have a forwarding port on a network segment! This leaves us with the Fa0/2 port on SB. Because it isn't a root port or designated forwarding port, it will be placed into blocking mode, which will prevent looks in our network.

Let's take a look at this example network when it has converged in Figure 1.11.

FIGURE 1.11 RSTP example 1 answer

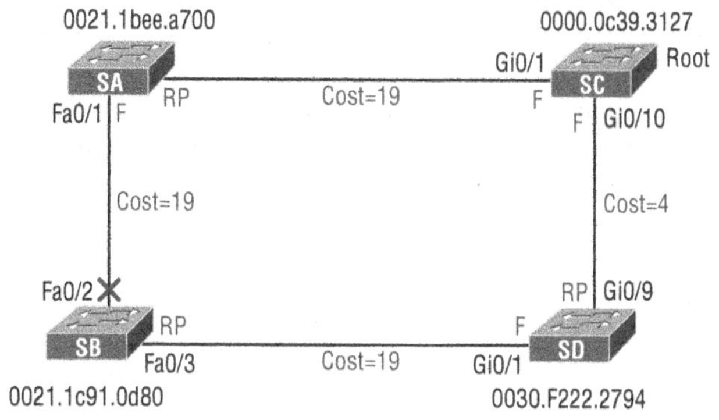

If this isn't clear or still seems confusing, just remember to always tackle this process following these three steps:

1. Find your root bridge by looking at bridge IDs.
2. Determine your root ports by finding the lowest path cost to the root bridge.
3. Find your designated ports by looking at bridge IDs.

As usual, the best way to nail this down is to practice, so let's explore another scenario, shown in Figure 1.12.

FIGURE 1.12 RSTP example 2

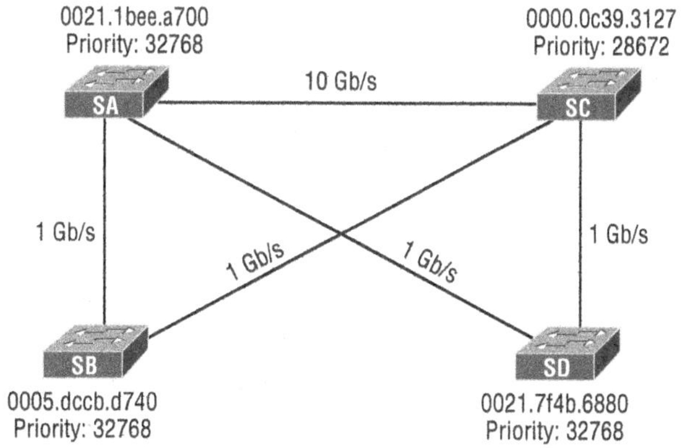

So, which bridge is our root bridge? Checking priorities first tells us that SC is the root bridge, which means all ports on SC are designated forwarding ports. Now, we need to find our root ports.

We can quickly see that SA has a 10-gigabit port to SC, so that would be a port cost of 2, and it would be our root port. SD has a direct Gigabit Ethernet port to SC, so that would be the root port for SD with a port cost of 4. SB's best path would also be the direct Gigabit Ethernet port to SC with a port cost of 4.

Now that we've determined our root bridge and found the three root ports we need, we've got to find our designated ports next. Whatever is left over simply goes into the discarding role. Let's take a look at Figure 1.13 and see what we have.

FIGURE 1.13 RSTP example 2, answer 1

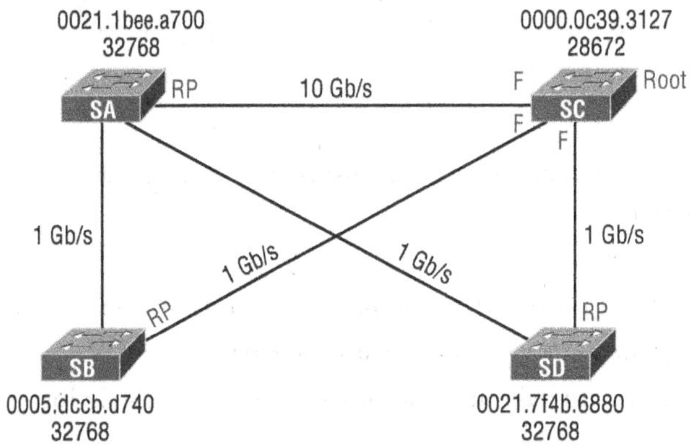

All right, it looks like there are two links to choose between to find one designated port per segment. Let's start with the link between SA and SD. Which one has the best bridge ID? They're both running the same default priority, so by looking at the MAC address, we can see that SD has the better bridge ID (lower), so the SA port toward SD will go into a discarding role—or will it? The SD port will go into discarding mode because the link from SA to the root has the lowest accumulated path costs to the root bridge, and that is used before the bridge ID in this circumstance. It makes sense to let the bridge with the fastest path to the root bridge be a designated forwarding port. Let's talk about this in a little more depth.

As you know, once your root bridge and root ports have been chosen, you're left with finding your designated ports. Anything left over goes into the discarding role. But how are the designated ports chosen? Is it just bridge ID? Here are the rules:

1. To choose the switch that will forward on the segment, we select the switch with the lowest accumulated path cost to the root bridge. We want the fast path to the root bridge.
2. If there is a tie on the accumulated path cost from both switches to the root bridge, then we'll use bridge ID, which was what we used in our previous example (but not with this latest RSTP example; not with a 10-Gigabit Ethernet link to the root bridge available!).
3. Port priorities can be set manually if we want a specific port chosen. The default priority is 32, but we can lower that if needed.

4. If there are two links between switches, and the bridge ID and priority are tied, the port with the lowest number will be chosen—for example, Fa0/1 would be chosen over Fa0/2.

Let's take a look at our answer now, but before we do, can you find the forwarding port between SA and SB? Take a look at Figure 1.14 for the answer.

FIGURE 1.14 RSTP example 2, answer 2

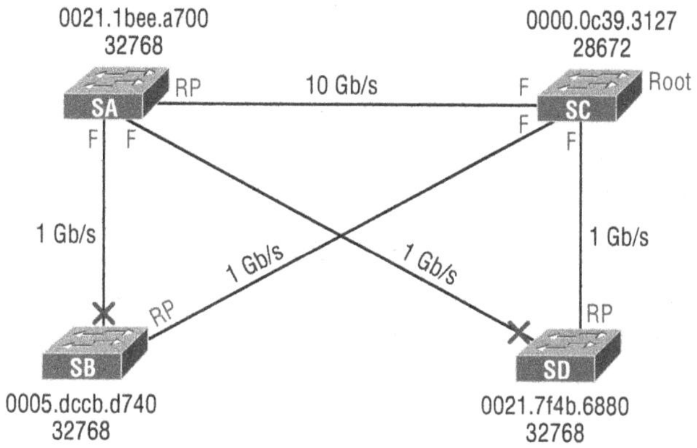

Again, to get the right answer to this question, we're going to let the switch on the network segment with the lowest accumulated path cost to the root bridge forward on that segment. This is definitely SA, meaning the SB port goes into discarding role—not so hard at all!

Modifying and Verifying the Bridge ID

To verify the spanning tree on a Cisco switch, just use the command `show spanning-tree`. From its output, we can determine our root bridge, priorities, root ports, and designated and blocking/discarding ports.

Let's use the same simple three-switch network we used earlier as the base to play around with the configuration of STP. Figure 1.15 shows the network we'll work with in this section.

FIGURE 1.15 Our simple three-switch network

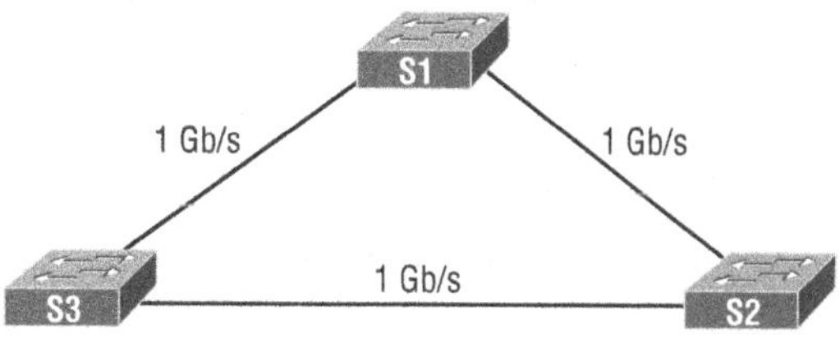

Let's start by taking a look at the output from S1:

```
S1#sh spanning-tree vlan 1
VLAN0001
  Spanning tree enabled protocol ieee
  Root ID    Priority    32769
             Address     0001.42A7.A603
             This bridge is the root
             Hello Time  2 sec  Max Age 20 sec  Forward Delay 15 sec

  Bridge ID  Priority    32769  (priority 32768 sys-id-ext 1)
             Address     0001.42A7.A603 him
             Hello Time  2 sec  Max Age 20 sec  Forward Delay 15 sec
             Aging Time  20

Interface        Role Sts Cost      Prio.Nbr Type
---------------- ---- --- --------- -------- --------------------------------
Gi1/1            Desg FWD 4         128.25   P2p
Gi1/2            Desg FWD 4         128.26   P2p
```

First, we can see that we're running the IEEE 802.1d STP version by default, and don't forget that this is really 802.1d PVST+! Looking at the output, we can see that S1 is the root bridge for VLAN 1. When you use this command, the top information is about the root bridge, and the Bridge ID output refers to the bridge you're looking at. In this example, they are one and the same. Notice the `sys-id-ext 1 (for VLAN 1)`. This is the 12-bit PVST+ field that is placed into the BPDU so it can carry multiple-VLAN information. You add the priority and `sys-id-ext` to come up with the true priority for the VLAN. We can also see from the output that both Gigabit Ethernet interfaces are designated forwarding ports. You will not see a blocked/discarding port on a root bridge. Now, let's take a look at S3's output:

```
S3#sh spanning-tree
VLAN0001
  Spanning tree enabled protocol ieee
  Root ID    Priority    32769
             Address     0001.42A7.A603
             Cost        4
             Port        26(GigabitEthernet1/2)
             Hello Time  2 sec  Max Age 20 sec  Forward Delay 15 sec

  Bridge ID  Priority    32769  (priority 32768 sys-id-ext 1)
             Address     000A.41D5.7937
             Hello Time  2 sec  Max Age 20 sec  Forward Delay 15 sec
             Aging Time  20

Interface        Role Sts Cost      Prio.Nbr Type
---------------- ---- --- --------- -------- --------------------------------
Gi1/1            Desg FWD 4         128.25   P2p
Gi1/2            Root FWD 4         128.26   P2p
```

Looking at the Root ID, it's easy to see that S3 isn't the root bridge, but the output tells us it's a cost of 4 to get to the root bridge and also that it's located out port 26 of the switch (Gi1/2). This tells us that the root bridge is one Gigabit Ethernet link away, which we already know is S1, but we can confirm this with the `show cdp neighbors` command:

```
Switch#sh cdp nei
Capability Codes: R - Router, T - Trans Bridge, B - Source Route Bridge
                  S - Switch, H - Host, I - IGMP, r - Repeater, P - Phone
Device ID     Local Intrfce    Holdtme    Capability   Platform    Port ID
S3            Gig 1/1           135           S        2960        Gig 1/1
S1            Gig 1/2           135           S        2960        Gig 1/1
```

That's how simple it is to find your root bridge if you don't have the nice figure we do. Use the `show spanning-tree` command, find your root port, and then use the `show cdp neighbors` command. Let's see what S2's output has to tell us now:

```
S2#sh spanning-tree
VLAN0001
  Spanning tree enabled protocol ieee
  Root ID    Priority    32769
             Address     0001.42A7.A603
             Cost        4
             Port        26(GigabitEthernet1/2)
             Hello Time  2 sec  Max Age 20 sec  Forward Delay 15 sec

  Bridge ID  Priority    32769  (priority 32768 sys-id-ext 1)
             Address     0030.F222.2794
             Hello Time  2 sec  Max Age 20 sec  Forward Delay 15 sec
             Aging Time  20

Interface        Role Sts Cost      Prio.Nbr Type
---------------- ---- --- --------- -------- --------------------------------
Gi1/1            Altn BLK 4         128.25   P2p
Gi1/2            Root FWD 4         128.26   P2p
```

We're certainly not looking at a root bridge because we're seeing a blocked port, which is S2's connection to S3!

Let's have some fun by making S2 the root bridge for VLAN 2 and for VLAN 3. Here's how easy that is to do:

```
S2#sh spanning-tree vlan 2
VLAN0002
  Spanning tree enabled protocol ieee
  Root ID    Priority    32770
             Address     0001.42A7.A603
             Cost        4
             Port        26(GigabitEthernet1/2)
             Hello Time  2 sec  Max Age 20 sec  Forward Delay 15 sec
```

```
  Bridge ID  Priority    32770  (priority 32768 sys-id-ext 2)
             Address     0030.F222.2794
             Hello Time  2 sec  Max Age 20 sec  Forward Delay 15 sec
             Aging Time  20

Interface        Role Sts Cost      Prio.Nbr Type
---------------- ---- --- --------- -------- --------------------------------
Gi1/1            Altn BLK 4         128.25   P2p
Gi1/2            Root FWD 4         128.26   P2p
```

We can see that the root bridge cost is 4, meaning that the root bridge is one gigabit link away. One more key factor I want to talk about before making S2 the root bridge for VLANs 2 and 3 is the `sys-id-ext`, which shows up as 2 in this output because this output is for VLAN 2. This `sys-id-ext` is added to the bridge priority, which, in this case, is 32768 + 2, which makes the priority 32770. Now that you understand what that output is telling us let's make S2 the root bridge:

```
S2(config)#spanning-tree vlan 2 ?
  priority  Set the bridge priority for the spanning tree
  root      Configure switch as root
  <cr>
S2(config)#spanning-tree vlan 2 priority ?
  <0-61440>  bridge priority in increments of 4096
S2(config)#spanning-tree vlan 2 priority 16384
```

You can set the priority to any value from 0 through 61440 in increments of 4096. Setting it to zero (0) means that the switch will always be a root as long as it has a lower MAC address than another switch that also has its bridge ID set to 0. If you want to set a switch to be the root bridge for every VLAN in your network, then you have to change the priority for each VLAN, with 0 being the lowest priority you can use. But trust me—it's never a good idea to set all switches to a priority of 0!

Furthermore, you don't actually need to change priorities because there is yet another way to configure the root bridge. Take a look:

```
S2(config)#spanning-tree vlan 3 root ?
  primary    Configure this switch as primary root for this spanning tree
  secondary  Configure switch as secondary root
S2(config)#spanning-tree vlan 3 root primary
```

Notice that you can set a bridge to either primary or secondary—very cool! Let's check to see if S2 is actually the root bridge for VLANs 2 and 3 now:

```
S2#sh spanning-tree vlan 2
VLAN0002
  Spanning tree enabled protocol ieee
  Root ID    Priority    16386
```

```
            Address     0030.F222.2794
            This bridge is the root
            Hello Time  2 sec  Max Age 20 sec  Forward Delay 15 sec

  Bridge ID Priority    16386  (priority 16384 sys-id-ext 2)
            Address     0030.F222.2794
            Hello Time  2 sec  Max Age 20 sec  Forward Delay 15 sec
            Aging Time  20

Interface        Role Sts Cost      Prio.Nbr Type
---------------- ---- --- --------- -------- --------------------------------
Gi1/1            Desg FWD 4         128.25   P2p
Gi1/2            Desg FWD 4         128.26   P2p
```

Nice—S2 is the root bridge for VLAN 2, with a priority of 16386 (16384 + 2). Let's take a look to see the root bridge for VLAN 3. I'll use a different command for that this time. Check it out:

```
S2#sh spanning-tree summary
Switch is in pvst mode
Root bridge for: VLAN0002 VLAN0003
Extended system ID           is enabled
Portfast Default             is disabled
PortFast BPDU Guard Default  is disabled
Portfast BPDU Filter Default is disabled
Loopguard Default            is disabled
EtherChannel misconfig guard is disabled
UplinkFast                   is disabled
BackboneFast                 is disabled
Configured Pathcost method used is short

Name                   Blocking Listening Learning Forwarding STP Active
---------------------- -------- --------- -------- ---------- ----------
VLAN0001                      1         0        0          1          2
VLAN0002                      0         0        0          2          2
VLAN0003                      0         0        0          2          2
---------------------- -------- --------- -------- ---------- ----------
3 vlans                       1         0        0          5          6
```

The preceding output tells us that S2 is the root for the two VLANs, but we can see we have a blocked port for VLAN 1 on S2, so it's not the root bridge for VLAN 1. This is because there's another bridge with a better bridge ID for VLAN 1 than S2's.

One last burning question: how do you enable RSTP on a Cisco switch? Well, doing that is actually the easiest part of this chapter! Take a look:

```
S2(config)#spanning-tree mode rapid-pvst
```

Is that really all there is to it? Yes, because it's a global command, not per VLAN. Let's verify we're running RSTP now:

```
S2#sh spanning-tree
VLAN0001
  Spanning tree enabled protocol rstp
  Root ID     Priority    32769
              Address     0001.42A7.A603
              Cost        4
              Port        26(GigabitEthernet1/2)
              Hello Time  2 sec  Max Age 20 sec  Forward Delay 15 sec
[output cut
S2#sh spanning-tree summary
Switch is in rapid-pvst mode
Root bridge for: VLAN0002 VLAN0003
```

Looks like we're set! We're running RSTP, S1 is our root bridge for VLAN 1, and S2 is the root bridge for VLANs 2 and 3. I know this doesn't seem hard, and it really isn't, but you still need to practice what we've covered so far in this chapter to really get your skills solid!

Spanning-Tree Failure Consequences

Clearly, there will be consequences when a routing protocol fails on a single router, but mainly, you'll just lose connectivity to the networks directly connected to that router, and it usually does not affect the rest of your network. This definitely makes it easier to troubleshoot and fix the issue!

There are two failure types with STP. One of them causes the same type of issue I mentioned with a routing protocol: when certain ports have been placed in a blocking state, they should be forwarding on a network segment instead. This situation makes the network segment unusable, but the rest of the network will still be working. But what happens when blocked ports are placed into forwarding state when they should be blocking? Let's work through this second failure issue now, using the same layout we used in the last section. Let's start with Figure 1.16 and then find out what happens when STP fails. Squeamish readers, be warned—this isn't pretty!

Looking at Figure 1.16, what do you think will happen if SD transitions its blocked port to the forwarding state? Clearly, the consequences to the entire network will be pretty

FIGURE 1.16 STP stopping loops

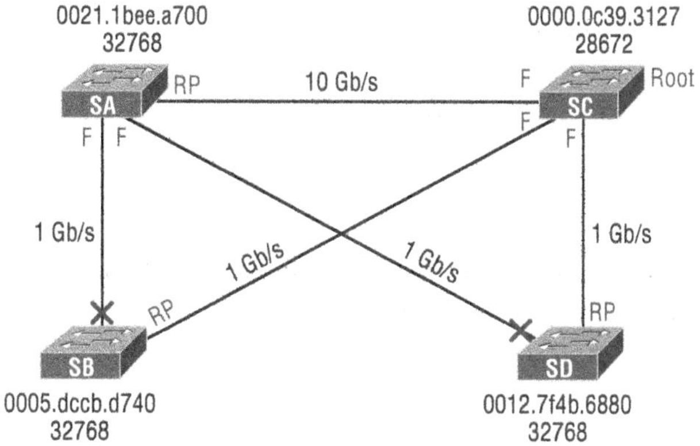

devastating! Frames that already had a destination address recorded in the MAC address table of the switches are forwarded to the port they're associated with; however, any broadcast, multicast, and unicasts not in the CAM are now in an endless loop.

Figure 1.17 shows us the carnage—when you see all the lights on each port blinking super-fast amber/green, this means serious errors are occurring, and lots of them!

FIGURE 1.17 STP failure

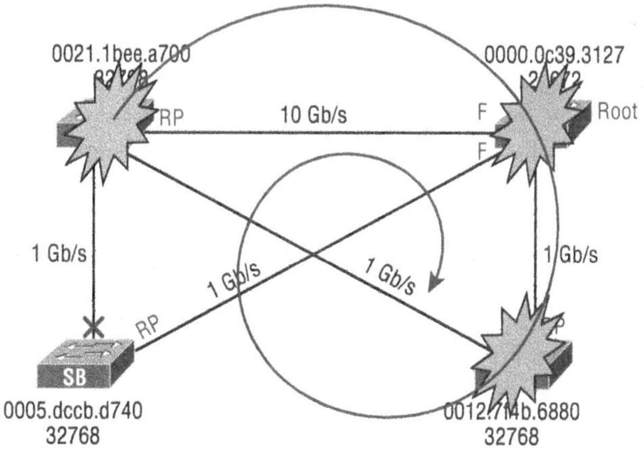

As frames begin building up on the network, the bandwidth starts getting saturated. The CPU percentage goes way up on the switches until they'll just give up and stop working completely, and all this within a few seconds!

Here is a list of the problems that will occur in a failed STP network that you must be aware of and be able to find in your production network—and, of course, you must know them to meet the exam objectives:

- The load on all links begins increasing, and more and more frames enter the loop. Remember, this loop affects all the other links in the network because these frames are always flooded out all ports. This scenario is a little less dire if the loop occurs within a single VLAN. In that case, the snag will be isolated to ports only in that VLAN membership, plus all trunk links that carry information for that VLAN.
- If you have more than one loop, traffic will increase on the switches because all the circling frames actually get duplicated. Switches basically receive a frame, make a copy of it, and send it out all ports. And they do this over and over and over again with the same frame, as well as for any new ones!
- The MAC address table is now completely unstable. It no longer knows where any source MAC address hosts are actually located because the same source address comes in via multiple ports on the switch.
- With the overwhelmingly high load on the links and the CPUs, now possibly at 100% or close to that, the devices become unresponsive, making it impossible to troubleshoot—it's a terrible thing!

At this point, your only option is to systematically remove every redundant link between switches until you can find the source of the problem. And don't freak because, eventually, your ravaged network will calm down and come back to life after STP converges. Your fried switches will regain consciousness, but the network will need some serious therapy, so you're not out of the woods yet!

Now is when you start troubleshooting to find out what caused the disaster in the first place. A good strategy is to place the redundant links back into your network one at a time and wait to see when a problem begins to occur. You could have a failing switch port or even a dead switch. Once you've replaced all your redundant links, you need to carefully monitor the network and have a back-out plan to quickly isolate the problem if it reoccurs. You don't want to go through this again!

You're probably wondering how to prevent these STP problems from ever darkening your doorstep in the first place. Well, just hang on because, after the next section, I'll tell you all about EtherChannel, which can stop ports from being placed in the blocked/discarding state on redundant links to save the day! But before we add more links to our switches and then bundle them, let's talk about PortFast.

PortFast and BPDU Guard

If you have a server or other devices connected into your switch that you're totally sure won't create a switching loop if STP is disabled, you can use a Cisco proprietary extension to the 802.1d standard called PortFast on these ports. With this tool, the port won't spend the usual 50 seconds to come up into forwarding mode while STP is converging, which is what makes it so cool.

Because ports will transition from blocking to forwarding state immediately, PortFast can prevent our hosts from being potentially unable to receive a DHCP address due to STP's slow convergence. If the host's DHCP request times out, or if every time you plug a host in, you're just tired of looking at the switch port being amber for almost a minute before it transitions to forwarding state and turns green, PortFast can really help you out!

Figure 1.18 illustrates a network with three switches, each with a trunk to each of the others and a host and server off the S1 switch.

FIGURE 1.18 PortFast

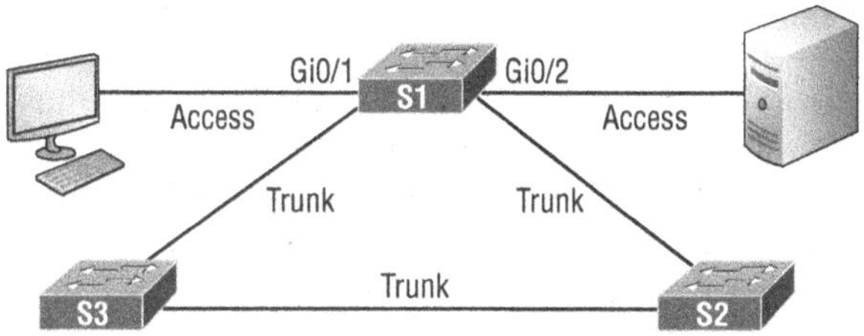

We can use PortFast on the ports on S1 to help them transition to the STP forwarding state immediately upon connecting to the switch.

Here are the commands, first from global config mode—they're pretty simple:

```
S1(config)#spanning-tree portfast ?
  bpdufilter  Enable portfast bdpu filter on this switch
  bpduguard   Enable portfast bpdu guard on this switch
  default     Enable portfast by default on all access ports
```

If you were to type `spanning-tree portfast default`, you would enable all nontrunking ports with PortFast. From interface mode, you can be more specific, which is the better way to go:

```
S1(config-if)#spanning-tree portfast ?
  disable  Disable portfast for this interface
  trunk    Enable portfast on the interface even in trunk mode
  <cr>
```

From interface mode, you can actually configure PortFast on a trunk port, but you would do that only if the port connects to a server or router, not to another switch, so we won't use that here. So, let's take a look at the message I get when I turn on PortFast on an interface Gi0/1:

```
S1#config t
S1#config)#int range gi0/1 - 2
S1(config-if)#spanning-tree portfast
```

```
%Warning: portfast should only be enabled on ports connected to a single
 host. Connecting hubs, concentrators, switches, bridges, etc... to this
 interface  when portfast is enabled can cause temporary bridging loops.
 Use with CAUTION

%Portfast has been configured on GigabitEthernet0/1 but will only
 have an effect when the interface is in a non-trunking mode.
Switch(config-if)#
```

PortFast is enabled on port Gi0/1 and Gi0/2, but notice that you get a pretty long message that's essentially telling you to be careful. This is because when using PortFast, you definitely don't want to create a network loop by plugging another switch or hub into a port that's also configured with PortFast! Why? Because if you let this happen, even though the network may still sort of work, data will pass super slowly, and worse, it could take you a really long time to find the source of the problem, making you very unpopular. So, proceed with caution!

At this juncture, you will be happy to know that there are some safeguard commands to have handy when using PortFast just in case someone causes a loop in a port that's configured with PortFast enabled. Let's talk about a key safeguard command now.

BPDU Guard

If you turn on PortFast for a switch port, it's a good idea to turn on BPDU Guard as well. In fact, it's such a great idea, I personally feel that it should be enabled by default whenever a port is configured with PortFast!

This is because if a switch port that has PortFast enabled receives a BPDU on that port, it will place the port into error disabled (shutdown) state, effectively preventing anyone from accidentally connecting another switch or hub port into a switch port configured with PortFast. Basically, you're preventing (guarding) your network from being severely crippled or even brought down. So, let's configure our S1 interface, which is already configured with PortFast, with BPDU Guard now—it's easy!

Here's how to set it globally:

```
S1(config)# spanning-tree portfast bpduguard default
```

And specifically on an interface:

```
S1(config-if)#spanning-tree bpduguard enable
```

It's important to know that you would only configure this command on your access layer switches—switches where users are directly connected.

Real World Scenario

Hedging My Bets Created Bad Switch Ports During the Super Bowl

A junior admin called me frantically, telling me all switch ports had just gone bad on the core switch, which was located at the data center where I was the lead consultant for a data center upgrade. Now, these things happen, but keep in mind that I just happened to be at a Super Bowl party having a great time watching my favorite team play in the "Big One" when I received this call! So, I took a deep breath to refocus. I needed to find out some key information to determine just how bad the situation really was, and my client was in as big a hurry as I was to get to a solution!

First, I asked the junior admin exactly what he did. Of course, he said, "Nothing, I swear!" I figured that's what he'd say, so I pressed him for more info and finally asked for stats on the switch. The admin told me that all the ports on the 10/100/1000 line card went amber at the same time—finally, some information I could use! I confirmed that, as suspected, these ports trunked to uplink distribution switches. Wow—this was not good!

At this point, though, I found it hard to believe that all 24 ports would suddenly go bad, but it was possible, so I asked if he had a spare card to try. He told me that he had already put in the new card, but the same thing was still happening. Well, okay—it's not the card or the ports, but maybe something happened with the other switches. I knew there were a lot of switches involved, so someone must have screwed something up to make this catastrophe happen! Or, maybe the fiber distribution closet went down somehow. If so, how? Was there a fire in the closet or something? Some serious internal shenanigans would be the only answer if that were the cause!

So, remaining ever-patient (because, to quote Dr. House, "Patients lie"), I again had to ask the admin exactly what he did, and sure enough, he finally admitted that he tried to plug his personal laptop into the core switch so he could watch the Super Bowl—and quickly added, ". . .but that's it, I didn't do anything else!" I'll skip over the fact that this guy was about to have the ugliest Monday ever, but something still didn't make sense, and here's why.

Knowing that the ports on that card would all connect to distribution switches, I configured the ports with PortFast so they wouldn't have to transition through the STP process. And because I wanted to make sure no one plugged a switch into any of those ports, I enabled BPDU Guard on the entire line card.

But a host would not bring down those ports, so I asked him if he had plugged in the laptop directly or used something in between. He admitted that he had indeed used another switch because, it turns out, there were lots of people from the office who wanted to plug into the core switch and watch the game, too. Was he kidding me? The security policy wouldn't allow connecting from their offices, so wouldn't you think they'd consider the core even more off-limits? Some people!

But wait. . . This doesn't explain all ports turning amber, because only the one he plugged into should be doing that. It took me a second, but I figured out what he did and finally got him to confess. When he plugged the switch in, the port turned amber, so he thought it went bad. So, what do you think he did? Well, if at first you don't succeed, try, try again, and that's just what he did—he actually kept trying ports—all 24 of them, to be exact! Now that's what I call determined!

Sad to say, I got back to the party in time just to watch my team lose in the last few minutes. A dark day, indeed!

EtherChannel

Know that almost all Ethernet networks today will typically have multiple links between switches because this kind of design provides redundancy and resiliency. On a physical design that includes multiple links between switches, STP will do its job and put a port or ports into blocking mode. In addition to that, routing protocols like OSPF and EIGRP could see all these redundant links as individual ones, depending on the configuration, which can mean an increase in routing overhead.

We can gain the benefits from multiple links between switches by using port channeling. EtherChannel is a port channel technology that was originally developed by Cisco as a switch-to-switch technique for grouping several Fast Ethernet or Gigabit Ethernet ports into one logical channel.

Also important to note is that once your port channel (EtherChannel) is up and working, layer 2 STP and layer 3 routing protocols will treat those bundled links as a single one, which would stop STP from performing blocking. An additional nice result is that because the routing protocols now only see this as a single link, a single adjacency across the link can be formed—elegant!

Figure 1.19 shows how a network would look if we had four connections between switches before and after configuring port channels.

FIGURE 1.19 Before and after port channels

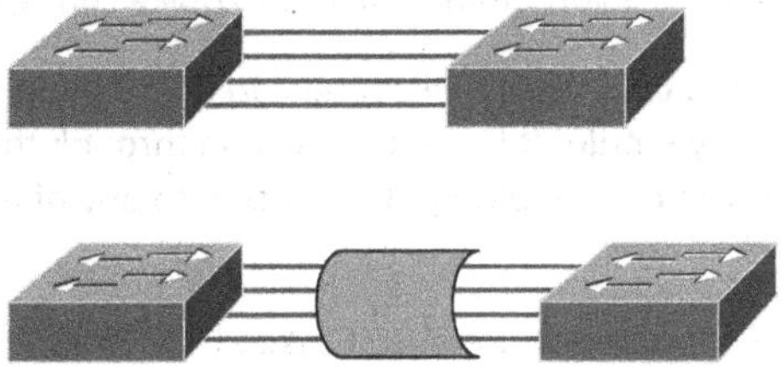

Now as usual, there's the Cisco version and the IEEE version of port channel negotiation protocols to choose from—take your pick. Cisco's version is called Port Aggregation Protocol (PAgP), and the IEEE 802.3ad standard is called Link Aggregation Control Protocol (LACP). Both versions work equally well, but the way you configure each is slightly different. Keep in mind that both PAgP and LACP are negotiation protocols and that EtherChannel can actually be statically configured without PAgP or LACP. Still, it's better to use one of these protocols to help with compatibility issues as well as to manage link additions and failures between two switches.

Cisco EtherChannel allows us to bundle up to eight ports active between switches. The links must have the same speed, duplex setting, and VLAN configuration—in other words, you can't mix interface types and configurations into the same bundle.

There are a few differences in configuring PAgP and LACP, but first, let's go over some terms so you don't get confused:

Port channeling Refers to combining two to eight Fast Ethernet or two Gigabit Ethernet ports together between two switches into one aggregated logical link to achieve more bandwidth and resiliency.

EtherChannel Cisco's proprietary term for port channeling.

PAgP This is a Cisco proprietary port channel negotiation protocol that aids in the automatic creation of EtherChannel links. All links in the bundle must match the same parameters (speed, duplex, VLAN info), and when PAgP identifies matched links, it groups the links into an EtherChannel. This is then added to STP as a single bridge port. At this point, PAgP's job is to send packets every 30 seconds to manage the link for consistency, any link additions, and failures.

LACP (802.3ad) This has the exact same purpose as PAgP but is nonproprietary, so it can work between multi-vendor networks.

`Channel-group` This is a command on Ethernet interfaces used to add the specified interface to a single EtherChannel. The number following this command is the port channel ID.

`Interface port-channel` Here's a command that creates the bundled interface. Ports can be added to this interface with the `channel-group` command. Keep in mind that the interface number must match the group number.

Now, let's see if you can make some sense of all these terms by actually configuring something!

Configuring and Verifying Port Channels

Let's use Figure 1.20 for our simple example of how to configure port channels.

FIGURE 1.20 EtherChannel example

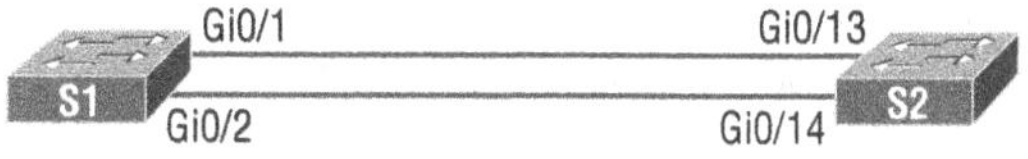

You can enable your `channel-group` for each channel by setting the channel mode for each interface to either `active` or `passive` if using LACP. When a port is configured in `passive` mode, it will respond to the LACP packets it receives, but it won't initiate an LACP negotiation. When a port is configured for `active` mode, the port initiates negotiations with other ports by sending LACP packets.

Let me show you a simple example of configuring port channels and then verifying them. First, I'll go to global configuration mode and create a port channel interface, and then I'll add this port channel to the physical interfaces.

Remember, all parameters and configurations of the ports must be the same, so I'll start by trunking the interfaces before I configure EtherChannel, like this:

```
S1(config)#int range g0/1 - 2
S1(config-if-range)#switchport trunk encapsulation dot1q
S1(config-if-range)#switchport mode trunk
```

All ports in your bundles must be configured the same, so I'll configure both sides with the same trunking configuration. Now I can assign these ports to a bundle:

```
S1(config-if-range)#channel-group 1 mode ?
  active      Enable LACP unconditionally
  auto        Enable PAgP only if a PAgP device is detected
  desirable   Enable PAgP unconditionally
  on          Enable Etherchannel only
  passive     Enable LACP only if a LACP device is detected
S1(config-if-range)#channel-group 1 mode active
S1(config-if-range)#exit
```

To configure the IEEE nonproprietary LACP, I'll use the `active` or `passive` command; if I wanted to use Cisco's PAgP, I'd use the `auto` or `desirable` command. You can't mix and match these on either end of the bundle, and really, it doesn't matter which one you use in a pure Cisco environment as long as you configure them the same on both ends (setting the mode to on would be statically configuring your EtherChannel bundle). At this point in the configuration, I'd have to set the mode to `active` on the S2 interfaces if I wanted the bundle to come up with LACP because, again, all parameters must be the same on both ends of the link. Let's create our port channel interface now with the `interface port-channel` command:

```
S1(config)#int port-channel 1
S1(config-if)#switchport trunk encapsulation dot1q
S1(config-if)#switchport mode trunk
S1(config-if)#switchport trunk allowed vlan 1,2,3
```

Notice that I set the same trunking method under the port channel interface as I did the physical interfaces, as well as VLAN information.

Time to configure the interfaces, channel groups, and port channel interface on the S2 switch:

```
S2(config)#int range g0/13 - 14
S2(config-if-range)#switchport trunk encapsulation dot1q
S2(config-if-range)#switchport mode trunk
S2(config-if-range)#channel-group 1 mode active
```

```
S2(config-if-range)#exit
S2(config)#int port-channel 1
S2(config-if)#switchport trunk encapsulation dot1q
S2(config-if)#switchport mode trunk
S2(config-if)#switchport trunk allowed vlan 1,2,3
```

On each switch, I configured the ports I wanted to bundle with the same configuration and then created the port channel. After that, I added the ports into the port channel with the `channel-group` command.

Let's verify our EtherChannel with a few commands. We'll start with the `show etherchannel port-channel` command to see information about a specific port channel interface:

```
S2#sh etherchannel port-channel
                Channel-group listing:
                ----------------------
Group: 1
----------
                Port-channels in the group:
                ---------------------------
Port-channel: Po1    (Primary Aggregator)
------------
Age of the Port-channel   = 00d:00h:46m:49s
Logical slot/port      = 2/1       Number of ports = 2
GC                     = 0x00000000      HotStandBy port = null
Port state             = Port-channel
Protocol               =   LACP
Port Security          = Disabled

Ports in the Port-channel:

Index   Load   Port     EC state        No of bits
------+------+------+------------------+-----------
  0     00     Gig0/2   Active             0
  0     00     Gig0/1   Active             0
Time since last port bundled:    00d:00h:46m:47s    Gig0/1
S2#
```

Notice that we have one group and that we're running the IEEE LACP version of port channeling. We're in `Active` mode, and that `Port-channel: Po1` interface has two physical interfaces. The heading `Load` is not the load over the interfaces; it's a hexadecimal value that decides which interface will be chosen to specify the flow of traffic.

The show etherchannel summary command displays one line of information per port channel:

```
S2#sh etherchannel summary
Flags:  D - down        P - in port-channel
        I - stand-alone s - suspended
        H - Hot-standby (LACP only)
        R - Layer3      S - Layer2
        U - in use      f - failed to allocate aggregator
        u - unsuitable for bundling
        w - waiting to be aggregated
        d - default port
Number of channel-groups in use: 1
Number of aggregators:           1

Group  Port-channel  Protocol    Ports
------+-------------+-----------+-----------------------------------------------
1      Po1(SU)          LACP   Gig0/1(P) Gig0/2(P)
```

This command shows that we have one group, that we're running LACP and Gig0/1 and Gig0/2 or (P), which means these ports are in port-channel mode. This command isn't really all that helpful unless you have multiple channel groups, but it does tell us our group is working well!

Summary

This chapter was all about switching technologies, with a particular focus on the Spanning Tree Protocol (STP) and its evolution to newer versions like RSTP and then Cisco's PVST+.

You learned about the problems that can occur if you have multiple links between bridges (switches) and the solutions attained with STP.

I also talked about and demonstrated issues that can occur if you have multiple links between bridges (switches), plus how to solve these problems by using STP.

I covered a detailed configuration of Cisco's Catalyst switches, including verifying the configuration, setting the Cisco STP extensions, and changing the root bridge by setting a bridge priority.

Finally, we discussed, configured, and verified the EtherChannel technology that helps us bundle multiple links between switches.

Exam Essentials

Understand the main purpose of the Spanning Tree Protocol in a switched LAN. The main purpose of STP is to prevent switching loops in a network with redundant switched paths.

Remember the states of STP. The purpose of the blocking state is to prevent the use of looped paths. A port in listening state prepares to forward data frames without populating the MAC address table. A port in learning state populates the MAC address table but doesn't forward data frames. A port in forwarding state sends and receives all data frames on the bridged port. Also, a port in the disabled state is virtually nonoperational.

Remember the command `show spanning-tree`. You must be familiar with the command `show spanning-tree` and how to determine the root bridge of each VLAN. Also, you can use the `show spanning-tree summary` command to help you get a quick glimpse of your STP network and root bridges.

Understand what PortFast and BPDU Guard provide. PortFast allows a port to transition to the forwarding state immediately upon a connection. Because you don't want other switches connecting to this port, BPDU Guard will shut down a PortFast port if it receives a BPDU.

Understand what EtherChannel is and how to configure it. EtherChannel allows you to bundle links to get more bandwidth instead of allowing STP to shut down redundant ports. You can configure Cisco's PAgP or the IEEE version, LACP, by creating a port channel interface and assigning the port channel group number to the interfaces you are bundling.

Written Lab

The answers to this lab can be found in Appendix A, "Answers to the Written Labs."

Write the answers to the following questions:

1. Which of the following is Cisco proprietary: LACP or PAgP?
2. What command will show you the STP root bridge for a VLAN?
3. What standard is RSTP PVST+ based on?
4. Which protocol is used in a layer 2 network to maintain a loop-free network?
5. Which proprietary Cisco STP extension would put a switch port into error-mode disabled mode if a BPDU is received on this port?
6. You want to configure a switch port to not transition through the STP port states but to go immediately to forwarding mode. What command will you use on a per-port basis?
7. What command will you use to see information about a specific port channel interface?
8. What command can you use to set a switch so that it will be the root bridge for VLAN 3 over any other switch?
9. You need to find the VLANs for which your switch is the root bridge. What two commands can you use?
10. What are the two modes you can set with LACP?

Review Questions

NOTE The following questions are designed to test your understanding of this chapter's material. For more information on how to get additional questions, please see this book's introduction.

The answers to these questions can be found in Appendix B, "Answers to the Review Questions."

1. You receive the following output from a switch:

```
S2#sh spanning-tree
VLAN0001
  Spanning tree enabled protocol rstp
  Root ID    Priority    32769
             Address     0001.42A7.A603
             Cost        4
             Port        26(GigabitEthernet1/2)
             Hello Time  2 sec  Max Age 20 sec  Forward Delay 15 sec
 [output cut]
```

   Which are true regarding this switch? (Choose two.)

   A. The switch is a root bridge.

   B. The switch is a non-root bridge.

   C. The root bridge is four switches away.

   D. The switch is running 802.1w.

   E. The switch is running STP PVST+.

2. If you want to effectively disable STP on a port connected to a server, which command would you use?

   A. `disable spanning-tree`

   B. `spanning-tree off`

   C. `spanning-tree security`

   D. `spanning-tree portfast`

3. Which of the following would you use to find the VLANs for which your switch is the root bridge? (Choose two.)

   A. `show spanning-tree`

   B. `show root all`

   C. `show spanning-tree port root VLAN`

   D. `show spanning-tree summary`

4. You want to run the new 802.1w on your switches. Which of the following would enable this protocol?
   A. `Switch(config)#spanning-tree mode rapid-pvst`
   B. `Switch#spanning-tree mode rapid-pvst`
   C. `Switch(config)#spanning-tree mode 802.1w`
   D. `Switch#spanning-tree mode 802.1w`
5. Which of the following is a layer 2 protocol used to maintain a loop-free network?
   A. VTP
   B. STP
   C. RIP
   D. CDP
6. Which statement describes a spanning-tree network that has converged?
   A. All switch and bridge ports are in the forwarding state.
   B. All switch and bridge ports are assigned as either root or designated ports.
   C. All switch and bridge ports are in either the forwarding or blocking state.
   D. All switch and bridge ports are either blocking or looping.
7. Which of the following modes enable LACP EtherChannel? (Choose two.)
   A. On
   B. Prevent
   C. Passive
   D. Auto
   E. Active
   F. Desirable
8. Which of the following are true regarding RSTP? (Choose three.)
   A. RSTP speeds the recalculation of the spanning tree when the layer 2 network topology changes.
   B. RSTP is an IEEE standard that redefines STP port roles, states, and BPDUs.
   C. RSTP is extremely proactive and very quick, and therefore it absolutely needs the 802.1 delay timers.
   D. RSTP (802.1w) supersedes 802.1d while remaining proprietary.
   E. All of the 802.1d terminology and most parameters have been changed.
   F. 802.1w is capable of reverting to 802.1d to interoperate with traditional switches on a per-port basis.

9. What does BPDU Guard perform?
   - A. Makes sure the port is receiving BPDUs from the correct upstream switch.
   - B. Makes sure the port is not receiving BPDUs from the upstream switch, only the root.
   - C. If a BPDU is received on a BPDU Guard port, PortFast is used to shut down the port.
   - D. Shuts down a port if a BPDU is seen on that port.

10. How many bits is the sys-id-ext field in a BPDU?
    - A. 4
    - B. 8
    - C. 12
    - D. 16

11. There are four connections between two switches running RSTP PVST+, and you want to figure out how to achieve higher bandwidth without sacrificing the resiliency that RSTP provides. What can you configure between these two switches to achieve higher bandwidth than the default configuration is already providing?
    - A. Set PortFast and BPDU Guard, which provides faster convergence.
    - B. Configure unequal cost load balancing with RSTP PVST+.
    - C. Place all four links into the same EtherChannel bundle.
    - D. Configure PPP and use multilink.

12. In which circumstance are multiple copies of the same unicast frame likely to be transmitted in a switched LAN?
    - A. During high-traffic periods
    - B. After broken links are reestablished
    - C. When upper-layer protocols require high reliability
    - D. In an improperly implemented redundant topology

13. You want to configure LACP. Which of the following to you need to use the make sure LACP is configured exactly the same on all switch interfaces you are using? (Choose three.)
    - A. Virtual MAC address
    - B. Port speeds
    - C. Duplex
    - D. PortFast enabled
    - E. VLAN information

14. Which of the following modes enable PAgP EtherChannel? (Choose two.)
    - A. On
    - B. Prevent
    - C. Passive
    - D. Auto
    - E. Active
    - F. Desirable

15. For this question, refer to the following illustration. SB's RP to the root bridge has failed.

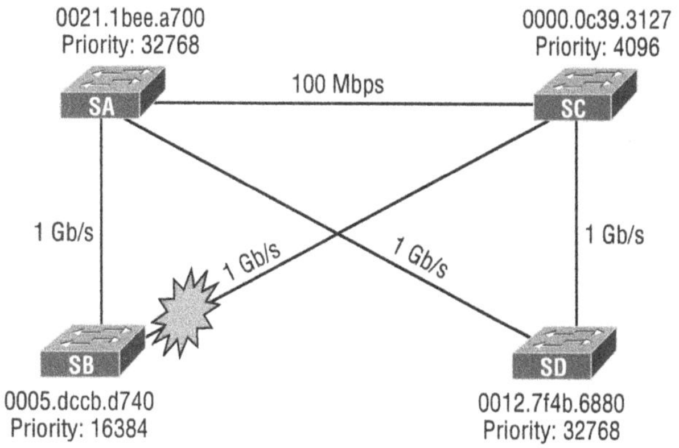

What is the new cost for SB to make a single path to the root bridge?

A. 4

B. 8

C. 23

D. 12

16. Which of the following would put switch interfaces into EtherChannel port number 1, using LACP? (Choose two.)

A. `Switch(config)#interface port-channel 1`

B. `Switch(config)#channel-group 1 mode active`

C. `Switch#interface port-channel 1`

D. `Switch(config-if)#channel-group 1 mode active`

17. Which two commands would guarantee your switch to be the root bridge for VLAN 30? (Choose two.)

A. `spanning-tree vlan 30 priority 0`

B. `spanning-tree vlan 30 priority 16384`

C. `spanning-tree vlan 30 root guarantee`

D. `spanning-tree vlan 30 root primary`

18. Why does Cisco use its proprietary extension of PVST+ with STP and RSTP?

A. Root bridge placement enables faster convergence as well as optimal path determination.

B. Non-root bridge placement clearly enables faster convergence as well as optimal path determination.

C. PVST+ allows for faster discarding of non-IP frames.

D. PVST+ is actually an IEEE standard called 802.1w.

19. Which are states in 802.1d? (Choose all that apply.)
    A. Blocking
    B. Discarding
    C. Listening
    D. Learning
    E. Forwarding
    F. Alternate

20. Which of the following are roles in STP? (Choose all that apply.)
    A. Blocking
    B. Discarding
    C. Root
    D. Non-designated
    E. Forwarding
    F. Designated

Chapter 2

Security with ACLs

THE FOLLOWING CCNA EXAM TOPICS ARE COVERED IN THIS CHAPTER:

✓ **5.0 Security Fundamentals**

5.6 Configure and verify access control lists

If you're a sys admin, I guess that shielding sensitive, critical data, as well as your network's resources, from every possible evil exploit is your top priority, right? Good to know you're on the right page, because Cisco has some really effective security solutions to equip you with the tools you'll need to make this happen in a very real way!

The first power tool I'm going to hand you is known as the access control list (ACL). Being able to execute an ACL proficiently is an integral part of Cisco's security solution, so I'm going to begin by showing you how to create and implement simple ACLs. From there, I'll move to demonstrating more advanced ACLs and describe how to implement them strategically to provide serious armor for an internetwork in today's challenging, high-risk environment.

The proper use and configuration of access lists is a vital part of router configuration because access lists are such versatile networking accessories. Contributing mightily to the efficiency and operation of your network, access lists give network managers a huge amount of control over traffic flow throughout the enterprise. With access lists, we can gather basic statistics on packet flow, and security policies can be implemented. These dynamic tools also enable us to protect sensitive devices from the dangers of unauthorized access.

In this chapter, we'll cover ACLs for TCP/IP as well as explore effective ways available to us for testing and monitoring how well applied access lists are functioning. We'll begin now by discussing key security measures deployed using hardware devices and VLANs, and then I'll introduce you to ACLs.

NOTE To find up-to-the-minute updates for this chapter, please see `www.lammle.com/ccna`.

Perimeter, Firewall, and Internal Routers

You see this a lot—typically, in medium to large enterprise networks—the various strategies for security are based on some mix of internal and perimeter routers plus firewall devices. Internal routers provide additional security by screening traffic to various parts of the protected corporate network, and they achieve this using access lists. You can see where each of these types of devices would be found in Figure 2.1.

FIGURE 2.1 A typical secured network

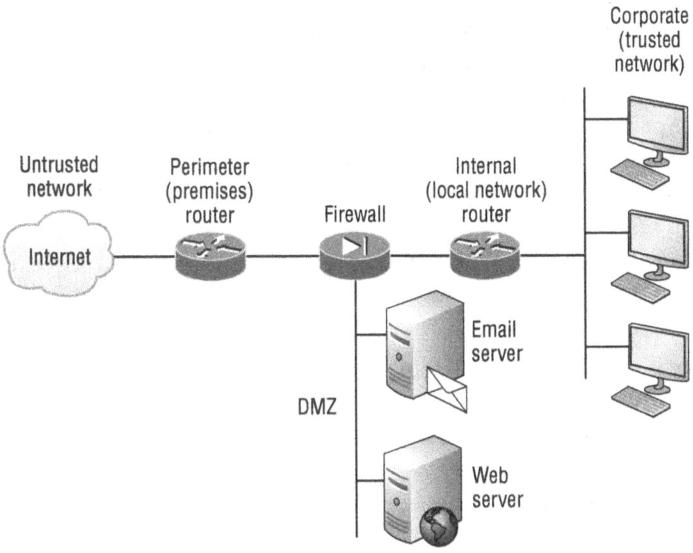

I'll use the terms *trusted network* and *untrusted network* throughout this chapter, as well as in Chapter 5, "Network Address Translation (NAT)," so it's important that you can see where they're found in a typical secured network. The demilitarized zone (DMZ) can be global (real) Internet addresses or private addresses, depending on how you configure your firewall, but this is typically where you'll find the HTTP, DNS, email, and other Internet-type corporate servers.

As you now know, instead of using routers, we can create VLANs with switches on the inside trusted network. Multilayer switches containing their own security features can sometimes replace internal (LAN) routers to provide higher performance in VLAN architectures.

Let's look at some ways of protecting the internetwork using access lists.

Introduction to Access Lists

An *access list* is essentially a list of conditions that categorize packets, and they really come in handy when you need to exercise control over network traffic. An ACL would be your tool of choice for decision-making in these situations.

One of the most common and easiest-to-understand uses of access lists is to filter unwanted packets when implementing security policies. For example, you can set them up to make very specific decisions about regulating traffic patterns so they'll allow only certain hosts to access web resources on the Internet while restricting others. With the right combination of access lists, network managers arm themselves with the power to enforce nearly any security policy they can invent.

Creating access lists is really a lot like programming a series of if-then statements—if a given condition is met, then a given action is taken. If the specific condition isn't met, nothing happens, and the next statement is evaluated. Access-list statements are basically packet filters that packets are compared against, categorized by, and acted upon accordingly. Once the lists are built, they can be applied to either inbound or outbound traffic on any interface. Applying an access list causes the router to analyze every packet crossing that interface in the specified direction and take the appropriate action.

There are three important rules that a packet follows when it's being compared with an access list:

- The packet is always compared with each line of the access list in sequential order—it will always start with the first line of the access list, move on to line 2, then line 3, and so on.
- The packet is compared with lines of the access list only until a match is made. Once it matches the condition on a line of the access list, the packet is acted upon, and no further comparisons take place.
- There is an implicit "deny" at the end of each access list—this means that if a packet doesn't match the condition on any of the lines in the access list, the packet will be discarded.

Each of these rules has some powerful implications when filtering IP packets with access lists, so keep in mind that creating effective access lists definitely takes some practice.

There are two main types of access lists:

Standard access lists These ACLs use only the source IP address in an IP packet as the condition test. All decisions are made based on the source IP address. This means that standard access lists basically permit or deny an entire suite of protocols. They don't distinguish between any of the many types of IP traffic such as Web, Telnet, UDP, and so on.

Extended access lists Extended access lists can evaluate many of the other fields in the layer 3 and layer 4 headers of an IP packet. They can evaluate source and destination IP addresses, the Protocol field in the Network layer header, and the port number at the Transport layer header. This gives extended access lists the ability to make much more granular decisions when controlling traffic.

Named access lists Hey, wait a minute—I said there were only two types of access lists but listed three! Well, technically there really are only two because *named access lists* are either standard or extended and not actually a distinct type. I'm just distinguishing them because they're created and referred to differently than standard and extended access lists, but they're still functionally the same.

NOTE We'll cover these types of access lists in more depth later in the chapter.

Once you create an access list, it's not really going to do anything until you apply it. Yes, it's there on the router, but it's inactive until you tell that router what to do with it. To use an access list as a packet filter, you need to apply it to an interface on the router where you want the traffic filtered. And you've got to specify which direction of traffic you want the access list applied to. There's a good reason for this—you may want different controls in place for traffic leaving your enterprise destined for the Internet than for traffic coming into your enterprise from the Internet. So, by specifying the direction of traffic, you can and must use different access lists for inbound and outbound traffic on a single interface:

Inbound access lists When an access list is applied to inbound packets on an interface, those packets are processed through the access list before being routed to the outbound interface. Any packets that are denied won't be routed because they're discarded before the routing process is invoked.

Outbound access lists When an access list is applied to outbound packets on an interface, packets are routed to the outbound interface and then processed through the access list before being queued.

There are some general access-list guidelines that you should keep in mind when creating and implementing access lists on a router:

- You can assign only one access list per interface per protocol per direction. This means that when applying IP access lists, you can have only one inbound access list and one outbound access list per interface.

NOTE When you consider the implications of the implicit deny at the end of any access list, it makes sense that you can't have multiple access lists applied on the same interface in the same direction for the same protocol. That's because any packets that don't match some condition in the first access list would be denied, and there wouldn't be any packets left over to compare against a second access list!

- Organize your access lists so that the more specific tests are at the top.
- Anytime a new entry is added to the access list, it will be placed at the bottom of the list, which is why I highly recommend using a text editor for access lists.
- You can't remove one line from an access list. If you try to do this, you will remove the entire list. This is why it's best to copy the access list to a text editor before trying to edit the list. The only exception is when you're using named access lists.

NOTE You can edit, add, or delete a single line from a named access list. I'll show you how shortly.

- Unless your access list ends with a `permit any` command, all packets will be discarded if they do not meet any of the list's tests. This means every list should have at least one `permit` statement or it will deny all traffic.
- Create access lists and then apply them to an interface. Any access list applied to an interface without access-list test statements present will not filter traffic.
- Access lists are designed to filter traffic going through the router. They will not filter traffic that has originated from the router.

- Place IP standard access lists as close to the destination as possible. This is the reason we don't really want to use standard access lists in our networks. You can't put a standard access list close to the source host or network because you can only filter based on the source address and all destinations would be affected as a result.
- Place IP extended access lists as close to the source as possible. Because extended access lists can filter on very specific addresses and protocols, you don't want your traffic to traverse the entire network just to be denied. By placing this list as close to the source address as possible, you can filter traffic before it uses up precious bandwidth.

Before I move on to demonstrate how to configure basic and extended ACLs, let's talk about how they can be used to mitigate the security threats I mentioned earlier.

Mitigating Security Issues with ACLs

The most common attack is a denial of service (DoS) attack. Although ACLs can help with a DoS, you really need an intrusion detection system (IDS) and intrusion prevention system (IPS) to help prevent these common attacks. Cisco sells the Adaptive Security Appliance (ASA), which has IDS/IPS modules, but lots of other companies also sell IDS/IPS products.

Here's a list of the many security threats you can mitigate with ACLs:

- IP address spoofing, inbound
- IP address spoofing, outbound
- DoS TCP SYN attacks, blocking external attacks
- DoS TCP SYN attacks, using TCP Intercept
- DoS smurf attacks
- Denying/filtering ICMP messages, inbound
- Denying/filtering ICMP messages, outbound
- Denying/filtering Traceroute

NOTE This is not an "introduction to security" book, so you may have to research some of the preceding terms if you don't understand them.

It's generally a bad idea to allow into a private network any external IP packets that contain the source address of any internal hosts or networks—just don't do it!

Here's a list of rules to live by when configuring ACLs from the Internet to your production network to mitigate security problems:

- Deny any source addresses from your internal networks.
- Deny any local host addresses (127.0.0.0/8).
- Deny any reserved private addresses (RFC 1918).
- Deny any addresses in the IP multicast address range (224.0.0.0/4).

None of these source addresses should ever be allowed to enter your internetwork. Finally, let's get our hands dirty and configure some basic and advanced access lists!

Standard Access Lists

Standard IP access lists filter network traffic by examining the source IP address in a packet. You create a *standard IP access list* by using the access-list numbers 1–99 or in the expanded range of 1300–1999 because the type of ACL is generally differentiated using a number. Based on the number used when the access list is created, the router knows which type of syntax to expect as the list is entered. By using numbers 1–99 or 1300–1999, you're telling the router that you want to create a standard IP access list, so the router will expect syntax specifying only the source IP address in the test lines.

The following output displays a good example of the many access-list number ranges that you can use to filter traffic on your network. The IOS version delimits the protocols you can specify access for:

```
Corp(config)#access-list ?
  <1-99>            IP standard access list
  <100-199>         IP extended access list
  <1000-1099>       IPX SAP access list
  <1100-1199>       Extended 48-bit MAC address access list
  <1200-1299>       IPX summary address access list
  <1300-1999>       IP standard access list (expanded range)
  <200-299>         Protocol type-code access list
  <2000-2699>       IP extended access list (expanded range)
  <300-399>         DECnet access list
  <600-699>         Appletalk access list
  <700-799>         48-bit MAC address access list
  <800-899>         IPX standard access list
  <900-999>         IPX extended access list
  dynamic-extended  Extend the dynamic ACL absolute timer
  rate-limit        Simple rate-limit specific access list
```

Wow—there certainly are a lot of old protocols listed in that output! IPX, AppleTalk, or DECnet would no longer be used in any of today's networks. Let's take a look at the syntax used when creating a standard IP access list:

```
Corp(config)#access-list 10 ?
  deny    Specify packets to reject
  permit  Specify packets to forward
  remark  Access list entry comment
```

As I said, by using the access-list numbers 1–99 or 1300–1999, you're telling the router that you want to create a standard IP access list, which means you can only filter on the source IP address.

Once you've chosen the access-list number, you need to decide whether you're creating a `permit` or `deny` statement. I'm going to create a `deny` statement now:

```
Corp(config)#access-list 10 deny ?
  Hostname or A.B.C.D  Address to match
  any                  Any source host
  host                 A single host address
```

The next step is more detailed because there are three options available in it:

1. The first option is the `any` parameter used to permit or deny any source host or network.
2. The second choice is to use an IP address to specify either a single host or a range of them.
3. The last option is to use the `host` command to specify a specific host only.

The `any` command is pretty obvious—any source address matches the statement, so every packet compared against this line will match. The `host` command is relatively simple too, as you can see here:

```
Corp(config)#access-list 10 deny host ?
  Hostname or A.B.C.D  Host address
Corp(config)#access-list 10 deny host 172.16.30.2
```

This tells the list to deny any packets from host 172.16.30.2. The default parameter is `host`. In other words, if you type **`access-list 10 deny 172.16.30.2`**, the router assumes you mean host 172.16.30.2, and that's exactly how it will show in your running-config.

But there's another way to specify either a particular host or a range of hosts, and it's known as wildcard masking. In fact, to specify any range of hosts, you must use wildcard masking in the access list.

So, exactly what is wildcard masking? Coming up, I'm going to show you using a standard access list example. I'll also guide you through controlling access to a virtual terminal. We'll use the same wildcard masks we used in the Configuring OSPF section of Book 1, Chapter 10, "Open Shortest Path First (OSPF)."

Wildcard Masking

Wildcards are used with access lists to specify an individual host, a network, or a specific range of a network or networks. The block sizes you learned about earlier used to specify a range of addresses are key to understanding wildcards.

Let me pause here for a quick review of block sizes before we go any further. I'm sure you remember that the different block sizes available are 64, 32, 16, 8, and 4. When you need to specify a range of addresses, you choose the next-largest block size for your needs. So, if you need to specify 34 networks, you need a block size of 64. If you want to specify 18 hosts, you need a block size of 32. If you specify only two networks, then go with a block size of 4.

Wildcards are used with the host or network address to tell the router a range of available addresses to filter. To specify a host, the address would look like this:

```
172.16.30.5 0.0.0.0
```

The four zeros represent each octet of the address. Whenever a zero is present, it indicates that the octet in the address must match the corresponding reference octet exactly. To specify that an octet can be any value, use the value 255. Here's an example of how a /24 subnet is specified with a wildcard mask:

```
172.16.30.0 0.0.0.255
```

This tells the router to match up the first three octets exactly, but the fourth octet can be any value.

That was the easy part. But what if you want to specify only a small range of subnets? This is where block sizes come in. You have to specify the range of values in a block size, so you can't choose to specify 20 networks. You can only specify the exact amount that the block size value allows. This means that the range would have to be either 16 or 32, but not 20.

Let's say you want to block access to the part of the network that ranges from 172.16.8.0 through 172.16.15.0. To do that, you would go with a block size of 8, your network number would be 172.16.8.0, and the wildcard would be 0.0.7.255. The 7.255 equals the value the router will use to determine the block size. So together, the network number and the wildcard tell the router to begin at 172.16.8.0 and go up a block size of eight addresses to network 172.16.15.0.

This really is easier than it looks! I could certainly go through the binary math for you, but no one needs that kind of pain because all you have to do is remember that the wildcard is always one number less than the block size. So, in our example, the wildcard would be 7 because our block size is 8. If you used a block size of 16, the wildcard would be 15. Easy, right?

Just to make sure you've got this, we'll go through some examples that will definitely help you nail it down. The following example tells the router to match the first three octets exactly but that the fourth octet can be anything:

```
Corp(config)#access-list 10 deny 172.16.10.0 0.0.0.255
```

The next example tells the router to match the first two octets and that the last two octets can be any value:

```
Corp(config)#access-list 10 deny 172.16.0.0 0.0.255.255
```

Now, try to figure out this next line:

```
Corp(config)#access-list 10 deny 172.16.16.0 0.0.3.255
```

This configuration tells the router to start at network 172.16.16.0 and use a block size of 4. The range would then be 172.16.16.0 through 172.16.19.255, and by the way, the Cisco objectives seem to really like this one!

Let's keep practicing. What about this next one?

```
Corp(config)#access-list 10 deny 172.16.16.0 0.0.7.255
```

This example reveals an access list starting at 172.16.16.0 going up a block size of 8 to 172.16.23.255.

Let's keep at it... What do you think the range of this one is?

```
Corp(config)#access-list 10 deny 172.16.32.0 0.0.15.255
```

This one begins at network 172.16.32.0 and goes up a block size of 16 to 172.16.47.255.

You're almost done practicing! After a couple more, we'll configure some real ACLs.

```
Corp(config)#access-list 10 deny 172.16.64.0 0.0.63.255
```

This example starts at network 172.16.64.0 and goes up a block size of 64 to 172.16.127.255.

What about this last example?

```
Corp(config)#access-list 10 deny 192.168.160.0 0.0.31.255
```

This one shows us that it begins at network 192.168.160.0 and goes up a block size of 32 to 192.168.191.255.

Here are two more things to keep in mind when working with block sizes and wildcards:

- Each block size must start at 0 or a multiple of the block size. For example, you can't say that you want a block size of 8 and then start at 12. You must use 0–7, 8–15, 16–23, etc. For a block size of 32, the ranges are 0–31, 32–63, 64–95, etc.
- The command `any` is the same thing as writing out the wildcard 0.0.0.0 255.255.255.255.

> **NOTE** Wildcard masking is a crucial skill to master when creating IP access lists, and it's used identically when creating standard and extended IP access lists.

Standard Access List Example

In this section, you'll learn how to use a standard access list to stop specific users from gaining access to the Finance department LAN.

In Figure 2.2, a router has three LAN connections and one WAN connection to the Internet. Users on the Sales LAN should not have access to the Finance LAN, but they should be able to access the Internet and the Marketing department files. The Marketing LAN needs to access the Finance LAN for application services.

FIGURE 2.2 IP access list example with three LANs and a WAN connection

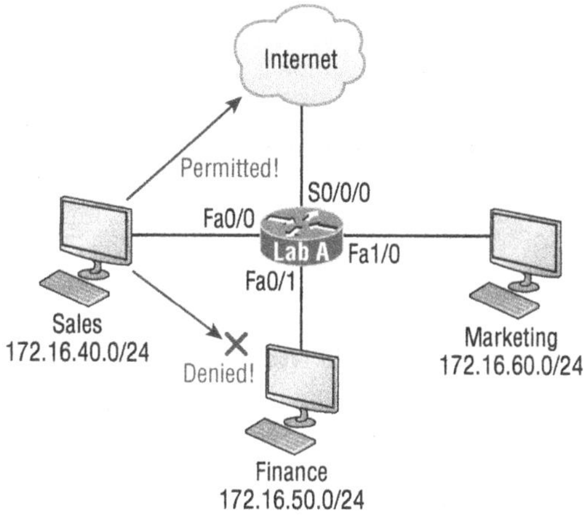

We can see that the following standard IP access list is configured on the router:

```
Lab_A#config t
Lab_A(config)#access-list 10 deny 172.16.40.0 0.0.0.255
Lab_A(config)#access-list 10 permit any
```

It's very important to remember that the any command is the same thing as saying the following using wildcard masking:

```
Lab_A(config)#access-list 10 permit 0.0.0.0 255.255.255.255
```

Because the wildcard mask says that none of the octets are to be evaluated, every address matches the test condition, so this is functionally doing the same as using the any keyword.

At this point, the access list is configured to deny source addresses from the Sales LAN to the Finance LAN and to allow everyone else. But remember, no action will be taken until the access list is applied on an interface in a specific direction!

But where should this access list be placed? If you place it as an incoming access list on Fa0/0, you might as well shut down the FastEthernet interface because all of the Sales LAN devices will be denied access to all networks attached to the router. The best place to apply this access list is on the Fa0/1 interface as an outbound list:

```
Lab_A(config)#int fa0/1
Lab_A(config-if)#ip access-group 10 out
```

Doing this completely stops traffic from 172.16.40.0 from getting out FastEthernet0/1. It has no effect on the hosts from the Sales LAN accessing the Marketing LAN and the Internet because traffic to those destinations doesn't go through interface Fa0/1. Any packet trying to exit out Fa0/1 will have to go through the access list first. If there were an inbound list placed on F0/0, then any packet trying to enter interface F0/0 would have to go through the access list before being routed to an exit interface.

Now, let's take a look at another standard access list example. Figure 2.3 shows an internetwork of two routers with four LANs.

FIGURE 2.3 IP standard access list example 2

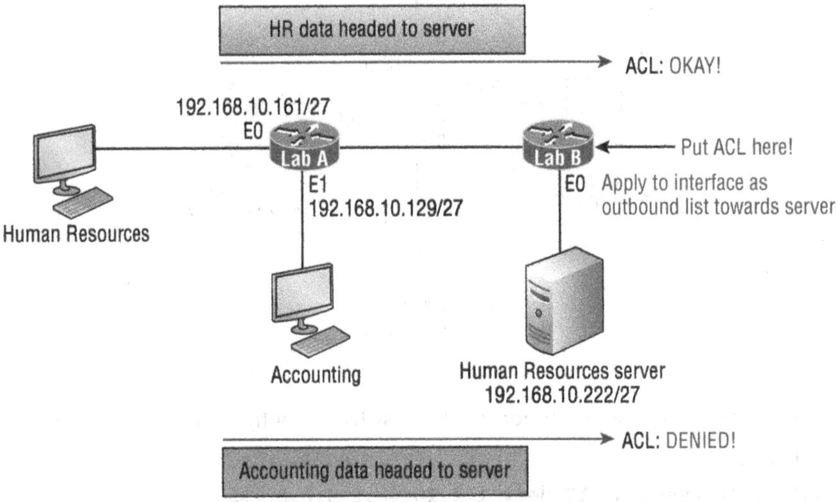

Now we're going to stop the Accounting users from accessing the Human Resources server attached to the Lab_B router but allow all other users access to that LAN using a standard ACL. What kind of standard access list would we need to create, and where would we place it to achieve our goals?

The real answer is that we should use an extended access list and place it closest to the source! But this question specifies using a standard access list, and as a rule, standard ACLs are placed closest to the destination. In this example, Ethernet 0 is the outbound interface on the Lab_B router, and here's the access list that should be placed on it:

```
Lab_B#config t
Lab_B(config)#access-list 10 deny 192.168.10.128 0.0.0.31
Lab_B(config)#access-list 10 permit any
Lab_B(config)#interface Ethernet 0
Lab_B(config-if)#ip access-group 10 out
```

Keep in mind that to be able to answer this question correctly, you really need to understand subnetting, wildcard masks, and how to configure and implement ACLs. The accounting subnet is 192.168.10.128/27, which is 255.255.255.224, with a block size of 32 in the fourth octet.

With all this in mind, and before we move on to restricting Telnet access on a router, let's take a look at one more standard access list example. This one is going to require some thought. In Figure 2.4, you have a router with four LAN connections and one WAN connection to the Internet.

FIGURE 2.4 IP standard access list example 3

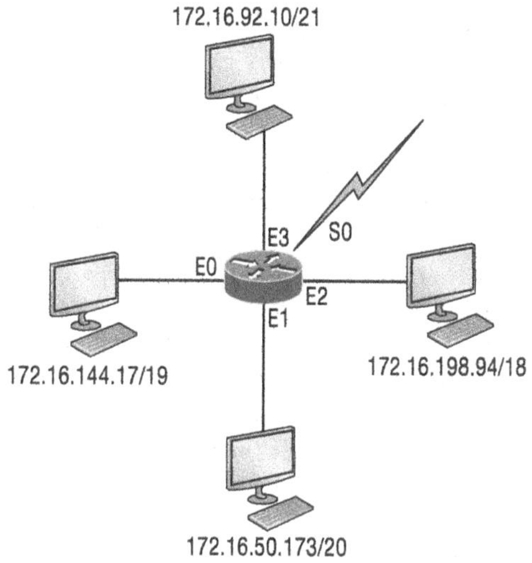

You need to write an access list that will stop access from each of the four LANs shown in the diagram to the Internet. Each of the LANs reveals a single host's IP address, which you need to use to determine the subnet and wildcards of each LAN to configure the access list.

Here is an example of what your answer should look like, beginning with the network on E0 and working through to E3:

```
Router(config)#access-list 1 deny 172.16.128.0 0.0.31.255
Router(config)#access-list 1 deny 172.16.48.0 0.0.15.255
Router(config)#access-list 1 deny 172.16.192.0 0.0.63.255
Router(config)#access-list 1 deny 172.16.88.0 0.0.7.255
Router(config)#access-list 1 permit any
Router(config)#interface serial 0
Router(config-if)#ip access-group 1 out
```

Sure, you could have done this with one line:

```
Router(config)#access-list 1 deny 172.16.0.0 0.0.255.255
```

But what fun is that?

And remember the reasons for creating this list. If you actually applied this ACL on the router, you'd effectively shut down access to the Internet, so why even have an Internet connection? I included this exercise so you can practice how to use block sizes with access lists, which is vital for succeeding when you take the Cisco exam!

Controlling VTY (Telnet/SSH) Access

Trying to stop users from telnetting or trying to SSH to a router is really challenging because any active interface on a router is fair game for VTY/SSH access. Creating an extended IP ACL that limits access to every IP address on the router may sound like a solution, but if you did that, you'd have to apply it inbound on every interface, which really wouldn't scale well if you happen to have dozens, even hundreds, of interfaces, now would it? And think of all the latency dragging down your network as a result of each and every router checking every packet just in case the packet was trying to access your VTY lines—horrible!

Don't give up—there's always a solution! And in this case, a much better one, which employs a standard IP access list to control access to the VTY lines themselves.

Why does this work so well? Because when you apply an access list to the VTY lines, you don't need to specify the protocol because access to the VTY already implies terminal access via the Telnet or SSH protocols. You also don't need to specify a destination address because it really doesn't matter which interface address the user used as a target for the Telnet session. All you really need control of is where the user is coming from, which is betrayed by their source IP address.

You need to do these two things to make this happen:

1. Create a standard IP access list that permits only the host or hosts you want to be able to telnet into the routers.
2. Apply the access list to the VTY line with the `access-class in` command.

Here, I'm allowing only host 172.16.10.3 to telnet into a router:

```
Lab_A(config)#access-list 50 permit host 172.16.10.3
Lab_A(config)#line vty 0 4
Lab_A(config-line)#access-class 50 in
```

Because of the implied `deny any` at the end of the list, the ACL stops any host from telnetting into the router except the host 172.16.10.3, regardless of the individual IP address on the router being used as a target. It's a good idea to include an admin subnet address as the source instead of a single host, but the reason I demonstrated this was to show you how to create security on your VTY lines without adding latency to your router.

Real World Scenario

Should You Secure Your VTY Lines on a Router?

You're monitoring your network and notice that someone has telnetted into your core router by using the `show users` command. You use the `disconnect` command and they're disconnected from the router, but you notice that they're right back in there a few minutes later. You consider putting an ACL on the router interfaces, but you don't want to add latency on each interface because your router is already pushing a lot of packets. At this point, you think about putting an access list on the VTY lines themselves, but not having done this before, you're not sure if this is a safe alternative to putting an ACL on each interface. Would placing an ACL on the VTY lines be a good idea for this network?

Yes—absolutely! And the `access-class` command covered in this chapter is the way to do it. Why? Because it doesn't use an access list that just sits on an interface looking at every packet, resulting in unnecessary overhead and latency.

When you put the `access-class in` command on the VTY lines, only packets trying to telnet into the router will be checked and compared, providing easy-to-configure yet solid security for your router!

TIP

Just a reminder—Cisco recommends using Secure Shell (SSH) instead of Telnet on the VTY lines of a router, as we cover in Book 1, Chapter 6, "Cisco's Internetworking Operating System (IOS)," so review that chapter if you need a refresher on SSH and how to configure it on your routers and switches.

Extended Access Lists

Let's go back to the standard IP access list example where you had to block all access from the Sales LAN to the Finance department and add a new requirement. You now must allow Sales to gain access to a certain server on the Finance LAN but not to other network services for security reasons. What's the solution? Applying a standard IP access list won't allow users to get to one network service but not another because a standard ACL won't allow you to make decisions based on both source and destination addresses. It makes decisions based only on source address, so we need another way to achieve our new goal—but what is it?

Using an *extended access list* will save the day because extended ACLs allow us to specify source and destination addresses as well as the protocol and port number that identify the upper-layer protocol or application. An extended ACL is just what we need to effectively allow users access to a physical LAN while denying them access to specific hosts—even specific services on those hosts!

We're going to take a look at the commands we have in our arsenal, but first, you need to know that you must use the extended access-list range from 100 to 199. The 2000–2699 range is also available for extended IP access lists.

After choosing a number in the extended range, you need to decide what type of list entry to make. For this example, I'm going with a `deny` list entry:

```
Corp(config)#access-list 110 ?
  deny     Specify packets to reject
  dynamic  Specify a DYNAMIC list of PERMITs or DENYs
  permit   Specify packets to forward
  remark   Access list entry comment
```

And once you've settled on the type of ACL, you then need to select a protocol field entry:

```
Corp(config)#access-list 110 deny ?
  <0-255>   An IP protocol number
  ahp       Authentication Header Protocol
  eigrp     Cisco's EIGRP routing protocol
  esp       Encapsulation Security Payload
  gre       Cisco's GRE tunneling
  icmp      Internet Control Message Protocol
  igmp      Internet Gateway Message Protocol
  ip        Any Internet Protocol
  ipinip    IP in IP tunneling
  nos       KA9Q NOS compatible IP over IP tunneling
  ospf      OSPF routing protocol
  pcp       Payload Compression Protocol
  pim       Protocol Independent Multicast
  tcp       Transmission Control Protocol
  udp       User Datagram Protocol
```

NOTE

If you want to filter by Application layer protocol, you have to choose the appropriate layer 4 transport protocol after the permit or deny statement. For example, to filter Telnet or FTP, choose TCP because both Telnet and FTP use TCP at the Transport layer. Selecting IP wouldn't allow you to specify a particular application protocol later and only filter based on source and destination addresses.

So now, let's filter an Application layer protocol that uses TCP by selecting TCP as the protocol and indicating the specific destination TCP port at the end of the line. Next, we'll be prompted for the source IP address of the host or network, and we'll choose the any command to allow any source address:

```
Corp(config)#access-list 110 deny tcp ?
  A.B.C.D   Source address
  any       Any source host
  host      A single source host
```

After we've selected the source address, we can then choose the specific destination address:

```
Corp(config)#access-list 110 deny tcp any ?
  A.B.C.D   Destination address
  any       Any destination host
  eq        Match only packets on a given port number
  gt        Match only packets with a greater port number
```

```
  host     A single destination host
  lt       Match only packets with a lower port number
  neq      Match only packets not on a given port number
  range    Match only packets in the range of port numbers
```

In this output, you can see that any source IP address that has a destination IP address of 172.16.30.2 has been denied:

```
Corp(config)#access-list 110 deny tcp any host 172.16.30.2 ?
  ack          Match on the ACK bit
  dscp         Match packets with given dscp value
  eq           Match only packets on a given port number
  established  Match established connections
  fin          Match on the FIN bit
  fragments    Check non-initial fragments
  gt           Match only packets with a greater port number
  log          Log matches against this entry
  log-input    Log matches against this entry, including input interface
  lt           Match only packets with a lower port number
  neq          Match only packets not on a given port number
  precedence   Match packets with given precedence value
  psh          Match on the PSH bit
  range        Match only packets in the range of port numbers
  rst          Match on the RST bit
  syn          Match on the SYN bit
  time-range   Specify a time-range
  tos          Match packets with given TOS value
  urg          Match on the URG bit
  <cr>
```

And once we have the destination host addresses in place, we just need to specify the type of service to deny using the `equal to` command, entered as eq. The following help screen reveals the options available now. You can choose a port number or use the application name:

```
Corp(config)#access-list 110 deny tcp any host 172.16.30.2 eq ?
  <0-65535>    Port number
  bgp          Border Gateway Protocol (179)
  chargen      Character generator (19)
  cmd          Remote commands (rcmd, 514)
  daytime      Daytime (13)
  discard      Discard (9)
  domain       Domain Name Service (53)
```

```
drip           Dynamic Routing Information Protocol (3949)
echo           Echo (7)
exec           Exec (rsh, 512)
finger         Finger (79)
ftp            File Transfer Protocol (21)
ftp-data       FTP data connections (20)
gopher         Gopher (70)
hostname       NIC hostname server (101)
ident          Ident Protocol (113)
irc            Internet Relay Chat (194)
klogin         Kerberos login (543)
kshell         Kerberos shell (544)
login          Login (rlogin, 513)
lpd            Printer service (515)
nntp           Network News Transport Protocol (119)
pim-auto-rp    PIM Auto-RP (496)
pop2           Post Office Protocol v2 (109)
pop3           Post Office Protocol v3 (110)
smtp           Simple Mail Transport Protocol (25)
sunrpc         Sun Remote Procedure Call (111)
syslog         Syslog (514)
tacacs         TAC Access Control System (49)
talk           Talk (517)
telnet         Telnet (23)
time           Time (37)
uucp           Unix-to-Unix Copy Program (540)
whois          Nicname (43)
www            World Wide Web (HTTP, 80)
```

Now, let's block Telnet (port 23) to host 172.16.30.2 only. If the users want to use FTP, fine—that's allowed. The `log` command is used to log messages every time the access-list entry is hit. This can be an extremely cool way to monitor inappropriate access attempts, but be careful because in a large network, this command can overload your console's screen with messages!

Here's our result:

```
Corp(config)#access-list 110 deny tcp any host 172.16.30.2 eq 23 log
```

This line says to deny any source host trying to telnet to destination host 172.16.30.2. Keep in mind that the next line is an implicit deny by default. If you apply this access list to an interface, you might as well just shut the interface down, because by default, there's an implicit `deny all` at the end of every access list. So, we've got to follow up the access list with the following command:

```
Corp(config)#access-list 110 permit ip any any
```

The IP in this line is important because it will permit the IP stack. If TCP was used instead of IP in this line, then UDP, etc., would all be denied. Remember, the `0.0.0.0 255.255.255.255` is the same command as `any`, so the command could also look like this:

```
Corp(config)#access-list 110 permit ip 0.0.0.0 255.255.255.255
0.0.0.0 255.255.255.255
```

But if you did this, when you looked at the running-config, the commands would be replaced with the `any any`. I like efficiency, so I'll just use the `any` command because it requires less typing.

As always, once our access list is created, we must apply it to an interface with the same command used for the IP standard list:

```
Corp(config-if)#ip access-group 110 in
```

Or this:

```
Corp(config-if)#ip access-group 110 out
```

Next, we'll check out some examples of how to use an extended access list.

Extended Access List Example 1

For our first scenario, we'll use Figure 2.5. What do we need to do to deny access to a host at 172.16.50.5 on the Finance department LAN for both Telnet and FTP services? All other services on this and all other hosts are acceptable for the Sales and Marketing departments to access.

FIGURE 2.5 Extended ACL example 1

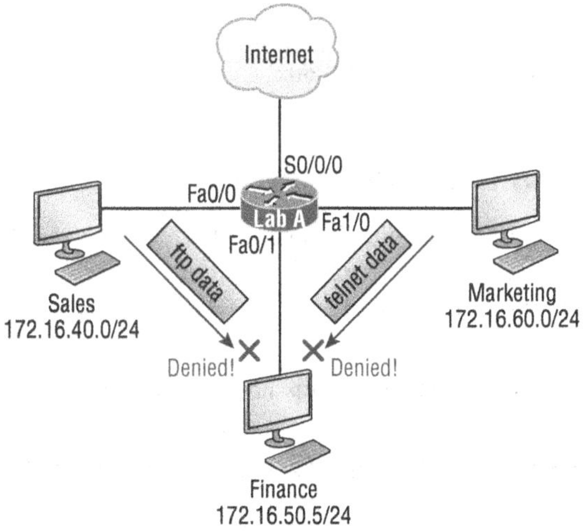

Here's the ACL we must create:

```
Lab_A#config t
Lab_A(config)#access-list 110 deny tcp any host 172.16.50.5 eq 21
Lab_A(config)#access-list 110 deny tcp any host 172.16.50.5 eq 23
Lab_A(config)#access-list 110 permit ip any any
```

The `access-list 110` tells the router we're creating an extended IP ACL. The `tcp` is the protocol field in the Network layer header. If the list doesn't say `tcp` here, you cannot filter by TCP port numbers 21 and 23, as shown in the example. Remember that these values indicate FTP and Telnet, which both use TCP for connection-oriented services. The `any` command is the source, which means any source IP address, and the `host` is the destination IP address. This ACL says that all IP traffic will be permitted from any host except FTP and Telnet to host 172.16.50.5 from any source.

> **NOTE** Remember, instead of the `host 172.16.50.5` command when we created the extended access list, we could have entered `172.16.50.5 0.0.0.0`. There would be no difference in the result other than the router would change the command to `host 172.16.50.5` in the running-config.

After the list is created, it must be applied to the FastEthernet 0/1 interface outbound because we want to block all traffic from getting to host 172.16.50.5 and performing FTP and Telnet. If this list was created to block access only from the Sales LAN to host 172.16.50.5, then we'd have put this list closer to the source or on FastEthernet 0/0. In that situation, we'd apply the list to inbound traffic. This highlights the fact that you really need to analyze each situation carefully before creating and applying ACLs!

Now let's go ahead and apply the list to interface Fa0/1 to block all outside FTP and Telnet access to the host 172.16.50.5:

```
Lab_A(config)#int fa0/1
Lab_A(config-if)#ip access-group 110 out
```

Extended Access List Example 2

We're going to use Figure 2.4 again, which has four LANs and a serial connection. We need to prevent Telnet access to the networks attached to the E1 and E2 interfaces.

The configuration on the router would look something like this, although the answer can vary:

```
Router(config)#access-list 110 deny tcp any 172.16.48.0 0.0.15.255
eq 23
Router(config)#access-list 110 deny tcp any 172.16.192.0 0.0.63.255
eq 23
Router(config)#access-list 110 permit ip any any
Router(config)#interface Ethernet 1
Router(config-if)#ip access-group 110 out
```

```
Router(config-if)#interface Ethernet 2
Router(config-if)#ip access-group 110 out
```

Here are the key factors to understand from this list:

- First, you need to verify that the number range is correct for the type of access list you are creating. In this example, it's extended, so the range must be 100–199.
- Second, you must verify that the protocol field matches the upper-layer process or application, which in this case, is TCP port 23 (Telnet).

> **TIP** The protocol parameter must be TCP because Telnet uses TCP. If it were TFTP instead, then the protocol parameter would have to be UDP because TFTP uses UDP at the Transport layer.

- Third, verify that the destination port number matches the application you're filtering for. In this case, port 23 matches Telnet, which is correct, but know that you can also type **telnet** at the end of the line instead of 23.
- Finally, the test statement `permit ip any any` is important to have there at the end of the list because it means to enable all packets other than Telnet packets destined for the LANs connected to Ethernet 1 and Ethernet 2.

Extended Access List Example 3

I want to guide you through one more extended ACL example before we move on to named ACLs. Figure 2.6 displays the network we're going to use for this last scenario.

FIGURE 2.6 Extended ACL example 3

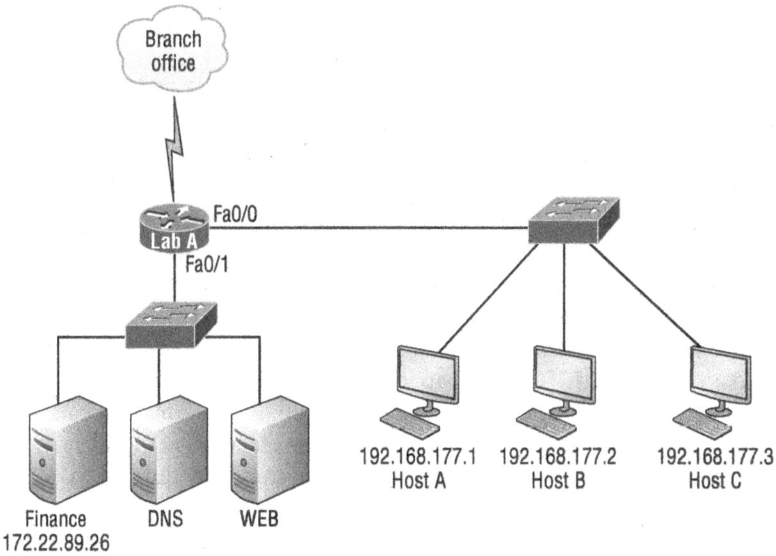

In this example, we're going to allow HTTP access to the Finance server from source Host B only. All other traffic will be permitted. We need to be able to configure this in only three test statements, and then we'll need to add the interface configuration.

Let's take what we've learned and knock this one out:

```
Lab_A#config t
Lab_A(config)#access-list 110 permit tcp host 192.168.177.2 host
172.22.89.26 eq 80
Lab_A(config)#access-list 110 deny tcp any host 172.22.89.26 eq 80
Lab_A(config)#access-list 110 permit ip any any
```

This is really pretty simple! First, we need to permit Host B HTTP access to the Finance server. But because all other traffic must be allowed, we must detail who cannot HTTP to the Finance server, so the second test statement is there to deny anyone else from using HTTP on the Finance server. Finally, now that Host B can HTTP to the Finance server and everyone else can't, we'll permit all other traffic with our third test statement.

Not so bad—this just takes a little thought! But wait, we're not done yet because we still need to apply this to an interface. Because extended access lists are typically applied closest to the source, we should simply place this inbound on Fa0/0, right? Well, this is one time we're not going to follow the rules. Our challenge required us to allow only HTTP traffic to the Finance server from Host B. If we apply the ACL inbound on Fa0/0, then the branch office would be able to access the Finance server and perform HTTP. So in this example, we need to place the ACL closest to the destination:

```
Lab_A(config)#interface fastethernet 0/1
Lab_A(config-if)#ip access-group 110 out
```

Perfect! Now let's get into how to create ACLs using names.

Named ACLs

As I said earlier, *named* access lists are just another way to create standard and extended access lists. In medium to large enterprises, managing ACLs can become a real hassle over time! A handy way to make things easier is to copy the access list to a text editor, edit the list, and then paste the new list back into the router, which would work pretty well if it weren't for the "pack rat" mentality. It's really common to think things like, "What if I find a problem with the new list and need to back out of the change?" This and other factors cause people to hoard unapplied ACLs, and over time, they can seriously build up on a router, leading to more questions like, "What were these ACLs for? Are they important? Do I need them?" All good questions, and named access lists are the answer to this problem!

And, of course, this kind of thing can also apply to access lists that are up and running. Let's say you come into an existing network and are looking at access lists on a router. Suppose you find an access list 177, which happens to be an extended access list that's a whopping 93 lines long. This leads to more of the same bunch of questions and can even lead to needless existential despair! Instead, wouldn't it be a whole lot easier to identify an access list with a name like "FinanceLAN" rather than one mysteriously dubbed "177"?

To our collective relief, named access lists allow us to use names for creating and applying either standard or extended access lists. There's really nothing new or different about these ACLs aside from being readily identifiable in a way that makes sense to humans, but there are some subtle changes to the syntax. So let's re-create the standard access list we created earlier for our test network in Figure 2.2 using a named access list:

```
Lab_A#config t
Lab_A(config)# ip access-list ?
  extended     Extended Access List
  log-update   Control access list log updates
  logging      Control access list logging
  resequence   Resequence Access List
  standard     Standard Access List
```

Notice that I started by typing **ip access-list**, not **access-list**. Doing this allows me to enter a named access list. Next, I'll need to specify it as a standard access list:

```
Lab_A(config)#ip access-list standard ?
  <1-99>       Standard IP access-list number
  <1300-1999>  Standard IP access-list number (expanded range)
  WORD         Access-list name

Lab_A(config)#ip access-list standard BlockSales
Lab_A(config-std-nacl)#
```

I've specified a standard access list and then added the name, BlockSales. I definitely could've used a number for a standard access list, but instead, I chose to use a nice, clear, descriptive name. And notice that after entering the name, I hit Enter, and the router prompt changed. This confirms that I'm now in named access list configuration mode and that I'm entering the named access list:

```
Lab_A(config-std-nacl)#?
Standard Access List configuration commands:
  default  Set a command to its defaults
  deny     Specify packets to reject
  exit     Exit from access-list configuration mode
  no       Negate a command or set its defaults
  permit   Specify packets to forward

Lab_A(config-std-nacl)#deny 172.16.40.0 0.0.0.255
Lab_A(config-std-nacl)#permit any
Lab_A(config-std-nacl)#exit
Lab_A(config)#^Z
Lab_A#
```

So, I've entered the access list and then exited configuration mode. Next, I'll take a look at the running configuration to verify that the access list is indeed in the router:

```
Lab_A#sh running-config | begin ip access
ip access-list standard BlockSales
 deny   172.16.40.0 0.0.0.255
 permit any
!
```

And there it is: the BlockSales access list has truly been created and is in the running-config of the router. Next, I'll need to apply the access list to the correct interface:

```
Lab_A#config t
Lab_A(config)#int fa0/1
Lab_A(config-if)#ip access-group BlockSales out
```

Clear skies! At this point, we've re-created the work done earlier using a named access list. But let's take our IP extended example, shown in Figure 2.6, and redo that list using a named ACL instead as well.

Same business requirements: allow HTTP access to the Finance server from source Host B only. All other traffic is permitted.

```
Lab_A#config t
Lab_A(config)#ip access-list extended 110
Lab_A(config-ext-nacl)#permit tcp host 192.168.177.2 host 172.22.89.26 eq 80
Lab_A(config-ext-nacl)#deny tcp any host 172.22.89.26 eq 80
Lab_A(config-ext-nacl)#permit ip any any
Lab_A(config-ext-nacl)#int fa0/1
Lab_A(config-if)#ip access-group 110 out
```

It's true—I named the extended list with a number, but sometimes it's okay to do that! I'm guessing that named ACLs don't seem all that exciting or different to you, do they? Maybe not in this configuration, except that I don't need to start every line with `access-list 110`, which is nice. But where named ACLs really shine is that they allow us to insert, delete, or edit a single line. That isn't just nice, it's wonderful! Numbered ACLs just can't compare with that, and I'll demonstrate this in a minute.

Remarks

The `remark` keyword is really important because it arms you with the ability to include comments—remarks—regarding the entries you've made in both your IP standard and extended ACLs. Remarks are very cool because they efficiently increase your ability to examine and understand your ACLs to superhero level! Without them, you'd be caught in a quagmire of potentially meaningless numbers without anything to help you recall what all those numbers mean.

Even though you have the option of placing your remarks either before or after a `permit` or `deny` statement, I totally recommend that you choose to position them consistently so you don't get confused about which remark is relevant to a specific `permit` or `deny` statement.

To get this going for both standard and extended ACLs, just use the `access-list` *`access-list number`* `remark` *`remark`* global configuration command like this:

```
R2#config t
R2(config)#access-list 110 remark Permit Bob from Sales Only To Finance
R2(config)#access-list 110 permit ip host 172.16.40.1 172.16.50.0 0.0.0.255
R2(config)#access-list 110 deny ip 172.16.40.0 0.0.0.255 172.16.50.0 0.0.0.255
R2(config)#ip access-list extended No_Telnet
R2(config-ext-nacl)#remark Deny all of Sales from Telnetting to Marketing
R2(config-ext-nacl)#deny tcp 172.16.40.0 0.0.0.255 172.16.60.0 0.0.0.255 eq 23
R2(config-ext-nacl)#permit ip any any
R2(config-ext-nacl)#do show run
[output cut]
!
ip access-list extended No_Telnet
 remark Stop all of Sales from Telnetting to Marketing
 deny   tcp 172.16.40.0 0.0.0.255 172.16.60.0 0.0.0.255 eq telnet
 permit ip any any
!
access-list 110 remark Permit Bob from Sales Only To Finance
access-list 110 permit ip host 172.16.40.1 172.16.50.0 0.0.0.255
access-list 110 deny   ip 172.16.40.0 0.0.0.255 172.16.50.0 0.0.0.255
access-list 110 permit ip any any
!
```

Sweet—I was able to add a `remark` to both an extended list and a named access list. Keep in mind that you cannot see these remarks in the output of the `show access-list` command, which we'll cover next because they only show up in the running-config.

Speaking of ACLs, I still need to show you how to monitor and verify them. This is an important topic, so pay attention!

Monitoring Access Lists

It's always good to be able to verify a router's configuration. Table 2.1 lists the commands that we can use to achieve that.

TABLE 2.1 Commands used to verify access-list configuration

Command	Effect
`show access-list`	Displays all access lists and their parameters configured on the router. Also shows statistics about how many times the line either permitted or denied a packet. This command does not show you which interface the list is applied on.
`show access-list 110`	Reveals only the parameters for access list 110. Again, this command will not reveal the specific interface the list is set on.
`show ip access-list`	Shows only the IP access lists configured on the router.
`show ip interface`	Displays which interfaces have access lists set on them.
`show running-config`	Shows the access lists and the specific interfaces that have ACLs applied on them.

We've already used the `show running-config` command to verify that a named access list was in the router, so now let's take a look at the output from some of the other commands.

The `show access-list` command will list all ACLs on the router, whether they're applied to an interface or not:

```
Lab_A#show access-list
Standard IP access list 10
    10 deny   172.16.40.0, wildcard bits 0.0.0.255
    20 permit any
Standard IP access list BlockSales
    10 deny   172.16.40.0, wildcard bits 0.0.0.255
    20 permit any
Extended IP access list 110
    10 deny tcp any host 172.16.30.5 eq ftp
    20 deny tcp any host 172.16.30.5 eq telnet
    30 permit ip any any
    40 permit tcp host 192.168.177.2 host 172.22.89.26 eq www
    50 deny tcp any host 172.22.89.26 eq www
Lab_A#
```

First, notice that access list 10 as well as both of our named access lists appear on this list—remember, my extended named ACL was named 110! Second, notice that even though I entered actual numbers for TCP ports in access list 110, the `show` command gives us the protocol names rather than TCP ports for serious clarity.

But wait! The best part is those numbers on the left side: 10, 20, 30, etc. Those are called sequence numbers, and they allow us to edit our named ACL. Here's an example where I added a line into the named extended ACL 110:

```
Lab_A (config)#ip access-list extended 110
Lab_A (config-ext-nacl)#21 deny udp any host 172.16.30.5 eq 69
Lab_A#show access-list
[output cut]
Extended IP access list 110
    10 deny tcp any host 172.16.30.5 eq ftp
    20 deny tcp any host 172.16.30.5 eq telnet
    21 deny udp any host 172.16.30.5 eq tftp
    30 permit ip any any
    40 permit tcp host 192.168.177.2 host 172.22.89.26 eq www
    50 deny tcp any host 172.22.89.26 eq www
```

You can see that I added line 21. I could have deleted a line or edited an existing line as well—very nice!

Here's the output of the `show ip interface` command:

```
Lab_A#show ip interface fa0/1
FastEthernet0/1 is up, line protocol is up
  Internet address is 172.16.30.1/24
  Broadcast address is 255.255.255.255
  Address determined by non-volatile memory
  MTU is 1500 bytes
  Helper address is not set
  Directed broadcast forwarding is disabled
  Outgoing access list is 110
  Inbound access list is not set
  Proxy ARP is enabled
  Security level is default
  Split horizon is enabled
[output cut]
```

Be sure to notice the bold line indicating that the outgoing list on this interface is 110, yet the inbound access list isn't set. What happened to BlockSales? I had configured that outbound on Fa0/1! That's true, I did, but I configured my extended named ACL 110 and applied it to Fa0/1 as well. You can't have two lists on the same interface in the same direction, so what happened here is that my last configuration overwrote the BlockSales configuration.

And as I've already mentioned, you can use the `show running-config` command to see any and all access lists.

Summary

In this chapter, you learned how to configure standard access lists to properly filter IP traffic. You discovered what a standard access list is and how to apply it to a Cisco router to add security to your network. You also learned how to configure extended access lists to further filter IP traffic. We also covered the key differences between standard and extended access lists as well as how to apply them to Cisco routers.

Moving on, you found out how to configure named access lists and apply them to interfaces on the router and learned that named access lists offer the huge advantage of being easily identifiable and, therefore, a whole lot easier to manage than mysterious access lists that are simply referred to by obscure numbers.

The chapter wrapped up by showing you how to monitor and verify selected access-list configurations on a router.

Exam Essentials

Remember the standard and extended IP access-list number ranges. The number ranges you can use to configure a standard IP access list are 1–99 and 1300–1999. The number ranges for an extended IP access list are 100–199 and 2000–2699.

Understand the term *implicit deny*. At the end of every access list is an *implicit deny*. What this means is that if a packet does not match any of the lines in the access list, it will be discarded. Also, if you have nothing but `deny` statements in your list, the list will not permit any packets.

Understand the standard IP access-list configuration command. To configure a standard IP access list, use the access-list numbers 1–99 or 1300–1999 in global configuration mode. Choose `permit` or `deny`, then choose the source IP address you want to filter on using one of the three techniques covered in this chapter.

Understand the extended IP access-list configuration command. To configure an extended IP access list, use the access-list numbers 100–199 or 2000–2699 in global configuration mode. Choose `permit` or `deny`, the Network layer protocol field, the source IP address you want to filter on, the destination address you want to filter on, and finally, the Transport layer port number if TCP or UDP has been specified as the protocol.

Remember the command to verify an access list on a router interface. To see whether an access list is set on an interface and in which direction it is filtering, use the `show ip interface` command. This command will not show you the contents of the access list, merely which access lists are applied on the interface.

Remember the command to verify the access-list configuration. To see the configured access lists on your router, use the `show access-list` command. This command will not show you which interfaces have an access list set.

Written Lab

The answers to this lab can be found in Appendix A, "Answers to the Written Labs."

Write the answers to the following questions:

1. What command would you use to configure a standard IP access list to prevent all machines on network 172.16.0.0/16 from accessing your Ethernet network?
2. What command would you use to apply the access list you created in question 1 to an Ethernet interface outbound?
3. What command(s) would you use to create an access list that denies host 192.168.15.5 access to an Ethernet network?
4. Which command verifies that you've entered the access list correctly?
5. What two tools can help notify and prevent DoS attacks?
6. What command(s) would you use to create an extended access list that stops host 172.16.10.1 from telnetting to host 172.16.30.5?
7. What command would you use to set an access list on a VTY line?
8. Write the same standard IP access list you wrote in question 1 but this time as a named access list.
9. Write the command to apply the named access list you created in question 8 to an Ethernet interface outbound.
10. Which command verifies the placement and direction of an access list?

Review Questions

NOTE The following questions are designed to test your understanding of this chapter's material. For more information on how to get additional questions, please see this book's introduction.

The answers to these questions can be found in Appendix B, "Answers to the Review Questions."

1. Which of the following statements is false when a packet is being compared to an access list?
   - **A.** It's always compared with each line of the access list in sequential order.
   - **B.** Once the packet matches the condition on a line of the access list, the packet is acted upon and no further comparisons take place.
   - **C.** There is an implicit "deny" at the end of each access list.
   - **D.** Until all lines have been analyzed, the comparison is not over.

2. You need to create an access list that will prevent hosts in the network range of 192.168.160.0 to 192.168.191.0. Which of the following lists will you use?
   - **A.** `access-list 10 deny 192.168.160.0 255.255.224.0`
   - **B.** `access-list 10 deny 192.168.160.0 0.0.191.255`
   - **C.** `access-list 10 deny 192.168.160.0 0.0.31.255`
   - **D.** `access-list 10 deny 192.168.0.0 0.0.31.255`

3. You have created a named access list called Blocksales. Which of the following is a valid command for applying this to packets trying to enter interface Fa0/0 of your router?
   - **A.** `(config)#ip access-group 110 in`
   - **B.** `(config-if)#ip access-group 110 in`
   - **C.** `(config-if)#ip access-group Blocksales in`
   - **D.** `(config-if)#Blocksales ip access-list in`

4. Which access list statement will permit all HTTP sessions to network 192.168.144.0/24 containing web servers?
   - **A.** `access-list 110 permit tcp 192.168.144.0 0.0.0.255 any eq 80`
   - **B.** `access-list 110 permit tcp any 192.168.144.0 0.0.0.255 eq 80`
   - **C.** `access-list 110 permit tcp 192.168.144.0 0.0.0.255 192.168.144.0 0.0.0.255 any eq 80`
   - **D.** `access-list 110 permit udp any 192.168.144.0 eq 80`

5. Which of the following access lists will allow only HTTP traffic into network 196.15.7.0?
   - **A.** `access-list 100 permit tcp any 196.15.7.0 0.0.0.255 eq www`
   - **B.** `access-list 10 deny tcp any 196.15.7.0 eq www`
   - **C.** `access-list 100 permit 196.15.7.0 0.0.0.255 eq www`
   - **D.** `access-list 110 permit ip any 196.15.7.0 0.0.0.255`
   - **E.** `access-list 110 permit www 196.15.7.0 0.0.0.255`

6. What router command allows you to determine whether an IP access list is enabled on a particular interface?
   - A. `show ip port`
   - B. `show access-lists`
   - C. `show ip interface`
   - D. `show access-lists interface`

7. An administrator configures an extended ACL to prevent devices on the 192.168.1.0 subnet from accessing the remote server at 10.1.1.5. Where should the administrator place this ACL for the most efficient use of network resources?
   - A. Closest to the hosts in the 192.168.1.0 subnet with an outbound list
   - B. Closest to the hosts in the 192.168.1.0 subnet with an inbound list
   - C. Furthest router interface closest to the remote server 10.1.1.5 with an inbound list
   - D. Furthest router interface to the remote server 10.1.1.5 with an outbound list

8. If you wanted to deny all Telnet connections to only network 192.168.10.0, which command could you use?
   - A. `access-list 100 deny tcp 192.168.10.0 255.255.255.0 eq telnet`
   - B. `access-list 100 deny tcp 192.168.10.0 0.255.255.255 eq telnet`
   - C. `access-list 100 deny tcp any 192.168.10.0 0.0.0.255 eq 23`
   - D. `access-list 100 deny 192.168.10.0 0.0.0.255 any eq 23`

9. If you want to deny FTP access from network 200.200.10.0 to network 200.199.11.0 but allow everything else, which of the following command strings is valid?
   - A. `access-list 110 deny 200.200.10.0 to network 200.199.11.0 eq ftp`
     `access-list 111 permit ip any 0.0.0.0 255.255.255.255`
   - B. `access-list 1 deny ftp 200.200.10.0 200.199.11.0 any any`
   - C. `access-list 100 deny tcp 200.200.10.0 0.0.0.255 200.199.11.0 0.0.0.255 eq ftp`
   - D. `access-list 198 deny tcp 200.200.10.0 0.0.0.255 200.199.11.0 0.0.0.255 eq ftp`
     `access-list 198 permit ip any 0.0.0.0 255.255.255.255`

10. You want to create an extended access list that denies the subnet of the following host: 172.16.50.172/20. Which of the following would you start your list with?
    - A. `access-list 110 deny ip 172.16.48.0 255.255.240.0 any`
    - B. `access-list 110 udp deny 172.16.0.0 0.0.255.255 ip any`
    - C. `access-list 110 deny tcp 172.16.64.0 0.0.31.255 any eq 80`
    - D. `access-list 110 deny ip 172.16.48.0 0.0.15.255 any`

11. Which of the following is the wildcard (inverse) version of a /27 mask?
    - A. 0.0.0.7
    - B. 0.0.0.31
    - C. 0.0.0.27
    - D. 0.0.31.255

12. You want to create an extended access list that denies the subnet of the following host: 172.16.198.94/19. Which of the following would you start your list with?
    - A. `access-list 110 deny ip 172.16.192.0 0.0.31.255 any`
    - B. `access-list 110 deny ip 172.16.0.0 0.0.255.255 any`
    - C. `access-list 10 deny ip 172.16.172.0 0.0.31.255 any`
    - D. `access-list 110 deny ip 172.16.188.0 0.0.15.255 any`

13. The following access list has been applied to an interface on a router:

```
access-list 101 deny tcp 199.111.16.32 0.0.0.31 host 199.168.5.60
```

    Which of the following IP addresses will be blocked because of this single rule in the list? (Choose all that apply.)
    - A. 199.111.16.67
    - B. 199.111.16.38
    - C. 199.111.16.65
    - D. 199.11.16.54

14. Which of the following commands connects access list 110 inbound to interface Ethernet0?
    - A. `Router(config)#`**`ip access-group 110 in`**
    - B. `Router(config)#`**`ip access-list 110 in`**
    - C. `Router(config-if)#`**`ip access-group 110 in`**
    - D. `Router(config-if)#`**`ip access-list 110 in`**

15. What is the effect of this single-line access list?

```
access-list 110 deny ip 172.16.10.0 0.0.0.255 host 1.1.1.1
```

    - A. Denies only the computer at 172.16.10
    - B. Denies all traffic
    - C. Denies the subnet 172.16.10.0/26
    - D. Denies the subnet 172.16.10.0/25

16. You configure the following access list. What will the result of this access list be?

```
access-list 110 deny tcp 10.1.1.128 0.0.0.63 any eq smtp
access-list 110 deny tcp any any eq 23
int ethernet 0
ip access-group 110 out
```

A. Email and Telnet will be allowed out E0.

B. Email and Telnet will be allowed in E0.

C. Everything but email and Telnet will be allowed out E0.

D. No IP traffic will be allowed out E0.

17. Which of the following series of commands will restrict Telnet access to the router?

A.
```
Lab_A(config)#access-list 10 permit 172.16.1.1
Lab_A(config)#line con 0
Lab_A(config-line)#ip access-group 10 in
```

B.
```
Lab_A(config)#access-list 10 permit 172.16.1.1
Lab_A(config)#line vty 0 4
Lab_A(config-line)#access-class 10 out
```

C.
```
Lab_A(config)#access-list 10 permit 172.16.1.1
Lab_A(config)#line vty 0 4
Lab_A(config-line)#access-class 10 in
```

D.
```
Lab_A(config)#access-list 10 permit 172.16.1.1
Lab_A(config)#line vty 0 4
Lab_A(config-line)#ip access-group 10 in
```

18. While examining excessive traffic on the network, it is noted that all incoming packets on an interface appear to be allowed even though an IPv4 ACL is applied to the interface. Which misconfigurations cause this behavior? (Choose two.)

A. The ACL is empty.

B. A matching permit statement is too broadly defined.

C. The packets fail to match any permit statement.

D. A matching deny statement is too high in the access list.

E. A matching permit statement is too high in the access list.

19. An engineer is configuring remote access to a router from IP subnet 10.19.8.0/28. The domain name, crypto keys, and SSH have been configured. Which configuration enables the traffic on the destination router?

A.
```
line vty 0 15
access-class 120 in
!
ip access-list extended 120
permit tcp 10.19.8.0 0.0.0.15 any eq 22
```

B.
```
interface FastEthernet0/0
ip address 10.122.49.1 255.255.255.252
ip access-group 10 in
!
ip access-list standard 10
permit udp 10.139.58.0 0.0.0.7 host 10.122.49.1 eq 22
```

C.
```
interface FastEthernet0/0
ip address 10.122.49.1 255.255.255.252
ip access-group 110 in
!
ip access-list standard 110
permit tcp 10.139.58.0 0.0.0.15 eq 22 host 10.122.49.1
```

D.
```
line vty 0 15
access-group 120 in
!
ip access-list extended 120
permit tcp 10.139.58.0 0.0.0.15 any eq 22
```

20. What are the two numbered ranges you can use to create an extended access-list?

A. 1–99 and 1300–1999

B. 100–199 and 2000–2699

C. 200–299 and 3000–3699

D. 300–399 and 4000–4699

Chapter 3

Internet Protocol Version 6 (IPv6)

THE FOLLOWING CCNA EXAM TOPICS ARE COVERED IN THIS CHAPTER:

✓ **1.0 Network Fundamentals**

- 1.8 Configure and verify IPv6 addressing and prefix
- 1.9 Describe IPv6 address types
  - 1.9.a Unicast (global, unique local, and link local)
  - 1.9.b Anycast
  - 1.9.c Multicast
  - 1.9.d Modified EUI 64

✓ **3.0 IP Connectivity**

- 3.3 Configure and verify IPv4 and IPv6 static routing

We've covered a lot of ground in this book series so far, and although the journey has been tough at times, it's been well worth it! But our networking expedition isn't quite over yet because we still have the vastly important frontier of IPv6 to explore. There's still some expansive territory to cover with this subject, so gear up and get ready to discover all you need to know about IPv6. Understanding IPv6 is vital now, so you'll be much better equipped and prepared to meet today's real-world networking challenges as well as ace the exam. This chapter is packed and brimming with all the IPv6 information you'll need to complete your Cisco exam trek successfully, so get psyched—we're in the home stretch!

I probably don't need to say this, but I will because I really want to go the distance and do everything I can to ensure that you arrive and achieve success. You must have a solid hold on IPv4 by now, but if you're still not confident with it or feel you could use a refresher, just page back to the chapters on TCP/IP and subnetting in book 1.

People refer to IPv6 as "the next-generation Internet protocol," and it was originally created as the solution to IPv4's inevitable and impending address-exhaustion crisis. Although you've probably heard a thing or two about IPv6 already, it has been improved even further in the quest to bring us the flexibility, efficiency, capability, and optimized functionality that can effectively meet our world's seemingly insatiable thirst for ever-evolving technologies and increasing access. The capacity of its predecessor, IPv4, pales wan and ghostly in comparison, which is why IPv4 is destined to fade into history completely, making way for IPv6 and the future.

The IPv6 header and address structure have been completely overhauled, and many of the features that were basically just afterthoughts and addenda in IPv4 are now included as full-blown standards in IPv6. It's power-packed, well equipped with robust and elegant features, poised and prepared to manage the mind-blowing demands of the Internet to come!

After an introduction like that, I understand if you're a little apprehensive, but I promise—really—to make this chapter and its VIP topic pretty painless for you. You might even find yourself enjoying it—I definitely did! Because IPv6 is so complex, while still being so elegant, innovative, and powerful, it fascinates me like some weird combination of a sleek, new Aston Martin and a riveting futuristic novel. Hopefully, you'll experience this chapter as an awesome ride and enjoy reading it as much as I did writing it!

NOTE

To find your included bonus material, as well as Todd Lammle videos, practice questions, and hands-on labs, please see `www.lammle.com/ccna`.

Why Do We Need IPv6?

Well, the short answer is that we need to communicate, and our current system isn't really cutting it anymore. It's kind of like the Pony Express trying to compete with airmail! Consider how much time and effort we've been investing for years while we scratch our heads to resourcefully come up with slick new ways to conserve bandwidth and IP addresses. Sure, variable-length subnet masks (VLSMs) are wonderful and cool, but they're really just another invention to help us cope while we desperately struggle to overcome the worsening address drought.

I'm not exaggerating at all about how dire things are getting, because it's simply reality. The number of people and devices that connect to networks increases dramatically each and every day, which is not a bad thing. We're just finding new and exciting ways to communicate with more people more often, which is a good thing. And it's not likely to go away or even decrease in the littlest bit because communicating and making connections are, in fact, basic human needs—they're in our very nature. But with our numbers increasing along with the rising tide of people joining the communications party increasing as well, the forecast for our current system isn't exactly clear skies and smooth sailing. IPv4, on which our ability to do all this connecting and communicating is presently dependent, is quickly running out of addresses for us to use.

IPv4 has only about 4.3 billion addresses available—in theory—and we know that we don't even get to use most of those! Sure, the use of Classless Inter-Domain Routing (CIDR) and Network Address Translation (NAT) has helped to extend the inevitable dearth of addresses, but we will still run out of them, and it's going to happen within a few years. China is barely online, and we know there's a huge population of people and corporations there that surely want to be. Myriad reports give us all kinds of numbers, but all you really need to think about to realize that I'm not just being an alarmist is this: there are about 7 billion people in the world today, and it's estimated that only just under half of the population is currently connected to the Internet—wow!

That statistic is basically screaming at us the ugly truth that based on IPv4's capacity, every person can't even have a computer, let alone all the other IP devices we use with them! I have more than one computer, and it's pretty likely that you do too, and I'm not even including in the mix the phones, laptops, game consoles, fax machines, routers, switches, and mother lode of other devices we use every day. So, I think I've made it pretty clear that we've got to do something before we run out of addresses and lose the ability to connect with each other as we know it. And that "something" just happens to be implementing IPv6.

The Benefits and Uses of IPv6

What's so fabulous about IPv6? Is it really the answer to our coming dilemma? Is it really worth it to upgrade from IPv4? All good questions—you may even think of a few more. Of course, there's going to be that group of people with the time-tested "resistance to change syndrome," but don't listen to them. If we had done that years ago, we'd still be waiting weeks, even months, for our mail to arrive via horseback. Instead, just know that the answer is a resounding *yes*, it is really the answer, and it is worth the upgrade! Not only does IPv6 give us lots of addresses (3.4×10^{38} = definitely enough), but there are tons of other features built into this version that make it well worth the cost, time, and effort required to migrate to it.

Today's networks, as well as the Internet, have a ton of unforeseen requirements that simply weren't even considerations when IPv4 was created. We've tried to compensate with a collection of add-ons that can actually make implementing them more difficult than they would be if they were required by a standard. By default, IPv6 has improved on and included many of those features as standard and mandatory. One of these sweet new standards is IPsec—a feature that provides end-to-end security.

But it's the efficiency features that are really going to rock the house! For starters, the headers in an IPv6 packet have half the fields, and they are aligned to 64 bits, which gives us some seriously souped-up processing speed. Compared to IPv4, lookups happen at light speed! Most of the information that used to be bound into the IPv4 header was taken out, and now you can choose to put it, or parts of it, back into the header in the form of optional extension headers that follow the basic header fields.

And of course there's that whole new universe of addresses—the 3.4×10^{38} I just mentioned—but where did we get them? Did some genie just suddenly arrive and make them magically appear? That huge proliferation of addresses had to come from somewhere! Well, it just so happens that IPv6 gives us a substantially larger address space, meaning the address itself is a whole lot bigger—four times bigger, as a matter of fact. An IPv6 address is actually 128 bits in length, and no worries—I'm going to break down the address piece by piece and show you exactly what it looks like in the section "IPv6 Addressing and Expressions." For now, let me just say that all that additional room permits more levels of hierarchy inside the address space and a more flexible addressing architecture. It also makes routing much more efficient and scalable because the addresses can be aggregated a lot more effectively. And IPv6 also allows multiple addresses for hosts and networks. This is especially important for enterprises veritably drooling for enhanced access and availability. Plus, the new version of IP now includes expanded use of multicast communication—one device sending to many hosts or to a select group—that joins in to seriously boost efficiency on networks because communications will be more specific.

IPv4 uses broadcasts prolifically, causing a bunch of problems, the worst of which is of course the dreaded broadcast storm. This is that uncontrolled deluge of forwarded broadcast traffic that can bring an entire network to its knees and devour every last bit of bandwidth! Another nasty thing about broadcast traffic is that it interrupts each and every device on the network. When a broadcast is sent out, every machine has to stop what it's doing and respond to the traffic, whether the broadcast is relevant to it or not.

But smile assuredly, everyone. There's no such thing as a broadcast in IPv6 because it uses multicast traffic instead. And there are two other types of communications as well: unicast, which is the same as it is in IPv4, and a new type called *anycast*. Anycast communication allows the same address to be placed on more than one device so that when traffic is sent to the device service addressed in this way, it's routed to the nearest host that shares the same address. And this is just the beginning—we'll get into the various types of communication later in the section called "Address Types."

IPv6 Addressing and Expressions

Just as understanding how IP addresses are structured and used is critical with IPv4 addressing, it's also vital when it comes to IPv6. You've already read about the fact that at 128 bits, an IPv6 address is much larger than an IPv4 address. Because of this, as well as the new ways the addresses can be used, you've probably guessed that IPv6 will be more complicated to manage. But no worries! As I said, I'll break down the basics and show you what the address looks like and how you can write it as well as many of its common uses. It's going to be a little weird at first, but before you know it, you'll have it nailed!

So let's take a look at Figure 3.1, which has a sample IPv6 address broken down into sections.

FIGURE 3.1 IPv6 address example

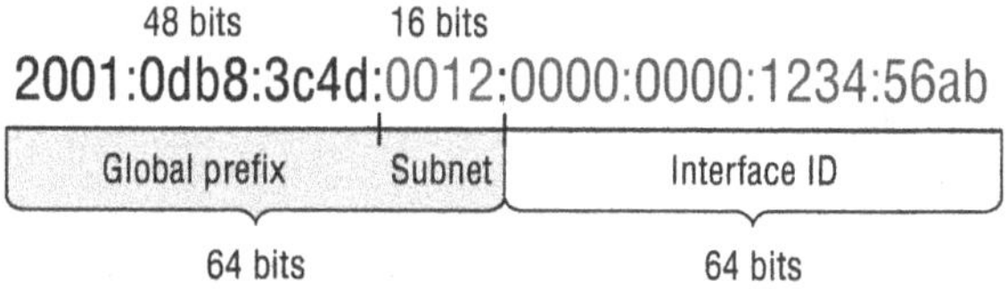

As you can clearly see, the address is definitely much larger. But what else is different? Well, first, notice that it has eight groups of numbers instead of four and also that those groups are separated by colons instead of periods. And hey, wait a second—there are letters in that address! Yep, the address is expressed in hexadecimal, just like a MAC address is, so you could say this address has eight 16-bit hexadecimal colon-delimited blocks. That's already quite a mouthful, and you probably haven't even tried to say the address out loud yet!

NOTE There are four hexadecimal characters (16 bits) in each IPv6 field (with eight fields total), separated by colons.

Shortened Expression

The good news is that there are a few tricks to help rescue us when writing these monster addresses. For one thing, you can actually leave out parts of the address to abbreviate it, but to get away with doing that, you have to follow a couple of rules. First, you can drop any leading zeros in each of the individual blocks. After you do that, the sample address from Figure 3.1 looks like this:

```
2001:db8:3c4d:12:0:0:1234:56ab
```

That's a definite improvement—at least we don't have to write all those extra zeros! But what about whole blocks that don't have anything in them except zeros? Well, we can kind of lose those, too—at least some of them. Again referring to our sample address, we can remove the two consecutive blocks of zeros by replacing them with a doubled colon, like this:

```
2001:db8:3c4d:12::1234:56ab
```

Cool—we replaced the blocks of all zeros with a doubled colon. The rule you have to follow to get away with this is that you can replace only one contiguous block of such zeros in an address. So if my address has four blocks of zeros and each of them are separated, I don't get to replace them all because I can replace only one contiguous block with a doubled colon. Check out this example:

```
2001:0000:0000:0012:0000:0000:1234:56ab
```

And just know that you *can't* do this:

```
2001::12::1234:56ab
```

Instead, the best you can do is this:

```
2001::12:0:0:1234:56ab
```

The reason the preceding example is our best shot is that if we remove two sets of zeros, the device looking at the address will have no way of knowing where the zeros go back in. Basically, the router would look at the incorrect address and say, "Well, do I place two blocks into the first set of doubled colons and two into the second set, or do I place three blocks into the first set and one block into the second set?" And on and on it would go because the information the router needs just isn't there.

Address Types

We're all familiar with IPv4's unicast, broadcast, and multicast addresses that basically define who or at least how many other devices we're talking to. But as I mentioned, IPv6 modifies that trio and introduces the anycast. Broadcasts, as we know them, have been eliminated in IPv6 because of their cumbersome inefficiency and basic tendency to drive us insane!

So, let's find out what each of these types of IPv6 addressing and communication methods do for us:

Unicast Packets addressed to a unicast address are delivered to a single interface. For load balancing, multiple interfaces across several devices can use the same address, but we'll call that an anycast address. There are a few different types of unicast addresses, but we don't need to get further into that here.

Global unicast addresses (2000::/3) These are your typical publicly routable addresses and they're the same as in IPv4. Global addresses start at 2000::/3. Figure 3.2 shows how a unicast address breaks down. The ISP can provide you with a minimum /48 network ID, which in turn provides you 16 bits to create a unique 64-bit router interface address. The last 64 bits are the unique host ID.

FIGURE 3.2 IPv6 global unicast addresses

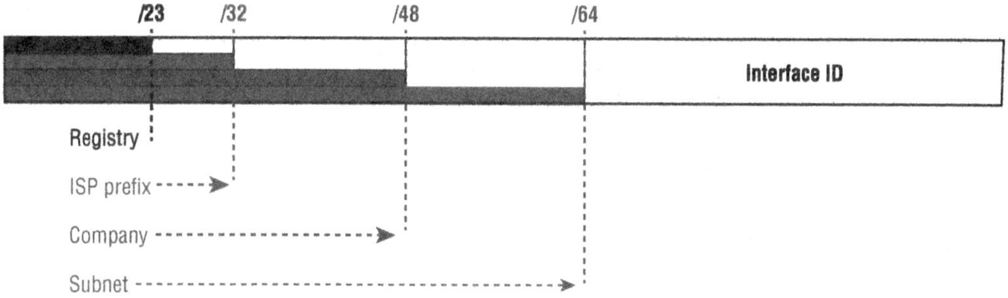

Link-local addresses (FE80::/10) Link-local addresses are only used for communications within the local subnet. These are like the Automatic Private IP Address (APIPA) addresses that Microsoft uses to automatically provide addresses in IPv4 in that they're not meant to be routed. In IPv6, they start with FE80::/10, as shown in Figure 3.3. Think of these addresses as handy tools that give you the ability to throw a temporary LAN together for meetings or create a small LAN that's not going to be routed but still needs to share and access files and services locally.

FIGURE 3.3 IPv6 link local FE80::/10: The first 10 bits define the address type.

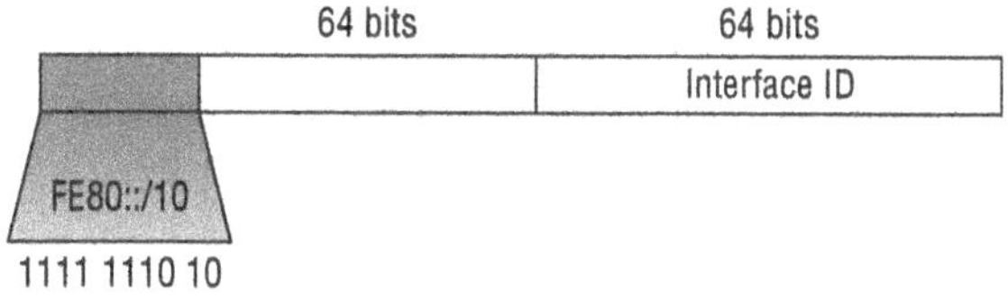

Unique local addresses (FC00::/7) These addresses are also intended for nonrouting purposes over the Internet, but they are nearly globally unique, so it's unlikely you'll ever have one of them overlap. Unique local addresses were designed to replace site-local addresses, so they basically do almost exactly what IPv4 private addresses (RFC 1918) do: allow communication throughout a site while being routable to multiple local networks. Site-local addresses were deprecated as of September 2004.

Multicast (FF00::/8) Again, as in IPv4, packets addressed to a multicast address are delivered to all interfaces tuned into the multicast address. Sometimes people call them "one-to-many" addresses because the FF00::/8 IPv6 address block sends packets to a group address rather than a single address. It's really easy to spot a multicast address in IPv6 because they always start with *FF*. We'll get deeper into multicast operation coming up in "How IPv6 Works in an Internetwork."

NOTE When an interface is configured with an IPv6 address, it automatically joins the all-nodes (FF02::1) and solicited-node (FF02::1:FFxx:xxxx) multicast groups. The all-nodes group is used to communicate with all interfaces on the local link, and the solicited-nodes multicast group is required for link-layer address resolution. Routers also join a third multicast group, the all-routers group (FF02::2).

Anycast Like multicast addresses, an anycast address identifies multiple interfaces on multiple devices. These IPv6 addresses are global and can be assigned to more than one interface, unlike an IPv6 unicast address. But there's a big difference: the anycast packet is delivered to only one device—actually, to the closest one it finds defined in terms of routing distance. This address is special because you can apply a single address to more than one host. These are referred to as "one-to-nearest" addresses because the anycast is designed to send a packet to the nearest interface that is part of that anycast group. Anycast addresses are typically only configured on routers, never hosts, and a source address could never be an anycast address. Of note is that the IETF did reserve the top 128 addresses for each /64 for use with anycast addresses.

You're probably wondering if there are any special, reserved addresses in IPv6 because you know they're there in IPv4. Well, there are—plenty of them! Let's go over those now.

Special Addresses

I'm going to list some of the addresses and address ranges (in Table 3.1) that you should definitely make sure to remember because you'll eventually use them. They're all special or reserved for a specific use, but unlike IPv4, IPv6 gives us a galaxy of addresses, so reserving a few here and there doesn't hurt at all!

NOTE When you run IPv4 and IPv6 on a router, you have what is called "dual-stack."

Let me show you how IPv6 actually works in an internetwork. We all know how IPv4 works, so let's see what's new!

TABLE 3.1 Special IPv6 addresses

Address	Meaning
0:0:0:0:0:0:0:0	Equals ::. This is the equivalent of IPv4's 0.0.0.0 and is typically the source address of a host before the host receives an IP address when you're using DHCP-driven stateful configuration.
0:0:0:0:0:0:0:1	Equals ::1. The equivalent of the loopback address 127.0.0.1 in IPv4.
0:0:0:0:0:0:192.168.100.1	This is how an IPv4 address would be written in a mixed IPv6/IPv4 network environment.
2000::/3	The global unicast address range. It's important to note that global unicast addresses are not the same as link-local addresses, which are used for communication within a single network segment or link and are not intended to be routable over the Internet.
FC00::/7	The unique local unicast range. These addresses are also intended for nonrouting purposes over the Internet.
FE80::/10	The link-local unicast range. Link-local addresses are only used for communications within the local subnet.
FF00::/8	The multicast range. Multicast addresses are delivered to all interfaces tuned into the multicast address. FF00://8 IPv6 address block forwards packets to a multicast address rather than a unicast address.
3FFF:FFFF::/32	Reserved for examples and documentation.
2001:0DB8::/32	Also reserved for examples and documentation.
2002::/16	Used with 6-to-4 tunneling, which is an IPv4-to-IPv6 transition system. The structure allows IPv6 packets to be transmitted over an IPv4 network without the need to configure explicit tunnels.

How IPv6 Works in an Internetwork

It's time to explore the finer points of IPv6. A great place to start is by showing you how to address a host and what gives it the ability to find other hosts and resources on a network.

I'll also demonstrate a device's ability to automatically address itself—something called stateless autoconfiguration—plus another type of autoconfiguration known as stateful. Keep in mind that stateful autoconfiguration uses a DHCP server in a very similar way to how it's used in an IPv4 configuration. I'll also show you how Internet Control Message Protocol (ICMP) and multicasting work for us in an IPv6 network environment.

Manual Address Assignment

To enable IPv6 on a router, you have to use the ipv6 unicast-routing global configuration command:

```
Corp(config)#ipv6 unicast-routing
```

By default, IPv6 traffic forwarding is disabled, so using this command enables it. Also, as you've probably guessed, IPv6 isn't enabled by default on any interfaces either, so we have to go to each interface individually and enable it.

There are a few different ways to do this, but a really easy way is to just add an address to the interface. You use the interface configuration command ipv6 address *<ipv6prefix>/<prefix-length>* [eui-64]to get this done.

Here's an example:

```
Corp(config-if)#ipv6 address 2001:db8:3c4d:1:0260:d6FF.FE73:1987/64
```

You can specify the entire 128-bit global IPv6 address, as I just demonstrated with the preceding command, or you can use the EUI-64 option. Remember, the EUI-64 (extended unique identifier) format allows the device to use its MAC address and pad it to make the interface ID. Check it out:

```
Corp(config-if)#ipv6 address 2001:db8:3c4d:1::/64 eui-64
```

As an alternative to typing in an IPv6 address on a router, you can enable the interface instead to permit the application of an automatic link-local address.

To configure a router so that it uses only link-local addresses, use the ipv6 enable interface configuration command:

```
Corp(config-if)#ipv6 enable
```

> **NOTE** Remember, if you have only a link-local address, you can communicate only on that local subnet.

Stateless Autoconfiguration (eui-64)

Autoconfiguration, also referred to as SLACC (Stateless Address Autoconfiguration), is an especially useful solution because it allows devices on a network to address themselves with a link-local unicast address as well as with a global unicast address. This process happens by first learning the prefix information from the router and then appending the device's own interface address as the interface ID.

But where does it get that interface ID? Well, you know every device on an Ethernet network has a physical MAC address, which is exactly what's used for the interface ID. But because the interface ID in an IPv6 address is 64 bits in length and a MAC address is only 48 bits, where do the extra 16 bits come from? The MAC address is padded in the middle with the extra bits—it's padded with FFFE.

NOTE

Each IPv6 node on the network needs a globally unique address to communicate outside its local segment. Here are a few options to assign this address to an interface:

Manual assignment: An administrator can manually configure every node with an IPv6 address.

DHCPv6 (Dynamic Host Configuration Protocol version 6): The most widely adopted protocol for dynamically assigning host addresses.

SLAAC (Stateless Address Autoconfiguration): This was designed to be a simpler and more straightforward approach to IPv6 auto-addressing.

For example, let's say I have a device with a MAC address that looks like this: 0060:d673:1987. After it's been padded, it would look like this: 0260:d6FF:FE73:1987. Figure 3.4 illustrates what an EUI-64 address looks like.

FIGURE 3.4 EUI-64 interface ID assignment

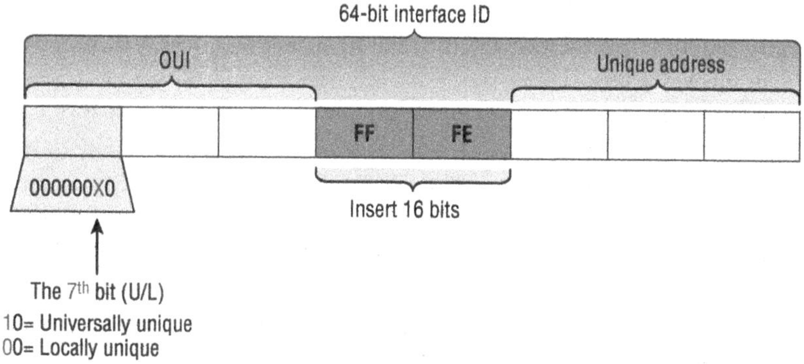

So, where did that 2 in the beginning of the address come from? Another good question. You see that part of the process of padding, called modified EUI-64 format, changes a bit to specify if the address is locally unique or globally unique. And the bit that gets changed is the seventh bit in the address.

The reason for modifying the U/L bit is that when using manually assigned addresses on an interface, it means you can assign the address 2001:db8:1:9::1/64 instead of the much longer 2001:db8:1:9:0200::1/64.

Also, suppose you are going to assign a link-local address manually. In that case, you can assign the short address fe80::1 instead of the long fe80::0200:0:0:1 or fe80:0:0:0:0200::1. So, even though at first glance it seems the IETF made this harder for you to understand IPv6 addressing by flipping the seventh bit, in reality, this made addressing much simpler. Also, because most people don't typically override the burned-in address, the U/L bit is a 0, which means that you'll see this inverted to a 1 most of the time. But because you're studying the Cisco exam objectives, you'll need to look at inverting it both ways.

Here are a few examples:

- MAC address 0090:2716:fd0f
- IPv6 EUI-64 address: 2001:0db8:0:1:0290:27ff:fe16:fd0f

That one was easy! Too easy for the Cisco exam, so let's do another:

- MAC address aa12:bcbc:1234
- IPv6 EUI-64 address: 2001:0db8:0:1:a812:bcff:febc:1234

10101010 represents the first 8 bits of the MAC address (aa), which, when inverting the seventh bit, becomes 10101000. The answer becomes A8. I can't tell you how important this is for you to understand, so bear with me and work through a couple more!

- MAC address 0c0c:dede:1234
- IPv6 EUI-64 address: 2001:0db8:0:1:0e0c:deff:fede:1234

0c is 00001100 in the first 8 bits of the MAC address, which then becomes 00001110 when flipping the seventh bit. The answer is then 0e. Let's practice one more:

- MAC address 0b34:ba12:1234
- IPv6 EUI-64 address: 2001:0db8:0:1:0934:baff:fe12:1234

0b in binary is 00001011, the first 8 bits of the MAC address, which then becomes 00001001. The answer is 09.

To perform autoconfiguration, a host goes through a basic two-step process:

1. The host needs the prefix information, similar to the network portion of an IPv4 address, to configure its interface, so it sends a router solicitation (RS) request for it. This RS is then sent out as a multicast to all routers (FF02::2). The actual information being sent is a type of ICMP message, and like everything in networking, this ICMP message has a number that identifies it. The RS message is ICMP type 133.
2. The router answers with the required prefix information via a router advertisement (RA). An RA message also happens to be a multicast packet that's sent to the all-nodes multicast address (FF02::1) and is ICMP type 134. RA messages are sent on a periodic basis, but the host sends the RS for an immediate response so it doesn't have to wait until the next scheduled RA to get what it needs.

These two steps are shown in Figure 3.5.

FIGURE 3.5 Two steps to IPv6 autoconfiguration

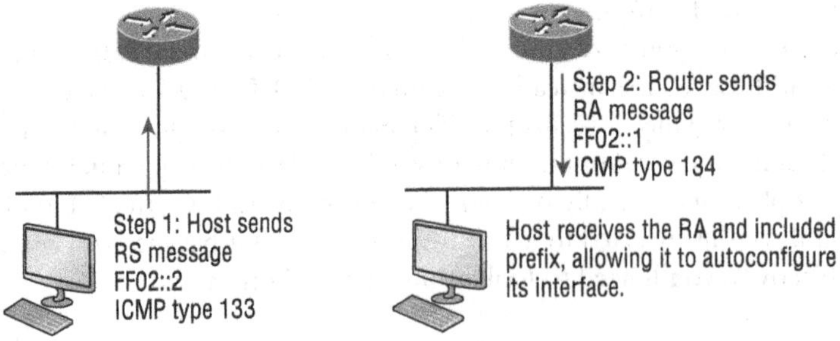

By the way, this type of autoconfiguration is also known as stateless autoconfiguration because it doesn't contact or connect to and receive any further information from the other device. We'll get to stateful configuration when we talk about DHCPv6 next.

But before we do that, first take a look at Figure 3.6. In this figure, the Branch router needs to be configured, but I just don't feel like typing in an IPv6 address on the interface connecting to the Corp router. I also don't feel like typing in any routing commands, but I need more than a link-local address on that interface, so I'm going to have to do something! So basically, I want to have the Branch router work with IPv6 on the internetwork with the least amount of effort from me. Let's see if I can get away with that.

FIGURE 3.6 IPv6 autoconfiguration example

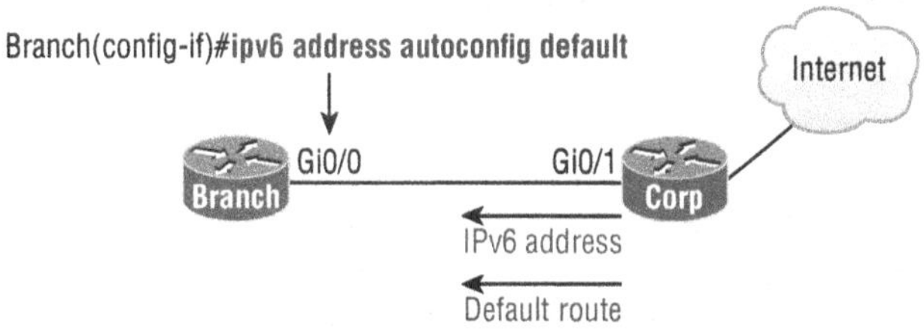

Aha—there is an easy way! I love IPv6 because it allows me to be relatively lazy when dealing with some parts of my network, yet it still works really well. By using the command `ipv6 address autoconfig`, the interface will listen for RAs and then, via the EUI-64 format, assign itself a global address—sweet!

This is all really great, but you're hopefully wondering what that `default` is doing there at the end of the command. If so, good catch! It happens to be a wonderful, optional part of the command that smoothly delivers a default route received from the Corp router, which will be automatically injected into my routing table and set as the default route—so easy!

DHCPv6 (Stateful)

DHCPv6 works pretty much the same way DHCP does in v4, with the obvious difference that it supports IPv6's new addressing scheme. And it might come as a surprise, but there are a couple of other options that DHCP still provides for us that autoconfiguration doesn't. And no, I'm not kidding—in autoconfiguration, there's absolutely no mention of DNS servers, domain names, or many of the other options that DHCP has always generously provided for us via IPv4. This is a big reason that the odds favor DHCP's continued use into the future in IPv6 at least partially—maybe even most of the time!

On booting up in IPv4, a client sends out a DHCP Discover message, looking for a server to give it the information it needs. But remember, in IPv6, the RS and RA process happens first, so if there's a DHCPv6 server on the network, the RA that comes back to the client will tell it if DHCP is available for use. If a router isn't found, the client will respond by sending out a DHCP Solicit message, which is actually a multicast message addressed with a destination of ff02::1:2 that calls out, "All DHCP agents, both servers and relays."

It's good to know that there's some support for DHCPv6 in the Cisco IOS, even though it's limited. This rather miserly support is reserved for stateless DHCP servers and tells us it doesn't offer any address management of the pool or the options available for configuring that address pool other than the DNS, domain name, default gateway, and SIP servers.

This means that you're definitely going to need another server around to supply and dispense all the additional required information—maybe even to manage the address assignment, if needed!

TIP Remember for the objectives that both stateless and stateful autoconfiguration can dynamically assign IPv6 addresses.

IPv6 Header

An IPv4 header is 20 bytes long, so because an IPv6 address is four times the size of an IPv4 address at 128 bits, its header must then be 80 bytes long, right? That makes sense and is totally intuitive, but it's also completely wrong! When the IPv6 designers devised the header, they created fewer, streamlined fields that would also result in a faster routed protocol at the same time.

Let's take a look at the streamlined IPv6 header using Figure 3.7.

FIGURE 3.7 IPv6 header

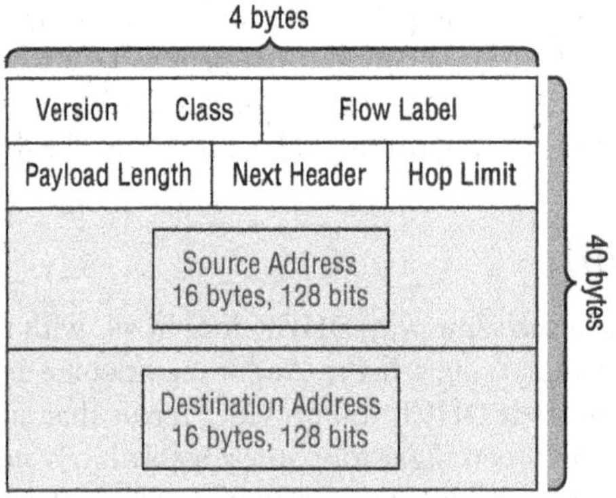

The basic IPv6 header contains eight fields, making it only twice as large as an IP header at 40 bytes. Let's zoom in on these fields:

Version This 4-bit field contains the number 6, instead of the number 4 as in IPv4.

Traffic Class This 8-bit field is like the Type of Service (ToS) field in IPv4.

Flow Label This new field, which is 24 bits long, is used to mark packets and traffic flows. A flow is a sequence of packets from a single source to a single destination host, an anycast or multicast address. The field enables efficient IPv6 flow classification.

Payload Length IPv4 had a total length field delimiting the length of the packet. IPv6's payload length describes the length of the payload only.

Next Header Because there are optional extension headers with IPv6, this field defines the next header to be read. This is in contrast to IPv4, which demands static headers with each packet.

Hop Limit This field specifies the maximum number of hops that an IPv6 packet can traverse.

TIP

For objectives, remember that the Hop Limit field is equivalent to the TTL field in IPv4's header, and the Extension header (after the destination address and not shown in the figure) is used instead of the IPv4 Fragmentation field.

Source Address This field of 16 bytes, or 128 bits, identifies the source of the packet.

Destination Address This field of 16 bytes, or 128 bits, identifies the destination of the packet.

There are also some optional extension headers following these eight fields, which carry other Network layer information. These header lengths are not a fixed number—they're of variable size.

So, what's different in the IPv6 header from the IPv4 header? Let's look at that:

- The Internet Header Length field was removed because it is no longer required. Unlike the variable-length IPv4 header, the IPv6 header is fixed at 40 bytes.
- Fragmentation is processed differently in IPv6 and does not need the Flags field in the basic IPv4 header. In IPv6, routers no longer process fragmentation; the host is responsible for fragmentation.
- The Header Checksum field at the IP layer was removed because most Data Link layer technologies already perform checksum and error control, which forces formerly optional upper-layer checksums (UDP, for example) to become mandatory.

TIP

For the objectives, remember that unlike IPv4 headers, IPv6 headers have a fixed length, use an extension header instead of the IPv4 Fragmentation field, and eliminate the IPv4 checksum field.

It's time to move on to talk about another IPv4 familiar face and find out how a certain very important, built-in protocol has evolved in IPv6.

ICMPv6

IPv4 used the ICMP workhorse for lots of tasks, including error messages like destination unreachable and troubleshooting functions like Ping and Traceroute. ICMPv6 still does those things for us, but unlike its predecessor, the v6 flavor isn't implemented as a separate layer 3 protocol. Instead, it's an integrated part of IPv6 and is carried after the basic IPv6 header information as an extension header. And ICMPv6 gives us another really cool feature—by default, it prevents IPv6 from doing any fragmentation through an ICMPv6 process called path MTU discovery. Figure 3.8 shows how ICMPv6 has evolved to become part of the IPv6 packet itself.

FIGURE 3.8 ICMPv6

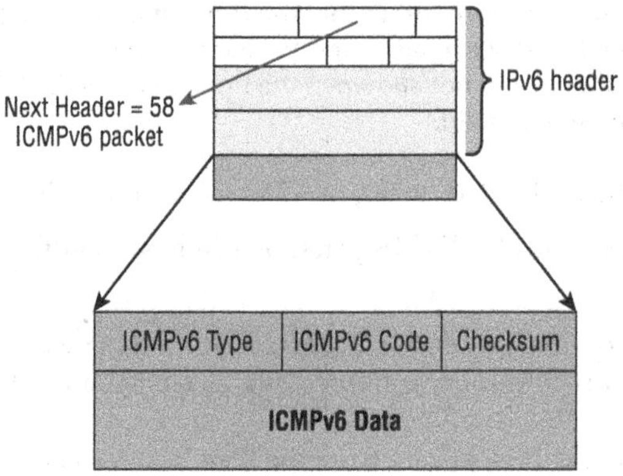

The ICMPv6 packet is identified by the value 58 in the Next Header field, located inside the ICMPv6 packet. The Type field identifies the particular kind of ICMP message that's being carried, and the Code field further details the specifics of the message. The Data field contains the ICMPv6 payload.

Table 3.2 shows the ICMP Type codes.

And this is how it works: the source node of a connection sends a packet that's equal to the MTU size of its local link's MTU. As this packet traverses the path toward its destination, any link that has an MTU smaller than the size of the current packet will force the intermediate router to send a "packet too big" message back to the source machine. This message tells the source node the maximum size the restrictive link will allow and asks the source to send a new, scaled-down packet that can pass through. This process will continue until the destination is finally reached, with the source node now sporting the new path's MTU. So now, when the rest of the data packets are transmitted, they'll be protected from fragmentation.

TABLE 3.2 ICMPv6 types

ICMPv6 Type	Description
1	Destination Unreachable
128	Echo Request
129	Echo Reply
133	Router Solicitation
134	Router Advertisement
135	Neighbor Solicitation
136	Neighbor Advertisement

ICMPv6 is used for router solicitation and advertisement, for neighbor solicitation and advertisement (i.e., finding the MAC data addresses for IPv6 neighbors), and for redirecting the host to the best router (default gateway).

Neighbor Discovery (NDP)

ICMPv6 also takes over the task of finding the address of other devices on the local link. The Address Resolution Protocol is used to perform this function for IPv4, but that's been renamed neighbor discovery (ND) in ICMPv6. This process is now achieved via a multicast address called the solicited-node address because all hosts join this multicast group upon connecting to the network.

Neighbor discovery enables these functions:

- Determining the MAC address of neighbors
- Router solicitation (RS) FF02::2 type code 133
- Router advertisements (RA) FF02::1 type code 134
- Neighbor solicitation (NS) Type code 135
- Neighbor advertisement (NA) Type code 136
- Duplicate address detection (DAD)

The part of the IPv6 address designated by the 24 bits farthest to the right is added to the end of the multicast address FF02:0:0:0:0:1:FF/104 prefix and is referred to as the *solicited-node address*. When this address is queried, the corresponding host will send back its layer 2 address.

Devices can find and keep track of other neighbor devices on the network in pretty much the same way. When I talked about RA and RS messages earlier and told you that they use multicast traffic to request and send address information, that too is actually a function of ICMPv6—specifically, neighbor discovery.

In IPv4, the protocol IGMP was used to allow a host device to tell its local router that it was joining a multicast group and would like to receive the traffic for that group. This IGMP function has been replaced by ICMPv6, and the process has been renamed multicast listener discovery.

With IPv4, our hosts could have only one default gateway configured, and if that router went down, we had to either fix the router, change the default gateway, or run some type of virtual default gateway with other protocols created as a solution for this inadequacy in IPv4. Figure 3.9 shows how IPv6 devices find their default gateways using neighbor discovery.

FIGURE 3.9 Router solicitation (RS) and router advertisement (RA)

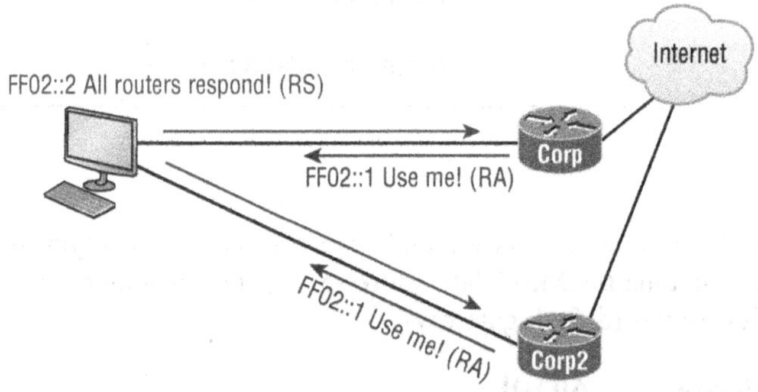

IPv6 hosts send a router solicitation (RS) onto their data link, asking for all routers to respond, and they use the multicast address FF02::2 to achieve this. Routers on the same link respond with a unicast to the requesting host or with a router advertisement (RA) using FF02::1.

But that's not all! Hosts can also send solicitations and advertisements between themselves using a neighbor solicitation (NS) and neighbor advertisement (NA), as shown in Figure 3.10. Remember, RA and RS gather or provide information about routers, and NS and NA gather information about hosts. Remember that a "neighbor" is a host on the same data link or VLAN.

FIGURE 3.10 Neighbor solicitation (NS) and neighbor advertisement (NA)

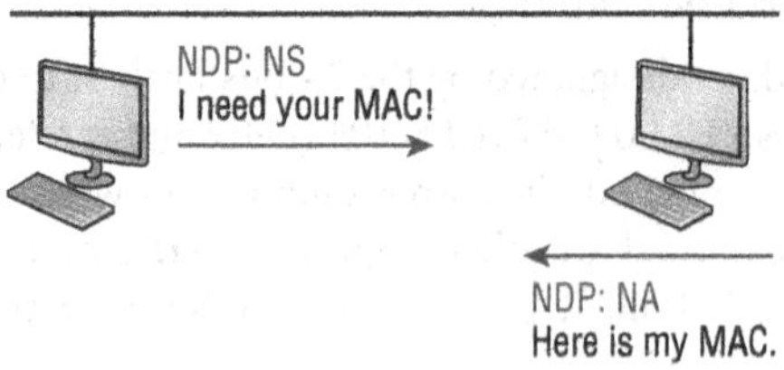

Solicited-Node and Multicast Mapping over Ethernet

If an IPv6 address is known, then the associated IPv6 solicited-node multicast address is known, and if an IPv6 multicast address is known, then the associated Ethernet MAC address is known.

For example, the IPv6 address 2001:DB8:2002:F:2C0:10FF:FE18:FC0F will have a known solicited-node address of FF02::1:FF18:FC0F.

Now we'll form the multicast Ethernet addresses by adding the last 32 bits of the IPv6 multicast address to 33:33.

For example, if the IPv6 solicited-node multicast address is FF02::1:FF18:FC0F, the associated Ethernet MAC address is 33:33:FF:18:FC:0F and is a virtual address.

Duplicate Address Detection (DAD)

So, what do you think the odds are that two hosts will assign themselves the same random IPv6 address? Personally, I think you could probably win the lotto every day for a year and still not come close to the odds against two hosts on the same data link duplicating an IPv6 address! Still, to make sure this doesn't ever happen, DAD was created, which isn't an actual protocol but a function of the NS/NA messages.

FIGURE 3.11 Duplicate address detection (DAD)

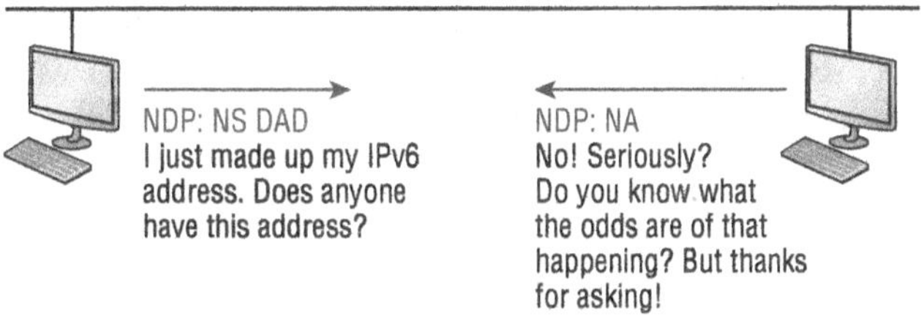

Figure 3.11 shows how a host sends an NDP NS when it receives or creates an IPv6 address.

When hosts make up or receive an IPv6 address, they send out three DADs via NDP NS, asking if anyone has this same address. The odds are unlikely that this will ever happen, but they ask anyway.

TIP: Remember for the objectives that ICMPv6 uses type 134 for router advertisement messages, and the advertised prefix must be 64 bits in length.

IPv6 Routing Protocols

All of the routing protocols we've already discussed have been tweaked and upgraded for use in IPv6 networks, so it figures that many of the functions and configurations you've already learned will be used almost the same way they are now. Knowing that broadcasts have been eliminated in IPv6, it's safe to conclude that any protocols relying entirely on broadcast traffic will go the way of the dodo. But unlike with the dodo, it'll be really nice to say goodbye to these bandwidth-hogging, performance-annihilating little gremlins!

The routing protocols we'll still use in IPv6 have been renovated and given new names. Even though this chapter's focus is on the Cisco exam objectives, which cover only static and default routing, I want to discuss a few of the more important ones, too.

First on the list is the IPv6 RIPng (next generation). Those of you who've been in IT for a while know that RIP has worked pretty well for us on smaller networks. This happens to be the very reason it didn't get whacked and will still be around in IPv6. And we still have EIGRPv6 because EIGRP already had protocol-dependent modules and all we had to do was add a new one to it to fit in nicely with the IPv6 protocol. Rounding out our group of protocol survivors is OSPFv3—that's not a typo; it really is v3! OSPF for IPv4 was actually v2, so when it got its upgrade to IPv6, it became OSPFv3. Finally, for the new objectives, we'll list MP-BGP4 as a multiprotocol BGP-4 protocol for IPv6. Please understand that for the objectives at this point in the book, we only need to understand static and default routing.

Static Routing with IPv6

Okay, don't let the heading of this section scare you into looking on `Monster.com` for some job that has nothing to do with networking! I know that static routing has always run a chill up our collective spines because it's cumbersome, difficult, and really easy to screw up. And I won't lie to you—it's certainly not any easier with IPv6's longer addresses, but you can do it!

We know that to make static routing work, whether in IP or IPv6, you need these three tools:

- An accurate, up-to-date network map of your entire internetwork
- Next-hop address and exit interface for each neighbor connection
- All the remote subnet IDs

Of course, we don't need to have any of these for dynamic routing, which is why we mostly use dynamic routing. It's just so awesome to have the routing protocol do all that work for us by finding all the remote subnets and automatically placing them into the routing table!

Figure 3.12 shows a really good example of how to use static routing with IPv6. It really doesn't have to be that hard, but just as with IPv4, you absolutely need an accurate network map to make static routing work!

FIGURE 3.12 IPv6 static and default routing

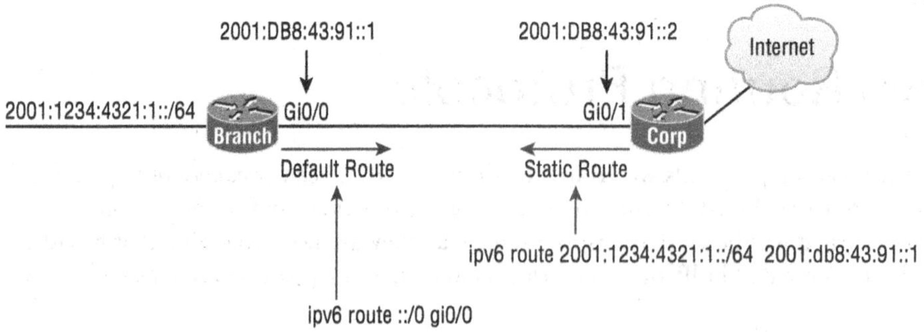

So, here's what I did: First, I created a static route on the Corp router to the remote network 2001:1234:4321:1::/64 using the next-hop address. I could've just as easily used the Corp router's exit interface. Next, I just set up a default route for the Branch router with ::/0 and the Branch exit interface of Gi0/0—not so bad!

Configuring IPv6 on Our Internetwork

We're going to continue working on the same internetwork we've been configuring throughout this book, as shown in Figure 3.13. Let's add IPv6 to the Corp, SF, and LA routers by using a simple subnet scheme of 11, 12, 13, 14, and 15. After that, we'll add the OSPFv3 routing protocol. Notice in Figure 3.13 how the subnet numbers are the same on each end of the WAN links. Keep in mind that we'll finish this chapter by running through some verification commands.

FIGURE 3.13 Our internetwork

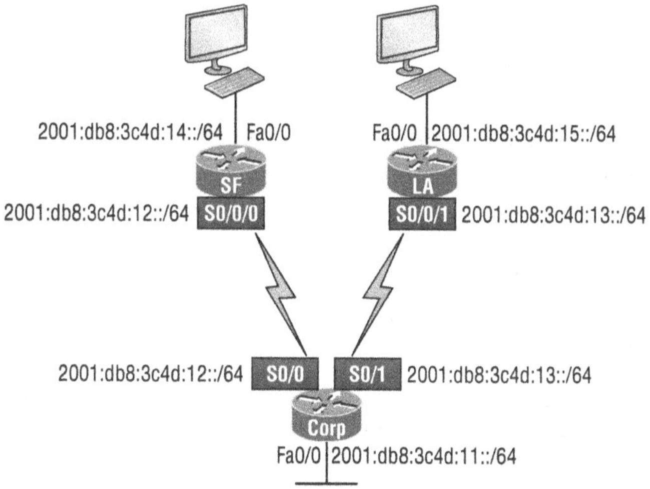

As usual, I'll start with the Corp router:

```
Corp#config t
Corp(config)#ipv6 unicast-routing
Corp(config)#int f0/0
Corp(config-if)#ipv6 address 2001:db8:3c4d:11::/64 eui-64
Corp(config-if)#int s0/0
Corp(config-if)#ipv6 address 2001:db8:3c4d:12::/64 eui-64
```

```
Corp(config-if)#int s0/1
Corp(config-if)#ipv6 address 2001:db8:3c4d:13::/64 eui-64
Corp(config-if)#^Z
Corp#copy run start
Destination filename [startup-config]?[enter]
Building configuration...
[OK]
```

Pretty simple! In the previous configuration, I only changed the subnet address for each interface slightly. Let's take a look at the routing table now:

```
Corp(config-if)#do sho ipv6 route
C 2001:DB8:3C4D:11::/64 [0/0]
via ::, FastEthernet0/0
L 2001:DB8:3C4D:11:20D:BDFF:FE3B:D80/128 [0/0]
via ::, FastEthernet0/0
C 2001:DB8:3C4D:12::/64 [0/0]
via ::, Serial0/0
L 2001:DB8:3C4D:12:20D:BDFF:FE3B:D80/128 [0/0]
via ::, Serial0/0
C 2001:DB8:3C4D:13::/64 [0/0]
via ::, Serial0/1
L 2001:DB8:3C4D:13:20D:BDFF:FE3B:D80/128 [0/0]
via ::, Serial0/1
L FE80::/10 [0/0]
via ::, Null0
L FF00::/8 [0/0]
via ::, Null0
Corp(config-if)#
```

All right, but what's up with those two addresses for each interface? One shows C for connected, one shows L. The connected address indicates the IPv6 address I configured on each interface, and the L is the link-local that's been automatically assigned. Notice in the link-local address that the FF:FE is inserted into the address to create the EUI-64 address.

Let's configure the SF router now:

```
SF#config t
SF(config)#ipv6 unicast-routing
SF(config)#int s0/0/0
SF(config-if)#ipv6 address 2001:db8:3c4d:12::/64
% 2001:DB8:3C4D:12::/64 should not be configured on Serial0/0/0, a subnet
router anycast
```

```
SF(config-if)#ipv6 address 2001:db8:3c4d:12::/64 eui-64
SF(config-if)#int fa0/0
SF(config-if)#ipv6 address 2001:db8:3c4d:14::/64 eui-64
SF(config-if)#^Z
SF#show ipv6 route
C 2001:DB8:3C4D:12::/64 [0/0]
via ::, Serial0/0/0
L 2001:DB8:3C4D:12::/128 [0/0]
via ::, Serial0/0/0
L 2001:DB8:3C4D:12:21A:2FFF:FEE7:4398/128 [0/0]
via ::, Serial0/0/0
C 2001:DB8:3C4D:14::/64 [0/0]
via ::, FastEthernet0/0
L 2001:DB8:3C4D:14:21A:2FFF:FEE7:4398/128 [0/0]
via ::, FastEthernet0/0
L FE80::/10 [0/0]
via ::, Null0
L FF00::/8 [0/0]
via ::, Null0
```

Did you notice that I used the exact IPv6 subnet addresses on each side of the serial link? Good... but wait—what's with that anycast error I received when trying to configure the interfaces on the SF router? I didn't mean to create that error; it happened because I forgot to add the `eui-64` at the end of the address. Still, what's behind that error? An anycast address is a host address of all 0s, meaning the last 64 bits are all off, but by typing in `/64` without the `eui-64`, I was telling the interface that the unique identifier would be nothing but zeros, and that's not allowed!

Let's configure the LA router now:

```
SF#config t
SF(config)#ipv6 unicast-routing
SF(config)#int s0/0/1
SF(config-if)#ipv6 address 2001:db8:3c4d:13::/64 eui-64
SF(config-if)#int f0/0
SF(config-if)#ipv6 address 2001:db8:3c4d:15::/64 eui-64
SF(config-if)#do show ipv6 route
C 2001:DB8:3C4D:13::/64 [0/0]
via ::, Serial0/0/1
L 2001:DB8:3C4D:13:21A:6CFF:FEA1:1F48/128 [0/0]
via ::, Serial0/0/1
```

```
C 2001:DB8:3C4D:15::/64 [0/0]
via ::, FastEthernet0/0
L 2001:DB8:3C4D:15:21A:6CFF:FEA1:1F48/128 [0/0]
via ::, FastEthernet0/0
L FE80::/10 [0/0]
via ::, Null0
L FF00::/8 [0/0]
via ::, Null0
```

This looks good, but I want you to notice that I used the exact same IPv6 subnet addresses on each side of the links from the Corp router to the SF router as well as from the Corp to the LA router.

Configuring Routing on Our Internetwork

I'll start at the Corp router and add simple static routes. Check it out:

```
Corp(config)#ipv6 route 2001:db8:3c4d:14::/64
2001:DB8:3C4D:12:21A:2FFF:FEE7:4398 150
Corp(config)#ipv6 route 2001:DB8:3C4D:15::/64 s0/1 150
Corp(config)#do sho ipv6 route static
[output cut]
S 2001:DB8:3C4D:14::/64 [150/0]
via 2001:DB8:3C4D:12:21A:2FFF:FEE7:4398
```

Okay—I agree that the first static route line was pretty long because I used the next-hop address, but notice that I used the exit interface on the second entry. But it still wasn't really all that hard to create the longer static route entry. I just went to the SF router, used the command `show ipv6 int brief`, and then copied and pasted the interface address used for the next hop. You'll get used to IPv6 addresses. (You'll get used to doing a lot of copy/paste moves!)

Now, because I put an AD of 150 on the static routes, once I configure a routing protocol such as OSPF, they'll be replaced with an OSPF injected route because it has a lower AD (remember, this is called a floating static route). Let's go to the SF and LA routers and put a single entry in each router to get to remote subnet 11:

```
SF(config)#ipv6 route 2001:db8:3c4d:11::/64 s0/0/0 150
```

That's it! I'm going to head over to LA and put a default route on that router now:

```
LA(config)#ipv6 route ::/0 s0/0/1
```

Let's take a peek at the Corp router's routing table and see if our static routes are in there.

```
Corp#sh ipv6 route static
[output cut]
S 2001:DB8:3C4D:14::/64 [150/0]
via 2001:DB8:3C4D:12:21A:2FFF:FEE7:4398
S 2001:DB8:3C4D:15::/64 [150/0]
via ::, Serial0/1
```

Voilà! I can see both of my static routes in the routing table, so IPv6 can now route to those networks. But we're not done, because we still need to test our network! First, I'm going to go to the SF router and get the IPv6 address of the Fa0/0 interface:

```
SF#sh ipv6 int brief
FastEthernet0/0 [up/up]
FE80::21A:2FFF:FEE7:4398
2001:DB8:3C4D:14:21A:2FFF:FEE7:4398
FastEthernet0/1 [administratively down/down]
Serial0/0/0 [up/up]
FE80::21A:2FFF:FEE7:4398
2001:DB8:3C4D:12:21A:2FFF:FEE7:4398
```

Next, I'm going to go back to the Corp router and ping that remote interface by copying and pasting in the address. No sense doing all that typing when copy/paste works great!

```
Corp#ping ipv6 2001:DB8:3C4D:14:21A:2FFF:FEE7:4398
Type escape sequence to abort.
Sending 5, 100-byte ICMP Echos to 2001:DB8:3C4D:14:21A:2FFF:FEE7:4398, timeout
is 2 seconds:
!!!!!
Success rate is 100 percent (5/5), round-trip min/avg/max = 0/0/0 ms
Corp#
```

We can see that the static route worked, so next, I'll go get the IPv6 address of the LA router and ping that remote interface as well:

```
LA#sh ipv6 int brief
FastEthernet0/0 [up/up]
FE80::21A:6CFF:FEA1:1F48
2001:DB8:3C4D:15:21A:6CFF:FEA1:1F48
Serial0/0/1 [up/up]
FE80::21A:6CFF:FEA1:1F48
2001:DB8:3C4D:13:21A:6CFF:FEA1:1F48
```

It's time to head over to Corp and ping LA:

```
Corp#ping ipv6 2001:DB8:3C4D:15:21A:6CFF:FEA1:1F48

Type escape sequence to abort.
Sending 5, 100-byte ICMP Echos to 2001:DB8:3C4D:15:21A:6CFF:FEA1:1F48, timeout
is 2 seconds:
!!!!!
Success rate is 100 percent (5/5), round-trip min/avg/max = 4/4/4 ms
Corp#
```

Now let's use one of my favorite commands:

```
Corp#sh ipv6 int brief
FastEthernet0/0 [up/up]
FE80::20D:BDFF:FE3B:D80
2001:DB8:3C4D:11:20D:BDFF:FE3B:D80
Serial0/0 [up/up]
FE80::20D:BDFF:FE3B:D80
2001:DB8:3C4D:12:20D:BDFF:FE3B:D80
FastEthernet0/1 [administratively down/down]
unassigned
Serial0/1 [up/up]
FE80::20D:BDFF:FE3B:D80
2001:DB8:3C4D:13:20D:BDFF:FE3B:D80
Loopback0 [up/up]
unassigned
Corp#
```

What a nice output! All our interfaces are up/up, and we can see the link-local and assigned global address.

Static routing really isn't so bad with IPv6! I'm not saying I'd like to do this in a ginormous network—no way—I wouldn't want to opt for doing that with IPv4, either. But you can see that it can be done. Also, notice how easy it was to ping an IPv6 address. Copy/paste really is your friend!

Before we finish the chapter, let's add another router to our network and connect it to the Corp Fa0/0 LAN. For our new router, I really don't feel like doing any work, so I'll just type this:

```
Boulder#config t
Boulder(config)#int f0/0
Boulder(config-if)#ipv6 address autoconfig default
```

Nice and easy! This configures stateless autoconfiguration on the interface, and the `default` keyword will advertise itself as the default route for the local link.

I hope you found this chapter as rewarding as I did. The best thing you can do to learn IPv6 is to get some routers and just go at it. Don't give up because it's seriously worth your time!

Summary

This chapter introduced you to some very key IPv6 structural elements as well as how to make IPv6 work within a Cisco internetwork. You now know that even when covering and configuring IPv6 basics, there's still a great deal to understand—and we just scratched the surface! But you're still well equipped with all you need to meet the Cisco exam objectives.

You learned the vital reasons why we need IPv6 and the benefits associated with it. I covered IPv6 addressing and the importance of using shortened expressions. As I covered addressing with IPv6, I also showed you the different address types, plus the special addresses reserved in IPv6.

IPv6 will mostly be deployed automatically, meaning hosts will employ autoconfiguration. I demonstrated how IPv6 utilizes autoconfiguration and how it comes into play when configuring a Cisco router. You also learned that in IPv6, we can and still should use a DHCP server to the router to provide options to hosts just as we've been doing for years with IPv4—not necessarily IPv6 addresses, but other mission-critical options like providing a DNS server address.

From there, I discussed the evolution of the more integral and familiar protocol like ICMP. They've been upgraded to work in the IPv6 environment, but these networking workhorses are still vital and relevant to operations, and I detailed how ICMP works with IPv6.

I wrapped up this pivotal chapter by demonstrating key methods to use when verifying that all is running correctly in your IPv6 network.

Exam Essentials

Understand why we need IPv6. Without IPv6, the world would be depleted of IP addresses.

Understand link-local. Link-local is like an IPv4 APIPA IP address, and it can't be routed at all, not even in your organization.

Understand unique local. This, like link-local, is like a private IP address in IPv4 and cannot be routed to the Internet. However, the difference between link-local and unique local is that unique local can be routed within your organization or company.

Remember IPv6 addressing. IPv6 addressing is not like IPv4 addressing. IPv6 addressing has much more address space, is 128 bits long, and is represented in hexadecimal, unlike IPv4, which is only 32 bits long and represented in decimal.

Understand and be able to read an EUI-64 address with the seventh bit inverted. Hosts can use autoconfiguration to obtain an IPv6 address, and one of the ways they can do that is through what is called EUI-64. This takes the unique MAC address of a host and inserts FF:FE in the middle of the address to change a 48-bit MAC address to a 64-bit interface ID. In addition to inserting the 16 bits into the interface ID, the seventh bit of the 1st byte is inverted, typically from a 0 to a 1.

Written Lab

The answers to this lab can be found in Appendix A, "Answers to the Written Labs."

Write the answers to the following questions:

1. Which type of packet is addressed and delivered to only a single interface?
2. Which type of address is used just like a regular public routable address in IPv4?
3. Which type of address is not meant to be routed?
4. Which type of address is not meant to be routed to the Internet but is still globally unique?
5. Which type of address is meant to be delivered to multiple interfaces?
6. Which type of address identifies multiple interfaces, but packets are delivered only to the first address it finds?
7. Which routing protocol uses multicast address FF02::5?
8. IPv4 had a loopback address of 127.0.0.1. What is the IPv6 loopback address?
9. What does a link-local address always start with?
10. What does a unique local unicast range start with?

Review Questions

NOTE The following questions are designed to test your understanding of this chapter's material. For more information on how to get additional questions, please see this book's introduction.

The answers to these questions can be found in Appendix B, "Answers to the Review Questions."

1. How is an EUI-64 format interface ID created from a 48-bit MAC address?
   - **A.** By appending 0xFF to the MAC address
   - **B.** By prefixing the MAC address with 0xFFEE
   - **C.** By prefixing the MAC address with 0xFF and appending 0xFF to it
   - **D.** By inserting 0xFFFE between the upper 3 bytes and the lower 3 bytes of the MAC address

2. Which option is a valid IPv6 address?
   - **A.** 2001:0000:130F::099a::12a
   - **B.** 2002:7654:A1AD:61:81AF:CCC1
   - **C.** FEC0:ABCD:WXYZ:0067::2A4
   - **D.** 2004:1:25A4:886F::1

3. Which statements about IPv6 prefixes are true? (Choose three.)
   - **A.** FF00:/8 is used for IPv6 multicast.
   - **B.** FE80::/10 is used for link-local unicast.
   - **C.** FC00::/7 is used in private networks.
   - **D.** 2001::1/127 is used for loopback addresses.
   - **E.** FE80::/8 is used for link-local unicast.
   - **F.** FEC0::/10 is used for IPv6 broadcast.

4. What are the approaches used when migrating from an IPv4 addressing scheme to an IPv6 scheme? (Choose three.)
   - **A.** Enable dual-stack routing.
   - **B.** Configure IPv6 directly.
   - **C.** Configure IPv4 tunnels between IPv6 islands.
   - **D.** Use proxying and translation to translate IPv6 packets into IPv4 packets.
   - **E.** Use DHCPv6 to map IPv4 addresses to IPv6 addresses.

5. Which statements about IPv6 router advertisement messages are true? (Choose two.)
   A. They use ICMPv6 type 134.
   B. The advertised prefix length must be 64 bits.
   C. The advertised prefix length must be 48 bits.
   D. They are sourced from the configured IPv6 interface address.
   E. Their destination is always the link-local address of the neighboring node.

6. Which of the following are true when describing an IPv6 anycast address? (Choose three.)
   A. One-to-many communication model
   B. One-to-nearest communication model
   C. Any-to-many communication model
   D. A unique IPv6 address for each device in the group
   E. The same address for multiple devices in the group
   F. Delivery of packets to the group interface that is closest to the sending device

7. You want to ping the loopback address of your IPv6 local host. What will you type?
   A. `ping 127.0.0.1`
   B. `ping 0.0.0.0`
   C. `ping ::1`
   D. `trace 0.0.::1`

8. What are the features of the IPv6 protocol? (Choose three.)
   A. Optional IPsec
   B. Autoconfiguration
   C. No broadcasts
   D. Complicated header
   E. Plug-and-play
   F. Checksums

9. Which statements describe characteristics of IPv6 unicast addressing? (Choose two.)
   A. Global addresses start with 2000::/3.
   B. Link-local addresses start with FE00:/12.
   C. Link-local addresses start with FF00::/10.
   D. There is only one loopback address, and it is ::1.
   E. If a global address is assigned to an interface, then that is the only allowable address for the interface.

10. A host sends a router solicitation (RS) on the data link. What destination address is sent with this request?
    A. FF02::A
    B. FF02::9
    C. FF02::2
    D. FF02::1
    E. FF02::5

11. When configuring IPv6 on an interface, which IPv6 multicast groups are joined? (Choose two.)
    A. 2000::/3
    B. 2002::5
    C. FC00::/7
    D. FF02::1
    E. FF02::2

12. Which IPv6 address type communicates between subnets and cannot route on the Internet?
    A. Link-local
    B. Unique local
    C. Multicast
    D. Global unicast

13. Which IPv6 address block sends packets to a group address rather than a single address?
    A. 2000::/3
    B. FC00::/7
    C. FE80::/10
    D. FF00::/8

14. Which command automatically generates an IPv6 address from a specified IPv6 prefix and MAC address of an interface?
    A. ipv6 address dhcp
    B. ipv6 address 2001:DB8:5:112::/64 eui-64
    C. ipv6 address autoconfig
    D. ipv6 address 2001:DB8:5:112::2/64 link-local

15. Which option is a valid IPv6 address?
    A. 2001:0000:130F::099a::12a
    B. 2002:7654:A1AD:61:81AF:CCC1
    C. FEC0:ABCD:WXYZ:0067::2A4
    D. 2004:1:25A4:886F::1

16. Which are characteristics of an IPv6 anycast address? (Choose three.)
    - A. One-to-many communication model
    - B. One-to-nearest communication model
    - C. Any-to-many communication model
    - D. A unique IPv6 address for each device in the group
    - E. The same address for multiple devices in the group
    - F. Delivery of packets to the group interface that is closest to the sending device
17. Which statements describe characteristics of IPv6 Global addressing?
    - A. Global addresses start with 2000::/3.
    - B. Link-local addresses start with FE00:/12.
    - C. Link-local addresses start with FF00::/10.
    - D. There is only one loopback address, and it is ::1.
    - E. If a global address is assigned to an interface, then that is the only allowable address for the interface.
18. Which action must be taken to assign a global unicast IPv6 address on an interface derived from that interface's MAC address?
    - A. Explicitly assign a link-local address
    - B. Disable the EUI-64 bit process
    - C. Enable SLAAC on an interface
    - D. Configure a stateful DHCPv6 server on the network
19. Which IPv6 address block forwards packets to a multicast address rather than a unicast address?
    - A. 2000::/3
    - B. FC00::/7
    - C. FE80::/10
    - D. FF00::/12
20. Which type of IPv6 address is publicly routable in the same way as IPv4 public addresses?
    - A. Multicast
    - B. Unique local
    - C. Link-local
    - D. Global unicast

Chapter 4

Troubleshooting IP, IPv6, and VLANs

✓ **1.0 Network Fundamentals**

1.6 Configure and verify IPv4 addressing and subnetting

1.8 Configure and verify IPv6 addressing and prefix

1.10 Verify IP parameters for Client OS (Windows, Mac OS, Linux)

✓ **2.0 Network Access**

2.1 Configure and verify VLANs (normal range) spanning multiple switches

✓ **3.0 IP Connectivity**

3.1 Interpret the components of routing table

3.3 Configure and verify IPv4 and IPv6 static routing

In this chapter, especially at first, it's going to seem like we're going over a lot of the same ground and concepts already covered in other chapters. The reason for this is that troubleshooting is such a major focus of the Cisco CCNA objectives that I've got to make sure I've guided you through this vital topic in depth. If not, then I just haven't done all I can to really set you up for success! So, to make that happen, we're now going to thoroughly examine troubleshooting with IP, IPv6, and *virtual LANs (VLANs)*. And I can't stress the point enough that you absolutely must have a solid, fundamental understanding of IP and IPv6 routing as well as a complete understanding of VLANs and trunking nailed down tight if you're going to win at this!

To help you do that, I'll be using different scenarios to walk you through the Cisco troubleshooting steps to correctly solve the problems you're likely to be faced with. Although it's hard to tell exactly what the CCNA exam will throw at you, you can read and completely understand the objectives so that no matter what, you'll be prepared, equipped, and up to the challenge. The way to do this is by building on a really strong foundation, including being skilled at troubleshooting. This chapter is precisely designed and exactly what you need to seriously help solidify your troubleshooting foundation.

In this chapter, we'll concentrate solely on IP, IPv6, and VLAN troubleshooting.

> **NOTE** To find your included bonus material, as well as Todd Lammle videos, practice questions, and hands-on labs, please see `www.lammle.com/ccna`

Troubleshooting IP Network Connectivity

Let's start by taking a moment for a short and sweet review of IP routing. Always remember that when a host wants to transmit a packet, IP looks at the destination address and determines if it's a local or remote request. If it's determined to be a local request, IP just broadcasts a frame out on the local network looking for the local host using an ARP request. If it's a remote request, the host sends an ARP request to the default gateway to discover the MAC address of the router.

Once the hosts have the default gateway address, they'll send each packet that needs to be transmitted to the Data Link layer for framing, and newly framed packets are then sent out on the local collision domain. The router will receive the frame and remove the packet from the frame, and IP will then parse the routing table, looking for the exit interface on the router. If the destination is found in the routing table, it will packet-switch the packet to the exit interface. At this point, the packet will be framed with new source and destination MAC addresses.

Okay, with that short review in mind, what would you say to someone who called you saying they weren't able to get to a server on a remote network? What's the first thing you would have this user do (besides reboot Windows) or that you would do yourself to test network connectivity? If you came up with using the Ping program, that's a great place to start. The Ping program is a great tool for finding out if a host is alive on the network with a simple ICMP echo request and echo reply. But being able to ping the host as well as the server doesn't guarantee that all is well in the network! Keep in mind that there's more to the Ping program than just being used as a quick and simple testing protocol.

To be prepared for the exam objectives, it's a great idea to get used to connecting to various routers and pinging from them. Of course, pinging from a router is not as good as pinging from the host reporting the problem, but that doesn't mean we can't isolate problems from the routers themselves.

Let's use Figure 4.1 as a basis to run through some troubleshooting scenarios.

FIGURE 4.1 Troubleshooting scenario

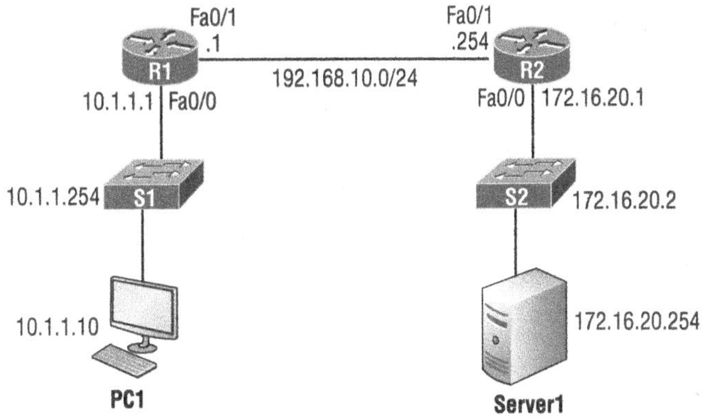

In this first scenario, a manager calls you and says they cannot log in to Server1 from PC1. Your job is to find out why and fix it. The Cisco objectives are clear on the troubleshooting steps you need to take when a problem has been reported, and here they are:

1. Check the cables to find out if there's a faulty cable or interface in the mix and verify the interface's statistics.
2. Make sure that devices are determining the correct path from the source to the destination. Manipulate the routing information if needed.
3. Verify that the default gateway is correct.

4. Verify that name resolution settings are correct.
5. Verify that there are no *access control lists (ACLs)* blocking traffic.

To effectively troubleshoot this problem, we'll narrow down the possibilities by process of elimination. We'll start with PC1 and verify that it's configured correctly and also that IP is working correctly.

There are four steps for checking the PC1 configuration:

1. Test that the local IP stack is working by pinging the loopback address.
2. Test that the local IP stack is talking to the Data Link layer (LAN driver) by pinging the local IP address.
3. Test that the host is working on the LAN by pinging the default gateway.
4. Test that the host can get to remote networks by pinging remote Server1.

Let's check out the PC1 configuration by using the `ipconfig` command or `ifconfig` on a Mac:

```
C:\Users\Todd Lammle>ipconfig

Windows IP Configuration

Ethernet adapter Local Area Connection:

   Connection-specific DNS Suffix  . : localdomain
   Link-local IPv6 Address . . . . . : fe80::64e3:76a2:541f:ebcb%11
   IPv4 Address. . . . . . . . . . . : 10.1.1.10
   Subnet Mask . . . . . . . . . . . : 255.255.255.0
   Default Gateway . . . . . . . . . : 10.1.1.1
```

We can also check the route table on the host with the `route print` command to see if it truly does know the default gateway:

```
C:\Users\Todd Lammle>route print
[output cut]
IPv4 Route Table
=======================================================================
Active Routes:
Network Destination        Netmask          Gateway       Interface  Metric
          0.0.0.0          0.0.0.0          10.1.1.10     10.1.1.1   10
[output cut]
```

Between the output of the `ipconfig` command and the `route print` command, we can be assured that the hosts are aware of the correct default gateway.

NOTE For the Cisco objectives, it's extremely important to be able to check and verify the default gateway on a host and also that this address matches the router's interface!

So, let's verify that the local IP stack is initialized by pinging the loopback address now:

```
C:\Users\Todd Lammle>ping 127.0.0.1

Pinging 127.0.0.1 with 32 bytes of data:
Reply from 127.0.0.1: bytes=32 time<1ms TTL=128
Reply from 127.0.0.1: bytes=32 time<1ms TTL=128
Reply from 127.0.0.1: bytes=32 time<1ms TTL=128
Reply from 127.0.0.1: bytes=32 time<1ms TTL=128

Ping statistics for 127.0.0.1:
    Packets: Sent = 4, Received = 4, Lost = 0 (0% loss),
Approximate round trip times in milli-seconds:
    Minimum = 0ms, Maximum = 0ms, Average = 0ms
```

This first output confirms the IP address and configured default gateway of the host, and then I verified that the local IP stack is working. Our next move is to verify that the IP stack is talking to the LAN driver by pinging the local IP address:

```
C:\Users\Todd Lammle>ping 10.1.1.10

Pinging 10.1.1.10 with 32 bytes of data:
Reply from 10.1.1.10: bytes=32 time<1ms TTL=128
Reply from 10.1.1.10: bytes=32 time<1ms TTL=128
Reply from 10.1.1.10: bytes=32 time<1ms TTL=128
Reply from 10.1.1.10: bytes=32 time<1ms TTL=128

Ping statistics for 10.1.1.10:
    Packets: Sent = 4, Received = 4, Lost = 0 (0% loss),
Approximate round trip times in milli-seconds:
    Minimum = 0ms, Maximum = 0ms, Average = 0ms
```

And now that we know the local stack is solid and the IP stack is communicating to the LAN driver, it's time to check our local LAN connectivity by pinging the default gateway:

```
C:\Users\Todd Lammle>ping 10.1.1.1

Pinging 10.1.1.1 with 32 bytes of data:
Reply from 10.1.1.1: bytes=32 time<1ms TTL=128
Reply from 10.1.1.1: bytes=32 time<1ms TTL=128
Reply from 10.1.1.1: bytes=32 time<1ms TTL=128
Reply from 10.1.1.1: bytes=32 time<1ms TTL=128

Ping statistics for 10.1.1.1:
    Packets: Sent = 4, Received = 4, Lost = 0 (0% loss),
Approximate round trip times in milli-seconds:
    Minimum = 0ms, Maximum = 0ms, Average = 0ms
```

Looking good! I'd say our host is in good shape. Let's try to ping the remote server next to see if our host is actually getting off the local LAN to communicate remotely:

```
C:\Users\Todd Lammle>ping 172.16.20.254

Pinging 172.16.20.254 with 32 bytes of data:
Request timed out.
Request timed out.
Request timed out.
Request timed out.

Ping statistics for 172.16.20.254:
    Packets: Sent = 4, Received = 0, Lost = 4 (100% loss),
```

Well, looks like we've confirmed local connectivity but not remote connectivity, so we're going to have to dig deeper to isolate our problem. But first, and just as important, it's key to make note of what we can rule out at this point:

1. The PC is configured with the correct IP address, and the local IP stack is working.
2. The default gateway is configured correctly, and the PC's default gateway configuration matches the router interface IP address.
3. The local switch is working because we can ping through the switch to the router.
4. We don't have a local LAN issue, meaning our Physical layer is good because we can ping the router. If we couldn't ping the router, we would need to verify our physical cables and interfaces.

Let's see if we can narrow the problem down further using the `traceroute` command:

```
C:\Users\Todd Lammle>tracert 172.16.20.254

Tracing route to 172.16.20.254 over a maximum of 30 hops
  1     1 ms     1 ms    <1 ms  10.1.1.1
  2     *        *        *     Request timed out.
  3     *        *        *     Request timed out.
```

Well, we didn't get beyond our default gateway, so let's go over to R2 and see if we can talk locally to the server:

```
R2#ping 172.16.20.254

Pinging 172.16.20.254 with 32 bytes of data:
Reply from 172.16.20.254: bytes=32 time<1ms TTL=128
Reply from 172.16.20.254: bytes=32 time<1ms TTL=128
Reply from 172.16.20.254: bytes=32 time<1ms TTL=128
Reply from 172.16.20.254: bytes=32 time<1ms TTL=128

Ping statistics for 172.16.20.254:
    Packets: Sent = 4, Received = 0, Lost = 4 (100% loss),
```

Okay, we just eliminated a local LAN problem by connecting to Server1 from the R2 router, so we're good there. Let's summarize what we know so far:

1. PC1 is configured correctly.
2. The switch located on the 10.1.1.0 LAN is working.
3. PC1's default gateway is configured correctly.
4. R2 can communicate with Server1, so we don't have a remote LAN issue.

But something is still clearly wrong, so what should we check next? Now would be a great time to verify the Server1 IP configuration and make sure the default gateway is configured correctly. Let's take a look:

```
C:\Users\Server1>ipconfig

Windows IP Configuration

Ethernet adapter Local Area Connection:

   Connection-specific DNS Suffix  . : localdomain
   Link-local IPv6 Address . . . . . : fe80::7723:76a2:e73c:2acb%11
   IPv4 Address. . . . . . . . . . . : 172.16.20.254
   Subnet Mask . . . . . . . . . . . : 255.255.255.0
   Default Gateway . . . . . . . . . : 172.16.20.1
```

Okay—the Server1 configuration looks good, and the R2 router can ping the server, so it seems that the server's local LAN is solid, the local switch is working, and there are no cable or interface issues. But let's zoom in on interface Fa0/0 on R2 and talk about what to expect if there were errors on this interface:

```
R2#sh int fa0/0
FastEthernet0/0 is up, line protocol is up
[output cut]
  Full-duplex, 100Mb/s, 100BaseTX/FX] ARP type: ARPA, ARP Timeout 04:00:00
  Last input 00:00:05, output 00:00:01, output hang never
  Last clearing of "show interface" counters never
  Input queue: 0/75/0/0 (size/max/drops/flushes); Total output drops: 0
  Queueing strategy: fifo
  Output queue: 0/40 (size/max)
  5 minute input rate 0 bits/sec, 0 packets/sec
  5 minute output rate 0 bits/sec, 0 packets/sec
     1325 packets input, 157823 bytes
     Received 1157 broadcasts (0 IP multicasts)
     0 runts, 0 giants, 0 throttles
     0 input errors, 0 CRC, 0 frame, 0 overrun, 0 ignored
     0 watchdog
```

```
0 input packets with dribble condition detected
2294 packets output, 244630 bytes, 0 underruns
0 output errors, 0 collisions, 3 interface resets
347 unknown protocol drops
0 babbles, 0 late collision, 0 deferred
4 lost carrier, 0 no carrier
0 output buffer failures, 0 output buffers swapped out
```

You've got to be able to analyze interface statistics to find problems there if they exist, so let's pick out the important factors now relevant to effectively meeting that challenge:

Speed and duplex settings Good to know that the most common cause of interface errors is a mismatched duplex mode between two ends of an Ethernet link. This is why it's so important to make sure that the switch and its hosts (PCs, router interfaces, etc.) have the same speed setting. If not, they just won't connect. And if they have mismatched duplex settings, you'll receive a legion of errors, which cause nasty performance issues, intermittent connectivity—even total loss of communication!

Using autonegotiation for speed and duplex is a very common practice, and it's enabled by default. But if this fails for some reason, you'll have to set the configuration manually like this:

```
Switch(config)#int gi0/1
Switch(config-if)#speed ?
  10    Force 10 Mbps operation
  100   Force 100 Mbps operation
  1000  Force 1000 Mbps operation
  auto  Enable AUTO speed configuration
Switch(config-if)#speed 1000
Switch(config-if)#duplex  ?
  auto  Enable AUTO duplex configuration
  full  Force full duplex operation
  half  Force half-duplex operation
Switch(config-if)#duplex  full
```

If you have a duplex mismatch, a telling sign is that the late collision counter will increment.

Input queue drops If the input queue drops counter increments, this signifies that more traffic is being delivered to the router than it can process. If this is consistently high, try to determine exactly when these counters are increasing and how the events relate to CPU usage. You'll see the ignored and throttle counters increment as well.

Output queue drops This counter indicates that packets were dropped due to interface congestion, leading to packet drops and queuing delays. When this occurs, applications like VoIP will experience performance issues. If you observe this constantly incrementing, consider QoS.

Input errors Input errors often indicate high errors such as CRCs. This can point to cabling problems, hardware issues, or duplex mismatches.

Output errors This is the total number of frames that the port tried to transmit when an issue such as a collision occurred.

We're going to move on in our troubleshooting process of elimination by analyzing the routers' actual configurations. Here's R1's routing table:

```
R1>sh ip route
[output cut]
Gateway of last resort is 192.168.10.254 to network 0.0.0.0

S*    0.0.0.0/0 [1/0] via 192.168.10.254
      10.0.0.0/8 is variably subnetted, 2 subnets, 2 masks
C        10.1.1.0/24 is directly connected, FastEthernet0/0
L        10.1.1.1/32 is directly connected, FastEthernet0/0
      192.168.10.0/24 is variably subnetted, 2 subnets, 2 masks
C        192.168.10.0/24 is directly connected, FastEthernet0/1
L        192.168.10.1/32 is directly connected, FastEthernet0/1
```

This actually looks pretty good! Both of our directly connected networks are in the table, and we can confirm that we have a default route going to the R2 router. So now let's verify the connectivity to R2 from R1:

```
R1>sh ip int brief
Interface              IP-Address      OK? Method Status                Protocol
FastEthernet0/0        10.1.1.1        YES manual up                      up
FastEthernet0/1        192.168.10.1    YES manual up                      up
Serial0/0/0            unassigned      YES unset  administratively down down
Serial0/1/0            unassigned      YES unset  administratively down down
R1>ping 192.168.10.254
Type escape sequence to abort.
Sending 5, 100-byte ICMP Echos to 192.168.10.254, timeout is 2 seconds:
!!!!!
Success rate is 100 percent (5/5), round-trip min/avg/max = 1/2/4 ms
```

This looks great, too! Our interfaces are correctly configured with the right IP address, and the Physical and Data Link layers are up. By the way, I also tested layer 3 connectivity by pinging the R2 Fa0/1 interface.

Because everything looks good so far, our next step is to check into the status of R2's interfaces:

```
R2>sh ip int brief
Interface              IP-Address      OK? Method Status                Protocol
FastEthernet0/0        172.16.20.1     YES manual up                      up
FastEthernet0/1        192.168.10.254  YES manual up                      up
```

```
R2>ping 192.168.10.1
Type escape sequence to abort.
Sending 5, 100-byte ICMP Echos to 192.168.10.1, timeout is 2 seconds:
!!!!!
Success rate is 100 percent (5/5), round-trip min/avg/max = 1/2/4 ms
```

Well, everything still checks out at this point. The IP addresses are correct, and the Physical and Data Link layers are up. I also tested the layer 3 connectivity with a ping to R1, so we're all good so far. We'll examine the routing table next:

```
R2>sh ip route
[output cut]
Gateway of last resort is not set

      10.0.0.0/24 is subnetted, 1 subnets
S        10.1.1.0 is directly connected, FastEthernet0/0
      172.16.0.0/16 is variably subnetted, 2 subnets, 2 masks
C        172.16.20.0/24 is directly connected, FastEthernet0/0
L        172.16.20.1/32 is directly connected, FastEthernet0/0
      192.168.10.0/24 is variably subnetted, 2 subnets, 2 masks
C        192.168.10.0/24 is directly connected, FastEthernet0/1
L        192.168.10.254/32 is directly connected, FastEthernet0/1
```

Okay—we can see that all our local interfaces are in the table, as well as a static route to the 10.1.1.0 network. But do you see the problem? Look closely at the static route. The route was entered with an exit interface of Fa0/0, and the path to the 10.1.1.0 network is out Fa0/1! Aha! We've found our problem! Let's fix R2:

```
R2#config t
R2(config)#no ip route 10.1.1.0 255.255.255.0 fa0/0
R2(config)#ip route 10.1.1.0 255.255.255.0 192.168.10.1
```

That should do it. Let's verify from PC1:

```
C:\Users\Todd Lammle>ping 172.16.20.254

Pinging 172.16.20.254 with 32 bytes of data:
Reply from 172.16.20.254: bytes=32 time<1ms TTL=128
Reply from 172.16.20.254: bytes=32 time<1ms TTL=128
Reply from 172.16.20.254: bytes=32 time<1ms TTL=128
Reply from 172.16.20.254: bytes=32 time<1ms TTL=128

Ping statistics for 172.16.20.254
    Packets: Sent = 4, Received = 4, Lost = 0 (0% loss),
Approximate round trip times in milli-seconds:
    Minimum = 0ms, Maximum = 0ms, Average = 0ms
```

Our snag appears to be solved, but just to make sure, we really need to verify with a higher-level protocol like Telnet:

```
C:\Users\Todd Lammle>telnet 172.16.20.254
Connecting To 172.16.20.254...Could not open connection to the host, on
port 23: Connect failed
```

Okay, that's not good! We can ping to the Server1, but we can't telnet to it. In the past, I've verified that telnetting to this server worked, but it's still possible that we have a failure on the server side. To find out, let's verify our network first, starting at R1:

```
R1>ping 172.16.20.254
Type escape sequence to abort.
Sending 5, 100-byte ICMP Echos to 172.16.20.254, timeout is 2 seconds:
!!!!!
Success rate is 100 percent (5/5), round-trip min/avg/max = 1/1/4 ms
R1>telnet 172.16.20.254
Trying 172.16.20.254 ...
% Destination unreachable; gateway or host down
```

This is some pretty ominous output! Let's try from R2 and see what happens:

```
R2#telnet 172.16.20.254
Trying 172.16.20.254 ... Open

User Access Verification

Password:
```

Oh my—I can ping the server from a remote network, but I can't telnet to it, but the local router R2 can! These factors eliminate the server being a problem because I can telnet to the server when I'm on the local LAN.

And we know we don't have a routing problem because we fixed that already. So what's next? Let's check to see if there's an ACL on R2:

```
R2>sh access-lists
Extended IP access list 110
    10 permit icmp any any (25 matches)
```

Seriously? What a loopy access list to have on a router! This ridiculous list permits ICMP, but that's it. It denies everything except ICMP due to the implicit `deny ip any any` at the end of every ACL. But before we uncork the champagne, we need to see if this foolish list has been applied to our interfaces on R2 to confirm that this is really our problem:

```
R2>sh ip int fa0/0
FastEthernet0/0 is up, line protocol is up
  Internet address is 172.16.20.1/24
  Broadcast address is 255.255.255.255
  Address determined by setup command
```

```
  MTU is 1500 bytes
  Helper address is not set
  Directed broadcast forwarding is disabled
  Outgoing access list is 110
  Inbound  access list is not set
```

There it is—that's our problem, all right! In case you're wondering why R2 could telnet to Server1, it's because an ACL filters only packets trying to go through the router—not packets generated at the router. Let's get to work and fix this:

```
R2#config t
R2(config)#no access-list 110
```

I just verified that I can telnet from PC1 to Server1, but let's try telnetting from R1 again:

```
R1#telnet 172.16.20.254
Trying 172.16.20.254 ... Open

User Access Verification

Password:
```

Nice—looks like we're set, but what about using the name?

```
R1#telnet Server1
Translating "Server1"...domain server (255.255.255.255)

% Bad IP address or host name
```

Well, we're not all set just yet. Let's fix R1 so that it can provide name resolution:

```
R1(config)#ip host Server1 172.16.20.254
R1(config)#^Z
R1#telnet Server1
Trying Server1 (172.16.20.254)... Open

User Access Verification

Password:
```

Great—things are looking good from the router, but if the customer can't telnet to the remote host using the name, we've got to check the DNS server to confirm connectivity and for the correct entry to the server. Another option would be to configure the local host table manually on PC1.

The last thing to do is to check the server to see if it's responding to HTTP requests via the `telnet` command, believe it or not! Here's an example:

```
R1#telnet 172.16.20.254 80
Trying 172.16.20.254, 80 ... Open
```

Yes—finally! Server1 is responding to requests on port 80, so we're in the clear. Now, let's mix things up a little by adding IPv6 to our network and working through the same troubleshooting steps.

Troubleshooting IPv6 Network Connectivity

I'm going to be straight with you: there isn't a lot that's going to be much different between this section and the process you just went through with the IPv4 troubleshooting steps. Except regarding the addressing, of course! So other than that key factor, we'll take the same approach, using Figure 4.2, specifically because I really want to highlight the differences associated with IPv6. So, the problem scenario I'm going to use will also stay the same: PC1 cannot communicate with Server1.

I want to point out that this is not an "introduction to IPv6" chapter, so I'm assuming you've got some IPv6 fundamentals down.

FIGURE 4.2 IPv6 troubleshooting scenario

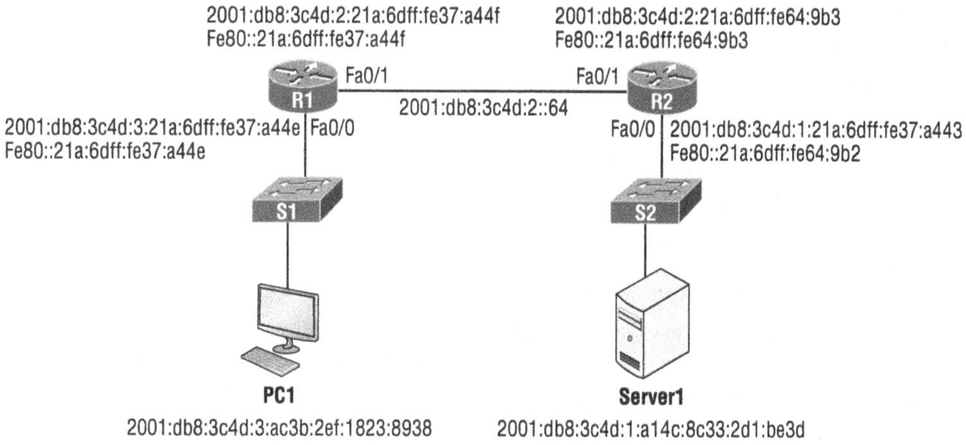

Notice that I documented both the *link-local* and *global addresses* assigned to each router interface in Figure 4.2. We need both to troubleshoot, so right away, you can see that things get a bit more complicated because of the longer addresses and the fact that there are multiple addresses per interface involved!

But *before* we start troubleshooting the IPv6 network in Figure 4.2, I want to refresh your memory on the ICMPv6 protocol, which is an important protocol in our troubleshooting arsenal.

ICMPv6

IPv4 used the ICMP workhorse for lots of tasks, including error messages like destination unreachable and troubleshooting functions like Ping and Traceroute. ICMPv6 still does those things for us, but unlike its predecessor, the v6 flavor isn't implemented as a separate layer 3 protocol. Instead, it's an integrated part of IPv6 and is carried after the basic IPv6 header information as an extension header.

ICMPv6 is used for router solicitation and advertisement, for neighbor solicitation and advertisement (i.e., finding the MAC addresses for IPv6 neighbors), and for redirecting the host to the best router (default gateway).

Neighbor Discovery (NDP)

ICMPv6 also takes over the task of finding the address of other devices on the local link. The Address Resolution Protocol is used to perform this function for IPv4, but that's been renamed Neighbor Discovery (ND or NDP) in ICMPv6. This process is now achieved via a multicast address called the solicited node address because all hosts join this multicast group upon connecting to the network.

Neighbor discovery enables these functions:

- Determining the MAC address of neighbors
- Router solicitation (RS) FF02::2
- Router advertisements (RA) FF02::1
- Neighbor solicitation (NS)
- Neighbor advertisement (NA)
- Duplicate address detection (DAD)

The part of the IPv6 address designated by the 24 bits farthest to the right is added to the end of the multicast address FF02:0:0:0:0:1:FF/104. When this address is queried, the corresponding host will send back its layer 2 address. Devices can find and keep track of other neighbor devices on the network in pretty much the same way.

RA and RS multicast traffic request and send address information, which, too, is actually a function of ICMPv6—specifically, neighbor discovery.

In IPv4, the protocol IGMP was used to allow a host device to tell its local router that it was joining a multicast group and would like to receive the traffic for that group. This IGMP function has been replaced by ICMPv6, and the process has been renamed multicast listener discovery.

With IPv4, our hosts could have only one default gateway configured, and if that router went down, we had to fix the router, change the default gateway, or run some type of virtual default gateway with other protocols created as a solution for this inadequacy in IPv4. Figure 4.3 shows how IPv6 devices find their default gateways using neighbor discovery.

FIGURE 4.3 Router solicitation (RS) and router advertisement (RA)

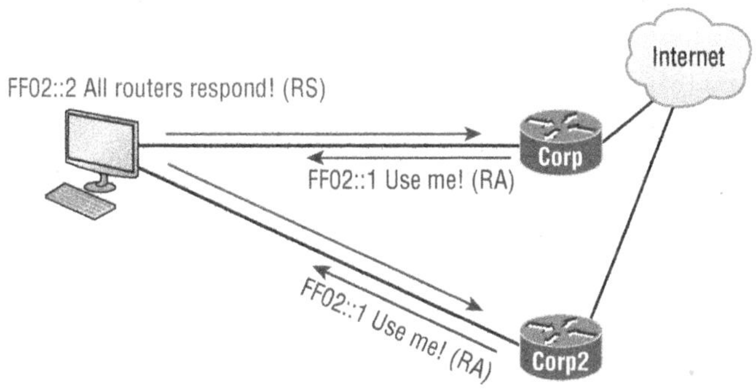

IPv6 hosts send a router solicitation (RS) onto their data link, asking for all routers to respond, and they use the multicast address FF02::2 to achieve this. Routers on the same link respond with a unicast to the requesting host or with a router advertisement (RA) using FF02::1.

But that's not all! Hosts can also send solicitations and advertisements between themselves using a neighbor solicitation (NS) and neighbor advertisement (NA), as shown in Figure 4.4.

FIGURE 4.4 Neighbor solicitation (NS) and neighbor advertisement (NA)

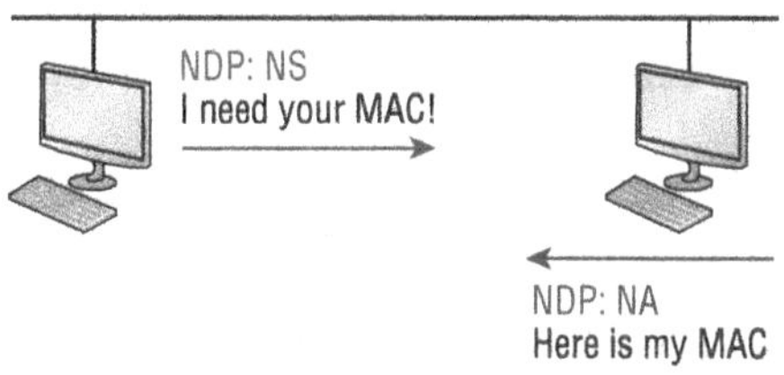

Remember that RA and RS gather or provide information about routers, and NS and NA gather information about hosts. Also, remember that a "neighbor" is a host on the same data link or VLAN.

With that foundation review in mind, here are the troubleshooting steps we'll progress through in our investigation:

1. Check the cables because there might be a faulty cable or interface. Verify interface statistics.
2. Make sure that devices are determining the correct path from the source to the destination. Manipulate the routing information if needed.
3. Verify that the default gateway is correct.
4. Verify that name resolution settings are correct, and especially for IPv6, make sure the DNS server is reachable via IPv4 and IPv6.
5. Verify that there are no ACLs that are blocking traffic.

To troubleshoot this problem, we'll use the same process of elimination, beginning with PC1. We must verify that it's configured correctly and that IP is working properly. Let's start by pinging the loopback address to verify the IPv6 stack:

```
C:\Users\Todd Lammle>ping ::1

Pinging ::1 with 32 bytes of data:
Reply from ::1: time<1ms
Reply from ::1: time<1ms
Reply from ::1: time<1ms
Reply from ::1: time<1ms
```

Well, the IPv6 stack checks out, so let's ping the Fa0/0 of R1, which PC1 is directly connected to on the same LAN, starting with the link-local address:

```
C:\Users\Todd Lammle>ping fe80::21a:6dff:fe37:a44e

Pinging fe80:21a:6dff:fe37:a44e with 32 bytes of data:
Reply from fe80::21a:6dff:fe37:a44e: time<1ms
Reply from fe80::21a:6dff:fe37:a44e: time<1ms
Reply from fe80::21a:6dff:fe37:a44e: time<1ms
Reply from fe80::21a:6dff:fe37:a44e: time<1ms
```

Next, we'll ping the global address on Fa0/0:

```
C:\Users\Todd Lammle>ping 2001:db8:3c4d:3:21a:6dff:fe37:a44e

Pinging 2001:db8:3c4d:3:21a:6dff:fe37:a44e with 32 bytes of data:
Reply from 2001:db8:3c4d:3:21a:6dff:fe37:a44e: time<1ms
Reply from 2001:db8:3c4d:3:21a:6dff:fe37:a44e: time<1ms
Reply from 2001:db8:3c4d:3:21a:6dff:fe37:a44e: time<1ms
Reply from 2001:db8:3c4d:3:21a:6dff:fe37:a44e: time<1ms
```

Okay—looks like PC1 is configured and working on the local LAN to the R1 router, so we've confirmed the Physical, Data Link, and Network layers between the PC1 and the R1 router Fa0/0 interface.

Our next move is to check the local connection on Server1 to the R2 router to verify that LAN. First, we'll ping the link-local address of the router from Server1:

```
C:\Users\Server1>ping fe80::21a:6dff:fe64:9b2

Pinging fe80::21a:6dff:fe64:9b2  with 32 bytes of data:
Reply from fe80::21a:6dff:fe64:9b2: time<1ms
Reply from fe80::21a:6dff:fe64:9b2: time<1ms
Reply from fe80::21a:6dff:fe64:9b2: time<1ms
Reply from fe80::21a:6dff:fe64:9b2: time<1ms
```

And next, we'll ping the global address of Fa0/0 on R2:

```
C:\Users\Server1>ping 2001:db8:3c4d:1:21a:6dff:fe37:a443

Pinging 2001:db8:3c4d:1:21a:6dff:fe37:a443 with 32 bytes of data:
Reply from 2001:db8:3c4d:1:21a:6dff:fe37:a443: time<1ms
Reply from 2001:db8:3c4d:1:21a:6dff:fe37:a443: time<1ms
Reply from 2001:db8:3c4d:1:21a:6dff:fe37:a443: time<1ms
Reply from 2001:db8:3c4d:1:21a:6dff:fe37:a443: time<1ms
```

Let's quickly summarize what we know at this point:

1. By using the `ipconfig /all` command on PC1 and Server1, I was able to document their global and link-local IPv6 addresses.
2. We know the IPv6 link-local addresses of each router interface.
3. We know the IPv6 global address of each router interface.
4. We can ping from PC1 to router R1's Fa0/0 interface.
5. We can ping from Server1 to router R2's Fa0/0 interface.
6. We can eliminate a local problem on both LANs.

From here, we'll go to PC1 and see if we can route to Server1:

```
C:\Users\Todd Lammle>tracert 2001:db8:3c4d:1:a14c:8c33:2d1:be3d

Tracing route to 2001:db8:3c4d:1:a14c:8c33:2d1:be3d over a maximum of 30 hops

  1     Destination host unreachable.
```

Okay, that's not good. Looks like we might have a routing problem. And on this little network, we're doing static IPv6 routing, so getting to the bottom of things will definitely take some effort! But before we start looking into our potential routing issue, let's check the link between R1 and R2. We'll ping R2 from R1 to test the directly connected link.

The first thing you need to do before attempting to ping between routers is verify your addresses—yes, verify them again! Let's check out both routers and then try pinging from R1 to R2:

```
R1#sh ipv6 int brief
FastEthernet0/0              [up/up]
    FE80::21A:6DFF:FE37:A44E
    2001:DB8:3C4D:3:21A:6DFF:FE37:A44E
FastEthernet0/1              [up/up]
    FE80::21A:6DFF:FE37:A44F
    2001:DB8:3C4D:2:21A:6DFF:FE37:A44F

R2#sh ipv6 int brief
FastEthernet0/0              [up/up]
    FE80::21A:6DFF:FE64:9B2
    2001:DB8:3C4D:1:21A:6DFF:FE37:A443
```

```
FastEthernet0/1              [up/up]
    FE80::21A:6DFF:FE64:9B3
    2001:DB8:3C4D:2:21A:6DFF:FE64:9B3
R1#ping 2001:DB8:3C4D:2:21A:6DFF:FE64:9B3
Type escape sequence to abort.
Sending 5, 100-byte ICMP Echos to ping 2001:DB8:3C4D:2:21A:6DFF:FE64:9B3,
timeout
is 2 seconds:
!!!!!
Success rate is 100 percent (5/5), round-trip min/avg/max = 0/2/8 ms
```

In the preceding output, you can see that I now have the IPv6 addresses for both the R1 and R2 directly connected interfaces. The output also shows that I used the Ping program to verify layer 3 connectivity. Just as with IPv4, we need to resolve the logical (IPv6) address to a MAC address to communicate on the local LAN. But unlike IPv4, IPv6 doesn't use ARP—it uses ICMPv6 neighbor solicitations instead—so after the successful ping, we can now see the neighbor resolution table on R1:

```
R1#sh ipv6 neighbors
IPv6 Address                              Age Link-layer Addr State Interface
FE80::21A:6DFF:FE64:9B3                     0 001a.6c46.9b09  DELAY Fa0/1
2001:DB8:3C4D:2:21A:6DFF:FE64:9B3           0 001a.6c46.9b09  REACH Fa0/1
```

Let's take a minute to talk about the possible states that a resolved address shows us:

INCMP (incomplete) Address resolution is being performed on the entry. A neighbor solicitation message has been sent, but the neighbor message has not yet been received.

REACH (reachable) Positive confirmation has been received, confirming that the path to the neighbor is functioning correctly. REACH is good!

STALE The state is STALE when the interface has not communicated within the neighbor reachable time frame. The next time the neighbor communicates, the state will change back to REACH.

DELAY Occurs after the STALE state, when no reachability confirmation has been received within what's known as the DELAY_FIRST_PROBE_TIME. This means that the path was functioning but it hasn't had communication within the neighbor reachable time frame.

PROBE When in PROBE state, the configured interface is resending a neighbor solicitation and waiting for a reachability confirmation from a neighbor.

We can verify our default gateway with IPv6 with the `ipconfig` command like this:

```
C:\Users\Todd Lammle>ipconfig
   Connection-specific DNS Suffix  . : localdomain
   IPv6 Address. . . . . . . . . . . : 2001:db8:3c4d:3:ac3b:2ef:1823:8938
```

```
Temporary IPv6 Address. . . . . . : 2001:db8:3c4d:3:2f33:44dd:211:1c3d
Link-local IPv6 Address . . . . . : fe80::ac3b:2ef:1823:8938%11
IPv4 Address. . . . . . . . . . . : 10.1.1.10
Subnet Mask . . . . . . . . . . . : 255.255.255.0
Default Gateway . . . . . . . . . : Fe80::21a:6dff:fe37:a44e%11
   10.1.1.1
```

It's important to understand that the default gateway will be the link-local address of the router, and in this case, we can see that the address the host learned is truly the link-local address of the Fa0/0 interface of R1. The `%11` is just used to identify an interface and isn't used as part of the IPv6 address.

Temporary IPv6 Addresses

The temporary IPv6 address, listed under the unicast IPv6 address as **2001:db8:3c4d:3:2f33:44dd:211:1c3d**, was created by Windows to provide privacy from the EUI-64 format. This creates a global address from your host without using your MAC address by generating a random number for the interface and hashing it, which is then appended to the /64 prefix from the router. You can disable this feature with the following commands:

```
netsh interface ipv6 set global randomizeidentifiers=disabled
netsh interface ipv6 set privacy state-disabled
```

In addition to the `ipconfig` command, we can use the command `netsh interface ipv6 show neighbor` to verify our default gateway address:

```
C:\Users\Todd Lammle>netsh interface ipv6 show neighbor
[output cut]

Interface 11: Local Area Connection

Internet Address                              Physical Address   Type
--------------------------------------------  -----------------  -----------
2001:db8:3c4d:3:21a:6dff:fe37:a44e            00-1a-6d-37-a4-4e  (Router)
Fe80::21a:6dff:fe37:a44e                      00-1a-6d-37-a4-4e  (Router)
ff02::1                                       33-33-00-00-00-01  Permanent
ff02::2                                       33-33-00-00-00-02  Permanent
ff02::c                                       33-33-00-00-00-0c  Permanent
ff02::16                                      33-33-00-00-00-16  Permanent
ff02::fb                                      33-33-00-00-00-fb  Permanent
ff02::1:2                                     33-33-00-01-00-02  Permanent
ff02::1:3                                     33-33-00-01-00-03  Permanent
ff02::1:ff1f:ebcb                             33-33-ff-1f-eb-cb  Permanent
```

NOTE I've checked the default gateway addresses on Server1, and they are correct. They should be because this is provided directly from the router with an ICMPv6 RA (router advertisement) message. However, the output for that verification is not shown.

Let's establish the information we have right now:

1. Our PC1 and Server1 configurations are working and have been verified.
2. The LANs are working and verified, so there is no Physical layer issue.
3. The default gateways are correct.
4. The link between the R1 and R2 routers is working and verified.

So, all this tells us is that it's now time to check our routing tables! We'll start with the R1 router:

```
R1#sh ipv6 route
C   2001:DB8:3C4D:2::/64 [0/0]
     via FastEthernet0/1, directly connected
L   2001:DB8:3C4D:2:21A:6DFF:FE37:A44F/128 [0/0]
     via FastEthernet0/1, receive
C   2001:DB8:3C4D:3::/64 [0/0]
     via FastEthernet0/0, directly connected
L   2001:DB8:3C4D:3:21A:6DFF:FE37:A44E/128 [0/0]
     via FastEthernet0/0, receive
L   FF00::/8 [0/0]
     via Null0, receive
```

All we can see in the output are the two directly connected interfaces configured on the router, and that won't help us send IPv6 packets to the 2001:db8:3c4d:1::/64 subnet off of Fa0/0 on R2. So, let's find out what R2 can tell us:

```
R2#sh ipv6 route
C   2001:DB8:3C4D:1::/64 [0/0]
     via FastEthernet0/0, directly connected
L   2001:DB8:3C4D:1:21A:6DFF:FE37:A443/128 [0/0]
     via FastEthernet0/0, receive
C   2001:DB8:3C4D:2::/64 [0/0]
     via FastEthernet0/1, directly connected
L   2001:DB8:3C4D:2:21A:6DFF:FE64:9B3/128 [0/0]
     via FastEthernet0/1, receive
S   2001:DB8:3C4D:3::/64 [1/0]
     via 2001:DB8:3C4D:2:21B:D4FF:FE0A:539
L   FF00::/8 [0/0]
     via Null0, receive
```

Now we're talking—that tells us a lot more than R1's table did! We have both of our directly connected configured LANs, Fa0/0 and Fa0/1, right there in the routing table, as well as a static route to 2001:DB8:3C4D:3::/64, which is the remote LAN Fa0/0 off of R1, which is good. Now, let's fix the route problem on R1 by adding a route that gives us access to the Server1 network and then move on to VLANs and trunking:

```
R1(config)#ipv6 route ::/0 fastethernet 0/1 FE80::21A:6DFF:FE64:9B3
```

I want to point out that I didn't need to make the default route as difficult as I did. I entered both the exit interface and next-hop link-local address when just the exit interface or next-hop global addresses would be mandatory, but not the link-local.

Next, we'll verify that we can now ping from PC1 to Server1:

```
C:\Users\Todd Lammle>ping 2001:db8:3c4d:1:a14c:8c33:2d1:be3d

Pinging 2001:db8:3c4d:1:a14c:8c33:2d1:be3d with 32 bytes of data:
Reply from 2001:db8:3c4d:1:a14c:8c33:2d1:be3d: time<1ms
Reply from 2001:db8:3c4d:1:a14c:8c33:2d1:be3d: time<1ms
Reply from 2001:db8:3c4d:1:a14c:8c33:2d1:be3d: time<1ms
Reply from 2001:db8:3c4d:1:a14c:8c33:2d1:be3d: time<1ms
```

Sweet—we're looking golden with this particular scenario! But know that it is still possible to have name-resolution issues. If that were the case, you would just need to check your DNS server or local host table.

Moving on in the same way we did in the IPv4 troubleshooting section, it's a good time to check into your ACLs, especially if you're still having a problem after troubleshooting all your local LANs and all other potential routing issues. To do that, just use the `show ipv6 access-lists` command to verify all configured ACLs on a router and the `show ipv6 interface` command to verify if an ACL is attached to an interface. Once you've confirmed that your ACLs all make sense, you're good to go!

Troubleshooting VLAN Connectivity

You know by now that VLANs are used to break up broadcast domains in a layer 2 switched network. You've also learned that we assign ports on a switch into a VLAN broadcast domain by using the `switchport access vlan` command.

The access port carries traffic for a single VLAN that the port is a member of. If members of one VLAN want to communicate with members in the same VLAN that are located on a different switch, then a port between the two switches needs to be either configured to be a member of this single VLAN or configured as a trunk link, which passes information on all VLANs by default.

We're going to reference Figure 4.5 as we go through the procedures for troubleshooting VLAN and trunking.

FIGURE 4.5 VLAN connectivity

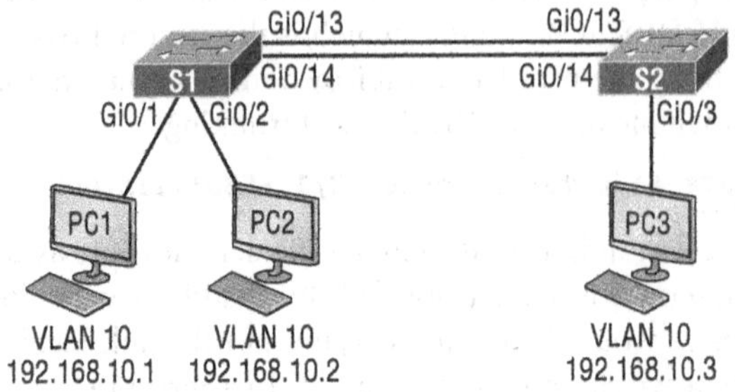

I'm going to begin with VLAN troubleshooting and then move on to trunk troubleshooting.

VLAN Troubleshooting

A couple of key times to troubleshoot VLANs are when and if you lose connectivity between hosts and when you're configuring new hosts into a VLAN but they're not working.

Here are the steps we'll follow to troubleshoot VLANs:

1. Verify the VLAN database on all your switches.
2. Verify your *content addressable memory (CAM)* table.
3. Verify that your port VLAN assignments are configured correctly.

And here's a list of the commands we'll be using in the following sections:

- show vlan
- show mac address-table
- show interfaces *interface* switchport
- switchport access vlan *vlan*

VLAN Troubleshooting Scenario

A manager calls and says they can't communicate with the new sales team member who just connected to the network. How would you proceed to solve this issue? Well, because the sales hosts are in VLAN 10, we'll begin with step 1 and verify that our databases on both switches are correct.

First, I'll use the `show vlan` or `show vlan brief` command to check if the expected VLAN is actually in the database. Here's a look at the VLAN database on S1:

```
S1#sh vlan
```

```
VLAN Name                             Status    Ports
---- -------------------------------- --------- -------------------------------
1    default                          active    Gi0/3, Gi0/4, Gi0/5, Gi0/6
                                                Gi0/7, Gi0/8, Gi0/9, Gi0/10
                                                Gi0/11, Gi0/12, Gi0/13, Gi0/14
                                                Gi0/15, Gi0/16, Gi0/17, Gi0/18
                                                Gi0/19, Gi0/20, Gi0/21, Gi0/22
                                                Gi0/23, Gi0/24, Gi0/25, Gi0/26
                                                Gi0/27, Gi0/28
10   Sales                            active    Gi0/1, Gi0/2
20   Accounting                       active
26   Automation10                     active
27   VLAN0027                         active
30   Engineering                      active
170  VLAN0170                         active
501  Private501                       active
502  Private500                       active
[output cut]
```

This output shows that VLAN 10 is in the local database and that Gi0/1 and Gi0/2 are associated with VLAN 10.

So next, we'll go to step 2 and verify the CAM with the `show mac address-table` command:

```
S1#sh mac address-table
          Mac Address Table
-------------------------------------------
Vlan    Mac Address       Type        Ports
----    -----------       --------    -----
 All    0100.0ccc.cccc    STATIC      CPU
[output cut]
   1    000d.2830.2f00    DYNAMIC     Gi0/24
   1    0021.1c91.0d8d    DYNAMIC     Gi0/13
   1    0021.1c91.0d8e    DYNAMIC     Gi0/14
   1    b414.89d9.1882    DYNAMIC     Gi0/17
   1    b414.89d9.1883    DYNAMIC     Gi0/18
   1    ecc8.8202.8282    DYNAMIC     Gi0/15
   1    ecc8.8202.8283    DYNAMIC     Gi0/16
  10    001a.2f55.c9e8    DYNAMIC     Gi0/1
  10    001b.d40a.0538    DYNAMIC     Gi0/2
Total Mac Addresses for this criterion: 29
```

Okay—know that your switch will show quite a few MAC addresses assigned to the CPU at the top of the output; those MAC addresses are used by the switch to manage the ports. The very first MAC address listed is the base MAC address of the switch and used by STP in the bridge ID. In the preceding output, we can see that there are two MAC addresses associated with VLAN 10 and that it was dynamically learned. We can also establish that this MAC address is associated with Gi0/1. S1 looks really good!

Let's take a look at S2 now. First, let's confirm that port PC3 is connected and check its configuration. I'll use the command `show interfaces` *`interface`* `switchport` command to do that:

```
S2#sh interfaces gi0/3 switchport
Name: Gi0/3
Switchport: Enabled
Administrative Mode: dynamic desirable
Operational Mode: static access
Administrative Trunking Encapsulation: negotiate
Operational Trunking Encapsulation: native
Negotiation of Trunking: On
Access Mode VLAN: 10 (Inactive)
Trunking Native Mode VLAN: 1 (default)
[output cut]
```

Okay—we can see that the port is enabled and that it's set to dynamic desirable. This means that if it connects to another Cisco switch, it will desire to trunk on that link. But keep in mind that we're using it as an access port, which is confirmed by the operational mode of static access. At the end of the output, the text shows `Access Mode VLAN: 10 (Inactive)`. This is not a good thing! Let's examine S2's CAM and see what we find out:

```
S2#sh mac address-table
          Mac Address Table
-------------------------------------------

Vlan    Mac Address       Type        Ports
----    -----------       --------    -----
 All    0100.0ccc.cccc    STATIC      CPU
 [output cut]
   1    001b.d40a.0538    DYNAMIC     Gi0/13
   1    0021.1bee.a70d    DYNAMIC     Gi0/13
   1    b414.89d9.1884    DYNAMIC     Gi0/17
   1    b414.89d9.1885    DYNAMIC     Gi0/18
   1    ecc8.8202.8285    DYNAMIC     Gi0/16
Total Mac Addresses for this criterion: 26
```

Referring back to Figure 4.5, we can see that the host is connected to Gi0/3. The problem here is that we don't see a MAC address dynamically associated with Gi0/3 in the MAC address table. What do we know so far that can help us? Well, first, we can see that Gi0/3 is configured into VLAN 10, but that VLAN is inactive. Second, the host off Gi0/3 doesn't appear in the CAM table. Now would be a good time to take a look at the VLAN database like this:

```
S2#sh vlan brief
VLAN Name                             Status    Ports
---- -------------------------------- --------- -------------------------------
1    default                          active    Gi0/1, Gi0/2, Gi0/4, Gi0/5
                                                Gi0/6, Gi0/7, Gi0/8, Gi0/9
                                                Gi0/10, Gi0/11, Gi0/12, Gi0/13
                                                Gi0/14, Gi0/15, Gi0/16, Gi0/17
                                                Gi0/18, Gi0/19, Gi0/20, Gi0/21
                                                Gi0/22, Gi0/23, Gi0/24, Gi0/25
                                                Gi0/26, Gi0/27, Gi0/28
26   Automation10                     active
27   VLAN0027                         active
30   Engineering                      active
170  VLAN0170                         active
[output cut]
```

Look at that: there is no VLAN 10 in the database! Clearly the problem, but also an easy one to fix by simply creating the VLAN in the database:

```
S2#config t
S2(config)#vlan 10
S2(config-vlan)#name Sales
```

That's all there is to it. Now let's check the CAM again:

```
S2#sh mac address-table
          Mac Address Table
-------------------------------------------
Vlan    Mac Address       Type        Ports
----    -----------       --------    -----
 All    0100.0ccc.cccc    STATIC      CPU
[output cut]
   1    0021.1bee.a70d    DYNAMIC     Gi0/13
  10    001a.6c46.9b09    DYNAMIC     Gi0/3
Total Mac Addresses for this criterion: 22
```

We're good to go—the MAC address off Gi0/3 shows in the MAC address table configured into VLAN 10.

That was pretty straightforward, but if the port had been assigned to the wrong VLAN, I would have used the `switch access vlan` command to correct the VLAN membership. Here's an example of how to do that:

```
S2#config t
S2(config)#int gi0/3
S2(config-if)#switchport access vlan 10
S2(config-if)#do sh vlan

VLAN Name                             Status    Ports
---- -------------------------------- --------- -------------------------------
1    default                          active    Gi0/1, Gi0/2, Gi0/4, Gi0/5
                                                Gi0/6, Gi0/7, Gi0/8, Gi0/9
                                                Gi0/10, Gi0/11, Gi0/12, Gi0/13
                                                Gi0/14, Gi0/15, Gi0/16, Gi0/17
                                                Gi0/18, Gi0/19, Gi0/20, Gi0/21
                                                Gi0/22, Gi0/23, Gi0/24, Gi0/25
                                                Gi0/26, Gi0/27, Gi0/28
10   Sales                            active    Gi0/3
```

Okay, great—we can see that our port Gi0/3 is in the VLAN 10 membership. Now, let's try to ping from PC1 to PC3:

```
PC1#ping 192.168.10.3
Type escape sequence to abort.
Sending 5, 100-byte ICMP Echos to 192.168.10.3, timeout is 2 seconds:
.....
Success rate is 0 percent (0/5)
```

No luck, so let's see if PC1 can ping PC2:

```
PC1#ping 192.168.10.2
Type escape sequence to abort.
Sending 5, 100-byte ICMP Echos to 192.168.10.2, timeout is 2 seconds:
!!!!!
Success rate is 100 percent (5/5), round-trip min/avg/max = 1/2/4 ms
PC1#
```

That worked! I can ping a host that's a member of the same VLAN connected to the same switch, but I can't ping a host on another switch that's a member of the same VLAN, which is VLAN 10. To get to the bottom of this, let's quickly summarize what we've learned so far:

1. We know that the VLAN database is now correct on each switch.
2. The MAC address table shows the ARP entries for each host as well as a connection to each switch.
3. We've verified that our VLAN memberships are now correct on all the ports we're using.

But because we still can't ping a host on another switch, we need to start checking out the connections between our switches.

Trunk Troubleshooting

You'll need to troubleshoot trunk links when you lose connectivity between hosts that are in the same VLAN but are located on different switches. Cisco refers to this as "VLAN leaking." Seems to me that we are leaking VLAN 10 between switches somehow.

These are the steps we'll take to troubleshoot VLANs:

1. Verify that the interface configuration is set to the correct trunk parameters.
2. Verify that the ports are configured correctly.
3. Verify the native VLAN on each switch.

And here are the commands we'll use to perform trunk troubleshooting:

```
Show interfaces trunk
Show vlan
Show interfaces interface trunk
Show interfaces interface switchport
Show dtp interface interface
switchport mode
switchport mode dynamic
switchport trunk native vlan vlan
```

Okay, let's get started by checking ports Gi0/13 and Gi0/14 on each switch because these are what the figure shows as forming the connection between our switches. We'll start with the `show interfaces trunk` command:

```
S1>sh interfaces trunk

S2>sh interfaces trunk
```

Not a scrap of output—that's definitely a bad sign! Let's take another look at the `show vlan` output on S1 and see what we can find out:

```
S1>sh vlan brief
VLAN Name                             Status    Ports
---- -------------------------------- --------- -------------------------------
1    default                          active    Gi0/3, Gi0/4, Gi0/5, Gi0/6
                                                Gi0/7, Gi0/8, Gi0/9, Gi0/10
                                                Gi0/11, Gi0/12, Gi0/13, Gi0/14
                                                Gi0/15, Gi0/16, Gi0/17, Gi0/18
                                                Gi0/19, Gi0/20, Gi0/21, Gi0/22
                                                Gi0/23, Gi0/24, Gi0/25, Gi0/26
                                                Gi0/27, Gi0/28
10   Sales                            active    Gi0/1, Gi0/2
20   Accounting                       active
[output cut]
```

Nothing new from when we checked it a few minutes ago, but look there under VLAN 1—we can see interfaces Gi/013 and Gi0/14. This means that our ports between switches are members of VLAN 1 and will pass only VLAN 1 frames!

Typically, I'll tell my students that if you type the `show vlan` command, you're really typing the nonexistent "show access ports" command because this output shows interfaces in access mode but doesn't show the trunk interfaces. This means that our ports between switches are access ports instead of trunk ports, so they'll pass information about only VLAN 1.

Let's go back over to the S2 switch to verify and see which port interfaces Gi0/13 and Gi0/14 are members of:

```
S2>sh vlan brief

VLAN Name                             Status    Ports
---- -------------------------------- --------- -------------------------------
1    default                          active    Gi0/1, Gi0/2, Gi0/4, Gi0/5
                                                Gi0/6, Gi0/7, Gi0/8, Gi0/9
                                                Gi0/10, Gi0/11, Gi0/12, Gi0/13
                                                Gi0/14, Gi0/15, Gi0/16, Gi0/17
                                                Gi0/18, Gi0/19, Gi0/20, Gi0/21
                                                Gi0/22, Gi0/23, Gi0/24, Gi0/25
                                                Gi0/26, Gi0/27, Gi0/28
10   Sales                            active    Gi0/3
```

Again, as with S1, the links between switches are showing in the output of the `show vlan` command, which means that they are not trunk ports. We can use the `show interfaces` *interface* `switchport` command to verify this as well:

```
S1#sho interfaces gi0/13 switchport
Name: Gi0/13
Switchport: Enabled
Administrative Mode: dynamic auto
Operational Mode: static access
Administrative Trunking Encapsulation: negotiate
Operational Trunking Encapsulation: native
Negotiation of Trunking: On
Access Mode VLAN: 1 (default)
Trunking Native Mode VLAN: 1 (default)
```

This output tells us that interface Gi0/13 is in dynamic auto mode. But its operational mode is static access, meaning it's not a trunk port. We can look closer at its trunking capabilities with the `show interfaces` *interface* `trunk` command:

```
S1#sh interfaces gi0/1 trunk

Port        Mode         Encapsulation  Status        Native vlan
Gi0/1       auto         negotiate      not-trunking  1
[output cut]
```

Sure enough—the port is not trunking, but we already knew that. Now we know it again. Notice that we can see that native VLAN is set to VLAN 1, which is the default native VLAN. This means that VLAN 1 is the default VLAN for untagged traffic.

Now, before we check the native VLAN on S2 to verify that there isn't a mismatch, I want to point out a key fact about trunking and how we would get these ports between switches to do that.

Many Cisco switches support the Cisco proprietary *Dynamic Trunking Protocol (DTP)*, which is used to manage automatic trunk negotiation between switches. Cisco recommends that you don't allow this and configure your switch ports manually instead. I agree!

Okay, with that in mind, let's check out our switch port Gi0/13 on S1 and view its DTP status. I'll use the `show dtp interface` *`interface`* command to view the DTP statistics:

```
S1#sh dtp interface gi0/13
DTP information for GigabitEthernet0/13:
  TOS/TAS/TNS:                               ACCESS/AUTO/ACCESS
  TOT/TAT/TNT:                               NATIVE/NEGOTIATE/NATIVE
  Neighbor address 1:                        00211C910D8D
  Neighbor address 2:                        000000000000
  Hello timer expiration (sec/state):        12/RUNNING
  Access timer expiration (sec/state):       never/STOPPED
```

Did you notice that our port GI0/13 from S1 to S2 is an access port configured to autonegotiate using DTP? That's interesting, and I want to delve a bit deeper into the different port configurations and how they affect trunking capabilities to clarify why:

Access Trunking is not allowed on a port set to access mode.

Auto Will trunk to neighbor switch only if the remote port is set to on or to desirable mode. This creates the trunk based on the DTP request from the neighboring switch.

Desirable This will trunk with all port modes except access. Ports set to dynamic desirable will communicate via DTP that the interface is attempting to become a trunk if the neighboring switch interface is able to become a trunk.

Nonegotiate No DTP frames are generated from the interface. Can only be used if the neighbor interface is manually set as trunk or access.

Trunk (on) Trunks with all switch port modes except access. Automatically enables trunking regardless of the state of the neighboring switch and regardless of any DTP requests.

Let's check out the different options available on the S1 switch with the `switchport mode dynamic` command:

```
S1(config-if)#switchport mode ?
  access         Set trunking mode to ACCESS unconditionally
  dot1q-tunnel   set trunking mode to TUNNEL unconditionally
  dynamic        Set trunking mode to dynamically negotiate access or trunk mode
  private-vlan   Set private-vlan mode
  trunk          Set trunking mode to TRUNK unconditionally
```

```
S1(config-if)#switchport mode dynamic ?
  auto       Set trunking mode dynamic negotiation parameter to AUTO
  desirable  Set trunking mode dynamic negotiation parameter to DESIRABLE
```

From interface mode, use the `switch mode trunk` command to turn on trunking. You can also use the `switch mode dynamic` command to set the port to auto or desirable trunking modes. To turn off DTP and any type of negotiation, use the `switchport nonegotiate` command.

Let's take a look at S2 and see if we can figure out why our two switches didn't create a trunk:

```
S2#sh int gi0/13 switchport
Name: Gi0/13
Switchport: Enabled
Administrative Mode: dynamic auto
Operational Mode: static access
Administrative Trunking Encapsulation: negotiate
Operational Trunking Encapsulation: native
Negotiation of Trunking: On
```

Okay—we can see that the port is in `dynamic auto` and that it's operating as an access port. Let's look into this further:

```
S2#sh dtp interface gi0/13
DTP information for GigabitEthernet0/3:
  DTP information for GigabitEthernet0/13:
  TOS/TAS/TNS:                              ACCESS/AUTO/ACCESS
  TOT/TAT/TNT:                              NATIVE/NEGOTIATE/NATIVE
  Neighbor address 1:                       000000000000
  Neighbor address 2:                       000000000000
  Hello timer expiration (sec/state):       17/RUNNING
  Access timer expiration (sec/state):      never/STOPPED
```

Do you see the problem? Don't be fooled—it's not that they're running in access mode; it's because two ports in `dynamic auto` will not form a trunk! This is a really common problem to look for because most Cisco switches ship in `dynamic auto`. The other issue you need to be aware of, as well as check for, is the frame-tagging method. Some switches run 802.1q, and some run both 802.1q and *Inter-Switch Link (ISL) routing*, so be sure the tagging method is compatible between all of your switches!

It's time to fix our problem on the trunk ports between S1 and S2. All we need to do is just fix one side of each link because `dynamic auto` will trunk with a port set to `desirable` or on:

```
S2(config)#int gi0/13
S2(config-if)#switchport mode dynamic desirable
23:11:37:%LINEPROTO-5-UPDOWN:Line protocol on Interface GigabitEthernet0/13,
changed state to down
```

```
23:11:37:%LINEPROTO-5-UPDOWN:Line protocol on Interface Vlan1, changed
state to down
23:11:40:%LINEPROTO-5-UPDOWN:Line protocol on Interface GigabitEthernet0/13,
changed state to up
23:12:10:%LINEPROTO-5-UPDOWN:Line protocol on Interface Vlan1, changed
state to up
S2(config-if)#do show int trunk

Port        Mode         Encapsulation  Status        Native vlan
Gi0/13      desirable    n-isl          trunking      1
[output cut]
```

Nice—it worked! With one side in `Auto` and the other now in `Desirable`, DTPs will be exchanged, and they will trunk. Notice in the preceding output that the mode of S2's Gi0/13 link is `desirable` and that the switches actually negotiated ISL as a trunk encapsulation—go figure! But don't forget to notice the native VLAN. We'll work on the frame-tagging method and native VLAN in a minute, but first, let's configure our other link:

```
S2(config-if)#int gi0/14
S2(config-if)#switchport mode dynamic desirable
23:12:%LINEPROTO-5-UPDOWN:Line protocol on Interface GigabitEthernet0/14,
changed state to down
23:12:%LINEPROTO-5-UPDOWN:Line protocol on Interface GigabitEthernet0/14,
changed state to up
S2(config-if)#do show int trunk

Port        Mode         Encapsulation  Status        Native vlan
Gi0/13      desirable    n-isl          trunking      1
Gi0/14      desirable    n-isl          trunking      1

Port        Vlans allowed on trunk
Gi0/13      1-4094
Gi0/14      1-4094
[output cut]
```

Great, we now have two trunked links between switches. But I've got to say, I really don't like the ISL method of frame tagging because it can't send untagged frames across the link. So, let's change our native VLAN from the default of 1 to 392. The number 392 just randomly sounded good at the moment. Here's what I entered on S1:

```
S1(config-if)#switchport trunk native vlan 392
S1(config-if)#
23:17:40: Port is not 802.1Q trunk, no action
```

See what I mean? I tried to change the native VLAN, and ISL basically responded with, "What's a native VLAN?" Very annoying, so I'm going to take care of that now!

```
S1(config-if)#int range gi0/13 - 14
S1(config-if-range)#switchport trunk encapsulation ?
  dot1q      Interface uses only 802.1q trunking encapsulation when trunking
  isl        Interface uses only ISL trunking encapsulation when trunking
  negotiate  Device will negotiate trunking encapsulation with peer on
             interface

S1(config-if-range)#switchport trunk encapsulation dot1q
23:23:%LINEPROTO-5-UPDOWN:Line protocol on Interface GigabitEthernet0/13,
changed state to down
23:23:%LINEPROTO-5-UPDOWN: Line protocol on Interface GigabitEthernet0/14,
changed state to down
23:23:%CDP-4-NATIVE_VLAN_MISMATCH: Native VLAN mismatch discovered on
GigabitEthernet0/13 (392), with S2 GigabitEthernet0/13 (1).
23:23:%LINEPROTO-5-UPDOWN: Line protocol on Interface GigabitEthernet0/14,
changed state to up
23:23:%LINEPROTO-5-UPDOWN: Line protocol on Interface GigabitEthernet0/13,
changed state to up
23:23:%CDP-4-NATIVE_VLAN_MISMATCH: Native VLAN mismatch discovered on
GigabitEthernet0/13 (392), with S2 GigabitEthernet0/13 (1).
```

Okay, that's more like it! As soon as I changed the encapsulation type on S1, DTP frames changed the frame-tagging method between S2 to 802.1q. Because I had already changed the native VLAN on port Gi0/13 on S1, the switch lets us know via CDP that we now have a native VLAN mismatch. Let's proceed to deal with this by verifying our interfaces with the `show interface trunk` command:

```
S1#sh int trunk
Port      Mode        Encapsulation  Status      Native vlan
Gi0/13    auto        802.1q         trunking    392
Gi0/14    auto        802.1q         trunking    1

S2#sh int trunk

Port      Mode        Encapsulation  Status      Native vlan
Gi0/13    desirable   n-802.1q       trunking    1
Gi0/14    desirable   n-802.1q       trunking    1
```

Now notice that both links are running 802.1q and that S1 is in `auto` mode and S2 is in `desirable` mode. And we can see a native VLAN mismatch on port Gi0/13. We can also see the mismatched native VLAN with the show `interfaces` *interface* `switchport` command by looking at both sides of the link like this:

```
S2#sh interfaces gi0/13 switchport
Name: Gi0/13
Switchport: Enabled
Administrative Mode: dynamic desirable
Operational Mode: trunk
Administrative Trunking Encapsulation: negotiate
Operational Trunking Encapsulation: dot1q
Negotiation of Trunking: On
Access Mode VLAN: 1 (default)
Trunking Native Mode VLAN: 1 (default)
```

```
S1#sh int gi0/13 switchport
Name: Gi0/13
Switchport: Enabled
Administrative Mode: dynamic auto
Operational Mode: trunk
Administrative Trunking Encapsulation: dot1q
Operational Trunking Encapsulation: dot1q
Negotiation of Trunking: On
Access Mode VLAN: 1 (default)
Trunking Native Mode VLAN: 392 (Inactive)
```

So, this has got to be bad, right? I mean really—are we sending any frames down that link or not? Let's see if we solved our little problem of not being able to ping hosts from S1 to S2 and find out:

```
PC1#ping 192.168.10.3
Type escape sequence to abort.
Sending 5, 100-byte ICMP Echos to 192.168.10.3, timeout is 2 seconds:
!!!!!
Success rate is 100 percent (5/5), round-trip min/avg/max = 1/1/4 ms
```

Yes, it works! Not so bad after all. We've solved our problem, or at least most of it. Having a native VLAN mismatch only means you can't send untagged frames down the link, which are essentially management frames like CDP, for example. So, although it's not the end of the world, it will prevent us from being able to remotely manage the switch or even sending any other types of traffic down just that one VLAN.

Am I saying you can just leave this issue the way it is? Well, you could, but you won't. No, you'll fix it because if you don't, CDP will send you a message every minute telling you that there's a mismatch, which will drive you mad! So, this is how we'll stop that from happening:

```
S2(config)#int gi0/13
S2(config-if)#switchport trunk native vlan 392
S2(config-if)#^Z
S2#sh int trunk

Port        Mode          Encapsulation  Status      Native vlan
Gi0/13      desirable     n-802.1q       trunking       392
Gi0/14      desirable     n-802.1q       trunking       1
[output cut]
```

All better! Both sides of the same link between switches are now using native VLAN 392 on Gigabit Ethernet 0/13. I want you to know that it's fine to have different native VLANs for each link if that's what works best for you. Each network is different, and you have to make choices between options that will end up meeting your particular business requirements in the most optimal way.

Summary

This chapter covered troubleshooting techniques from basic to advanced. Although most chapters in this book cover troubleshooting, this chapter focused purely on IPv4, IPv6, and VLAN/trunk troubleshooting.

You learned how to troubleshoot step-by-step from a host to a remote device. Starting with IPv4, you learned the steps to test the host and the local connectivity and then how to troubleshoot remote connectivity.

We then moved on to IPv6 and proceeded to troubleshoot using the same techniques that you learned with IPv4. It's important that you can use the verification commands I used in each step of this chapter.

Last, I covered VLAN and trunk troubleshooting and how to go step-by-step through a switched network using verification commands and narrowing down the problem.

Exam Essentials

Remember the Cisco steps in troubleshooting an IPv4 and IPv6 network.

1. Check the cables to find out if there's a faulty cable or interface in the mix, and verify the interface's statistics.
2. Make sure that devices are determining the correct path from the source to the destination. Manipulate the routing information if needed.

3. Verify that the default gateway is correct.
4. Verify that name resolution settings are correct.
5. Verify that there are no ACLs blocking traffic.

Remember the commands to verify and troubleshoot IPv4 and IPv6. You need to remember and practice the commands used in this chapter, especially `ping` and `traceroute` (`tracert` on Windows). But we also used the Windows commands `ipconfig` and `route print` and Cisco's commands `show ip int brief`, `show interface`, and `show route`.

Remember how to verify an ARP cache with IPv6. The command `show ipv6 neighbors` shows the IP-to-MAC-address resolution table on a Cisco router.

Remember to look at the statistics on a router and switch interface to determine problems. You've got to be able to analyze interface statistics to find problems if they exist, and this includes speed and duplex settings, input queue drops, output queue drops, and input and output errors.

Understand what a native VLAN is and how to change it. A native VLAN works with only 802.1q trunks and allows untagged traffic to traverse the trunk link. This is VLAN 1 by default on all Cisco switches, but it can be changed for security reasons with the `switchport native vlan` *`vlan`* command.

Written Lab

The answers to this lab can be found in Appendix A, "Answers to the Written Labs."

Write the answers to the following questions:

1. If your IPv6 ARP cache shows an entry of INCMP, what does this mean?
2. You want traffic from VLAN 66 to traverse a trunked link untagged. Which command will you use?
3. What are the five modes you can set a switch port to?
4. You are having a network problem and have checked the cables to find out if there's a faulty cable or interface in the mix and also verified the interface's statistics, made sure that devices are determining the correct path from the source to the destination, and verified that you don't need to manipulate the routing. What are your next troubleshooting steps?
5. You need to find out if the local IPv6 stack is working on a host. What command will you use?

Review Questions

NOTE The following questions are designed to test your understanding of this chapter's material. For more information on how to get additional questions, please see this book's introduction.

The answers to these questions can be found in Appendix B, "Answers to the Review Questions."

1. You need to verify the IPv6 ARP cache on a router and see that the state of an entry is REACH. What does REACH mean?
   - **A.** The router is reaching out to get the address.
   - **B.** The entry is incomplete.
   - **C.** The entry has reached the end of life and will be discarded from the table.
   - **D.** A positive confirmation has been received by the neighbor, and the path to it is functioning correctly.
2. What is the most common cause of interface errors?
   - **A.** Speed mismatch
   - **B.** Duplex mismatch
   - **C.** Buffer overflows
   - **D.** Collisions between a dedicated switch port and an NIC
3. Which command will verify the DTP status on a switch interface?
   - **A.** `sh dtp status`
   - **B.** `sh dtp status interface` *`interface`*
   - **C.** `sh interface` *`interface`* `dtp`
   - **D.** `sh dtp interface` *`interface`*
4. What mode will not allow DTP frames generated from a switch port?
   - **A.** Nonegotiate
   - **B.** Trunk
   - **C.** Access
   - **D.** Auto
5. The following output was generated by which command?

```
IPv6 Address                        Age Link-layer Addr State Interface
FE80::21A:6DFF:FE64:9B3                   0 001a.6c46.9b09  DELAY Fa0/1
2001:DB8:3C4D:2:21A:6DFF:FE64:9B3         0 001a.6c46.9b09  REACH Fa0/1
```

   - **A.** `show ip arp`
   - **B.** `show ipv6 arp`
   - **C.** `show ip neighbors`
   - **D.** `show ipv6 neighbors`

6. Which of the following states tells you that an interface has not communicated within the neighbor-reachable time frame?
   A. REACH
   B. STALE
   C. TIMEOUT
   D. CLEARED

7. You receive a call from a user who says they cannot log in to a remote server, which only runs IPv6. Based on the output, what could the problem be?

```
C:\Users\Todd Lammle>ipconfig
   Connection-specific DNS Suffix  . : localdomain
   IPv6 Address. . . . . . . . . . . : 2001:db8:3c4d:3:ac3b:2ef:1823:8938
   Temporary IPv6 Address. . . . . . : 2001:db8:3c4d:3:2f33:44dd:211:1c3d
   Link-local IPv6 Address . . . . . : fe80::ac3b:2ef:1823:8938%11
   IPv4 Address. . . . . . . . . . . : 10.1.1.10
   Subnet Mask . . . . . . . . . . . : 255.255.255.0
   Default Gateway . . . . . . . . . : 10.1.1.1
```

   A. The global address is in the wrong subnet.
   B. The IPv6 default gateway has not been configured or received from the router.
   C. The link-local address has not been resolved, so the host cannot communicate with the router.
   D. There are two IPv6 global addresses configured. One must be removed from the configuration.

8. Your host cannot reach remote networks. Based on the output, what is the problem?

```
C:\Users\Server1>ipconfig

Windows IP Configuration

Ethernet adapter Local Area Connection:

   Connection-specific DNS Suffix  . : localdomain
   Link-local IPv6 Address . . . . . : fe80::7723:76a2:e73c:2acb%11
   IPv4 Address. . . . . . . . . . . : 172.16.20.254
   Subnet Mask . . . . . . . . . . . : 255.255.255.0
   Default Gateway . . . . . . . . . : 172.16.2.1
```

   A. The link-local IPv6 address is wrong.
   B. The IPv6 global address is missing.
   C. There is no DNS server configuration.
   D. The IPv4 default gateway address is misconfigured.

9. Which commands will show you if you have a native VLAN mismatch? (Choose two.)
   A. `show interface native vlan`
   B. `show interface trunk`
   C. `show interface` *`interface`* `switchport`
   D. `show switchport interface`

10. You connect two new Cisco 3560 switches together and expect them to use DTP and create a trunk. However, when you check statistics, you find that they are access ports and didn't negotiate. Why didn't DTP work on these Cisco switches?
   A. The ports on each side of the link are set to auto trunking.
   B. The ports on each side of the link are set to on.
   C. The ports on each side of the link are set to dynamic.
   D. The ports on each side of the link are set to desirable.

Chapter 5

Network Address Translation (NAT)

THE FOLLOWING CCNA EXAM TOPICS ARE COVERED IN THIS CHAPTER:

✓ **4.0 IP Services**

4.1 Configure and verify inside source NAT using static and pools

In this chapter, we're going to dig into Network Address Translation (NAT), Dynamic NAT, and Port Address Translation (PAT), also known as NAT Overload. Of course, I'll demonstrate all the NAT commands.

It's important to understand the Cisco objectives for this chapter. They are very straightforward: You have hosts on your inside Corporate network using RFC 1918 addresses, and you need to allow those hosts access to the Internet by configuring NAT translations. With that objective in mind, that will be my direction with this chapter.

Because we'll be using ACLs in our NAT configurations, it's important that you're really comfortable with the skills you learned in Chapter 2 before proceeding with this one.

NOTE

To find your included bonus material, as well as Todd Lammle videos, practice questions, and hands-on labs, please see `www.lammle.com/ccna`.

When Do We Use NAT?

Network Address Translation (NAT) is similar to Classless Inter-Domain Routing (CIDR) in that the original intention for NAT was to slow the depletion of available IP address space by allowing multiple private IP addresses to be represented by a much smaller number of public IP addresses.

Since then, it's been discovered that NAT is also a useful tool for network migrations and mergers, server load sharing, and creating "virtual servers." So in this chapter, I'm going to describe the basics of NAT functionality and the terminology common to NAT.

Because NAT really decreases the overwhelming number of public IP addresses required in a networking environment, it comes in handy when two companies that have duplicate internal addressing schemes merge. NAT is also a great tool to use when an organization changes its Internet service provider (ISP) but the networking manager needs to avoid the hassle of changing the internal address scheme.

Here's a list of situations when NAT can be especially helpful:

- When you need to connect to the Internet and your hosts don't have globally unique IP addresses
- When you've changed to a new ISP that requires you to renumber your network
- When you need to merge two intranets with duplicate addresses

You typically use NAT on a border router. For example, in Figure 5.1, NAT is used on the Corporate router connected to the Internet.

FIGURE 5.1 Where to configure NAT

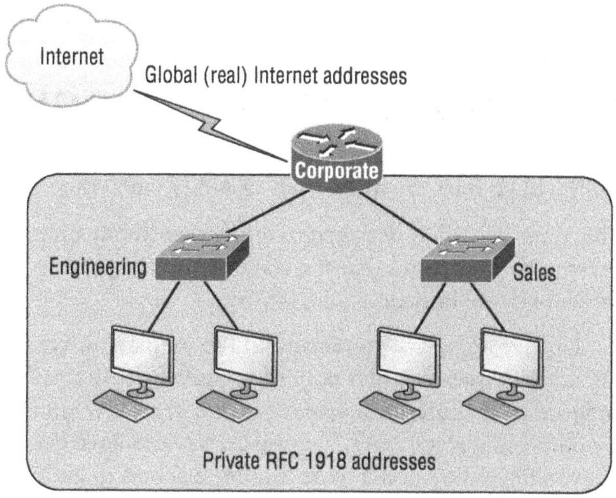

Now you may be thinking, "NAT's totally cool, and I just gotta have it!" But don't get too excited yet because there are some serious snags related to using NAT that you need to understand first. Don't get me wrong—it can truly be a lifesaver sometimes, but NAT has a bit of a dark side you need to know about, too. For the pros and cons linked to using NAT, check out Table 5.1.

TABLE 5.1 Advantages and disadvantages of implementing NAT

Advantages	Disadvantages
Conserves legally registered addresses	Translation results in switching path delays
Remedies address overlap events	Causes loss of end-to-end IP traceability
Increases flexibility when connecting to the Internet	Certain applications will not function with NAT enabled
Eliminates address renumbering as a network evolves	

NOTE The most obvious advantage associated with NAT is that it allows you to conserve your legally registered address scheme. But a version of it known as PAT is also why we've only just recently run out of IPv4 addresses. Without NAT/PAT, we'd have run out of IPv4 addresses more than a decade ago!

Types of Network Address Translation

In this section, I'm going to go over the three types of NATs with you:

Static NAT This type of NAT is designed to allow one-to-one mapping between local and global addresses. Keep in mind that the static version requires you to have one real Internet IP address for every host on your network.

Dynamic NAT This version gives you the ability to map an unregistered IP address to a registered IP address from out of a pool of registered IP addresses. You don't have to statically configure your router to map each inside address to an individual outside address as you would using static NAT, but you do have to have enough real, bona fide IP addresses for everyone who's going to be sending packets to and receiving them from the Internet at the same time.

Overloading This is the most popular type of NAT configuration. Understand that overloading really is a form of dynamic NAT that maps multiple unregistered IP addresses to a single registered IP address (many-to-one) by using different source ports. Now, why is this so special? Well, because it's also known as *Port Address Translation (PAT)*, which is also commonly referred to as NAT Overload. Using PAT allows you to permit thousands of users to connect to the Internet using only one real global IP address—pretty slick, right? Seriously, NAT Overload is the real reason we haven't run out of valid IP addresses on the Internet. Really—I'm not joking!

NAT Names

The names we use to describe the addresses used with NAT are fairly straightforward. Addresses used after NAT translations are called *global addresses*. These are usually the public addresses used on the Internet, which you don't need if you aren't going on the Internet.

Local addresses are the ones we use before NAT translation. This means that the inside local address is actually the private address of the sending host that's attempting to get to the Internet. The outside local address would typically be the router interface connected to your ISP and is also usually a public address used as the packet begins its journey.

After translation, the inside local address is then called the *inside global address*, and the outside global address then becomes the address of the destination host.

Check out Table 5.2, which lists all this terminology and offers a clear picture of the various names used with NAT. Keep in mind that these terms and their definitions can vary somewhat based on implementation. The table shows how they're used according to the Cisco exam objectives.

TABLE 5.2 NAT terms

Names	Meaning
Inside local	Source host inside address before translation—typically an RFC 1918 address.
Outside local	Address from which source host is known on the Internet. This is usually the address of the router interface connected to the ISP—the actual Internet address.
Inside global	Source host address used after translation to get onto the Internet. This is also the actual Internet address.
Outside global	Address of outside destination host and, again, the real Internet address.

How NAT Works

It's time to look at how this whole NAT thing works. I'm going to start by using Figure 5.2 to describe basic NAT translation.

FIGURE 5.2 Basic NAT translation

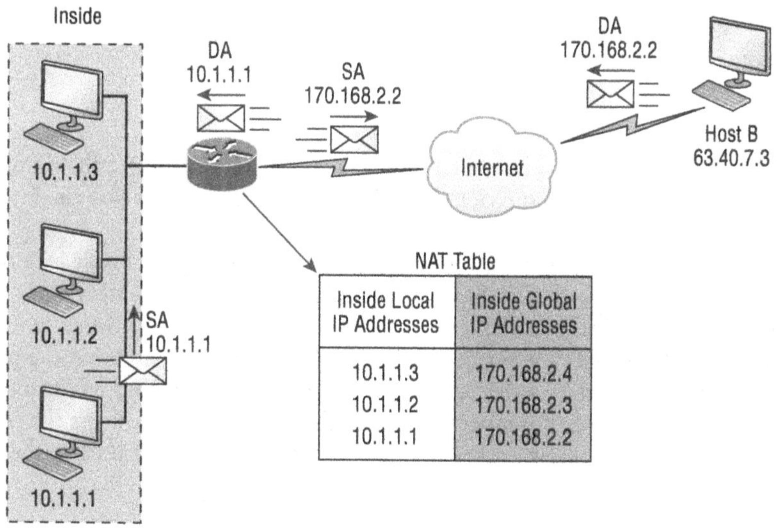

In this figure, we can see host 10.1.1.1 sending an Internet-bound packet to the border router configured with NAT. The router identifies the source IP address as an inside local IP address destined for an outside network, translates the source IP address in the packet, and documents the translation in the NAT table.

The packet is sent to the outside interface with the new translated source address. The external host returns the packet to the destination host and the NAT router translates the inside global IP address back to the inside local IP address using the NAT table. This is as simple as it gets!

Let's take a look at a more complex configuration using overloading, also referred to as PAT. I'll use Figure 5.3 to demonstrate how PAT works by having an inside host HTTP to a server on the Internet.

FIGURE 5.3 NAT overloading example (PAT)

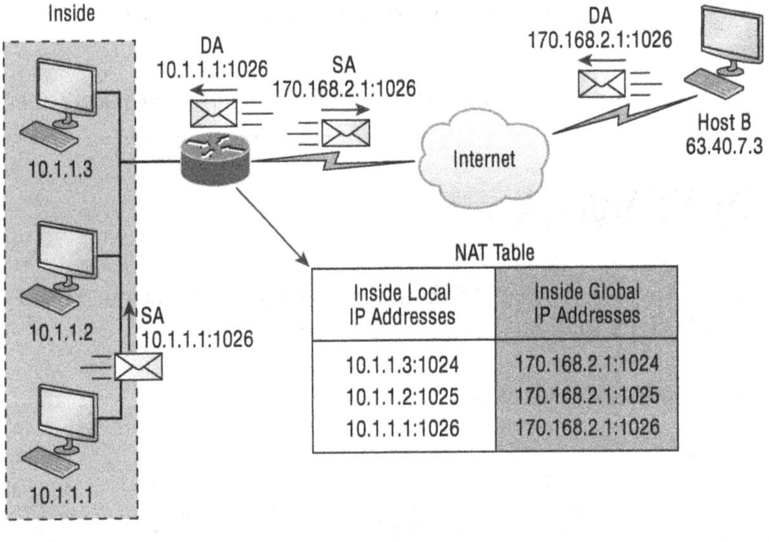

With PAT, all inside hosts get translated to one single IP address, hence the term *overloading*. Again, the reason we've just run out of available global IP addresses on the Internet is because of overloading (PAT).

Take a look at the NAT table in Figure 5.3 again. In addition to the inside local IP address and inside global IP address, we now have port numbers. These port numbers help the router identify which host should receive the return traffic. The router uses the source port number from each host to differentiate the traffic from each of them. Understand that the packet has a destination port number of 80 when it leaves the router, and the HTTP server sends back the data with a destination port number of 1026 in this example. This allows the NAT translation router to differentiate between hosts in the NAT table and then translate the destination IP address back to the inside local address.

Port numbers are used at the Transport layer to identify the local host in this example. If we had to use real global IP addresses to identify the source hosts, that's called *static NAT* and we would run out of addresses. PAT allows us to use the Transport layer to identify the hosts, which in turn, allows us to theoretically use up to about 65,000 hosts with only one real IP address!

Static NAT Configuration

Let's take a look at a simple example of a basic static NAT configuration:

```
ip nat inside source static 10.1.1.1 170.46.2.2
!
interface Ethernet0
 ip address 10.1.1.10 255.255.255.0
 ip nat inside
!
interface Serial0
 ip address 170.46.2.1 255.255.255.0
 ip nat outside
!
```

In the preceding router output, the `ip nat inside source` command identifies which IP addresses will be translated. In this configuration example, the `ip nat inside source` command configures a static translation between the inside local IP address 10.1.1.1 to the outside global IP address 170.46.2.2.

Scrolling further down in the configuration, we find an `ip nat` command under each interface. The `ip nat inside` command identifies that interface as the inside interface. The `ip nat outside` command identifies that interface as the outside interface. When you look back at the `ip nat inside source` command, you can see that the command is referencing the inside interface as the source or starting point of the translation. You could also use the command like this: `ip nat outside source`. This option indicates the interface that you designated as the outside interface should become the source or starting point for the translation.

Dynamic NAT Configuration

Basically, dynamic NAT really means we have a pool of addresses that we'll use to provide real IP addresses to a group of users on the inside. Because we don't use port numbers, we must have real IP addresses for every user who's trying to get outside the local network simultaneously.

Here is a sample output of a dynamic NAT configuration:

```
ip nat pool todd 170.168.2.3 170.168.2.254
    netmask 255.255.255.0
ip nat inside source list 1 pool todd
!
```

```
interface Ethernet0
 ip address 10.1.1.10 255.255.255.0
 ip nat inside
!
interface Serial0
 ip address 170.168.2.1 255.255.255.0
 ip nat outside
!
access-list 1 permit 10.1.1.0 0.0.0.255
!
```

The `ip nat inside source list 1 pool todd` command tells the router to translate IP addresses that match `access-list 1` to an address found in the IP NAT pool named todd. Here the ACL isn't there to filter traffic for security reasons by permitting or denying traffic. In this case, it's there to select or designate what we often call interesting traffic. When interesting traffic has been matched with the access list, it's pulled into the NAT process to be translated. This is actually a common use for access lists, which aren't always stuck with the dull job of just blocking traffic at an interface!

The command `ip nat pool todd 170.168.2.3 192.168.2.254 netmask 255.255.255.0` creates a pool of addresses that will be distributed to the specific hosts that require global addresses. When troubleshooting NAT for the Cisco objectives, always check this pool to confirm that there are enough addresses in it to provide translation for all the inside hosts. Last, check to make sure the pool names match exactly on both lines, remembering that they are case sensitive; if they don't, the pool won't work!

PAT (Overloading) Configuration

This last example shows how to configure inside global address overloading. This is the typical form of NAT that we would use today. It's actually now rare to use static or dynamic NAT unless it is for something like statically mapping a server, for example.

Here is a sample output of a PAT configuration:

```
ip nat pool globalnet 170.168.2.1 170.168.2.1 netmask 255.255.255.0
ip nat inside source list 1 pool globalnet overload
!
interface Ethernet0/0
 ip address 10.1.1.10 255.255.255.0
 ip nat inside
!
interface Serial0/0
 ip address 170.168.2.1 255.255.255.0
 ip nat outside
!
access-list 1 permit 10.1.1.0 0.0.0.255
```

The nice thing about PAT is that these are the only differences between this configuration and the previous dynamic NAT configuration:

- Our pool of addresses has shrunk to only one IP address.
- We included the `overload` keyword at the end of our `ip nat inside source` command.

A key factor in the example is that the one IP address in the pool for us to use is the IP address of the outside interface. This is perfect if you are configuring NAT Overload for yourself at home or for a small office that only has one IP address from your ISP. You could, however, use an additional address such as 170.168.2.2 if you had that address available to you as well, and doing that could prove very helpful in a large implementation where you've got such an abundance of simultaneously active internal users that you need to have more than one overloaded IP address on the outside!

Simple Verification of NAT

Okay—as always, once you've chosen and configured the type of NAT you're going to run, which is typically PAT, you must be able to verify your configuration.

To see basic IP address translation information, use the following command:

```
Router#show ip nat translations
```

When looking at the IP NAT translations, you may see many translations from the same host to the corresponding host at the destination. Understand that this is typical when there are many connections to the same server.

You can also verify your NAT configuration via the `debug ip nat` command. This output will show the sending address, the translation, and the destination address on each debug line:

```
Router#debug ip nat
```

But wait—how do you clear your NAT entries from the translation table? Just use the `clear ip nat translation` command, and if you want to clear all entries from the NAT table, just use an asterisk (`*`) at the end of the command.

Testing and Troubleshooting NAT

Cisco's NAT gives you some serious power—and it does so without much effort because the configurations are really pretty simple. But we all know nothing's perfect, so in case something goes wrong, you can figure out some of the more common culprits by running through this list of potential causes:

- Check the dynamic pools. Are they composed of the right scope of addresses?
- Check to see if any dynamic pools overlap.

- Check to see if the addresses used for static mapping and those in the dynamic pools overlap.
- Ensure that your access lists specify the correct addresses for translation.
- Make sure there aren't any addresses left out that need to be there, and ensure that none are included that shouldn't be.
- Check to make sure you've got both the inside and outside interfaces delimited properly.

A key thing to keep in mind is that one of the most common problems with a new NAT configuration often isn't specific to NAT at all—it usually involves a routing blooper. So, because you're changing a source or destination address in a packet, make sure your router still knows what to do with the new address after the translation!

The first command you should typically use is the `show ip nat translations` command:

```
Router#show ip nat trans
Pro   Inside global    Inside local    Outside local    Outside global
---   192.2.2.1        10.1.1.1        ---              ---
---   192.2.2.2        10.1.1.2        ---              ---
```

After checking out this output, can you tell me if the configuration on the router is static or dynamic NAT? The answer is yes, either static or dynamic NAT is configured because there's a one-to-one translation from the inside local to the inside global. Basically, by looking at the output, you can't tell if it's static or dynamic per se, but you can absolutely tell that you're not using PAT because there are no port numbers.

Let's take a look at another output:

```
Router#sh ip nat trans
Pro Inside global        Inside local        Outside local       Outside global
tcp 170.168.2.1:11003  10.1.1.1:11003      172.40.2.2:23       172.40.2.2:23
tcp 170.168.2.1:1067   10.1.1.1:1067       172.40.2.3:23       172.40.2.3:23
```

You can easily see that the above output is using NAT Overload (PAT). The protocol in this output is TCP, and the inside global address is the same for both entries.

Supposedly, the sky's the limit regarding the number of mappings the NAT table can hold. But this is reality, so things like memory and CPU, or even the boundaries set in place by the scope of available addresses or ports, can cause limitations on the actual number of entries. Consider that each NAT mapping devours about 160 bytes of memory. And sometimes the number of entries must be limited for the sake of performance or because of policy restrictions, which doesn't happen very often. In situations like these, just go to the `ip nat translation max-entries` command for help.

Another handy command for troubleshooting is `show ip nat statistics`. Deploying this gives you a summary of the NAT configuration, and it will count the number of active translation types, too. Also counted are hits to an existing mapping as well as any misses, with the latter causing an attempt to create a mapping. This command will also reveal expired translations. If you want to check into dynamic pools, their types, the total available addresses, how many addresses have been allocated and how many have failed, plus the number of translations that have occurred, just use the `pool` keyword.

Here is an example of the basic NAT debugging command:

```
Router#debug ip nat
NAT: s=10.1.1.1->192.168.2.1, d=172.16.2.2 [0]
NAT: s=172.16.2.2, d=192.168.2.1->10.1.1.1 [0]
NAT: s=10.1.1.1->192.168.2.1, d=172.16.2.2 [1]
NAT: s=10.1.1.1->192.168.2.1, d=172.16.2.2 [2]
NAT: s=10.1.1.1->192.168.2.1, d=172.16.2.2 [3]
NAT*: s=172.16.2.2, d=192.168.2.1->10.1.1.1 [1]
```

Notice the last line in the output and how the `NAT` at the beginning of the line has an asterisk (`*`). This means the packet was translated and fast-switched to the destination. What's fast-switched? Well, in brief, fast-switching has gone by several aliases such as cache-based switching and the nicely descriptive name "route one switch many." The fast-switching process is used on Cisco routers to create a cache of layer 3 routing information to be accessed at layer 2 so packets can be forwarded quickly through a router without the routing table having to be parsed for every packet. As packets are packet-switched (looked up in the routing table), this information is stored in the cache for later use if needed for faster routing processing.

Let's get back to verifying NAT. Did you know you can manually clear dynamic NAT entries from the NAT table? You can, and doing this can come in seriously handy if you need to get rid of a specific rotten entry without sitting around waiting for the timeout to expire! A manual clear is also useful when you want to clear the whole NAT table to reconfigure a pool of addresses.

You also need to know that the Cisco IOS software won't allow you to change or delete an address pool if any of that pool's addresses are mapped in the NAT table. The `clear ip nat translations` command clears entries—you can indicate a single entry via the global and local address and through TCP and UDP translations, including ports, or you can just type in an asterisk (`*`) to wipe out the entire table. But know that if you do that, only dynamic entries will be cleared because this command won't remove static entries.

Oh, and there's more—any outside device's packet destination address that happens to be responding to any inside device is known as the inside global (IG) address. This means that the initial mapping has to be held in the NAT table so that all packets arriving from a specific connection get translated consistently. Holding entries in the NAT table also cuts down on repeated translation operations happening each time the same inside machine sends packets to the same outside destinations on a regular basis.

Let me clarify: when an entry is placed into the NAT table the first time, a timer begins ticking, and its duration is known as the translation timeout. Each time a packet for a given entry translates through the router, the timer gets reset. If the timer expires, the entry will be unceremoniously removed from the NAT table, and the dynamically assigned address will then be returned to the pool. Cisco's default translation timeout is 86,400 seconds (24 hours), but you can change that with the `ip nat translation timeout` command.

Before we move on to the configuration section and actually use the commands I just talked about, let's go through a couple of NAT examples and see if you can figure out the best configuration to go with. To start, look at Figure 5.4 and ask yourself two things: Where would you implement NAT in this design? What type of NAT would you configure?

FIGURE 5.4 NAT example

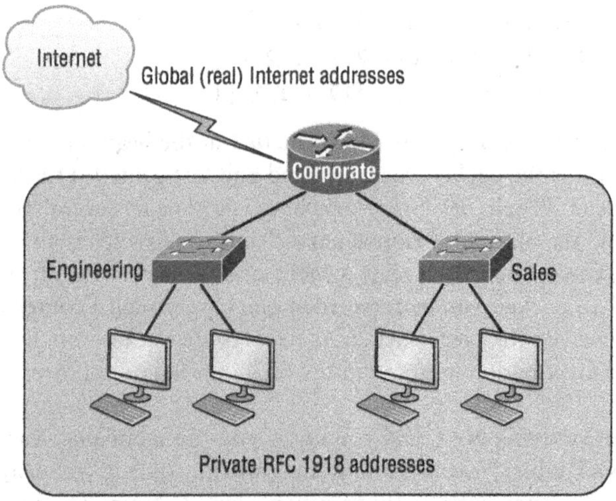

In Figure 5.4, the NAT configuration would be placed on the corporate router, just as I demonstrated with Figure 5.1, and the configuration would be dynamic NAT with overload (PAT). In this next NAT example, what type of NAT is being used?

```
ip nat pool todd-nat 170.168.10.10 170.168.10.20 netmask 255.255.255.0
ip nat inside source list 1 pool todd-nat
```

The preceding command uses dynamic NAT without PAT. The `pool` in the command gives the answer away as dynamic, plus there's more than one address in the pool, and there is no `overload` command at the end of our `ip nat inside source` command. This means we are not using PAT!

In the next NAT example, refer to Figure 5.5, and see if you can create the necessary configuration.

Figure 5.5 shows a border router that needs to be configured with NAT and allow the use of six public IP addresses to the inside locals, 192.1.2.109 through 192.1.2.114. However, on the inside network, you have 62 hosts that use the private addresses of 192.168.10.65 through 192.168.10.126. What would your NAT configuration be on the border router?

FIGURE 5.5 Another NAT example

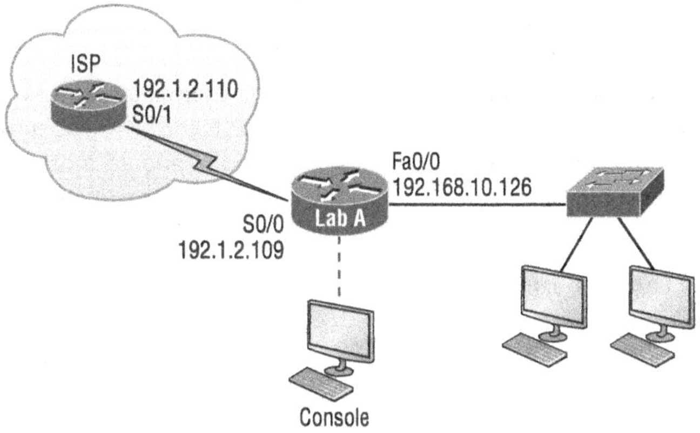

Two different answers would both work here, but the following would be my first choice based on the exam objectives:

```
ip nat pool Todd 192.1.2.109 192.1.2.109 netmask 255.255.255.248
access-list 1 permit 192.168.10.64 0.0.0.63
ip nat inside source list 1 pool Todd overload
```

The command `ip nat pool Todd 192.1.2.109 192.1.2.109 netmask 255.255.255.248` sets the pool name as Todd and creates a dynamic pool of only one address using NAT address 192.1.2.109. Instead of the `netmask` command, you can use the `prefix-length 29` statement. Just in case you're wondering, no, you cannot do this on router interfaces as well!

The second answer would get you the exact same result of having only 192.1.2.109 as your inside global, but you can type this in, and it will also work: `ip nat pool Todd 192.1.2.109 192.1.2.114 netmask 255.255.255.248`. But this option really is a waste because the second through sixth addresses would only be used if there was a conflict with a TCP port number. You would use something like what I've shown in this example if you literally had about 10,000 hosts with one Internet connection! You would need it to help with the TCP-Reset issue when two hosts are trying to use the same source port number and get a negative acknowledgment (NAK). But in our example, we've only got up to 62 hosts connecting to the Internet at the same time, so having more than one inside global gets us nothing!

If you're fuzzy on the second line where the access list is set in the NAT configuration, do a quick review of Chapter 2, "Security with ACLs." But this isn't difficult to grasp because it's easy to see in this access-list line that it's just the *`network number`* and *`wildcard`* used with that command. I always say, "Every question is a subnet question," and this one is no exception. The inside locals in this example were 192.168.10.65–126, which is a block of 64 or a 255.255.255.192 mask. As I've said in pretty much every chapter, you really need to be able to subnet quickly!

The command `ip nat inside source list 1 pool Todd overload` sets the dynamic pool to use PAT by using the `overload` command.

And be sure to add the `ip nat inside` and `ip nat outside` statements on the appropriate interfaces.

Okay, one more example, and then you are off to the written labs, and review questions.

The network in Figure 5.6 is already configured with IP addresses, as shown in the figure, and there is only one configured host. However, you need to add 25 more hosts to the LAN. Now, all 26 hosts must be able to get to the Internet at the same time.

FIGURE 5.6 Last NAT example

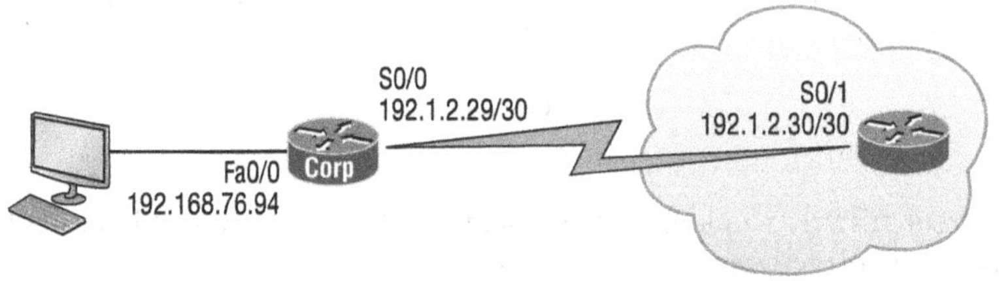

By looking at the configured network, use only the following inside addresses to configure NAT on the Corp router to allow all hosts to reach the Internet:

- Inside globals: 198.18.41.129 through 198.18.41.134
- Inside locals: 192.168.76.65 through 192.168.76.94

This one is a bit more challenging because all we have to help us figure out the configuration are the inside globals and the inside locals. But even meagerly armed with these crumbs of information, plus the IP addresses of the router interfaces shown in the figure, we can still configure this correctly.

To do that, we must first determine what our block sizes are so we can get our subnet mask for our NAT pool. This will also equip us to configure the wildcard for the access list.

You should easily be able to see that the block size of the inside globals is 8 and the block size of the inside locals is 32. Know that it's critical not to stumble on this foundational information!

Okay, so we can configure NAT now that we have our block sizes:

```
ip nat pool Corp 198.18.41.129 198.18.41.134 netmask 255.255.255.248
ip nat inside source list 1 pool Corp overload
access-list 1 permit 192.168.76.64 0.0.0.31
```

Because we had a block of only 8 for our pool, we had to use the `overload` command to make sure all 26 hosts can get to the Internet at the same time.

There is one other simple way to configure NAT, and I use this command at my home office to connect to my ISP. One command line, and it's done! Here it is:

```
ip nat inside source list 1 int s0/0/0 overload
```

I can't say enough how much I love efficiency, and being able to achieve something cool using one measly line always makes me happy! My one little powerfully elegant line essentially says, "Use my outside local as my inside global and overload it." Nice! Of course, I still had to create ACL 1 and add the inside and outside interface commands to the configuration, but this is a really nice, fast way to configure NAT if you don't have a pool of addresses to use.

Summary

Now this really was a fun chapter. Come on—admit it! You learned a lot about Network Address Translation (NAT) and how it's configured as static and dynamic, as well as with Port Address Translation (PAT), also called NAT Overload.

I also described how each flavor of NAT is used in a network as well as how each type is configured.

We finished up by going through some verification and troubleshooting commands. Don't forget to practice all the wonderfully written review questions until you've got them nailed down tight!

Exam Essentials

Understand the term *NAT*. This may come as news to you because I didn't—okay, failed to—mention it earlier, but NAT has a few nicknames. In the industry, it's referred to as network masquerading, IP masquerading, and (for those who are besieged with OCD and compelled to spell everything out) Network Address Translation. Whatever you want to dub it, basically, they all refer to the process of rewriting the source/destination addresses of IP packets when they go through a router or firewall. Just focus on the process that's occurring and your understanding of it (i.e., the important part) and you're on it for sure!

Remember the three methods of NAT. The three methods are static, dynamic, and overloading; the latter is also called PAT.

Understand static NAT. This type of NAT is designed to allow one-to-one mapping between local and global addresses.

Understand dynamic NAT. This version gives you the ability to map a range of unregistered IP addresses to a registered IP address from a pool of registered IP addresses.

Understand overloading. Overloading really is a form of dynamic NAT that maps multiple unregistered IP addresses to a single registered IP address (many-to-one) by using different ports. It's also known as *PAT*.

Written Lab

The answers to this lab can be found in Appendix A, "Answers to the Written Labs."

In this section, write the answers to the following questions:

1. What type of address translation can use only one address to allow thousands of hosts to be translated globally?
2. What command can you use to show the NAT translations as they occur on your router?
3. What command will show you the translation table?
4. What command will clear all your NAT entries from the translation table?
5. An inside local is before or after translation?
6. An inside global is before or after translation?
7. Which command can be used for troubleshooting and displays a summary of the NAT configuration as well as counts of active translation types and hits to an existing mapping?
8. What commands must be used on your router interfaces before NAT will translate addresses?
9. In the following output, what type of NAT is being used?

   ```
   ip nat pool todd-nat 170.168.10.10 170.168.10.20 netmask 255.255.255.0
   ```

10. Instead of the `netmask` command, you can use the ___________ statement.

Review Questions

NOTE The following questions are designed to test your understanding of this chapter's material. For more information on how to get additional questions, please see this book's introduction.

The answers to these questions can be found in Appendix B, "Answers to the Review Questions."

1. Which of the following are the disadvantages of using NAT? (Choose three.)
   - A. Translation introduces switching path delays.
   - B. NAT conserves legally registered addresses.
   - C. NAT causes loss of end-to-end IP traceability.
   - D. NAT increases flexibility when connecting to the Internet.
   - E. Certain applications will not function with NAT enabled.
   - F. NAT reduces address overlap occurrence.
2. Which of the following are advantages of using NAT? (Choose three.)
   - A. Translation introduces switching path delays.
   - B. NAT conserves legally registered addresses.
   - C. NAT causes loss of end-to-end IP traceability.
   - D. NAT increases flexibility when connecting to the Internet.
   - E. Certain applications will not function with NAT enabled.
   - F. NAT remedies address overlap occurrence.
3. Which command will allow you to see real-time translations on your router?
   - A. `show ip nat translations`
   - B. `show ip nat statistics`
   - C. `debug ip nat`
   - D. `clear ip nat translations *`
4. Which command will show you all the translations active on your router?
   - A. `show ip nat translations`
   - B. `show ip nat statistics`
   - C. `debug ip nat`
   - D. `clear ip nat translations *`

5. Which command will clear all the translations active on your router?
   A. `show ip nat translations`
   B. `show ip nat statistics`
   C. `debug ip nat`
   D. `clear ip nat translations *`
6. Which command will show you the summary of the NAT configuration?
   A. `show ip nat translations`
   B. `show ip nat statistics`
   C. `debug ip nat`
   D. `clear ip nat translations *`
7. Which command will create a dynamic pool named Todd that will provide you with 30 global addresses?
   A. `ip nat pool Todd 171.16.10.65 171.16.10.94 net 255.255.255.240`
   B. `ip nat pool Todd 171.16.10.65 171.16.10.94 net 255.255.255.224`
   C. `ip nat pool Todd 171.16.10.65 171.16.10.94 net 255.255.255.224`
   D. `ip nat pool Todd 171.16.10.1 171.16.10.254 net 255.255.255.0`
8. Which statement about the nature of NAT overload is true?
   A. Applies a one-to-many relationship to internal IP addresses
   B. Applies a one-to-one relationship to internal IP addresses
   C. Applies a many-to-many relationship to internal IP addresses
   D. Can be configured only on a Gigabit interface
9. Which type of address is the public IP address of a NAT device?
   A. Outside global
   B. Outside local
   C. Inside global
   D. Inside local
   E. Outside public
   F. Inside public
10. Which of the following would be a good starting point for troubleshooting if your router is not translating?
    A. Reboot.
    B. Call Cisco.
    C. Check your interfaces for the correct configuration.
    D. Run the `debug all` command.

11. Which of the following would be good reasons to run NAT? (Choose three.)

    A. You need to connect to the Internet, and your hosts don't have globally unique IP addresses.

    B. You change to a new ISP that requires you to renumber your network.

    C. You don't want any hosts connecting to the Internet.

    D. You require two intranets with duplicate addresses to merge.

12. Which of the following is considered to be the inside host's address after translation?

    A. Inside local

    B. Outside local

    C. Inside global

    D. Outside global

13. Which of the following is considered to be the inside host's address before translation?

    A. Inside local

    B. Outside local

    C. Inside global

    D. Outside global

14. By looking at the following output, which of the following commands would allow dynamic translations?

```
Router#show ip nat trans
Pro  Inside global    Inside local    Outside local  Outside global
---  1.1.128.1        10.1.1.1        ---            ---
---  1.1.130.178      10.1.1.2        ---            ---
---  1.1.129.174      10.1.1.10       ---            ---
---  1.1.130.101      10.1.1.89       ---            ---
---  1.1.134.169      10.1.1.100      ---            ---
---  1.1.135.174      10.1.1.200      ---            ---
```

A. `ip nat inside source pool todd 1.1.128.1 1.1.135.254 prefix-length 19`

B. `ip nat pool todd 1.1.128.1 1.1.135.254 prefix-length 19`

C. `ip nat pool todd 1.1.128.1 1.1.135.254 prefix-length 18`

D. `ip nat pool todd 1.1.128.1 1.1.135.254 prefix-length 21`

15. Your inside locals are not being translated to the inside global addresses. Which of the following commands will show you if your inside globals are allowed to use the NAT pool?

```
ip nat pool Corp 198.18.41.129 198.18.41.134 netmask 255.255.255.248
ip nat inside source list 100 int pool Corp overload
```

A. `debug ip nat`

B. `show access-list`

C. `show ip nat translation`

D. `show ip nat statistics`

16. Which command would you place on the interface of a private network?
    A. `ip nat inside`
    B. `ip nat outside`
    C. `ip outside global`
    D. `ip inside local`

17. Which command would you place on an interface connected to the Internet?
    A. `ip nat inside`
    B. `ip nat outside`
    C. `ip outside global`
    D. `ip inside local`

18. Which NAT term is defined as a group of addresses available for NAT use?
    A. NAT pool
    B. Dynamic NAT
    C. Static NAT
    D. One-way NAT

19. What does the asterisk (*) represent in the following output?

```
NAT*: s=172.16.2.2, d=192.168.2.1->10.1.1.1 [1]
```

    A. The packet was destined for a local interface on the router.
    B. The packet was translated and fast-switched to the destination.
    C. The packet attempted to be translated but failed.
    D. The packet was translated but there was no response from the remote host.

20. Which of the following needs to be added to the configuration to enable PAT?

```
ip nat pool Corp 198.18.41.129 198.18.41.134 netmask 255.255.255.248
access-list 1 permit 192.168.76.64 0.0.0.31
```

    A. `ip nat pool inside overload`
    B. `ip nat inside source list 1 pool Corp overload`
    C. `ip nat pool outside overload`
    D. `ip nat pool Corp 198.41.129 net 255.255.255.0 overload`

Chapter 6

IP Services

THE FOLLOWING CCNA EXAM TOPICS ARE COVERED IN THIS CHAPTER:

✓ **2.0 Network Access**

2.3 Configure and verify Layer 2 discovery protocols (Cisco Discovery Protocol and LLDP)

✓ **4.0 IP Services**

4.2 Configure and verify NTP operating in a client and server mode

4.4 Explain the function of SNMP in network operations

4.5 Describe the use of syslog features, including facilities and levels

4.8 Configure network devices for remote access using SSH

We're going to start off the chapter talking about how to find neighbor device information using the proprietary Cisco Discovery Protocol (CDP) and the industry-standard Link Layer Discovery Protocol (LLDP). Next, I'll show you how to make sure our times are synchronized with our devices using Network Time Protocol (NTP). After that, we'll look at Simple Network Management Protocol (SNMP) and the type of alerts sent to the network management station (NMS). You'll learn about the all-so-important Syslog logging and configuration, and finally, I'll cover how to configure Secure Shell (SSH).

I know we discussed SSH and syslog in the first book, but I'm going to delve into it more in-depth in this chapter. In addition, we'll cover Cisco NetFlow and how it works in the internetwork.

> **NOTE** To find your included bonus material, as well as Todd Lammle videos, practice questions, and hands-on labs, please see `www.lammle.com/ccna`.

Exploring Connected Devices Using CDP and LLDP

Cisco Discovery Protocol (CDP) is a proprietary protocol designed by Cisco to help us collect information about locally attached devices. Using CDP, we can gather hardware and protocol information about neighbor devices—vital information for documenting and troubleshooting the network! Another dynamic discovery protocol is Link Layer Discovery Protocol (LLDP), but it's not proprietary like CDP.

We'll start by covering the CDP timer and other CDP commands used to verify our network.

Getting CDP Timers and Holdtime Information

The `show cdp` command (`sh cdp` for short) is great for getting information about two CDP global parameters typically configured on Cisco devices:

- *CDP timer* delimits how often CDP packets are transmitted out of all active interfaces.
- *CDP holdtime* delimits the amount of time that the device will hold packets received from neighbor devices.

Both Cisco routers and switches use the same parameters. Figure 6.1 shows how CDP works within a switched network.

FIGURE 6.1 Cisco Discovery Protocol

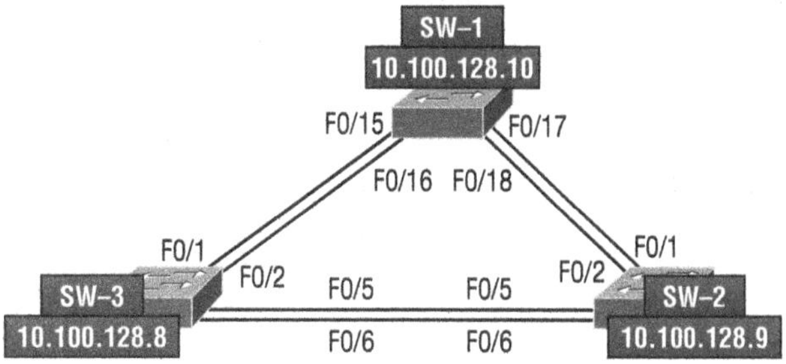

The output on my 3560 SW-3 looks like this:

```
SW-3#sh cdp
Global CDP information:
        Sending CDP packets every 60 seconds
        Sending a holdtime value of 180 seconds
        Sending CDPv2 advertisements is enabled
```

This output tells us that the default transmits every 60 seconds and will hold packets from a neighbor in the CDP table for 180 seconds. I can use the global commands `cdp holdtime` and `cdp timer` to configure the CDP holdtime and timer on a router like this:

```
SW-3(config)#cdp ?
  advertise-v2  CDP sends version-2 advertisements
  holdtime      Specify the holdtime (in sec) to be sent in packets
  run           Enable CDP
  timer         Specify the rate at which CDP packets are sent (in sec)
  tlv           Enable exchange of specific tlv information

SW-3(config)#cdp holdtime ?
  <10-255>  Length  of time  (in sec) that the receiver must keep this packet

SW-3(config)#cdp timer ?
  <5-254>  Rate at which CDP packets are sent (in  sec)
```

You can turn off CDP completely with the `no cdp run` command from the global configuration mode of a router and enable it with the `cdp run` command:

```
SW-3(config)#no cdp run
SW-3(config)#cdp run
```

To turn CDP off or on for an interface, use the `no cdp enable` and `cdp enable` commands.

Gathering Neighbor Information

The `show cdp neighbor` command (`sh cdp nei` for short) delivers information about directly connected devices. It's important to remember that CDP packets aren't passed through a Cisco switch and that you only see what's directly attached. This means that if your router is connected to a switch, you won't see any of the Cisco devices connected to that switch!

This output shows the `show cdp neighbor` command I used on SW-3:

```
SW-3#sh cdp neighbors
Capability Codes: R - Router, T - Trans Bridge, B - Source Route Bridge
S - Switch, H - Host, I - IGMP, r - Repeater, P - Phone,
D - Remote, C - CVTA, M - Two-port Mac Relay Device ID Local Intrfce Holdtme
Capability Platform Port ID
SW-1 Fas 0/1 150 S I WS-C3560- Fas 0/15
SW-1 Fas 0/2 150 S I WS-C3560- Fas 0/16
SW-2 Fas 0/5 162 S I WS-C3560- Fas 0/5
SW-2 Fas 0/6 162 S I WS-C3560- Fas 0/6
```

Okay—we can see that I'm directly connected with a console cable to the SW-3 switch and also that SW-3 is directly connected to two other switches. But do we really need the figure to draw out our network? We don't! CDP allows me to see who my directly connected neighbors are and gather information about them. From the SW-3 switch, you can see that there are two connections to SW-1 and two connections to SW-2. SW-3 connects to SW-1 with ports Fas 0/1 and Fas 0/2, and there are connections to SW-2 with local interfaces Fas 0/5 and Fas 0/6. Both the SW-1 and SW-2 switches are 3650 switches. SW-1 is using ports Fas 0/15 and Fas 0/16 to connect to SW-3. SW-2 is using ports Fas 0/5 and Fas 0/6.

To sum this up, the device ID shows the configured hostname of the connected device, that the local interface is our interface, and the port ID is the remote device's directly connected interface. Remember that all you get to view are directly connected devices!

Table 6.1 summarizes the information displayed by the `show cdp neighbor` command for each device.

TABLE 6.1 Output of the `show cdp neighbors` command

Field	Description
Device ID	The hostname of the device directly connected.
Local Interface	The port or interface that you're receiving CDP packets on.
Holdtime	The amount of time the router will hold the information before discarding it if no more CDP packets are received.
Capability	The capability of the neighbor—the router, switch, or repeater. The capability codes are listed at the top of the command output.
Platform	The type of Cisco device directly connected. In the previous output, the SW-3 shows it's directly connected to two 3560 switches.
Port ID	The neighbor device's port or interface that CDP packets are multicast from.

> **NOTE** You must be able to look at the output of a `show cdp neighbors` command and understand the information it's given you about the neighbor device's capability. It tells you whether it's a router or switch, the model number (platform) of the port connecting to that device (local interface), and the port of the neighbor connecting to you (port ID).

Another command that will deliver the goods on neighbor information is the `show cdp neighbors detail` command (`show cdp nei de` for short). This command can be run on both routers and switches, and it displays detailed information about each device connected to the device you're running the command on. Check out the router output:

```
SW-3#sh cdp neighbors detail
-------------------------
Device ID: SW-1

Device ID: SW-1
Entry address(es):
  IP address: 10.100.128.10
Platform: cisco WS-C3560-24TS,  Capabilities: Switch IGMP
Interface: FastEthernet0/1,  Port ID (outgoing port): FastEthernet0/15
Holdtime : 135 sec

Version :
Cisco IOS Software, C3560 Software (C3560-IPSERVICESK9-M), Version 12.2(55)
SE5, RELEASE SOFTWARE (fc1)
Technical Support: http://www.cisco.com/techsupport
Copyright (c) 1986-2013 by Cisco Systems, Inc.
Compiled Mon 28-Jan-13 10:10 by prod_rel_team

advertisement version: 2
Protocol Hello:  OUI=0x00000C, Protocol ID=0x0112; payload len=25,
value=00000000FFFFFFFF010221FF000000000000001C555EC880Fc00f000
VTP Management Domain: 'NULL'
Native VLAN: 1
Duplex: full
Power Available TLV:

    Power request id: 0, Power management id: 1, Power available: 0, Power
management level: -1
Management address(es):
  IP address: 10.100.128.10
-------------------------

[ouput cut]

-------------------------
```

```
Device ID: SW-2
Entry address(es):
  IP address: 10.100.128.9
Platform: cisco WS-C3560-8PC,  Capabilities: Switch IGMP
Interface: FastEthernet0/5,  Port ID (outgoing port): FastEthernet0/5
Holdtime : 129 sec

Version :
Cisco IOS Software, C3560 Software (C3560-IPBASE-M), Version 12.2(35)SE5,
RELEASE SOFTWARE (fc1)
Copyright (c) 1986-2005 by Cisco Systems, Inc.
Compiled Thu 19-Jul-05 18:15 by nachen

advertisement version: 2
Protocol Hello:  OUI=0x00000C, Protocol ID=0x0112; payload len=25,
value=00000000FFFFFFFF010221FF000000000000B41489D91880Fc00f000
VTP Management Domain: 'NULL'
Native VLAN: 1
Duplex: full
Power Available TLV:

    Power request id: 0, Power management id: 1, Power available: 0, Power
management level: -1
Management address(es):
  IP address: 10.100.128.9
[output cut]
```

So, what do we see here? First, we've been given the hostname and IP address of all directly connected devices. In addition to the same information displayed by the `show cdp neighbors` command, the `show cdp neighbors detail` command tells us the IOS version and IP address of the neighbor device—nice!

The `show cdp entry *` command displays the same information as the `show cdp neighbors detail` command. There really isn't any difference between these commands.

Real World Scenario

CDP Can Save Lives!

Karen has just been hired as a senior network consultant at a large hospital in Dallas, Texas, so she's expected to be able to take care of any and all problems that crop up. As if that weren't enough pressure, she also has to worry about the awful possibility that people won't receive correct healthcare solutions—even the correct medications—if the network goes down. . . a potentially life-or-death situation!

But Karen is confident and begins optimistically. Of course, it's not long before the network reveals that it has a few problems. Unfazed, she asks one of the junior administrators for a network map so she can troubleshoot the network. This person tells her that the old senior administrator, whom she replaced, had the maps with him, and no one can find them! The sky begins to darken a bit.

Doctors are now calling every couple of minutes because they can't get the necessary information they need to take care of their patients. What should she do?

It's CDP to the rescue! And it's a gift that this hospital happens to be running Cisco routers and switches exclusively, because CDP is enabled by default on all Cisco devices. Karen is also in luck because the disgruntled former administrator didn't turn off CDP on any devices before he left!

So, all Karen has to do now is to use the `show CDP neighbor detail` command to find all the information she needs about each device to help draw out the hospital's network. With the command's critical information, she brings the network back up to speed, and the personnel relying so heavily on it can get back to the important business of saving lives!

The only snag to nailing this in your own network is if you don't know the passwords of all those devices. Your only hope then is to somehow find out the access passwords or to perform password recovery on them.

So, use CDP—you never know when you may end up saving someone's life.

By the way, this is a true story!

Documenting a Network Topology Using CDP

With that real-life scenario in mind, I'm going to show you how to document a sample network by using CDP. You'll learn to determine the appropriate router types, interface types, and IP addresses of various interfaces using only CDP commands and the `show running-config` command. Our rules for this exercise are as follows:

- We can only console into the Lab_A router to document the network.
- We'll have to assign any remote routers the next IP address in each range.

We'll use a different figure for this example—Figure 6.2—to help us complete the required documentation.

FIGURE 6.2 Documenting a network topology using CDP

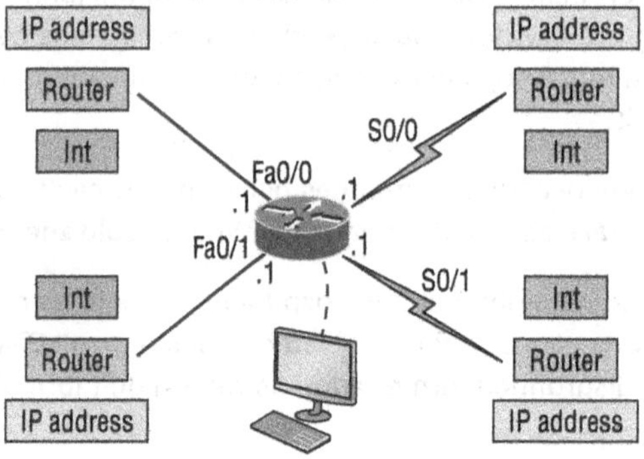

In this output, you can see we have a router with four interfaces: two Fast Ethernet and two serial. So first, let's find out the IP addresses of each interface using the `show running-config` command like this:

```
Lab_A#sh running-config
Building configuration...
Current configuration : 960 bytes
!
version 12.2
service timestamps debug uptime
service timestamps log uptime
no service password-encryption
!
hostname Lab_A
!
ip subnet-zero
!
!
interface FastEthernet0/0
ip address 192.168.21.1 255.255.255.0
duplex auto
!
interface FastEthernet0/1
ip address 192.168.18.1 255.255.255.0
duplex auto
!
interface Serial0/0
ip address 192.168.23.1 255.255.255.0
!
```

```
interface Serial0/1
ip address 192.168.28.1 255.255.255.0
!
ip classless
!
line con 0
line aux 0
line vty 0 4
!
end
```

With this step completed, we can document the IP addresses of the Lab_A router's four interfaces. Next, we've got to determine the type of device on the other end of each of these interfaces. For that, we'll use the `show cdp neighbors` command:

```
Lab_A#sh cdp neighbors
Capability Codes: R - Router, T - Trans Bridge, B - Source Route Bridge
S - Switch, H - Host, I - IGMP, r - Repeater
Device ID Local Intrfce Holdtme Capability Platform Port ID
Lab_B Fas 0/0 158 R 2501 E0
Lab_C Fas 0/1 135 R 2621 Fa0/0
Lab_D Ser 0/0 158 R 2514 S1
Lab_E Ser 0/1 135 R 2620 S0/1
```

Wow—looks like we're connected to some old routers! It's not our job to judge—our mission is to draw out the network, and now we've got some nice information to meet that challenge with. Using both the `show running-config` and `show cdp neighbors` commands, we have the IP addresses of the Lab_A router, the types of routers connected to each of the Lab_A router's links, plus all the interfaces of the remote routers.

Equipped with all the information gathered via `show running-config` and `show cdp neighbors`, we can accurately create the topology in Figure 6.3.

FIGURE 6.3 Network topology documented

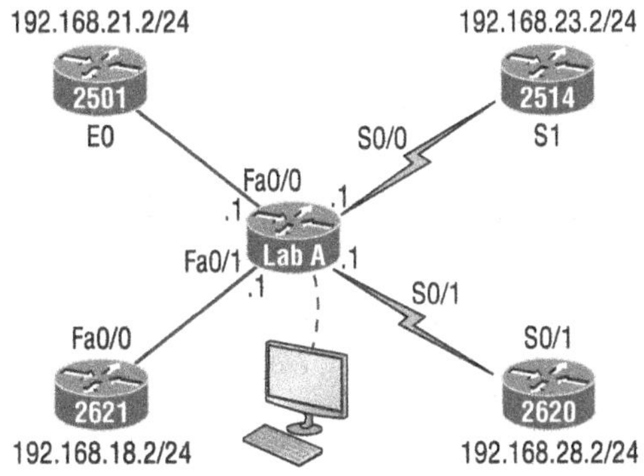

If we needed to, we could've also used the `show cdp neighbors detail` command to view the neighbor's IP addresses. But because we know the IP addresses of each link on the Lab_A router, we already know what the next available IP address is going to be.

Link Layer Discovery Protocol (LLDP)

Before moving on from CDP, I want to tell you about a nonproprietary discovery protocol that provides pretty much the same information as CDP but works in multivendor networks.

The IEEE created a new standardized discovery protocol called 802.1AB for Station and Media Access Control Connectivity Discovery. We'll call it *Link Layer Discovery Protocol (LLDP)*.

LLDP defines basic discovery capabilities, but it was also enhanced to address voice applications specifically. This version is called LLDP-MED (Media Endpoint Discovery). An important factor to remember is that LLDP and LLDP-MED are not compatible!

LLDP has the following configuration guidelines and limitations:

- LLDP must be enabled on the device before you can enable or disable it on any interface.
- LLDP is supported only on physical interfaces.
- LLDP can discover up to one device per port.
- LLDP can discover Linux servers.

You can turn off LLDP completely with the `no lldp run` command from global configuration mode and enable it with the `lldp run` command. Doing this enables it on all interfaces:

```
SW-3(config)#no lldp run
SW-3(config)#lldp run
```

To turn LLDP off or on for an interface, use the `lldp transmit` and `lldp receive` commands:

```
SW-3(config-if)#no lldp transmit
SW-3(config-if)#no lldp receive

SW-3(config-if)#lldp transmit
SW-3(config-if)#lldp receive
```

Next, we'll make sure that all our devices are in sync with the same time by covering Network Time Protocol.

Network Time Protocol (NTP)

Network Time Protocol provides pretty much what it describes: time to all your network devices. More specifically, NTP synchronizes the clocks of computer systems over packet-switched, variable-latency data networks.

Typically you'll have an NTP server that connects through the Internet to an atomic clock. This time can then be synchronized throughout the network to keep all routers, switches, servers, etc., receiving the same time information and in synch.

Correct network time within the network is important because

- It allows the tracking of events in the network in the correct order.
- Clock synchronization is critical for the correct interpretation of events within the syslog data.
- Clock synchronization is critical for digital certificates.

Having all your devices synchronized with the correct time is critical to your routers and switches for analyzing logs to find security issues or other maintenance tasks. These devices issue log messages when different events take place, like when an interface goes down and back up or not. You already know that all messages generated by the IOS go only to the console port by default; however, those console messages can be directed to a syslog server.

A syslog server saves copies of console messages and can time-stamp them so you can view them later. And this is actually really easy to do. Here would be your configuration on the SF router:

```
SF(config)#service timestamps log datetime msec
```

So, even though I had the messages time-stamped with the command `service timestamps log datetime msec`, this doesn't mean that we'll know the exact time using default clock sources.

To make sure all devices are synchronized with the same time information, I'm going to configure our devices to get accurate time information from a centralized server, as shown here, in Figure 6.4:

```
SF(config)#ntp server 172.16.10.1 version 4
```

FIGURE 6.4 Synchronizing time information

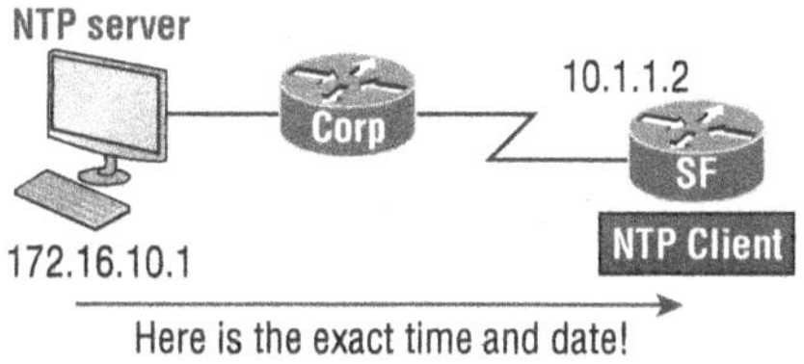

Just use that single command on all your devices, and each of them will accurately receive the same, exact time and date information. You can also make your router or switch an NTP server with the `ntp master` command.

To verify that our NTP client is receiving clocking information, use the following commands:

```
SF#sh ntp ?
  associations  NTP associations
  status        NTP status  status      VTP domain status

SF#sh ntp status
Clock is unsynchronized, stratum 16, no reference clock
nominal freq is 119.2092 Hz, actual freq is 119.2092 Hz, precision is 2**18
reference time is 00000000.00000000 (00:00:00.000 UTC Mon Jan 1 1900)
clock offset is 0.0000 msec, root delay is 0.00 msec
S1#sh ntp associations

address     ref clock      st  when  poll reach  delay  offset    disp
 ~172.16.10.1   0.0.0.0          16     -    64    0      0.0     0.00  16000.
 * master (synced), # master (unsynced), + selected, - candidate, ~ configured
```

In this example, we can see that the NTP client in SF isn't synchronized with the server via the `show ntp status` command. The stratum value is a number from 1 to 15, and a lower stratum value indicates a higher NTP priority—16 means there's no clocking being received.

There are a bunch of additional ways to configure an NTP client, like NTP authentication, making a router or switch foolproof against things like an intruder being able to change the time of an attack.

Secure Shell (SSH)

I'm strongly recommending that you use Secure Shell (SSH) instead of Telnet to connect to your devices because it creates a more secure session. Telnet uses an unencrypted data stream, whereas SSH uses encryption keys to send data so your username and password aren't sent in the clear, vulnerable to poaching!

Here are the steps for setting up SSH on your Cisco devices:

1. Set your hostname:

   ```
   Router(config)#hostname Todd
   ```

2. Set the domain name—both the hostname and domain name are required for the encryption keys to be generated:

   ```
   Todd(config)#ip domain-name Lammle.com
   ```

3. Set the username to allow SSH client access:

   ```
   Todd(config)#username Todd password Lammle
   ```

4. Generate the encryption keys for securing the session:

```
Todd(config)#crypto key generate rsa
The name for the keys will be: Todd.Lammle.com
Choose the size of the key modulus in the range of 360 to
4096 for your General Purpose Keys. Choosing a key modulus
Greater than 512 may take a few minutes.
How many bits in the modulus [512]: 1024
% Generating 1024 bit RSA keys, keys will be non-exportable...
[OK] (elapsed time was 6 seconds)
Todd(config)#
1d14h: %SSH-5-ENABLED: SSH 1.99 has been enabled*June 24
19:25:30.035: %SSH-5-ENABLED: SSH 1.99 has been enabled
```

5. Enable SSH version 2 on the device—not mandatory, but strongly suggested:

```
Todd(config)#ip ssh version 2
```

6. Connect to the VTY lines of the switch or router:

```
Todd(config)#line vty 0 15
```

7. Tell the lines to use the local database for passwords:

```
Todd(config-line)#login local
```

8. Configure your access protocols:

```
Todd(config-line)#transport input ?
all All protocols
none No protocols
ssh TCP/IP SSH protocol
telnet TCP/IP Telnet protocol
```

Beware of this next line, and make sure you never use it in production because it's a horrendous security risk:

```
Todd(config-line)#transport input all
```

I recommend using the next line instead to secure your VTY lines with SSH:

```
Todd(config-line)#transport input ssh ?
telnet TCP/IP Telnet protocol
<cr>
```

I actually do use Telnet once in a while when a situation arises that specifically calls for it. It just doesn't happen very often. But if you want to go with SSH and Telnet on a device, here's how you do that:

```
Todd(config-line)#transport input ssh telnet
```

Know that if you don't use the keyword `telnet` at the end of the command string, only SSH will work on the device. You can go with either, as long as you understand that SSH is way more secure than Telnet.

Syslog

Reading system messages from a switch's or router's internal buffer is the most popular and efficient method of seeing what's going on with your network at a particular time. But the best way is to log messages to a *syslog* server, which stores messages from you and can even time-stamp and sequence them for you—and it's easy to set up and configure!

Syslog allows you to display, sort, and even search messages, all of which make it a really great troubleshooting tool. The search feature is especially powerful because you can use keywords and even severity levels. Plus, the server can email admins based on the severity level of the message.

Network devices can be configured to generate a syslog message and forward it to various destinations. These four examples are popular ways to gather messages from Cisco devices:

- Logging buffer (on by default)
- Console line (on by default)
- Terminal lines (using the `terminal monitor` command)
- Syslog server

As you already know, all system messages and debug output generated by the IOS go out only the console port by default and are also logged in buffers in RAM. And you also know that Cisco routers aren't exactly shy about sending messages! To send a message to the VTY lines, use the `terminal monitor` command. We'll also add a small configuration needed for syslog, which I'll show you soon in the configuration section.

Okay, so by default, we'd see something like this on our console line:

```
*Oct 21 17:33:50.565:%LINK-5-CHANGED:Interface FastEthernet0/0, changed
state to administratively down
*Oct 21 17:33:51.565:%LINEPROTO-5-UPDOWN:Line protocol on Interface
FastEthernet0/0, changed state to down
```

And the Cisco router would send a general version of the message to the syslog server that would be formatted into something like this:

```
Seq no:timestamp: %facility-severity-MNEMONIC:description
```

The system message format can be broken down in this way:

seq no This stamp logs messages with a sequence number, but not by default. If you want this output, you've got to configure it.

Timestamp Data and time of the message or event, which again will show up only if configured.

Facility The facility to which the message refers.

Severity A single-digit code from 0 to 7 that indicates the severity of the message.

MNEMONIC Text string that uniquely describes the message.

Description Text string containing detailed information about the event being reported.

The severity levels, from the most severe level to the least severe, are explained in Table 6.2. Informational is the default and will result in all messages being sent to the buffers and console.

TABLE 6.2 Severity levels

Severity level	Explanation
Emergency (severity 0)	System is unusable.
Alert (severity 1)	Immediate action is needed.
Critical (severity 2)	Critical condition.
Error (severity 3)	Error condition.
Warning (severity 4)	Warning condition.
Notification (severity 5)	Normal but significant condition.
Information (severity 6)	Normal information message.
Debugging (severity 7)	Debugging message.

TIP If you are studying for your Cisco exam, you must memorize Table 6.2.

Understand that only emergency-level messages will be displayed if you've configured severity level 0. But if, for example, you opt for level 4 instead, levels 0 through 4 will be displayed, giving you emergency, alert, critical, error, and warning messages, too.

Level 7 is the highest-level security option and displays everything, but be warned that going with it could have a serious impact on the performance of your device. So always use debugging commands carefully with an eye on the messages you really need to meet your specific business requirements!

Configuring and Verifying Syslog

As I said, Cisco devices send all log messages of the severity level you've chosen to the console. They'll also go to the buffer, and both happen by default. Because of this, it's good to know that you can disable and enable these features with the following commands:

```
Router(config)#logging ?
  Hostname or A.B.C.D  IP address of the logging host
  buffered             Set buffered logging parameters
```

```
  buginf              Enable buginf logging for debugging
  cns-events          Set CNS Event logging level
  console             Set console logging parameters
  count               Count every log message and timestamp last occurrence
  esm                 Set ESM filter restrictions
  exception           Limit size of exception flush output
  facility            Facility parameter for syslog messages
  filter              Specify logging filter
  history             Configure syslog history table
  host                Set syslog server IP address and parameters
  monitor             Set terminal line (monitor) logging parameters
  on                  Enable logging to all enabled destinations
  origin-id           Add origin ID to syslog messages
  queue-limit         Set logger message queue size
  rate-limit          Set messages per second limit
  reload              Set reload logging level
  server-arp          Enable sending ARP requests for syslog servers when
                      first configured
  source-interface    Specify interface for source address in logging
                      transactions
  trap                Set syslog server logging level
  userinfo            Enable logging of user info on privileged mode enabling
Router(config)#logging console
Router(config)#logging buffered
```

Wow—as you can see in this output, there are plenty of options you can use with the `logging` command! The preceding configuration enabled the console and buffer to receive all log messages of all severities, and don't forget that this is the default setting for all Cisco IOS devices. If you want to disable the defaults, use the following commands:

```
Router(config)#no logging console
Router(config)#no logging buffered
```

I like leaving the `console` and `buffers` commands on to receive the logging info, but that's up to you. You can see the buffers with the `show logging` command here:

```
Router#sh logging
Syslog logging: enabled (11 messages dropped, 1 messages rate-limited,
                0 flushes, 0 overruns, xml disabled, filtering disabled)
    Console logging: level debugging, 29 messages logged, xml disabled,
                     filtering disabled
    Monitor logging: level debugging, 0 messages logged, xml disabled,
                     filtering disabled
```

```
    Buffer logging: level debugging, 1 messages logged, xml disabled,
                    filtering disabled
    Logging Exception size (4096 bytes)
    Count and timestamp logging messages: disabled
No active filter modules.

    Trap logging: level informational, 33 message lines logged

Log Buffer (4096 bytes):
*Jun 21 23:09:37.822: %SYS-5-CONFIG_I: Configured from console by console
Router#
```

Notice that the default trap (message from device to NMS) level is `informational`, but you can change this, too.

And now that you've seen the default system message format on a Cisco device, I want to show you how you can also control the format of your messages via sequence numbers and time stamps, which aren't enabled by default.

We'll begin with a basic, very simple example of how to configure a device to send messages to a syslog server, demonstrated in Figure 6.5.

FIGURE 6.5 Messages sent to a syslog server

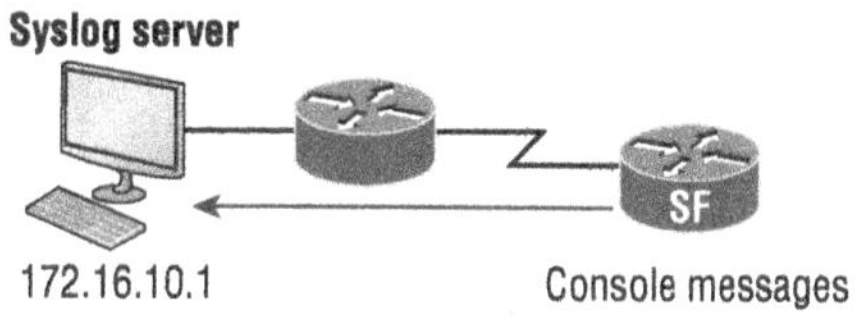

A syslog server saves copies of console messages and can time-stamp them for viewing at a later time. This is actually pretty easy to configure, and here's how doing that would look on the SF router:

```
SF(config)#logging 172.16.10.1
SF(config)#service timestamps log datetime msec
```

This is awesome—now all the console messages will be stored in one location to be viewed at your convenience! I typically use the `logging host ip_address` command, but the `logging IP_address` command without the `host` keyword gets the same result.

I want to point out that even though I had the messages time-stamped in the configuration associated with Figure 6.5, the command `service timestamps log datetime msec` doesn't mean that I'll know the messages' exact time if I'm using default clock sources. To make sure all devices are synchronized with the same time information, be sure you use an NTP server.

We can limit the number of messages sent to the syslog server, based on severity, with the following command:

```
SF(config)#logging trap ?
  <0-7>          Logging severity level
  alerts         Immediate action needed                (severity=1)
  critical       Critical conditions                    (severity=2)
  debugging      Debugging messages                     (severity=7)
  emergencies    System is unusable                     (severity=0)
  errors         Error conditions                       (severity=3)
  informational  Informational messages                 (severity=6)
  notifications  Normal but significant conditions (severity=5)
  warnings       Warning conditions                     (severity=4)
  <cr>
SF(config)#logging trap warnings
```

Notice that we can use either the number or the actual severity level name—and they are in alphabetical order, not severity order, which makes it even harder to memorize the order! (Thanks, Cisco!) Because I went with severity level 4, I'll receive messages for levels 0 through 4. Now, let's configure the router to use sequence numbers:

```
SF(config)#no service timestamps
SF(config)#service sequence-numbers
SF(config)#^Z
000038: %SYS-5-CONFIG_I: Configured from console by console
```

When you exit configuration mode, the router will send a message like the one shown in the preceding code lines. Without the time stamps enabled, we'll no longer see a time and date, but we will see a sequence number.

So we now have the following:

- Sequence number: 000038
- Facility: %SYS
- Severity level: 5
- MNEMONIC: CONFIG_I
- Description: Configured from console by console

Of all of these, the security level is what you need to pay the most attention to for the Cisco exams and to control the number of messages sent to the syslog server!

NOTE

If a notice-level messaging is sent to a syslog server, a routing instance has flapped.

SNMP

Although *Simple Network Management Protocol (SNMP)* certainly isn't the oldest protocol ever, it's still pretty old, considering it was created way back in 1988 (RFC 1065)!

SNMP is an Application layer protocol that provides a message format for agents on a variety of devices to communicate with network management stations (NMSs)—for example, Cisco Prime or HP Openview. These agents send messages to the NMS station, which then either reads or writes information in the database stored on the NMS that's called a Management Information Base (MIB).

NOTE Agents send information about MIB variables in response to requests from the NMS.

The NMS periodically queries or polls the SNMP agent on a device to gather and analyze statistics via GET messages. End devices running SNMP agents will send an SNMP trap to the NMS if a problem occurs. This is demonstrated in Figure 6.6.

FIGURE 6.6 SNMP GET and TRAP messages

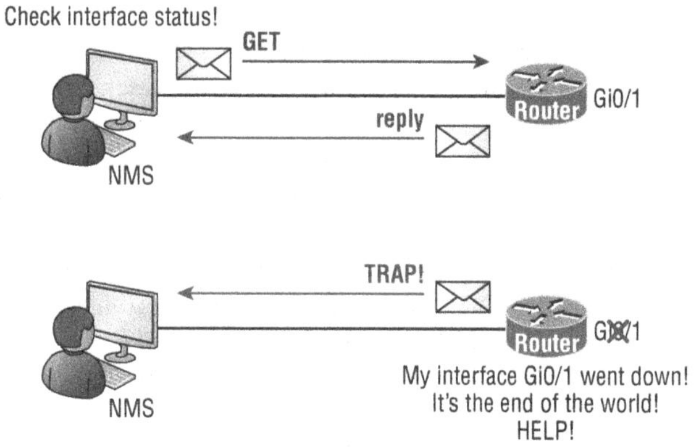

Admins can also use SNMP to provide some configurations to agents as well, called SET messages. This can be done in bulk to routers, for example, to back up multiple routers simultaneously.

NOTE The SNMP *inform* message type is considered reliable and precedes an acknowledgment response from the SNMP manager.

In addition to polling to obtain statistics, SNMP can be used for analyzing information and compiling the results in a report or even a graph. Thresholds can be used to trigger a notification process when exceeded.

Graphing tools are used to monitor the CPU statistics of Cisco devices like a core router. The CPU should be monitored continuously, and the NMS can graph the statistics. Notification will be sent when any threshold you've set has been exceeded.

SNMP has three versions, with version 1 being rarely, if ever, implemented today. Here's a summary of these three versions:

SNMPv1 Supports plaintext authentication with community strings and uses only UDP.

SNMPv2c Supports plaintext authentication with MD5 or SHA with no encryption but provides GET BULK, which is a way to gather many types of information at once and minimize the number of GET requests. It offers a more detailed error message reporting method, but it's not more secure than v1. It uses UDP even though it can be configured to use TCP.

SNMPv3 Supports strong authentication with MD5 or SHA, providing confidentiality (encryption) and data integrity of messages via DES or DES-256 encryption between agents and managers. GET BULK is a supported feature of SNMPv3, and this version also uses TCP.

Management Information Base (MIB)

With so many kinds of devices and so much data that can be accessed, there needed to be a standard way to organize this plethora of data, so MIB to the rescue!

A *management information base (MIB)* is a collection of information that's organized hierarchically and can be accessed by protocols like SNMP. RFCs define some common public variables, but most organizations define their own private branches along with basic SNMP standards.

Organizational IDs (OIDs) are laid out as a tree with different levels assigned by different organizations, with top-level MIB OIDs belonging to various standards organizations.

Vendors assign private branches in their own products. Let's take a look at Cisco's OIDs, which are described in words or numbers to locate a particular variable in the tree, as shown in Figure 6.7.

Luckily, you don't need to memorize the OIDs in Figure 6.7 for the Cisco exams!

I'll use CPU as an example of a key thing to check at least every 5 minutes. We'll examine output from an SNMP application. It's called `snmpget`, and it comes from an NMS station.

Here's the command from an NMS prompt on a Linux box running the SNMP application:

```
[14:11][admin@nms]$~snmpget -v2c -c community 192.168.10.12
.1.3.6.1.4.1.9.2.1.58.0
SNMPv2-SMI::enterprises.9.2.1.58.0=INTEGER: 19
```

You must specify the version, the correct community string, the IP address of the network device you're querying, plus the OID number. The community string will authenticate your

FIGURE 6.7 Cisco's MIB OIDs

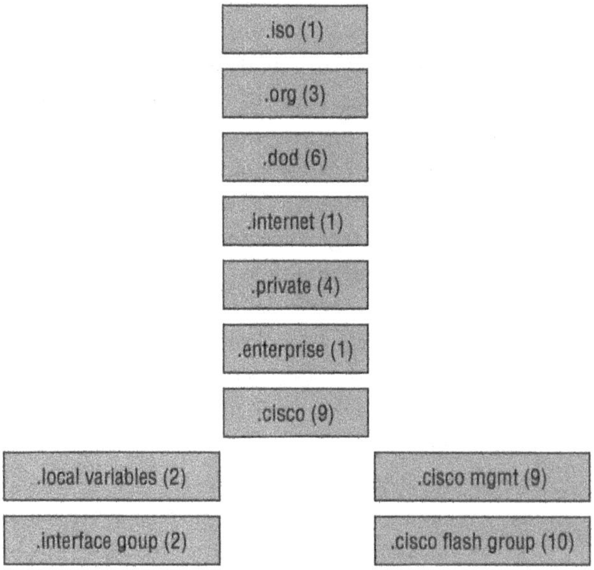

access to the MIB database; so the NMS can access the switch, the community string definition on the NMS must match at least one of the three community string definitions on the network devices.

Configuring SNMP

Configuring SNMP is a pretty straightforward process for which you only need a few commands. These four steps are all you need to run through to configure a Cisco device for SNMP access:

1. Enable SNMP read-write access to the router.
2. Configure SNMP contact information.
3. Configure SNMP location.
4. Configure an ACL to restrict SNMP access to the NMS hosts.

The only required configuration is the community string because the other three are optional. Here's an example of a typical SNMP router configuration:

```
Router(config)#snmp-server ?
  chassis-id          String to uniquely identify this chassis
  community           Enable SNMP; set community string and access privs
  contact             Text for mib object sysContact
  context             Create/Delete a context apart from default
```

```
  drop               Silently drop SNMP packets
  enable             Enable SNMP Traps or Informs
  engineID           Configure a local or remote SNMPv3 engineID
  group              Define a User Security Model group
  host               Specify hosts to receive SNMP notifications
  ifindex            Enable ifindex persistence
  inform             Configure SNMP Informs options
  location           Text for mib object sysLocation
  manager            Modify SNMP manager parameters
  packetsize         Largest SNMP packet size
  queue-length       Message queue length for each TRAP host
  source-interface   Assign an source interface
  system-shutdown    Enable use of the SNMP reload command
  tftp-server-list   Limit TFTP servers used via SNMP
  trap               SNMP trap options
  trap-source        Assign an interface for the source address of all traps
  trap-timeout       Set timeout for TRAP message retransmissions
  user               Define a user who can access the SNMP engine
  view               Define an SNMP MIB view
Router(config)#snmp-server community ?
  WORD  SNMP community string
Router(config)#snmp-server community Todd ?
  <1-99>       Std IP accesslist allowing access with this community string
  <1300-1999>  Expanded IP accesslist allowing access with this community
               string
  WORD         Access-list name
  ipv6         Specify IPv6 Named Access-List
  ro           Read-only access with this community string
  rw           Read-write access with this community string
  view         Restrict this community to a named MIB view
  <cr>
Router(config)#snmp-server community Todd rw
Router(config)#snmp-server location Boulder
Router(config)#snmp-server contact Todd Lammle
Router(config)#service sequence-numbers
Router(config)#ip access-list standard Protect_NMS_Station
Router(config-std-nacl)#permit host 192.168.10.254
```

Entering the `snmp-server` command enables SNMPv1 on the Cisco device. The command `service sequence-numbers` adds a sequence number to each system message.

You can efficiently restrict the read-only function of a requesting SNMP management station based on the IP address by entering an ACL directly in the SNMP configuration to provide security, using either a number or a name. Here is an example:

```
Router(config)#snmp-server community Todd Protect_NMS_Station rw
```

Notice that even though there's a boatload of configuration options under SNMP, you only really need to work with a few of them to configure a basic SNMP trap setup on a router. First, I chose the community name of `Todd` with RW access (read-write), which means the NMS will be able to retrieve and modify MIB objects from the router. Location and contact information comes in handy for troubleshooting the configuration. Make sure you understand that the ACL protects the NMS from access, not the devices with the agents!

Let's define the SNMP read and write options:

Read-only (RO) Gives authorized management stations read-access to all objects in the MIB except the community strings and doesn't allow write-access

Read-write (RW) Gives authorized management stations read- and write-access to all objects in the MIB but doesn't allow access to the community strings

There are still more ways to gather information from Cisco devices, and next, we'll explore a Cisco proprietary method of gathering statistics on internetwork devices.

NetFlow

SNMP can be a powerful tool to help you manage and troubleshoot your network, but Cisco knew it would be very helpful for engineers to be able to track TCP/IP flows within the network as well.

That's why we have NetFlow as an application for collecting IP traffic information. Cisco compares NetFlow informational reports to receiving a phone bill with detailed call information to track calls, call frequency, and even calls that shouldn't have been made at all. A more current analogy would be the IRS and certain additional government "alphabet agencies" watching who has talked to whom, when, and for how long!

Cisco IOS NetFlow efficiently provides a key set of services for IP applications, including network traffic accounting for baselining, usage-based network billing for consumers of network services, network design and planning, general network security, and DoS and DDoS monitoring capabilities as well as general network monitoring.

Figure 6.8 shows basic flow monitoring via Cisco NetFlow with the latest version, version 9, which is called Flexible NetFlow.

In Figure 6.8, let's assume that a host has connected to a server located in the fictitious Sales VLAN using Telnet. NetFlow can monitor the application by counting packets, bytes sent and received, and so on, and then send this information to a NetFlow collector.

FIGURE 6.8 Flexible NetFlow output

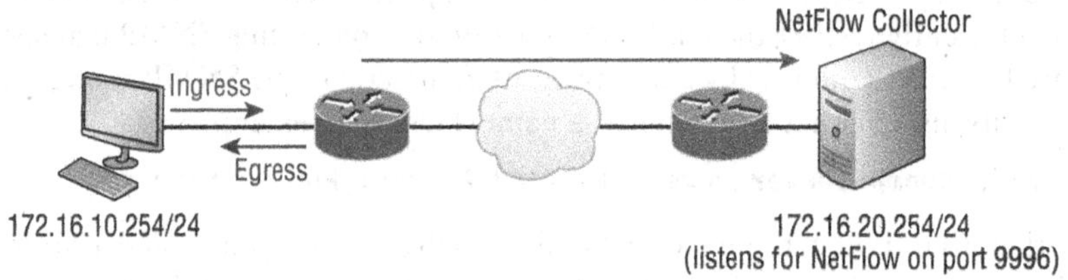

NetFlow Overview and Flows

Understand that NetFlow is completely transparent to the users in the network, including all end stations and applications, and you don't need to run it on all your routers.

Actually, you shouldn't—there's definitely overhead when using NetFlow because it requires memory for storing information in cache on the device.

NetFlow enables near real-time visualization and analysis of recorded and aggregated flow data. You can specify the router, the aggregation scheme, and the time interval for when you want to view and then retrieve the relevant data and sort it into bar charts, pie charts, and so on.

The components used with NetFlow include a router enabled with NetFlow and a NetFlow collector.

Service providers use NetFlow to do the following:

- Efficiently measuring who is using network service and for which purpose
- Accounting and charging back according to the resource utilization level
- Using the measured information for more effective network planning so that resource allocation and deployment are well aligned with customer requirements
- Using the information to better structure and customize the set of available applications and services to meet user needs and customer service requirements

  Moreover, there are different types of analyzers available to gather NetFlow statistics and analyze the traffic on your network by showing the following:

- Major users of the network, meaning top talkers, top listeners, top protocols, and so on
- Websites that are routinely visited, plus what's been downloaded
- Who's generating the most traffic and using excessive bandwidth
- Descriptions of bandwidth needs for an application as well as your available bandwidth

NetFlow is built around TCP/IP communication for statistical record-keeping using the concept of a flow. A flow is a unidirectional stream of packets between a source and destination host or system. With an understanding of TCP/IP, you can figure out that NetFlow is using socket information, meaning source and destination IP addresses and source and destination port numbers. But there are a few more fields that NetFlow uses. Here is a list of commonly used NetFlow flows:

- Source IP address
- Destination IP address

- Source port number
- Destination port number
- Layer 3 protocol field
- Type of Service (ToS) marking
- Input logical interface

As mentioned, the first four listings are the sockets used between the source and destination host, which identify the application. The protocol field identifies the data the packet is carrying, and ToS in the IPv4 header describes how QoS rules are applied to the packets in the flow. If a packet has a key field that's different from another packet, it's considered to belong to another flow. You configure NetFlow on the router's interfaces, and that's exactly what I'll show you next—how to configure and then verify NetFlow.

Configuring NetFlow

These four factors must be completed to properly implement NetFlow on a router:

- Configure NetFlow data capture by configuring ingress (incoming) and egress (outgoing) packets.
- Configure NetFlow data export by specifying the IP address of the NetFlow collector and the UDP port the collector listens for.
- Configure the NetFlow data export version by specifying the version of NetFlow, with version 9 being the most current.
- Verify NetFlow by analyzing the exported data on a host running a NetFlow collection engine or by using `show` command on the NetFlow router.

Here's an example of configuring NetFlow on the SF router:

```
SF(config)#int fa0/0
SF(config-if)#ip flow ingress
SF(config-if)#ip flow egress
SF(config-if)#exit
SF(config)#ip flow-export destination 172.16.20.254 9996
SF(config)#ip flow-export version ?
  1
  5
  9
SF(config)#ip flow-export version 9
SF(config)#ip flow-export source loopback 0
```

First, I configured the Fast Ethernet 0/0 interface of the Corp router as both my ingress and egress interface, which tells the router to capture NetFlow data for flows on the interface. After that, I configured the NetFlow collector's IP address as well as the version.

Notice that I could opt to configure only versions 1, 5, and 9. Version 9 includes all the fields I mentioned already, plus MPLS and IPv6 information and ports. The loopback interface defines the source IP address of packets sent to the collector.

To verify NetFlow, you need to verify that the correct interfaces in the correct direction have been configured, starting with the `show ip flow interface` command like this:

```
SF#sh ip flow interface
FastEthernet0/0
  ip flow ingress
  ip flow egress
```

Sure enough! The correct interface of Fast Ethernet 0/0 is configured with the `ingress` and `egress` commands. Now, I'll check that I've correctly configured the export parameters via the `show ip flow export` command:

```
SF#sh ip flow export
Flow export v9 is enabled for main cache
  Exporting flows to 172.16.20.254 (9996) 172.16.20.254 (9996)
  Exporting using source interface Loopback0
  Version 9 flow records
  43 flows exported in 15 udp datagrams
[output cut]
```

Notice that the destination port is 9996. This is the Cisco default port number on which the NetFlow collectors listen for NetFlow packets. I can use the `sh ip cache flow` command to verify my flows by examining the information stored on a router directly, which will show that I'm actually collecting packets:

```
SF#sh ip cache flow
IP packet size distribution (161 total packets):
[output cut]
IP Flow Switching Cache, 278544 bytes
  1 active, 4095 inactive, 1 added
  215 ager polls, 0 flow alloc failures
  Active flows timeout in 30 minutes
  Inactive flows timeout in 15 seconds
IP Sub Flow Cache, 21640 bytes
  1 active, 1023 inactive, 1 added, 1 added to flow
  0 alloc failures, 0 force free
  1 chunk, 1 chunk added
  last clearing of statistics never
Protocol         Total    Flows    Packets Bytes  Packets Active(Sec) Idle(Sec)
--------         Flows     /Sec     /Flow  /Pkt     /Sec      /Flow     /Flow
TCP-Telnet       14        0.0      19      58      0.1       6.5      11.7
TCP-WWW           8        0.0       9     108      0.1       2.5       1.7
SrcIf         SrcIPaddress     DstIf       DstIPaddress    Pr SrcP DstP  Pkts
Fa0/0         172.16.10.1      gig0/1      255.255.255.255 11 0044 0050  1161
```

Nice: you can see that packets are truly being received—1,161 so far—and the bottom lines show that the router is collecting flow for Telnet and HTTP. You can also see the source interface, source IP, destination interface, and source and destination ports in hex (50 is 80 in hex). It's important to remember that the `show ip cache flow` command provides a summary of the NetFlow statistics, including which protocols are in use.

Summary

I began this chapter by providing detailed information on how to find neighbor device information using the proprietary Cisco Discovery Protocol (CDP) and industry-standard Link Layer Discovery Protocol (LLDP).

We then synchronized the time for our devices using Network Time Protocol (NTP).

After that, I walked you through Simple Network Management Protocol (SNMP), an Application layer protocol that provides a message format for agents on a variety of devices to communicate to network management stations (NMSs). I discussed the basic information you need to use syslog and SNMP: configuration and verification.

You also learned about the type of alerts sent to the network management station (NMS). We then moved on to the very important Syslog, which was covered in depth, and finally, I demonstrated how to configure SSH.

Last, I discussed Cisco NetFlow. Cisco IOS NetFlow efficiently provides a key set of services for IP applications, including network traffic accounting for baselining, usage-based network billing for consumers of network services, network design and planning, general network security, and DoS and DDoS monitoring capabilities, as well as general network monitoring.

Exam Essentials

Describe the value of CDP and LLDP. Cisco Discovery Protocol can be used to help you document and troubleshoot your network. LLDP is a nonproprietary protocol that can provide the same information as CDP.

Understand the information provided by the output of the `show cdp neighbors` command. The `show cdp neighbors` command provides the following information: device ID, local interface, holdtime, capability, platform, and port ID (remote interface).

List Understand how to configure NTP. It's pretty simple to configure NTP, and you don't have to remember all of the options! Most important are configuring syslog to mark the time and date and enabling NTP:

```
SF(config)#service timestamps log datetime msec
SF(config)#ntp server 172.16.10.1 version 4
```

Understand the various levels of syslog. Although it's simple to configure syslog, there are a bunch of options you have to remember for the exam. Use the mnemonic "Every Awesome Cisco Engineer Will Need Icecream Daily" to remember this table:

Severity Level	Explanation
Emergency (severity 0)	System is unusable.
Alert (severity 1)	Immediate action is needed.
Critical (severity 2)	Critical condition.
Error (severity 3)	Error condition.
Warning (severity 4)	Warning condition.
Notification (severity 5)	Normal but significant condition.
Informational (severity 6)	Normal information message.
Debugging (severity 5)	Debugging message.

Remember the differences between SNMPv2 and SNMPv3. SNMPv2 uses UDP but can use TCP. SNMPv2 still sends data to the NMS station in clear text, exactly like SNMPv1. SNMPv2 implemented GETBULK and INFORM messages. SNMPv3 uses TCP and authenticates users, plus it can use ACLs in the SNMP strings to protect the NMS station from unauthorized use.

Describe the advantages of using Secure Shell, and list its requirements. Secure Shell (SSH) uses encrypted keys to send data so that usernames and passwords are not sent in the clear. It requires that a hostname and domain name be configured for encryption keys to be generated.

Understand what Cisco's NetFlow is used for. Cisco IOS NetFlow efficiently provides a key set of services for IP applications, including network traffic accounting for baselining, usage-based network billing for consumers of network services, network design and planning, general network security, and DoS and DDoS monitoring capabilities as well as general network monitoring.

Written Lab

The answers to this lab can be found in Appendix A, "Answers to the Written Labs."

1. Which Cisco protocol can efficiently provide a key set of services for IP applications, including network traffic accounting?
2. Which function does an SNMP agent perform?

3. Which protocol can request and receive information from a monitored device on the network?
4. Which syslog severity level results in warning-level messages?
5. Which technology must be implemented to configure network device monitoring with the highest security?
6. What command is used to configure a host to send messages to a syslog server?
7. A network administrator enters the following command on a router: logging trap 3. What are three message types that will be sent to the syslog server?
8. Which protocol does the logging level define for the severity of a particular message?
9. Which protocol is used for secure remote CLI access?
10. Which syslog message logging level displays interface line protocol up/down events?

Review Questions

NOTE The following questions are designed to test your understanding of this chapter's material. For more information on how to get additional questions, please see this book's introduction.

The answers to these questions can be found in Appendix B, "Answers to the Review Questions."

1. How can you efficiently restrict the read-only function of a requesting SNMP management station based on the IP address?
   - **A.** Place an ACL on the logical control plane.
   - **B.** Place an ACL on the line when configuring the RO community string.
   - **C.** Place an ACL on the VTY line.
   - **D.** Place an ACL on all router interfaces.
2. You want to add a sequence number on your console message on a Cisco router. Which command will you use?
   - **A.** `service sequence-numbers`
   - **B.** `service timestamps`
   - **C.** `service number-sequence`
   - **D.** `sequence service messages`
3. Which configuration is needed to generate an RSA key for SSH on a router?
   - **A.** Configure VTY access.
   - **B.** Configure the version of SSH.
   - **C.** Assign a DNS domain name.
   - **D.** Create a user with a password.
4. You want to send a console message to a syslog server, but you only want to send status messages of 4 and lower. Which of the following commands will you use?
   - **A.** `logging trap emergencies`
   - **B.** `logging trap errors`
   - **C.** `logging trap debugging`
   - **D.** `logging trap notifications`
   - **E.** `logging trap critical`
   - **F.** `logging trap warnings`
   - **G.** `logging trap alerts`

5. Which command enables you to view a summary of the NetFlow statistics of the protocols on a router?

   A. `show ip flow`

   B. `show ip cache flow`

   C. `show ip netflow`

   D. `show ip flow interface gi0/1`

6. Which SNMP message type is reliable and precedes an acknowledgment response from the SNMP manager?

   A. Get

   B. Inform

   C. Traps

   D. Set

7. You want to send a console message to a syslog server, but you only want to send status messages of 5 and lower. Which of the following commands will you use?

   A. `logging trap emergencies`

   B. `logging trap errors`

   C. `logging trap debugging`

   D. `logging trap notifications`

   E. `logging trap critical`

   F. `logging trap warnings`

   G. `logging trap alerts`

8. What are the pieces needed for NetFlow to gather data? (Choose two.)

   A. An SNMP NMS station

   B. Collector

   C. Syslog configured

   D. NetFlow-configured router

9. You want to send a console message to a syslog server, but you only want to send status messages of 3 and lower. Which of the following commands will you use?

   A. `logging trap emergencies`

   B. `logging trap errors`

   C. `logging trap debugging`

   D. `logging trap notifications`

   E. `logging trap critical`

   F. `logging trap warnings`

   G. `logging trap alerts`

10. You want to send a console message to a syslog server, but you only want to send status messages of 7 and lower. Which of the following commands will you use?
    A. `logging trap emergencies`
    B. `logging trap errors`
    C. `logging trap debugging`
    D. `logging trap notifications`
    E. `logging trap critical`
    F. `logging trap warnings`
    G. `logging trap alerts`
11. You want to send a console message to a syslog server, but you only want to send status messages of 6 and lower. Which of the following commands will you use?
    A. `logging trap emergencies`
    B. `logging trap errors`
    C. `logging trap debugging`
    D. `logging trap notifications`
    E. `logging trap critical`
    F. `logging trap warnings`
    G. `logging trap informational`
12. Which SNMP version provides authentication, data integrity, and encryption?
    A. SNMPv1
    B. SNMPv2
    C. SNMPv3
    D. SNMPv4
    E. SNMPv6
13. If notice-level messaging is sent to a Syslog server, which event has occurred?
    A. A network device has restarted.
    B. A debug operation is running.
    C. A routing instance has flapped.
    D. An ARP inspection has failed.
14. A network engineer must back up 10 network router configurations globally within a customer environment. Which protocol allows the engineer to perform this function using the Cisco IOS MIB?
    A. ARP
    B. SNMP
    C. IOS TCP
    D. CDP
    E. SMTP

15. What event has occurred if a router sends a notice-level message to a syslog server?
    A. A certificate has expired.
    B. An interface line has changed status.
    C. A TCP connection has been torn down.
    D. An ICMP connection has been built.
16. An engineering team asks an implementer to configure syslog for warning and error conditions. Which command does the implementer configure to achieve the desired result?
    A. logging trap 5
    B. logging trap 2
    C. logging trap 4
    D. logging trap 3
17. What is a syslog facility?
    A. Host that is configured for the system to send log messages
    B. Password that authenticates a Network Management System to receive log messages
    C. Group of log messages associated with the configured severity level
    D. Set of values that represent the processes that can generate a log message
18. Which condition must be met before an NMS handles an SNMP trap from an agent?
    A. The NMS software must be loaded with the MIB associated with the trap.
    B. The NMS must be configured on the same router as the SNMP agent.
    C. The NMS must receive a trap and an inform message from the SNMP agent within a configured interval.
    D. The NMS must receive the same trap from two different SNMP agents to verify that it is reliable.
19. Which fact must the engineer consider when implementing syslog on a new network?
    A. Syslog defines the software or hardware component that triggered the message.
    B. There are 16 different logging levels (0–15).
    C. The logging level defines the severity of a particular message.
    D. By default, all message levels are sent to the syslog server.
20. Which conditions must be met before SSH can operate normally on a Cisco IOS switch? (Choose two.)
    A. IP routing must be enabled on the switch.
    B. A console password must be configured on the switch.
    C. Telnet must be disabled on the switch.
    D. The switch must be running a k9 (crypto) IOS image.
    E. The `ip domain-name` command must be configured on the switch.

Chapter 7

Security Fundamentals

THE FOLLOWING CCNA EXAM TOPICS ARE COVERED IN THIS CHAPTER:

✓ **5.0 Security Fundamentals**

5.1 Define key security concepts (threats, vulnerabilities, exploits, and mitigation techniques)

5.2 Describe security program elements (user awareness, training, and physical access control)

5.3 Configure device access control using local passwords

5.4 Describe security password policy elements, such as management, complexity, and password alternatives (multifactor authentication, certificates, and biometrics)

5.7 Configure Layer 2 security features (DHCP snooping, dynamic ARP inspection, and port security)

5.8 Compare authentication, authorization, and accounting concepts

Network security has grown from a critical consideration into an essential one. In an age of increasing use and dependence on the Internet, nearly everyone—from individuals and small businesses to huge corporations, institutions, and worldwide organizations—is now a potential victim of hackers and E-crime. And although our defense techniques continue to improve with time, so do the sophistication and weaponry used by the bad guys.

Today's tightest security will be laughably transparent three years from now, making it absolutely necessary for administrators to stay up with the industry's quickly evolving security trends.

Among additional important technologies, this chapter will cover authentication, authorization, and accounting (AAA). AAA is a technology that gives us substantial control over users and what they're permitted to do inside of our networks. That's just the beginning—there are more tools in the box! RADIUS and TACACS+ security servers like Identity Services Engine (ISE) help us implement a centralized security plan by recording network events to the security server or to a syslog server via logging.

Solid security hasn't just become imperative; it's also becoming increasingly complex. Cisco continues to develop and extend its features to meet these demands by providing us with a whole suite of hardware and software solutions.

ISE (Identity Security Engine), Cisco Prime, Tetration, ACI, and other powerful tools like Next Generation Firewall (NGFW), also called Cisco Firepower & Firepower Threat Defense (FTD), will be covered in my new CCNP Security books. For now, just know that the new FTD and even older ASA devices can be used to send authentication to the server.

In this chapter, we'll also be covering user accounts, password security, and user authentication methods, and we'll finish up by demonstrating how to set passwords on your Cisco devices.

I know all of this sounds pretty complicated, and truthfully, it is. That's why I'm devoting a whole chapter to these crucial topics!

So, let's look into the specific types of threats your network is probably vulnerable to now.

NOTE To find your included bonus material, as well as Todd Lammle videos, practice questions, and hands-on labs, please see `www.lammle.com/ccna`.

Network Security Threats

There are four primary threats to network security you must be familiar with as well as being able to define the type of attacker:

Unstructured threats These threats typically originate from curious people who have downloaded information from the Internet and want to feel the sense of power this provides them. Sure, some of these types, called Script Kiddies, can be pretty nasty, but most of them are just doing it for the rush, thrills, and bragging rites. They're not talented, experienced hackers.

Structured threats This kind of hacker is much more sophisticated, technically competent, and calculating. They're dedicated to their work and usually understand network design and how to exploit routing and network vulnerabilities. They can create hacking scripts that allow them to penetrate deep into the network's systems and tend to be repeat offenders. Both structured and unstructured threats typically come from the Internet.

External threats These typically come from people on the Internet or from someone who has found a hole in your network from the outside. These serious threats have become ubiquitous now that all companies have an Internet presence. External threats generally make their way into your network via the Internet.

Internal threats These come from users on your network, typically employees. These are probably the scariest of all threats because they're really hard to catch and stop. Worse, because these hackers are authorized to be on the network, they can do some serious damage in less time because they're already in and know their way around. Add that to the profile of an angry, disgruntled employee or contractor out for revenge, and you've got a real problem! We all know doing this is illegal, but some of us also know it's pretty easy to cause a lot of damage really fast, and the odds aren't bad that they'll get away with it!

Three Primary Network Attacks

Now you know your enemy, but what, exactly, are they up to? The better you understand that, the more equipped you'll be to handle anything an attacker may throw at you. Most network attacks fall into these three categories:

Reconnaissance attacks *Reconnaissance attacks* are basically an unauthorized familiarization session. An attacker on reconnaissance is out for discovery—mapping the network and its resources, systems, and vulnerabilities. This is often preliminary. The information gathered will often be used to attack the network later.

Access Attacks *Access attacks* are waged against networks or systems to retrieve data, gain access, and/or escalate their access privilege. This can be as easy as finding network shares with no passwords. Some access attacks are just for the intellectual challenge, but beware. Darker motivations include actual theft, corporate espionage, or using you as camouflage, making their dirty work appear to originate from your network!

Denial of service (DoS) attacks *Denial of service (DoS) attacks* are always vile. Their sole purpose is to disable or corrupt network services. The result of a DoS attack will usually be to either crash a system or slow it down to the point that it's rendered useless. DoS attacks are usually aimed at web servers and are surprisingly easy to carry out.

Network Attacks

There are a bunch of ways to gather information about a network, compromise corporate information, or destroy corporate web servers and services. Most of them are pretty common. TCP/IP teams up with operating systems to provide lots of weak, exploitable spots into our networks, and some are so bad they're almost like an outright invitation!

Here's a list of the most common threats:

- Eavesdropping
- DoS attacks
- Unauthorized access
- WareZ
- Masquerade attack (IP spoofing)
- Session replaying or hijacking
- Rerouting
- Repudiation
- Smurfing
- Password attacks
- Man-in-the-middle attacks
- Application-layer attacks
- HTML attacks

It's your job to protect your company's network from these attacks. You've got to effectively prevent the theft, destruction, and corruption of sensitive corporate information, as well as block the introduction of corrupt information that can cause irreparable damage.

Eavesdropping

Eavesdropping, otherwise known as network snooping and packet sniffing, is the act of a hacker "listening in" to your system. There's a really cool product called a *packet sniffer* that enables us to read packets of information sent across a network. Because a network's packets aren't encrypted by default, you can just imagine how helpful sniffers can be when trying to optimize or troubleshoot a network! But it's not a stretch to imagine hackers using them for evil and breaking into a network to gather up sensitive corporate info, right?

And gather they can! Some applications send all information across the network in cleartext, an especially convenient feature for someone striving to nick usernames and passwords to gain access to corporate resources. A bad guy only needs to jack the right account and they've got the run of your network. Worse, if they manage to gain admin or root access, they can even create a new user ID to use at any time as a back door into your network and its resources. The network belongs to the hacker—kiss it goodbye!

Simple Eavesdropping

Here's an example of eavesdropping when I was checking my email that demonstrates how easy it is to find usernames and passwords!

The network analyzer I'm using shows the first packet has the username in cleartext in the following output:

```
  Source Port:            3207
  Destination Port:       110  pop3
  Sequence Number:        1904801173
  Ack Number:             1883396251
  Offset:                 5  (20  bytes)
  Reserved:               %000000
  Flags:                  %011000
                          0. .... (No Urgent pointer)
                          .1 .... Ack
                          .. 1... Push
                          .. .0.. (No Reset)
                          .. ..0. (No SYN)
                          .. ...0 (No FIN)
  Window:                 64166
  Checksum:               0x078F
  Urgent Pointer:         0
  No TCP Options
POP - Post Office Protocol
  Line  1:                USER tlammle1<CR><LF>
FCS - Frame Check Sequence
  FCS (Calculated):       0x0CFCA80E
```

This next packet has the password. Everything needed to break into the system is seen in this packet! In this case, it's an email address and username/password):

```
  Source Port:            3207
  Destination Port:       110  pop3
```

```
  Sequence Number:        1904801188
  Ack Number:             1883396256
  Offset:                 5  (20  bytes)
  Reserved:               %000000
  Flags:                  %011000
                          0. .... (No Urgent pointer)
                          .1 .... Ack
                          .. 1... Push
                          .. .0.. (No Reset)
                          .. ..0. (No SYN)
                          .. ...0 (No FIN)
  Window:                 64161
  Checksum:               0x078F
  Urgent Pointer:         0
  No TCP Options
POP - Post Office Protocol
  Line  1:                PASS secretpass<CR><LF>
```

Both the username, "tlammle1," and the password, "secretpass," are right there in cleartext for everyone's viewing pleasure!

So, worse yet, eavesdropping is also used to steal information and identities. Imagine the intruder hacking into some financial institution, snaking credit card numbers, accounts, and other personal information from the institution's network computers or data crossing its network. Voilà! The hacker now has everything needed for some serious identity theft.

Of course, there's something we can do about this, and again, the solution stems from having a nice, tight network security policy in place. To counteract eavesdropping, create a policy forbidding the use of protocols with known susceptibilities to eavesdropping and make sure all sensitive, important network traffic is encrypted.

Denial-of-Service Attacks

The most debilitating of all, denial-of-service (DoS) attacks can force a corporation to its knees by crippling its ability to conduct business.

And unfortunately, these attacks are alarmingly simple in design and execution. The basic idea is to keep open all available connections supported by the key server. This locks out valid attempts to gain access because legitimate users like customers and employees are shut out due to all services being overwhelmed and all bandwidth consumed.

DoS attacks are often implemented using common Internet protocols like TCP and ICMP—TCP/IP weaknesses for which Cisco offers some safeguards, but nothing we could call bulletproof.

TCP attacks are carried out when a hacker opens up more sessions than the targeted server can handle, rendering it inaccessible to anyone else.

ICMP attacks, sometimes called "The Ping of Death," are executed by an attacker in one of two ways: The first way is by sending so many pings to a server that it's thoroughly overwhelmed dealing with pings instead of serving its corporation. The second method is achieved by modifying the IP portion of a header, making the server believe there's more data in the packet than there really is. If enough of these packets are sent, they'll overwhelm and crash the server.

Here's a list describing some of the other kinds of DoS attacks you should know about:

Chargen Massive amounts of UDP packets are sent to a device, resulting in tremendous congestion on the network.

SYN flood Randomly opens up lots of TCP ports, tying up the network equipment with bogus requests and denying sessions to real users.

Packet fragmentation and reassembly This attack exploits the buffer overrun bug in hosts or internetwork equipment, creating fragments that can't be reassembled and crashing the system. Having packet reassembly on an interface is very efficient for your network; however, you should disable this on your outside interface/zone.

Accidental DoS of service attacks can happen by legitimate users using misconfigured network devices.

E-mail bombs Many free programs exist that allow users to send bulk e-mails to individuals, groups, lists, or domains, taking up all the e-mail service.

Land.c Uses the TCP SYN packet that specifies the target host's address as both the source and destination. Land.c also uses the same port on the target host as source and destination, causing the target to crash.

The Cisco IOS gives us some nice firewall features to help stop DoS attacks, but you just can't prevent them completely right now without cutting off legitimate users. Here's a list of Cisco's safeguards:

Context-Based Access Control (CBAC) CBAC provides advanced traffic filtering services and can be used as an integral part of your network's firewall.

Java blocking Helps stop hostile Java applet attacks.

DoS detection and monitoring You really have to understand exactly how much protective power your network actually needs from this feature because going with too much will keep out attackers as well as legitimate users! Carefully assess your specific network needs and weigh the pros and cons of using the DoS monitoring system wisely.

Audit trails Audit trails are great for keeping track of who's attacking you, which is awesome because you can then send those logs to the FBI.

Real-time alerts log Keeping a log of the attacks in real time is helpful in exactly the same way audit trails are: for helping the authorities go after the bad guys.

NOTE The Cisco TCP intercept feature implements software to protect TCP servers from a type of DoS attack called *TCP SYN-flooding.*

Unauthorized Access

Intruders love gaining access to the root or administrator because they can exploit that access to powerful privileges. The /etc/password file on the UNIX host allows them to view important passwords. Adding additional accounts to use as backdoors permits them access any time they want.

Sometimes intruders gain access to a network so they can place unauthorized files or resources on another system for ready access by other intruders. Other goals could be to steal software and distribute it if possible—more on that in a bit.

Again, the Cisco IOS offers us help with something called *Lock and Key.* Another tool is a *Terminal Access Controller Access Control System* (TACACS+) server—a remote authentication server. There's also an authentication protocol called Challenge Handshake Authentication Protocol (CHAP). All of these technologies provide additional security against unauthorized access attempts.

In addition to a TACACS+ server and CHAP, you can implement a mechanism that authenticates a user beyond an IP network address. It supports things like password token cards and creates other challenges to gaining access. This mechanism also requires remote reauthorization during periods of inactivity—another safeguard!

WareZ

WareZ applies to the unauthorized distribution of software. The intruder's goal is theft and piracy—they want to either sell someone else's software or distribute unlicensed versions of it for free on the Internet. It's a favorite of present or former employees but could be executed by anyone on the Internet with a cracked version of the software. As you can imagine, WareZ is a huge problem!

There are many ways to provide free software on the Internet, and a legion of servers in the Far East offer blatantly pirated downloads of free software because they know there is nothing anyone can do about it. The only thing that can protect products from a WareZ is to include some type of activation key and licensing preventing illegal use.

Masquerade Attack (IP Spoofing)

Masquerading or *IP spoofing* is pretty easy to prevent once you understand how it works. An IP spoofing attack happens when someone outside your network pretends to be a trusted computer by using an IP address that's within the range of your network's IP addresses. The attacker's plan is to steal an IP address from a trusted source for use in gaining access to network resources. A trusted computer is one that you either have administrative control over or one you've decided to trust on your network.

You can head off this attack by placing an access control list (ACL) on the corporate router's interface to the Internet, denying access to your internal addresses from that interface. This approach easily stops IP spoofing, but only if the attacker is coming in from outside the network.

To spoof a network ID, a hacker would need to change the routing tables in your router to receive any packets. Once they do that, the odds are good that they'll gain access to user accounts and passwords. And if your hacker happens to understand messaging protocols, they just might add a little twist and send e-mail messages from some poor employee's company e-mail account to other users in the company. That way, it looks like that user sent the messages, and many hackers get a real kick out of embarrassing corporate users. IP spoofing helps them achieve that goal.

Session Hijacking or Replaying

When two hosts communicate, they typically use the TCP protocol at the Transport layer to set up a reliable session. This session can be "hijacked" by making the hosts believe that they are sending packets to a valid host when in fact they're delivering their packets to a hijacker.

You don't see this so much anymore because a network sniffer can gather much more information, but it still happens now and then, so you should still be aware of it. You can protect yourself from *session hijacking* or *replaying* by using a strongly authenticated, encrypted management protocol.

Rerouting

A *rerouting* attack is launched by a hacker who understands IP routing. The hacker breaks into the corporate router and then changes the routing table to alter the course of IP packets so they'll go to the attacker's unauthorized destination instead. Some types of cookies and Java or Active X scripts can also be used to manipulate routing tables on hosts.

To stop a rerouting attack, you can use access control with a PIX firewall or the Cisco IOS Firewall Feature Set.

Repudiation

Repudiation is a denial of a transaction so that no communications can be traced by erasing or altering logs to hide the trail, providing deniability. Doing this can prevent a third party from being able to prove that a communication between two other parties ever took place.

Non-repudiation is the opposite—a third party can prove that a communication between two other parties took place. So because you generally want the ability to trace your communications, as well as prove they actually did take place, non-repudiation is the preferred transaction.

Attackers who want to create a repudiation attack can use Java or Active X scripts to do so. They can also use scanning tools that confirm TCP ports for specific services, network or system architectures, and OSs. Once information is obtained, the attacker will try to find vulnerabilities associated with those entities.

To stop repudiation, set your browser security to "high," You can also block any corporate access to public e-mail sites. In addition, add access control and authentication on your network. Non-repudiation can be used with digital signatures.

Smurfing

The latest trend in the attacker game is the *smurf attack*. This attack sends a large amount of ICMP (Internet Control Message Protocol) echo (ping) traffic to IP broadcast addresses from a supposedly valid host that is traceable. The framed host then gets blamed for the attack. The target IP address is used as the source address in the ping, and all systems reply to the target, eating up its resources.

Smurf attacks send a layer 2 (Data-Link layer) broadcast. Most hosts on the attacked IP network will reply to each ICMP echo request with an echo reply, multiplying the traffic by the number of hosts responding. This eats up tons of bandwidth and results in a denial of service to valid users because the network traffic is so high.

The smurf attack's cousin is called *fraggle*, which uses UDP echo packets in the same fashion as the ICMP echo packets. Fraggle is a simple rewrite of smurf to use a layer 4 (Transport layer) broadcast.

To stop a smurf attack, all networks should perform filtering either at the edge of the network where customers connect (the access layer) or at the edge of the network with connections to the upstream providers. Your goal is to prevent source-address-spoofed packets from entering from downstream networks or leaving for upstream ones.

Password Attacks

These days, it's a rare user who isn't aware of password issues, but you can still depend on them to pick the name of their dog, significant other, or child because those things are nice and easy to remember. But you've been wise and set policies to stop these easy-to-guess passwords, so no worries—right?

Well, almost. You've definitely saved yourself a good bit of grief. It's just that even if your users pick really great passwords, programs that record a username and password can still be used to gather them up. If a hacker creates a program that repeatedly attempts to identify a user account and/or password, it's called a *brute-force attack*. And if it's successful, the hacker will gain access to all resources the stolen username and password usually provides to the now ripped-off corporate user. As you can imagine, it's an especially dark day when the bad guy manages to jack the username and password of an administrator account.

Man-in-the-Middle Attacks

A *man-in-the-middle* attack is just that: a person between you and the network you are connected to, gathering everything you send and receive. For a man-in-the-middle attack to be possible, the attacker must have access to network packets traveling across the networks. This means your middleman could be an internal user, someone who spoofed—even someone who works for an Internet service provider (ISP). Man-in-the-middle attacks are usually implemented by using network packet sniffers, routing protocols, or even Transport layer protocols.

Your middleman attacker's goal is any or all of the following:

- Theft of information
- Hijacking of an ongoing session to gain access to your internal network resources
- Traffic analysis to derive information about your network and its users
- Denial of service
- Corruption of transmitted data
- Introduction of new information into network sessions

Application-Layer Attacks

An *Application-layer attack* involves an application with well-known weaknesses that can be easily exploited. Sendmail, PostScript, and FTP are a few really good examples. The idea here is to gain access to a computer with the permissions of the account running the application, which is usually a privileged, system-level account.

Trojan Horse Programs, Viruses, and Worms

I hate to admit this, but the *Trojan horse attack* is actually very cool—that is, if you look at the way it's implemented and, more importantly, if it's not happening to you. See, the Trojan horse creates a substitute for a common program, duping users into thinking they are in a valid program when they're not. They're in the horse. This gives the attacker the power to monitor login attempts and to capture user account and password information. This attack can even take it up a notch and allow the horse's rider to modify application behavior and receive all your corporate e-mail messages instead of you. Pretty stylin', huh? I told you it was cool.

Both worms and viruses spread and infect multiple systems. The differentiator between the two is that viruses require some form of human intervention to spread, and worms do that on their own. Because viruses, Trojan horses, and worms are conceptually alike, they're all considered the same form of attack. They're all software programs created for and aimed at destroying your data. And some variants of these weapons can also deny legitimate users access to resources that can consume bandwidth, memory, disk space, and CPU cycles.

So be smart—use a virus program and update it regularly!

HTML Attacks

Another new attack on the Internet scene exploits several new technologies: the Hypertext Markup Language (HTML) specification, web browser functionality, and HTTP.

HTML attacks can include Java applets and ActiveX controls, and their modus operandi is to pass destructive programs across the network and load them through a user's browser.

Microsoft promotes an Authenticode technology for ActiveX, only it doesn't do much except provide a false sense of security to users. This is because attackers can use a properly signed and totally bug-free ActiveX control to create a Trojan horse!

This particular approach is unique because it's teamwork—the attacker and you. Part one of this attack—the bad guy's part—is to modify a program and set it up so you, the user, actually initiate the attack when you either start the program or choose a function within it. And these attacks aren't hardware dependent. They're very flexible because of the portability of the programs.

Security Program Elements

A security program backed by a security policy is one of the best ways to maintain a secure posture at all times. Solid programs cover many elements, but three are key:

- User awareness
- Training
- Physical security

User Awareness

Attacks are often successful because users aren't wise to the type of social engineering attacks confronting them. Moving beyond figuring out they're being played, users must also be skilled enough to avoid being set up and trapped as the inevitable dangers are encountered. Social engineering attacks and attackers use believable language, manipulation, and user gullibility to get the goods they're after, like user credentials or other sensitive, confidential information. Common threats that you want your people to be able to identify and understand include phishing/pharming, shoulder surfing, identity theft, and dumpster diving.

Phishing/Pharming

When phishing, attackers try to learn personal information, including credit card information and financial data. A very popular phishing technique is to put up a mock website that closely resembles a legitimate one. Users visit the site and enter their data, including credentials, essentially handing the bad guys facets of their valuable identity! Spear phishing is when an attack is carried out against a specific target by learning about the chosen mark's habits and likes. Because of the detailed background information required, these attacks take longer to carry out.

Pharming is similar to phishing, only pharming actually pollutes the contents of a computer's DNS cache so that requests to a legitimate site are routed to an alternate one.

Malware

Malicious software, or malware, is any software designed to perform malicious acts.

Here are the four classes of malware you should understand:

- *Virus:* Any malware that attaches itself to another application to replicate or distribute itself
- *Worm:* Any malware that replicates itself but doesn't need another application or human interaction to propagate
- *Trojan horse:* Any malware that disguises itself as a needed application while carrying out malicious actions
- *Spyware:* Any malware that collects private user data, including browsing history or keyboard input

The best defense against malicious software is to implement antivirus and anti-malware software. Today, most vendors package these two types of protection together. Keeping antivirus and anti-malware software up to date is vital, especially ensuring that the latest virus and malware definitions have been installed.

Training

The best countermeasure against social engineering threats is to provide user security awareness training. This training should be required and must occur on a regular basis because social engineering techniques evolve constantly.

Caution users against using any links embedded in e-mail messages, even if the message appears to have come from a legitimate entity. Users should also scrutinize a site's address bar any time they access a site where their personal information is required, to verify that the site is genuine and SSL is being used. The latter is indicated by either a padlock icon or an HTTPS designation at the beginning of the URL address.

Physical Access Control

With no physical security, logical or technical methods are pretty useless. For example, if someone can physically access your routers and switches, they can erase your configuration and take ownership of the devices! Likewise, physical access to a workstation can permit a hacker to boot to an operating system on a flash drive and access data.

Physical security is a grab bag of elements added to an environment to aid in securing it. Let's look at a few examples now.

Mantrap

Think of a mantrap like a series of two doors with a small room between them. The person who wants in is authenticated at the first door and then allowed into the room. Next, additional verification, like a guard visually identifying them, is required to permit them through the second door. Most of the time, mantraps are used only in very high-security situations and typically require the first door to be closed before opening the second one.

Figure 7.1 shows a mantrap design.

FIGURE 7.1 Aerial view of a mantrap

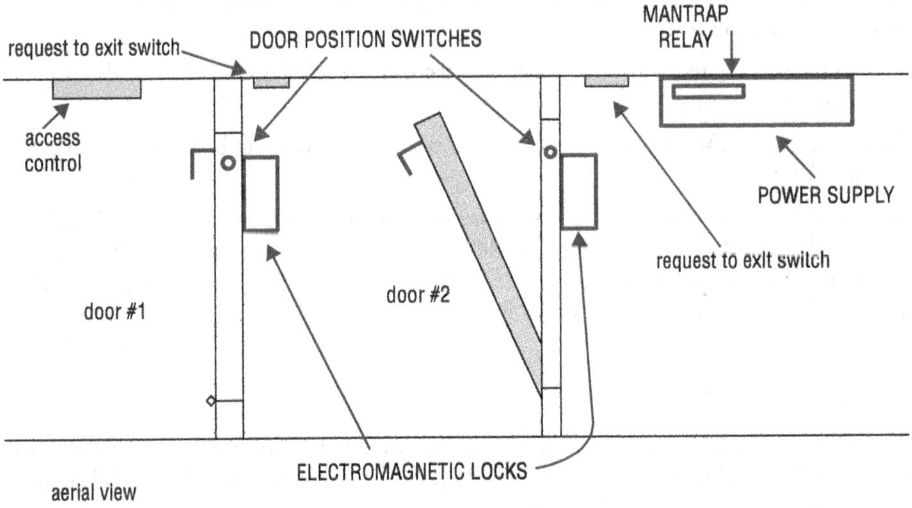

Badge Reader

Radio frequency identification (RFID) is a wireless, no-contact technology used with badges or cards and their accompanying reader. The reader is connected to the workstation and validates against the security system. This is an upgrade for authentication process security because the user must be in physical possession of the badge to access resources. An obvious drawback here is if the card is lost or stolen, anybody with the card can access those resources! Badge readers are used to provide access to devices and to open doors as well.

Smart Card

A smart card is basically a fancy badge or card that gives you access to myriad resources, including buildings, parking lots, and computers. It's embedded with your identity and access privilege information, and each area or device you access has a card scanner to insert your card into or swipe.

Smart cards are tough to counterfeit but easy to steal, and once a thief has it, they can access anything the card allows. To counteract this, most organizations avoid placing identifying marks on their smart cards, which definitely does make it harder for thieves to use them. Taking things further, a modern smart card often requires a password or PIN to activate it, plus encryption to protect the card's contents.

Security Guard

Sometimes, nothing takes the place of a human being. Security guards rely on the training, intuition, and common sense that automated systems lack to head off intruders. They can even be armed.

Door Lock

One of the easiest ways to prevent people with bad intentions from physically entering your environment is to lock your doors. Door locks are the most universal form of physical barrier and are a key point of access control for protecting network systems and devices. One door is good, but more doors are better, and the most effective physical barrier implementations are called *multiple-barrier systems*.

Ideally, you should have a minimum of three physical barriers to be effective. The first one is the external entrance to the building, called the *perimeter*, which is protected by alarms, external walls, fencing, surveillance, and so on. Keep an accurate access list of who can enter and be verified by a guard or someone else in authority. The second barrier is the actual entrance into the building. Use things like ID badges verified by security guards to permit access here. The third barrier is the entrance to the computer room itself. Here's where things like fobs and smart cards are used to gain access. (If sufficiently paranoid and loaded with cash, you could even go with a biometric system!) Of course, each of these entrances should be individually secured, monitored, and protected with alarm systems.

TIP Think of the three barriers this way: Outer = fence; Middle = guards, locks, and mantraps; Inner = key fobs/smart cards.

Yes, the truly determined can still break in, but these three barriers will probably slow an intruder down enough for law enforcement to respond before they can get away!

Layer 2 Security Features

The Cisco hierarchical model is a great reference for designing, implementing, and maintaining scalable, reliable, and cost-effective internetwork.

The bottom layer of this model, the Access layer, controls user and workgroup access to internetwork resources. Sometimes, it's referred to as the Desktop layer. The network resources most users need are available locally because the Distribution layer above handles traffic for remote services.

Here's a list of some of Access layer functions:

- Continued use of access control lists and policies from the Distribution layer
- Creation of separate collision domains with microsegmentation
- Workgroup connectivity into the Distribution layer

- Device connectivity
- Resiliency and security services
- Advanced technological capabilities (voice/video, PoE, port security, QoS, etc.)
- Gigabit switching

The Access layer is where user devices connect to the network, and it's also the connection point between the network and the client device. So clearly, safeguarding this layer is vital to protecting users, applications, and the network itself from attacks.

Some ways to protect the access layer are pictured in Figure 7.2.

FIGURE 7.2 Mitigating threats at the Access layer

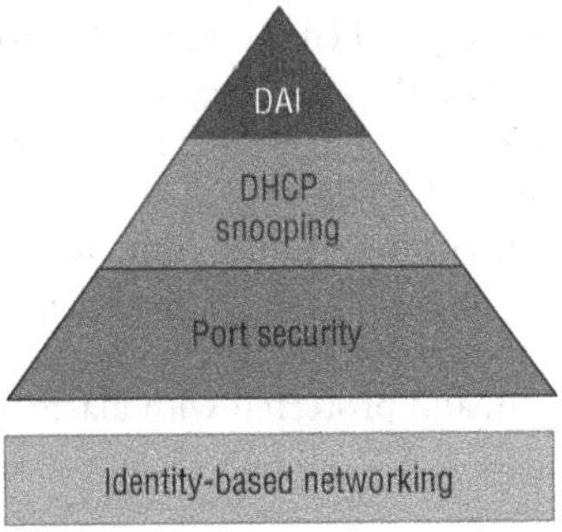

Port security Yes—you're already familiar with port security. It's the most common way to defend the access layer by restricting a port to a specific set of MAC addresses.

DHCP snooping DHCP snooping is a layer 2 security feature that validates DHCP messages by acting like a firewall between trusted hosts and untrusted DHCP servers.

To stop rogue DHCP servers within the network, switch interfaces are configured as trusted or untrusted. Trusted interfaces allow all types of DHCP messages, but untrusted interfaces only permit requests. Trusted interfaces connect to a legitimate DHCP server or an uplink toward the legitimate DHCP server, as shown in Figure 7.3.

With DHCP snooping enabled, a switch also builds a DHCP snooping binding database. Each entry includes the MAC and IP address of the host, as well as the DHCP lease time, binding type, VLAN, and interface. Dynamic ARP inspection also uses the DHCP snooping binding database.

Dynamic ARP inspection (DAI) DAI, used with DHCP snooping, tracks IP-to-MAC bindings from DHCP transactions to protect against ARP poisoning. You need DHCP snooping to build the MAC-to-IP bindings for DAI validation.

FIGURE 7.3 DHCP snooping

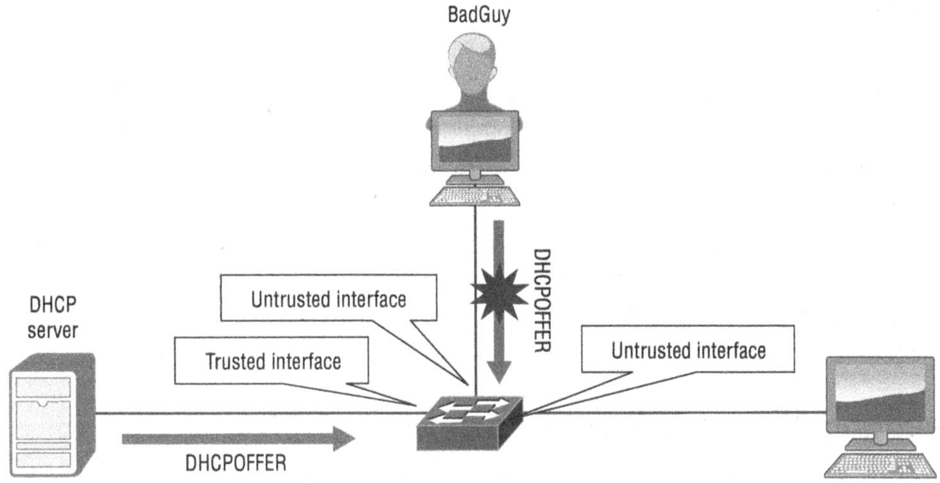

Identity-based networking Identity-based networking is a concept that ties together several authentication, access control, and user policy components to provide users with only the network services you want them to access.

In the past, for a user to connect to Finance services, they had to be plugged into the Finance LAN or VLAN. But with user mobility as one of the core requirements of modern networks, this is no longer practical, nor does it provide sufficient security.

Identity-based networking allows us to verify users when they connect to a switch port by authenticating them, placing them in the right VLAN, and applying security and QoS policies based on their identity. Users who fail to pass the authentication process might be placed in a guest VLAN, but their access can be rejected, too!

Figure 7.4 illustrates this process.

FIGURE 7.4 Identity-based networking

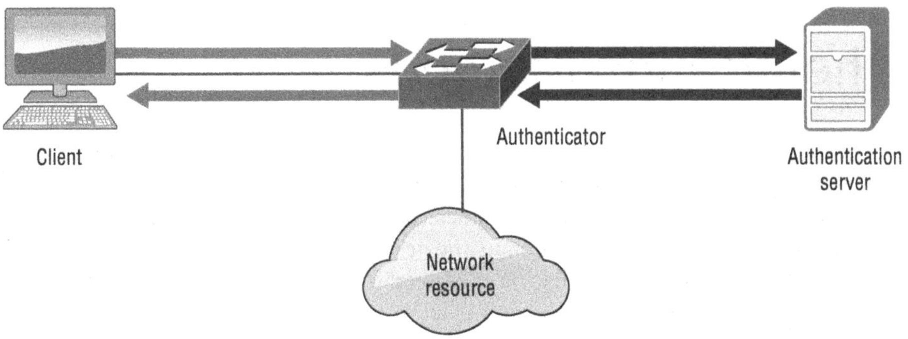

NOTE ISE and DNA Center are identity-based networking products from Cisco.

The IEEE 802.1x standard permits the implementation of identity-based networking on wired and wireless hosts by using client-server access control. There are three roles:

- Client: also referred to as a supplicant; software that runs on a client, which is 802.1x compliant
- Authenticator: Typically a switch, VPN server, or wireless AP controls physical access to the network and is a proxy between the client and the authentication server
- Authentication server (RADIUS): Server that authenticates each client before making any services available

Securing Network Access with Cisco AAA

A really nice feature of the authentication, authorization, and accounting (AAA) architecture is that it enables systematic access security both locally and remotely. AAA technologies work within the remote client system and the security server to secure access. Here's a definition of each of the "A"s in AAA:

- **Authentication** requires users to prove that they are who they say they are in one of these three ways:
  - Name and password
  - Challenge and response
  - Token cards
- **Authorization** only takes place after authentication is validated. Authorization provides the needed resources specifically allowed to a certain user and permits the operations that specific user is allowed to perform.
- **Accounting** and auditing records what the user actually did on the network as well as which resources they accessed. It also keeps track of how much time they spent using network resources.

Authentication Methods

With a terminal server configuration, a router authenticates a user coming in on it by ensuring that the person attempting to connect is valid and truly permitted access. The most common way the router determines that is either via a password or a combination of a username and a password. First, the user submits the needed information to the router, and then the router checks to see if that information is correct. If so, the user is then authenticated and allowed access to the console.

But that's only one way for routers to authenticate users from outside its boundaries. There are several different authentication methods you can apply that involve the operating system, security server, PAP, and CHAP authentication. CHAP is rarely in use today. I'm going to tell you about all of these techniques shortly, but first, I want to go into more detail about the way authentication is achieved most often—via usernames and passwords.

Username/password methods range from weak to strong in their authentication power—it depends on how vigilant you want to be. A database of usernames and passwords is employed at the simpler and least secure end of the range, whereas more advanced methods utilize one-time passwords, multi-factor, certificates, and biometrics.

The following list begins with the least secure authentication and progresses through to the most:

- **No username or password:** Obviously, this is the least secure method. It provides ease of connectivity but absolutely no security to network equipment or network resources. An attacker simply has to find the server or network address to gain access.
- **Username/password (static):** Set up by a network administrator and remains in place and unchanged until the network administrator changes it. It's better than nothing, but hackers can easily decipher usernames and passwords using snooping devices.
- **Aging username/password:** These expire after a set time (usually between 30 and 90 days) and must be reset—most often, by the user. The administrator configures the time period. This is tighter than the static usernames and password method, but it's still susceptible to playback attacks, eavesdropping, theft, and password cracking.
- **One-time passwords (OTP):** This is a very secure username/password method. Most OTP systems are based on a "secret pass-phrase," which is used to generate a list of passwords. They're only good for one login, so they're useless to anyone who manages to eavesdrop and capture them. A list of accessible passwords is typically generated by S/KEY server software and is then distributed to users.
- **Token cards/soft tokens:** This is the most secure authentication method. An administrator passes out a token card and a personal identification number (PIN) to each user. Token cards are typically the size of a credit card and are provided by a vendor to the administrator when they buy a token card server. This type of security usually consists of a remote client computer, a security device such as the Cisco ASA/FTD, and a security server running token security software.

Figure 7.5 shows a typical RSA token card, although an authenticator app on a smartphone is common today as well.

FIGURE 7.5 RSA token card

Token cards and servers generally work like this:

- An OTP is generated by the user with the token card using a security algorithm.
- The user enters this password into the authentication screen generated on the client.
- The password is sent to the token server via the network and a device.
- On the token server, an algorithm is used—the same one running on the client—to verify the password and authenticate the user.

The network security policy you've created provides you with the guidelines you need to determine the kind of authentication method you choose to implement on your network.

Windows Authentication

Everyone knows that Microsoft graciously includes many captivating bugs and flaws with its OS, but at least it does manage to provide an initial authentication screen, and users need to authenticate to log into Windows!

If those users happen to be local, they log in to the device via the Windows logon dialog box. If they're remote, they log in to the Windows remote dialog box using PPP (Point to Point Protocol) and TCP/IP over the communication line to the security server.

Generally, that security server is responsible for authenticating users, but it doesn't have to be. A user's identity (username and password) can also be validated using an AAA security server.

The AAA server can then access the MS AD server's user database.

Security Server Authentication

Cisco AAA access control gives you options—it provides either a local security database or a remote one. Your Cisco devices, such as the ASA or the new Cisco FTD, run the local database for a small group of users, and if you simply have one or two devices, you can opt for local authentication through it. All the remote security data is on a separate server that runs the AAA security protocol, which provides services for both network equipment and a big group of users.

Although it's true that local authentication and line security offer an adequate level of security, you're way better off going there if you have a fairly small network. That's because they require a whole bunch of administration. Picture a huge network with, say, 300 routers. Every time a password needs to be changed, the entire roost of routers—that's all 300—must be modified individually to reflect that change. That's right—*individually* by the administrator—YOU!

This is exactly why it's so much smarter to use security servers if your network is even somewhat large. Security servers provide centralized management of usernames and passwords, and this is how they work: when a router wants to authenticate a user, it collects the username and password information from them and submits that information to the ISE security server. The security server then compares the information it's been given to the user database to see if the user should be allowed access to the router. All usernames and passwords are stored centrally on a single or redundant pair of security servers.

This AAA four-step process is pictured in Figure 7.6.

FIGURE 7.6 External authentication options

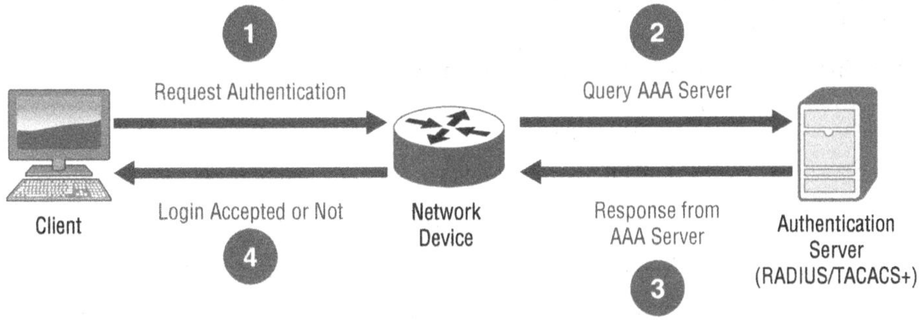

With administration consolidated on a single device like this, managing millions of users is a day at the beach!

Three types of security server protocols are supported by Cisco routers: RADIUS, TACACS+, and Kerberos. Let's take a look at each of these now.

External Authentication Options

Of course, we only want authorized IT folks to have administrative access to our network devices, such as routers and switches, and in a small to medium-sized network, using just local authentication is sufficient.

But if you have hundreds of devices, managing administrative connectivity would be nearly impossible because you'd have to configure each device by hand. So, if you changed just one password, it could take hours to update your network!

Because maintaining the local database for each network device individually in a very large network is unwise, you can use an external AAA server to manage all user and administrative access needs for an entire network.

The two most popular options for external AAA are RADIUS and TACACS+.

RADIUS

Remote Authentication Dial-In User Service (*RADIUS*) was developed by the Internet Engineering Task Force—the IETF. It's basically a security system that works to guard the network against unauthorized access. RADIUS, which uses only UDP, is an open standard implemented by most major vendors. It's one of the most popular types of security servers around because it combines authentication and authorization services into a single process. So, after users are authenticated, they are then authorized for network services.

RADIUS implements a client/server architecture, where the typical client is a router, switch, or AP, and the typical server: a Windows or Unix device that's running RADIUS software.

The authentication process has three distinct stages:

- First, the user is prompted for a username and password.
- Second, the username and encrypted password are sent over the network to the RADIUS server.
- And finally, the RADIUS server replies with one of the following:

Response	Meaning
Accept	The user has been successfully authenticated.
Reject	The username and password are not valid.
Challenge	The RADIUS server requests additional information.
Change Password	The user should select a new password.

It's important to remember that RADIUS encrypts only the password in the access-request packet from the client to the server. The remainder of the packet is unencrypted.

Configuring RADIUS

To configure a RADIUS server for console and VTY access, you first need to enable AAA services so you can configure all the AAA commands. Configure the **aaa new-model** command in global configuration mode:

```
Router(config)# aaa new-model
```

The **aaa new-model** command immediately applies local authentication to all lines and interfaces—except `line con 0`. So, to avoid being locked out of the router or switch, you should define a local username and password before starting the AAA configuration.

Now, configure a local user:

```
Router(config)#username Todd password Lammle
```

Creating this user is super important because you can use this same locally created user to gain access if the external authentication server fails! If you don't do this and you can't get to the server, you're going to end up doing a password recovery.

Next, configure a RADIUS server of any name and the RADIUS key that is configured on the server:

```
Router(config)#radius server SecureLogin
Router(config-radius-server)#address ipv4 10.10.10.254
Router(config-radius-server)#key MyRadiusPassword
```

Now, add your newly created RADIUS server to a AAA group of any name:

```
Router(config)#aaa group server radius MyRadiusGroup
Router(config-sg-radius)#server name SecureLogin
```

Finally, configure this newly created group to be used for AAA login authentication. If the RADIUS server fails, the fallback to local authentication should be set:

```
Router(config)# aaa authentication login default group MyRadiusGroup local
```

TACACS+

Terminal Access Controller Access Control System (TACACS+) is also a Cisco proprietary security server that uses TCP. It's really similar in many ways to RADIUS and does all RADIUS does, only more, including multiprotocol support.

TACACS+ was developed by Cisco Systems and was later released as an open standard, so it was originally designed specifically to interact with Cisco's AAA services. If you're using TACACS+, the entire menu of AAA features is available to you, and it handles each security aspect separately, unlike RADIUS:

- Authentication includes messaging support in addition to login and password functions.
- Authorization enables explicit control over user capabilities.
- Accounting supplies detailed information about user activities.

NOTE Understand that authentication and authorization are treated as separate processes.

Configuring TACACS+

This is pretty much identical to the RADIUS configuration.

To configure a TACACS+ server for console and VTY access, first you need to enable AAA services and configure all the AAA commands. Configure the **aaa new-model** command in the global configuration mode if it isn't already enabled:

```
Router(config)# aaa new-model
```

Now, configure a local user if you haven't already:

```
Router(config)#username Todd password Lammle
```

Next, configure a TACACS+ server of any name and the key that is configured on the server:

```
Router(config)#tacacs-server SecureLoginTACACS+
Router(config-radius-server)#address ipv4 10.10.10.254
Router(config-radius-server)#key MyTACACS+Password
```

Add your newly created TACACS+ server to a AAA group of any name:

```
Router(config)#aaa group server tacacs+ MyTACACS+Group
Router(config-sg-radius)#server name SecureLoginTACACS+
```

Finally, configure this newly created group to be used for AAA login authentication. If the TACACS+ server fails, the fallback to local authentication should be set:

```
Router(config)# aaa authentication login default group MyTACACS+Group local
```

Managing User Accounts

A whole bunch of authentication schemes are used today, and although it's important to know about them and how they work, all that knowledge doesn't equal power if your network's users aren't schooled on how to manage their account names and passwords correctly.

Clearly, if the wrong people get their hands on usernames and passwords, they've got a way to get into your network. Worse, if a hacker gains the administrator account name and password for your network, it doesn't matter what authentication protocol or server you're using. That hacker is going to get in with the escalated rights that type of account allows and can do some serious damage!

So, let's look at some solid ways to manage user accounts and passwords and follow that up by talking about the key authentication methods in use today.

Usernames and passwords are vital to network security because their whole purpose is to control initial access to a device. Even if the system administrator assigns individuals their usernames and passwords, users can and often do change them, so you need to make sure your network's users know the difference between a good password and a bad one and how to keep their passwords safe from theft.

Your first step in managing access to network resources is through user accounts and the rights you assign to the network resources. System administrators usually maintain user accounts on a daily basis, doing things like renaming account groups and setting the number of simultaneous connections. You can also designate where users can log in, how often, and when, plus adjust how often their passwords and accounts expire.

Disabling Accounts

This is important—when a user leaves the organization, you have these three options:

- Leave the account in place.
- Delete the account.
- Disable the account.

The first option isn't so good because if you just leave the account in place, anyone (including the user to whom it belonged) can still log in as that user if they know the password. But deleting the account presents its own set of problems because if you delete an account and then create a new one, the numeric ID associated with that user (UID in Unix, SID in Windows Server) will be lost. It's through this magic number that passwords and rights to network resources are associated with the user account. This can be good, but if you create a new user account with the same name as the one you deleted, the identification number of the new account will be different from the old one, so all of its settings will be removed for the new account.

This leaves you with disabling an account until you've made a decision about what should happen to it. It's really your best bet because you'll probably just want to rename the account when someone new is hired. When you disable an account, it still exists, but no one can use it to log in. Another good time to disable an account is when someone will be gone for an extended period when taking a leave, going on sabbatical, or even an extended vacation.

Another scenario that's fairly common is if a company employs contract and temporary employees. These people will need temporary accounts that are used for only a short time and then disabled. So, knowing how to manage them is important! If you know it in advance, just set the employee's account to expire on their expected last day of work.

Setting Up Anonymous Accounts

Anonymous accounts allow only extremely limited access for a large number of users who all log in with the same username—for instance, *anonymous* or *guest*. These logins are frequently used to access public Wi-Fi service and FTP files—access is gained when you log in with the username *anonymous* and enter your email address as the password.

It's a very bad idea to use anonymous accounts for regular network access because you just can't track them. All Windows Server products from Windows NT onward come with the anonymous account Guest disabled, and it's usually good to leave it that way. When you want to enable that account, like at a public Wi-Fi kiosk, make sure you carefully manage what it's able to access by implementing strict group policies.

Some web servers create an Internet user account to allow anonymous access to the website through which a user is allowed to access the web server over the network. The password is always blank, and you never see a request to log in to the server because it's done automatically. Without this kind of account, no one would be able to access your web pages!

Limiting Connections

It's smart to limit how many times a user can connect to the network. Because they can only be in one place at a time, users should normally be logged in to the network for one instance only. So, if your system is telling you that someone is logged in from more than one place, it's probably because someone else is using their account. By limiting simultaneous connections to one, only a single user at a single workstation can gain access to the network using a specific user account.

There are times when some users need to log in multiple times to use certain applications or perform certain tasks, and you can allow that specific user to have multiple concurrent connections.

Some people limit a particular user to logging in from a specific location from their own workstations. Sounds good, but I wouldn't usually do this because users move around without taking their computers with them and sometimes log in at someone else's machine to get their jobs done or collaborate. So unless you require extra tight security, this rule will just complicate your job because it requires a lot of administration. Windows Server products can limit which station(s) a user is allowed to log in from, but they don't do so by default. A Windows feature that's enabled by default is preventing average users from logging in at the server console. Some serious damage can be done even by accident!

Renaming the Maintenance Account

Network operating systems automatically give the network maintenance (administration) account a default name. On Windows servers, it's Administrator, and for Unix, it's root. Clearly, if you don't change this account name, bad guys already have half the information they need to break into your network. The only thing missing is the password!

So yes, definitely rename that account to something cool and creative that you'll remember but that would be really hard for someone to guess—and don't write it on a Post-it and stick it to the server. Here's a "do not use" list of names:

- Admin
- Administrator
- Analyst
- Audit
- Comptroller
- Controller
- Manager
- Root
- Super
- Superuser
- Supervisor
- Wizard
- Any variation on the above

Security Password Policy Elements

Managing passwords is one of the most important parts of access management. In this section, we'll discuss common considerations and offer some alternatives to simple passwords.

Password Management

One of the strongest ways to keep a system safe is to employ strong passwords and educate your users about the best security practices. In this section, we'll explore various techniques that can enhance the security of your user passwords.

Setting Strong Passwords

Passwords should be as long as possible. Most security experts believe a password of 10 characters is the minimum that should be used if security is a real concern. If you use only the lowercase letters of the alphabet, you have 26 characters with which to work. If you add the numeric values 0 through 9, you'll get another 10 characters. If you go one step further and add the uppercase letters, you'll then have an additional 26 characters, giving you a total of 62 characters with which to construct a password.

> **TIP** Most vendors recommend that you use nonalphabetical characters such as #, $, and % in your password, and some go so far as to require it.

If you used a four-character password, this would be 62 × 62 × 62 × 62 (62^4), or approximately 14 million password possibilities. If you used five characters in your password, this would give you 62 to the fifth power (62^5), or approximately 920 million password possibilities. If you used a 10-character password, this would give you 62 to the tenth power (62^{10}) or 8.4×10^{17} (a very big number) possibilities.

As you can see, these numbers increase exponentially with each character added to the password. The 4-digit password could probably be broken in a fraction of a day, whereas the 10-digit password would take considerably longer and consume much more processing power.

If your password used only the 26 lowercase letters from the alphabet, the 4-digit password would have 26 to the fourth power or 456,000 password combinations. A 5-character password would have 26 to the fifth power, or more than 11 million, and a 10-character password would have 26 to the tenth power, or 1.4×10^{14}. This is still a big number, but it would take considerably less time to break.

NIST now considers password length more important than complexity.

Password Expiration

The longer that a password is used, the more likely it is that it will be compromised in some way. It is for this reason that requiring users to change their passwords at certain intervals increases the security of their passwords. You should require users to set a new password every 30 days (more frequently for higher-security networks), and you must also prevent them from reusing old passwords. Most password management systems have the ability to track previously used passwords and to disallow users from recycling old passwords.

Password Complexity

You can set up many different parameters and standards to force the people in your organization to conform to security practices. In establishing these parameters, it's important that you consider the capabilities of the people who will be working with these policies. If you're working in an environment where people aren't computer savvy, you may spend a lot of time helping them remember and recover passwords. Many organizations have had to reevaluate their security guidelines after they've invested great time and expense to implement high-security systems.

Setting authentication security, especially in supporting users, can become a high-maintenance activity for network administrators. On the one hand, you want people to be able to authenticate themselves easily; on the other hand, you want to establish security that protects your company's resources. In a Windows server domain, password policies can be configured at the domain level using Group Policy objects. Variables you can configure include password complexity, length, and time between allowed changes.

A good password includes both uppercase and lowercase letters as well as numbers and symbols. In the past, an accepted practice was to make passwords complex (using at least three of the four character types: uppercase, lowercase, numbers, and non-numeric figures), but recently, as mentioned previously, NIST has recommended that longer and simpler passwords are more secure than shorter and more complex ones.

Screensaver Required Password

A screensaver should automatically start after a short period of idle time, and that screensaver should require a password before the user can begin the session again. This method of locking the workstation adds one more level of security.

BIOS/UEFI Passwords

Passwords should be configured and required to access either the BIOS or UEFI settings on all devices. If this is not the case, it would be possible for someone to reboot a device, enter the settings, change the boot order, boot to an operating system residing on a USB or optical drive, and use that OS as a platform to access data located on the other drives. Although this is a worst-case scenario, there is also less significant mayhem a malicious person could cause in the BIOS and UEFI.

Requiring Passwords

Make absolutely certain you require passwords (such a simple thing to overlook in a small network) for all accounts, and change the default passwords on system accounts.

Managing Passwords

Like any other aspect of network security, passwords must be managed, and doing that involves ensuring that all passwords for user accounts follow security guidelines so black hats can't easily crack them. You've also got to implement certain features of your network operating system to prevent unauthorized access.

A strong password is some combination of alphanumeric and special characters that's easy for you to remember but really hard for someone else to guess. Like server account names, they should never be written down on anything that is then put into your desk or stuck onto your machines. In a perfect world, everyone is smart and avoids doing those things, but users tend to make things easy by choosing passwords that are also easy to guess. Let's look at some characteristics of strong passwords.

Minimum Length

Strong passwords should be at least 8 characters (the more, the merrier), but they shouldn't be any longer than 15 characters to make them easier to remember. You absolutely must specify a minimum length for passwords because a short password is easily cracked—after all, there are only so many combinations of three characters, right? The upper limit depends on the capabilities of your operating system and the ability of your users to remember complex passwords. Here's what I call "The Weak List" for passwords—never use them!

- The word *password* (not kidding—people actually still do this!)
- Proper names
- Your pet's name
- Your spouse's name
- Your children's names
- Any word in the dictionary
- A license plate number
- Birth dates
- Anniversary dates
- Your username
- The word *server*
- Any text or label on the PC or monitor
- Your company's name
- Your occupation
- Your favorite color
- Any of the above with a leading number
- Any of the above with a trailing number
- Any of the above spelled backward

There are more, but you get the idea!

Real World Scenario

Security Audits

A great way to begin a basic security audit and get a feel for any potential threats to your network is to simply take a walk through the company's halls and offices. I've done this a lot, and it always pays off because invariably, I happen on some new and different way that people are trying to "beat the system" regarding security. This doesn't necessarily indicate that a given user is trying to cause damage on purpose. It's just that following the rules can be inconvenient—especially when it comes to adhering to strict password policies. Your average user just doesn't get how important their role is in maintaining the security of the network (maybe even their job security as well) by sticking to the network's security policy, so you have to make sure they do.

Think about it. If you can easily discover user passwords just by taking a little tour of the premises, so can someone else, and once they have a username and a password, it's pretty easy to hack into resources. I wasn't kidding about people slapping sticky notes with their usernames and/or passwords right on their monitors—this happens a lot more than you would think. Some users, thinking they're actually being really careful, glue them to the back of their keyboards instead, but you don't have to be Sherlock Holmes to think about looking there either, right? People wouldn't think of leaving their cars unlocked with the windows down and the keys in the ignition, but that's exactly what they're doing by leaving sensitive info anywhere on or near their workstations.

Even though it might not make you Mr. or Ms. Popularity when you search workspaces or even inside desks for notes with interesting or odd words written on them, do it anyway. People will try to hide these goodies anywhere. Sometimes, not so much. . . I had a user who actually wrote his password on the border of his monitor with a Sharpie, and when his password expired, he just crossed it off and wrote the new one underneath it. Sheer genius! But my personal favorite was when I glanced at this one guy's keyboard and noticed that some of the letter keys had numbers written on them. All you had to do was follow the numbers that (surprise!) led straight to his password. Oh sure—he'd followed the policy to the, ahem, letter by choosing random letters and numbers, but a lot of good that did—he had to draw himself a little map in plain sight on his keyboard to remember the password.

So, like it or not, you have to walk your beat to find out if users are managing their accounts properly. If you find someone doing things the right way, praise them for it openly. If not, it's time for more training—or, maybe worse, termination.

Using Characters to Make a Strong Password

The good news is that solid passwords don't have to be in ancient Mayan to be hard to crack. They just need to include a combination of numbers, letters, and special characters—that's it. Special characters aren't letters or numbers but symbols like $ % ^ # @). Here's an example of a strong password: tqbf4#jotld. Looks like gibberish, but remember that famous sentence, "The quick brown fox jumped over the lazy dog"? Well, this particular password uses the first letter of each word in that sentence with a 4# thrown in the middle of it. Sweet, solid, and easy to remember! You can do this with favorite quotes, song lyrics, and so on, with a couple of numbers and symbols stuck in the middle. Just make sure you don't actually sing the song every time you log in!

If you want to test the strength of passwords to make sure they're nice and tight, you can use auditing tools like crack programs that try to guess passwords. Clearly, if that program has a really tough time or even fails to crack the password, you have a good one. By the way, don't just use a regular word preceded by or ending with a special character because good crack programs strip off the leading and trailing characters during decryption attempts.

Password-Management Features

All network operating systems include built-in features for managing passwords to help ensure that your system remains secure and that passwords cannot be easily hacked with crack programs. These features usually include automatic account lockouts and password expiration.

Automatic Account Lockouts

Hackers, and even people who forget their passwords, usually try to log in by guessing passwords. This is why most network operating systems will lock you out after a few unsuccessful attempts. Some will even disable the account. Once that happens, the user won't be able to log in to that account even if they enter the correct password. This feature prevents a potential hacker from running an automated script to crack account passwords by continuously attempting to log in using different character combinations.

When an account is on lockdown, guards—I mean, network staff—will have to unlock the account if the network operating system doesn't unlock it after a preset period. In any high-security network, it's a good idea to require an administrator to manually unlock every locked account instead of setting the network operating system to do it automatically. This way, you will be sure to know about any possible security breaches.

WARNING

Be careful not to lock yourself out! With many network operating systems, only administrators can reset passwords, so if you happen to be the administrator and lock yourself out, only another administrator can unlock your account. Embarrassing, yes, but what if you're the only administrator? That's real trouble because even though many network operating system vendors have solutions to this humiliating issue, the cost of those solutions isn't cheap!

TIP

It's good to know that Windows-based servers allow you to configure accounts to be locked out after a number of bad login attempts, yet the default Administrator account is exempt from this happening. This might sound convenient for you, but it's actually a security risk. You should definitely rename this account, and it's also a good idea not to use it for day-to-day administration. Create a new administrator account (with a different name, of course) and use it for management instead.

Password Expiration and Password Histories

Unlike a good wine, even really good passwords don't age well over time; they just become more likely to be cracked. This is why it's good to set passwords so that they expire after a specific amount of time. Most organizations set up passwords to expire every 30 to 45 days, after which the network's users all must reset their passwords either immediately or during a preset grace period. The grace period is usually limited to a specific number of login attempts, or it may allow a couple of days.

TIP By default, each network operating system delimits a specific password-expiration period, and any hacker with skills knows about it. So make sure you reset that time period to something other than the default!

Older network OSs allowed users to reset their passwords back to their original form after using an intermediary password for a while. Today's network OSs prevent this via password histories—a record of the past several passwords used by a specific user, which prevents them from using recent passwords stored in the history. If they try, the password will fail, and the operating system will then request a password change. What this means to you is that if your security policy dictates that passwords be reset every two weeks, you should make sure your password history can hold at least 20 passwords. This prevents a user from reusing a password until the password is at least 10 months old (two changes per month)!

By the way, your more experienced users know about this history feature, and because coming up with a tight password takes a little thought, when savvy users create ones they really like, they may have a hard time letting go. Maybe they just want to avoid the hassle of creating a tight new password and remembering it, so they'll try to find ways to get out of doing that by getting around the password history feature. I knew one guy who actually admitted that he just changed his password as many times as it took to defeat the history log and then changed it one last time to his beloved, original password, which only took him only about five minutes!

You can force users to change their passwords to ones that are unique because the latest operating systems require unique passwords and can, depending on the network operating system, store more than 20 passwords. This feature makes it a whole lot harder to revert to any previous passwords. But it's still possible for users to beat the system by beating the minimum password age setting, so don't rely completely on it.

Single Sign-On

In today's modern enterprises, users sometimes get overwhelmed by the number of points in the network where they're required to identify themselves. Most have to log on to the domain to have network access at all, and there are company websites requiring an authentication process to access databases, SharePoint sites, secured drives, personal folders, and so on.

When users have to remember multiple passwords, as the number increases, they begin to resort to unsafe security practices like writing passwords on sticky notes, hiding passwords in their drawers, and even sharing them with coworkers. All of these practices undermine the security of the network.

Single sign-on (SSO) solves this problem because when the user logs into the domain, the domain controller issues them an access token. This access token contains a list of all the resources, including folders, drives, websites, databases, etc., to which they're permitted access. As a result, anytime the user accesses a resource, the token is verified behind the scenes, shielding users from having to provide multiple passwords!

Local Authentication

Users authenticate to either a domain or to the local machine. When local authentication is performed, the user's local account and password are verified with the local user database. This local user database is called Security Accounts Manager (SAM), and it's located in c:\windows\system32\config\.

In Linux, the database is a text file, */etc/passwd* (called the *password file*), which lists all valid usernames and their associated information.

LDAP

Microsoft Active Directory is a common user database designed to centralize data management regarding network subjects and objects. A typical directory contains a hierarchy including users, groups, systems, servers, client workstations, and so on. Because the directory service contains data about users and other network entities, it can be used by many applications that require access to that information. A common directory service standard is Lightweight Directory Access Protocol (LDAP), which is based on the earlier standard X.500.

X.500 uses Directory Access Protocol (DAP). In X.500, the distinguished name (DN) provides the full path in the X.500 database where the entry is found. The relative distinguished name (RDN) in X.500 is an entry's name without the full path.

LDAP is simpler than X.500. LDAP supports DN and RDN, but it includes more attributes, such as the common name (CN), domain component (DC), and organizational unit (OU) attributes. Using a client/server architecture, LDAP uses TCP port 389 to communicate. If advanced security is needed, LDAP over SSL communicates via TCP port 636.

Password Alternatives

Passwords are considered the lowest form of authentication but can be effective when combined with other methods. Let's look at some of these.

Certificates

Instead of clunky usernames and passwords, we'll use certificates as a key to unlock the door.

A digital *certificate* provides an entity, usually a user, with the credentials to prove its identity and associates that identity with a public key. At a minimum, a digital certification must provide the serial number, the issuer, the subject (owner), and the public key.

A certificate is a text document that ties a user account to a public and private key pair created by a certificate server or certificate authority (CA).

An X.509 certificate contains the following fields:

- Version
- Serial Number
- Algorithm ID
- Issuer

- Validity
- Subject
- Subject Public Key Info
- Public Key Algorithm
- Subject Public Key
- Issuer Unique Identifier (optional)
- Subject Unique Identifier (optional)
- Extensions (optional)

VeriSign first introduced the following digital certificate classes:

- Class 1: For individuals; intended for e-mail. These certificates get saved by web browsers.
- Class 2: For organizations that must provide proof of identity.
- Class 3: For servers and software signing in when independent verification and identity and authority checking are done by the issuing CA.

Multifactor Authentication

Multifactor authentication is designed to add an additional level of security to the authentication process by verifying more than one characteristic of a user before allowing access to a resource. Users can be identified in one of three ways:

- By something they know (password)
- By something they are (retinas, fingerprint, facial recognition)
- By something they possess (smart card)
- By somewhere they are (location)
- By something they do (behavior)

Two-factor authentication is when two of these factors are being tested, whereas multifactor is when more than two of these factors are being tested. An example of two-factor authentication would be requiring both a smart card and a PIN to log onto the network. The possession of either by itself would not be sufficient to authenticate. This protects against the loss and theft of the card as well as the loss of the password. An example of multifactor would be when three items are required, such as a smart card, a PIN, and a fingerprint scan.

This process can get as involved as the security requires. In an extremely high-security situation, you might require a smart card, a password, a retina scan, and a fingerprint scan. The trade-off to all the increased security is an inconvenient authentication process for the user and the high cost of biometric authentication devices.

Biometrics

For high-security scenarios that warrant the additional cost and administrative effort involved, biometrics is a viable option. Biometric devices use physical characteristics to identify the user. Such devices are becoming more common in the business environment. Biometric systems include hand scanners, retinal scanners, and soon, possibly, DNA scanners.

To gain access to resources, you must pass a physical screening process. In the case of a hand scanner, this may include identifying fingerprints, scars, and markings on your hand. Retinal scanners compare your eye's retinal pattern, which is as unique as fingerprints, to a stored retinal pattern to verify your identity. DNA scanners will examine a unique portion of your DNA structure to verify that you are who you say you are.

With the passing of time, the definition of *biometrics* is expanding from simply identifying physical attributes about a person to being able to describe patterns in their behavior. Recent advances have been made in the ability to authenticate someone based on the key pattern they use when entering their password (how long they pause between each key, the amount of time each key is held down, and so forth). A company adopting biometric technologies needs to consider the controversy they may face (some authentication methods are considered more intrusive than others). It also needs to consider the error rate and that errors can include both false positives and false negatives.

User-Authentication Methods

There are a number of authentication systems in use today, but I'm going to focus on the ones you're likely to be confronted with in the objectives.

Public Key Infrastructure (PKI)

Public Key Infrastructure (PKI) is a system that links users to public keys and verifies a user's identity by using a *certificate authority (CA)*. Think of a CA as an online notary public—an organization that's responsible for validating user IDs and issuing unique identifiers to confirmed individuals to certify that their identity can really be trusted. Figure 7.7 shows how the CA process works in relation to two users.

FIGURE 7.7 The certificate authority process

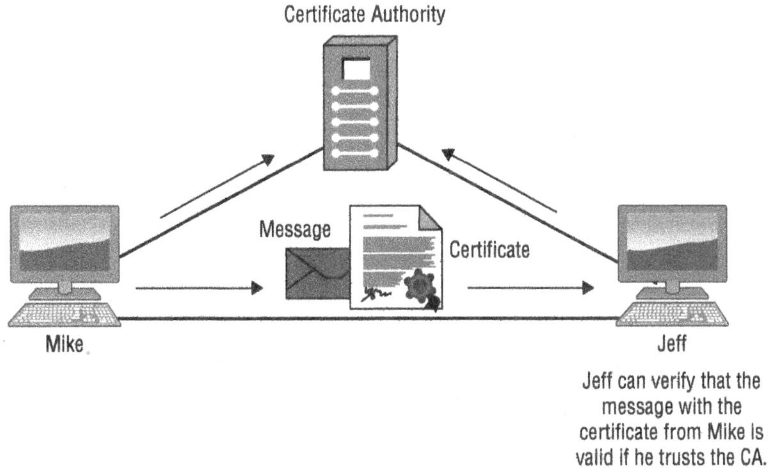
Certificate Authority
Message
Certificate
Mike
Jeff
Jeff can verify that the message with the certificate from Mike is valid if he trusts the CA.

PKI allows people to communicate with each other with the confidence that they're talking to whom they think they are talking to. It's used to establish confidentiality and to ensure message integrity without knowing anything about the other party prior to the conversation. It's also used to verify the digital signature of a private key's owner.

Public-key encryption operates through asymmetric cryptography, meaning that a different key is used to encrypt and decrypt the message, respectively. Symmetric cryptography uses the same key to encrypt and decrypt, so it's a lot less secure. Here's how it works: if I sent you a message using PKI, I'd use your public key to encrypt the message. When you received the message, you would use your private key, which is theoretically the only thing that can be used to decrypt the message back into something readable by humans. If a digital signature was required, you would use a hash algorithm to generate a message digest of the message and then encrypt the hash with your private key; anyone with access to your public key would be able to verify that only you could have encrypted the hash, and then the hash could be used to verify the integrity of the message itself. So clearly, you should be the only one who has access to your private key.

Figure 7.8 illustrates what I just described.

FIGURE 7.8 PKI encryption process in action

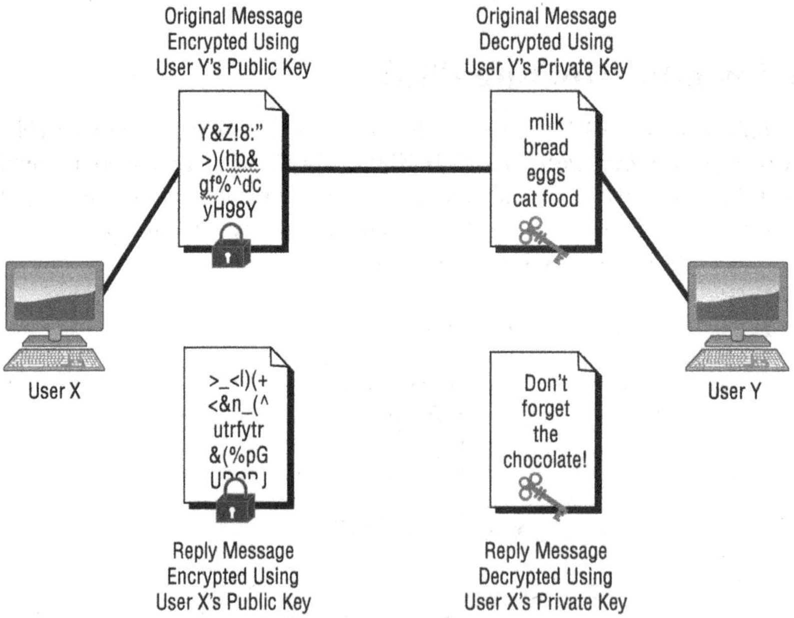

This type of authentication is often hidden in the background of websites that perform transactions. You've probably experienced shopping online and having an error message pop up notifying you that a certain site's certificate or key has expired and asking if you want to proceed with the transaction. If you do, it's time to rethink things—you're probably way too trusting. Just say no!

Kerberos

Kerberos, created at MIT, isn't just a protocol; it's an entire security system that establishes a user's identity when they first log on to a system running it. It employs strong encryptions for all transactions and communication, and it's readily available. The source code for Kerberos can be freely downloaded from many places on the Internet.

Figure 7.9 shows the five steps that Kerberos uses to authenticate a user.

FIGURE 7.9 The Kerberos authentication process

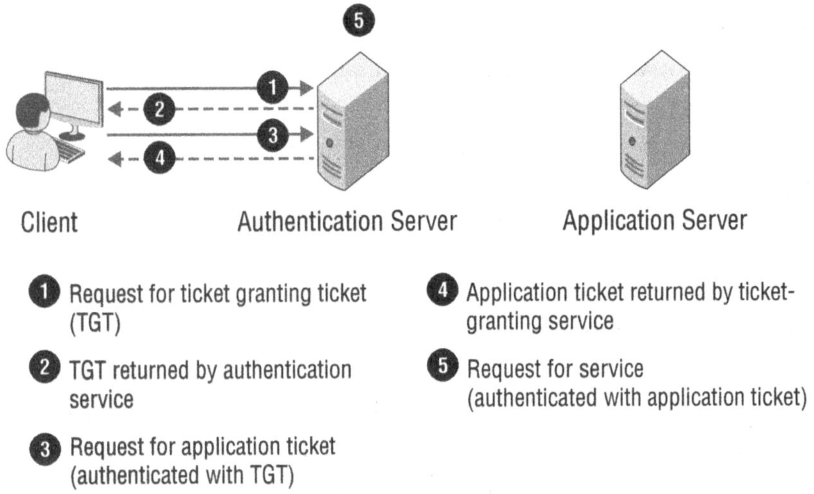
5
1
2
3
4
Client
Authentication Server
Application Server
1 Request for ticket granting ticket (TGT)
2 TGT returned by authentication service
3 Request for application ticket (authenticated with TGT)
4 Application ticket returned by ticket-granting service
5 Request for service (authenticated with application ticket)

Kerberos works by issuing tickets to users who log in, kind of like going to an amusement park—as long as you have your ticket to ride, you're good to go. Even though the tickets expire quickly, they're automatically refreshed as long as you remain logged in. Because of this refresh feature, all systems participating in a Kerberos domain must have synchronized clocks. This synchronicity is a bit complicated to set up, although in Microsoft servers and domains, the process is automatic, requiring only access to a recognized time server (which Microsoft also operates). The real negative hits come if you have only one Kerberos authentication server—if it goes down, no one can log in to the network!

So, when running Kerberos, having redundant servers is vital. You should also know that because all users' secret keys are stored in one centralized database, if that's compromised, you have a security tsunami on your hands. Luckily, these keys are stored in an encrypted state.

Setting Passwords

There are five passwords you'll need to secure your Cisco routers: console, auxiliary, telnet (VTY), enable password, and enable secret. The enable secret and enable password are the ones used to set the password for securing privileged mode. Once the `enable` commands are set, users will be prompted for a password when entering privileged mode.

The other three are used to configure a password when user mode is accessed through the console port, through the auxiliary port, or via Telnet.

The most common form of router authentication is line authentication, also called *character-mode access*. It uses different passwords to authenticate users depending on the line the user is connecting through.

Let's start by configuring a Cisco device with the enable password.

Enable Passwords

You set the enable passwords from global configuration mode like this:

```
Todd(config)#enable ?
last-resort Define enable action if no TACACS servers
respond
password Assign the privileged level password
secret Assign the privileged level secret
use-tacacs Use TACACS to check enable passwords
```

The following list describes the enable password parameters:

`last-resort` This allows you to still enter the device if you set up authentication through a TACACS server and it's not available. It won't be used if the TACACS server is working.

`password` This sets the enable password on older, pre-10.3 systems and isn't ever used if an enable secret is set.

`secret` The newer, encrypted password that overrides the enable password if it has been set.

`use-tacacs` This tells the router or switch to authenticate through a TACACS server. It comes in really handy when you have lots of routers because changing the password on a multitude of them can be insanely tedious. It's much easier to simply go through the TACACS server and change the password only once!

Here's an example that shows how to set the enable passwords:

```
Todd(config)#enable secret todd
Todd(config)#enable password todd
The enable password you have chosen is the same as your
enable secret. This is not recommended. Re-enter the
enable password.
```

If you try to set the enable secret and enable passwords the same, the device will give you a polite warning to change the second password. Make a note to yourself that if there aren't any old legacy routers involved, you don't even bother to use the enable password!

User-mode passwords are assigned via the line command like this:

```
Todd(config)#line ?
<0-16> First Line number
console Primary terminal line
vty Virtual terminal
```

And these three lines are especially important for the exam objectives:

console Sets a console user-mode password.

vty Sets a Telnet password on the device. If this password isn't set, then by default, Telnet can't be used.

Aux Sets a password on the Aux line, used for modem connections.

To configure user-mode passwords, choose the line you want and configure it using the `login` command to make the switch prompt for authentication. Let's focus on the configuration of individual lines now.

Console Password

We set the console password with the `line console 0` command, but look at what happened when I tried to type **line console ?** from the `(config-line)#` prompt—I received an error! Here's the example:

```
Todd(config-line)#line console ?
% Unrecognized command
Todd(config-line)#exit
Todd(config)#line console ?
<0-0> First Line number
Todd(config)#line console 0
Todd(config-line)#password console
Todd(config-line)#login
```

You can still type **line console 0** and that will be accepted, but the help screens just don't work from that prompt. Type **exit** to go back one level, and you'll find that your help screens now work. This is a "feature." Really.

Because there's only one console port, I can only choose line console 0. You can set all your line passwords to the same password, but doing this isn't exactly a brilliant security move!

And it's also important to remember to apply the `login` command, or the console port won't prompt for authentication. The way Cisco has this process set up means you can't set the `login` command before a password is set on a line because if you set it but don't then set a password, that line won't be usable. You'll actually get prompted for a password that doesn't exist, so Cisco's method isn't just a hassle; it makes sense and is a feature, after all!

> **NOTE** Definitely remember that although Cisco has this "password feature" on its routers starting with IOS 12.2 and above, it's not included in older IOSs.

Okay, there are a few other important commands you need to know regarding the console port.

For one, the `exec-timeout 0 0` command sets the time-out for the console EXEC session to zero, ensuring that it never times out. The default time-out is 10 minutes.

> **TIP** If you're feeling mischievous, try this on people at work: set the `exec-timeout` command to 0 1. This will make the console time out in 1 second, and to fix it, you have to continually press the down arrow key while changing the time-out time with your free hand!

`Logging synchronous` is such a cool command that it should be a default, but it's not. It's great because it's the antidote for those annoying console messages that disrupt the input you're trying to type. The messages will still pop up, but at least you get returned to your device prompt without your input being interrupted! This makes your input messages oh-so-much easier to read.

Here's an example of how to configure both commands:

```
Todd(config-line)#line con 0
Todd(config-line)#exec-timeout ?
<0-35791> Timeout in minutes
Todd(config-line)#exec-timeout 0 ?
<0-2147483> Timeout in seconds
<cr>
Todd(config-line)#exec-timeout 0 0
Todd(config-line)#logging synchronous
```

> **NOTE** You can set the console to go from never timing out (0 0) to timing out in 35,791 minutes and 2,147,483 seconds. Remember, the default is 10 minutes.

Telnet Password

It's hard to believe, but as I've mentioned before, a lot of my customers still use Telnet, even though I try hard to get them to move to SSH. Jump back to Chapter 12 real quick if you need to review the SSH configuration.

> **NOTE** Most people would not use Telnet in production, or so you'd think. I see a lot of customers who still use Telnet when they should be using SSH. Why do they still use Telnet? Because it's easy. . . Same reason I use it on my own private labs.

To set the user-mode password for Telnet access into the router or switch, use the line vty command. IOS switches typically have 16 lines, but routers running the Enterprise edition have considerably more. The best way to find out how many lines you have is to use that handy question mark like this:

```
Todd(config-line)#line vty 0 ?
% Unrecognized command
Todd(config-line)#exit
Todd(config)#line vty 0 ?
<1-15> Last Line number
<cr>
Todd(config)#line vty 0 15
Todd(config-line)#password telnet
Todd(config-line)#login
```

This output clearly shows that you cannot get help from your `(config-line)#` prompt. You must go back to global config mode to use the question mark (?).

As a reminder, to enable SSH, use the following command under your lines:

```
Todd(config)#line vty 0 15
Todd(config-line)#transport input ssh
```

This effectively disables Telnet and enables only SSH on your device.

So, what will happen if you try to telnet into a device that doesn't have a VTY password set? You'll receive an error saying the connection has been refused because the password isn't set. Suppose you telnet into a switch and receive a message like this one that I got from Switch B:

```
Todd#telnet SwitchB
Trying SwitchB (10.0.0.1)...Open
Password required, but none set
[Connection to SwitchB closed by foreign host]
Todd#
```

This means the switch doesn't have the VTY password set. But you can still get around this and tell the switch to allow Telnet connections without a password by using the no `login` command:

```
SwitchB(config-line)#line vty 0 15
SwitchB(config-line)#no login
```

WARNING

I definitely do not recommend using the `no login` command to allow Telnet connections without a password unless you're in a testing or classroom environment. In a production network, always set your VTY password!

After your IOS devices are configured with an IP address, you can use the Telnet program to configure and check your routers instead of having to use a console cable. You can use the Telnet program by typing `telnet` from any command prompt (DOS or Cisco).

Auxiliary Password

To configure the auxiliary password on a router, go into global configuration mode and type **`line aux ?`**. And by the way, you won't find these ports on a switch. This output shows that you only get a choice of 0–0, which is because there's only one port:

```
Todd#config t
Todd(config)#line aux ?
<0-0> First Line number
Todd(config)#line aux 0
Todd(config-line)#login
% Login disabled on line 1, until 'password' is set
Todd(config-line)#password aux
Todd(config-line)#login
```

Encrypting Your Passwords

Because only the enable secret password is encrypted by default, you'll need to manually configure the user-mode and enable passwords for encryption.

Notice that you can see all the passwords except the enable secret when performing a `show running-config` on a switch:

```
Todd#sh running-config
Building configuration...
Current configuration : 1020 bytes
!
! Last configuration change at 00:03:11 UTC Mon Mar 1 1993
!
version 15.0
no service pad
service timestamps debug datetime msec
service timestamps log datetime msec
no service password-encryption
!
hostname Todd
!
enable secret 4 ykw.3/tgsOuy9.6qmgG/EeYOYgBvfX4v.S8UNA9Rddg
enable password todd
!
[output cut]
!
```

```
line con 0
password console
login
line vty 0 4
password telnet
login
line vty 5 15
password telnet
login
!
end
```

To manually encrypt your passwords, use the `service password-encryption` command. Here's how:

```
Todd#config t
Todd(config)#service password-encryption
Todd(config)#exit
Todd#show run
Building configuration...
!
!
enable secret 4 ykw.3/tgsOuy9.6qmgG/EeYOYgBvfX4v.S8UNA9Rddg
enable password 7 1506040800
!
[output cut]
!
!
line con 0
password 7 050809013243420C
login
line vty 0 4
password 7 06120A2D424B1D
login
line vty 5 15
password 7 06120A2D424B1D
login
!
end
Todd#config t
Todd(config)#no service password-encryption
Todd(config)#^Z
Todd#
```

Nicely done—the passwords will now be encrypted. All you need to do is encrypt the passwords, perform a `show run`, and then turn off the command if you want. This output clearly shows us that the enable password and the line passwords are all encrypted.

Before we finish this chapter, I want to stress some points about password encryption. As I said, if you set your passwords and then turn on the service password-encryption command, you have to perform a `show running-config` before you turn off the encryption service, or your passwords won't be encrypted.

However, you don't have to turn off the encryption service at all—you'd only do that if your switch is running low on processes. And if you turn on the service before you set your passwords, then you don't even have to view them to have them encrypted.

Summary

This chapter started by covering understanding the security program elements. I then covered authentication, authorization, and accounting, or AAA services, which is a technology that gives us substantial control over users and what they're permitted to do inside of our networks.

In this chapter, I also covered user accounts, password security, and user authentication methods, and I finished by showing how to set passwords on your Cisco devices.

Exam Essentials

Know which attacks can occur because of TCP/IP's weakness. There are many attacks that can occur because of TCP/IP's inherent weaknesses. The most important to remember are spoofing, man-in-the-middle, and session replaying.

Understand security program elements. The three security program elements are user awareness, training, and physical security.

Remember the security password policy elements. Password management is important, and that goes without saying, but you may set strong passwords and have expirations, complexity, screen saver passwords, and BIOS passwords.

Practice setting Cisco passwords. On your Cisco devices, practice setting your console, Telnet, AUX, and enable secret passwords as shown in the chapter.

Understand how to mitigate threats at the Access layer. You can mitigate threats at the Access layer by using port security, DHCP snooping, dynamic ARP inspection, and identify-based networking.

Understand TACACS+ and RADIUS. TACACS+ is Cisco proprietary, uses TCP, and can separate services. RADIUS is an open standard, uses UDP, and cannot separate services.

Understand PKI. *Public Key Infrastructure (PKI)* is a system that links users to public keys and verifies a user's identity by using a *certificate authority (CA)*.

Understand Kerberos. *Kerberos*, created at MIT, isn't just a protocol; it's an entire security system that establishes a user's identity when they first log on to a system that's running it.

Written Lab

The answers to this lab can be found in Appendix A, "Answers to the Written Labs."

Write the answers to the following questions:

1. AAA stands for?
2. How do AAA operations compare regarding user identification, user services, and access control?
3. An organization secures its network with multifactor authentication using an authenticator app on employee smartphones. How is the application secured in the case of a user's smartphone being lost or stolen?
4. Which type of attack can be mitigated by dynamic ARP inspection?
5. Which security program element involves installing badge readers on data-center doors to allow workers to enter and exit based on their job roles?

Review Questions

NOTE The following questions are designed to test your understanding of this chapter's material. For more information on how to get additional questions, please see this book's introduction.

The answers to these questions can be found in Appendix B, "Answers to the Review Questions."

1. Which of the following commands will enable AAA on a router?
   - A. aaa enable
   - B. enable aaa
   - C. new-model aaa
   - D. aaa new-model
2. Which of the following will mitigate Access layer threats? (Choose two.)
   - A. Port security
   - B. Access lists
   - C. Dynamic ARP inspection
   - D. AAA
3. Which of the following is not true about DHCP snooping?
   - A. Validates DHCP messages received from untrusted sources and filters out invalid messages.
   - B. Builds and maintains the DHCP snooping binding database, which contains information about trusted hosts with leased IP addresses.
   - C. Rate-limits DHCP traffic from trusted and untrusted sources.
   - D. DHCP snooping is a layer 2 security feature that acts like a firewall between hosts.
4. Which of the following are true about TACACS+? (Choose two.)
   - A. TACACS+ is a Cisco proprietary security mechanism.
   - B. TACACS+ uses UDP.
   - C. TACACS+ combines authentication and authorization services as a single process—after users are authenticated, they are also authorized.
   - D. TACACS+ offers multiprotocol support.
5. Which of the following is not true about RADIUS?
   - A. RADIUS is an open standard protocol.
   - B. RADIUS separates AAA services.
   - C. RADIUS uses UDP.
   - D. RADIUS encrypts only the password in the access-request packet from the client to the server. The remainder of the packet is unencrypted.

6. You want to configure RADIUS so your network devices have external authentication, but you also need to make sure you can fall back to local authentication. Which command will you use?

   A. `aaa authentication login local group MyRadiusGroup`

   B. `aaa authentication login group MyRadiusGroup fallback local`

   C. `aaa authentication login default group MyRadiusGroup external local`

   D. `aaa authentication login default group MyRadiusGroup local`

7. Which is true about DAI?

   A. It must use TCP, BootP, and DHCP snooping to work.

   B. DHCP snooping is required to build the MAC-to-IP bindings for DAI validation.

   C. DAI is required to build the MAC-to-IP mapping that protects against man-in-the-middle attacks.

   D. DAI tracks ICMP-to-MAC bindings from DHCP

8. The IEEE 802.1x standard allows you to implement identity-based networking on wired and wireless hosts by using client-server access control. There are three roles. Which of the following are these? (Choose three.)

   A. Client

   B. Forwarder

   C. Security access control

   D. Authenticator

   E. Authentication server

9. Which of the following is *not* a password alternative?

   A. Multifactor authentication (MFA)

   B. Malware lookups

   C. Biometrics

   D. Certificates

10. Security awareness is *not* defined by which of the following?

    A. Smart card

    B. User awareness

    C. Training

    D. Physical security

11. Which of the following are examples of TCP/IP weaknesses? (Choose three.)

    A. Trojan horse

    B. HTML attack

    C. Session replaying

    D. Application-layer attack

    E. SNMP

    F. SMTP

12. Which Cisco IOS feature would you use to protect the TCP server from TCP SYN-flooding attacks?
    A. Rerouting
    B. TCP intercept
    C. Access control lists
    D. Encryption

13. Which of the following can be used to counter an unauthorized access attempt? (Choose three.)
    A. Encrypted data
    B. Cisco Lock and Key
    C. Access lists
    D. PAP
    E. CHAP
    F. IKE
    G. TACACS

14. Which one of the following threats is an example of snooping and network sniffing?
    A. Repudiation
    B. Masquerade threats
    C. Eavesdropping
    D. DoS

15. In a masquerade attack, what does an attacker steal when pretending to come from a trusted host?
    A. Account identification
    B. User group
    C. IP address
    D. CHAP password

16. What is the primary difference between AAA authentication and authorization?
    A. Authentication identifies and verifies a user attempting to access a system, and authorization controls the tasks the user can perform.
    B. Authentication controls the system processes a user can access, and authorization logs the activities the user initiates.
    C. Authentication verifies a username and password, and authorization handles the communication between the authentication agent and the user database.
    D. Authentication identifies a user who is attempting to access a system, and authorization validates the user's password.

17. Which set of actions satisfy the requirement for multifactor authentication?
    - **A.** The user enters a username and password and then re-enters the credentials on a second screen.
    - **B.** The user swipes a key fob and then clicks through an email link.
    - **C.** The user enters a username and password and then clicks a notification in an authentication app on a mobile device.
    - **D.** The user enters a PIN into an RSA token and then enters the displayed RSA key on a login screen.

18. In which ways does a password manager reduce the chance of a hacker stealing a user's password? (Choose two.)
    - **A.** It automatically provides a second authentication factor that is unknown to the original user.
    - **B.** It uses an internal firewall to protect the password repository from unauthorized access.
    - **C.** It protects against keystroke logging on a compromised device or website.
    - **D.** It stores the password repository on the local workstation with built-in antivirus and anti-malware functionality.
    - **E.** It encourages users to create stronger passwords.

19. An organization secures its network with multifactor authentication using an authenticator app on employee smartphones. How is the application secured in the case of a user's smartphone being lost or stolen?
    - **A.** The application requires the user to enter a PIN before it provides the second factor.
    - **B.** The application challenges a user by requiring an administrator password to reactivate when the smartphone is rebooted.
    - **C.** The application requires an administrator password to reactivate after a configured interval.
    - **D.** The application verifies that the user is in a specific location before it provides the second factor.

20. Which security program element involves installing badge readers on data-center doors to allow workers to enter and exit based on their job roles?
    - **A.** Role-based access control
    - **B.** Biometrics
    - **C.** Multifactor authentication
    - **D.** Physical access control

Chapter 8

First-Hop Redundancy Protocol (FHRP)

THE FOLLOWING CCNA EXAM TOPIC IS COVERED IN THIS CHAPTER:

✓ **3.0 IP Connectivity**

3.5 Describe the purpose of first-hop redundancy protocol

You're about to learn how to build redundancy and load-balancing features into your network elegantly with routers that you might even have already. You really don't need to buy some overpriced load-balancing device when you know how to configure and use Hot Standby Router Protocol (HSRP).

I'm going to get started by telling you the reasons why we need a layer 3 redundancy protocol.

NOTE: To find your included bonus material, as well as Todd Lammle videos, practice questions, and hands-on labs, please see `www.lammle.com/ccna`.

Client Redundancy Issues

How could it be possible to configure a client to send data off its local link when its default gateway router has gone down? It usually isn't because most host operating systems don't allow you to change data routing. Sure, if a host's default gateway router goes down, the rest of the network will still converge, but it won't share that information with the hosts!

Take a look at Figure 8.1 to see what I am talking about.

There are actually two routers available to forward data for the local subnet, but the hosts only know about one of them. They learn about this router when you provide them with the default gateway either statically or through DHCP.

But is there another way to use the second active router? The answer is a bit complicated, so bear with me. There is a feature that's enabled by default on Cisco routers called Proxy Address Resolution Protocol (Proxy ARP). Proxy ARP enables hosts, which have no knowledge of routing options to obtain the MAC address of a gateway router that can forward packets for them.

You can see how this happens in Figure 8.2. If a Proxy ARP–enabled router receives an ARP request for an IP address that it knows isn't on the same subnet as the requesting host, it will respond with an ARP reply packet to the host.

FIGURE 8.1 Default gateway

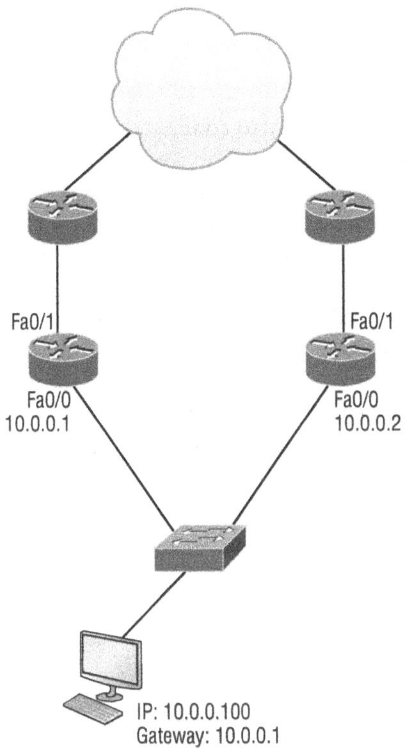

FIGURE 8.2 Proxy ARP

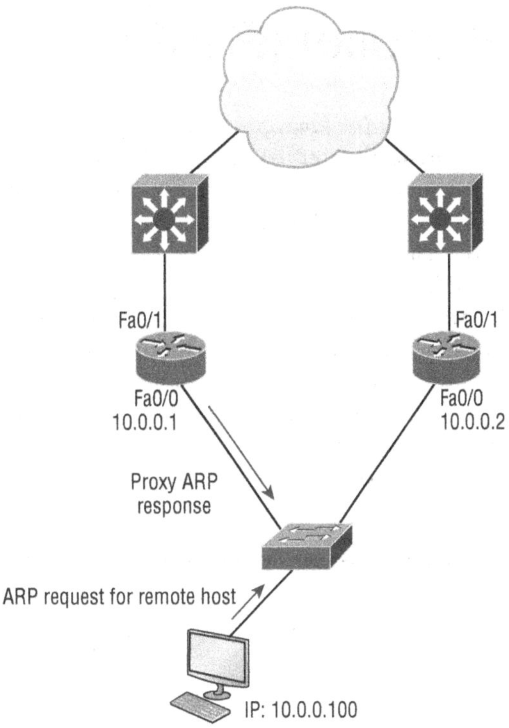

The router will give its own local MAC address—the MAC address of its interface on the host's subnet—as the destination MAC address for the IP address that the host is seeking to be resolved. After receiving the destination MAC address, the host will send all the packets to the router, not knowing that what it thinks is the destination host is really a router. The router will then forward the packets toward the intended host.

So with Proxy ARP, the host device sends traffic as if the destination device were located on its own network segment. If the router that responded to the ARP request fails, the source host continues to send packets for that destination to the same MAC address. But because they're being sent to a failed router, the packets will be sent to the other router that is also responding to ARP requests for remote hosts.

After the time-out period on the host, the proxy ARP MAC address ages out of the ARP cache. The host can then make a new ARP request for the destination and get the address of another proxy ARP router. Keep in mind that the host cannot send packets off of its subnet during the failover time. This isn't exactly ideal, so there's got to be a better way, right? There is! Our solution is found through the use of redundancy protocols.

Introducing First-Hop Redundancy Protocol (FHRP)

First-hop redundancy protocols (FHRPs) work by giving you a way to configure more than one physical router to appear as if they were only a single logical one. This makes client configuration and communication easier because you can simply configure a single default gateway, and the host machine can use its standard protocols to communicate. *First hop* is a reference to the default router being the first router, or first router hop, that a packet will pass through.

So, how does a redundancy protocol get this done? Basically by presenting a virtual router to all of the clients. The virtual router has its own IP and MAC addresses. The virtual IP address is the address that's configured on each of the host machines as the default gateway. The virtual MAC address is the address that will be returned when an ARP request is sent by a host. The hosts don't know or care which physical router is actually forwarding the traffic, as you can see in Figure 8.3.

FIGURE 8.3 FHRPs use a virtual router with a virtual IP address and virtual MAC address.

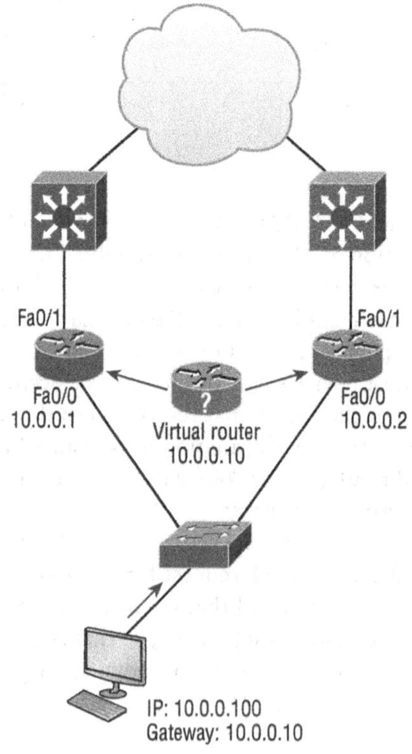

It's the responsibility of the redundancy protocol to decide which physical router will actively forward traffic and which one will be placed on standby in case the active router fails. Even if the active router fails, the transition to the standby router will be transparent to the hosts because the virtual router that's identified by the virtual IP and MAC addresses is now used by the standby router. The hosts never change default gateway information, so traffic keeps flowing.

NOTE Fault-tolerant solutions ensure continued operation in the event of a device failure, and load-balancing solutions distribute the workload over multiple devices.

There are three important redundancy protocols, but only one is covered in the CCNA objectives now:

Hot Standby Router Protocol (HSRP) HSRP has to be Cisco's favorite protocol ever! Don't buy just one router; buy up to eight routers to provide the same service and keep seven as backup in case of failure! HSRP is a Cisco proprietary protocol that provides a redundant gateway for hosts on a local subnet. The drawback here is that this isn't a load-balanced solution. HSRP allows you to configure two or more routers into a standby group that shares an IP and MAC address and provides a default gateway. When the IP and MAC addresses are independent of the routers' physical addresses—on a virtual interface and not tied to a specific interface—they can swap control of an address if the current active forwarding router fails. There is actually a way you can sort of achieve load balancing with HSRP: by using multiple VLANs and designating a specific router active for one VLAN and then an alternate router as active for the other VLAN via trunking. This is really just rigging things and still isn't a true load-balancing solution. It's not nearly as solid as what you can achieve using Gateway Load Balancing Protocol!

Virtual Router Redundancy Protocol (VRRP) Also provides a redundant gateway for hosts on a local subnet, but again, not a load-balanced one. It's an open standard protocol that functions almost identically to HSRP, meaning that it allows two or more routers to act as a default gateway, which enables normal operations to continue after a member failure without requiring a change in a host ARP cache. The MAC address used with VRRP as a virtual address is 00-00-5E-00-01-0a.

Gateway Load Balancing Protocol (GLBP) For the life of me, I can't figure out how GLBP isn't a CCNA objective anymore! GLBP doesn't stop at providing us with a redundant gateway; it's a true load-balancing solution for routers. GLBP allows a maximum of four routers in each forwarding group. By default, the active router directs the traffic from hosts to each successive router in the group using a round-robin algorithm. The hosts are directed to send their traffic toward a specific router by being given the MAC address of the next router in line for deployment.

Hot Standby Router Protocol (HSRP)

So again, HSRP is a Cisco proprietary protocol that can be run on most, but not all of Cisco's router and multilayer switch models. It defines a standby group, and each standby group that you define includes the following routers:

- Active router
- Standby router
- Virtual router
- Any other routers that may be attached to the subnet

The problem with HSRP is that with it, only one router is active, and two or more routers just sit there in standby mode and won't be used unless a failure occurs—not very cost-effective or efficient! Although I'm sure Cisco doesn't mind.

Figure 8.4 shows how only one router is used at a time in an HSRP group.

FIGURE 8.4 HSRP active and standby routers

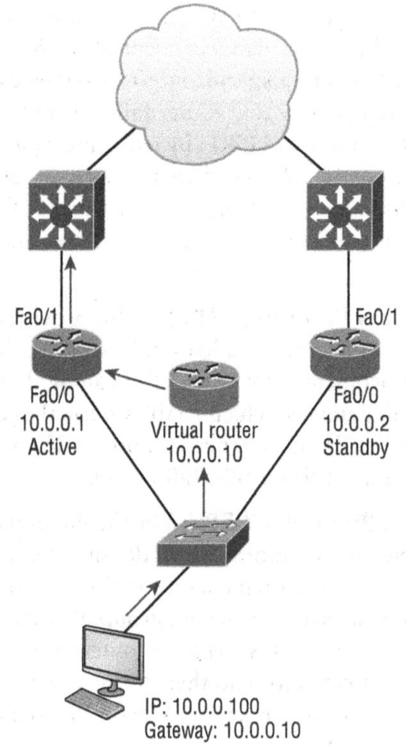

The standby group will always have at least two routers participating in it. The primary players in the group are the one active router and one standby router that communicate with each other using multicast Hello messages. The Hello messages provide all of the required communication for the routers. They contain the information required to accomplish the election, which determines the active and standby router positions. They also hold the key to the failover process. If the standby router stops receiving Hello packets from the active router, it then takes over the active router role, as shown in Figure 8.5.

FIGURE 8.5 Example of HSRP active and standby routers swapping interfaces

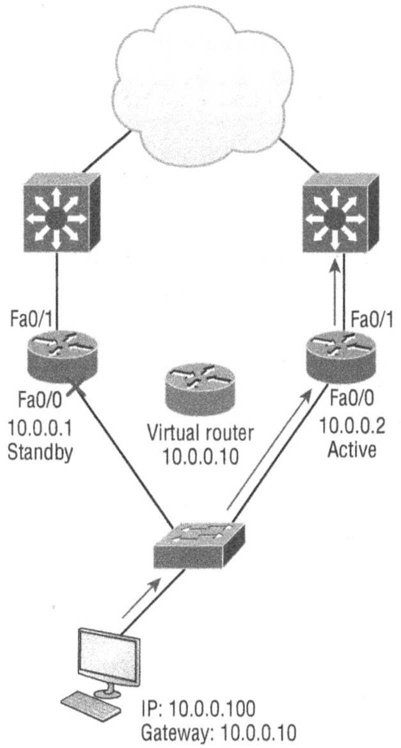

As soon as the active router stops responding to Hellos, the standby router automatically becomes the active router and starts responding to host requests.

> **NOTE** In HSRP version 1, HSRP messages are sent to the multicast IP address 224.0.0.2 and UDP port 1985. HSRP version 2 uses the multicast IP address 224.0.0.102 and UDP port 1985.

Virtual MAC Address

A virtual router in an HSRP group has a virtual IP address and a virtual MAC address. So where does that virtual MAC come from? The virtual IP address isn't that hard to figure out; it just has to be a unique IP address on the same subnet as the hosts defined in the configuration. But MAC addresses are a little different, right? Or are they? The answer is yes—sort of. With HSRP, you create a totally new, made-up MAC address in addition to the IP address.

The HSRP MAC address has only one variable piece in it. The first 24 bits still identify the vendor that manufactured the device (the organizationally unique identifier, or OUI). The next 16 bits in the address tell us that the MAC address is a well-known HSRP MAC address. Finally, the last 8 bits of the address are the hexadecimal representation of the HSRP group number.

Let me clarify all this with a picture of what an HSRP MAC address would look like:

```
0000.0c07.ac0a
```

- The first 24 bits (0000.0c) are the vendor ID of the address; in the case of HSRP being a Cisco protocol, the ID is assigned to Cisco.
- The next 16 bits (07.ac) are the well-known HSRP ID. This part of the address was assigned by Cisco in the protocol, so it's always easy to recognize that this address is for use with HSRP.
- The last 8 bits (0a) are the only variable bits and represent the HSRP group number that you assign. In this case, the group number is 10 and converted to hexadecimal when placed in the MAC address, where it becomes the 0a that you see.

You can see this displayed with every MAC address added to the ARP cache of every router in the HSRP group. There will be the translation from the IP address to the MAC address, as well as the interface it's located on.

HSRP Timers

Before we get deeper into the roles that each of the routers can have in an HSRP group, I want to define the HSRP timers. The timers are very important to HSRP function because they ensure communication between the routers, and if something goes wrong, they allow the standby router to take over. The HSRP timers include *hello*, *hold*, *active*, and *standby*:

Hello timer The hello timer is the defined interval during which each of the routers sends out Hello messages. Their default interval is 3 seconds, and they identify the state that each router is in. This is important because the particular state determines the specific role of each router and, as a result, the actions each will take within the group. Figure 8.6 shows the Hello messages being sent and the router using the hello timer to keep the network flowing in case of a failure.

FIGURE 8.6 HSRP Hellos

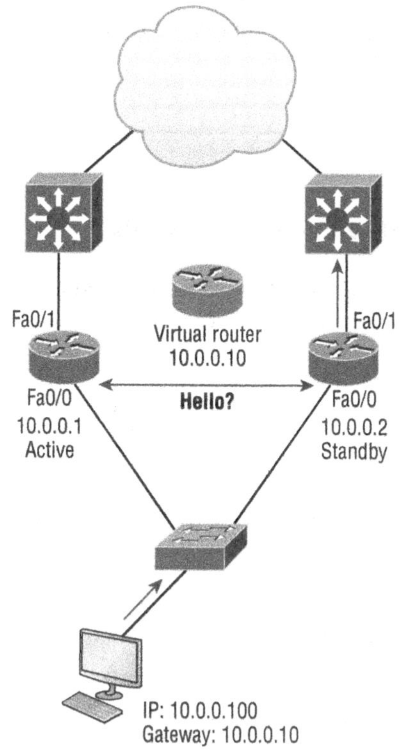

This timer can be changed, but people used to avoid doing so because it was thought that lowering the hello value would place an unnecessary load on the routers. That isn't true with most of the routers today; in fact, you can configure the timers in milliseconds, meaning the failover time can be in milliseconds! Keep in mind that increasing the value will make the standby router wait longer before taking over for the active router when it fails or can't communicate.

Hold timer The hold timer specifies the interval the standby router uses to determine whether the active router is offline or out of communication. By default, the hold timer is 10 seconds, roughly three times the default for the hello timer. If one timer is changed for some reason, I recommend using this multiplier to adjust the other timers, too. By setting the hold timer at three times the hello timer, you ensure that the standby router doesn't take over the active role every time there's a short break in communication.

Active timer The active timer monitors the state of the active router. The timer resets each time a router in the standby group receives a Hello packet from the active router. This timer expires based on the hold time value that's set in the corresponding field of the HSRP hello message.

Standby timer The standby timer is used to monitor the state of the standby router. The timer resets anytime a router in the standby group receives a Hello packet from the standby router and expires based on the hold time value that's set in the respective Hello packet.

Real World Scenario

Large Enterprise Network Outages with FHRPs

Years ago, when HSRP was all the rage and before VRRP and GLBP, enterprises used hundreds of HSRP groups. With the hello timer set to 3 seconds and a hold time of 10 seconds, these timers worked just fine, and we had great redundancy with our core routers.

But now, and certainly in the future, 10 seconds is a lifetime! Some of my customers have started complaining about the failover time and loss of connectivity to their virtual server farm.

So lately, I've been changing the timers to well below the defaults. Cisco changed the timers so you could use sub-second times for failover. Because these are multicast packets, the overhead seen on a current high-speed network is almost nothing.

The hello timer is typically set to 200 msec, and the hold time is 700 msec. The command is as follows:

```
(config-if)#Standby 1 timers msec 200 msec 700
```

This almost ensures that not even a single packet is lost when there's an outage!

Group Roles

Each of the routers in the standby group has a specific function and role to fulfill. The three main roles are virtual router, active router, and standby router. Additional routers can also be included in the group:

Virtual router As its name implies, the virtual router is not a physical entity. It really just defines the role that's held by one of the physical routers. The physical router that communicates as the virtual router is the current active router. The virtual router is nothing more than a separate IP address and MAC address that packets are sent to.

Active router The active router is the physical router that receives data sent to the virtual router address and routes it onward to its various destinations. As I mentioned, this router accepts all the data sent to the MAC address of the virtual router in addition to the data that's been sent to its own physical MAC address. The active router processes the data that's being forwarded and will also answer any ARP requests destined for the virtual router's IP address.

Standby router The standby router is the backup to the active router. Its job is to monitor the status of the HSRP group and quickly take over packet-forwarding responsibilities if the active router fails or loses communication. Both the active and standby routers transmit Hello messages to inform all other routers in the group of their role and status.

Other routers An HSRP group can include additional routers, which are members of the group but don't take the primary roles of either active or standby states. These routers monitor the Hello messages sent by the active and standby routers to ensure that an active and standby router exists for the HSRP group they belong to. They will forward data that's specifically addressed to their own IP addresses, but they will never forward data addressed to the virtual router unless elected to the active or standby state. These routers send "speak" messages based on the hello timer interval that informs other routers of their position in an election.

Interface Tracking

By now, you probably understand why having a virtual router on a LAN is a great idea. It's a very good thing that the active router can change dynamically, giving us much needed redundancy on our inside network. But what about the links to the upstream network or the Internet connection off of those HSRP-enabled routers? And how will the inside hosts know if an outside interface goes down or if they are sending packets to an active router that can't route to a remote network? Key questions and HSRP do provide a solution for them called interface tracking.

Figure 8.7 shows how HSRP-enabled routers can keep track of the interface status of the outside interfaces and how they can switch the inside active router as needed to keep the inside hosts from losing connectivity upstream.

If the outside link of the active router goes down, the standby router will take over and become the active router. There is a default priority of 100 on routers configured with an HSRP interface, and if you raise this priority, which we'll do in a bit, it means your router has a higher priority to become the active router. The reason I'm bringing this up now is because when a tracked interface goes down, it decrements the priority of this router.

Configuring and Verifying HSRP

Configuring and verifying the different FHRPs can be pretty simple, especially regarding the Cisco objectives, but as with most technologies, you can quickly get into advanced configurations and territory.

The Cisco objectives don't cover much about the configuration of FHRPs, but verification and troubleshooting are important, so I'll use a simple configuration on two routers here. Figure 8.8 shows the network I'll use to demonstrate HSRP.

FIGURE 8.7 Interface tracking setup

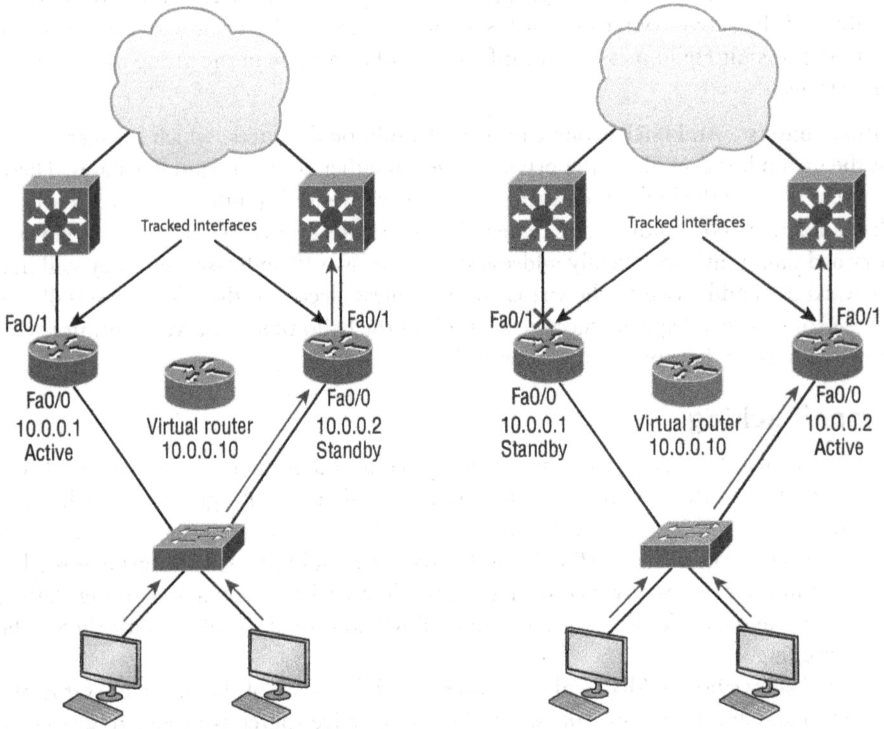

This is a simple configuration that you really need only one command for: `standby` *`group`* `ip` *`virtual_ip`*. After using this single mandatory command, I'll name the group and set the interface on router HSRP1 so it wins the election and becomes the active router by default:

```
HSRP1#config t
HSRP1(config)#int fa0/0
HSRP1(config-if)#standby ?
  <0-255>         group number
  authentication  Authentication
  delay           HSRP initialisation delay
  ip              Enable HSRP and set the virtual IP address
  mac-address     Virtual MAC address
  name            Redundancy name string
  preempt         Overthrow lower priority Active routers
  priority        Priority level
```

```
  redirect        Configure sending of ICMP Redirect messages with an HSRP
                  virtual IP address as the gateway IP address
  timers          Hello and hold timers
  track           Priority tracking
  use-bia         HSRP uses interface's burned in address
  version         HSRP version

HSRP1(config-if)#standby 1 ip 10.1.1.10
HSRP1(config-if)#standby 1 name HSRP_Test
HSRP1(config-if)#standby 1 priority ?
  <0-255>  Priority value

HSRP1(config-if)#standby 1 priority 110
000047: %HSRP-5-STATECHANGE: FastEthernet0/0 Grp 1 state Speak -> Standby
000048: %HSRP-5-STATECHANGE: FastEthernet0/0 Grp 1 state Standby -> Active110
```

FIGURE 8.8 HSRP configuration and verification

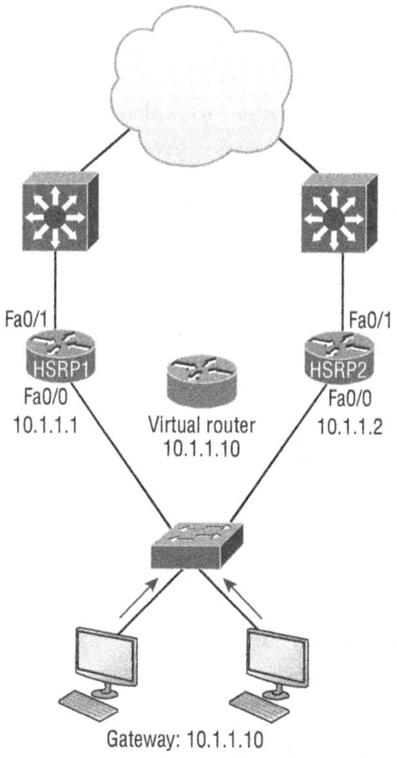

There are quite a few commands available to use in an advanced setting with the standby command, but we'll stick with the simple commands that follow the Cisco objectives. First, I numbered the group (1), which must be the same on all routers sharing HSRP duties; then I added the virtual IP address shared by all routers in the HSRP group. Optionally, I named the group and then set the priority of HSRP1 to 110, and I left HSRP2 to a default of 100. The router with the highest priority will win the election to become the active router. Let's configure the HSRP2 router now:

```
HSRP2#config t
HSRP2(config)#int fa0/0
HSRP2(config-if)#standby 1 ip 10.1.1.10
HSRP2(config-if)#standby 1 name HSRP_Test
*Jun 23 21:40:10.699:%HSRP-5-STATECHANGE:FastEthernet0/0 Grp 1 state
Speak -> Standby
```

I really only needed the first command—naming it was for administrative purposes only. Notice that the link came up, and the HSRP2 router became the standby router because it had the lower priority of 100 (the default). Make a note that this priority comes into play only if both routers were to come up at the same time. This means that HSRP2 would be the active router, regardless of priority, if it comes up first.

Preemption

According to the dictionary, *preempt* means "to replace with something considered to be of greater value or priority."

Using preemption, one router can take over another router only during an election, and preemption is the only way to force an election when a device hasn't gone down.

By using the command standby 1 preempt, you can have a particular device always be the active (forwarding) device. Because I want router 1 to always be the forwarding router if possible, our configuration of router 1 would now look like this:

```
HSRP1(config-if)#standby 1 ip 10.1.1.10
HSRP1(config-if)#standby 1 name HSRP_Test
HSRP1(config-if)#standby 1 priority 110
HSRP1(config-if)#standby 1 prempt
```

HSRP Verification

Let's take a look at the configurations with the show standby and show standby brief commands:

```
HSRP1(config-if)#do show standby
FastEthernet0/0 - Group 1
  State is Active
    2 state changes, last state change 00:03:40
  Virtual IP address is 10.1.1.10
```

```
  Active virtual MAC address is 0000.0c07.ac01
    Local virtual MAC address is 0000.0c07.ac01 (v1 default)
  Hello time 3 sec, hold time 10 sec
    Next hello sent in 1.076 secs
  Preemption disabled
  Active router is local
  Standby router is 10.1.1.2, priority 100 (expires in 7.448 sec)
  Priority 110 (configured 110)
  IP redundancy name is "HSRP_Test" (cfgd)
HSRP1(config-if)#do show standby brief
                     P indicates configured to preempt.
                     |
Interface   Grp Prio P State    Active          Standby         Virtual IP
Fa0/0       1   110    Active   local           10.1.1.2        10.1.1.10
```

Notice the group number in each output—it's a key troubleshooting spot! Each router must be configured in the same group or they won't work. Also, you can see the virtual MAC and configured virtual IP address, as well as the hello time of 3 seconds. The standby and virtual IP addresses are also displayed.

HSRP2's output tells us that it's in standby mode:

```
HSRP2(config-if)#do show standby brief
                     P indicates configured to preempt.
                     |
Interface   Grp Prio P State    Active          Standby         Virtual IP
Fa0/0       1   100    Standby  10.1.1.1        local           10.1.1.10
HRSP2(config-if)#
```

Also notice that so far, you've seen HSRP states of Active and Standby, but watch what happens when I disable Fa0/0:

```
HSRP1#config t
HSRP1(config)#interface Fa0/0
HSRP1(config-if)#shutdown
*Nov 20 10:06:52.369: %HSRP-5-STATECHANGE: Ethernet0/0 Grp 1 state
Active -> Init
```

The HSRP state went into Init state, meaning it's trying to initialize with a peer. The possible interface states for HSRP are shown in Table 8.1.

TABLE 8.1 HSRP states

State	Definition
Initial (INIT)	This is the state at the start. This state indicates that HSRP does not run. This state is entered through a configuration change or when an interface first becomes available.
Learn	The router has not determined the virtual IP address and has not yet seen an authenticated hello message from the active router. In this state, the router still waits to hear from the active router.
Listen	The router knows the virtual IP address, but the router is neither the active router nor the standby router. It listens for hello messages from those routers.
Speak	The router sends periodic hello messages and actively participates in the election of the active and/or standby router. A router can't enter the speak state unless the router has the virtual IP address.
Standby	The router is a candidate to become the next active router and sends periodic hello messages. With the exclusion of transient conditions, there is at most one router in the group in standby state.
Active	The router currently forwards packets that are sent to the group's virtual MAC address. The router sends periodic hello messages. With the exclusion of transient conditions, there must be at most one router in active state in the group.

There's one other command that I want to cover. If you really want to understand HSRP, learn to use this debug command and have your active and standby routers move. You'll really get to see what's going on!

```
HSRP2#debug standby
*Sep 15 00:07:32.344:HSRP:Fa0/0 Interface UP
*Sep 15 00:07:32.344:HSRP:Fa0/0 Initialize swsb, Intf state Up
*Sep 15 00:07:32.344:HSRP:Fa0/0 Starting minimum intf delay (1 secs)
*Sep 15 00:07:32.344:HSRP:Fa0/0 Grp 1 Set virtual MAC 0000.0c07.ac01
type: v1 default
*Sep 15 00:07:32.344:HSRP:Fa0/0 MAC hash entry 0000.0c07.ac01, Added
Fa0/0 Grp 1 to list
*Sep 15 00:07:32.348:HSRP:Fa0/0 Added 10.1.1.10 to hash table
*Sep 15 00:07:32.348:HSRP:Fa0/0 Grp 1 Has mac changed? cur 0000.0c07.ac01
new 0000.0c07.ac01
*Sep 15 00:07:32.348:HSRP:Fa0/0 Grp 1 Disabled -> Init
*Sep 15 00:07:32.348:HSRP:Fa0/0 Grp 1 Redundancy "hsrp-Fa0/0-1" state
Disabled -> Init
```

```
*Sep 15 00:07:32.348:HSRP:Fa0/0 IP Redundancy "hsrp-Fa0/0-1" added
*Sep 15 00:07:32.348:HSRP:Fa0/0 IP Redundancy "hsrp-Fa0/0-1" update,
Disabled -> Init
*Sep 15 00:07:33.352:HSRP:Fa0/0 Intf min delay expired
*Sep 15 00:07:39.936:HSRP:Fa0/0 Grp 1 MAC addr update Delete from SMF
0000.0c07.ac01
*Sep 15 00:07:39.936:HSRP:Fa0/0 Grp 1 MAC addr update Delete from SMF
0000.0c07.ac01
*Sep 15 00:07:39.940:HSRP:Fa0/0 ARP reload
```

HSRP Load Balancing

As you know, HSRP doesn't really perform true load balancing, but it can be configured to use more than one router at a time for use with different VLANs. This is different from the true load balancing that's possible with GLBP, which I'll demonstrate in a minute, but HSRP still performs a load-balancing act of sorts.

Figure 8.9 shows how load balancing would look with HSRP.

FIGURE 8.9 HSRP load balancing per VLAN

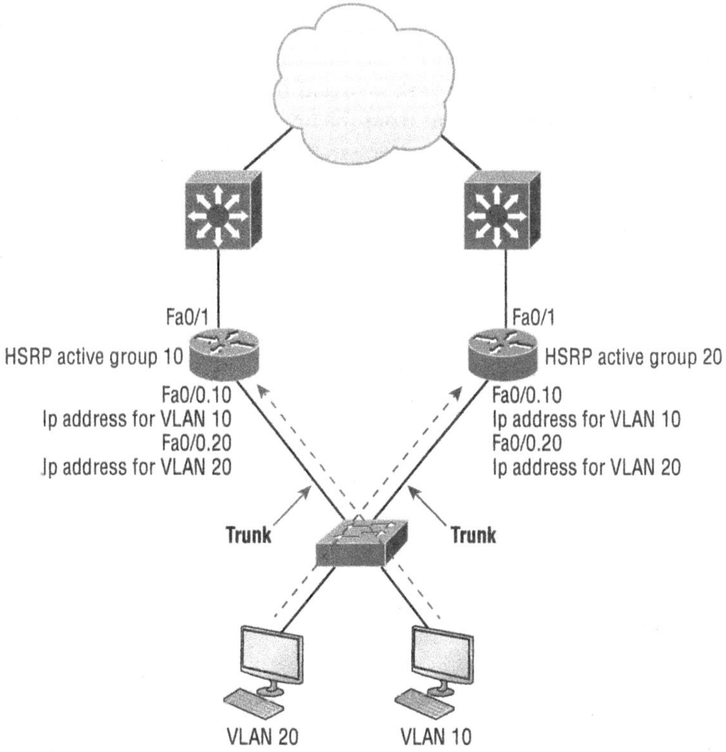

How can you get two HSRP routers active at the same time? Well, for the same subnet with this simple configuration, you can't, but by trunking the links to each router, they'll run and be configured with a "router on a stick" (ROAS) configuration. This means that each router can be the default gateway for different VLANs, but you still only have one active router per VLAN.

In a more advanced setting, you usually wouldn't go with HSRP for load balancing. Instead, you'd opt for GLBP. But you can do load-sharing with HSRP, which is the topic of an objective, so you'll remember that, right? It comes in handy because it prevents situations where a single point of failure causes traffic interruptions. This HSRP feature improves network resilience by allowing for load-balancing and redundancy capabilities between subnets and VLANs.

HSRP Troubleshooting

Besides the HSRP verification, troubleshooting HSRP is the Cisco objective hotspot, so let's explore that now.

Most of your HSRP misconfiguration issues can be solved by checking the output of the `show standby` command. In the output, you can see the active IP and the MAC address, the timers, the active router, and more, as shown in the earlier verification section.

There are several possible misconfigurations of HSRP, but the following are the focus for your CCNA:

Different HSRP virtual IP addresses configured on the peers Console messages will notify you about this, of course, but if you configure it this way and the active router fails, the standby router takes over with a virtual IP address. This is different from the one used previously and different from the one configured as the default gateway address for end devices, so your hosts stop working, defeating the purpose of an FHRP.

Different HSRP groups are configured on the peers This misconfiguration leads to both peers becoming active, and you'll start receiving duplicate IP address warnings. This seems easy to troubleshoot, but the next issue results in the same warnings.

Different HSRP versions are configured on the peers or ports blocked HSRP comes in 2 versions, 1 and 2. If there's a version mismatch, both routers will become active, and you'll get duplicate IP address warnings again.

In version 1, HSRP messages are sent to the multicast IP address 224.0.0.2 and UDP port 1985. HSRP version 2 uses the multicast IP address 224.0.0.102 and UDP port 1985. These IP addresses and ports need to be permitted in the inbound access lists. If the packets are blocked, the peers won't see each other, meaning there will be no HSRP redundancy.

Summary

We began this chapter with a talk about how to mitigate security threats at the Access layer and also discussed external authentication for our network devices for ease of management.

I showed you how to integrate redundancy and load-balancing features into your network with existing routers you probably already have. We explored the Cisco proprietary HSRP as well as GLBP, and you learned how to configure and use Hot Standby Router Protocol (HSRP).

Exam Essentials

Remember the three FHRPs. HSRP, VVRP, and GLBP are all FHRPs, with HSRP and GLBP being Cisco proprietary protocols.

Remember how load balancing works with HSRP and GLBP. HSRP load balances per VLAN's trunk links, and GLBP can perform per-host load balancing.

Remember how to verify HSRP and GLBP. Use the `show standby` command with HSRP and `show glbp` with GLBP.

Remember the HSRP virtual address. The HSRP MAC address has only one variable piece in it. The first 24 bits still identify the vendor who manufactured the device (the organizationally unique identifier, or OUI). The next 16 bits in the address tell us that the MAC address is a well-known HSRP MAC address. Finally, the last 8 bits of the address are the hexadecimal representation of the HSRP group number.

Here is an example of what an HSRP MAC address would look like:

`0000.0c07.ac0a`

Remember the MAC address used with VRRP as a virtual address. The MAC address used with VRRP as a virtual address is 00-00-5E-00-01-0a.

Written Lab

The answers to this lab can be found in Appendix A, "Answers to the Written Labs."

Write the answers to the following questions:

1. 224.0.0.102, UDP port 1985, is used for which FHRP version?
2. When the active router in an HSRP group fails, what router assumes the role and forwards packets?
3. Which virtual MAC address is used by VRRP group 1?
4. Which command should you enter to verify the priority of a router in an HSRP group?
5. In a more advanced setting, you usually wouldn't go with HSRP for load balancing. Instead, you'd opt for _____.

Review Questions

NOTE The following questions are designed to test your understanding of this chapter's material. For more information on how to get additional questions, please see this book's introduction.

The answers to these questions can be found in Appendix B, "Answers to the Review Questions."

1. What is the default priority setting on an HSRP router?
   - A. 25
   - B. 50
   - C. 100
   - D. 125
2. What is true regarding any type of FHRP?
   - A. The FHRP supplies hosts with routing information.
   - B. The FHRP is a routing protocol.
   - C. The FHRP provides default gateway redundancy.
   - D. The FHRP is only standards-based.
3. Which of the following are HSRP states? (Choose two.)
   - A. INIT
   - B. ACTIVE
   - C. ESTABLISHED
   - D. IDLE
4. Which command configures an interface to enable HSRP with the virtual router IP address 10.1.1.10?
   - A. **standby 1 ip 10.1.1.10**
   - B. **ip hsrp 1 standby 10.1.1.10**
   - C. **hsrp 1 ip 10.1.1.10**
   - D. **standby 1 hsrp ip 10.1.1.10**
5. Which command displays the status of all HSRP groups on a Cisco router or layer 3 switch?
   - A. show ip hsrp
   - B. show hsrp
   - C. show standby hsrp
   - D. show standby
   - E. show hsrp groups

6. Two routers are part of an HSRP standby group, and there's no priority configured for the routers for the HSRP group. Which of these statements is correct?
   A. Both routers will be in active state.
   B. Both routers will be in standby state.
   C. Both routers will be in listen state.
   D. One router will be active and the other standby.
7. Which of the following statements is true about the HSRP version 1 hello packet?
   A. HSRP hello packets are sent to multicast address 224.0.0.5.
   B. HSRP RP hello packets are sent to multicast address 224.0.0.2 with TCP port 1985.
   C. HSRP hello packets are sent to multicast address 224.0.0.2 with UDP port 1985.
   D. HSRP hello packets are sent to multicast address 224.0.0.10 with UDP port 1986.
8. Routers HSRP1 and HSRP2 are in HSRP group 1. HSRP1 is the active router with a priority of 120, and HSRP2 has the default priority. When HSRP1 reboots, HSRP2 will become the active router. Once HSRP1 comes back up, which of the following statements will be true? (Choose two.)
   A. HSRP1 will become the active router.
   B. HSRP2 will stay the active router.
   C. HSRP1 will become the active router if it is also configured to preempt.
   D. Both routers will go into speak state.
9. What's the multicast and port number used for HSRP version 2?
   A. 224.0.0.2, UDP port 1985
   B. 224.0.0.2. TCP port 1985
   C. 224.0.0.102, UDP port 1985
   D. 224.0.0.102, TCP port 1985
10. Which outcomes are predictable behaviors for HSRP? (Choose two.)
    A. The two routers negotiate one router as the active router and the other as the standby router.
    B. The two routers share the same interface IP address, and default gateway traffic is load-balanced between them.
    C. The two routers synchronize configurations to provide consistent packet forwarding.
    D. Each router has a different IP address; both routers act as the default gateway on the LAN, and traffic is load-balanced between them.
    E. The two routers share a virtual IP address that is used as the default gateway for devices on the LAN.

Chapter 9

Quality of Service (QoS)

THE FOLLOWING CCNA EXAM TOPIC IS COVERED IN THIS CHAPTER:

✓ **4.0 IP Services**

4.7 Explain the forwarding per-hop behavior (PHB) for QoS, such as classification, marking, queuing, congestion, policing, shaping

Quality of service (QoS) refers to the way resources are controlled so that the quality of services is maintained.

In this chapter, I'm going to cover how QoS solves problems by using classification and marking tools, policing, shaping and re-marking, providing congestion management and scheduling tools, and finally, link-specific tools.

NOTE To find your included bonus material, as well as Todd Lammle videos, practice questions, and hands-on labs, please see `www.lammle.com/ccna`.

Quality of Service

Quality of service (QoS) provides the ability to assign a different priority to one or more types of traffic over others for different applications, data flows, or users so a certain level of performance can be guaranteed. QoS is used to manage contention for network resources for a better end-user experience.

QoS methods focus on one of five problems that can affect data as it traverses network cable:

1. **Delay** Data can run into congested lines or take a less-than-ideal route to the destination, and delays like these can make some applications, such as VoIP, fail. This is the best reason to implement QoS when real-time applications are in use in the network—to prioritize delay-sensitive traffic.

2. **Dropped packets** Some routers will drop packets if they receive a packet while their buffers are full. If the receiving application is waiting for the packets but doesn't get them, it will usually request that the packets be retransmitted, another common cause of a service(s) delay. With QoS, when there is contention on a link, less important traffic is delayed or dropped in favor of delay-sensitive and/or otherwise prioritized traffic.

3. **Error** Packets can be corrupted in transit and arrive at the destination in an unacceptable format, again requiring retransmission and resulting in delays.

4. **Jitter** Not every packet takes the same route to the destination, so some will be more delayed than others if they travel through a slower or busier network connection. The variation in packet delay is called *jitter*, which can have a particularly negative impact on programs that communicate in real time.

5. Out-of-order delivery Out-of-order delivery is also a result of packets taking different paths through the network to their destination. The application at the receiving end needs to put them back together in the right order for the message to be completed. So if there are significant delays or the packets are reassembled out of order, users will experience decline in an application's quality.

QoS can ensure that applications with a required bit rate receive the necessary bandwidth to work properly. Clearly, this isn't a factor on networks with excess bandwidth, but the more limited your bandwidth is, the more important QoS becomes!

Traffic Characteristics

Today's networks will typically have a mix of data, voice, and video traffic traversing them. Each traffic type has different properties.

Figure 9.1 shows the different traffic characteristics for data, voice, and video.

FIGURE 9.1 Traffic characteristics

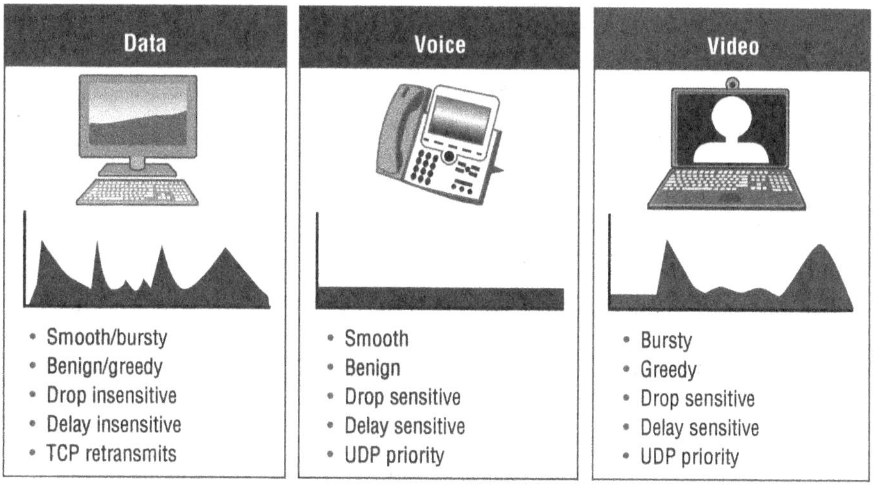

Data traffic is not real-time traffic. Data-packet traffic is bursty and unpredictable, making packet arrival vary by quite a bit.

The following are data characteristics we can see in Figure 9.1:

- Smooth/bursty
- Benign/greedy
- Drop insensate
- Delay insensitive
- TCP retransmits

Data traffic doesn't really require special handling in modern networks, especially if TCP is used. Voice traffic is real-time traffic that requires and consumes a consistent amount of bandwidth with known packet arrival times.

These are the characteristics of voice traffic on a network:

- Smooth
- Benign
- Drop sensitive
- Delay sensitive
- UDP priority

And these are the voice requirements for one-way traffic:

- Latency of less than or equal to 150 milliseconds
- Jitter of less than or equal to 30 milliseconds
- Loss of less than or equal to 1%
- Bandwidth of only 30–12,000Kbps

There's quite a variety of video traffic types around today on the Internet. Netflix, Hulu and other apps, gaming, and remote collaboration require streaming video, real-time interactive video, and video conferencing.

Video requirements for one-way traffic are

- Latency of less than or equal to 200–400 milliseconds
- Jitter of less than or equal to 30–50 milliseconds
- Loss of less than or equal to 0.1–1%
- Bandwidth 384 Kbps to 20 Mbps or greater

Trust Boundary

The trust boundary refers to a point in the network where packet markings aren't necessarily trusted and where we can create, remove, or rewrite markings. The borders of a trust domain are the network locations where packet markings are accepted and acted upon. Figure 9.2 illustrates some typical trust boundaries.

FIGURE 9.2 Trust boundary

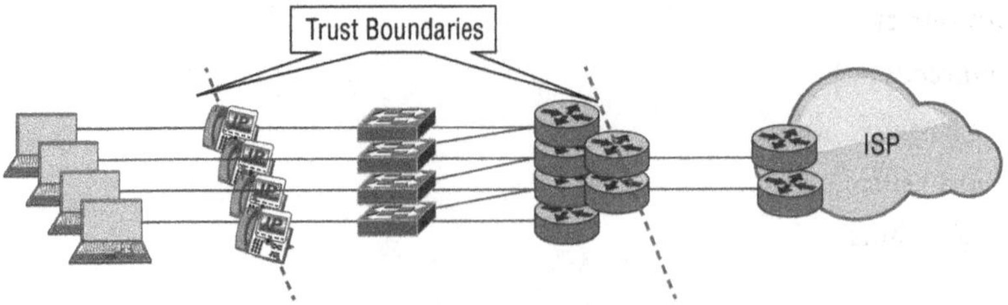

The figure shows that IP phones and router interfaces are typically trusted but not beyond a certain point. Those points are trust boundaries.

To meet the exam objectives, understand these three things:

Untrusted domain This is the part of the network you're not actively managing, populated by PCs, printers, etc.

Trusted domain This is the part of the network with only administrator-managed devices like switches, routers, etc.

Trust boundary Where packets are classified and marked in an enterprise campus network, the trust boundary is almost always at the edge switch. An IP phone and the boundary between the ISP and enterprise network are also common examples of trust boundaries.

So, traffic at the trust boundary is classified and marked before being forwarded to the trusted domain. Markings on traffic coming from an untrusted domain are usually ignored to prevent end-user-controlled markings from taking unfair advantage of the network QoS configuration.

QoS Mechanisms

Next, we're going to explore the following mechanisms:

- Classification and marking tools
- Policing, shaping, and re-marking tools
- Congestion management or scheduling tools
- Link-specific tools

Let's take a detailed look at each one now.

Classification and Marking

A classifier inspects a field with a packet to identify the type of traffic that the packet is carrying so that QoS can determine which traffic class it belongs to and how the packet should be treated. Traffic is then directed to a policy-enforcement mechanism called policing. It's important that this isn't a constant cycle for traffic because it takes up time and resources!

Policy enforcement mechanisms include marking, queuing, policing, and shaping, and there are various layer 2 and layer 3 fields in a frame and packet for marking traffic. Understanding these marking techniques is important for the objectives, so here you go:

Class of service (CoS) Class of service (CoS) is a term to describe designated fields in a frame or packet header. Considered an Ethernet frame marking at layer 2 containing 3 bits. This is called the Priority Code Point (PCP) within an Ethernet frame header when VLAN-tagged frames, as defined by IEEE 802.1Q, are used.

Type of service (ToS) ToS comprises 8 bits, 3 of which are designated as the IP precedence field in an IPv4 packet header. The IPv6 header field is called the Traffic Class.

Differentiated services code point (DSCP or DiffServ) One of the methods that can be used for classifying and managing network traffic and providing QoS on modern IP networks is DSCP. It uses a 6-bit differentiated services code point in the 8-bit differentiated services (DS) field within the IP header for packet classification. This permits us to create traffic classes needed for assigning priorities. Although IP precedence is the old way to mark ToS, DSCP is the new way. DSCP is backward-compatible with IP precedence.

Layer 3 packet marking with IP precedence and DSCP is the most widely deployed marking option because layer 3 packet markings have end-to-end significance.

Class selector Class selector uses the same 3 bits of the field as IP precedence and is used to indicate a 3-bit subset of DSCP values.

Traffic identifier (TID) TID is for wireless frames and describes a 3-bit field within the QoS control field in 802.11. Very similar to CoS—just remember that CoS is wired Ethernet, and TID is wireless.

Classification Marking Tools

As we talked about, the classification of traffic determines which type of traffic the packets or frames belong to. Once that's been determined, we can apply policies to it by marking, shaping, and policing. Always try to mark traffic as close to the trust boundary as possible.

We typically use three ways to classify traffic:

Markings This looks at header information on existing layer 2 or 3 settings. Classification is based on existing markings.

Addressing This classification technique looks at header information using the sources and destinations of interfaces, layer 2 and 3 addresses, and layer 4 port numbers. We can group traffic with the device using IP and by type using port numbers.

Application signatures This technique is the way to look at the information in the payload called deep packet inspection.

I'm going to dive a bit deeper into deep packet inspection by introducing you to network-based application recognition (NBAR).

NBAR is a classifier that provides deep-packet inspection on layers 4–7 on a packet. Compared to using addresses (IP or ports) or ACLs, using NBAR is the most CPU-intensive technique.

Because it's not always possible to identify applications by looking at just layers 3 and 4, NBAR looks deep into the packet payload and compares the payload content against its signature database called a packet description language model (PDLM).

There are two different modes of operation used with NBAR:

- **Passive mode:** Using passive mode will give you real-time statistics on applications by protocol or interface, as well as packet bit rate, packet, and byte counts.
- **Active mode:** Classifies applications for traffic marking so QoS policies can be applied.

Policing, Shaping, and Re-Marking

So, now that we've identified and marked traffic, it's time to put some action on our packet. We do this with bandwidth assignments, policing, shaping, queuing, or dropping. For example, if some traffic exceeds bandwidth, it might be delayed, dropped, or even re-marked to avoid congestion.

Policers and shapers are two tools that identify and respond to traffic problems. Both are rate-limiters, and Figure 9.3 shows how they differ.

FIGURE 9.3 Policing and Shaping rate limiters

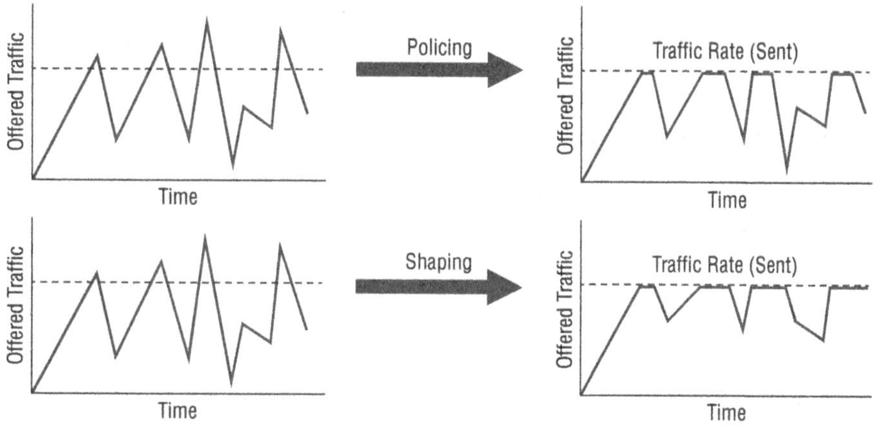

Policers and shapers identify traffic violations in a similar way, but they differ in their responses:

Policers Because policers make instant decisions, you want to deploy them on the ingress if possible—you want to drop traffic as soon as you receive it if it's going to be dropped anyway, right? Still, you can place policers on an egress to control the amount of traffic per class. When traffic is exceeded, policers don't delay it by introducing jitter or delay; they check the traffic and drop or re-mark it. Just know that you can end up with a whole bunch of TCP resends due to the higher drop probability. Use the police command to mark a packet with different quality of service (QoS) values based on conformance to the service-level agreement. Traffic policing allows you to control the maximum rate of traffic transmitted or received on an interface: Gold/Video, Silver/Best Effort (default), and Bronze/Background.

Shapers Shapers are usually deployed between an enterprise network and the ISPs on the egress side to ensure that you stay within the contract rate. If the rate is exceeded, it gets policed by the provider and dropped. This allows the traffic to meet the IP service level agreement (SLA). An IP SLA allows an IT professional to collect information about network performance in real time, which helps determine whether the QoS on the network is sufficient for IP services. Shaping introduces jitter and delay and results in fewer

TCP resends than policers. Traffic shaping retains excess packets in a queue and then schedules the excess for later transmission over increments of time.

> **TIP** Basically, remember that policers drop traffic and shapers delay it. Shapers introduce delay and jitter, but policers do not. Policers cause significant TCP resends, but shapers do not.

Tools for Managing Congestion

Next up are a couple of important sections on congestion issues. If traffic exceeds network resources, the traffic gets queued into the temporary storage of backed-up packets. Queuing is done to avoid dropping packets and isn't a bad thing because without it, packets that can't be processed immediately would be dropped. Also, traffic classes like VoIP are actually better off being immediately dropped unless you can somehow guarantee enough delay-free bandwidth for them!

When congestion occurs, two types of congestion management are activated, as shown in Figure 9.4.

FIGURE 9.4 Congestion management

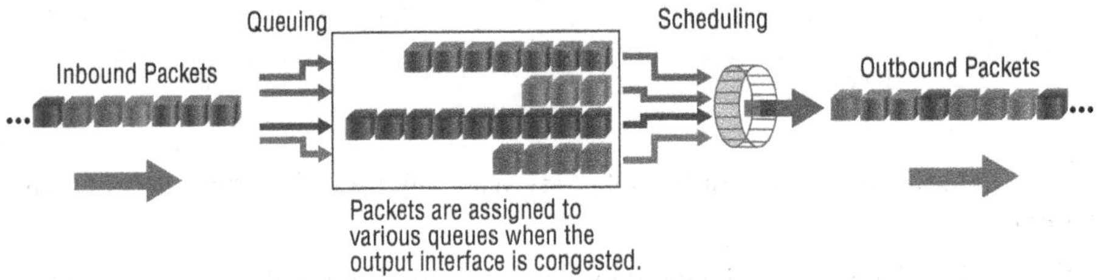

Let's take a closer look at congestion management:

Queuing (or buffering) Buffering is the logic of ordering packets in output buffers and is only activated when congestion occurs. When queues fill up, packets can be reordered so that the higher-priority ones are sent out of the exit interface sooner than lower-priority traffic.

Scheduling This is the process of deciding which packet should be sent out next and occurs whether or not there is congestion on the link. Make sure you're familiar with these three scheduling mechanisms:

Strict priority scheduling Scheduling low-priority queues only happens once the high-priority queues are empty. This is great if you're sending high-priority traffic, but it's possible for low-priority queues to never be processed. We call this traffic or queue starvation.

Round-robin scheduling This sounds like a fair technique because queues are serviced in a set sequence. You won't find starving queues here, but real-time traffic suffers badly!

Weighted fair scheduling By weighing the queues, the scheduling process will service some queues more often than others—an upgrade over round-robin. You won't find any starvation carnage here either, but unlike round-robin, you can give priority to real-time traffic. The inevitable disclaimer coming at us here is that we get no guarantees for actual bandwidth availability.

Okay, let's run back over and finish queueing. Queuing is typically a layer 3 process, but some queueing can occur at layer 2 or even layer 1. Interestingly, if a layer 2 queue fills up, the data can be pushed into layer 3 queues, and when layer 1—called the transmit ring or TX-ring queue, fills up—the data is pushed to layer 2 and 3 queues. This is when QoS becomes active on the device.

There are many different queuing mechanisms, with only two of them typically used today. Even so, it won't hurt to take a quick look at legacy queuing methods:

First in first out (FIFO) A single queue, with packets being processed in the exact order they arrived in.

Priority queuing (PQ) Similar to round-robin scheduling, lower-priority queues are only served when the higher-priority queues are empty. There are only four queues, and low-priority traffic may never be sent. PQ guarantees strict priority in that it ensures that one type of traffic will be sent, possibly at the expense of all others. Strict PQ allows delay-sensitive data, such as voice, to be dequeued and sent before packets in other queues are dequeued.

Custom queueing (CQ) With up to nine queues and round-robin scheduling, CQ prevents low-level queue starvation and gives us traffic guarantees. But it doesn't provide strict priority for real-time traffic so VoIP traffic could still end up being dropped.

Weighted fair queuing (WFQ) WFQ was actually a pretty popular way of queuing for a long time because it divided up the bandwidth by the number of flows. This provided bandwidth for all applications and worked great for real-time traffic, but there weren't any guarantees for a particular flow.

So now that you know about the queuing methods not to use, let's focus on the two newer queuing mechanisms recommended for today's rich-media networks—class-based weighted fair queuing (CBWFQ) and low-latency queuing (LLQ). Check out Figure 9.5.

FIGURE 9.5 Modern queuing mechanisms

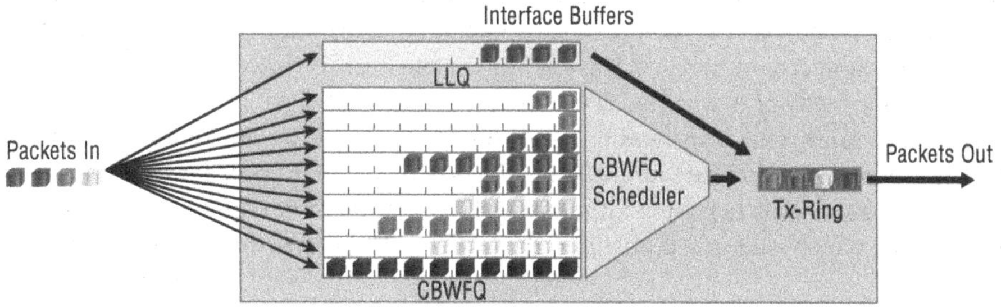

And here's a brief description of CBWFQ and LLQ:

Class-based weighted fair queuing (CBWFQ) Provides fairness and bandwidth guarantees for all traffic but doesn't provide a latency guarantee. It's typically only used for data traffic management.

Low-latency queuing (LLQ) LLQ is really the same thing as CBWFQ but with stricter priorities for real-time traffic. LLQ is great for both data and real-time traffic because it guarantees latency and bandwidth. LLQ is the preferred queuing policy for VoIP. Given the stringent delay/jitter-sensitive requirements of voice and video and the need to synchronize audio and video for CUVA, priority (LLQ) queuing is recommended for all video traffic as well. Note that for video, priority bandwidth is generally fudged up by 20% to account for the overhead.

In Figure 9.6, you can see the LLQ queuing mechanism working great for real-time traffic.

FIGURE 9.6 Queuing mechanisms

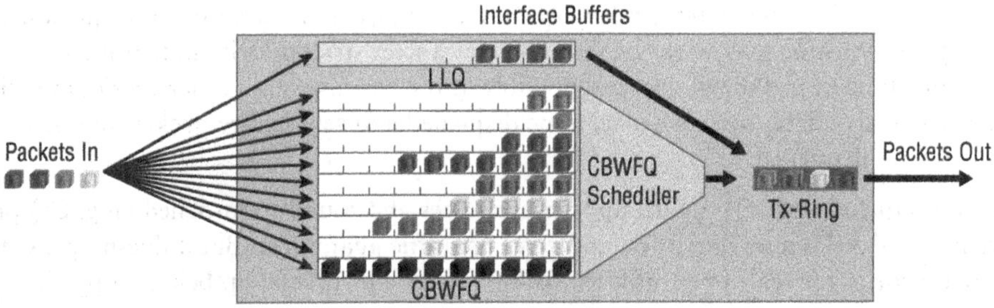

If you remove the LLQ (at the top), you're left with CBWFQ, which is only used for data-traffic networks!

Tools for Congestion Avoidance

TCP changed our networking world when it introduced sliding windows as a flow-control mechanism in the middle 1990s. Flow control is a way for the receiving device to control the amount of traffic from a transmitting device.

If a problem occurred during a data transmission, the previous flow control methods employed by TCP and other layer 4 protocols like SPX before sliding windows would just cut the transmission rate in half and leave it at the same rate, or lower, for the duration of the connection. Clearly, this was less than popular with users!

Sure, TCP certainly cuts transmission rates drastically if a flow control issue occurs, but it increases the transmission rate after the missing segments are resolved or when packets are finally processed. This behavior, although awesome at the time, can result in something called tail drop, which isn't acceptable in today's networks because bandwidth isn't used effectively.

What's tail drop? It's the dropping of packets as they arrive when the queues on the receiving interface are full. This is a terrible waste of bandwidth because TCP will just keep resending the data until it's happy again when it finally receives an ACK. Enter another new term—TCP global synchronization—wherein each sender reduces their transmission rate simultaneously when packet loss occurs.

Congestion avoidance starts dropping packets before a queue fills using traffic weights instead of just randomness. Cisco uses something called weighted random early detection (WRED), a queuing method that ensures high-precedence traffic has lower loss rates than other traffic during times of congestion. This prevents more important traffic, like VoIP, from being dropped by prioritizing it over less important traffic, like a connection to Facebook.

WRED drops packets selectively based on IP precedence. Edge routers assign IP precedence to packets as they enter the network.

When a packet arrives, the following events occur:

1. The average queue size is calculated.
2. The arriving packet is queued if the average is less than the minimum queue threshold.
3. If the average is between the minimum queue threshold for that type of traffic and the maximum threshold for the interface, the packet is either dropped or queued, depending on the packet drop probability for that type of traffic.
4. If the average queue size is greater than the maximum threshold, the packet is dropped.

TIP Queuing algorithms manage the front of the queue, and congestion mechanisms manage the back of the queue.

Figure 9.7 shows how congestion avoidance works.

FIGURE 9.7 Congestion avoidance

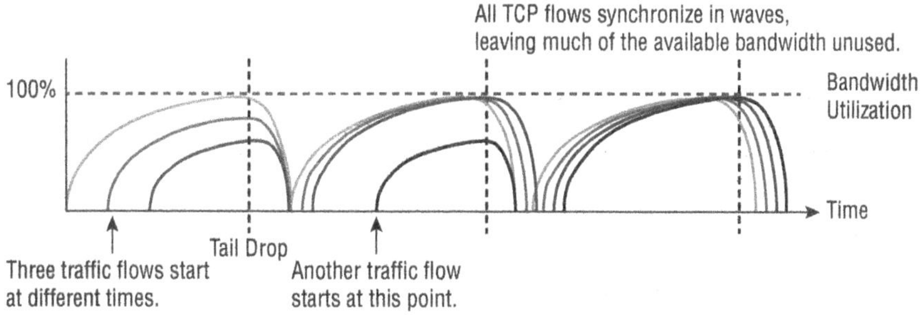

We can see three traffic flows beginning at different times, resulting in congestion. In a situation like this, TCP may cause a tail drop because it drops the traffic as soon as it's received if the buffers are full!

At that point, TCP would begin another traffic flow, synchronizing the TCP flows in waves, which sadly leaves much of the bandwidth unused.

Summary

Quality of service (QoS) refers to the way the resources are controlled so that the quality of services is maintained.

In this chapter, we discussed how QoS solves problems by using classification and marking tools, policing, shaping and re-marking, and providing congestion management and scheduling tools. We wrapped it up by covering link-specific tools.

Exam Essentials

Have a deep understanding of QoS. You must understand QoS, specifically marking, device trust, and prioritization for voice, video, and data. Also in the need-to-know category: shaping, policing, and congestion management. Understand all of these in detail.

Remember the two queuing mechanisms used in today's networks. The two queuing mechanisms you should now use in today's network are CBWFQ (class-based weighted fair queuing) and LLQ (low-latency queuing.)

Remember the two tools that identify and respond to traffic problems. Policers and shapers are two tools that identify and respond to traffic problems and are both rate-limiters.

Written Lab

The answers to this lab can be found in Appendix A, "Answers to the Written Labs."

Write the answers to the following questions:

1. Which QoS mechanism is a 6-bit value that is used to describe the meaning of the layer 3 IPv4 ToS field?
2. What does traffic shaping do?
3. Which QoS mechanism is a term that is used to describe a 3-bit field in the QoS control field of wireless frames?
4. What are the three general ways to classify traffic?
5. CoS is a layer 2 QoS ________?

6. A session is using more bandwidth than allocated. Which QoS mechanism will drop the traffic?
7. Which QoS feature drops traffic that exceeds the committed access rate?
8. What are two examples of newer queuing mechanisms that are recommended for rich-media networks?
9. What is a layer 4–7 deep-packet inspection classifier that is more CPU-intensive than marking?
10. What does traffic shaping do to reduce congestion in a network?

Review Questions

NOTE: The following questions are designed to test your understanding of this chapter's material. For more information on how to get additional questions, please see this book's introduction.

The answers to these questions can be found in Appendix B, "Answers to the Review Questions."

1. Which of the following is a congestion-avoidance mechanism?
   A. LMI
   B. WRED
   C. QPM
   D. QoS
2. Which features are properties and one-way requirements for voice traffic? (Choose three.)
   A. Bursty voice traffic.
   B. Smooth voice traffic.
   C. Latency should be below 400 ms.
   D. Latency should be below 150 ms.
   E. Bandwidth is roughly between 30 and 128 kbps.
   F. Bandwidth is roughly between 0.5 and 20 Mbps.
3. Which statement about QoS trust boundaries or domains is true?
   A. The trust boundary is always a router.
   B. PCs, printers, and tablets are usually part of a trusted domain.
   C. An IP phone is a common trust boundary.
   D. Routing will not work unless the service provider and the enterprise network are one single trust domain.
4. Which advanced classification tool can be used to classify data applications?
   A. NBAR
   B. MPLS
   C. APIC-EM
   D. ToS
5. The DSCP field constitutes how many fields in the IP header?
   A. 3 bits
   B. 4 bits
   C. 6 bits
   D. 8 bits

6. Which option is a layer 2 QoS marking?
   - A. EXP
   - B. QoS group
   - C. DSCP
   - D. CoS
7. Which QoS mechanism will drop traffic if a session uses more than the allotted bandwidth?
   - A. Congestion management
   - B. Shaping
   - C. Policing
   - D. Marking
8. Which QoS queuing method discards or marks packets that exceed the desired bit rate of traffic flow?
   - A. Shaping
   - B. Policing
   - C. CBWFQ
   - D. LLQ
9. Which actions are performed by the weighted random early detection mechanism? (Choose two.)
   - A. It supports protocol discovery.
   - B. It guarantees the delivery of high-priority packets.
   - C. It can identify different flows with a high level of granularity.
   - D. It can mitigate congestion by preventing the queue from filling up.
   - E. It drops lower-priority packets before it drops higher-priority packets.
10. What is the purpose of traffic shaping?
    - A. To provide fair queuing for buffered flows
    - B. To mitigate delays over slow links
    - C. To limit the bandwidth that a flow can use
    - D. To be a marking mechanism that identifies different flows
11. Which QoS tools provide congestion management? (Choose two.)
    - A. CAR
    - B. CBWFQ
    - C. PQ
    - D. PBR
    - E. FRTS

12. Which QoS tool can you use to optimize voice traffic on a network that is primarily intended for data traffic?
    A. FIFO
    B. WFQ
    C. PQ
    D. WRED

13. In QoS, which prioritization method is appropriate for interactive voice and video?
    A. Expedited forwarding
    B. Traffic policing
    C. Round-robin scheduling
    D. Low-latency queuing

14. Which feature or protocol determines whether the QOS on the network is sufficient to support IP services?
    A. LLDP
    B. CDP
    C. IP SLA
    D. EEM

15. Which QoS tools are used to guarantee minimum bandwidth to certain traffic? (Choose two.)
    A. FIFO
    B. LLC
    C. CBWFQ
    D. RSVP
    E. WFQ

16. Which QoS tools can provide congestion management? (Choose two.)
    A. CBWFQ
    B. FRTS
    C. CAR
    D. PQ
    E. PBR

17. Which QoS traffic-handling technique retains excess packets in a queue and reschedules these packets for later transmission when the configured maximum bandwidth has been surpassed?
    A. Traffic
    B. Weighted random early detection
    C. Traffic prioritization
    D. Traffic shaping

18. Which option is the main function of congestion management?
    - **A.** Discarding excess traffic
    - **B.** Queuing traffic based on priority
    - **C.** Classifying traffic
    - **D.** Providing long-term storage of buffered data
19. Which QoS per-hop behavior changes the value of the ToS field in the IPv4 packet header?
    - **A.** Shaping
    - **B.** Classification
    - **C.** Policing
    - **D.** Marking
20. Which of the following does traffic shaping use to reduce congestion in a network?
    - **A.** Buffers and queues packets
    - **B.** Buffers without queuing packets
    - **C.** Queues without buffering packets
    - **D.** Drops packets

Chapter 10

Wireless Technologies

THE FOLLOWING CCNA EXAM TOPICS ARE COVERED IN THIS CHAPTER:

✓ **1.0 Network Fundamentals**

- 1.1.d Access points
- 1.1.e Controllers

✓ **1.11 Describe wireless principles**

- 1.11.a Nonoverlapping Wi-Fi channels
- 1.11.b SSID
- 1.11.c RF
- 1.11.d Encryption

✓ **5.0 Security Fundamentals**

- 5.9 Describe wireless security protocols (WPA, WPA2, and WPA3)

Wireless connectivity is everywhere these days; to really get away recently, I vacationed to a beautiful spot with no cell or Internet service on purpose! I know, crazy, right? Although it's true that I definitely chilled out, most of the time, I wouldn't even think of checking in anywhere that doesn't offer these things!

So clearly, those of us already in or wishing to enter the IT field better have our chops down on wireless network components and installation factors, which brings us to a great starting point: if you want to understand the basic wireless LANs (WLANs) used today, just think Ethernet connectivity with hubs—except the wireless devices we connect to are called *access points* (APs). This means that our WLANs run half-duplex communication—everyone is sharing the same bandwidth with only one device communicating at a time per channel. This isn't necessarily bad; it's just not good enough. Not only do we want it fast, but we want it secure, too!

Because I know you've crushed all the previous chapters, you're ready to dive into this one! If that's not exactly you, know that chapters on switching (Volume 1's Chapter 12 and Chapter 13, and Volume 2's Chapter 1) provided a really nice review on switching and VLANs.

Why do you need a strong background in switching and VLANs? Because if you think about it for a minute, you come to the important realization that APs have to connect to something. If not, how else would all those hosts hanging around in a wireless network area be able to connect to your wired resources or the Internet?

You also might be surprised to hear that wireless security is basically nonexistent on APs and clients by default. That's because the original 802.11 committee just didn't foresee that wireless hosts would one day outnumber bounded media hosts. Same thing with the IPv4 routed protocol—unfortunately, engineers and scientists just didn't include wireless security standards robust enough to work in a corporate environment. These factors leave us to face this problem with proprietary solution add-ons to create a secure wireless network. The good news is that some of the standards actually do provide some solid wireless security. And they're also pretty easy to implement with a little practice.

So let's start this chapter by defining a basic wireless network as well as basic wireless principles. We'll talk about different types of wireless networks and the minimum devices required to create a simple wireless network, and we'll look at some basic wireless topologies as well. After that, I'll get into basic security by covering WPA, WPA2, and WPA3.

NOTE

To find your included bonus material, as well as Todd Lammle videos, practice questions, and hands-on labs, please see `www.lammle.com/ccna`.

Wireless Networks

Wireless networks come in many forms, cover various distances, and provide a wide range of bandwidth capacities depending on the type that's been installed. The typical wireless network today is an extension of an Ethernet LAN, with wireless hosts utilizing Media Access Control (MAC) addresses, IP addresses, and so forth, just like they would on a wired LAN.

Figure 10.1 shows a simple, typical WLAN.

FIGURE 10.1 Wireless LANs are an extension of our existing LANs.

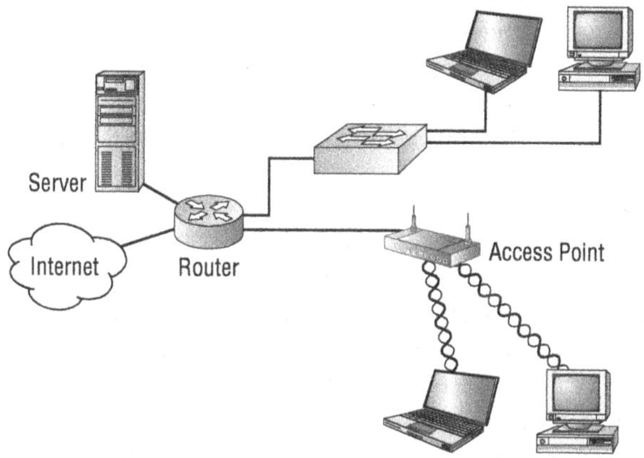

Wireless networks are more than just run-of-the-mill LANs because they're wireless, of course. They cover a range of distances, from short-range personal area networks to wide area networks (WANs) that really go the distance.

Figure 10.2 illustrates how different types of wireless networks look and the related distances they'll provide coverage for in today's world.

FIGURE 10.2 Today's wireless networks

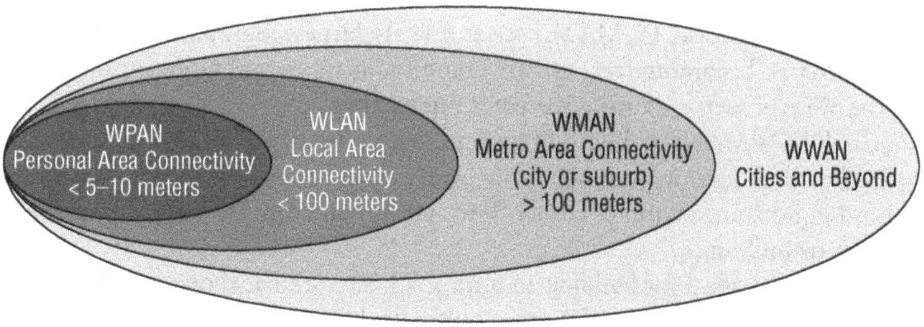

Now that you've got a mental picture, let's explore each of these networks in more detail.

Wireless Personal Area Networks

A wireless personal area network (PAN) works in a very small area and connects devices like mice, keyboards, PDAs, headsets, and cell phones to our computers. This conveniently eliminates the cabling clutter of the past. If you're thinking Bluetooth, you've got it, because it's by far the most popular type of PAN around.

PANs are low power, cover short distances, and are small. You can stretch one of these to cover about 30 feet max, but most devices on a PAN have a short reach, making them popular for small and/or home offices. Bigger isn't always better—you don't want your PAN's devices interfering with your other wireless networks or someone else's. Plus, you've got the usual security concerns to manage. So remember that PANs are the perfect solution for small devices you want to connect to your PC.

The standard use for PANs is unlicensed. This means that beyond initially purchasing PAN-typical devices, the users involved don't have to pay to use the type of devices in this network. This factor definitely encourages the development of devices that can use PAN frequencies.

Wireless LANs

Wireless LANs (WLANs) were created to cover longer distances and offer higher bandwidth than PANs. They're the most popular type of wireless network in use today.

The first WLAN had a data rate up to 2 Mbps, could stretch about 200–300 feet, depending on the area, and was called *802.11*. The typical rates in use today are higher—11 Mbps for IEEE 802.11b and 54 Mbps for 802.11g/a.

The ideal for a WLAN is to have many users connect to the network simultaneously, but this can cause interference and collisions because the network's users are all competing for the same bandwidth.

Like PANs, WLANs use an unlicensed frequency band, which means you don't have to pay for the frequency band to transmit. And again, this attribute has resulted in an explosion of new development in the WLAN arena.

Wireless Metro Area Networks

Wireless metro area networks (WMANs) cover a fairly large geographic area like a city or small suburb. They're becoming increasingly common as more and more products are introduced into the WLAN sector, causing the price tag to drop.

You can think of WMANs as low-budget bridging networks. They'll save you some real cash compared to shelling out for much more costly leased lines, but there's a catch: to get your discount long-distance wireless network to work, you've got to have a line of sight between each hub or building.

Fiber connections are ideal for building an ultra-solid network backbone, so go with them if they're available in your area. If your ISP doesn't offer the fiber option, or you just don't have the cash for it, a WMAN is a perfectly fine, economical alternative for covering something like a campus or another large area so long as you've got that vital line-of-sight factor in check!

Wireless Wide Area Networks

So far, it's very rare to come across a wireless wide area network (WWAN) that can provide you with WLAN speeds, but there sure is a lot of chatter about them. A good example of a WWAN would be the latest cellular networks that can transmit data at a pretty good clip. But even though WWANs can certainly cover plenty of areas, they're still not speedy enough to replace our ubiquitous WLANs.

Some people—especially those shilling stuff on TV—claim to adore their infallible, turbocharged cellular networks. These terminally happy people are usually watching high-speed video while uploading images and gaming on their smart phones, but I don't know anyone who lives outside the TV who actually gets that kind of speed. And as for that "coverage anywhere" schtick? Off the set, dead zones, and frozen phones are just reality for now.

It's possible we'll see more efficiency and growth for WWANs soon, but because WWANs are used to provide connectivity over a really large geographic area, it follows that implementing one will separate your cell service provider from a large quantity of cash. So it's going to come to motivation—as more people demand this type of service and are willing to pay for it, cellular companies will gain the resources to expand and improve upon these exciting networks.

Another set of positives in favor of WWAN growth and development: they meet a lot of business requirements, and technology is growing in such a direction that the need for this type of long-distance wireless network is getting stronger. So it's a fairly good bet that connectivity between a WLAN and a WWAN will be critical to many things in our future. For instance, when we have more IPv6 networks, the "pass-off" between these two types of networks may be seamless.

Basic Wireless Devices

Although it might not seem this way to you right now, *simple* WLANs are less complex than their wired cousins because they require fewer components. To make a basic wireless network work properly, all you need are two main devices: a wireless AP and a wireless network interface card (NIC). This also makes it a lot easier to install a wireless network because basically, you just need an understanding of these two components to make it happen.

Wireless Access Points

You'll find a central component like a hub or switch in the vast majority of wired networks, which is there to connect hosts together and allow them to communicate. Wireless also has a component that connects all wireless devices together, only that device is known as a wireless *access point* (AP). Wireless APs have at least one antenna. Usually there are two for better reception (referred to as *diversity*) and a port to connect them to a wired network.

Figure 10.3 gives you an example of a Cisco wireless AP, which just happens to be one of my personal favorites.

FIGURE 10.3 A wireless access point

APs have the following characteristics:

- APs function as a central junction point for the wireless stations, much like a switch or hub does within a wired network. Due to the half-duplex nature of wireless networking, the hub comparison is more accurate, even though hubs are rarely found in the wired world anymore.
- APs have at least one antenna—most likely two.
- APs function as a bridge to the wired network, giving the wireless station access to the wired network and/or the Internet.
- Small office, home office (SOHO) APs come in two flavors—the stand-alone AP and the wireless router. They can and usually do include functions like network address translation (NAT) and Dynamic Host Configuration Protocol (DHCP).

Even though it's not a perfect analogy, you can compare an AP to a hub because it doesn't create collision domains for each port like a switch does. But APs are definitely smarter than hubs. An AP is a portal device that can either direct network traffic to the wired backbone or back out into the wireless realm. If you look at Figure 10.1 again, you can see that the connection back to the wired network is called the *distribution system* (DS), and it also maintains MAC address information within the 802.11 frames. What's more, these frames are capable of holding as many as four MAC addresses, but only when a wireless DS is in use.

An AP also maintains an association table that you can view from the web-based software used to manage the AP. So what's an association table? It's basically a list of all workstations currently connected to or associated with the AP, which are listed by their MAC addresses. Another nice AP feature is that wireless routers can function as NAT routers, and they can carry out DHCP addressing for workstations as well.

In the Cisco world, there are two types of APs: autonomous and lightweight. An autonomous AP is one that's configured, managed, and maintained in isolation with regard to all the other APs that exist in the network. A lightweight AP gets its configuration from a central device called a *wireless controller*. In this scenario, the APs function as antennas, and all information is sent back to the wireless LAN controller (WLC). There are a bunch of advantages to this, like the capacity for centralized management and more seamless roaming. You'll learn all about using WLC and lightweight APs throughout this book.

You can think of an AP as a bridge between the wireless clients and the wired network. And depending on the settings, you can even use an AP as a wireless bridge for bridging two wired network segments together.

In addition to the stand-alone AP, there's another type of AP that includes a built-in router, which you can use to connect both wired and wireless clients to the Internet. These devices are usually employed as NAT routers, and they're the type shown in Figure 10.3.

Wireless Network Interface Card

Every host you want to connect to a wireless network needs a wireless *network interface card* to do so. Basically, a wireless NIC does the same job as a traditional NIC, only instead of having a socket/port to plug a cable into, the wireless NIC has a radio antenna.

Figure 10.4 gives you a picture of a wireless NIC.

FIGURE 10.4 Wireless NIC

The wireless card shown in Figure 10.4 is used in a laptop or desktop computer, and pretty much all laptops have wireless cards plugged into or built into the motherboard.

NOTE

These days, it's pretty rare to use an external wireless client card because all laptops come with them built in, and desktops can be ordered with them, too. But it's good to know that you can still buy the client card shown in Figure 10.4. Typically, you would use cards like the ones shown in the figure for areas of poor reception or use with a network analyzer because they can have better range—depending on the antenna you use.

Wireless Antennas

Wireless antennas work with both transmitters and receivers. There are two broad classes of antennas on the market today: *omnidirectional* (or point-to-multipoint) and *directional* (or point-to-point). An example of omni antennas is shown in Figure 10.3, attached to the Cisco 800 AP.

Yagi antennas usually provide greater range than omni antennas of equivalent gain. Why? Because yagis focus all their power in a single direction. Omnis must disperse the same amount of power in all directions at the same time, like a large donut.

A downside to using a directional antenna is that you've got to be much more precise when aligning communication points. It's also why most APs use omnis, because often, clients and other APs can be located in any direction at any given moment.

To get a picture of this, think of the antenna on your car. Yes, it's a non-networking example, but it's still a good one because it clarifies the fact that your car's particular orientation doesn't affect the signal reception of whatever radio station you happen to be listening to. Well, most of the time, anyway. If you're in the boonies, out of range, you're out of luck—something that also applies to the networking version of omnis.

Wireless Principles

Next up, we're going to cover different types of networks you'll run into and/or design and implement as your wireless networks grow:

- IBSS
- BSS
- ESS
- Workgroup bridges
- Repeater APs
- Bridging (point-to-point and point-to-multipoint)
- Mesh

Let's check out these networks in detail now.

Independent Basic Service Set (Ad Hoc)

This is the easiest way to install wireless 802.11 devices. In this mode, the wireless NICs (or other devices) can communicate directly without needing an AP. A good example of this is two laptops with wireless NICs installed. If both cards were set up to operate in ad hoc mode, they could connect and transfer files as long as the other network settings, like protocols, were set up to enable this as well. We'll also call this an *independent basic service set* (IBSS), which is born as soon as two wireless devices communicate.

To create an ad hoc network, all you need is two or more wireless-capable devices. Once you've placed them within a range of 20–40 meters of each other, they'll "see" each other and be able to connect—assuming they share some basic configuration parameters. One computer may be able to share the Internet connection with the rest of them in your group.

Figure 10.5 shows an example of an ad hoc wireless network. Notice that there's no AP!

FIGURE 10.5 A wireless network in ad hoc mode

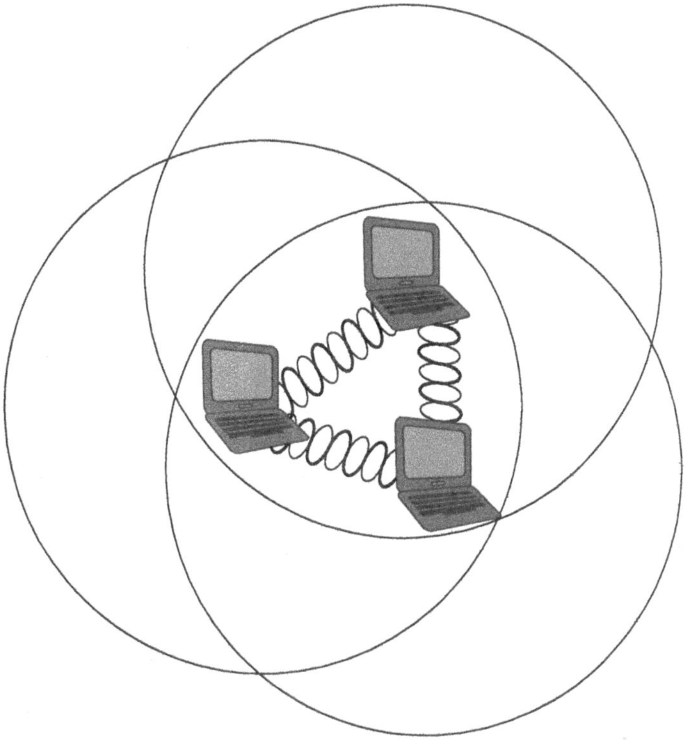

An ad hoc network, also known as peer to peer, doesn't scale well, and I wouldn't recommend it due to collision and organization issues in today's corporate networks. With the low cost of APs, you don't need this kind of network anymore anyway, except for maybe in your home—probably not even there.

Another con is that ad hoc networks are pretty insecure, so you really want to have the AdHoc setting turned off before connecting to your wired network.

Basic Service Set

A *basic service set* (BSS) is the area, or cell, defined by the wireless signal served by the AP. It can also be called a *basic service area* (BSA), and the two terms, BSS and BSA, can be interchangeable. Even so, BSS is the most common term that's used to define the cell area. Figure 10.6 shows an AP providing a BSS for hosts in the area and the basic service area (cell) that's covered by the AP.

FIGURE 10.6 Basic service set/basic service area

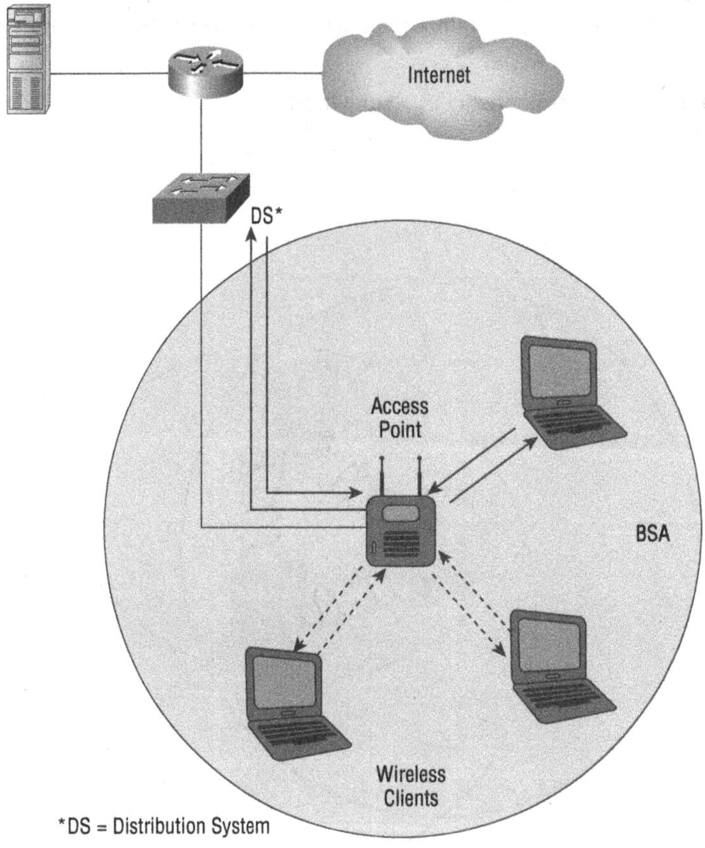

So the AP isn't connected to a wired network in this example, but it provides for the management of wireless frames so the hosts can communicate. Unlike the ad hoc network, this network will scale better, and more hosts can communicate in this network because the AP manages all network connections.

Infrastructure Basic Service Set

In infrastructure mode, wireless NICs only communicate with an AP instead of directly with each other like they do when they're in ad hoc mode. All communication between hosts, as well as any wired portion of the network, must go through the AP. Remember this important fact: in infrastructure mode, wireless clients appear to the rest of the network as though they were standard, wired hosts.

Figure 10.6 shows a typical infrastructure mode wireless network. Pay special attention to the AP and the fact that it's also connected to the wired network. This connection from the AP to the wired network is called the *distribution system (DS)* and is how the APs communicate with each other about hosts in the BSA. Basic standalone APs don't communicate with each other via the wireless network, only through the DS.

Before you configure a client to operate in wireless infrastructure mode, you need to understand SSIDs. The *service set identifier (SSID)* is the unique 32-character identifier that represents a particular wireless network and defines the BSS. And just so you know, lots of people use the terms *SSID* and *BSS* interchangeably, so don't let that confuse you! All devices involved in a particular wireless network can be configured with the same SSID. Sometimes APs even have multiple SSIDs.

Let's talk about that a little more now...

Service Set ID

Technically, an SSID is a basic name that defines the basic service area (BSA) transmitted from the AP. A good example of this is "Linksys" or "Netgear." You've probably seen that name pop up on our host when looking for a wireless network. This is the name the AP transmits out to identify which WLAN the client station can associate with.

The SSID can be up to 32 characters long. It normally consists of human-readable ASCII characters, but the standard doesn't require this. The SSID is defined as a sequence of 1–32 octets, each of which may take any value.

The SSID is configured on the AP and can be either broadcasted to the outside world or hidden. If the SSID is broadcasted, when wireless stations use their client software to scan for wireless networks, the network will appear in a list identified by its SSID. But if it's hidden, it either won't appear in the list at all, or it will show up as "unknown network," depending on the client's operating system.

Either way, a hidden SSID requires the client station to be configured with a wireless profile, including the SSID, to connect. And this requirement is above and beyond any other normal authentication steps or security essentials.

The AP associates a MAC address to this SSID. It can be the MAC address for the radio interface itself—called the *basic service set identifier* (BSSID)—or it can be derived from the MAC address of the radio interface if multiple SSIDs are used. The latter is sometimes called a *virtual MAC address*, and you would call it a *multiple basic service set identifier* (MBSSID), as shown in Figure 10.7.

There are two things you really want to make note of in this figure: first, there's a "Contractor BSSID" and a "Sales BSSID"; second, each of these SSID names is associated with a separate virtual MAC address, which was assigned by the AP.

These SSIDs are virtual and implementing things this way won't improve your wireless network's or AP's performance. You're not breaking up collision domains or broadcast

FIGURE 10.7 A network with MBSSIDs configured on an AP

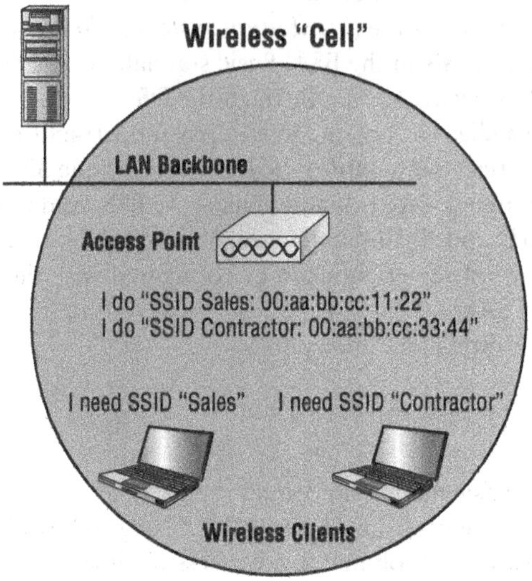

domains by creating more SSIDs on your AP; you just have more hosts sharing the same half-duplex radio. The reason for creating multiple SSIDs on your AP is so that you can set different levels of security for each client that's connecting to your AP(s).

Extended Service Set

A good thing to know is that if you set all your APs to the same SSID, mobile wireless clients can roam around freely within the same network. This is the most common wireless network design you'll find in today's corporate settings.

Doing this creates something called an *extended service set (ESS)*, which provides more coverage than a single AP and allows users to roam from one AP to another without having their host disconnected from the network. This design gives us the ability to move fairly seamlessly from one AP to another.

Figure 10.8 shows two APs configured with the same SSID in an office, thereby creating the ESS network.

For users to be able to roam throughout the wireless network—from AP to AP without losing their connection to the network—all APs must overlap by 20 percent of their signal or more to their neighbor's cells. To make this happen, be sure the channels (frequency) on each AP are set differently.

FIGURE 10.8 Extended service set (ESS)

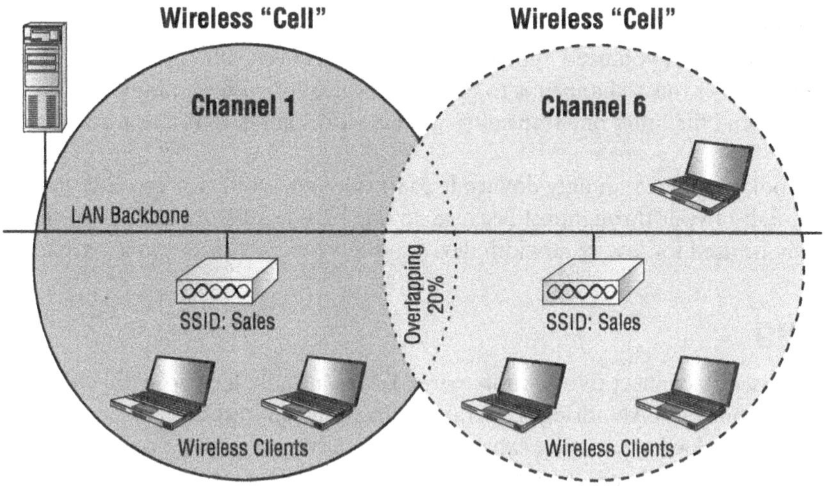

Repeaters

If you need to extend the coverage of an AP, you can either increase the gain of a directional antenna or add another AP into the area. If neither of those options solves your problem, try adding a repeater AP into the network and extending the range without having to pull an Ethernet cable for a new AP.

Figure 10.9 offers a picture of what this network design looks like.

FIGURE 10.9 An AP repeater network

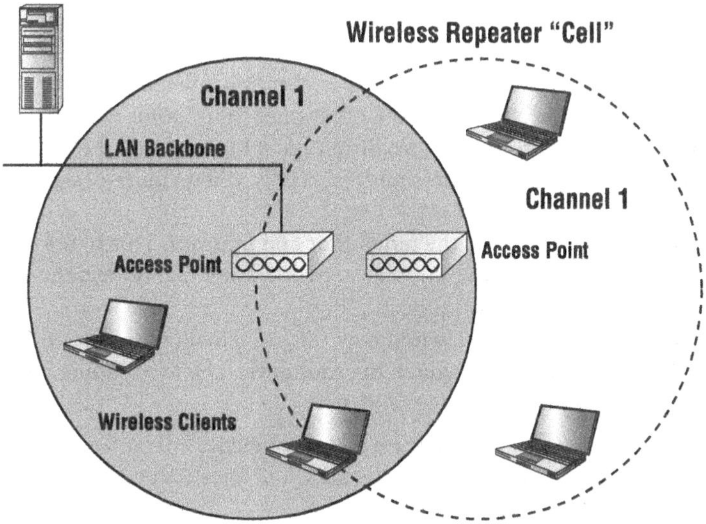

A wireless repeater AP isn't connected to the wired backbone. It uses its antenna to receive the signal from an AP that's directly connected to the network and repeats the signal for clients located too far away from it.

To make this work, you need appropriate overlap between APs, as shown in Figure 10.9. Another way to get this to happen is to place a repeater AP with two radios in use, with one receiving and the other one transmitting. This works somewhat like a dual half-duplex repeater.

Seems cool, but there's an ugly downside to this design—for every repeater installed, you lose about half of your throughput! Because no one likes less bandwidth, a repeater network should only be used for low-bandwidth devices, like a barcode reader in a warehouse.

Bridging

Bridges are used to connect two or more wired LANs, usually located within separate buildings, to create one big LAN. Bridges operate at the MAC address layer (Data Link layer), which means they have no routing capabilities. So you've got to put a router in place if you want to be able to do any IP subnetting within your network. Basically, you would use bridges to enlarge the broadcast domains on your network. Armed with a firm understanding of how bridging works, you can definitely improve your network's capacity.

To build wireless networks correctly, it's important to have a working knowledge of root and nonroot bridges, sometimes referred to as *parent* and *child* bridges. Some bridges allow clients to connect directly to them, but others don't, so make sure you understand your business requirements exactly before just randomly buying a wireless bridge.

Figure 10.10 shows the typical bridge scenarios used in today's networks.

A point-to-point wireless network is a popular design that's often used outdoors to connect two buildings or LANs together.

A point-to-multipoint design works well in a campus environment where you have a main building with a bunch of ancillary buildings you want to be able to connect to each other and back to the main one. Wireless bridges are commonly used to make these connections, and they just happen to be pricier than a traditional AP. The thing you want to remember about point-to-multipoint wireless networks is that each remote building won't be able to communicate directly with each other. To do that, they must first connect to the central main point (main building) and then to one of the other ones (multipoint buildings).

Okay—now let's get back to that root/nonroot issue I brought up a minute ago. This becomes really important to understand, especially when you're designing outdoor networks!

So look to Figure 10.10 and find the terms *root* and *nonroot*. This figure shows a traditional point-to-point and point-to-multipoint network when one bridge, the root, accepts communications only from nonroot devices.

Root devices are connected to the wired network, which allows nonroot devices, like clients, to access the wired resources through the root device. Here are some important guidelines to help you design your wireless networks:

- Nonroot devices can only communicate with root devices. Nonroot devices include nonroot bridges, workgroup bridges, repeater APs, and wireless clients.

FIGURE 10.10 Typical bridge scenarios

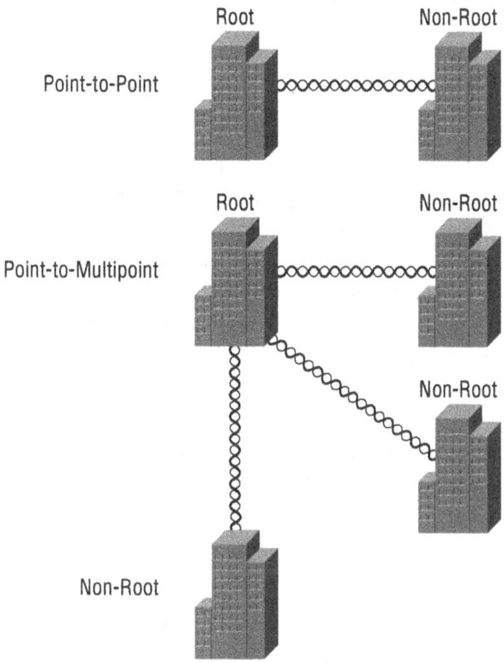

- Root devices cannot communicate with other root devices. Examples of devices that can be roots are APs and bridges.
- Nonroot devices cannot communicate with other nonroot devices.

But wait, there's one exception to that last bullet point. If you have a nonroot bridge set up as a repeater AP with two radios, the device must be configured as a nonroot device!

It will then repeat and extend the distance of your outdoor, bridged network, as shown in Figure 10.11.

FIGURE 10.11 A repeater AP bridge configured as a nonroot bridge

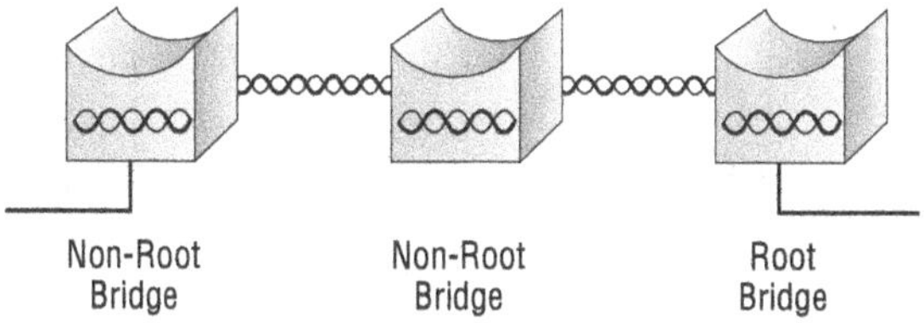

Figure 10.11 demonstrates that a nonroot bridge will communicate with another nonroot bridge only if one of the nonroot bridges has a root bridge in its uplink.

Mesh Networks

As more vendors migrate to a mesh hierarchical design and as larger networks are built using lightweight APs that are managed by a controller, you can see that we need a standardized protocol that governs how lightweight APs communicate with WLAN systems. This is exactly the role filled by one of the Internet Engineering Task Force's (IETF's) latest draft specifications, Lightweight Access Point Protocol (LWAPP).

Mesh networking infrastructure is decentralized and comparably inexpensive for all the nice amenities it provides because each host only needs to transmit as far as the next host. Hosts act as repeaters to transmit data from nearby hosts to peers that are too far away for a manageable cabled connection. The result is a network that can span a large area, especially over rough or difficult terrain.

Remember that mesh is a network topology in which devices are connected with many redundant connections between host nodes, and we can use this topology to our advantage in large wireless installations.

Figure 10.12 shows a large meshed environment using Cisco outdoor managed APs to "umbrella" an outdoor area with wireless connectivity.

FIGURE 10.12 Typical large mesh outdoor environment

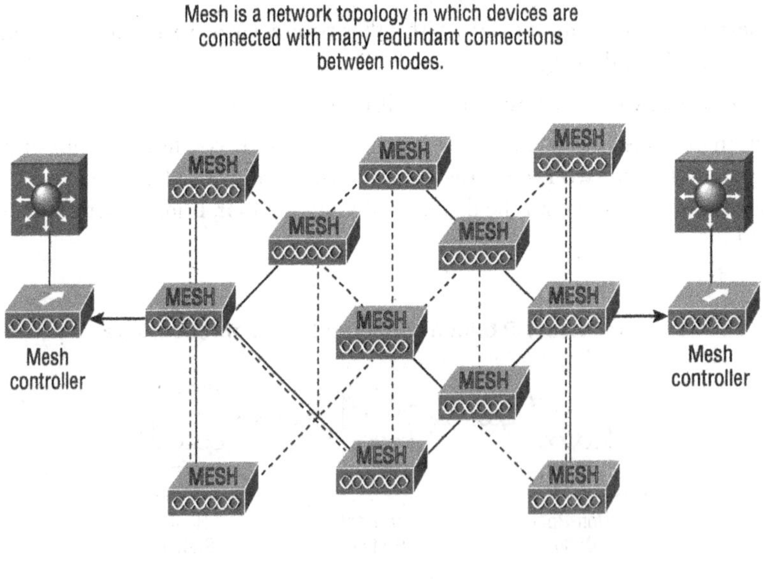

Oh, and did I mention that mesh networks also happen to be extremely reliable? Because each host can potentially be connected to several other hosts, if one of them drops out of the network because of hardware failure or something, its neighbors simply find another route. So you get extra capacity and fault tolerance automatically just by adding more hosts!

Wireless mesh connections between AP hosts are formed with a radio, providing many possible paths from a single host to other hosts. Paths through the mesh network can change in response to traffic loads, radio conditions, or traffic prioritization.

At this time, mesh networks just aren't a good solution for home use or small companies on a budget. As the saying goes, "If you have to ask. . ." As with most things in life, the more bells and whistles, the more it costs, and mesh networks are certainly no exception.

Nonoverlapping Wi-Fi Channels

In both the 2.4 GHz and the 5 GHz frequency bands, channels are defined by the standards. 802.11, 802.11b, and 802.11g use the 2.4 GHz band, also known as the industrial, scientific, and medical (ISM) band. 802.11a uses the 5 GHz band. When two APs are operating in the same area on the same channel or even an adjacent channel, they will interfere with each other. Interference lowers the throughput. Therefore, channel management to avoid interference is critical to ensure reliable operation. In this section, we will examine issues that impact channel management.

2.4 GHz Band

Within the 2.4 GHz (ISM) band are 11 channels approved for use in the United States, 13 in Europe, and 14 in Japan. Each channel is defined by its center frequency, but remember that the signal is spread across 22 MHz. There's 11 MHz on one side of the center frequency and 11 MHz on the other side, so each channel encroaches on the channel next to it—even others from it to a lesser extent.

Take a look at Figure 10.13.

FIGURE 10.13 2.4 GHz band 22 MHz wide channels

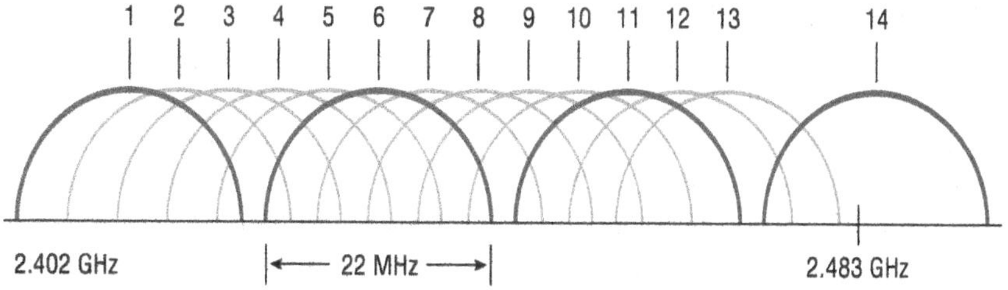

This means that consequently, within the United States, only channels 1, 6, and 11 are considered nonoverlapping. So when you have two APs in the same area that are operating on overlapping channels, the effect depends on whether they're on the same channel or on adjacent channels. Let's examine each scenario.

When APs are on the same channel, they will hear each other and defer to one another when transmitting. This is due to information sent in the header of each wireless packet that instructs all stations in the area (including any APs) to refrain from transmitting until the current transmission is received. The APs perform this duty based partially on the duration field. Anyway, the end result is that both networks will be slower because they'll be dividing their transmission into windows of opportunity to transmit between them.

When the APs are only one or two channels apart, things get a little tricky because in this case, they may not be able to hear each clearly enough to read the duration field. The ugly result of this is that they'll transmit at the same time, causing collisions that cause retransmissions and can seriously slow down your throughput—ugh! Therefore, although the two behaviors are different within these two scenarios, the end result is the same: greatly lowered throughput.

5 GHz Band

802.11a uses the 5 GHz frequency that's divided into three unlicensed bands called the *Unlicensed National Information Infrastructure* (UNII) bands. Two are adjacent to each other, but there is a frequency gap between the second and third. These bands are known as UNII-1, UNII-2, and UNII-3—the lower, middle, and upper UNII bands. Each of these bands hosts discrete channels, as in the ISM.

The 802.11a amendment specifies the location of the center point of each frequency, as well as the distance that must exist between the center point frequencies, but it fails to specify the exact width of each frequency. The good news is that the channels only overlap with the next adjacent channel, so it's easier to find nonoverlapping channels in 802.11a.

In the lower UNII band, the center points are 10 MHz apart, and in the other two, the center frequencies are 20 MHz apart. Figure 10.14 illustrates the overlap of the UNII bands (top and bottom) compared to the 2.4 GHz band (middle).

The channel numbers in the lower UNII are 36, 40, 44, and 48. In the middle UNII, the channels are 52, 56, 60, and 64. The channels in UNII-3 are 149, 153, 157, and 161.

Channel Overlap Techniques

Sometimes it becomes necessary to deploy multiple APs, and here are two scenarios that certainly scream for doing this:

- You have a large number of users in a relatively small area. Considering the nature of the contention method used by WLANs, the more users associated with a particular AP, the slower the performance. By placing multiple APs in the same area on different channels, the station-to-AP ratio improves, and performance improves accordingly.

FIGURE 10.14 5 GHz band 20 MHz wide channels

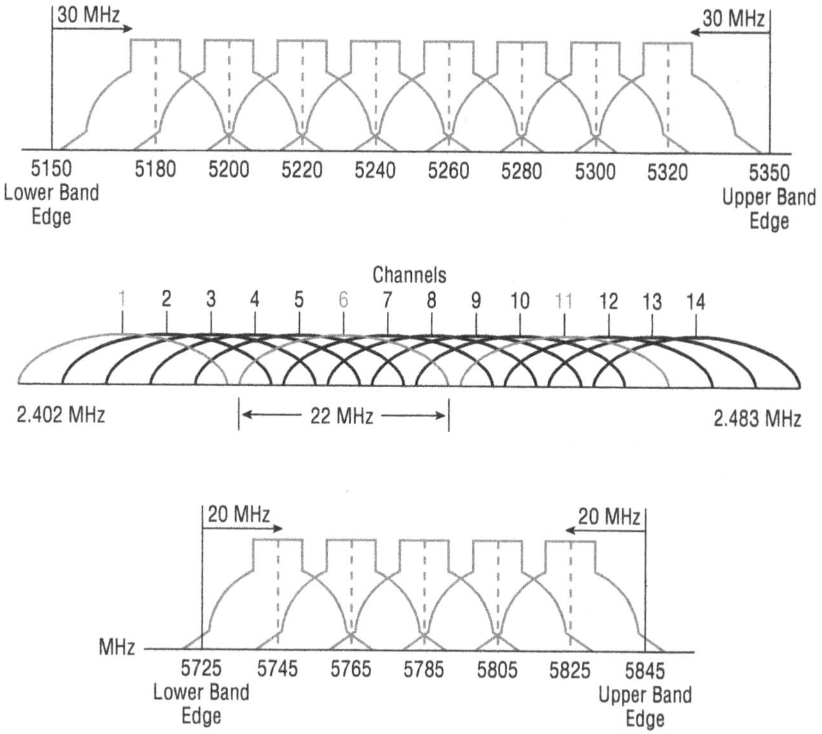

- The area to be covered exceeds the range of a single AP, and you would like to enable seamless roaming between the APs when users move around in the area.

Considering the channel overlap characteristics of both the 2.4 GHz and the 5 GHz bands, you must implement proper channel reuse when necessary to deploy multiple APs in the same area. It's also important if you want to deploy multiple APs within a large area to provide maximum coverage.

Multiple APs, Same Area

When deploying multiple APs in the same area, you need to choose channels that don't overlap. With the 2.4 GHz band, the channels must have at least four channels' space between them, and remember—only 1, 6, and 11 are nonoverlapping.

When deploying APs in the 5 GHz band (802.11a), the space between the channels can be two channels, given that there's no overlap.

Also vital to remember is that when choosing channels in a wide area, they can be reused if there's enough space between each channel's usage area or cell.

For example, in Figure 10.15, Channel 6 is used eight times, but no two areas using Channel 6 overlap.

FIGURE 10.15 Channel overlap in the 2.4 GHz range

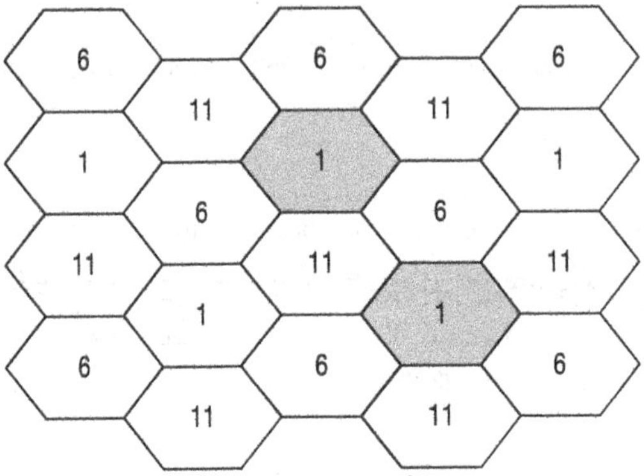

In the 5 GHz band, there are two cells between cells that use the same channel, as shown in Figure 10.16.

FIGURE 10.16 Channel overlap in the 5 GHz band

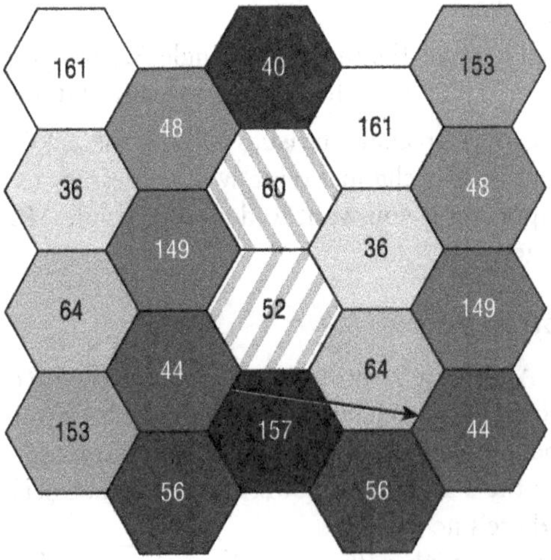

2.4 GHz/5 GHz (802.11n)

802.11n builds on previous 802.11 standards by adding *multiple-input multiple-output (MIMO)*, which uses multiple transmitters and receiver antennas to increase data throughput and range. 802.11n can allow up to eight antennas, but most of today's APs use only four to six. This setup permits considerably higher data rates than 802.11a/b/g does.

The following three vital items are combined in 802.11n to enhance performance:

- At the Physical layer, the way a signal is sent is changed, enabling reflections and interferences to become an advantage instead of a source of degradation.
- Two 20 MHz-wide channels are combined to increase throughput.
- At the MAC layer, a different way of managing packet transmission is used.

It's important to know that 802.11n isn't truly compatible with 802.11b, 802.11g, or even 802.11a, but it is designed to be backward compatible with them. How 802.11n achieves backward compatibility is by changing the way frames are sent so they can be understood by 802.11a/b/g.

Here's a list of some of the primary components of 802.11n that together sum up why people claim 802.11n is more reliable and predictable:

40 MHz channels 802.11g and 802.11a use 20 MHz channels and employ tones on the sides of each channel that are not used to protect the main carrier. This means that 11 Mbps goes unused and is basically wasted. 802.11n aggregates two carriers to double the speed from 54 Mbps to more than 108. Add in those wasted 11 Mbps rescued from the side tones, and you get a grand total of 119 Mbps!

MAC efficiency 802.11 protocols require acknowledgment of each and every frame. 802.11n can pass many packets before an acknowledgment is required, which saves you a huge amount of overhead. This is called *block acknowledgment*.

Multiple-input multiple-output (MIMO) Several frames are sent by several antennae over several paths and are then recombined by another set of antennae to optimize throughput and multipath resistance. This is called *spatial multiplexing*.

Okay—now that you've nailed down the a/b/g/n networks, it's time to move on and get into some detail about RF.

Radio Frequency

It all starts when an electrical signal like one that represents data from a LAN needs to be transmitted via radio waves. First, the signal is sent to an antenna where it is then radiated in a pattern that's determined by the particular type of antenna. The pattern radiated from an antenna is an electrical signal called an *alternating current*, and the direction of the signal's current changes cyclically. This cycle creates a pattern known as a waveform. The waveform has peaks and valleys that repeat in a pattern, and the distance between one peak or valley and the next is known as the wavelength. The wavelength determines certain properties of the signal—for example, the impact of obstacles in the environment.

Some AM radio stations use wavelengths that stretch well over a thousand feet, or 400–500 meters, but our wireless networks use a wavelength that's smaller than your outstretched hand. Believe it or not, satellites use tiny waves that only measure about one millimeter!

Because cable, fiber, and other physical media impose various limitations upon data transmission, the ultimate goal is for us to use radio waves to send information instead. A radio wave can be defined as an electromagnetic field that radiates from a sender, which hopefully gets to the intended receiver of the energy that's been sent. A good example of this concept is the electromagnetic energy we call light that our eyes can interpret and send to our brains, which then transform it into impressions of colors.

Figure 10.17 shows the RF spectrum that we use today to send our wireless data.

FIGURE 10.17 RF spectrum

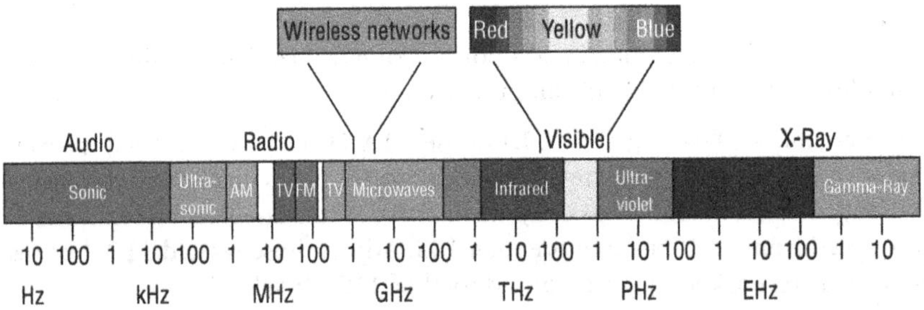

It is good that our eyes can't see these kinds of waves because if we could, we would be so bombarded with them that we wouldn't be able to see much else!

When traveling through the air, certain wave groups are more efficient than others depending on the type of information being sent because they have different properties. So, it follows that different terms are used to define different signals generated in the transmitter when they're sent to the antenna to create the movements of the electrons generated within an electric field. This process creates an electromagnetic wave, and we use the terms frequency and wavelength to define them.

The frequency determines how often a signal is "seen," with one frequency cycle called *1 hertz* (Hz). The size or distance of the cycle pattern is called the *wavelength*. The shorter the wavelength, the more often the signal repeats itself, and the more often it repeats, the higher its frequency is considered to be when compared with a wavelength that repeats itself less often in the same amount of time.

To get a picture of this, check out Figure 10.18.

FIGURE 10.18 Frequency

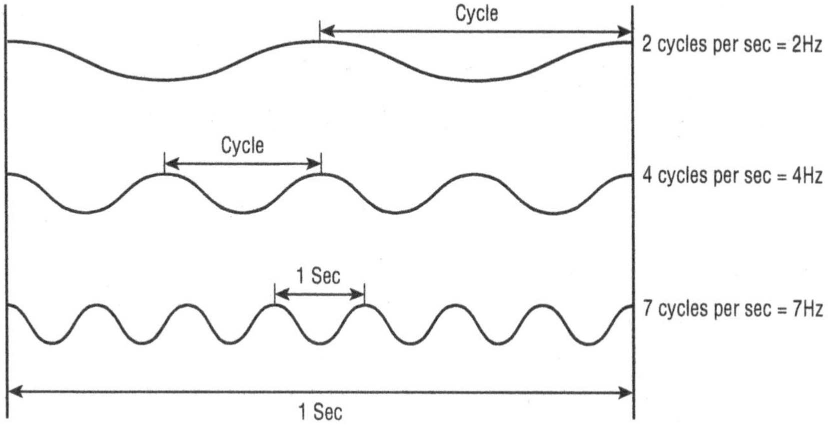

Here are some important RF terms to remember:

- 1 Hz = The RF signal cycle occurs once a second.
- 1 MHz = The signal cycle occurs 1 million times a second.
- 1 GHz = The signal cycle occurs 1 billion times a second.

Also good to know is that lower frequencies can travel farther but provide less bandwidth. Higher frequencies have a wavelength with fast repeat times, which means that although they can't travel long distances, they can carry higher bandwidth. Another important term to get cozy with before we move on and talk about how RF is affected by many factors is *amplitude*. Amplitude refers to the strength of the signal and is commonly represented by the Greek symbol α.

It has a profound effect on signal strength because it represents the level of energy injected into one cycle. The more energy injected in a cycle, the higher the amplitude. The term *gain* is used to describe an increase in the RF signal.

In Figure 10.19, the top signal has the least amplitude or signal strength, and the bottom example has the greatest amplitude or signal strength. By the way, that's the only difference among each of these signals—all three have the same frequency because the distance between the peaks and valleys in them is the same.

Okay, let's say you're playing an electric guitar that you've plugged into your amp. If you turn up the amp's volume knob, the increased or amplified signal will look like the one on the bottom. Of note, attenuation also happens naturally the farther the signal moves from the transmitter—another reason for the use of amplifiers. We can even use certain antennas to give us more gain, which, in combination with the transmitter power, can determine our signal's ability to go the distance.

FIGURE 10.19 Amplitude

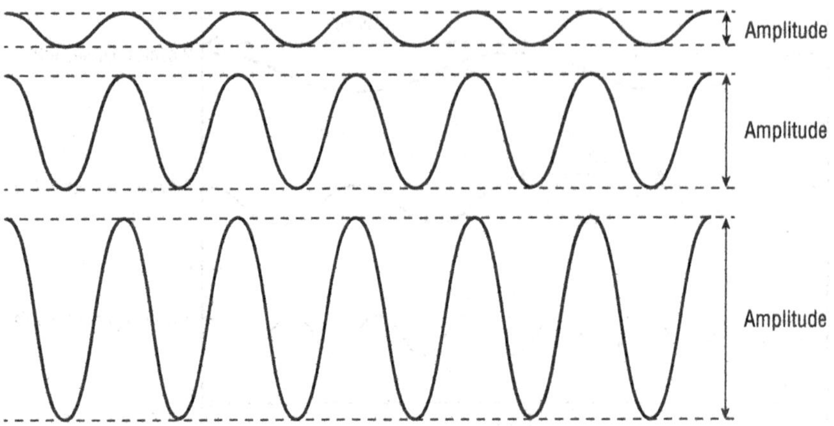

A downside to amps is that they can distort the signal and/or overload and damage the receiver if too much power is pushed into it. So finding the right balance takes experience, and yes, sometimes parting with some good ol' cash to score better equipment.

Radio Frequency Behaviors

When you're armed with a solid understanding of RF signals, the challenges inherent to wireless networking and the things you can do to mitigate factors that negatively affect transmissions become oh-so-much-easier to deal with! So, coming up next, I'm going to cover vital RF characteristics.

Free Space Path Loss

Attenuation is defined as the effect of a signal over the time or length of a cable or other medium. The signal is weakened the farther it travels from the transmitting device. Free space path loss is similar because it's a limiting factor with regard to the distance that RF signals can successfully travel and be received properly. We call it *free space path loss* because environmental obstacles don't cause it. Instead, it's simply a result of the normal attenuation that happens as the signal gradually weakens over the distance it travels.

Figure 10.20 shows an example of free space path loss.

There are two major factors on both ends of a transmission that determine the effects of free space path loss: the strength of the signal delivered to the antenna and the type of antenna it's delivered to. The AP can amplify the signal to a certain extent because with most APs and many client devices, signal strength can be controlled. This type of signal gain is called *active* gain.

FIGURE 10.20 Free space path loss

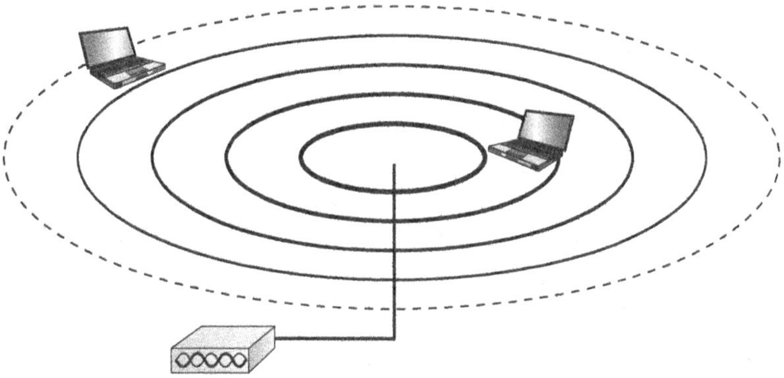

As the wave spreads away from the emitter, it gets weaker.

A directional antenna focuses the same amount of energy in one direction that an omnidirectional antenna sends horizontally in all directions. This results in a signal of the same strength being able to travel farther. In this scenario, the antenna provides what we call *passive* gain, which means that it comes from the particular shape of the antenna pattern itself.

On the receiving end, the same factors come into play. First, the receiver has a certain listening strength, called *received sensitivity*, and second, the shape of the receiving antenna has the same kind of effect on a signal that the shape of a sending antenna does. This means that two highly directional antennas that happen to be aimed perfectly at each other can carry a signal of the same strength much farther than two omnidirectional antennas.

Absorption

Because our world isn't flat and has lots of objects on it, as a signal radiates away from the antenna, it will invariably encounter obstacles like walls, ceilings, trees, people, buildings, cars—you get the idea. Even though the signal can pass through most of these obstacles, a price is paid when it does so in the form of decreased amplitude. Earlier, you learned that amplitude is the height and depth of each wave in the pattern that represents the signal strength.

So when the signal manages to pass through the object—which, surprisingly, in most cases it will—it always emerges weaker on the other side. This is what's referred to as *absorption* because the people and things the signal passes through actually absorb some of its energy as heat.

To get a picture of the absorption phenomenon, check out Figure 10.21.

FIGURE 10.21 Absorption

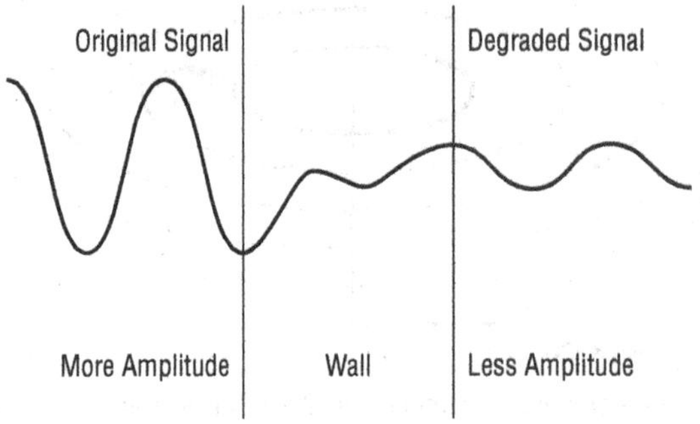

Important to note is that the amount of signal degradation depends on the nature of what it has passed through. Clearly, drywall is not going to cause the same amount of signal degradation that concrete will, and yes, there are some materials that will block the signal completely. This is why we perform site surveys—to define where the problem areas are and figure out how to get around them by strategically placing AP(s) where they will be able to function with the least amount of obstruction.

Reflection

Now you know that absorption occurs when a signal travels through an obstacle and loses some of its energy, right? Well, *reflection* occurs when a signal strikes an object at an angle instead of directly. When this happens, some of the energy will be absorbed, but some will reflect off at an angle equal to the angle at which it struck the object.

Figure 10.22 illustrates reflection.

The exact ratio of the amount absorbed to the amount reflected depends on how porous the material is that the signal ran into and the angle at which it hit the material. The more porous the material, the more of the signal's energy will be absorbed by it.

Another thing that influences how much of the signal is reflected and how much is absorbed is the signal's frequency. Signals in the 2.4 GHz range can behave differently than those in the 5 GHz range. So just remember that these three factors influence absorption/reflection ratio:

- Angle of the signal
- Frequency of the signal
- Nature of the surface

FIGURE 10.22 Reflection

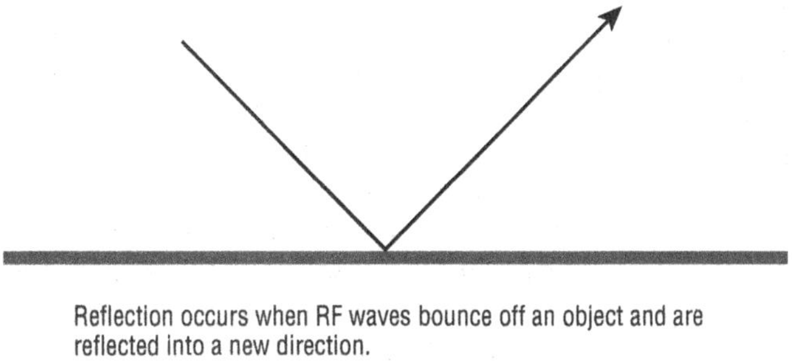

Reflection occurs when RF waves bounce off an object and are
reflected into a new direction.

One of the main problems reflection causes is a phenomenon called *multipath*.

Multipath

Multipath occurs when reflection is occurring. Remember, there's lots of stuff around that reflected signals can bounce off before they finally arrive at the receiver, and because these bounced signals took a longer path to get to the receiver than the ones that took a direct path, it makes sense that they typically arrive later.

This is illustrated in Figure 10.23.

FIGURE 10.23 Multipath

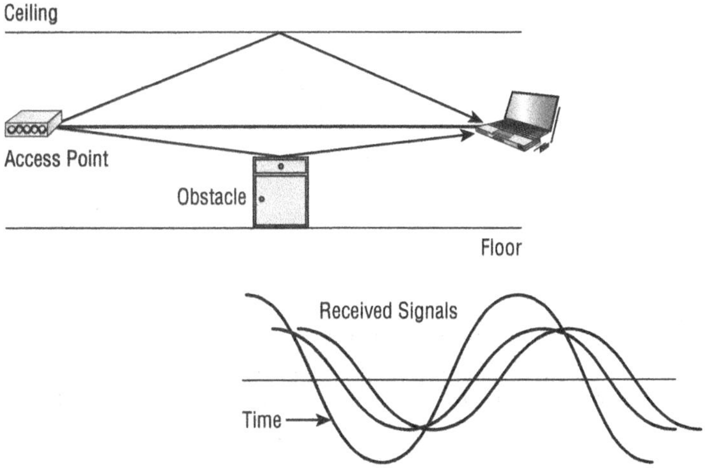

This is definitely not a good thing—because they arrive later, they'll be out of phase with the main signal, as shown in Figure 10.21. Remember how the signal wavelength has a recurring pattern? Well, if the pattern of the main signal doesn't line up with that of the reflected signal, they're out of phase—and how much they're out of phase varies in degrees.

This is ugly because out-of-phase signals are degraded signals, and if those signals are 120–170 degrees out, multipath can weaken them. This concept is known as *downfade*. It gets worse, too—if they arrive 180 degrees out, they cancel each other entirely, a nasty effect suitably called *nulling the signal*. If it's your lucky day and they go full circle, the rogue signals arrive 360 degrees out, and blam—they're right back in phase and arrive at the same time. This boosts the amplitude or signal and is known as *upfade*.

Clearly, being able to deal with multipath events well is an important skill, but for now, just one last thought: although I just said how bad multipath can be (and it can be!), IEEE 802.11n can take advantage of this to get higher speeds.

Refraction

Refraction refers to a change in the direction of a signal as a result of it passing through different mediums. Because this mostly happens when a signal passes from dry air to wet, or vice versa, it's more of a concern with long-range outdoor wireless links.

Figure 10.24 shows how refraction might look.

FIGURE 10.24 Refraction

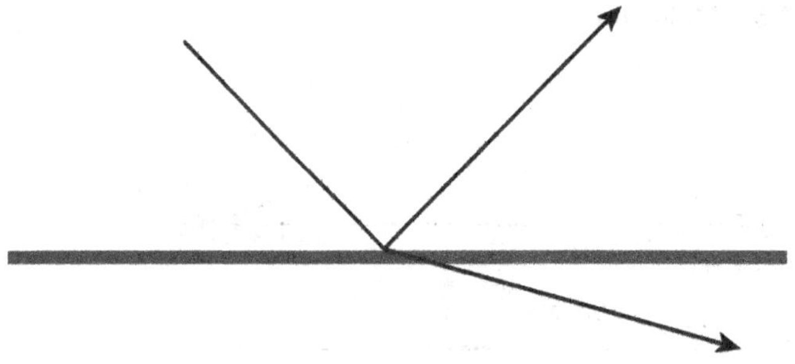

As the figure shows, refraction occurs when waves pass through a heterogeneous medium and some of the waves are reflected and others are bent. Drier air tends to bend the signal away from the Earth, whereas humid air tends to bend the signal toward Earth.

Diffraction

Diffraction happens when a signal bends around an object. Think about what happens when you throw a rock into a quiet pool of water. As soon as your rock plunks in, it sends perfect rings of waves radiating outward from where it sank in all directions. If these waves slam into an object in the pool, you can see the wave bend around the object and change direction. RF signals do this too, and when they do, we experience this in the form of dead spots in places behind, say, a building.

Figure 10.25 shows a simple example of what diffraction may look like with an RF signal.

FIGURE 10.25 Diffraction

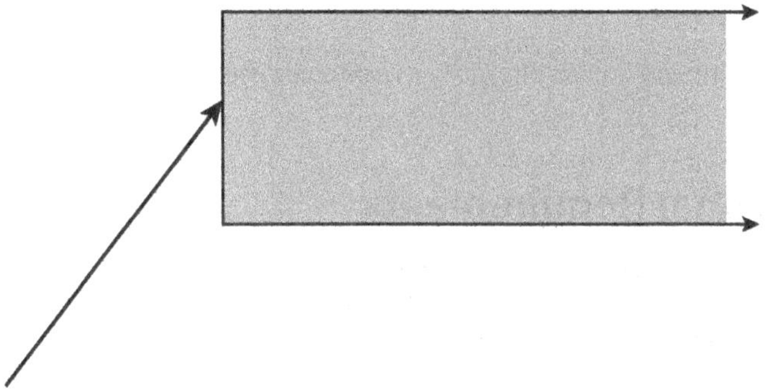

Diffraction is commonly confused with refraction, but the two are vastly dissimilar because diffraction bends the RF, whereas in refraction, the RF bounces.

Scattering

Scattering is a lot like refraction, but the difference is that when signals strike an object or objects, their scattered reflections bound off in many unpredictable directions instead of just bouncing back off at an angle pretty much equal to the angle at which it hit the object. This phenomenon is caused by the attributes of the object or objects. Here are some objects and conditions that can cause scattering:

- Dust, humidity, and microdroplets of water in the atmosphere and rain
- Density fluctuations within a given object and its surface irregularities
- Uneven surfaces like moving water and tree leaves

Figure 10.26 shows what scatter might look like to an RF signal.

The worst thing about scattering is—you guessed it—its unpredictable nature, which makes mitigation efforts more than just a little difficult!

All this brings me back to that all-important site survey. I'm repeating this because nothing is more important than performing a thorough one before and after you design a WLAN! There's just nothing else that can help you accurately identify, predict, and mitigate RF behaviors, determine proper AP placement, select the right type of antenna(s),

FIGURE 10.26 Scattering

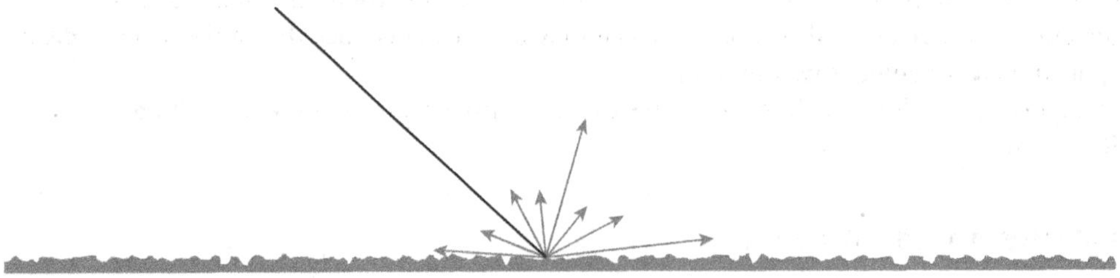

or even make adjustments to the physical environment itself if possible (like trimming some trees).

RF Operational Requirements

Even in WLAN environments that exist mostly in fantasy, where most or none of the aforementioned potential problems are present, there are still certain operational requirements if you want your WLAN to work well—or even at all.

Those absolute necessities that affect the performance of WLANs, and in some cases, directly affect whether or not they'll function at all, are what I'm going to cover next.

Line of Sight

Okay—so although it's true that in an indoor scenario, there are usually not as many things signals can bounce off of, they still exist there, too. So again, do that site survey! Whether your WLAN will only cover a small outside or inside area, signals can usually travel through and even bounce off a few objects and still reach the receiver in fine shape. But when you're dealing with a larger coverage area using omnidirectional and semidirectional antennas, like in an outdoor area—especially when creating a point-to-point wireless bridge between, say, two buildings—something known as *line of sight* becomes critical for success. And if you're faced with creating a long-distance wireless connection using highly directional and/or dish antennas, line of sight becomes even more critical.

I want you to understand that line of sight is not as simple as having the center of the two antennas properly lined up. That's a visual line of sight, and RF line of sight and visual line of sight are two different things. Regarding WLANs, RF line of sight is what you need, and to help you understand that, first, let's review how spread-spectrum technology works.

In narrowband RF, the signal is set to a single frequency and stays there. In the spread spectrum, although people talk about channels and the like, the signal is actually being spread across a range of frequencies.

What I mean by this is that when we say a device is using "Channel 6," that channel is actually 22 MHz wide, and the signal is spread across the entire 22 MHz range.

Furthermore, if a signal is spread out like this, it means that all of it, or at least a certain percentage of it, must be received in order for it to be interpreted well.

The following obstructions might obscure a line-of-sight link:

- Topographic features, such as mountains
- Curvature of the Earth
- Buildings and other man-made objects
- Trees

Even if the visual line of sight is perfect, the RF line of sight can still be lacking if the distance is so far that the curvature of the Earth gets in the way. Check out Figure 10.27.

FIGURE 10.27 Line of sight

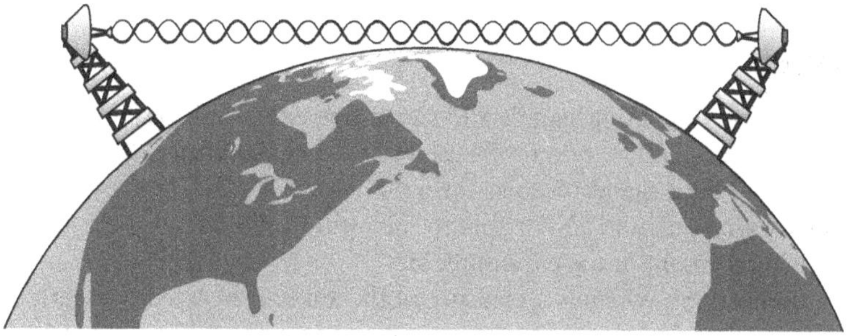

Line of sight disappears at 6 miles (9.7 km) because of the curvature of the earth.

Now, look ahead to Figure 10.28—see those trees?

Okay, I know they're not actual size, but what they signify is that objects can block even a small part of what we call the *Fresnel zone*, which is closely related to RF line of sight and is what you're going to learn about next.

Fresnel Zone

The Fresnel zone is an elliptical-shaped area between the transmitter and receiver that must be at least 60 percent clear for the signal to be received properly.

In Figure 10.28, even though a visual line of sight looks just great, there's a major blockage of the football-shaped area around the center line of the signal. This is very bad. You've personally experienced RF line-of-sight blocking if you've ever had a tree branch grow a lot over the summer and interfere with your satellite dish.

FIGURE 10.28 Fresnel zone

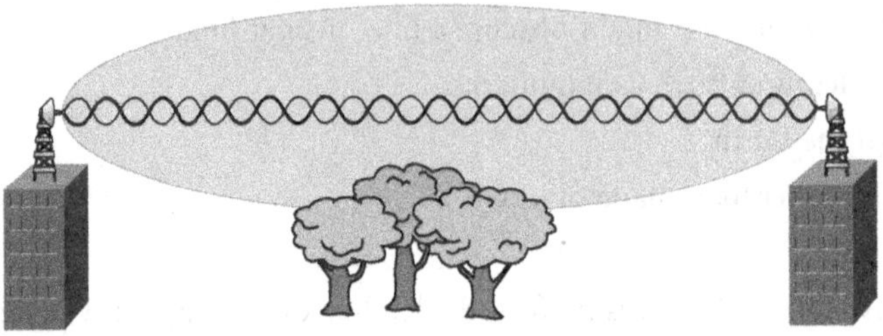

Interestingly, these zones are in alternating bands, with the inner band being in phase, the next being out of phase, and then the next one in phase again. So if one of us could figure out how to block only the out-of-phase band while leaving the in-phase bands alone, it just might be a technological breakthrough. (Hasn't happened yet!)

RSSI and SNR

We've logged a lot of ink discussing signals and signal strength, but so far, I haven't told you how these are measured. There are two terms used to discuss signal strength: received signal strength indicator (RSSI) and signal-to-noise ratio (SNR). RSSI is designed to describe the strength of the signal received, and SNR refers to the ratio of the signal to the surrounding RF noise that is always present in the environment.

First, let's talk about RSSI, which is a measure of the amount of signal strength that actually arrives at the receiving device. It has a grade value ranging from 0 to 255. For each grade value, an equivalent dBm (decibels relative to a milliwatt) value is displayed. For example, 0 on the scale may equal –95 dBm, and 100 might be –15 dBm. So 0 would equal a much greater loss of signal than 100 would.

I'll get into dBm in more detail soon, but for now understand that dBm is not an absolute measure; it's a relative one. What I mean by *relative* is that it's a value referenced against another value—in this case, milliwatts. Decibels are used to measure an increase or decrease in power as opposed to an absolute value, meaning that decibel values come through as positive (gain) and negative (loss). RSSI values are negative and represent the level of signal loss that can be experienced en route with the card still able to receive the signal correctly. Most manufacturers will have a table listing the RSSI that's required at each frequency.

RSSI values can't be compared from one card vendor to another because each company typically uses a different scale. For example, Company A might be using a scale of 0 to 100, whereas Company B is using a scale from 0 to 60. Because the scales are different, the resulting RSSI values can't be compared, right?

Figure 10.29 depicts the relationship between these values.

SNR is a critical comparison of the amount of signal as compared to the surrounding noise. If the level of noise is too close to the level of the signal, the signal can't be picked out

FIGURE 10.29 SNR

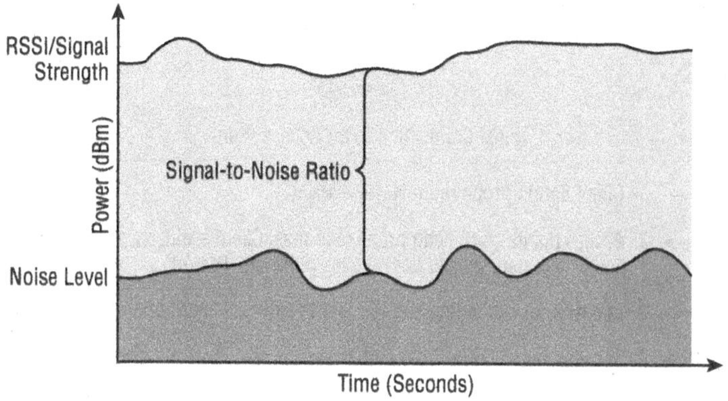

from the noise and understood. Think of this as someone whispering in a really loud room. A higher value is good for SNR.

Wireless Security

Now that we've covered the very basics of wireless devices used in today's networks, let's move on to wireless security.

At the foundational level, authentication uniquely identifies the user and/or machine. The encryption process protects the data or the authentication process by scrambling the information enough that it becomes unreadable by anyone trying to capture the raw frames.

Authentication and Encryption

Two types of authentication were specified by the IEEE 802.11 committee: open and shared-key authentication. Open authentication involves little more than supplying the right SSID, but it's the most common method in use today.

With shared-key authentication, the AP sends the client device a challenge-text packet that the client must then encrypt with the correct Wired Equivalent Privacy (WEP) key and return to the AP. Without the correct key, authentication will fail, and the client won't be allowed to associate with the AP.

Figure 10.30 shows shared-key authentication.

Shared-key authentication is still not considered secure because all a bad guy has to do to get around it is to detect both the clear-text challenge, the same challenge encrypted with a WEP key, and then decipher the WEP key. So it's no surprise that shared key isn't used in today's WLANs.

FIGURE 10.30 Open access process

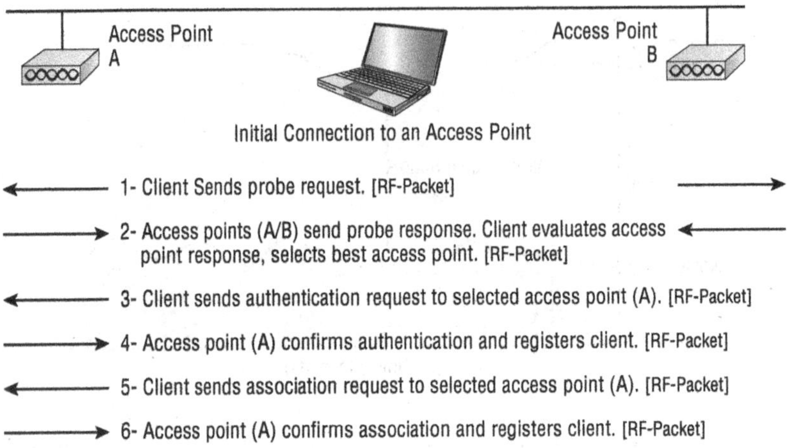

Access Point
A
Access Point
B
Initial Connection to an Access Point
1- Client Sends probe request. [RF-Packet]
2- Access points (A/B) send probe response. Client evaluates access point response, selects best access point. [RF-Packet]
3- Client sends authentication request to selected access point (A). [RF-Packet]
4- Access point (A) confirms authentication and registers client. [RF-Packet]
5- Client sends association request to selected access point (A). [RF-Packet]
6- Access point (A) confirms association and registers client. [RF-Packet]

All Wi-Fi certified wireless LAN products are shipped in "open access" mode, with their security features turned off. Although open access or no security sounds scary, it's totally acceptable for places like public hot spots. But it's definitely not an option for an enterprise organization, and it's probably not a good idea for your private home network, either!

Check out Figure 10.31 to see the open-access wireless process.

FIGURE 10.31 Open access process

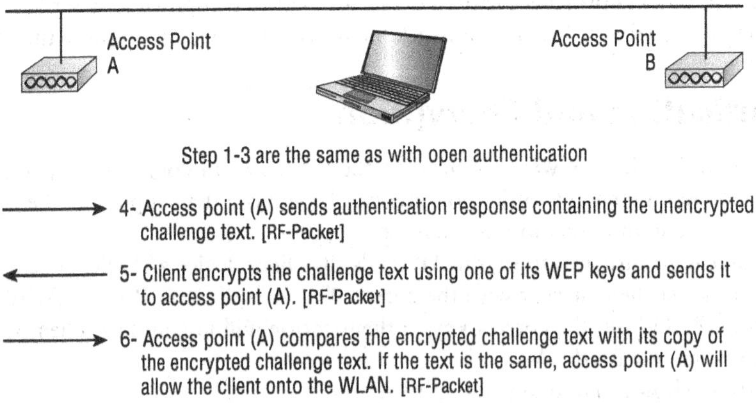

Access Point
A
Access Point
B
Step 1-3 are the same as with open authentication
4- Access point (A) sends authentication response containing the unencrypted challenge text. [RF-Packet]
5- Client encrypts the challenge text using one of its WEP keys and sends it to access point (A). [RF-Packet]
6- Access point (A) compares the encrypted challenge text with its copy of the encrypted challenge text. If the text is the same, access point (A) will allow the client onto the WLAN. [RF-Packet]

Here, you can see that an authentication request has been sent and "validated" by the AP. But when open authentication is used or set to "none" in the wireless controller, the request is pretty much guaranteed not to be denied. For now, understand that this authentication is done at the MAC layer (layer 2), so don't confuse this with the higher-layer authentication we'll cover later, which occurs after the client is associated with the AP.

With what I've told you so far, I'm sure you agree that security seriously needs to be enabled on wireless devices during their installation in enterprise environments. But believe it or not, a surprising number of companies don't enable any WLAN security features, dangerously exposing their valuable data networks and resources to tremendous risk!

The reason these products are shipped in open access mode is so anyone, even someone without any IT knowledge, can buy an AP, plug it into their cable or DSL modem, and voilà—they're up and running. It's marketing, plain and simple, and simplicity sells. But that doesn't mean you should leave the default settings there—unless you want to allow that network to be open to the public!

WEP

With open authentication, even if a client can complete authentication and associate with an AP, the use of WEP prevents the client from sending and receiving data from an AP unless the client has the correct WEP key.

A WEP key is composed of either 40 or 128 bits, and in its basic form, it's usually statically defined by the network administrator on the AP and on all clients that communicate with that AP. When static WEP keys are used, a network administrator must perform the tedious task of entering the same keys on every device in the WLAN.

Clearly, we now have fixes for this because tackling this manually would be administratively impossible in today's huge corporate wireless networks!

WPA and WPA2: An Overview

Wi-Fi Protected Access (WPA) and WPA2 were created in response to the shortcomings of WEP. WPA was a stopgap measure taken by the Wi-Fi Alliance to provide better security until the IEEE finalized the 802.11i standard. When 802.11i was ratified, WPA2 incorporated its improvements, so there are some significant differences between WPA and WPA2.

These are each essentially another form of basic security that is really just an add-on to the specifications. Even though you can totally lock the vault, WPA/WPA2 preshared key (PSK) is a better form of wireless security than any other basic wireless security method I've talked about so far. Still, keep in mind that I did say basic!

WPA is a standard developed by the Wi-Fi Alliance and provides a standard for authentication and encryption of WLANs that's intended to solve known security problems. The standard takes into account the well-publicized AirSnort and man-in-the-middle WLAN attacks. So, of course, we use WPA2 to help us with today's security issues because we can use AES encryption, which provides for better key caching than WPA does. WPA is only a software update, whereas WPA2 required a hardware update, but you'd be hard-pressed to find a laptop or any PC today that doesn't have WPA2 support built-in.

The PSK verifies users via a password or identifying code, often called a *passphrase*, on both the client machine and the AP. A client gains access to the network only if its password matches the AP's password. The PSK also provides keying material that TKIP or AES uses to generate an encryption key for each packet of transmitted data.

Although it's more secure than static WEP, the PSK method still has a lot in common with static WEP in that the PSK is stored on the client station and can be compromised if the client station is lost or stolen—even though finding this key isn't all that easy to do. This is exactly why I definitely recommend using a seriously strong PSK passphrase that includes a mixture of letters, numbers, cases, and nonalphanumeric characters. With WPA, it's still possible to specify the use of dynamic encryption keys that change each time a client establishes a connection.

NOTE The benefit of WPA keys over static WEP keys is that the WPA keys can change dynamically while the system is used.

WPA is a step toward the IEEE 802.11i standard and uses many of the same components, with the exception of encryption. 802.11i (WPA2) uses AES-CCMP encryption. The IEEE 802.11i standard replaced WEP with a specific mode of AES known as Counter Mode with Cipher Block Chaining Message Authentication Code Protocol (CCMP). This allows AES-CCMP to provide both data confidentiality (encryption) and data integrity—now we're getting somewhere!

Wi-Fi Protected Access

WPA was designed to offer two methods of authentication in implementation. The first, called *WPA Personal* or WPA (PSK), was designed to work using a passphrase for authentication, but it improves the level of protection for authentication and data encryption, too.

WPA PSK uses the exact same encryption as WPA Enterprise—the PSK just replaces the check to a RADIUS server for the authentication portion. PSK offers us these benefits:

- The IV is 48 bits and not 24 bits. This increases the number of vector values from over 16 million possibilities to 280 trillion values. Also, they must be used in order and not randomly, which, oddly enough, increases security because it eliminates the reuse of IVs—a condition referred to as *collisions*, not to be confused with collision domains.
- The key for each frame is changed for each packet; hence the term *temporal* or temporary. A serial number is applied to each frame, and the serial number, along with the temporal key and the IV, is used to create a key unique to each frame. Furthermore, each frame undergoes per-packet key hashing as well.
- Centralized key management by the AP, including broadcast and unicast keys. The broadcast keys are rotated to ensure they don't remain the same, even though at any particular point in time, they will be the same for all stations in the basic service set (BSS). When a PSK is used for authentication, it's used to derive the pairwise master key (PMK) as well as the resulting pairwise transient keys (PTKs). No worries—I'll tell you more about those concepts later!
- Finally, we get a new form of frame check sequence (FCS). The FCS refers to the part of any packet that's used to ensure that the integrity of the packet is maintained. It's also used to determine if anything changed in the packet. Here's a scenario: through an

attack called *bit flipping*, a hacker could generate a TCP resend message. The AP will forward this TCP resend to the wireless space, thereby generating a new initialization vector. A bit-flipping attack allows the attacker to artificially increase the number of IVs, thus speeding up a WEP attack by increasing the chance of duplicates or collisions occurring. TKIP uses a message integrity code (MIC) instead of a regular FCS. MIC can detect almost all changes to a bit in the frame, so it can bust bit flipping much more readily than FCS. If it detects a MIC failure, it will report this event to the AP. If the AP receives two of these failures in 60 seconds, it will respond by disassociating all stations and stopping all traffic for 60 seconds. This makes it impossible for the hacker to recover the key—nice!

The only known weakness of WPA PSK lies in the complexity of the password or key used on the AP and the stations. If it happens to be one that's easily guessed, it could be susceptible to something known as a dictionary attack. This type of attack uses a dictionary file that tries out a huge number of passwords until the correct match is found. Consequently, this is very time-consuming for the hacker. WPA3's big difference is how it can prevent a dictionary attack.

Because of this, WPA PSK should mainly be used in a SOHO environment, and an enterprise environment only when device restrictions, such as voice over IP (VoIP) phones, don't support RADIUS authentication.

WPA2 Enterprise

Regardless of whether WPA or WPA2 is used during the initial connection between the station and the AP, the two agree on common security requirements. Following that agreement, a series of important key related activities occur in this specific order:

1. The authentication server derives a key called the *pairwise master key* (PMK). This key will remain the same for the entire session. The same key is derived from the station. The server moves the PMK to the AP where it's needed.
2. The next step is called the four-way handshake. Its purpose is to derive another key called the *pairwise transient key* (PTK). This step occurs between the AP and the station and, of course, requires four steps to complete:
   a. The AP sends a random number known as a *nonce* to the station.
   b. Using this value along with the PMK, the station creates a key used to encrypt a nonce that's called the *snonce*, which is then sent to the AP. It includes a reaffirmation of the security parameters that were negotiated earlier. It also protects the integrity of this frame with a MIC. This bidirectional exchange of nonces is a critical part of the key-generation process.
   c. Now that the AP has the client nonce, it will generate a key for unicast transmission with the station. It sends the nonce back to the station along with a group key, commonly called a *group transient key*, as well as a confirmation of security parameters.
   d. The fourth message simply confirms to the AP that the temporal keys (TKs) are in place.

One final function performed by this four-way handshake is to confirm that the two peers are still "alive."

802.11i

Although WPA2 was built with the 802.11i standard in mind, some features were added when the standard was ratified:

- A list of EAP methods that can be used with the standard.
- AES-CCMP for encryption instead of RC4.
- Better key management; the master key can be cached, permitting a faster reconnect time for the station.

But wait, there's more! There is a new sheriff in town, and its name is WPA3.

WPA3

In 2018, the Wi-Fi Alliance announced the new WPA3, a Wi-Fi security standard to replace WPA2. The WPA2 standard has served us well, but it's been around since 2004! WPA3 will improve the WPA2 protocol with more security features, just like WPA2 was designed to fix WPA.

What's fun about WPA3 is the naming used to define the handshake as well as the exploits—yes, exploits are already out there! First, remember that WPA2 uses a PSK, but WPA3 has been upgraded to 128-bit encryption and uses a system called *simultaneous authentication of equals* (SAE). This is referred to as the *dragonfly handshake*. It forces network interaction on login so that hackers can't deploy a dictionary attack by downloading its cryptographic hash and then running cracking software to break it.

Even more fun, the known exploits of WPA3 are called *Dragonblood*. The reason these Dragonblood exploits are already out is that the protections in WPA2 haven't really changed that much in WPA3—at least not yet. Worse, WPA3 is backward compatible, meaning that if someone wants to attack you, they can just use WPA2 in an attack to effectively downgrade your WPA3-compatible system back to WPA2!

Like WPA2, the Wi-Fi Protected Access security includes solutions for personal and enterprise networks. But WPA3 offers up some very cool new goodies, which pave the way for more powerful authentication and enhanced cryptographic clout. It also helps to protect vital networks by preserving resiliency and offers a cleaner approach to security.

Here's a list of characteristics shared by all WPA3 networks:

- Use the latest security methods
- Don't allow outdated legacy protocols
- Require the use of protected management frames (PMFs)

Like us, our Wi-Fi networks have different levels of risk tolerance according to type and function. For the nonpublic home or enterprise variety, WPA3 gives us some cool tools to shut down password-guessing attacks. WPA3 also works with superior security protocols for networks that require or want a higher degree of protection.

As mentioned, WPA3 is backward compatible and provides interoperability with WPA2 devices, but this is really only an option for companies developing certified devices. I'm sure that it will become a required piece over time as market adoption grows.

WPA3-Personal

So, how does being able to seriously protect your individual users sound? WPA3-Personal gives us that ability by offering up powerful password-based authentication via simultaneous authentication of equals (SAE). This is a big upgrade from WPA2's preshared key (PSK) and works really well even when users choose simple, easy-to-crack passwords!

And as I said, WPA3 frustrates hackers' attempts to crack passwords via dictionary attacks, too. Some additional perks include:

- Natural password selection: Allows users to choose passwords that are easier to remember
- Ease of use: Delivers enhanced protections with no change to the way users connect to a network
- Forward secrecy: Protects data traffic even if a password is compromised after the data was transmitted

WPA3-Enterprise

Basically, wireless networks of all kinds gain a lot of security with WPA3, but those with sensitive data on them, like networks belonging to financial institutions, governments, and even enterprises, really get a boost! WPA3-Enterprise improves everything WPA2 offers, plus it streamlines how security protocols are applied throughout our networks.

WPA3-Enterprise even gives us the option to use 192-bit-minimum strength security protocols, plus some very cool cryptographic tools to lock things down tight!

Here's a list of the ways WPA3 beefs up security:

- **Sweet feature alert:** WPA3 uses a system called *Wi-Fi Device Provisioning Protocol* (DPP), which thankfully allows users to utilize NFC tags or QR codes to allow devices on the network. Like I said, sweet!
- **Authenticated encryption:** 256-bit Galois/Counter Mode Protocol (GCMP-256).
- **Key derivation and confirmation:** 384-bit hashed message authentication mode (HMAC) with secure hash algorithm (HMAC-SHA384).
- **Key establishment and authentication:** Elliptic curve Diffie-Hellman (ECDH) exchange and elliptic curve digital signature algorithm (ECDSA) using a 384-bit elliptic curve.
- **Robust management frame protection:** 256-bit Broadcast/Multicast Integrity Protocol Galois message authentication code (BIP-GMAC-256).
- The 192-bit security mode offered by WPA3-Enterprise ensures that the right combination of cryptographic tools is used and sets a consistent baseline of security within a WPA3 network.

WPA3 has also improved on 802.11's open authentication support by giving us something called *opportunistic wireless encryption* (OWE). The idea behind the OWE enhancement option is to offer encryption communication for networks without passwords, and it works by giving every device on the network its own unique key.

This implements something called *individualized data protection* (IDP), which happens to come in handy for password-protected networks, too, because even if an attacker gets a hold of the network password, they still can't access any other encrypted data!

All good—we've got WPA, WPA2, and now WPA3 covered. But how do they compare? Table 10.1 breaks them down.

TABLE 10.1 WPA, WPA2, and WPA3 Compared

Security TYPE	WPA	WPA2	WPA3
Enterprise mode: business, education, government	Authentication: IEEE 802.1X/EAP Encryption: TKIP/ MIC	Authentication: IEEE 802.1X/EAP Encryption: AES-CCMP	Authentication: IEEE 802.1X/EAP Encryption: GCMP-256
Personal mode: SOHO, home, and personal	Authentication: PSK Encryption: TKIP/ MIC	Authentication: PSK Encryption: AES-CCMP	Authentication: SAE Encryption: AES-CCMP
	128-bit RC4 w/TKIP encryption	128-bit AES encryption	128-bit AES encryption
	Ad hoc is not supported.	Ad hoc is not supported	Ad hoc is not supported

Summary

This chapter really packed a punch! Like rock 'n' roll, wireless technologies are here to stay, and for those of us who have come to depend on wireless technologies, it's actually pretty hard to imagine a world without wireless networks—what did we do before cell phones?

So we began this chapter by exploring the essentials and fundamentals of how wireless networks function.

Springing off that foundation, I then introduced you to the basics of wireless RF and the IEEE standards. We discussed 802.11 from its inception through its evolution to current and near-future standards and talked about the subcommittees that create them.

All of this led to a discussion of wireless security—or rather, nonsecurity for the most part, which logically directed us toward the WPA, WPA2, and WPA3 standards.

Exam Essentials

Understand the IEEE 802.11a specification. 802.11a runs in the 5 GHz spectrum, and if you use the 802.11h extensions, you have 23 nonoverlapping channels. 802.11a can run up to 54 Mbps, but only if you are less than 50 feet from an AP.

Understand the IEEE 802.11b specification. IEEE 802.11b runs in the 2.4 GHz range and has three nonoverlapping channels. It can handle long distances but with a maximum data rate of up to 11 Mpbs.

Understand the IEEE 802.11g specification. IEEE 802.11g is 802.11b's big brother and runs in the same 2.4 GHz range, but it has a higher data rate of 54 Mbps if you are less than 100 feet from an AP.

Understand the IEEE 802.11n components. 802.11n uses 40 MHz wide channels to provide more bandwidth, provides MAC efficiency with block acknowledgments, and uses MIMO to allow better throughput and distance at high speeds.

Understand the different encryption used between WPA, WPA2, and WPA3. WPA3 Enterprise uses GCMP-256 for encryption, WPA2 uses AES-CCMP for encryption, and WPA uses TKIP.

Written Lab

The answers to this lab can be found in Appendix A, "Answers to the Written Labs."

Write the answers to the following questions:

1. What is the maximum data rate of IEEE 802.11b?
2. What is the maximum data rate of IEEE 802.11g?
3. What is the maximum data rate of IEEE 802.11a?
4. What is the frequency range of IEEE 802.11b?
5. What is the frequency range of IEEE 802.11g?
6. What is the frequency range of IEEE 802.11a?
7. What is the possible bandwidth of 802.11ac?
8. Why would we use WPA instead of basic WEP?
9. Which IEEE committee has been sanctioned by WPA and is called WPA2?
10. The IEEE 802.11b/g basic standard has how many nonoverlapping channels?

Review Questions

NOTE: The following questions are designed to test your understanding of this chapter's material. For more information on how to get additional questions, please see this book's introduction.

The answers to these questions can be found in Appendix B, "Answers to the Review Questions."

1. Which encryption type does enterprise WPA3 use?
   A. AES-CCMP
   B. GCMP-256
   C. PSK
   D. TKIP/MIC
2. What is the frequency range of the IEEE 802.11b standard?
   A. 2.4 Gbps
   B. 5 Gbps
   C. 2.4 GHz
   D. 5 GHz
3. What is the frequency range of the IEEE 802.11a standard?
   A. 2.4 Gbps
   B. 5 Gbps
   C. 2.4 GHz
   D. 5 GHz
4. What is the frequency range of the IEEE 802.11g standard?
   A. 2.4 Gbps
   B. 5 Gbps
   C. 2.4 GHz
   D. 5 GHz
5. You've finished physically installing an access point on the ceiling of your office. At a minimum, which parameter must be configured on the access point to allow a wireless client to operate on it?
   A. AES
   B. PSK
   C. SSID
   D. TKIP
   E. WEP
   F. 802.11i

6. Which encryption type does WPA2 use?
   A. AES-CCMP
   B. PPK via IV
   C. PSK
   D. TKIP/MIC
7. How many nonoverlapping channels are available with 802.11b?
   A. 3
   B. 12
   C. 23
   D. 40
8. Which of the following has built-in resistance to dictionary attacks?
   A. WPA
   B. WPA2
   C. WPA3
   D. AES
   E. TKIP
9. What's the maximum data rate for the 802.11a standard?
   A. 6 Mbps
   B. 11 Mbps
   C. 22 Mbps
   D. 54 Mbps
10. What's the maximum data rate for the 802.11g standard?
    A. 6 Mbps
    B. 11 Mbps
    C. 22 Mbps
    D. 54 Mbps
11. What's the maximum data rate for the 802.11b standard?
    A. 6 Mbps
    B. 11 Mbps
    C. 22 Mbps
    D. 54 Mbps

12. WPA3 replaced the default open authentication with which of the following enhancements?
    - A. AES
    - B. OWL
    - C. OWE
    - D. TKIP
13. A wireless client can't connect to an 802.11b/g BSS with a b/g wireless card. And the client section of the access point doesn't list any active WLAN clients. What's a possible reason for this?
    - A. The incorrect channel is configured on the client.
    - B. The client's IP address is on the wrong subnet.
    - C. The client has an incorrect preshared key.
    - D. The SSID is configured incorrectly on the client.
14. Which features did WPA add to address the inherent weaknesses found in WEP? (Choose two.)
    - A. A stronger encryption algorithm
    - B. Key mixing using temporal keys
    - C. Shared key authentication
    - D. A shorter initialization vector
    - E. Per-frame sequence counter
15. Which wireless encryption methods are based on the RC4 encryption algorithm? (Choose two.)
    - A. WEP
    - B. CCKM
    - C. AES
    - D. TKIP
    - E. CCMP
16. Two workers have established wireless communication directly between their wireless laptops. What type of wireless topology has been created by these two employees?
    - A. BSS
    - B. SSID
    - C. IBSS
    - D. ESS

17. Which of the following describe the wireless security standard that WPA defines? (Choose two.)
    - **A.** It specifies the use of dynamic encryption keys that change throughout the user's connection time.
    - **B.** It requires that all devices must use the same encryption key.
    - **C.** It can use PSK authentication.
    - **D.** Static keys must be used.
18. Which wireless LAN design ensures that a mobile wireless client will not lose connectivity when moving from one access point to another?
    - **A.** Using adapters and access points manufactured by the same company
    - **B.** Overlapping the wireless cell coverage by at least 15%
    - **C.** Configuring all access points to use the same channel
    - **D.** Utilizing MAC address filtering to allow the client MAC address to authenticate with the surrounding APs
19. You're connecting your access point, and it's set to root. What does extended service set ID mean?
    - **A.** That you have more than one access point, and they are in the same SSID connected by a distribution system
    - **B.** That you have more than one access point, and they are in separate SSIDs connected by a distribution system
    - **C.** That you have multiple access points, but they are placed physically in different buildings
    - **D.** That you have multiple access points, but one is a repeater access point
20. What are the basic parameters to configure on a wireless access point? (Choose three.)
    - **A.** Authentication method
    - **B.** RF channel
    - **C.** RTS/CTS
    - **D.** SSID
    - **E.** Microwave interference resistance

Chapter 11

Configuring Legacy Wireless Controllers

THE FOLLOWING CCNA EXAM TOPICS ARE COVERED IN THIS CHAPTER:

✓ **2.0 Network Access**

2.6 Describe Cisco Wireless Architectures and AP modes

2.7 Describe physical infrastructure connections of WLAN components (AP, WLC, access/trunk ports, and LAG)

2.9 Interpret the wireless LAN GUI configuration for client connectivity, such as WLAN creation, security settings, QoS profiles, and advanced settings

✓ **5.0 Security Fundamentals**

5.10 Configure and verify WLAN within the GUI using WPA2 PSK

Now that you know how wireless works from the previous chapter, I will guide you through configuring a wireless network from beginning to end.

To start our journey, I'll explain the wireless deployment models we can use. After that, we will spend a lot of time getting into how to get a Cisco Wireless LAN Controller (WLC) up and running, including getting the network infrastructure ready and going over its various components.

Finally, we'll look at how to connect access points (APs) to our new WLC and create an SSID to connect a laptop to it! Cisco is in the process of switching everything to its new 9800 wireless controllers, so we will examine the traditional way of doing things in this chapter, and the new method in the next chapter.

NOTE To find your included bonus material, as well as Todd Lammle videos, practice questions, and hands-on labs, please see `www.lammle.com/ccna`.

WLAN Deployment Models

Cisco's Unified Wireless Networks (CUWN) was brought into this world to save our sanity by making it a lot less painful to tackle WLAN management issues like these:

- Integrating diverse device types into our WLANs while ensuring they play nicely and work together well.
- Maintaining a consistent security configuration with a constant onslaught of APs being added to the enterprise.
- Monitoring the environment for new sources of interference and redeploying existing devices as necessary.
- Properly managing channel allocation to minimize co-channel and adjacent channel interference while ensuring that enough APs are deployed in areas requiring high capacity.

To complicate things further, remember that all these issues must be managed within a three-dimensional environment that's constantly changing. An important key to this whole puzzle is that most of the challenges I just listed exist because of an outmoded deployment model we used back in the day called the *stand-alone* model, sometimes called the *autonomous* model or design. I'll tell you more about this model soon, but for now know that in it,

APs operate as separate entities with no centralized management capabilities! What could go wrong? It's not exactly much of a stretch to imagine the inherent weakness of this design.

A typical stand-alone design begins with a static site survey that's a snapshot of the radio frequency (RF) environment at a particular moment. Based on this snapshot, you would then deploy devices to mitigate any existing interference and provide coverage where needed. Because we all know that change is the constant within the RF space, the big snag lies in the word *static*. A common RF environment change is when a new company moves into the unoccupied office next door. That would change pretty much everything, but even tiny things like someone bringing a new metal object into the area can also bring you some serious grief!

Introducing the new lightweight model—*lightweight* is also used to describe the type of APs used within it. It not only puts the power of centralized administration in our hands, but it also brings some sweet new capabilities for addressing the snags I listed earlier to the table! Even more wonderful, this model can create an infrastructure that can react to changes in real time. Yes! In. Real. Time! Let's compare these two models now.

Stand-Alone Model

Not just any AP can operate in the stand-alone model—only the autonomous variety of APs can do this. I'll give you a list of all the different types soon. Figure 11.1 shows a standalone Cisco AP.

FIGURE 11.1 A standalone access point

Autonomous APs use the same internetworking operating system (IOS) that your Cisco routers do, except they also have more wireless features built into the code. You configure them individually, and there's no centralized administration point.

And let me tell you—managing several autonomous APs (AAPs) can get out of control quickly because you must keep the configuration consistent between the AAPs. You also must manually handle the security policies on each one and potentially tune the wireless channels and features to improve performance and reliability—no small thing! Cisco came up with a couple of solutions that focused on helping with configuration and management issues, but those fixes are nothing compared with the lightweight solution. I'll only talk about them briefly here.

You can configure a Wireless Domain Services (WDS) feature on an AP or Cisco switch, allowing at least some crumbs to centralize services for autonomous APs.

There's also an older solution called the Wireless Solution Engine (WLSE), which can provide limited centralized control and monitoring.

Lightweight Model

Practically, the issue with the standalone model can be solved with central management—no joke! With centralized management, a controller can push configurations to APs and intelligently tune the wireless performance for you because it can see the bigger picture of the wireless network.

The CUWN lightweight model requires centralized control, which we gained via Cisco WLAN controllers (WLCs). We'll discuss these in a bit. For now, know that the WLC controls and monitors APs. All clients and APs transmit information back to the WLC, including stats about coverage, interference, and even client data.

Figure 11.2 shows the lightweight model.

FIGURE 11.2 A lightweight AP

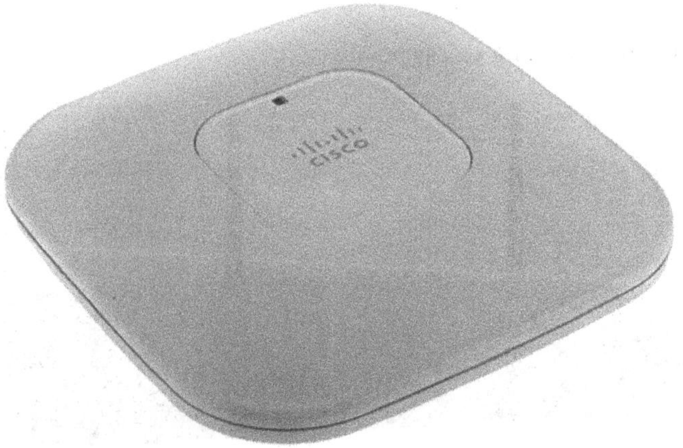

All transmitted data is sent between the APs and the WLCs via a mouthful of an encapsulation protocol called *Control And Provisioning of Wireless Access Point* (CAPWAP). CAPWAP carries and encapsulates control information between the APs and the WLC over an encrypted tunnel over UDP 5246 for control traffic and UDP 5247 for the data. Client data is encapsulated with a CAPWAP header that contains vital information about the client's received signal strength indicator (RSSI) and signal-to-noise ratio (SNR). Once the data arrives at the WLC, it can be forwarded as needed, which is how the real-time processes I discussed earlier become available. A few great benefits of centralized control are improved security and traffic conditioning. For example, traffic is redirected directly to the WLC, so you only need a central firewall to secure all wireless traffic instead of needing to secure each and every site!

Physical and logical security becomes much tighter in the CUWN because to ensure only authorized APs connect to the WLC, both devices exchange a certificate and mutually authenticate. Any APs found not to be capable of CAPWAP are classified as rogues. So basically, the network forces CAPWAP-capable APs to be authenticated before downloading any configuration from a WLC, which helps mitigate rogue APs. For physical security reasons, the configuration of the AP resides only in RAM while in operation and connected to the WLC. That way, the configuration can't be nicked from the AP once that device has been removed from the network.

The CUWN consists of five elements that work together to provide a unified enterprise solution:

- Client devices
- APs
- Network unification
- Network management
- Mobility services

Various devices support these elements, including Cisco Aironet client devices, the Cisco Secure Services Client (CSSC), and other Cisco-compatible devices. For APs, we can choose between the type configured and managed by a WLC and those that operate in standalone mode.

Although it's good to know that a single Cisco WLC can manage many APs, know that you'll savor a major increase in capacity with a few additional Cisco WLCs in the mix. You can incorporate other devices into your basic CUWN to add more features and management capabilities, like the Cisco Wireless Control System (WCS), which facilitates the centralized management of multiple WLCs. You also need WCS to add a Cisco Wireless Location Appliance. These cool tools provide features like real-time location tracking of clients and RFID tags.

And that's not all. Cisco also offers an Embedded Wireless Controller (EWC). This scaled-down wireless controller used to run on a Cisco switch like the 3850 when the solution was known as Mobility Express, but now it only runs on certain modern Cisco APs to provide virtual management. The newest type of Wireless Controller is the Cisco 9800, which is entirely built into IOS-XE instead of running AireOS like the legacy WLC uses.

Split MAC

Even more good news about lightweight architecture is that it allows for the splitting of 802.11 Data Link layer functions between the lightweight AP and the WLC.

The lightweight AP handles real-time communication portions, and the Cisco WLC handles non-time-sensitive items. This technology is typically referred to as *split MAC*.

Here's a list of the real-time portions of the protocol that the AP handles:

- Frame exchange handshake between the client and AP performed during each frame transfer
- Beacon frame transmission
- Handling of frames for clients operating in power save mode (including both buffering and transmission)
- Responses to probe request frames from clients and the relaying of received probe requests to the controller
- Transmission to the controller of real-time signal quality information for every received frame
- RF channel monitoring for noise, interference, other WLANs and rogue APs
- Encryption and decryption (layer 2 wireless only), with the exception of VPN and IPSec clients

The WLC handles the remaining tasks that aren't time sensitive. Some of the MAC-layer functions provided by WLC include

- 802.11 authentication
- 802.11 association and reassociation (mobility)
- 802.11 to 802.3 frame translation and bridging
- The termination of all 802.11 frames at the controller

NOTE Although the controller handles the authentication, wireless encryption keys for WPA2 or EAP will remain in both the AP and the client.

Cloud Model

A slick new way to manage your wireless infrastructure is to use Cisco Meraki. It is entirely managed by the cloud, so all you have to do is ensure that the APs can reach the Internet. You can now manage your entire Meraki network from a publicly accessible web interface.

This means you can make changes to your network from anywhere. Check out Figure 11.3.

A control plane is formed in the cloud to allow for management. This plane provides monitoring information to help with troubleshooting and other features. The cloud provides automatic firmware upgrades, analytics, security features, updates, and a central point for automation.

The data plane remains on the premises, so cloud management doesn't affect end-user traffic.

The downside to the cloud model is that APs don't offer much local management on the devices—they don't support command-line interfaces (CLI). So, if the Internet connection goes down at the office, you won't be able to make any changes to your network until the Meraki device can get back online!

FIGURE 11.3 Meraki Cloud model

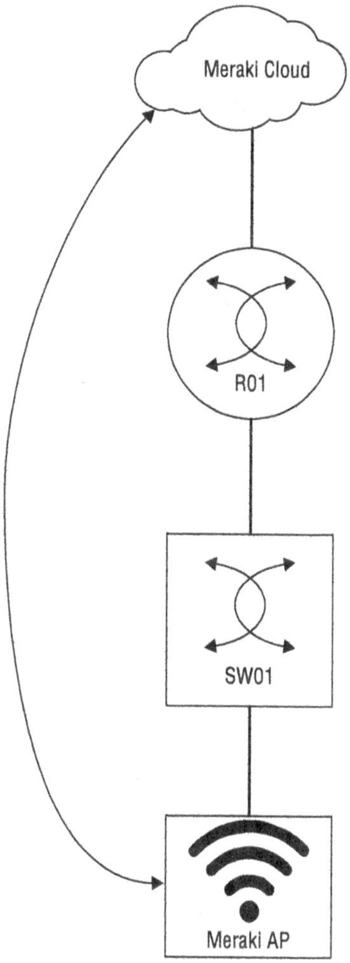

Another caveat with Meraki is that because its focus is on ease of use, it doesn't offer as many features as other Cisco controllers.

So, basically, Meraki can be a great tool for companies that lack a highly skilled IT team to deploy more complex solutions. It would also work for branches that lack IT staff to help with configurations or troubleshooting.

Figure 11.4 gives you a sample of the Meraki dashboard for configuring an SSID, though we don't need to go any further into how to do things in Meraki for the CCNA.

FIGURE 11.4 Meraki SSIDs

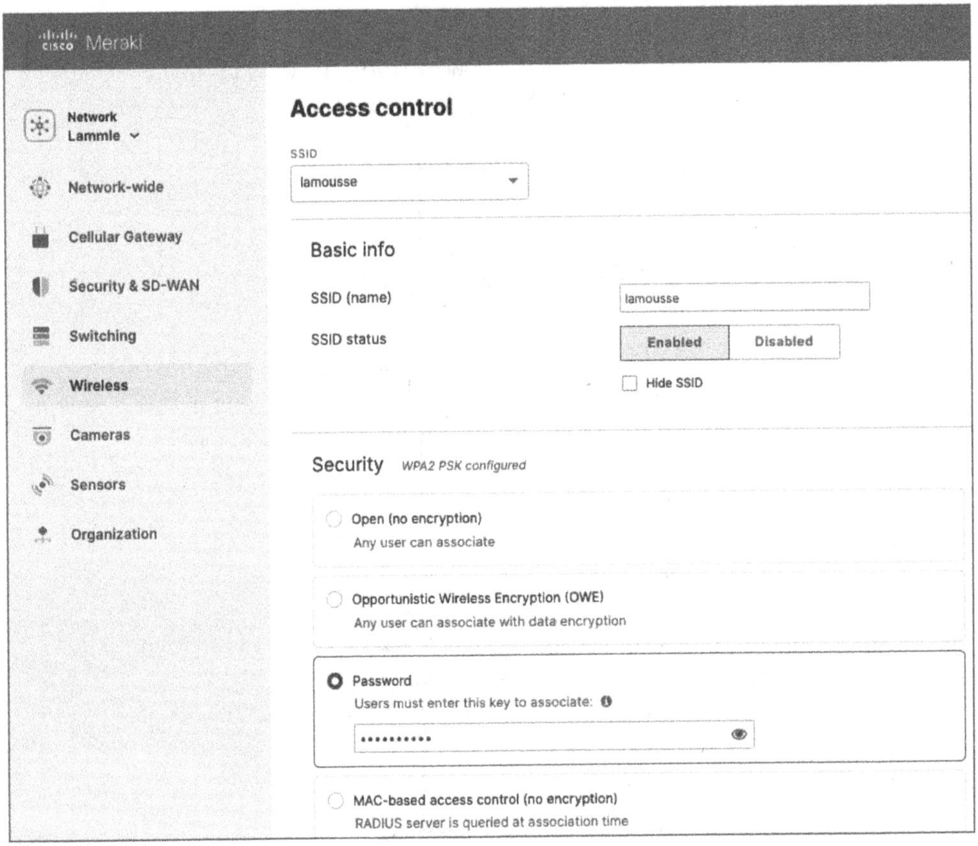

Configuring the Network

Now that you understand the different wireless deployment models, it's a good time to start laying the groundwork for our WLC configurations (see Figure 11.5). First, we'll need to create some VLANS, trunk ports that will eventually become a port channel later, and an access port so we can play around with the service port later in the chapter.

We will create the following VLANs on my switch:

VLAN ID	VLAN name
311	Wireless-Management
316	Wireless-ServicePort

FIGURE 11.5 WLC topology

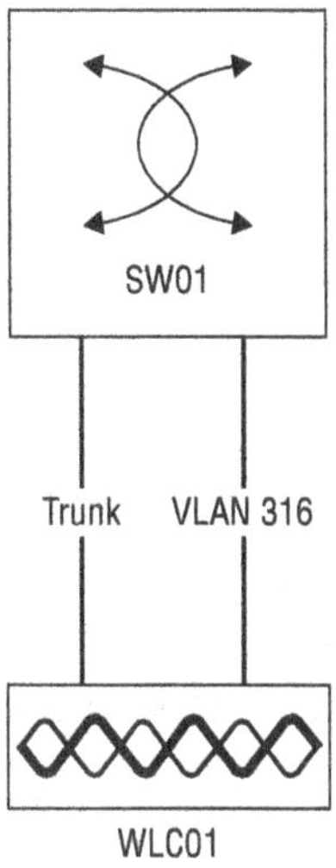

The Wireless-Management VLAN will be used for the WLC's management interface, and the Wireless-ServicePort VLAN will be used for the service port interface, which provides out-of-band (OOB) management:

```
C9200-SW01(config)#vlan 311
C9200-SW01(config-vlan)#name Wireless-Management
C9200-SW01(config-vlan)#vlan 316
C9200-SW01(config-vlan)#name Wireless-ServicePort
C9200-SW01(config-vlan)#exit
```

Because we are creating VLANs for the controller, we may as well create the VLANs we will need later when we make the WLANs. The WLC will use VLANs 101–103:

VLAN ID	VLAN name
101	WLAN101
102	WLAN102
103	WLAN103

I'll make the VLANs like so:

```
C9200-SW01(config)#vlan 101
C9200-SW01(config-vlan)#name WLAN101
C9200-SW01(config-vlan)#vlan 102
C9200-SW01(config-vlan)#name WLAN102
C9200-SW01(config-vlan)#vlan 103
C9200-SW01(config-vlan)#name WLAN103
```

Of course, the switch will also need SVIs for those new VLANs to actually provide IP connectivity to the WLC:

VLAN ID	IP address / mask
311	10.30.11.1/24
316	10.10.16.1/24
101	10.30.101.1/24
102	10.30.102.1/24
103	10.30.103.1/24

Creating the SVIs would look like this:

```
C9200-SW01(config)#interface vlan 311
C9200-SW01(config-if)#description Wireless Controller
C9200-SW01(config-if)#ip address 10.30.11.1 255.255.255.0
C9200-SW01(config-if)#no shut
C9200-SW01(config-if)#interface vlan 316
C9200-SW01(config-if)#description Wireless Service Port
C9200-SW01(config-if)#ip address 10.10.16.1 255.255.255.0
C9200-SW01(config-if)#no shut
C9200-SW01(config-if)#interface vlan 101
C9200-SW01(config-if)#description WLAN101
C9200-SW01(config-if)#ip address 10.30.101.1 255.255.255.0
C9200-SW01(config-if)#no shut
C9200-SW01(config-if)#interface vlan 102
C9200-SW01(config-if)#description WLAN102
C9200-SW01(config-if)#ip address 10.30.102.1 255.255.255.0
C9200-SW01(config-if)#no shut
C9200-SW01(config-if)#interface vlan 103
C9200-SW01(config-if)#description WLAN103
C9200-SW01(config-if)#ip address 10.30.103.1 255.255.255.0
C9200-SW01(config-if)#no shut
```

The last thing we need to do on the switch, for now, is to configure the switch ports. In my environment, I'm using

Interface	Mode
GigabitEthernet1/0/1	Trunk
GigabitEthernet1/0/2	Trunk
GigabitEthernet1/0/3	Access VLAN 316

We will start out by adding the interface descriptions on the ports.

```
C9200-SW01(config)#interface g1/0/1
C9200-SW01(config-if)#description Trunk to WLC01
C9200-SW01(config-if)#interface g1/0/2
C9200-SW01(config-if)#description Trunk to WLC01
C9200-SW01(config-if)#interface g1/0/3
C9200-SW01(config-if)#description Service Port to WLC01
C9200-SW01(config-if)#exit
```

Next, we will use the range command to speed up our trunk configuration. Because the WLC does not run STP, we can enable port fast to ensure the port always comes up quickly; because this is a trunk port, we will need to use the `spanning-tree portfast trunk` command:

```
C9200-SW01(config)#interface range g1/0/1-2
C9200-SW01(config-if-range)#switchport mode trunk
C9200-SW01(config-if-range)#spanning-tree portfast trunk
%Warning: portfast should only be enabled on ports connected to a single
 host. Connecting hubs, concentrators, switches, bridges, etc... to this
 interface  when portfast is enabled can cause temporary bridging loops.
 Use with CAUTION
C9200-SW01(config-if-range)#exit
```

Finally, we will configure our service port to be an access port, so let's put it in VLAN 316 and enable Portfast the usual way:

```
C9200-SW01(config)#interface g1/0/3
C9200-SW01(config-if)#switchport mode access
C9200-SW01(config-if)#switchport access vlan 316
C9200-SW01(config-if)#spanning portfast
%Warning: portfast should only be enabled on ports connected to a single
 host. Connecting hubs, concentrators, switches, bridges, etc... to this
 interface  when portfast is enabled, can cause temporary bridging loops.
 Use with CAUTION
%Portfast has been configured on GigabitEthernet1/0/3 but will only
 have an effect when the interface is in a non-trunking mode.
```

Configuring Legacy WLCs

In the vital world of wireless, there are two types of APs: autonomous and lightweight.

An autonomous AP is configured, managed, and maintained in isolation relative to all the other APs in the network. In other words, it is a standalone AP like the cheap D-Link or Netgear wireless router you might have in your home network, except it will have many more features. Because they are standalone, they don't scale well because you must add a WLAN by manually configuring each AP.

A lightweight AP gets its configuration from a central appliance called a *wireless controller*. In this scenario, the APs essentially function as antennas, with all information being sent back to the wireless LAN controller (WLC). There are several real advantages to this, with a couple of good examples being the capacity for centralized management and more seamless roaming.

When implementing the lightweight model, the centralized control system is the WLC. All device configurations are done at the WLC and then downloaded to the appropriate device. WLCs come with different features, price tags, and many form factors, from stand-alone physical or virtual appliances to modules that integrate into routers and multilayer switches. Depending on what model you pick for your network, a WLC can support up to 6,000 APs per controller! Figure 11.6 shows the Cisco Wireless LAN Controller.

FIGURE 11.6 Cisco WLC

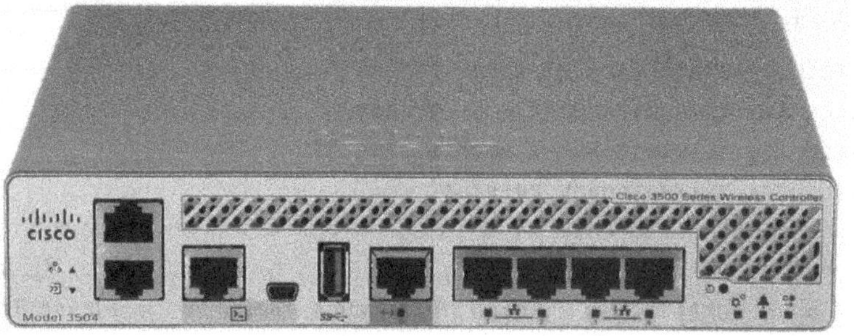

It's just so impressive that we can configure and control up to 16 WLANs for each AP on a single WLC! A WLAN is defined in the WLC a lot like a profile, and it has a separate WLAN ID (1–16) and a separate WLAN SSID (WLAN name). The WLAN SSID defines where we configure unique security and quality of service (QoS) settings.

If you have clients connected to one AP, they'll share the same RF space and channel, but if they're connected to different SSIDs, they're in a different logical network.

Of course, this means that clients in different SSIDs can be isolated from one another in the RF space and can have different VLAN and QoS tags. But they'll still be in the same collision domain as in autonomous AP configurations with VLANs. The SSIDs will be mapped to the VLANs in the WLC configuration.

As a reminder, we care about two types of Cisco wireless controllers for the CCNA: the now-legacy Wireless LAN Controller (WLC) and the new 9800 controllers. Because the exam can technically ask you about either model right now, we will focus on the WLC and then have a look at the shiny new 9800 in the next chapter.

NOTE Even though the CCNA does not exactly require it, I will include examples of the WLC command-line interface along with the web interface configurations throughout this chapter. I'm doing this because the WLC AireOS is very different from what you're used to with Cisco IOS, so it definitely won't hurt for you to get some exposure to it here!

WLC Initial Setup

Okay, now the switch is ready. I can console my WLC and power it up! After a few minutes, it will boot us into the setup wizard because I wiped the configuration:

```
(Cisco Controller)
Welcome to the Cisco Wizard Configuration Tool
Use the '-' character to backup

AUTO-INSTALL: starting now...
Would you like to terminate autoinstall? [yes]: yes
```

The wizard asks me to set a hostname and a username/password for the system:

```
System Name [Cisco_5e:ba:e4] (31 characters max): WLC01
Enter Administrative User Name (24 characters max): admin
Enter Administrative Password (3 to 24 characters):**********
Re-enter Administrative Password                 : **********
```

Next, it'll ask for the service port IP address. I promise we will talk about what that port does soon, but for now, it needs to be a separate subnet from the management port subnet, so I'm going to give it 10.10.16.220/24 in my lab.

```
Service Interface IP Address Configuration [static][DHCP]: static
Service Interface IP Address: 10.10.16.220
Service Interface Netmask: 255.255.255.0
```

At this point, the wizard will ask whether we want to use link aggregation. Later in our lab we will, but not at this point, so I will leave it disabled so I can show you how to enable it from the regular web interface:

```
Enable Link Aggregation (LAG) [yes][NO]: no
```

Aside from the username/password, the most important configuration is the management interface because you won't be able to do much if you can't reach the appliance. Let's give it an IP address of 10.30.11.40/24, and it will use the VLAN 311 SVI IP address as the default gateway or default router in this case. Because we are using trunk links to connect to the WLC, we also need to set the VLAN to 311 unless I want to change the interface's native VLAN instead.

It is also important to tell the wizard which port we are using for management; I will just go with port 1 for now:

```
Management Interface IP Address: 10.30.11.40
Management Interface Netmask: 255.255.255.0
Management Interface Default Router: 10.30.11.1
Management Interface VLAN Identifier (0 = untagged): 311
Management Interface Port Num [1 to 8]: 1
Management Interface DHCP Server IP Address: 10.30.11.1
```

You must also provide a virtual gateway IP, but more on that later! I'll also leave high availability off because that is way out of scope for what you need in a CCNA book, but in the real world, having a second controller for redundancy would be a good idea:

```
Enable HA [yes][NO]: no
Virtual Gateway IP Address: 192.0.2.1
```

The Mobility/RF Group Name is a feature that helps several WLCs work together. I'm not going to go into it here, but it is a mandatory field, so type any value you want. I'll go with Testlab:

```
Mobility/RF Group Name: Testlab
```

Sadly, the wizard requires us to configure an SSID, but we still have a lot to cover in this chapter before we get to that step. So, I will configure an SSID called Temp-SSID with the default options, and then we will delete it when the WLC is up and running:

```
Network Name (SSID): Temp-SSID
Configure DHCP Bridging Mode [yes][NO]:
Allow Static IP Addresses [YES][no]:
```

Once again, the WLC wizard wants to get ahead of us and have us configure a RADIUS server! Just say no for now; we'll be doing this manually later on:

```
Configure a RADIUS Server now? [YES][no]: no
```

Wireless controllers and APs need to know which country they are operating in because different countries handle wireless frequencies differently; in fact, quite a few laws govern wireless. I'm in Canada, so I'll use CA for the code:

```
Enter Country Code list (enter 'help' for a list of countries) [US]: CA
```

Get your Enter key finger ready, because we can accept the next few defaults; these concern what wireless radios we will enable for our WLANs. Since this book is basically just a large lab, I'm not overly concerned with performance, so I will allow everything:

```
Enable 802.11b Network [YES][no]:
Enable 802.11a Network [YES][no]:
Enable 802.11g Network [YES][no]:
Enable Auto-RF [YES][no]:
```

WLCs use certificates to allow APs to register themselves to the controller securely, so it is a good idea to ensure we have the proper system time on our appliance. Otherwise, the incorrect time may cause us a headache. I have an NTP server in my lab, so I will use 10.30.11.10 for my WLC:

```
Configure a NTP server now? [YES][no]:
Enter the NTP server's IP address: 10.30.11.10
Enter a polling interval between 3600 and 604800 secs: 3600
```

As cool as IPv6 is, I'm not going to enable it on the WLC; Cisco expects you to know the basics; in fact, showing this wizard is probably overkill as it is:

```
Would you like to configure IPv6 parameters[YES][no]: no
```

At least we have reached the end of the wizard; it will ask if everything is correct, so say yes—or you'll have to start over from the beginning! The WLC will restart and then be ready to go after a few minutes:

```
Configuration correct? If yes, system will save it and reset. [yes][NO]: yes
Cleaning up DHCP Server

Configuration saved!
Resetting system with new configuration...
```

Joining Access Points

Before we dive into the rest of the WLC topics, let's take a minute and explore how to join APs to the controller so we have them ready to go for later. You don't need to know how to join an AP to a WLC controller for the CCNA; however, our new WLC won't do us much good if we don't add some APs into the mix.

There is more than one way to make an AP register for our WLC, so I'll show you the most common methods: manually from the AP CLI, using a DNS record, and using DHCP options.

NOTE: You can use any join method discussed here with the WLC and the 9800 controllers.

Manual Method

The manual method is quick and easy, but it can get old fast if you have to log in to more than a couple of APs and point them to the controller.

If the Cisco AP has an IP address, you can connect to it through SSH; otherwise, you can use the serial port. Once connected, you can log in with **Cisco/Cisco** as the default username and password. The enable password is also Cisco:

```
AP7c69.f6ef.6d5f>enable
Password:
AP7c69.f6ef.6d5f#
```

The AP will set the hostname to AP followed by the device's MAC address. Assuming the AP has received an IP address from DHCP already, we need to point it to the controller like this:

```
AP7c69.f6ef.6d5f#capwap ap controller ip address 10.30.11.40
```

If there isn't any DHCP on the AP's VLAN, then you can set a static IP by entering these commands:

```
AP7c69.f6ef.6d5f#capwap ap ip address 10.30.20.101 255.255.255.0
AP7c69.f6ef.6d5f#capwap ap ip default-gateway 10.30.20.1
```

DNS Method

A more scalable way to configure APs is to create a DNS entry so the AP can locate the WLC and register to it.

I must create an "A" record on my DNS server to use the DNS method. The host record is CISCO-CAPWAP-CONTROLLER and points to the WLC's IP address, as demonstrated in Figure 11.7.

FIGURE 11.7 DNS record

I also need to ensure that the DHCP server assigns the AP the proper domain name so it can find the correct DNS record when it looks up the special DNS entry.

DHCP Method

The DHCP method is a bit harder because we need to work with hex to configure the feature—yes, we do use hex addressing outside of IPv6! To get this done, I'll build out the hex string like so:

1. It always starts with F1.
2. Next is either 04 for one controller (4 × 1) or 08 for two controllers (4 × 2).
3. Finally, we add the controller's IP in hex format; if we specified two controllers, we would add both IPs one after another.

For example, my WLC is 10.30.11.40, so the conversion would be

10 = 0A
30 = 1E
11 = 0B
40 = 28

Putting it all together, the resulting hex would be F1040A1E0B28.

Just for fun, if I had a second controller in my lab that had 10.30.12.40 as an IP, the conversion would be:

10 = 0A
30 = 1E
12 = 0C
40 = 28

The final hex would be F1080A1E0B280A1E0C28.

This isn't so bad once you do it a few times, but the DNS option is more popular because it is easier to understand. Anyway, now that I have my hex value, I can configure a DHCP server and have it provide that value to the APs. We do that by passing along option 43 and specifying that the value will be in hex.

For this example, I'm going to configure a DHCP server on my Cisco switch like this:

```
C9200-SW01(config)#ip dhcp pool Wireless-AP
C9200-SW01(dhcp-config)#network 10.30.20.0 255.255.255.0
C9200-SW01(dhcp-config)#default-router 10.30.20.1
C9200-SW01(dhcp-config)#domain-name testlab.com
C9200-SW01(dhcp-config)#dns-server 10.30.11.10 10.30.12.10
C9200-SW01(dhcp-config)#option 43 hex f104.0a1e.0b28
C9200-SW01(dhcp-config)#exit
C9200-SW01(config)#ip dhcp excluded-address 10.30.20.1 10.30.20.99
```

Configuring the VLAN

Because we created a DHCP range for the APs, we must also create a VLAN and SVI to complete the configuration. It is always a good idea to place your APs in a new VLAN so the traffic is separate from your client networks, plus putting the APs in a new subnet will help them stand out when you are troubleshooting because you can more easily notice the different IP range when looking at logs, etc.

I'll create VLAN 320 and an SVI with an IP address of 10.30.20.1/24:

```
C9200-SW01(config)#vlan 320
C9200-SW01(config-vlan)#name Wireless-AP
C9200-SW01(config-vlan)#exit
C9200-SW01(config)#interface vlan 320
C9200-SW01(config-if)#description Wireless APs
C9200-SW01(config-if)#ip add 10.30.20.1 255.255.255.0
C9200-SW01(config-if)#no shut
```

Configuring the Switchport

There isn't really anything special about configuring a Cisco AP on a switch when it is running in local mode. The AP will send all the wireless traffic back to the control through a CAPWAP tunnel so we can configure the interface to be an access port and put it in a VLAN that can reach the controller:

```
C9200-SW01(config)#int g1/0/6
C9200-SW01(config-if)#description AP01
C9200-SW01(config-if)#switchport mode access
C9200-SW01(config-if)#switchport access vlan 320
C9200-SW01(config-if)#spanning-tree portfast
%Warning: portfast should only be enabled on ports connected to a single
 host. Connecting hubs, concentrators, switches, bridges, etc... to this
 interface  when portfast is enabled, can cause temporary bridging loops.
 Use with CAUTION
%Portfast has been configured on GigabitEthernet1/0/6 but will only
 have effect when the interface is in a non-trunking mode.
```

The only complicating factor is if the AP is running in FlexConnect mode, because the AP will dump all the user traffic on the switch instead of tunneling it to the controller; therefore, we would need to make the switch port a trunk so it can handle the WLAN traffic in this scenario. Because trunks will use VLAN 1 as the native VLAN by default, a good trick is to change the native VLAN to our Wireless-AP one so that it can properly register to the WLC and also support the WLAN tags:

```
C9200-SW01(config)#interface g1/0/7
C9200-SW01(config-if)#description AP02
```

```
C9200-SW01(config-if)#switchport mode trunk
C9200-SW01(config-if)#switch trunk native vlan 320
C9200-SW01(config-if)#spanning portfast trunk
%Warning: portfast should only be enabled on ports connected to a single
 host. Connecting hubs, concentrators, switches, bridges, etc... to this
 interface  when portfast is enabled can cause temporary bridging loops.
 Use with CAUTION
```

NOTE We don't specify the trunk encapsulation in modern switches because ISL was removed from IOS quite some time ago.

WLC Port Types

The WLC has various port types that you use to connect the WLC to the network or deploy configurations. Here's a list of them:

- Console / Serial port
- Service port
- Redundancy port
- Distribution system port
- Management interface
- Redundancy management
- Virtual interface
- Service port interface
- Dynamic interface

Console / Serial Port

I'm guessing that you're already familiar with the console port because you learned about them when we talked about configuring routers and switches. But just in case, this port allows you to access the WLC's CLI unconditionally, even if it is still booting.

You can connect via a console cable and the following settings by default:

- 9600 baud
- 8 data bits
- 1 stop bit
- No Flow Control
- No Parity

You need to use the console port to initially set up the WLC, as we did when we walked through the setup wizard. You might also need the console port if the WLC loses its network access after you make a configuration error. To change the serial port settings, click Serial Port in the Management menu, as shown in Figure 11.8.

FIGURE 11.8 Serial port settings

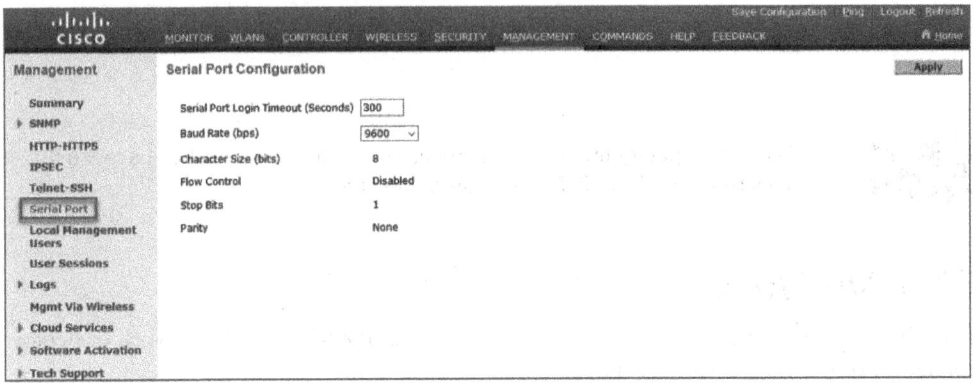

You can also adjust the baud rate with the following command:

```
(WLC01) >config serial baudrate
[1200/2400/4800/9600/19200/38400/57600/115200] Enter serial speed.

(WLC01) >config serial baudrate 115200
```

Service Port

This port is used for the WLC's out-of-band management. I've got to say that this port can be a bit annoying to use, though, because it uses a separate routing table and can't use a default gateway. This means you've got to add static routes to use the port so it knows how to reach your management network. Figure 11.9 shows the Add Route screen:

You can add routes through the CLI by using the following commands:

```
(WLC01) >config route add 192.168.124.0 255.255.255.0 10.10.16.1
(WLC01) >show route summary
Number of Routes................................. 5
Destination Network          Netmask              Gateway
-------------------    -------------------    -------------------
192.168.121.0          255.255.255.0          10.10.16.1
192.168.122.0          255.255.255.0          10.10.16.1
192.168.123.0          255.255.255.0          10.10.16.1
192.168.124.0          255.255.255.0          10.10.16.1
```

FIGURE 11.9 WLC Add Route

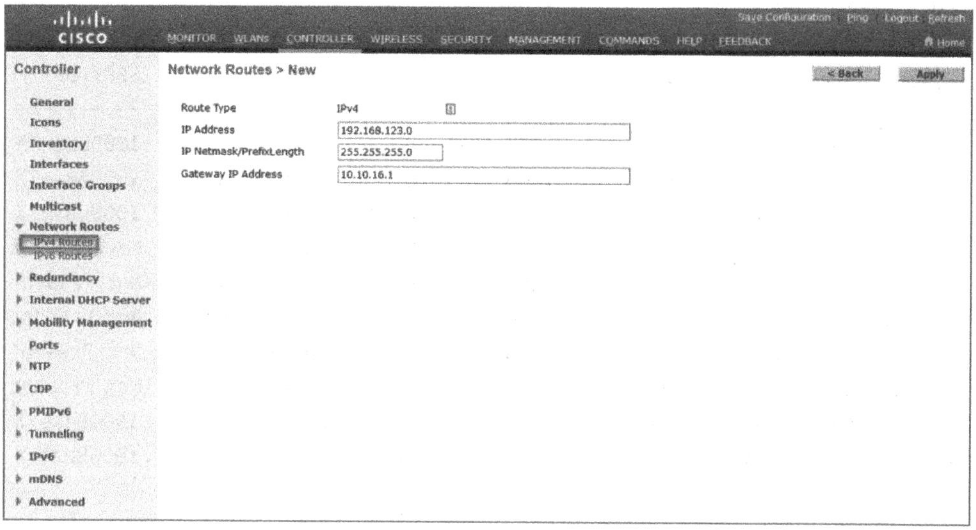

Redundancy Port

This port can connect to a second WLC to ensure high availability and that a WLC is always available to serve your wireless networking needs. I'll cover this one more deeply in the interface type section.

Distribution System Port

This is just a fancy name for regular interfaces on the WLC, which can be either Ethernet or SFP connections, depending on the type of WLC controller you've got. You can view the distribution system ports, or just ports for short, via the Controller page, where you click Ports, as shown in Figure 11.10.

FIGURE 11.10 Distribution system ports

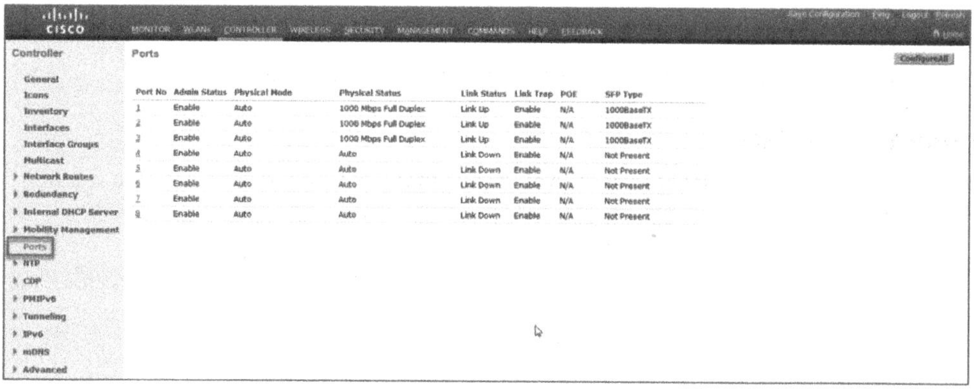

And you can also use the following CLI command to see the ports on the system:

```
(WLC01) >show port summary
    STP   Admin   Physical   Physical   Link   Link
Pr  Type   Stat   Mode      Mode       Status   Status  Trap     POE   SFPType
-- ------- ---- ------- ---------- ---------- ------ ------- -----  ----------
1  Normal  Forw Enable  Auto        1000 Full  Up      Enable  N/A    1000BaseTX
2  Normal  Forw Enable  Auto        1000 Full  Up      Enable  N/A    1000BaseTX
3  Normal  Forw Enable  Auto        1000 Full  Up      Enable  N/A    1000BaseTX
4  Normal  Disa Enable  Auto        Auto       Down    Enable  N/A    Not Present
5  Normal  Disa Enable  Auto        Auto       Down    Enable  N/A    Not Present
6  Normal  Disa Enable  Auto        Auto       Down    Enable  N/A    Not Present
7  Normal  Disa Enable  Auto        Auto       Down    Enable  N/A    Not Present
8  Normal  Disa Enable  Auto        Auto       Down    Enable  N/A    Not Present
RP Normal  Disa Enable  Auto        Auto       Down    Enable  N/A    1000BaseTX
SP Normal  Forw Enable  Auto        Auto       Up      Enable  N/A    1000BaseTX
```

Management interface

This interface is used for normal management traffic, including RADIUS user authentication, WLC-to-WLC communication, web-based and SSH sessions, SNMP, Network Time Protocol (NTP), syslog, etc. The management interface also terminates CAPWAP tunnels between the controller and its APs.

Redundancy Management

This is the management IP address of a redundant WLC that's part of a high-availability pair of controllers. The active WLC uses the management interface address, whereas the standby WLC uses the redundancy management address.

Virtual Interface

This is the IP address facing wireless clients when the controller relays client DHCP requests, performs client web authentication, and supports client mobility.

Service Port Interface

This is bound to the service port and used for out-of-band management.

Dynamic Interface

This is used to connect a VLAN to a WLAN. You would create a dynamic interface whenever you need to create a new VLAN on the WLC.

WLC Interface Types

The WLC also has different interface types that connect to the ports we just discussed and provide services to the wireless networks we'll be configuring soon.

You can view the interfaces on the WLC by selecting Interfaces under Controller, as shown in Figure 11.11.

FIGURE 11.11 WLC interfaces

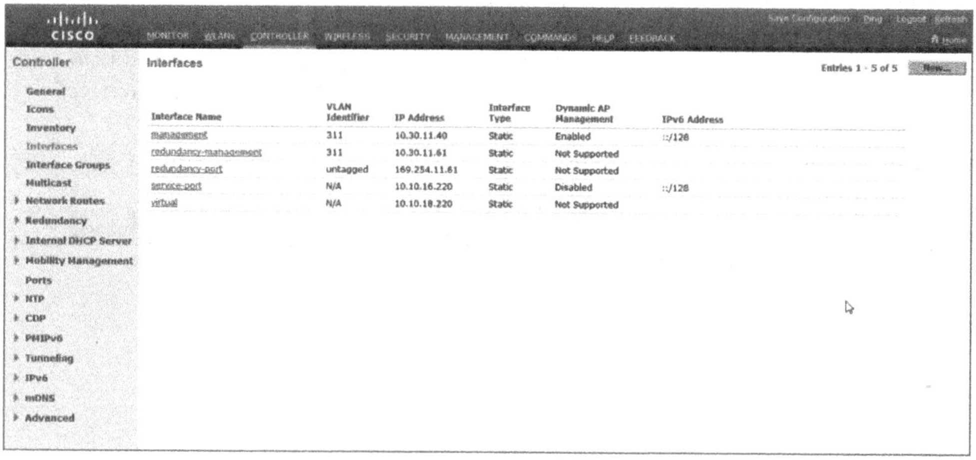

You can also check the interfaces with the following command:

```
(WLC01) >show interface summary
 Number of Interfaces.......................... 8
Interface Name                   Port Vlan Id  IP Address      Type Ap Mgr Guest
-------------------------------- ---- -------- -------------- ------- -----

management                       LAG  311      10.30.11.40     Static  Yes    No
redundancy-management            LAG  311      10.30.11.61     Static  No     No
redundancy-port                  -    untagged 169.254.11.61   Static  No     No
service-port                     N/A  N/A      10.10.16.220    Static  No     No
virtual                          N/A  N/A      192.0.2.1       Static  No     No
```

Management Interface

You'll usually connect to your WLC through the web interface or CLI by accessing the management interface. It needs to be given either an IPv4 or IPv6 address, and because we'll probably be trunking to the switch, we'll have to set a VLAN tag for the interface, too. Because wireless traffic is brought to the controller via a CAPWAP by default, we would also set up a DHCP helper on the interface so the wireless client can get its IP address.

In addition to allowing you to configure everything, the management interface also has the Dynamic AP Manager role enabled by default. This allows APs to register to the WLC and terminates CAPWAP tunnels to the controller.

If you want to move the role to another interface, you can disable the role by unchecking the Enable Dynamic AP Management box, but that isn't usually worth the effort due to complexities that are out of scope here. Figure 11.12 shows the WLC management interface.

FIGURE 11.12 WLC management interface

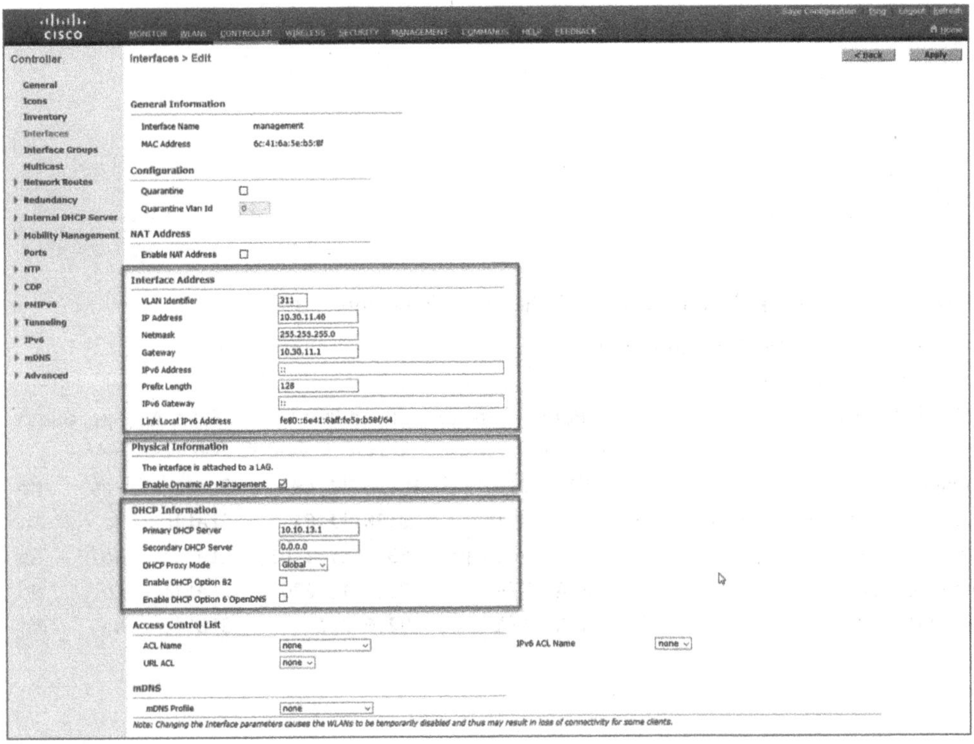

We can also configure this through the CLI with these commands:

```
(WLC01) >config interface address management 10.30.11.40

<netmask>       Enter the interface's netmask.
```

```
(WLC01) >config interface address management 10.30.11.40 255.255.255.0

<gateway>      Enter the interface's gateway address.

(WLC01) >config interface address management 10.30.11.40 255.255.255.0
10.30.11.1
```

Service Port Interface

This interface is how we configure the service port I discussed earlier. As shown in Figure 11.13, this interface has fewer options than the management interface. You can set an IPv4 or IPv6 address, or you can just use DHCP on the port to get an address.

The SP interface doesn't even support VLAN tagging, so you've got to configure the switch to use untagged VLANs as well.

FIGURE 11.13 WLC service port interface

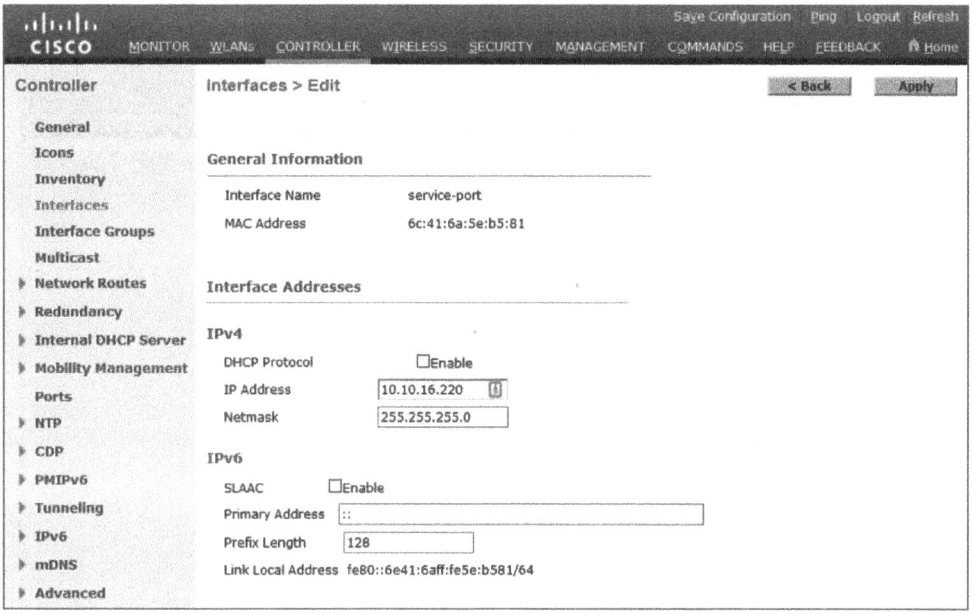

We can also configure the service port through the CLI:

```
(WLC01) >config interface address service-port

<IP address>   Enter the interface's IP Address.
```

```
(WLC01) >config interface address service-port 10.10.16.220
<netmask>       Enter the interface's netmask.
(WLC01) >config interface address service-port 10.10.16.220 255.255.255.0
```

Redundancy Management

The redundancy management interface is used to configure the redundancy port we talked about. It's actually the same as the service port, which is referenced in both places.

Anyway, this port is the one we use to set up high availability between two wireless controllers. Remember to configure an IP address in the same subnet as the management interface.

The rest of the steps are out of scope for this book, but you can probably guess the options by checking out the controller page. Figure 11.14 shows the WLC redundancy management interface.

FIGURE 11.14 WLC redundancy management interface

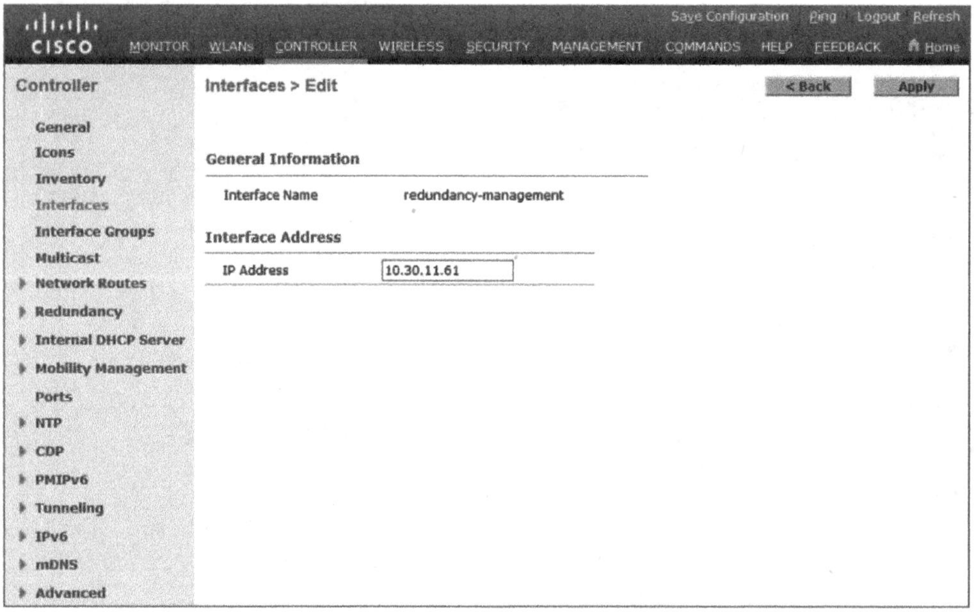

I won't show the CLI for this interface because it dives into the full-on high-availability configuration. Just know that it follows a pattern similar to the interfaces we just covered.

Virtual Interface

The virtual interface jumps into action when the WLC needs to redirect wireless client traffic back to the controller. Remember when you last connected to Wi-Fi at a hotel or a coffee shop, and a website asked you to agree to the rules or demanded that you fork over some money to get online? That's courtesy of the virtual interface!

Back in the day, we all used 1.1.1.1 as our redirection IP address because it was unlikely to be used by anything important. Well, Cloudflare launched a very popular DNS service that uses that IP!

So, after the IT community ranted about that online, it was finally decided that we'll use 192.0.2.1 as the new and preferred virtual IP for redirection. Figure 11.15 shows the WLC virtual interface configuration.

FIGURE 11.15 WLC virtual interface

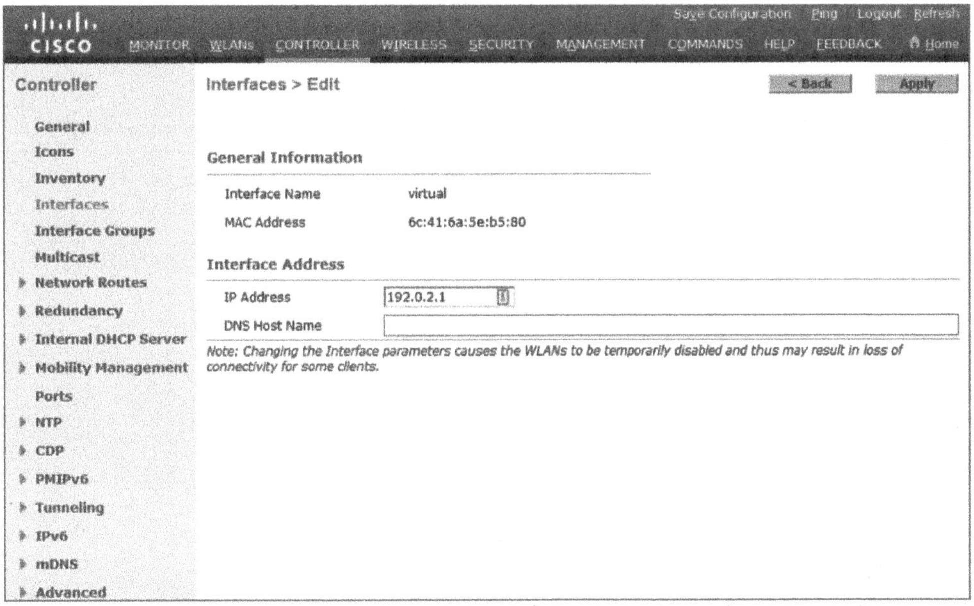

The CLI for configuring this interface is

```
(WLC01) >config interface address virtual 192.0.2.1
```

Dynamic Interface

When the WLC terminates the wireless traffic to the controller through CAPWAP, it will land on the management interface by default. This means that all wireless SSIDs will use the management interface's VLAN for IP addressing by default.

We can achieve more flexibility by choosing to create dynamic interfaces, which are like SVIs on a switch—logical interfaces that allow traffic to be terminated to different VLANs instead of just using the management.

You create a dynamic interface by clicking the New button on the Interfaces page, giving it a name that makes sense to you, and finally specifying the VLAN you want to use. In this case, I named the interface WLAN101 and used VLAN 101.

Depending on the controller model, the WLC can support between 16 and 4,096 dynamic interfaces! See Figure 11.16.

FIGURE 11.16 WLC dynamic interface

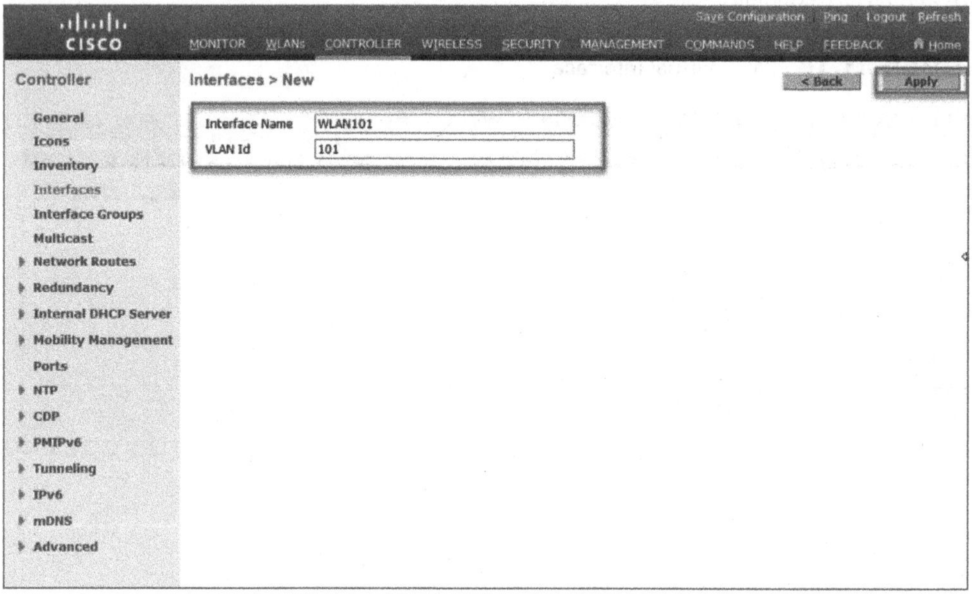

To do this in the CLI, I'm going to type the following:

```
(WLC01) >config interface create

<interface-name> Enter interface name.

(WLC01) >config interface create WLAN101

<vlan-id>       Enter VLAN Identifier.

(WLC01) >config interface create WLAN101 101
```

Once the interface is created, the configuration is really similar to the management interface, with the exception that dynamic AP management is disabled by default.

Because the WLC does not support dynamic routing and static routes are only for the service port, it's good to put the gateway IP on the switch network instead of directly on the WLC. After all, we can't easily advertise it to the network. Figure 11.17 shows the dynamic interface configuration.

FIGURE 11.17 WLC dynamic interface configuration

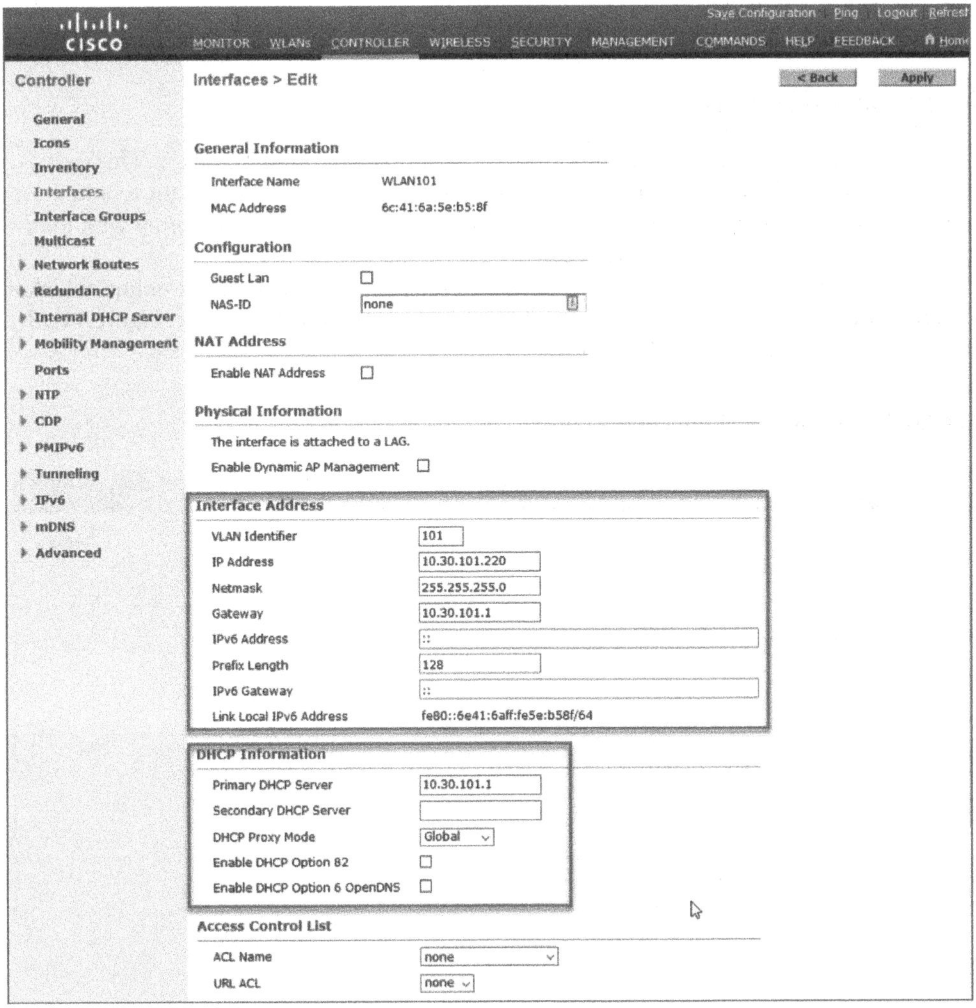

The CLI for configuring an IP on the dynamic interface looks like this:

```
(WLC01) >config interface address dynamic-interface wlan101 10.30.101.220

<netmask>        Enter the interface's netmask.

(WLC01) >config interface address dynamic-interface wlan101 10.30.101.220
255.255.255.0

<gateway>        Enter the interface's gateway address.

(WLC01) >config interface address dynamic-interface wlan101 10.30.101.220
255.255.255.0 10.30.101.1
```

Interface Groups

Interface groups are exactly what it sounds like—a way of grouping interfaces. This can come in really handy if your SSID is running out of IP addresses, and you want to add more without having to change the subnet mask on the interface. Instead of bothering with that, you can just add more dynamic interfaces!

You can even add the management interface to the pool so clients can get online, which is cool because it lets you keep subnet sizes smaller than issuing one big subnet. Figure 11.18 shows the interface groups configuration.

FIGURE 11.18 WLC interface groups

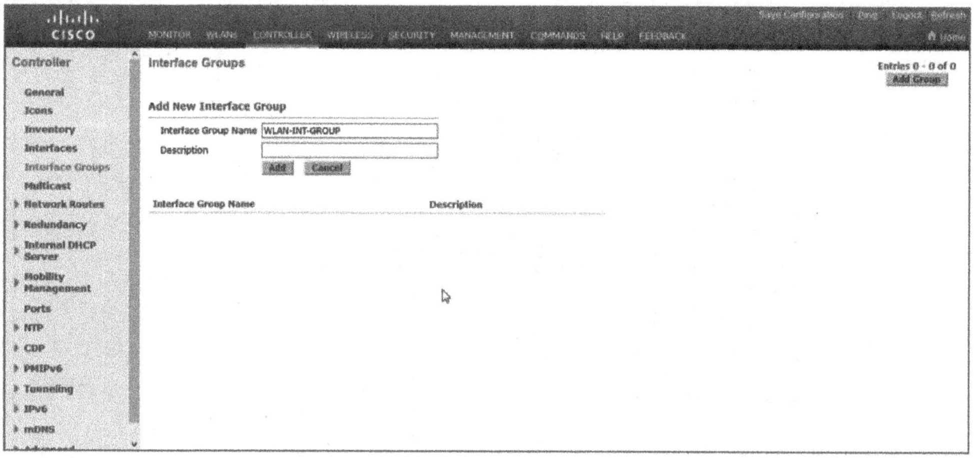

As usual, the command for getting this done is

```
<Interface Group name> Enter interface group name.
(WLC01) >config interface group create int-group
```

Next, you just need to pick the interfaces that will become part of the group. I'll create some more dynamic interfaces so you can see how this works when we create a WLAN. To do this, I need to select each interface and click the Add Interface button, as seen in Figure 11.19.

FIGURE 11.19 WLC interface group configuration

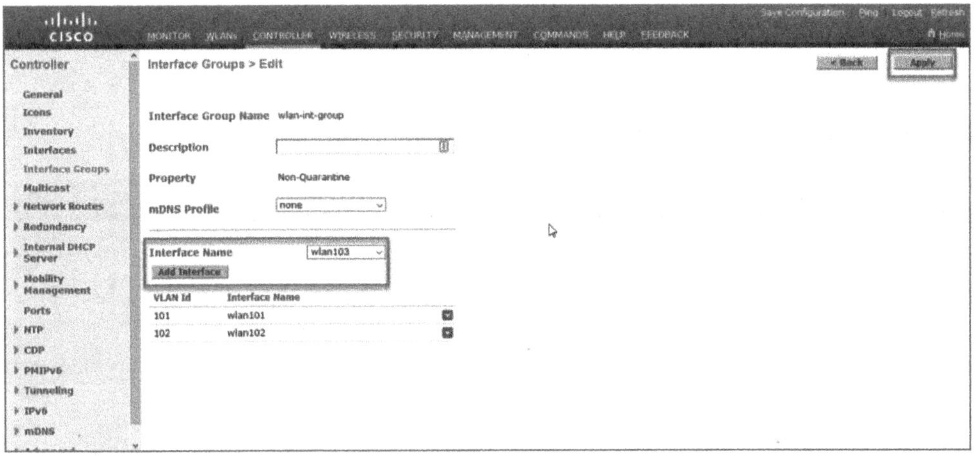

The CLI for adding interface groups is

```
WLC01) >config interface group interface add wlan-int-group wlan101
WLC01) >config interface group interface add wlan-int-group wlan102
WLC01) >config interface group interface add wlan-int-group wlan103
WLC01) >show interface group summary
Interface Group Name       Total Interfaces  Total Wlans  Total AP Groups
Quarantine
-------------------------- ----------------  -----------  ----------
wlan-int-group                    3               2             2          No
```

LAN Aggregation Group (LAG)

Because everybody wants a high-performance, reliable network, I'm going to show you how to increase fault tolerance and optimize our WLC's network connectivity by creating a port channel. It's too bad this isn't as flexible as it is on the modern 9800 controllers, but it's still worth doing.

On a WLC, all distributed system ports are added to the LAN aggregation group (LAG). Because the WLC doesn't support LACP or PAGP, we'll have to go with **channel-group #** `mode on` for switch side. Pro tip: you're going to reboot the WLC for the LAG to activate, so don't do this on a production system during the day!

We'll enable LAG from the Controller page, which thoughtfully reminds us to save our configuration and reboot the system.

Be warned that if you're using any untagged interfaces for wireless traffic, they'll be deleted after rebooting! Figure 11.20 shows the LAG configuration.

FIGURE 11.20 WLC LAN aggregation group

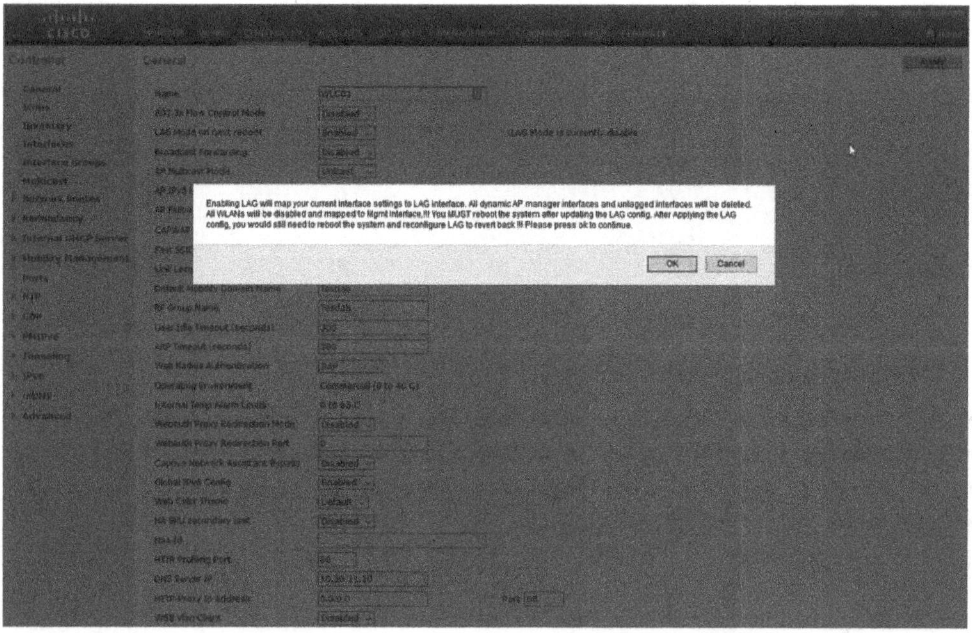

Just choose Save Configuration at top right on the page, and then go to Commands and click the Reboot page, where you'll click the Reboot button as in Figure 11.21.

FIGURE 11.21 WLC reboot

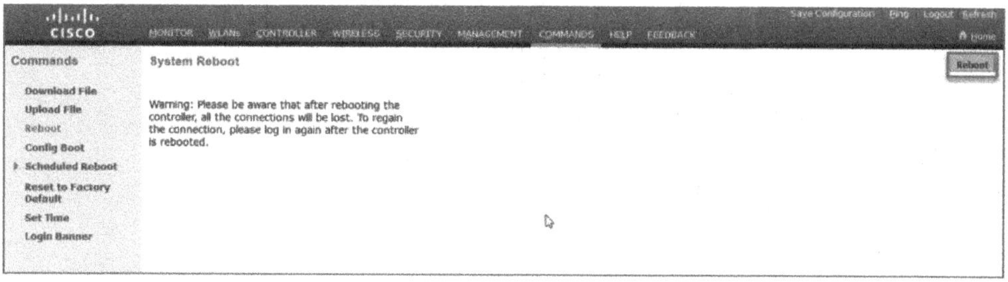

We get the same reminders if we configure this through the CLI:

```
(WLC01) >config lag enable
Enabling LAG will map your current interface setting to the LAG interface,
All dynamic AP Manager interfaces and Untagged interfaces will be deleted
All WLANs will be disabled and mapped to Mgmt interface
!!! You MUST reboot the system after updating the LAG config. !!!
!!! After Applying the LAG config, you would still need to    !!!
!!! reboot the system and reconfigure LAG to revert back      !!!
Are you sure you want to continue? (y/n) y
You MUST now save config and reset the system.
(WLC01) >save config
Are you sure you want to save? (y/n) y
Configuration Saved!
(WLC01) >reset system
Are you sure you would like to reset the system? (y/N) y
System will now restart!
```

Now, on my switch, I'm going to go ahead and configure a port channel on interfaces Gig1/0/1 through Gig1/0/2 that are connected to the WLC:

```
C9200-SW01(config)#int range GigabitEthernet 1/0/1-2
C9200-SW01(config-if-range)#channel-group 1 mode on
Creating a port-channel interface Port-channel 1
C9200-SW01(config-if-range)#
*Aug 24 19:06:12.829: %LINK-3-UPDOWN: Interface Port-channel1, changed
state to up
C9200-SW01(config-if-range)#
*Aug 24 19:06:13.830: %LINEPROTO-5-UPDOWN: Line protocol on Interface Port-
channel1, changed state to up
```

Because we are using on mode to create our port channel, it is simply going to be in an up/up state because it doesn't care if the WLC is ready or not. We can also finish our configuration by adding a description to our new port channel; also recall that the trunk and Portfast configuration will be inherited from earlier in the chapter:

```
C9200-SW01(config-if-range)#interface po1
C9200-SW01(config-if)#description Uplink to WLC01
C9200-SW01(config-if)#do sh run int po1
Building configuration...
Current configuration : 113 bytes
!
interface Port-channel1
 description Uplink to WLC01
 switchport mode trunk
 spanning-tree portfast trunk
```

Our port channel is ready to rock as soon as the WLC comes back up. Because all of the interfaces have been added to the LAG, we can add more links by connecting another cable and configuring the switch port to join the channel group—nice!

Configuring the AP

I've got two APs showing up on my WLC because we went through the join methods at the beginning of this chapter. I'm going to configure them by going to Wireless and then All APs, and then selecting the name of the AP I want to edit. Check out Figure 11.22.

FIGURE 11.22 WLC AP configuration screen

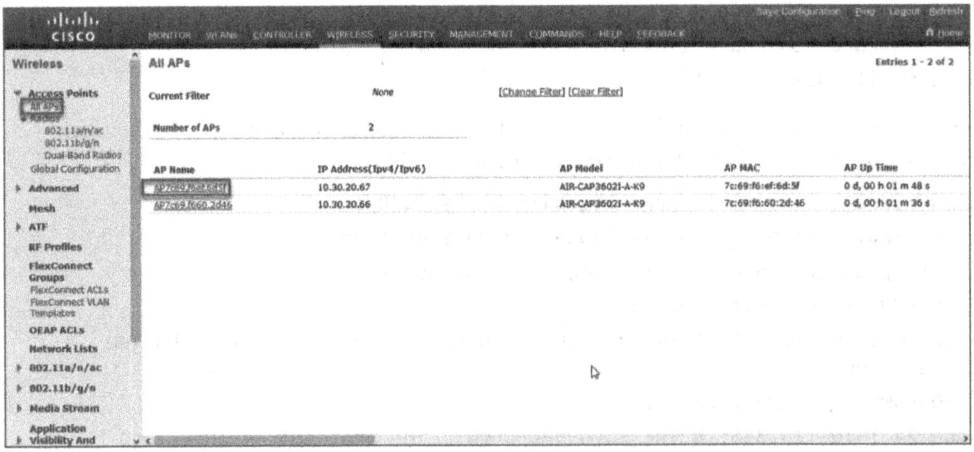

On the General page, I will pick an AP name that makes sense to me. I'm also changing the IP to static so I can better track the AP when I connect to things in my lab.

We won't be able to adjust the DNS address until we click Apply to commit the changes, as shown in Figure 11.23.

FIGURE 11.23 WLC AP IP addressing

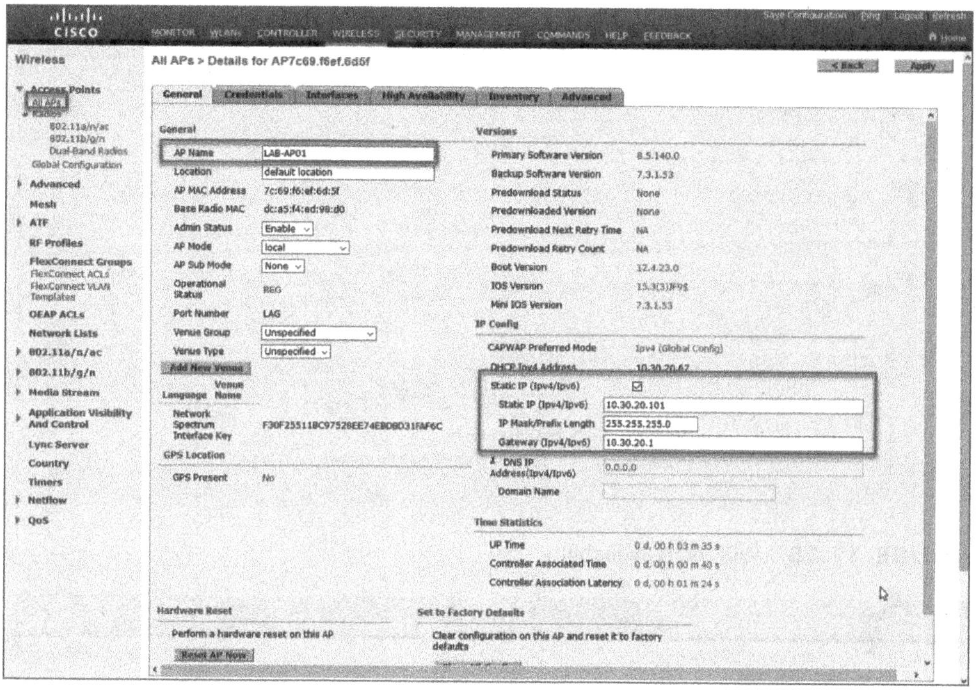

Now we can go ahead and enter the DNS server and tell the AP the domain name it should use, as shown in Figure 11.24.

Wow! There are many options here, but we will focus on the High Availability tab shown in Figure 11.25. This is where we can define up to three WLCs that the AP should try to connect to. This is really important because if an AP loses connection to the primary controller, it will try the next one on the list, and so on.

Figure 11.26 shows the configuration of the other AP; this is what the result looks like. I have a couple of other APs that I'll add, but the steps to do that will be the same.

FIGURE 11.24 WLC AP DNS configuration

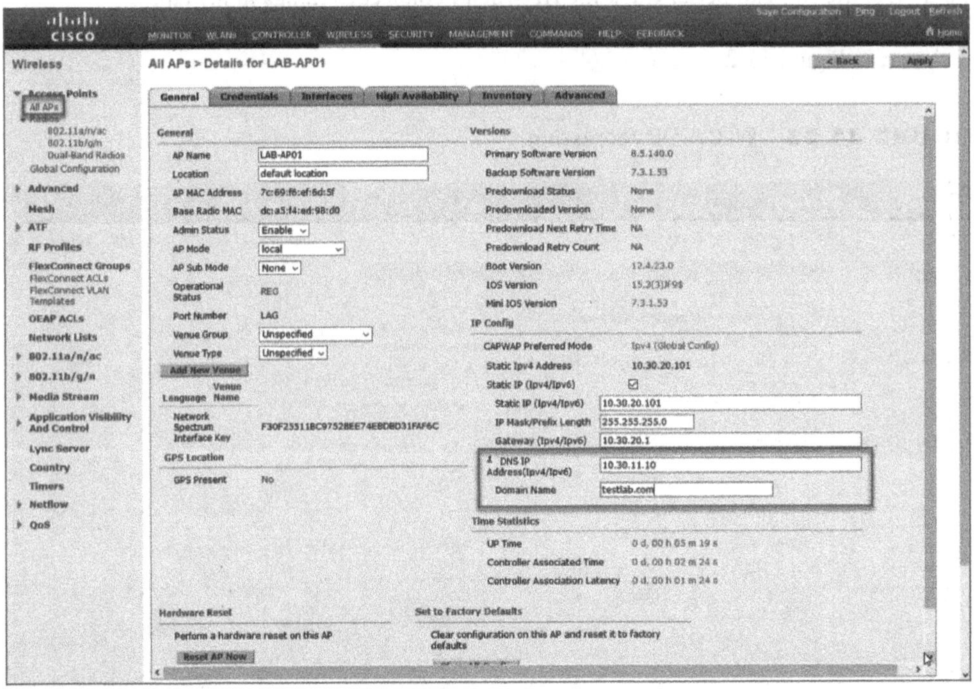

FIGURE 11.25 WLC high availability

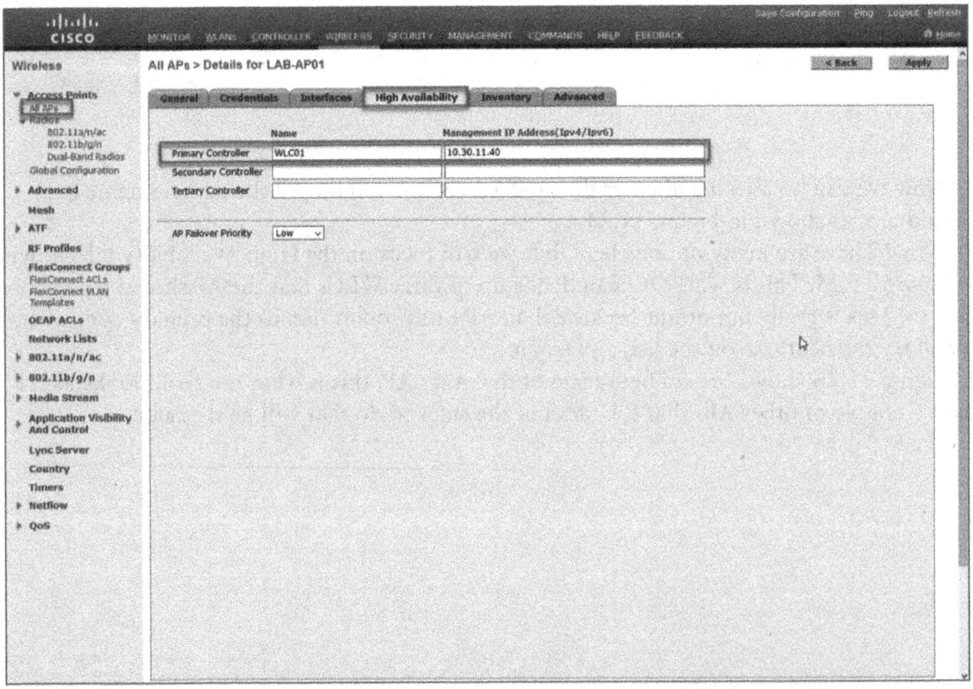

FIGURE 11.26 WLC finished AP configuration

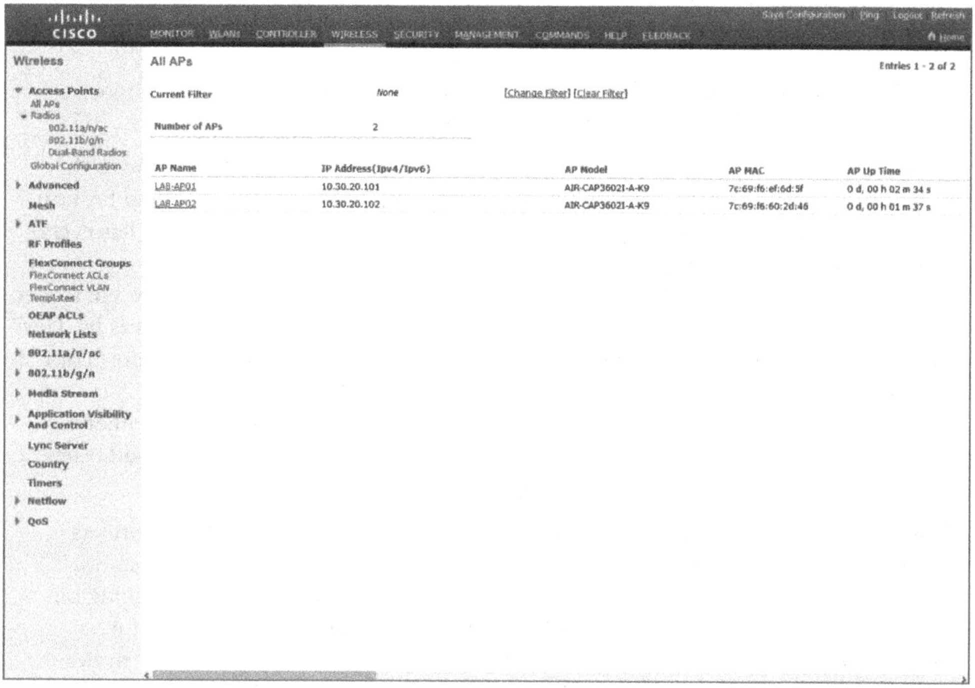

AP Modes

APs can do more than just connect you to wireless; they also support different functions and different ways of connecting. The various options available are called *modes*.

The WLC supports nine AP modes, depending on your specific AP model. I'll tell you about all the available options, but just know that local is the most important for the CCNA exam and beyond:

Local This is the default mode an AP will use and the only mode the CCNA expects you to know. All traffic will be carried back to the wireless controller through a CAP-WAP tunnel in this mode. This is handy if you want a central firewall at your main office to handle all wireless traffic for all your sites.

Also, when the AP isn't busy transmitting traffic, it'll keep itself busy by scanning the other channels for interference, measuring the noise level, checking for rogue devices, and looking for intrusion detection events. This mode can also run a Wireless Intrusion Prevention System submode, which enhances wireless security by comparing wireless traffic to IPS events and preventing bad traffic.

Monitor This mode doesn't send any wireless traffic at all. Instead, the AP acts as a dedicated sensor on your network. Like local mode, it will check the noise and interference for rogue devices and intrusion detection events. It will also try to provide location-based services by figuring out the location of endpoints on the network.

You should only enable this mode if you have spare APs or if you need more information to troubleshoot a performance issue.

FlexConnect The problem with local mode is that sending all wireless traffic to the wireless controller may be better for a site without an internet connection and firewall. However, sending traffic through the controller can be undesirable if the site has everything it needs to handle the traffic.

FlexConnect allows APs to switch traffic locally rather than send it to the controller, allowing the network to which the AP is connected to route the traffic as it sees fit. This mode is much more complex than local, but it offers more flexibility and performance if it suits your environment.

It can also run a Wireless Intrusion Prevention System submode, which enhances wireless security by comparing wireless traffic to IPS events and preventing bad traffic. We will have an in-depth look at this mode at the end of the chapter.

Sniffer This mode is great when you're troubleshooting an issue with the wireless network and need to do a packet capture. It doesn't serve traffic, but it does start a packet capture that can be sent to Wireshark so you can understand what's going on in the network. Once the AP is in sniffer mode, select what channel you want it to capture and give it a destination to send the captured traffic to. Figure 11.27 shows the sniffer screen.

FIGURE 11.27 WLC radio sniffer

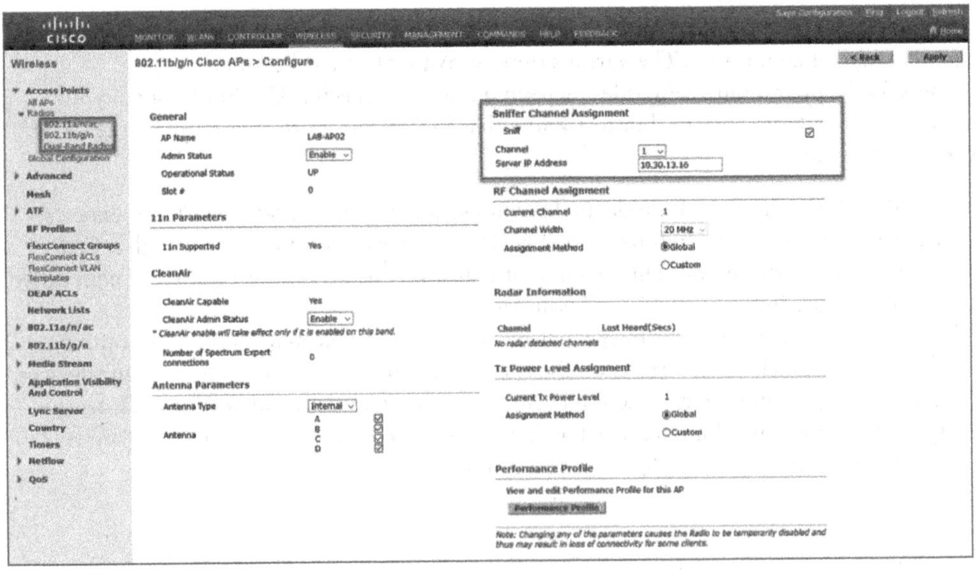

Rogue Detector This is another mode that doesn't send wireless traffic but dedicates itself to tracking APs that aren't joined to the WLC but are still possibly in your network.

An example would be an employee bringing in a cheap wireless router from home and connecting it to their office ethernet port because they don't like all that security that IT uses. Trust me—it happens! Once the WLC detects a rogue AP, it can notify you or try to contain the AP by spoofing deauthentication frames so clients can't connect to it anymore.

> **NOTE** In some areas, interfering with wireless connections can be illegal, so be sure to check with your company's legal team before implementing security features.

SE-Connect This mode lets you connect the AP to a spectrum analyzer to view the wireless spectrum. It's cool because it lets you determine if any noise or interference affects the channel and helps you find better channels for the wireless network to use instead.

Cisco has a tool called Spectrum Expert that you can use to connect to APs in this mode. However, it's pretty dated—the last update was in 2012! So, it's best to go with other solutions like Ekahau or a cheaper tool like Metageek's Chanalyzer tool. Once again, this mode doesn't serve wireless traffic.

Figure 11.28 gives you an example of a Cisco Spectrum Expert that's connected to one of the APs in SE-Connect mode.

FIGURE 11.28 Cisco Spectrum Expert

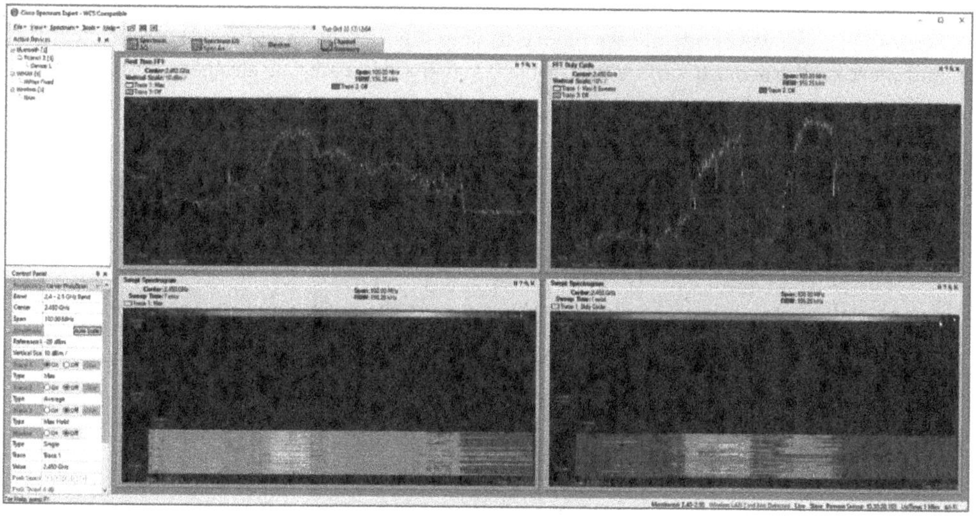

To compare, Figure 11.29 shows an example of Metageek's Chanalyzer tool connected to one of the APs in the same mode.

FIGURE 11.29 Metageek's Chanalyzer

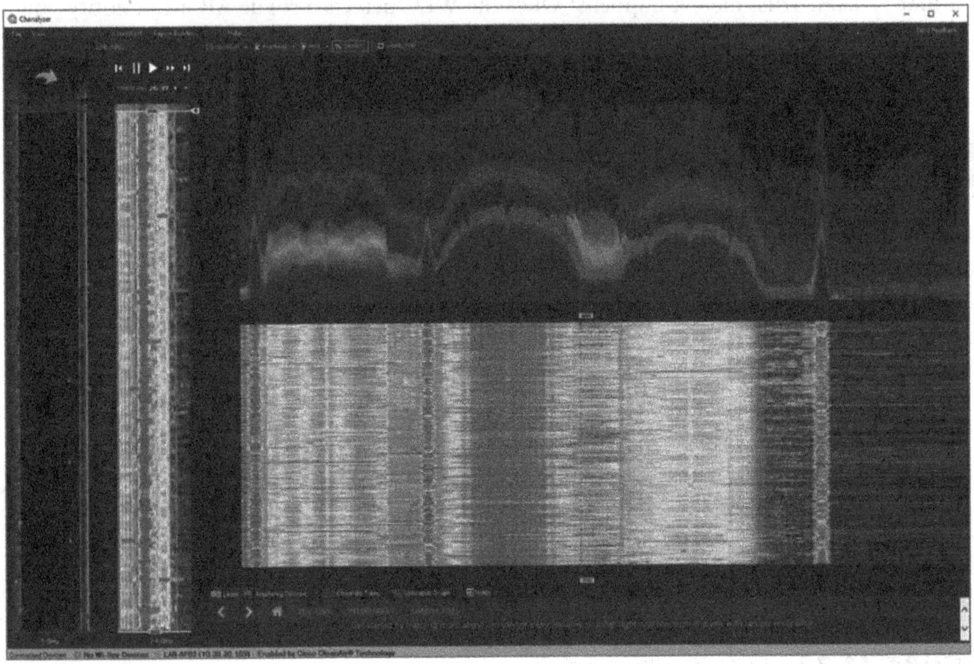

Sensor This newer mode allows the AP to help out Catalyst Center's Assurance feature and increase the accuracy of its decisions. It's also a dedicated mode that doesn't serve traffic. You can only use this mode on newer APs.

Bridge This mode, also known as a *mesh*, allows an AP to connect to another AP to form a point-to-point or point-to-multipoint connection. This helps you wirelessly connect areas if you can't run a cable between the sites because of distance or terrain.

The wireless mesh usually connects the site through ethernet to the switch, but you can also allow wireless SSIDs through the mesh. At the mesh network's top is the root

AP (RAP). When traffic reaches the RAP, it's sent to the controller through a CAPWAP tunnel, just like in the local mode. Figure 11.30 shows a bridge layout.

FIGURE 11.30 Bridge mode

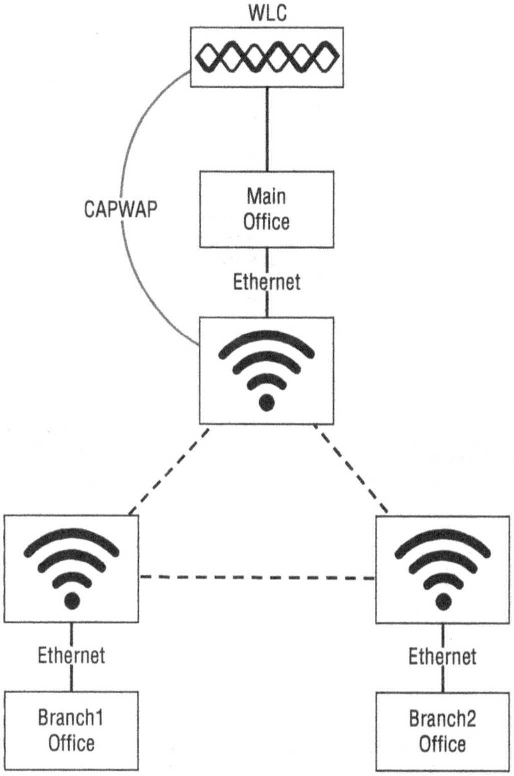

Flex+Bridge This mode adds FlexConnect to the mesh network. Traffic is locally switched from the RAP when it reenters the network. It can also support ethernet and wireless connections. Figure 11.31 shows the kind of layout wherein Flex+Bridge would come in handy.

FIGURE 11.31 FlexConnect layout

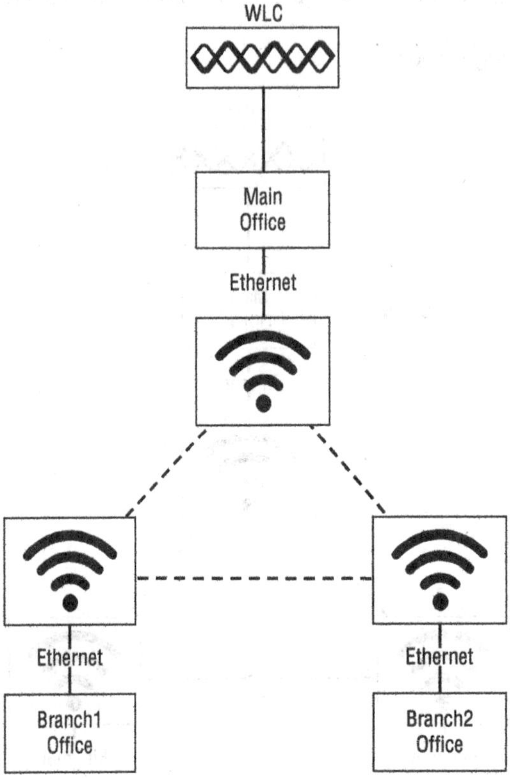

AP and WLC Management Access Connections

Okay—right now, we've got the WLC set up and some APs registered to it, so it's a great time to dive into the different kinds of management access connections available on the WLC and APs. Here's a list of the ones I'm going to cover with you:

- CDP
- Telnet
- SSH
- HTTP
- HTTPS
- Console
- RADIUS

CDP

Even though CDP doesn't technically provide management access, it's really useful if you're working on Cisco networks and need to figure out how the WLC and APs are connected to the Cisco switches.

Both the WLC and APs have CDP enabled by default, so you don't need to make any changes to make it work. But you can configure it by going to Controller and then CDP to tweak the settings, as seen in Figure 11.32.

FIGURE 11.32 WLC CDP configuration

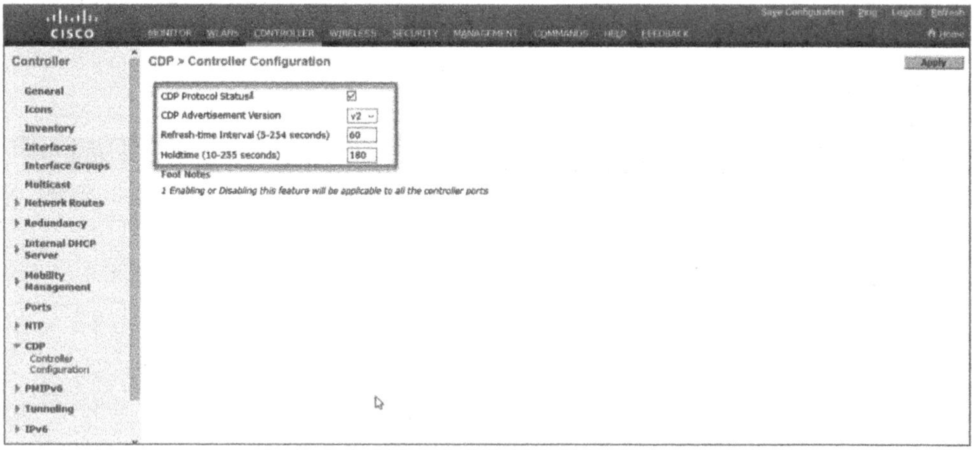

As usual, you can use the CLI to enable CDP if it is disabled for some reason:

```
(WLC01) >config cdp enable
```

From the WLC, you can check into CDP information from the Monitor page, then CDP Interface Neighbors, as shown in Figure 11.33.

FIGURE 11.33 WLC CDP verification

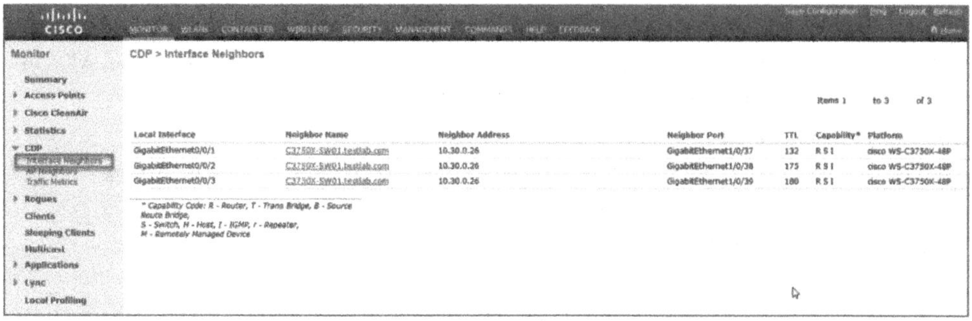

The command for this is the same one you use on a Cisco switch or router:

```
(WLC01) >show cdp neighbors
Capability Codes: R - Router, T - Trans Bridge, B - Source Route Bridge
        S - Switch, H - Host, I - IGMP, r - Repeater,
        M - Remotely Managed Device
Device ID          Local    Intrfce      Holdtme  Capability  Platform  Port ID
C9200-SW01.testlab.com Gig 0/0/1         176      R S I       C9KV-Q200 Gig 1/0/1
C9200-SW01.testlab.com Gig 0/0/2         152      R S I       C9KV-Q200 Gig 1/0/2
```

And again, just like on a switch or router, you can get more detail by clicking the neighbor on the page, as seen in Figure 11.34, or by entering **show cdp neighbor detail**.

FIGURE 11.34 Show CDP neighbors

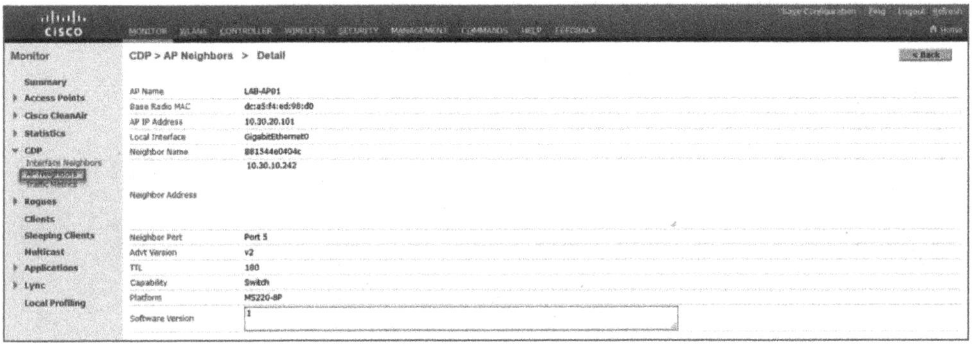

The command is also the same on Cisco APs:

```
LAB-AP03#show cdp neighbors
Capability Codes: R - Router, T - Trans Bridge, B - Source Route Bridge
        S - Switch, H - Host, I - IGMP, r - Repeater, P - Phone,
        D - Remote, C - CVTA, M - Two-port Mac Relay
Device ID          Local Intrfce     Holdtme    Capability  Platform  Port ID
C3750X-SW01.testlab.com Gig 0            148      R S I  WS-C3750X Gig 1/0/1
```

To give you the whole picture, check out the following output. I can also see the WLC and APs if I look at the CDP output on my switch. This makes it easy to track down APs on your switches when you need to locate their switch ports:

```
C9200-SW01#show cdp nei
Capability Codes: R - Router, T - Trans Bridge, B - Source Route Bridge
   S - Switch, H - Host, I - IGMP, r - Repeater, P - Phone,
   D - Remote, C - CVTA, M - Two-port Mac Relay
```

```
Device ID          Local Intrfce     Holdtme    Capability  Platform  Port ID
WLC01              Gig 1/0/1        128              H    AIR-CT550 Gig 0/0/1
WLC01              Gig 1/0/2        128              H    AIR-CT550 Gig 0/0/2
WLC01              Gig 1/0/3        128              H    AIR-CT550 Gig 0/0/3
LAB-AP03.testlab.com Gig 1/0/8       149           T B I  AIR-CAP37 Gig 0
LAB-AP02.testlab.com Gig 1/0/6       141           T B I  AIR-CAP36 Gig 0
LAB-AP01.testlab.com Gig 1/0/7       134           T B I  AIR-CAP36 Gig 0
Total cdp entries displayed : 11
```

Telnet

Using Telnet for management is a bad idea these days because it's plaintext, so the WLC turns it off by default! Most of the time, you want to leave this setting off so Telnet remains disabled.

But if you want to turn it on for your lab, go to the Management page, click Telnet-SSH on the menu, and set Allow New Telnet Sessions to Yes.

Figure 11.35 shows you the WLC Telnet configuration.

FIGURE 11.35 WLC Telnet configuration

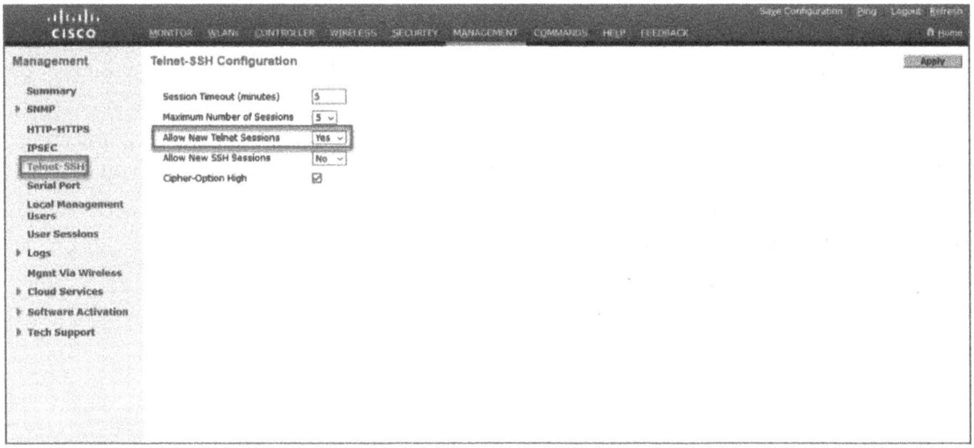

This can be configured through the CLI with the following:

```
(WLC01) >config network telnet
enable          Enables this setting.
disable         Disables this setting.
(WLC01) >config network telnet enable
```

SSH

SSH is already turned on by default, so you shouldn't need to change anything to make it work. If you do want to make any changes to it, go to the same page as Telnet, click Telnet-SSH, and make sure Allow New SSH Sessions is set to Yes, as shown in Figure 11.36.

FIGURE 11.36 WLC SSH configuration

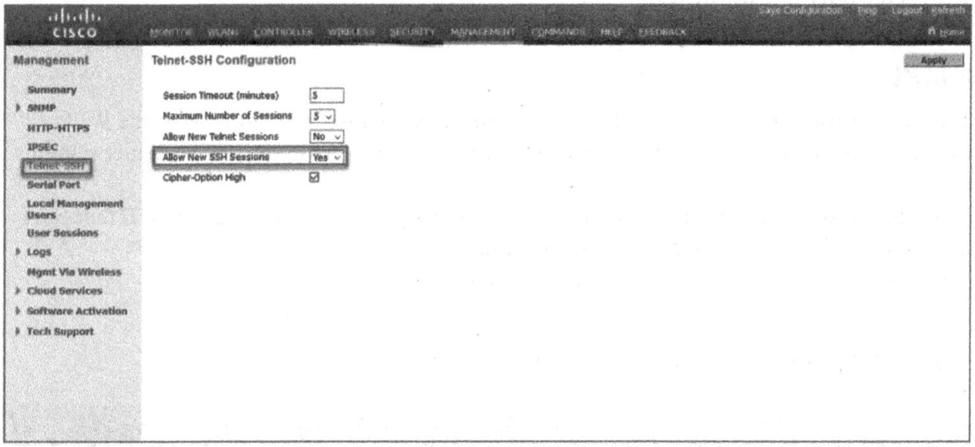

Of course, you can configure SSH with the CLI, but because you're probably connecting to the WLC CLI through SSH, make sure you have another way on the WLC if you decide to try out disabling SSH!

```
(WLC01) >config network ssh
cipher-option  Configure cipher requirements for SSH.
delete         delete ssh public keys .
disable        Disallow new ssh sessions.
enable         Allow new ssh sessions.
host-key       Configure SSH access host key
(WLC01) >config network ssh enable
```

HTTP

HTTP is also disabled by default because it's plaintext and should only be used in a lab setting. There's just not a great reason for using it at all. But so you know, HTTP can be enabled or disabled by clicking HTTP-HTTPs on the Management page and confirming that HTTP Access is either enabled or disabled, as shown in Figure 11.37.

FIGURE 11.37 WLC HTTP configuration

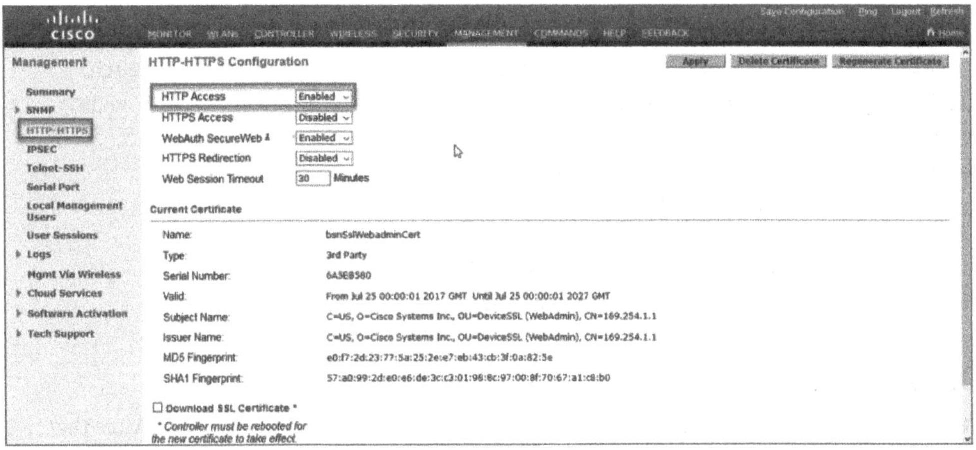

Back on the CLI, the command for this is a little less obvious than usual, because HTTP access is called webmode here:

```
(WLC01) >config network webmode
enable          Enables this setting.
disable         Disables this setting.
```

HTTPS

HTTPS is your shining star—it's the primary way to configure the WLC. You can also choose to enable HTTPS redirection so if you accidentally use HTTP to access the WLC, it will automatically switch you over to HTTPS—nice! You can configure HTTPS on the same page as HTTP, as shown in Figure 11.38.

FIGURE 11.38 WLC HTTPS configuration

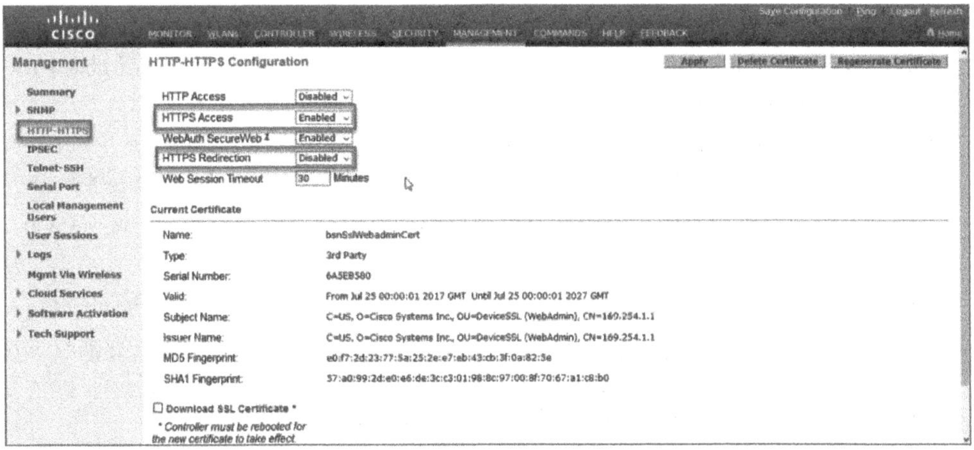

Once again, the command line uses a different keyword than you'd think; for HTTPS, it is secureweb:

```
(WLC01) >config network secureweb
cipher-option  Configure cipher requirements for web admin and web auth.
csrfcheck      Enable or disable Cross-Site Request Forgery for web mode.
disable        Disable the Secure Web (HTTPS) management interface.
enable         Enable the Secure Web (HTTPS) management interface.
ocsp           Configure OCSP requirements for web admin in format
http://<ip>/path
sslv3          Configure SSLv3 for web admin and web auth
(WLC01) >config network secureweb enable
```

Console

When the WLC is fresh out of the box, we use the console port to configure it. After that, it's mainly used for troubleshooting, as discussed earlier in this chapter.

RADIUS

Wireless commonly uses RADIUS servers to help secure wireless connections when using 802.1X for the SSID's security. The WLC supports up to 32 RADIUS servers, and each SSID lets us specify 6 RADIUS servers. This is cool because it gives us a lot of flexibility when we make our WLANs because we can use some RADIUS servers on one WLAN and different ones on another.

As you should know by now, AAA has three components: authentication, authorization, and accounting. The WLC needs us to configure authentication and accounting. Still, it gives us a break and doesn't have us configure an authorization section either because it is just built into the authentication part.

So, let's get started. To configure RADIUS, click the Security page, find RADIUS under AAA, and then click Authentication. Once there, click New to start adding a new server to the WLC.

We're going to configure two RADIUS authentication servers for this chapter, and the main fields you need to know about for the CCNA are as follows:

Server Index This is the RADIUS server's priority. It controls the order in which the server appears in the selection list. The server index must be unique, so after I pick 1 for the value, the next server will need to be 2.

Server IP Address This is just the RADIUS server's IP address, which can be IPv4 or IPv6. WLC does support DNS names, but they're a bit over the top for the CCNA.

Shared Secret Format This controls which format the shared secret will be in—ASCII text or hex.

Shared Secret The password that's used between the RADIUS server and the client.

Port Number This is a default field, but it is good to know that RADIUS will use 1812 for all modern connections. Some legacy RADIUS configurations might use port UDP 1645 because it's the legacy RADIUS authentication number.

Support for CoA CoA stands for change of authorization—optional for the CCNA. It allows an 802.1X server like a Cisco Identity Service Engine (ISE) to change a RADIUS session's authorization result.

The rest of the fields can be left as default at the CCNA level.

So now I'm going to add two RADIUS servers. The first one will be priority "1" and will use a server IP of 10.20.11.32, as shown in Figure 11.39.

The next server is going to use a priority of 2 and have a server IP of 10.20.12.32, as I configured in Figure 11.40.

FIGURE 11.39 WLC RADIUS configuration

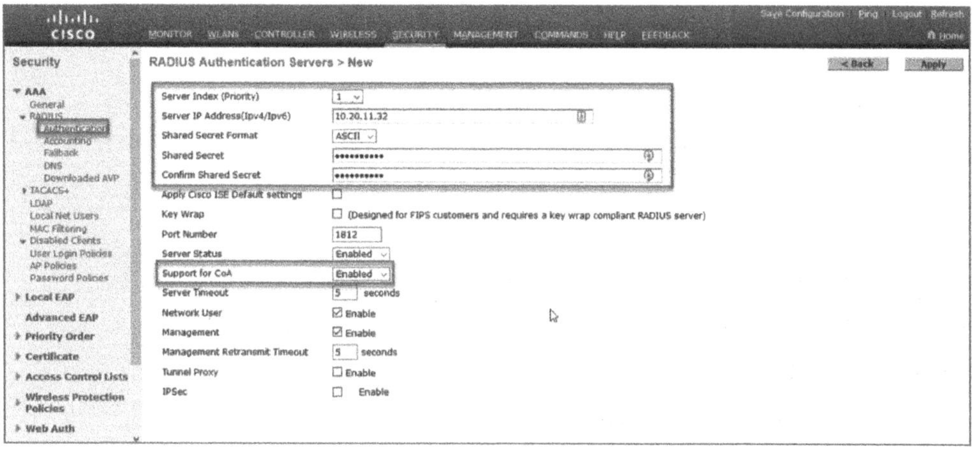

FIGURE 11.40 WLC second RADIUS configuration

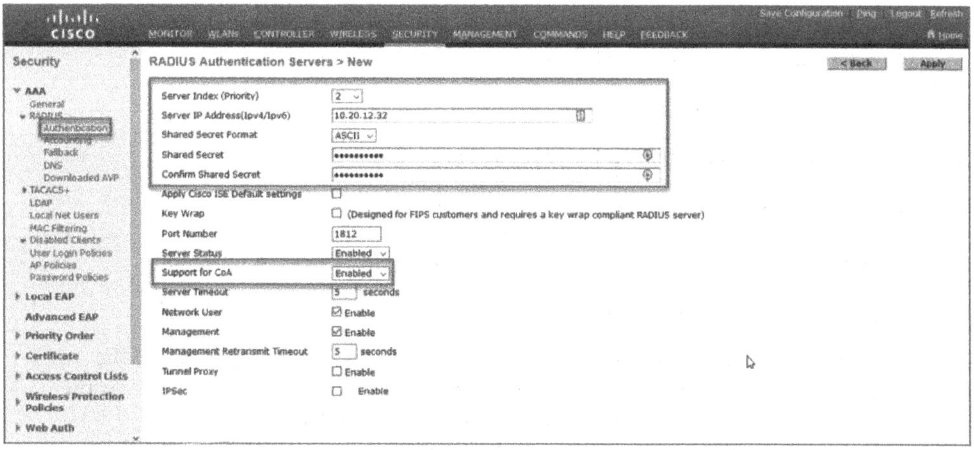

And now that I've added the servers, we can see a summary of what was configured on the Authentication page, shown in Figure 11.41.

FIGURE 11.41 RADIUS configuration summary

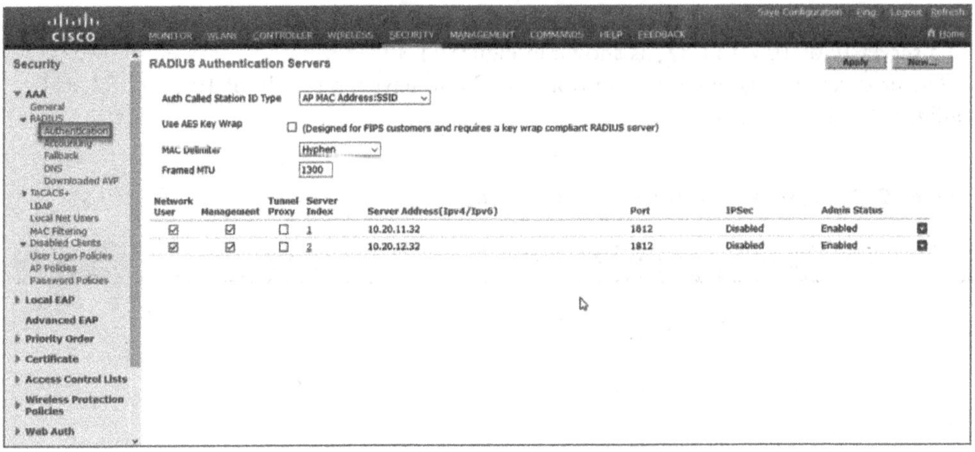

The CLI to configure the RADIUS authentication servers looks like this:

```
(WLC01) >config radius auth add 1

<IP addr>       Enter RADIUS Server IP (ipv4 or ipv6) Address.

(WLC01) >config radius auth add 1 10.20.11.32

<port>          Configures a RADIUS Server's UDP port.

(WLC01) >config radius auth add 1 10.20.11.32 1812

[ascii/hex]     The type of RADIUS Server's secret is ascii or hex.

(WLC01) >config radius auth add 1 10.20.11.32 1812 meowcatAAA

<secret>        Enter the RADIUS Server's secret.

(WLC01) >config radius auth add 1 10.20.11.32 1812 ascii

<secret>        Enter the RADIUS Server's secret.

(WLC01) >config radius auth add 1 10.20.11.32 1812 ascii meowcatAAA

(WLC01) >config radius auth add 2 10.20.12.32 1812 ascii meowcatAAA
```

Okay, great—the RADIUS authentication is set up, so now we've got to go to the RADIUS accounting side of things and configure that. This is vital because it allows the RADIUS server to track session details so it knows who did what and when!

To configure this, click Accounting under the RADIUS section, and then click New to get the configuration page shown in Figure 11.42.

FIGURE 11.42 WLC RADIUS accounting configuration

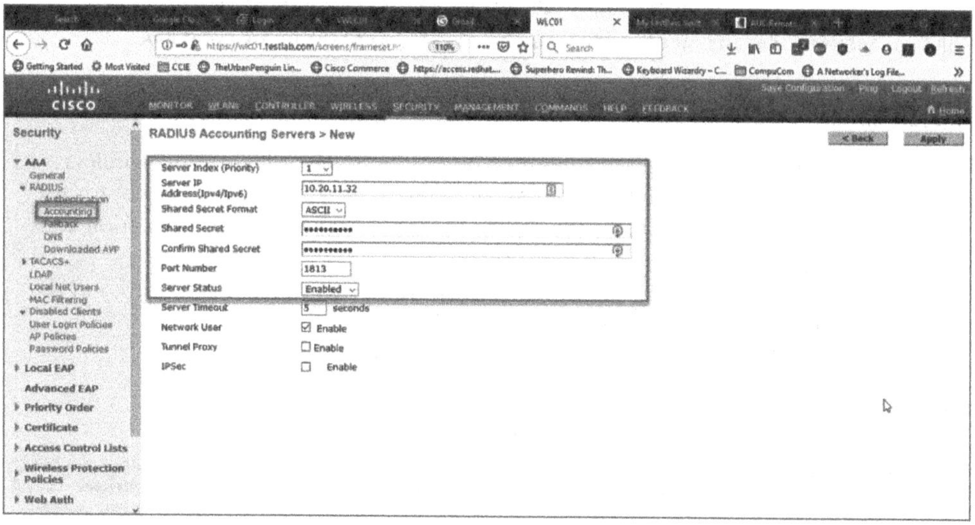

I will also configure two RADIUS accounting servers just like we did with authentication. The only real difference is that accounting uses UDP 1813 by default, but you could see UDP 1646 being used instead in legacy configs. The server IP is going to be the same as the authentication servers.

So here again, we can see the summary by looking at the Accounting page shown in Figure 11.43.

FIGURE 11.43 WLC RADIUS accounting summary

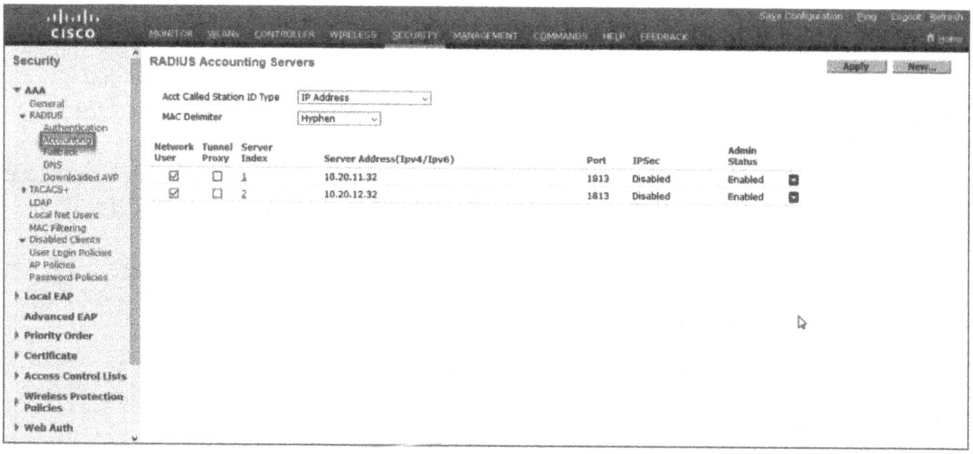

The CLI is a lot like the authentication config, except it uses the `acct` keyword:

```
(WLC01) >config radius acct add 1 10.20.11.32 1813 ascii meowcatAAA
(WLC01) >config radius acct add 2 10.20.12.32 1813 ascii meowcatAAA
```

TACACS+

TACACS+ is better suited for device administration rather than authenticating wireless users. Because of this, the WLC supports TACACS+ for management users but not for use in WLANs. The WLC supports up to three servers; we must configure authentication and authorization separately.

To create a TACACS+ authentication server, click Authentication under TACACS in the AAA section and then click New, as shown in Figure 11.44.

FIGURE 11.44 WLC TACACS+ configuration

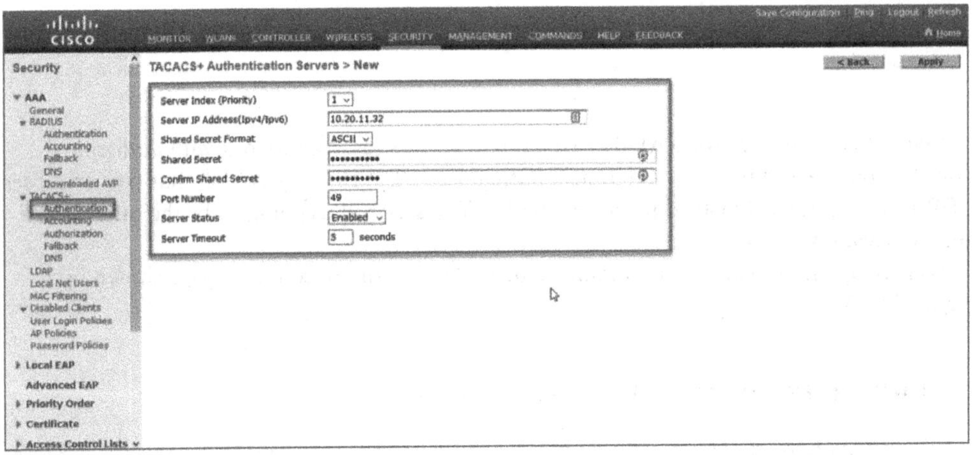

I mentioned all the fields you can configure on the new server page, but know that RADIUS is only available for a limited number of options. TACACS+ uses TCP 49 for its port number.

Because I'm using Cisco ISE, which supports both RADIUS and TACACS+, let's configure TACACS+ now using the same IPs we used for the RADIUS configuration: 10.20.11.32 and 10.20.12.32.

The CLI is the same as the RADIUS config, except it uses the `tacacs` keyword:

```
(WLC01) >config tacacs auth add

<1-3>          Enter the TACACS+ Server index.

(WLC01) >config tacacs auth add 1
```

```
<IP addr>       Enter TACACS+ Server IP (v4 or v6) Address.
(WLC01) >config tacacs auth add 1 10.20.11.32
<port>          Configures a TACACS+ Server's TCP port.
(WLC01) >config tacacs auth add 1 10.20.11.32 49
[ascii/hex]     The type of TACACS+ Server's secret is ascii or hex.
(WLC01) >config tacacs auth add 1 10.20.11.32 49 ascii
<secret>        Enter the TACACS+ Server's secret.
(WLC01) >config tacacs auth add 1 10.20.11.32 49 ascii meowcatAAA
```

And just like with RADIUS, we can view a summary by looking at the TACACS+ Authentication page shown in Figure 11.45.

FIGURE 11.45 WLC TACACS+ summary

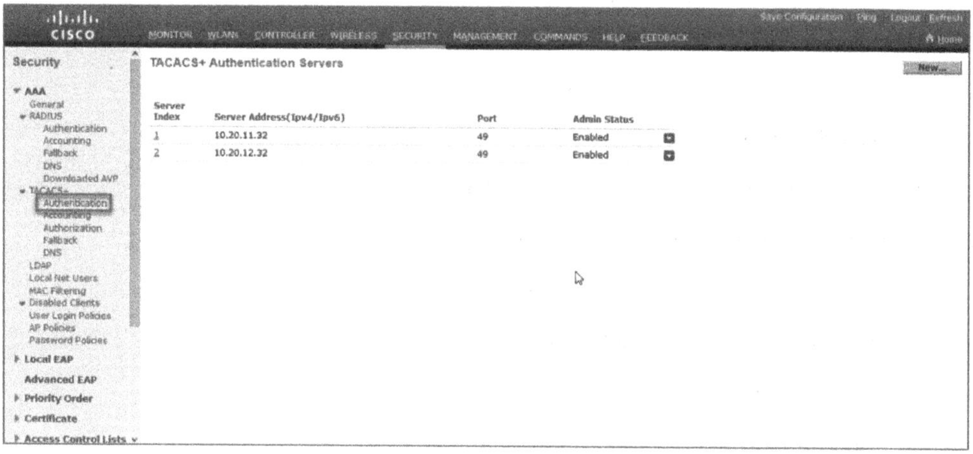

Finally, we need to configure the accounting servers, and I'll use the same IPs as previously. As mentioned, TACACS+ uses TCP 49 for all operations, as shown in Figure 11.46.

FIGURE 11.46 WLC TACACS+ accounting configuration

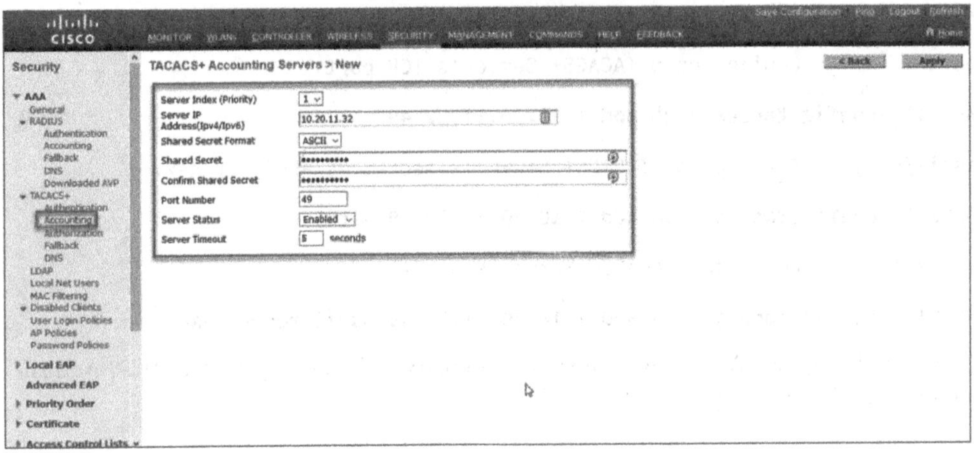

The CLI is the same, except it uses the `acct` keyword:

```
(WLC01) >config tacacs acct add

<1-3>          Enter the TACACS+ Server index.

(WLC01) >config tacacs acct add 1

<IP addr>      Enter TACACS+ Server IP (v4 or v6) Address.

(WLC01) >config tacacs acct add 1 10.20.11.32

<port>         Configures a TACACS+ Server's TCP port.

(WLC01) >config tacacs acct add 1 10.20.11.32 49

[ascii/hex]    The type of TACACS+ Server's secret is ascii or hex.

(WLC01) >config tacacs acct add 1 10.20.11.32 49 ascii

<secret>       Enter the TACACS+ Server's secret.

(WLC01) >config tacacs acct add 1 10.20.11.32 49 ascii meowcatAAA
```

Of course, we can verify our changes by looking at the Accounting page, as demonstrated in Figure 11.47.

To use TACACS+ for WLC management user authentications, click Management User on the Security page under Priority Order. Then, move TACACS+ from Not Used to Order Used for Authentication and adjust the order.

FIGURE 11.47 WLC TACACS+ Accounting Summary

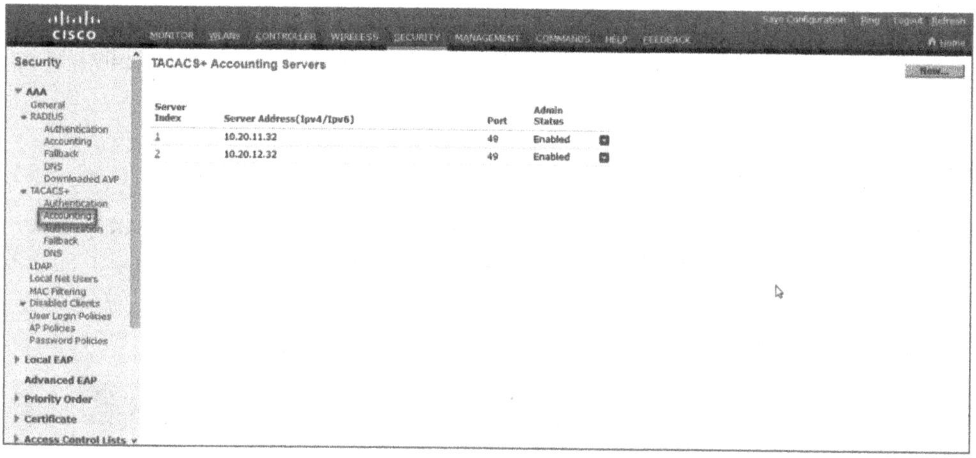

NOTE If you move LOCAL from the top of the order so that RADIUS or TACACS+ is first, LOCAL will only be used if all the remote servers are unavailable. So, if you have a configuration issue on the server that prevents you from logging in, you'll need to resolve it before you can log in to the WLC!

Figure 11.48 shows the authentication order that I configured.

FIGURE 11.48 WLC authentication order

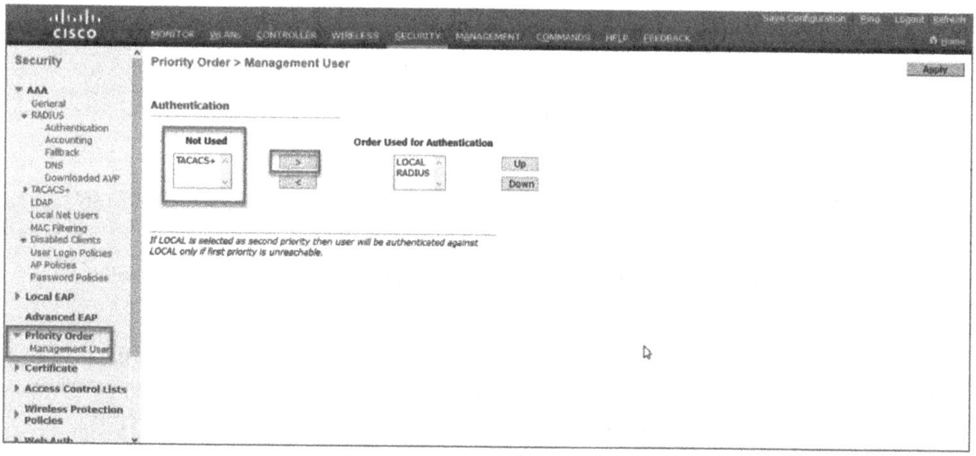

Configuring WLANs

Phew! Okay—it's finally time to create a Wireless LAN (WLAN) that we can actually connect a host to!

WLAN creation

To create a WLAN, we predictably head over to the WLAN page. Make sure Create New is at the top right of the screen, and then click Go, as shown in Figure 11.49.

FIGURE 11.49 WLC WLAN creation

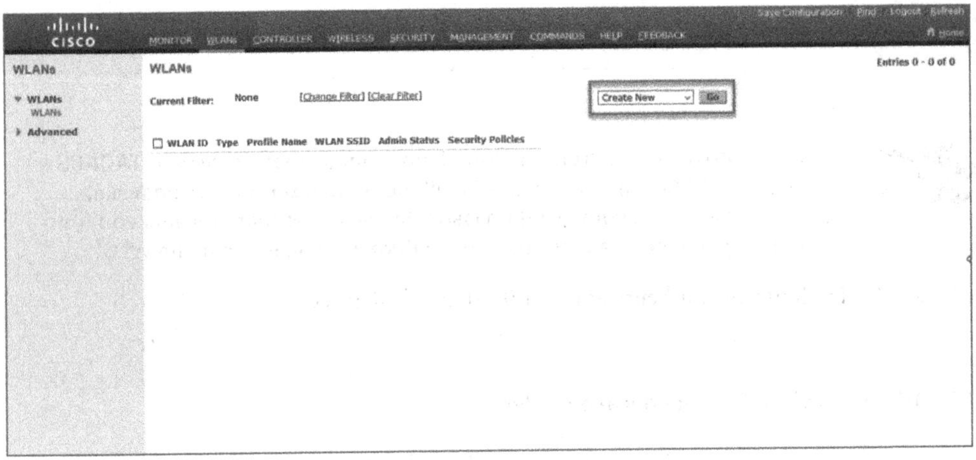

We will give the WLAN some information here on the New WLAN page.
Here are the options:

Type This controls the type of wireless network we will create—it will always be WLAN at the CCNA level.

Profile Name This is just a friendly name for our WLAN, and it can be whatever you want.

SSID This is the name of the actual SSID used by the WLAN, and most people just set it to be the same as the profile name. Again, you can pick any SSID name you want, but remember that people can see it when they connect to the wireless, so keep it office-friendly!

ID Every WLAN needs a unique ID that's between 1 and 512. Typically, you would leave this at the default unless you need it to be at a certain value.

Figure 11.50 shows the WLAN configuration.

FIGURE 11.50 WLC WLAN configuration

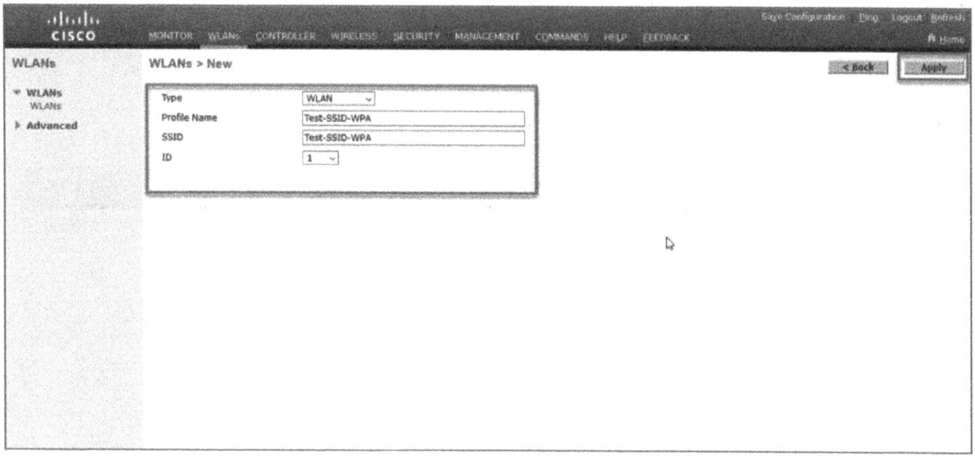

Lets configure a WLAN using ID of 1.

```
(WLC01) >config wlan create

<WLAN id>       Enter WLAN Identifier between 1 and 512.

(WLC01) >config wlan create 1

<name>          Enter Profile Name up to 32 alphanumeric characters.

(WLC01) >config wlan create 1 test-wlan-wpa

<ssid>          Enter SSID (Network Name) up to 32 alphanumeric characters.

(WLC01) >config wlan create 1 test-wlan-wpa test-wlan-wpa
```

General settings

The General Settings tab is where the more administrative features of the WLAN are configured. In addition to letting us change the profile and SSID name, we've got some other options available as well:

Status This is like the `shutdown` command on a Cisco router—you can turn the WLAN on or off if you need to.

Interface/Interface Group This option binds the WLAN to a WLC interface or interface group. It allows you to control which VLANs the client IP will be in when they connect.

Broadcast SSID This option controls whether the SSID is visible to everyone's wireless devices. It's more common to broadcast most SSIDs but not 802.1X wireless connections because they're usually pushed to the work laptop through Group Policy.

Figure 11.51 shows the General Tab on the WLC WLAN page.

FIGURE 11.51 WLC WLAN General tab

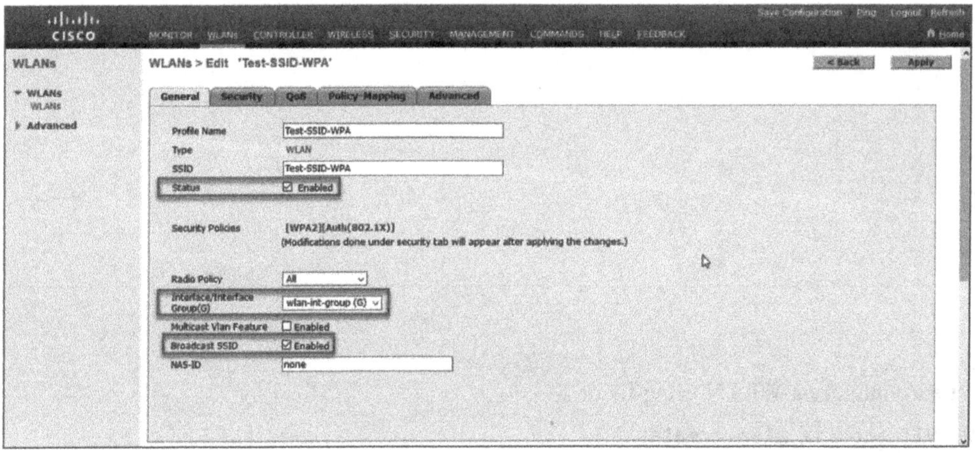

The CLI is a bit different this time from what you've been seeing. We'll use the keyword for the feature we want to configure and then reference the WLAN ID number to apply it to the right WLAN:

```
(WLC01) >config wlan broadcast-ssid enable 1
(WLC01) >config wlan interface 1 wlan-int-group
(WLC01) >config wlan enable 1
```

Security Settings—Layer 2

The Security tab is just what it sounds like—it controls the WLAN's security settings, and yes, there are many of them! Fortunately for you, the CCNA is only interested in a few of the options. The WLAN will default to supporting WPA2 connections, so you don't need to change the layer 2 security type. The main options you've got to adjust are under the Authentication Key Management section:

802.1X This allows you to use a Cisco ISE server to control the WLAN connections, but you won't use it in the CCNA. You do need to make sure it's turned off so PSK can work!

PSK This option tells the WLAN to use a preshared key to authenticate wireless clients.

PSK Format You can enter a preshared key in either ASCII format or hex. The PSK must be at least eight characters in length, as you can see in Figure 11.52.

FIGURE 11.52 WLC WLAN Security tab

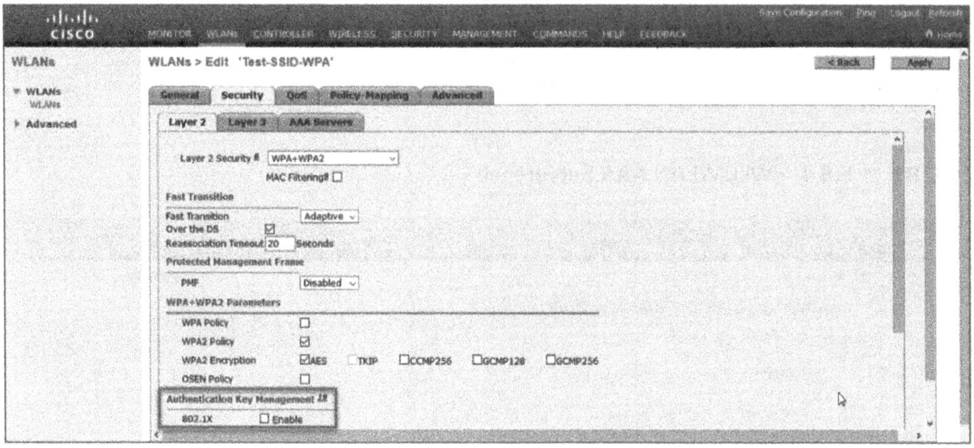

Figure 11.53 shows the PSK configuration.

FIGURE 11.53 WLC WLAN PSK configuration

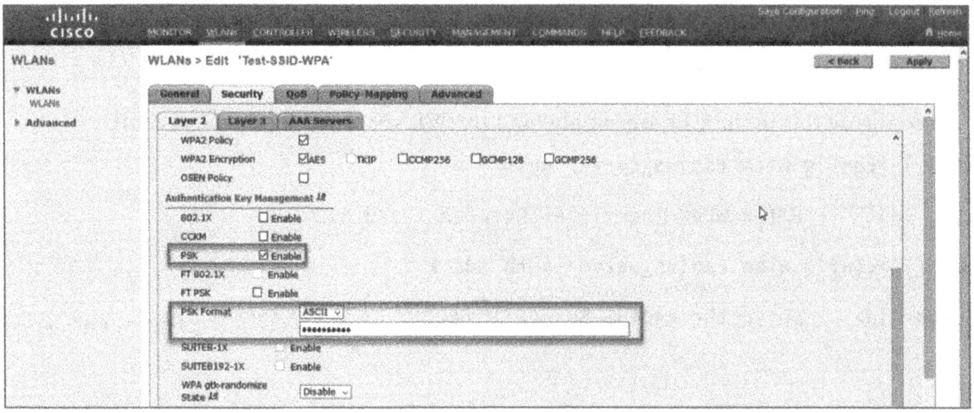

You handle PSK configuration with the following commands:

```
(WLC01) >config wlan security wpa akm psk enable 1
(WLC01) >config wlan security wpa akm psk set-key ascii meowcatPSK 1
```

Security Settings—AAA Servers

Now, if you want to use WPA2-Enterprise, the WLAN must talk to some RADIUS servers, and you can use the AAA Server subtab under Security to set that up. Because our WLAN is using a preshared key, it doesn't need AAA configuration to work, so I'll create a sample new WLAN to show you how to do that.

On this page, choose the RADIUS authentication and accounting servers we just created, and put them in the proper order. Server 1 is used before Server 2, and so on. Remember, the WLAN can support up to six servers.

The WLC will use the management interface to contact the RADIUS server unless you check the RADIUS Server Override Interface check box.

Figure 11.54 shows the AAA Servers tab.

FIGURE 11.54 WLC WLAN AAA Servers tab

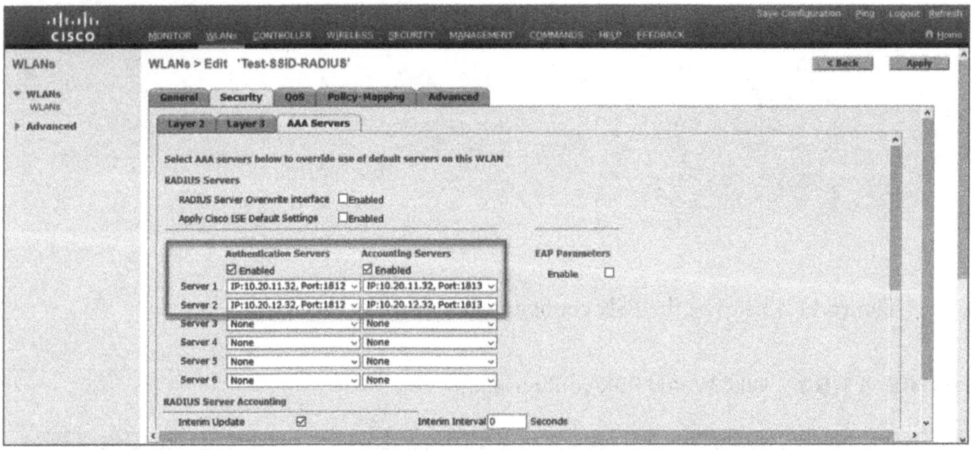

To configure this in the CLI, we simply bind the WLAN to the RADIUS server ID:

```
(WLC01) >config wlan radius_server auth add

<WLAN id>      Enter WLAN Identifier between 1 and 512.

(WLC01) >config wlan radius_server auth add 1

<Server id>    Enter the RADIUS Server Index.
```

```
(WLC01) >config wlan radius_server auth add 1 1
(WLC01) >config wlan radius_server auth add 1 2
(WLC01) >config wlan radius_server acct add 1 1
(WLC01) >config wlan radius_server acct add 1 2
```

QoS profiles

Wireless supports quality of service to help prioritize crucial wireless traffic like wireless phones. By default, it'll use the Best Effort queue. This means there's no QoS policy, but you can create one manually or via Catalyst Center if it's doing the QoS heavy lifting. I'll talk about this more in a later chapter.

There are four queues available for the WLC:

Bronze This provides the lowest level of bandwidth for things like guest services or unimportant traffic. It's also known as the *background queue.*

Silver This provides the normal level of bandwidth for clients and is the *best-effort queue.*

Gold This supports high-bandwidth video applications and is also known as the *video queue.*

Platinum This is the highest quality of service that is meant for voice traffic over wireless connections, also known as the *voice queue.*

The QoS tab also supports manually adjusting the bandwidth, WMM, Call Admission Control, and Lync support, which is Microsoft's Unified Communications solution commonly known as Skype for Business.

Figure 11.55 shows the QoS tab.

FIGURE 11.55 WLC WLAN QoS tab

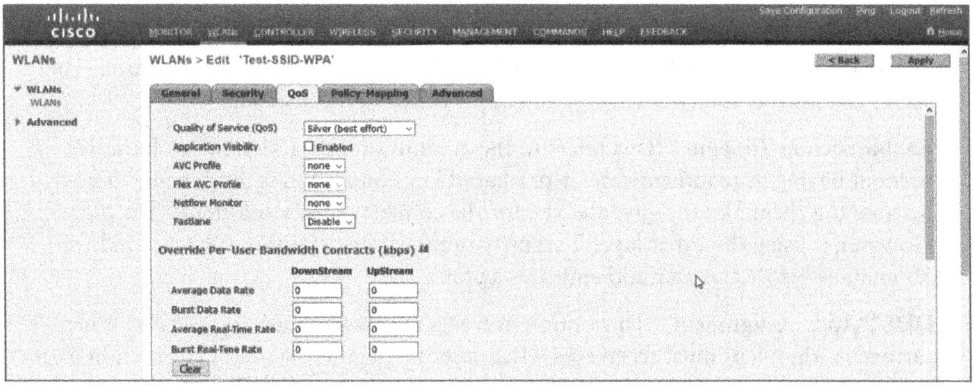

Policy Mapping Settings

We're going to skip over the Policy Mapping tab because it doesn't apply to the CCNA and there isn't much to look at right now. Basically, it allows you to treat different endpoint types differently, so an iPad can act differently from an Android phone.

Advanced WLAN Settings

As the name implies, the Advanced tab contains various advanced settings that can be applied to the WLAN. Figure 11.56 shows the Advanced tab.

FIGURE 11.56 WLC WLAN Advanced tab

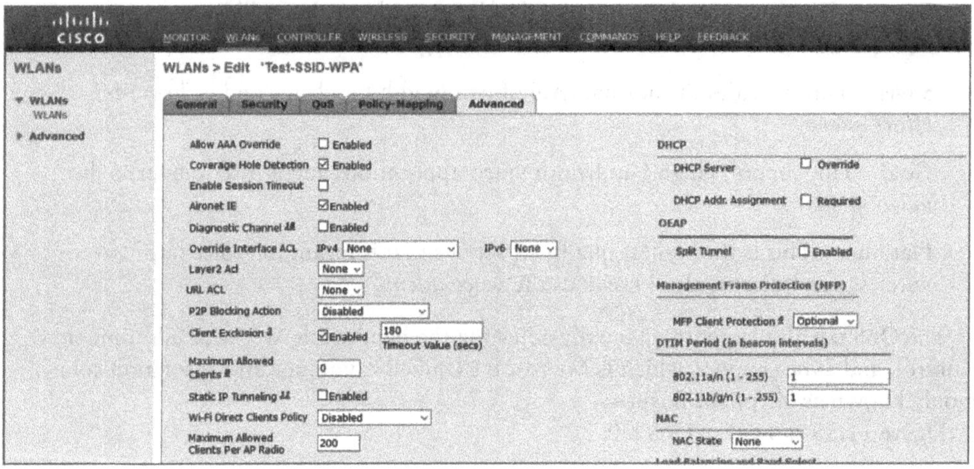

Most of these are beyond what you need to know for the CCNA exam, but they're interesting and important in real life:

Allow AAA Override This is used in connections that talk to RADIUS servers. It allows the server to tell WLC the right VLAN tagging to use for the connection. The server can also set the QoS settings and apply ACLs to the session.

Enable Session Timeout This refers to the amount of time a session can be active without having to reauthenticate. A preshared key connection is disabled by default because the client already gave the key for the connection to work in the first place. However, if using the other layer 2 security options, the default is 1,800 seconds or 30 minutes before the user authenticates again.

DHCP Addr. Assignment This option prevents clients from using static IPs. When turned on, the client must receive a DHCP offer through the wireless connection to get online. This little arrangement helps improve security if you have end users trying to outsmart your security policies!

DHCP/HTTP Profiling The WLC can determine which endpoints are connected to the WLAN. It does this by examining the DHCP process and watching HTTP packets to identify the connection.

Connecting the Client

Now that our WLAN has been created, I can finally connect to the wireless network with my laptop! Because it is a WPA2-PSK connection, I must enter the preshared key to log on to the network. Figure 11.57 shows a client connected to the WLAN.

FIGURE 11.57 Connect a client to the WLAN

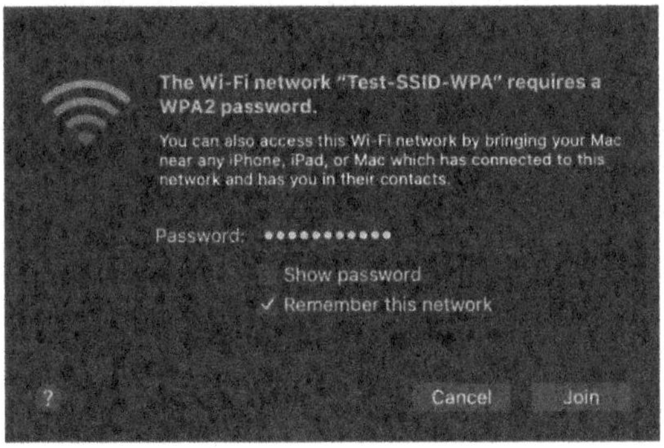

Because the WLAN uses an interface group for its IP assignment, I'm getting an IP address from the WLAN102 dynamic interface. If I connect my iPhone, I might get an IP from the WLAN103 dynamic interface because the WLC will try to load-balance the client traffic across all the interfaces in the interface group. Figure 11.58 shows a client configuration.

On the WLC, we can see many client session details, including a network diagram showing the CAPWAP tunnel being used by the connection and the connectivity state. Figure 11.59 illustrates the verification of a connected client.

The CLI can also give us a ton of information about the client:

```
(WLC01) >show client detail a4:83:e7:c4:e8:b8
Client MAC Address.............................. a4:83:e7:c4:e8:b8
Client Username ................................ N/A
Hostname: .......................................
Device Type: ................................... Unclassified
AP MAC Address.................................. 7c:95:f3:31:68:00
```

FIGURE 11.58 WLAN client configuration

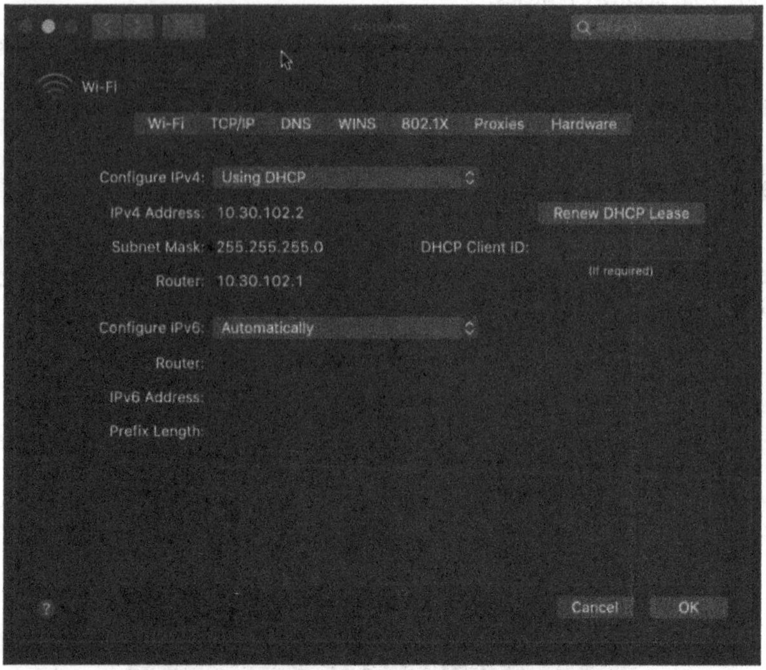

FIGURE 11.59 WLAN client verification

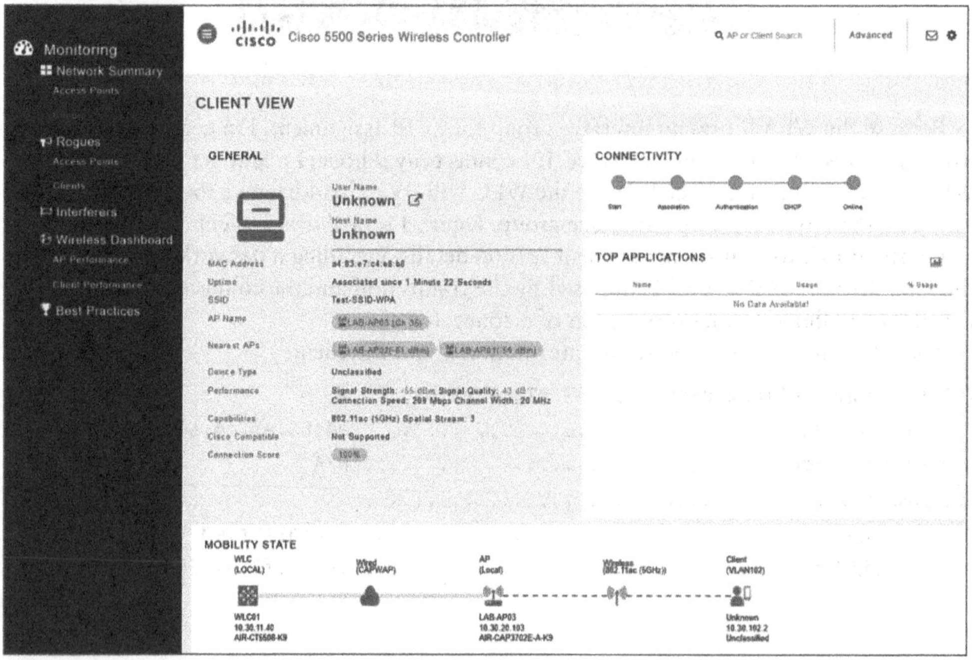

```
AP Name.......................................... LAB-AP02
AP radio slot Id................................. 1
Client State..................................... Associated
Client User Group................................
Client NAC OOB State............................. Access
Wireless LAN Id.................................. 1
Wireless LAN Network Name (SSID)................. Test-SSID-WPA
Wireless LAN Profile Name........................ Test-SSID-WPA
Hotspot (802.11u)................................ Not Supported
BSSID............................................ 7c:95:f3:31:68:0f
Connected For ................................... 476 secs
Channel.......................................... 52
IP Address....................................... 10.30.102.2
Gateway Address.................................. 10.30.102.1
Netmask.......................................... 255.255.255.0
IPv6 Address..................................... fe80::1073:3a59:a857:4647
Association Id................................... 1
Authentication Algorithm......................... Open System
Reason Code...................................... 1
Status Code...................................... 0
Session Timeout.................................. 0
Client CCX version............................... No CCX support

    Output Omitted for brevity
```

FlexConnect

Although the CCNA focuses on using local mode for WLANs, it can ask you about FlexConnect in the exam, so I decided to show you how FlexConnect works in detail! With FlexConnect mode, the AP locally switches the client traffic and dumps it on its switch port instead of tunneling it back to the controller.

Because the controller isn't doing the heavy lifting anymore, we need to push configurations like VLANs or ACLs directly to the AP, which means we must jump through a bunch of extra hoops compared to what we did in the previous example.

Consider the topology shown in Figure 11.60. We have a virtual wireless controller in the main office and an AP in the branch site called FLEX-AP01. Because the branch has a dedicated firewall with its own internet connection, we can safely terminate the wireless traffic at the BRANCH-SW01 switch, so we don't waste bandwidth bringing it back to CORE-SW01.

FIGURE 11.60 FlexConnect topology

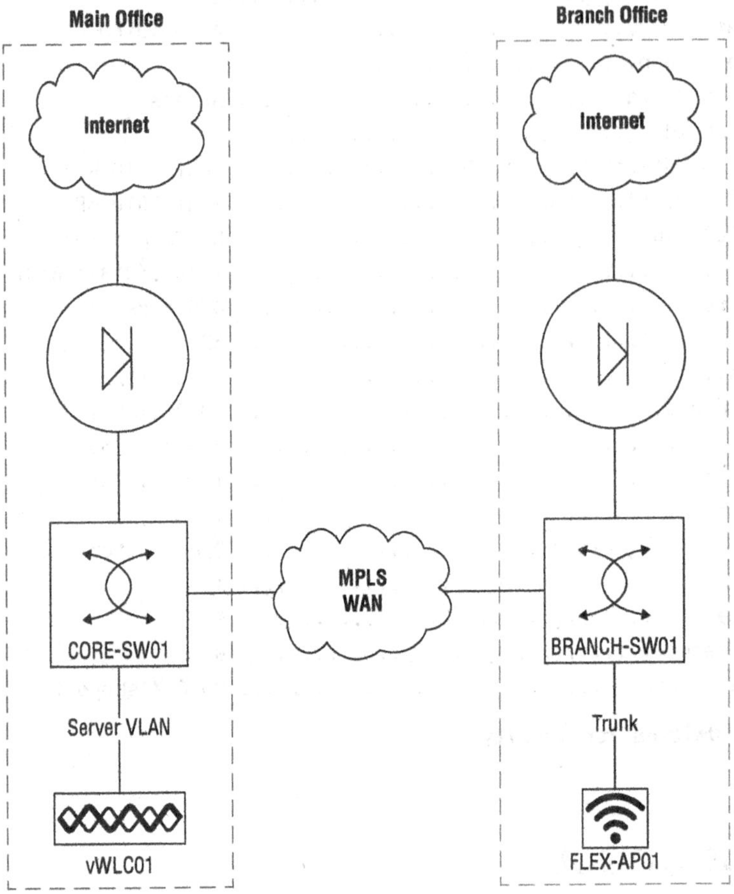

I already showed you how to configure a switch port for a FlexConnect configuration, but as a quick reminder, this is how we would set up the switch:

```
BRANCH-SW01(config)#vlan 320
BRANCH-SW01(config-vlan)#name Wireless-AP
BRANCH-SW01(config-vlan)#vlan 315
BRANCH-SW01(config-vlan)#name FLEXCONNECT-WLAN
BRANCH-SW01(config-vlan)#exit
BRANCH-SW01(config)#interface vlan 320
BRANCH-SW01(config-if)#description Wireless-AP
BRANCH-SW01(config-if)#ip address 10.30.20.1 255.255.255.0
BRANCH-SW01(config-if)#interface vlan 315
```

```
BRANCH-SW01(config-if)#description FLEXCONNECT-WLAN
BRANCH-SW01(config-if)#ip address 10.30.15.1 255.255.255.0
BRANCH-SW01(config-if)#exit
```

The easiest way to set up a FlexConnect AP is to set the interface mode to trunk and then change the native VLAN to the AP's management VLAN. This is a handy time saver because the interface will allow all VLANs by default to be in the right VLAN so the AP can register. You can also manually set the VLAN ID on the AP, which takes much more effort:

```
BRANCH-SW01(config)#interface g1/0/1
BRANCH-SW01(config-if)#description FLEXCONNECT-AP
BRANCH-SW01(config-if)#switchport mode trunk
BRANCH-SW01(config-if)#switchport trunk native vlan 320
BRANCH-SW01(config-if)#spanning-tree portfast trunk
```

Once the AP is registered to our Virtual Wireless Lan Controller (vWLC), we need to go into the AP configuration, change the AP mode to FlexConnect, as seen in Figure 11.61, and then apply the changes.

FIGURE 11.61 FlexConnect AP configuration

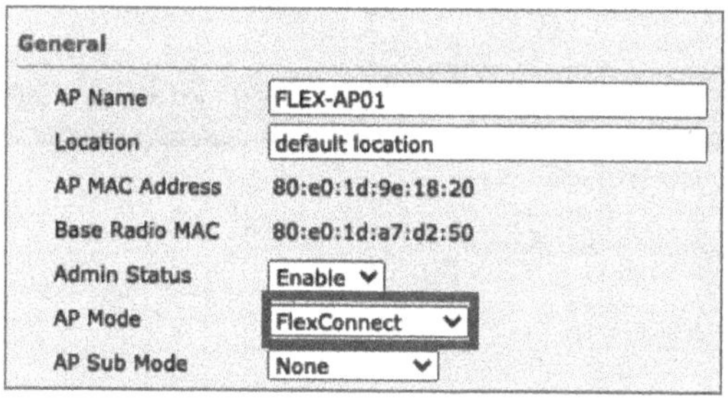

Then, we can move on to creating the actual WLAN. We will call it FLEXCONFIG-WLAN and use the same thing as the SSID. Figure 11.62 shows the WLAN creation.

FIGURE 11.62 WLAN creation

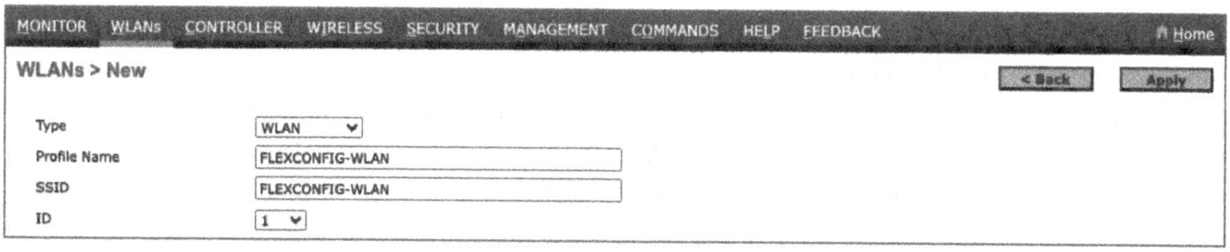

To actually enable the FlexConnect stuff, we need to go to the Advanced tab and check the FlexConnect Local Switching box in the FlexConnect section near the bottom, as seen in Figure 11.63.

FIGURE 11.63 WLAN advanced settings

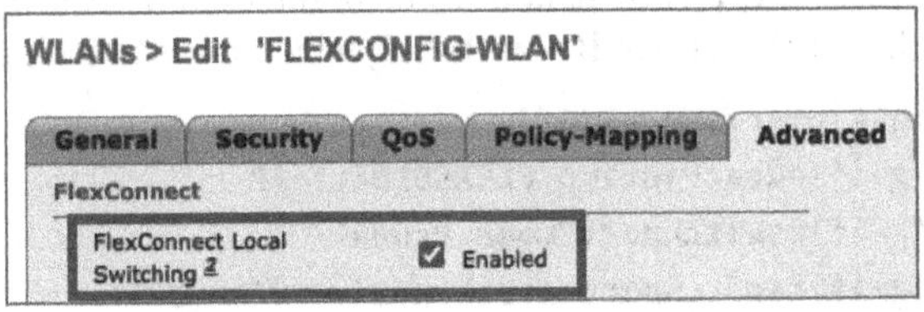

Next, we will move the FlexConnect Group section under wireless and create a new group called LAB-FLEX-GROUP. This group will contain the rest of the FlexConnect settings, which we can use when we create our new WLAN. Figure 11.64 shows the group creation page.

FIGURE 11.64 FlexConnect group configuration

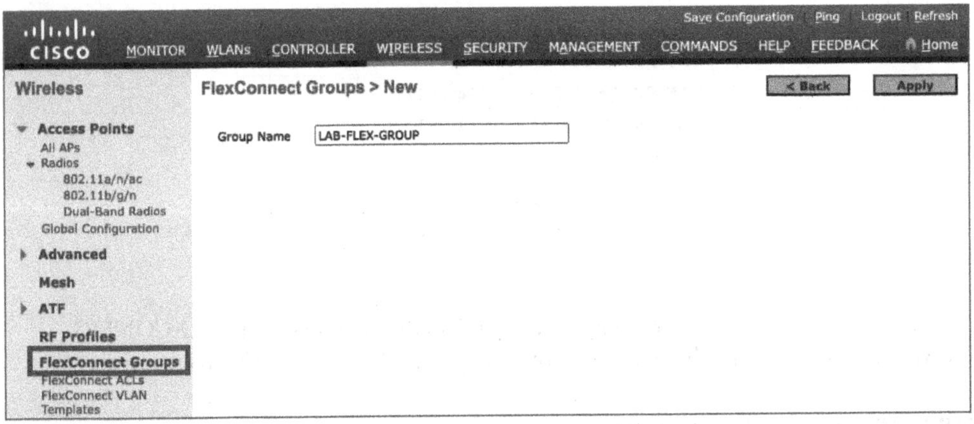

Figure 11.65 shows the General page of the group configuration. We must click the FlexConnect AP link to associate our AP with the group.

On the next page, check the Select APs from Current Controller box and add our FlexConnect APs to the list. If the APs haven't been registered to the WLC yet, you can manually type in some MAC addresses to preconfigure the group. Figure 11.66 shows the AP list.

Now that the AP has been associated, we must configure the AP's local switching on the WLAN VLAN mapping tab. Once there, we must check the VLAN Support box and

FIGURE 11.65 FlexConnect group—General

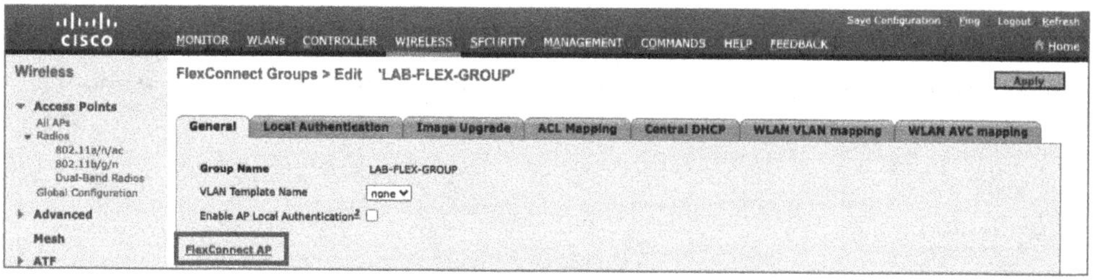

FIGURE 11.66 FlexConnect group—APs

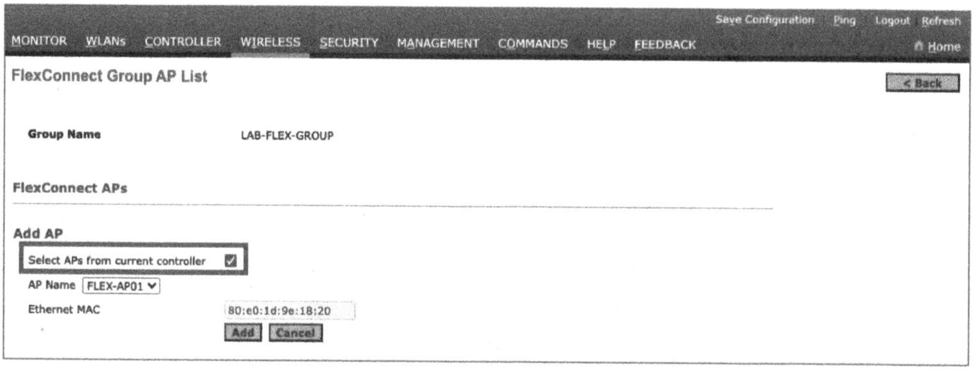

apply the changes. If you forget to click that Apply button, you won't be able to continue! Figure 11.67 shows the VLAN Support check box.

FIGURE 11.67 FlexConnect group—VLAN Support

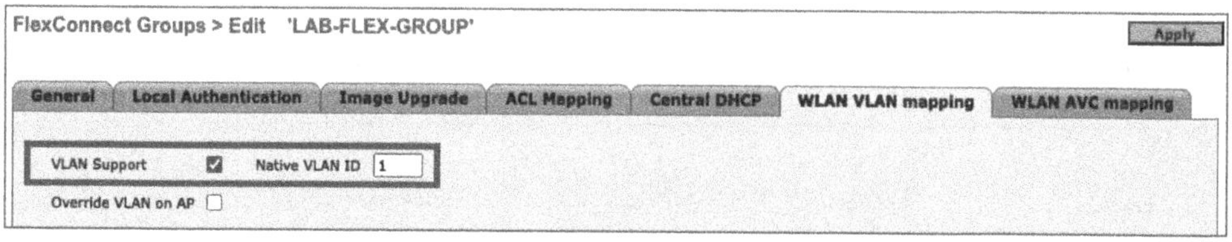

Finally, in our scenario, we need to bind our WLAN ID to the locally switched VLAN we want—WLAN ID 1 and VLAN 105—and then click Add. If we had multiple WLANs we wanted to switch locally, we could add the mappings as many times as necessary. Figure 11.68 shows the VLAN mapping in action.

FIGURE 11.68 FlexConnect group—VLAN Mapping

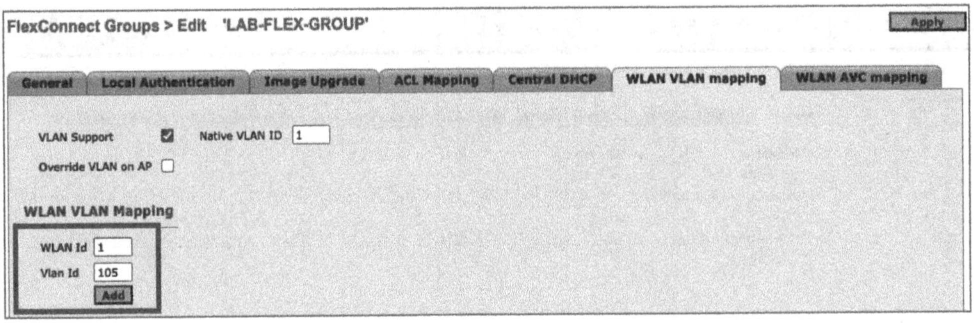

At this point, I can join the WLAN from my test computer that is running Windows 11, as seen in Figure 11.69.

FIGURE 11.69 Connecting to the WLAN

To finish this up, we can verify that FlexConnect is actually working a few different ways, but we'll have a look at the WLC's client page that shows the AP is running in FlexConnect mode. Figure 11.70 shows the final connection status.

FIGURE 11.70 Client dashboard

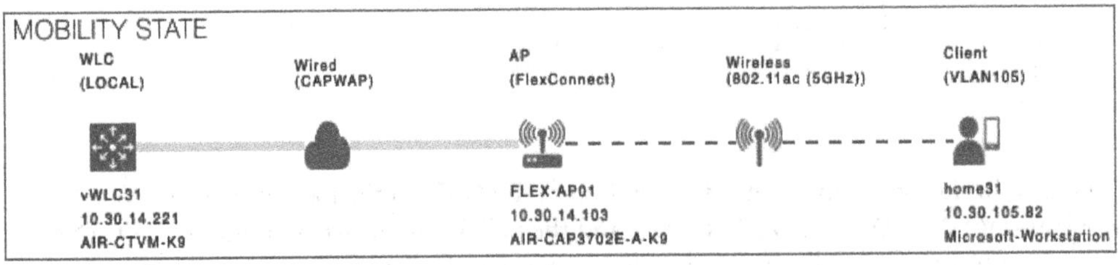

Summary

Wow, we covered a lot in this chapter! I talked about the various types of wireless controllers that Cisco offers and described some of the deployment models that wireless can use.

From there, I extensively covered all the ports and interfaces on the WLC. Because wireless controllers aren't very useful without access points, I described a few methods for joining APs to the WLC.

Once that was done, we discussed the different management access connections that can be used on the WLC before finally showing you how to configure a working WLAN in both local and FlexConnect modes!

Exam Essentials

Understand the three WLAN deployment models. Cisco uses three types of WLAN deployment models: standalone, where the access point acts independently and must be manually configured, and lightweight, where the access point registers to a controller via an encrypted CAPWAP tunnel that allows for central management and easier performance tuning. The last model we discussed is the cloud method, where the controller lives in the cloud, and APs need to get online to be managed. Meraki is Cisco's cloud-based networking solution.

Understand the WLC port types. The WLC has several port types, such as console ports for initial configuration, service ports for out-of-band management, a redundancy port to allow for high availability, and distributed system ports, which are just fancy names for regular interfaces.

Understand the WLC interface types. The WLC also has several interface types that provide services to the WLANs and other features. The service port interface provides access to the service port, and the redundancy management port provides access to the redundancy port. The management port is used to provide WLC access. It runs the AP-Manager by default, which allows APs to register to the interface and terminates CAPWAP tunnels. Finally, dynamic interfaces can be used to terminate WLANs to specific VLANs.

Understand the WLC and AP management access connections. Cisco wireless controllers and access points support several methods for providing management access, including telnet: SSH, HTTP, HTTPS, a console port, RADIUS, and TACACS+. CDP is also very useful for managing these systems.

Understand how to Join APs. Wireless controllers require APs to provide network access. We covered three methods for joining APs in the chapter: the manual method, where we log in to the AP and type some commands; the DNS method, where we make a DNS A record to allow the AP to find the wireless controller on its own; and the DHCP method, where we use our hex skills to provide the WLC address through option 43.

Understand how to configure WLANs. A large part of the WLC configuration is creating the WLANs that clients can connect to. This has several parts, including the SSID, security method, and myriad other options we can choose to enable when creating a wireless network.

Written Lab

The answers to this lab can be found in Appendix A, "Answers to the Written Labs."

1. How do you set up a Cisco wireless LAN controller (WLC) and create a basic wireless network?
2. What are the main differences between a standalone access point and a lightweight access point?
3. What steps do you follow to manually connect an access point (AP) to a WLC?
4. What is split MAC architecture in a lightweight wireless network, and how does it help?
5. What is the CAPWAP protocol, and why is it important in Cisco wireless networks?
6. How are VLANs used in WLC configurations, and what is the role of dynamic interfaces?
7. What is the difference between local mode and FlexConnect mode for APs, and when would you use FlexConnect?
8. How do you set up a RADIUS server on a WLC for WPA2-Enterprise security?
9. What are the different port types on a WLC, and what are they used for?
10. Why should you use HTTPS and SSH instead of HTTP and Telnet for managing a WLC?

Review Questions

NOTE The following questions are designed to test your understanding of this chapter's material. For more information on how to get additional questions, please see this book's introduction.

The answers to these questions can be found in Appendix B, "Answers to the Review Questions."

1. What AP mode is known as local switching?
   A. Local
   B. FlexConnect
   C. Monitor
   D. Sniffer
   E. Bridge

2. What's required to use the service port on a WLC? (Choose three.)
   A. The service port interface must be connected to a switch.
   B. The switchport must be configured to be a trunk
   C. You must add static routes to the WLC.
   D. The switchport must be configured to an access port.
   E. The service port interface must be configured with a subnet IP in the same subnet as the management port.

3. What DNS record do you need to create for APs to automatically discover the WLC.
   A. CISCO-WLC-CONTROLLER
   B. WLC-CONTROLLER
   C. CISCO-AP-CONTROLLER
   D. CISCO-DISCOVER-CONTROLLER
   E. CISCO-CAPWAP-CONTROLLER

4. What's the default QoS queue for a WLAN?
   A. Gold
   B. Platinum
   C. Bronze
   D. Silver
   E. Diamond

5. What's the QoS queue intended for Video?
   - A. Gold
   - B. Platinum
   - C. Bronze
   - D. Silver
   - E. Diamond
6. You've been informed that people are intermittently not able to connect to your office's WLAN. After some troubleshooting, you find that the VLAN is running out of IP addresses. What's the recommended solution?
   - A. Create a new WLAN and have half the employees connect to it instead.
   - B. Adjust the subnet mask to a larger value.
   - C. Create an additional dynamic interface and use an interface group with the WLAN.
   - D. Configure Session Timeout so idle connections will be dropped.
   - E. Add more access points to the area.
7. What are the requirements for enabling a LAG on the WLC? (Choose three.)
   - A. LACP must be configured on the directly connected Switch.
   - B. The WLC must be rebooted.
   - C. All distributed system interfaces must be added to the LAG.
   - D. No more than two interfaces can be in the LAG.
   - E. The switch must use **channel-group#** `mode on`.
8. What are the drawbacks to using autonomous APs? (Choose three.)
   - A. They require central management.
   - B. They are independently configured.
   - C. AAPs don't see the full picture of the wireless network.
   - D. Security policies are harder to maintain.
   - E. CAPWAP is supported.
9. Where can TACACS+ be used on a WLC?
   - A. WLAN configuration
   - B. Management users
   - C. Interface configuration
   - D. Port configuration
10. Which port does TACACS+ use for accounting?
    - A. UDP 49
    - B. UDP 1645
    - C. UDP 1812
    - D. UDP 1813
    - E. TCP 49

11. Which port does RADIUS use for authentication on modern servers?
    - A. UDP 1645
    - B. TCP 1645
    - C. UDP 1812
    - D. TCP 1812
    - E. UDP 1700
12. Which port does RADIUS use for authentication on legacy servers?
    - A. UDP 1645
    - B. TCP 1645
    - C. UDP 1812
    - D. TCP 1812
    - E. UDP 1700
13. What is the purpose of the virtual interface?
    - A. Management
    - B. Redirecting clients to the WLC
    - C. Registering APs
    - D. Terminating CAPWAP
    - E. Routing
14. Which IP address is recommended for the virtual interface?
    - A. 1.1.1.1
    - B. 2.2.2.2
    - C. 192.168.0.1
    - D. 192.0.2.1
    - E. 10.10.10.10
15. What QoS should be used with VoIP traffic?
    - A. Bronze
    - B. Silver
    - C. Gold
    - D. Platinum
    - E. EF
16. Telnet is enabled by default on the WLC.
    - A. True
    - B. False
    - C. Depends on version

17. A dynamic interface is similar to what kind of interface found on a Cisco switch?
    A. Ethernet
    B. Loopback
    C. Switched virtual interface
    D. Tunnel
    E. Port-channel

18. What is the DHCP option 43 hex value for a single WLC with the IP address 192.168.123.100?
    A. F104C0A87B64
    B. F102C0A87B64
    C. F102C0A99B70
    D. F104C0A99B70
    E. F10211BBCC88

19. What's the default AP mode?
    A. Local
    B. Monitor
    C. FlexConnect
    D. Sniffer
    E. SE-Connect

20. Which AP modes serve wireless traffic? (Choose two.)
    A. Local
    B. Monitor
    C. FlexConnect
    D. Sniffer
    E. SE-Connect

Chapter 12

Configuring Modern Wireless Controllers

THE FOLLOWING CCNA EXAM TOPICS ARE COVERED IN THIS CHAPTER:

✓ **2.0 Network Access**

2.7 Describe physical infrastructure connections of WLAN components (AP, WLC, access/trunk ports, and LAG)

2.8 Describe network device management access (Telnet, SSH, HTTP, HTTPS, console, TACACS+/RADIUS, and cloud managed)

2.9 Interpret the wireless LAN GUI configuration for client connectivity, such as WLAN creation, security settings, QoS profiles, and advanced settings

✓ **5 Security Fundamentals**

5.10 Configure and verify WLAN within the GUI using WPA2 PSK

We just finished extensively exploring how to make some basic wireless networks using Cisco's legacy wireless LAN controller (WLC). But the key word there is *legacy*; Cisco has switched to a new type of wireless controller based on IOS-XE instead of that annoying AireOS that we had to use! In this chapter, we will finish our wireless topics by looking at the new way of doing things, because the exam can technically ask you about both wireless controller platforms.

To start, I'll walk you through setting up a virtual Cisco 9800 controller and using port channels. Next, we will create a simple WPA2 WLAN using PSK, just as we did with the WLC. Then, we will join our new wireless network with my test PC to confirm that everything works as advertised!

Finally, we will finish up the chapter by exploring how to work with cloud-managed access points.

> **NOTE** To find your included bonus material, as well as Todd Lammle videos, practice questions, and hands-on labs, please see `www.lammle.com/ccna`.

Network Setup

The Cisco 9800 controller is based on IOS-XE instead of the AireOS that the WLC uses. This means that aside from some wireless-specific commands, the controller is really just a modern Cisco switch that doesn't run STP.

Because of this, a lot of the setup is the same stuff we do when configuring a normal switch, like creating VLANs, trunks, routing, and user accounts.

Let's take a minute to examine the topology shown in Figure 12.1. This is mostly the same as the previous chapter's FlexConnect lab, but it will allow us to explore all the features we need to examine. The virtual 9800 controller is on the main office site and has two links, so we can try the new way of making a port channel. Our LAB-AP01 access point is at the branch site.

On our controller, I will use the CLI to set up basic functionality. Notice that unlike the WLC, we don't have an exhaustive setup wizard we need to run through; however, there will be a streamlined one when we get to the GUI. First, I'll create some VLANs: VLAN200, named WIRELESS-MGMT, and VLAN201, named WLAN201:

```
C9800-WLC(config)#vlan 200
C9800-WLC(config-vlan)#name WIRELESS-MGMT
C9800-WLC(config-vlan)#vlan 201
C9800-WLC(config-vlan)#name WLAN201
C9800-WLC(config-vlan)#exit
```

FIGURE 12.1 Lab topology

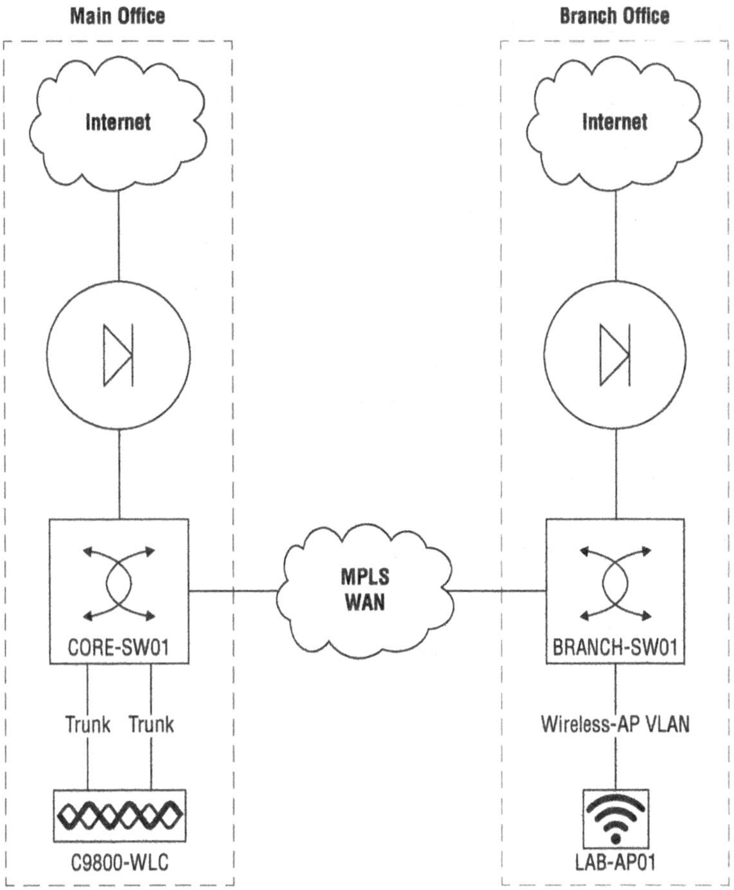

Next, I will make the first interface a trunk and create an SVI for the WIRELESS-MGMT VLAN so the controller will be reachable in my network:

```
C9800-WLC(config)#int g1
C9800-WLC(config-if)#switchport mode trunk
C9800-WLC(config-if)#exit

C9800-WLC(config)#interface vlan 200
C9800-WLC(config-if)#description WIRELESS-MGMT
C9800-WLC(config-if)#ip address 172.31.200.10 255.255.255.0
C9800-WLC(config-if)#no shut
C9800-WLC(config-if)#exit
```

Because this is really a layer 3 switch, we can enable routing and add a default route to allow for connectivity. Earlier versions of the 9800 allowed for full routing protocols like OSPF, but Cisco has settled on static routing for now:

```
C9800-WLC(config)#ip routing
C9800-WLC(config)#ip route 0.0.0.0 0.0.0.0 172.31.200.1
```

Finally, we must create a user account to log into the GUI. This is all stuff you have seen before in these books, except for `ip http authentication local`, which tells the controller's web server to use the local database for authentication:

```
C9800-WLC(config)#aaa new-model
C9800-WLC(config)#aaa authentication login default local
C9800-WLC(config)#username admin privilege 15 secret CCNA1sFun!
C9800-WLC(config)#enable secret CCNA1sFun!
C9800-WLC(config)#ip http authentication local
```

To save some time for later, I will also create a DHCP pool on CORE-SW01 to provide wireless clients with IP addresses:

```
CORE-SW01(config)#ip dhcp pool WLAN201
CORE-SW01(dhcp-config)#network 172.31.201.0 255.255.255.0
CORE-SW01(dhcp-config)#default-router 172.31.201.1
CORE-SW01(dhcp-config)#dns-server 10.30.11.10 10.30.12.10
CORE-SW01(dhcp-config)#domain testlab.com
CORE-SW01(dhcp-config)#exit
CORE-SW01(config)#ip dhcp excluded-address 172.31.201.1 172.31.201.99
```

9800 Controller Setup

After the initial network setup, I can now access the controller's web interface, where we will do most of the rest of the configuration. When you log in, you will be greeted with a simple wizard to do the basic setup, including setting the NTP servers, the time zone, and AAA servers if needed. Finally, it will have you confirm the actual IP and routing settings on the box, although we have already configured what we want using the CLI. Figure 12.2 shows the first page of the setup wizard.

The next page will let you create a wireless network; this is a nice change from the WLC because that platform forced us to make one, even if we were going to delete it right after. I'll skip making a WLAN now so I can show you another way of doing it later. Figure 12.3 shows the WLAN creation part of the wizard.

Next is the Advanced Settings page, as seen in Figure 12.4, and it has a few settings worth discussing. First off, we can see that the Virtual IP Address is set to 192.0.2.1 by default, so you don't need to worry about memorizing that address anymore unless you are studying for a certification exam!

FIGURE 12.2 Cisco 9800 setup wizard

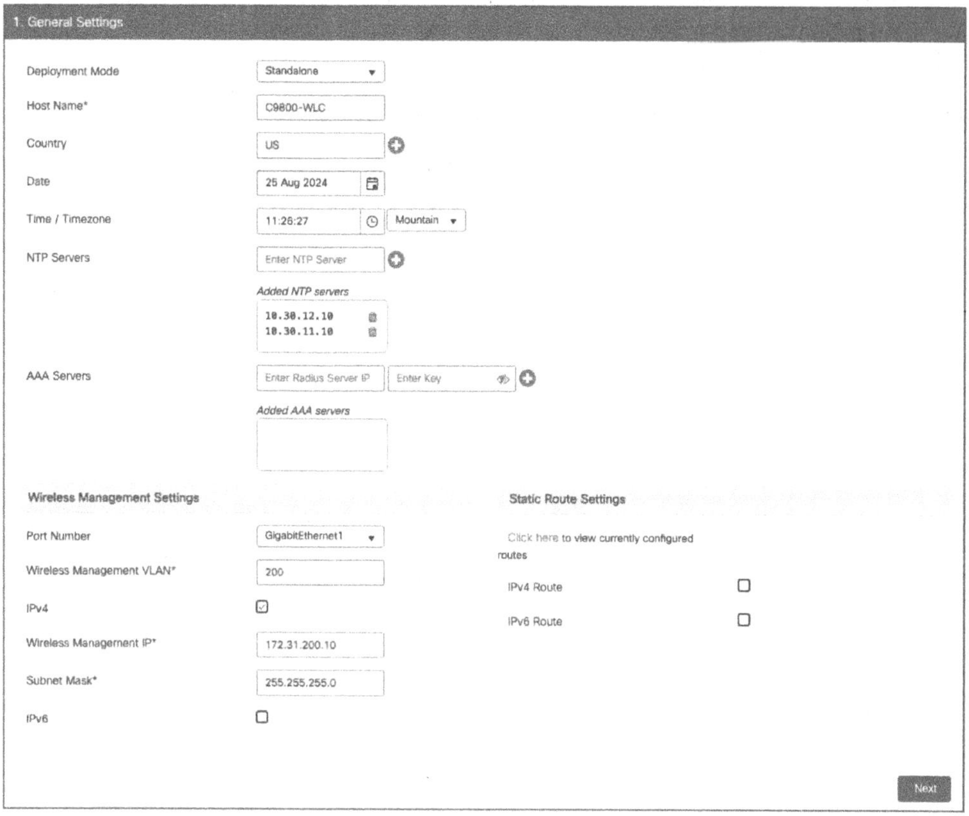

FIGURE 12.3 Cisco 9800 setup wizard—WLAN

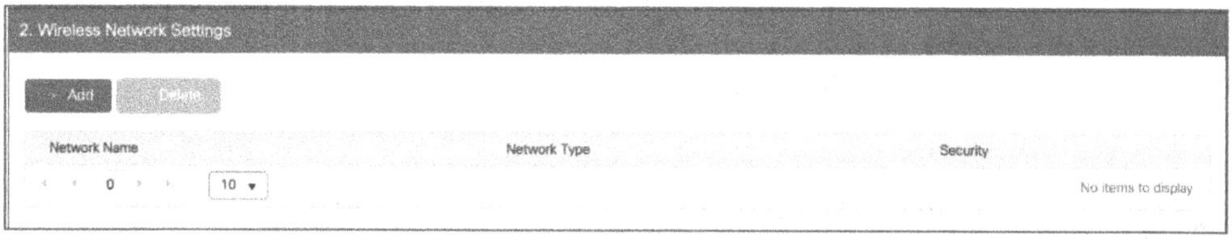

This section will also generate a self-signed certificate for the controller. I like using 4096 as the RSA key size, so I changed it from 2048. We also need to set a password for the certificate private key, so I went ahead and set one.

We also need to create a management user that will be pushed to the access points (APs) that join the controller; this is known as the AP management user and is really just Cisco's way of ensuring you aren't using the AP's default login in your environment. I used apuser for the username and my common lab password.

FIGURE 12.4 Cisco 9800 setup wizard—Advanced Settings

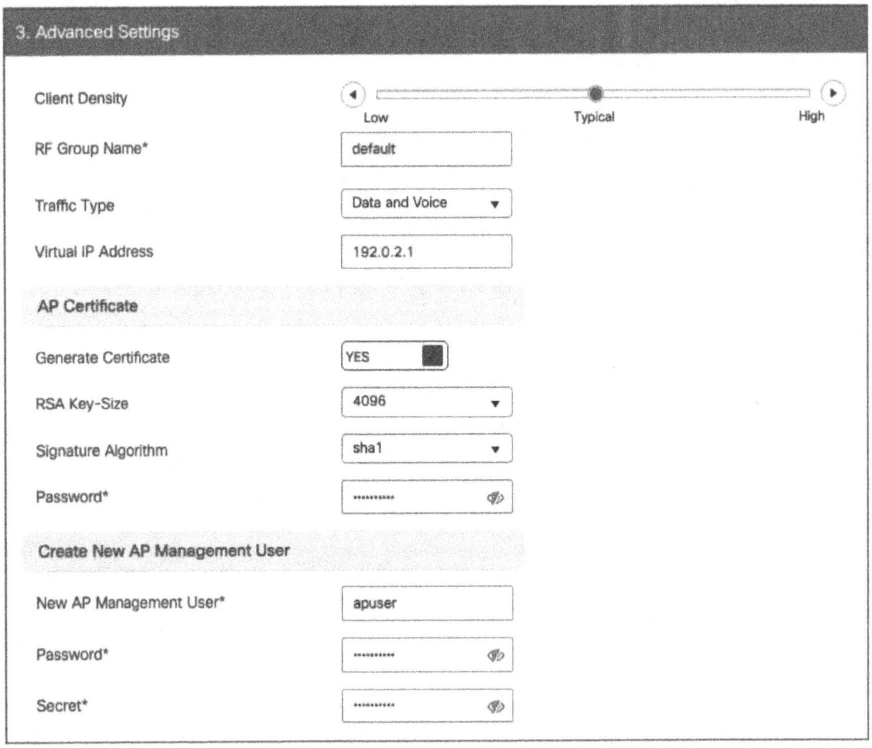

Figure 12.5 shows the Summary page with all the configurations that will be pushed when I click the Finish button. This will take a few minutes, and we will be kicked out of our web interface session while it does its magic.

NOTE The previous chapter covered how to join APs to a controller; those methods work with the 9800 as well.

Interfaces

Interfaces are a lot more straightforward on the 9800 because they are just standard interfaces that you encounter in regular IOS-XE. Instead of using a confusing service port that requires static routes to function, we instead utilize an out-of-band management port that

FIGURE 12.5 Cisco 9800 setup wizard—Summary

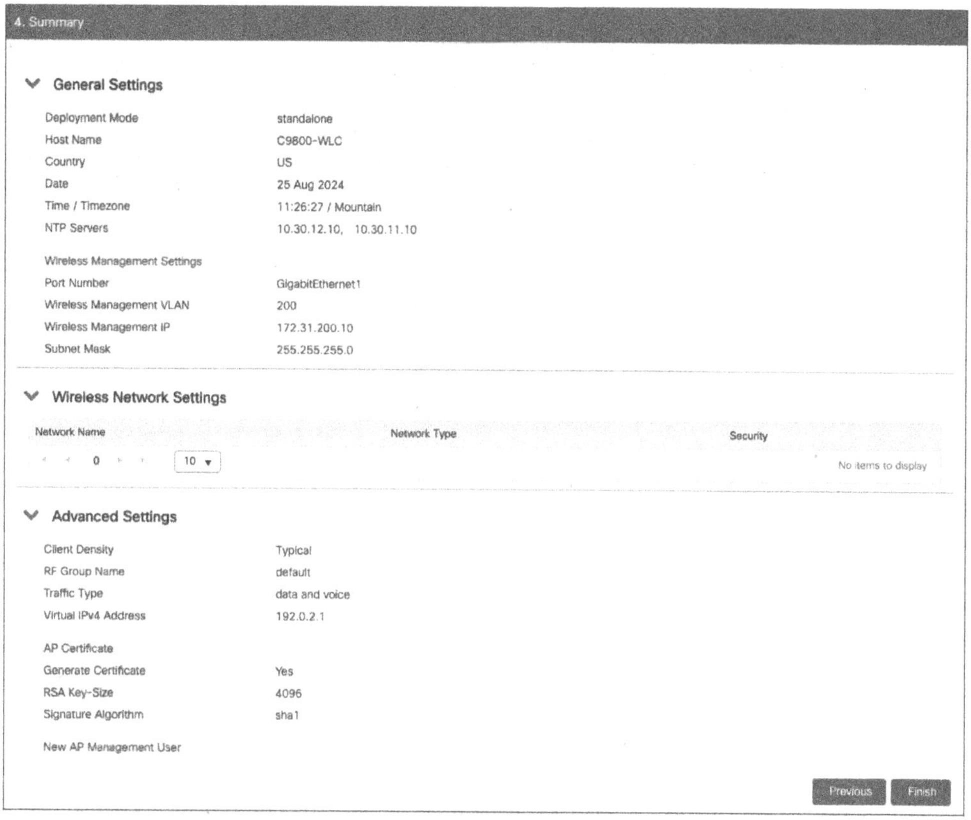

uses VRF-Lite to isolate the routing table—we will be looking more at VRFs in the next chapter.

Instead of using dynamic interfaces to terminate the VLANs on our wireless networks, we work directly with VLANs and reference them when we combine all the WLAN parts together in a profile.

Port Channel

Using LAGs was really annoying in the WLC because it didn't support LACP or PAgP. We had to switch over all our WLC data interfaces and reboot the WLC to enable them. Fortunately, the 9800 doesn't have any of those annoyances; because it is based on IOS-XE, we can create a port channel the usual way.

Figures 12.6 and 12.7 show the port channel creation screen in the web interface.

FIGURE 12.6 Port channel

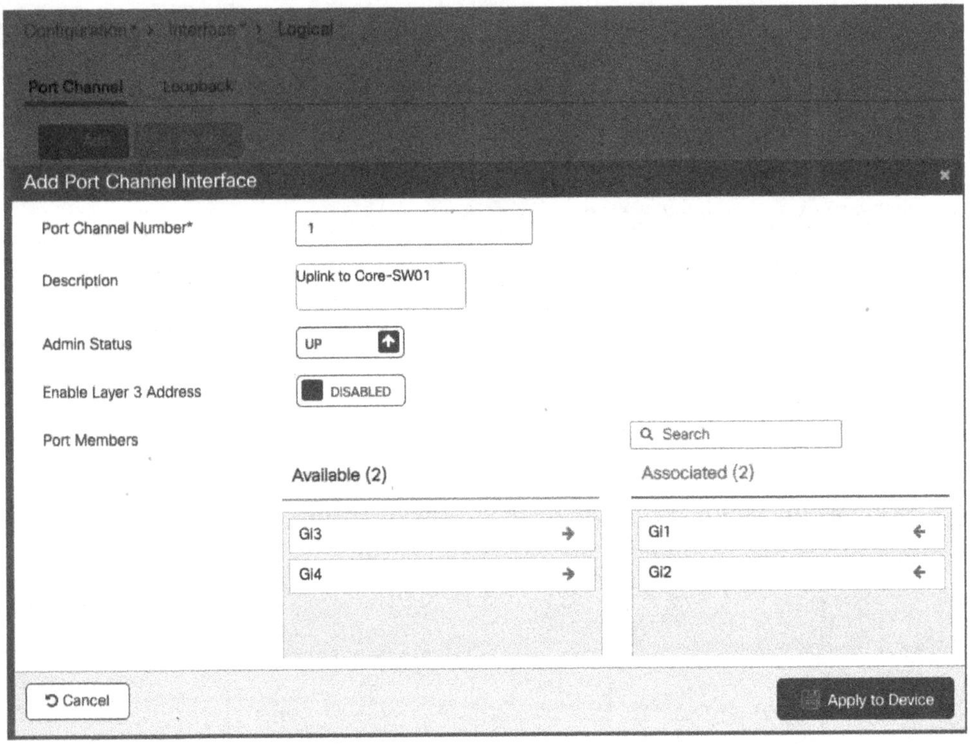

We can also go ahead and use the CLI to create it the same way we would if we were configuring a LAG between two switches:

```
C9800-WLC(config)#int range g1-2
C9800-WLC(config-if-range)#switchport mode trunk
C9800-WLC(config-if-range)#channel-group 1 mode active
Creating a port-channel interface Port-channel 1

C9800-WLC(config-if-range)#
Aug 25 19:38:23.221: %LINK-5-UPDOWN: Interface Port-channel1, changed
state to up
Aug 25 19:38:24.222: %LINEPROTO-5-UPDOWN: Line protocol on Interface Port-
channel1, changed state to up
C9800-WLC(config-if-range)#int po1
C9800-WLC(config-if)#description Uplink to Core-SW01
C9800-WLC(config-if)#exit
```

FIGURE 12.7 Port channel—options

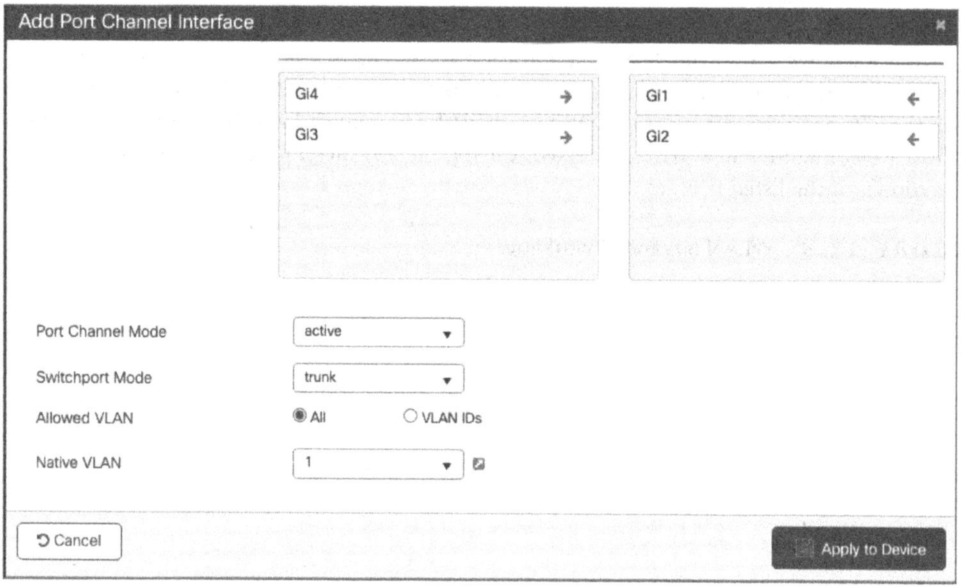

We can also verify that the port channel is running by using the command we always use!

```
C9800-WLC#show etherchannel summary
Flags:  D - down        P - bundled in port-channel
        I - stand-alone s - suspended
        H - Hot-standby (LACP only)
        R - Layer3      S - Layer2
        U - in use      f - failed to allocate aggregator

        M - not in use, minimum links not met
        u - unsuitable for bundling
        w - waiting to be aggregated
        d - default port

        A - formed by Auto LAG
Number of channel-groups in use: 1
Number of aggregators:           1
Group  Port-channel  Protocol    Ports
------+-------------+-----------+-----------------------------------------------
1      Po1(SU)          LACP       Gi1(P)          Gi2(P)
```

Creating a WLAN

One major change is that the 9800 configuration is extremely modular. We have to make several different profiles, then use tags to group them together, and finally associate them with the APs on which we want to advertise the WLAN. Figure 12.8 shows the full picture of how we configure a new wireless network using the advanced wizard. Following is a breakdown of the listed profiles.

FIGURE 12.8 WLAN advanced workflow

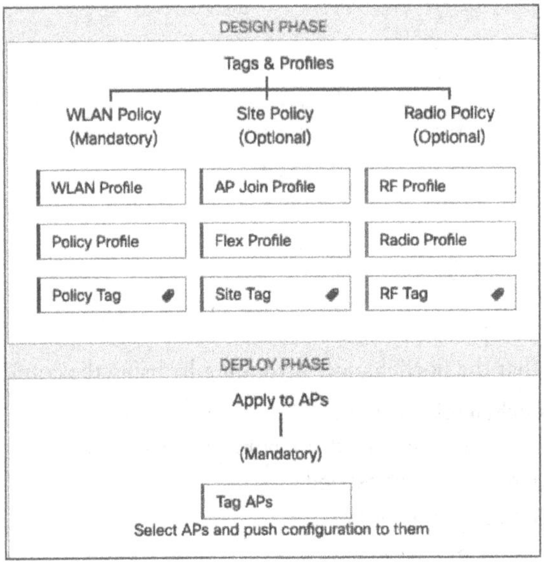

WLAN Profile

The WLAN profile contains various settings that control the overall WLAN, including the SSID, security settings, and other advanced features related to the actual connection. This is very similar to what we get when creating a WLAN in a WLC.

Policy Profile

The policy profile maps the WLAN to the VLAN we want to use and also provides other advanced settings such as profiling, ACLs, and QoS settings.

AP Join Profile

The AP join profile provides common settings for the APs that will be serving our WLAN, such as the country the AP is operating in and what controllers it should fail over to if our primary one goes offline.

Flex Profile

The Flex profile is the 9800 version of the FlexConnect group we looked at in the previous chapter; it controls how we map locally switched VLANs to WLANs in pretty much the same way we looked at before. However, we aren't going to be using FlexConnect in this example.

RF Profile

The RF profile is used to control the actual wireless settings, such as maximum bandwidth rates and RF thresholds.

Radio Profile

Finally, the radio profile controls the AP's actual radios and lets you make adjustments to support various wireless features that we don't need to discuss for the CCNA.

Tags

The 9800 controller uses the tag concept to bind profiles and APs together. For example, the Policy tag will bind the WLAN and policy profiles together, and then that tag will be referenced by the larger policy when it is pushed to the actual AP.

Basic Workflow

Wait—don't run away! We also have a basic workflow that is much more straightforward for getting us up and running. Let's go ahead and create our WLAN201 WLAN using the basic workflow seen in Figure 12.9.

FIGURE 12.9 WLAN basic workflow

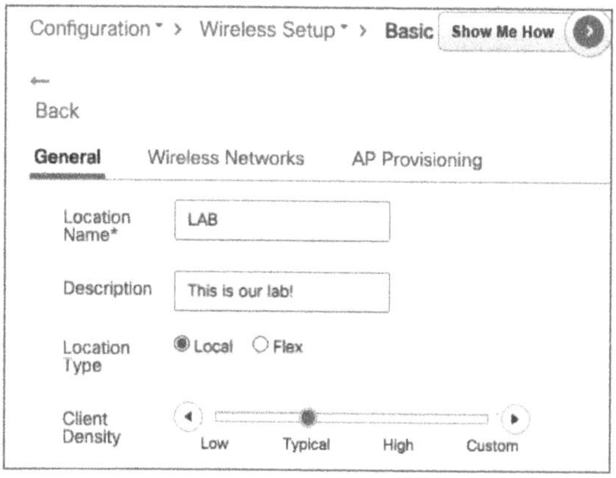

The first thing we need to do is give the location a name, so I'm just going to call it LAB, and I'll also give it a description. The most important choice is whether we are running the AP in local or flex mode; I'll leave it on local because we are just doing the defaults here.

On the wireless tab, we need to create our WLAN profile. Fortunately, they give us a handy link to create it directly from the workflow! Figure 12.10 shows how to create a WLAN profile.

FIGURE 12.10 Add WLAN shortcut

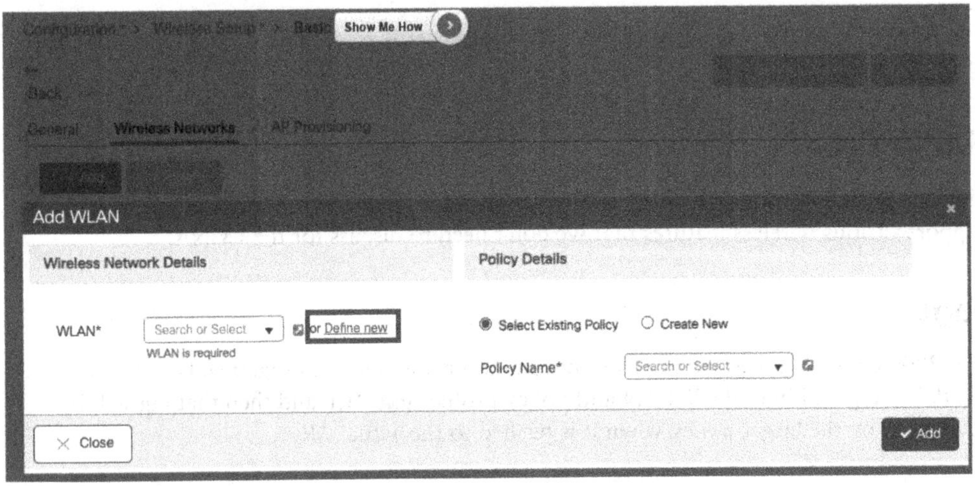

In the popup, we will create the WLAN profile; I'll go ahead and call the profile WLAN201, which will also autopopulate the SSID (see Figure 12.11). I will also enable the WLAN by setting Status to Enabled, and I will disable 6 GHz for the WLAN because my lab AP is really old and doesn't support the new stuff.

FIGURE 12.11 Add WLAN profile—General

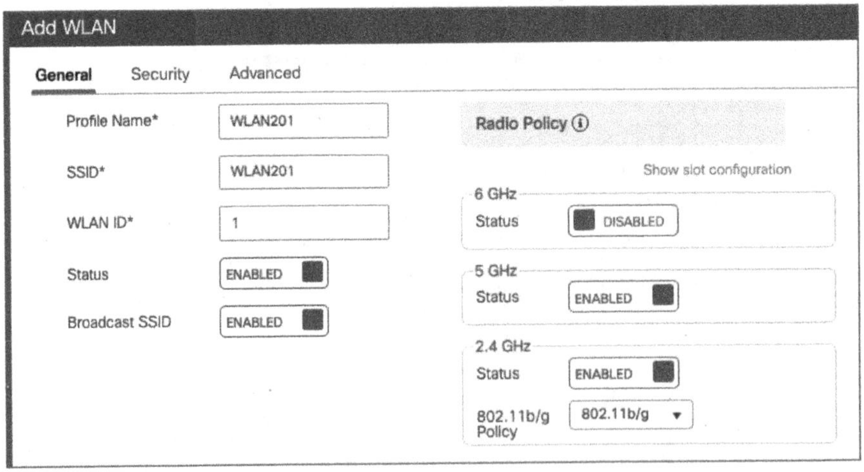

The Security tab is pretty close to the WLC version, although it is a bit cleaner than the old version. I will disable 802.1X because it is enabled by default and select PSK instead. Because WPA2 is already selected, I just need to scroll down and set the PSK passphrase. Figures 12.12 and 12.13 show the Security tab.

FIGURE 12.12 Add WLAN profile—Security

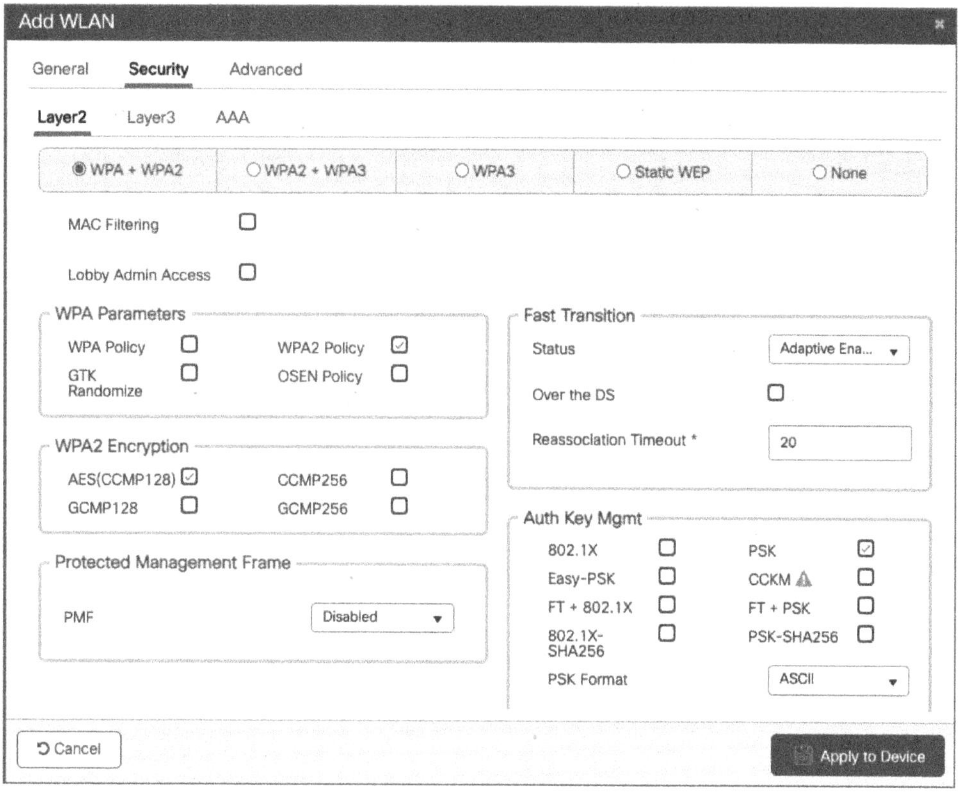

FIGURE 12.13 Add WLAN profile—Security—PSK

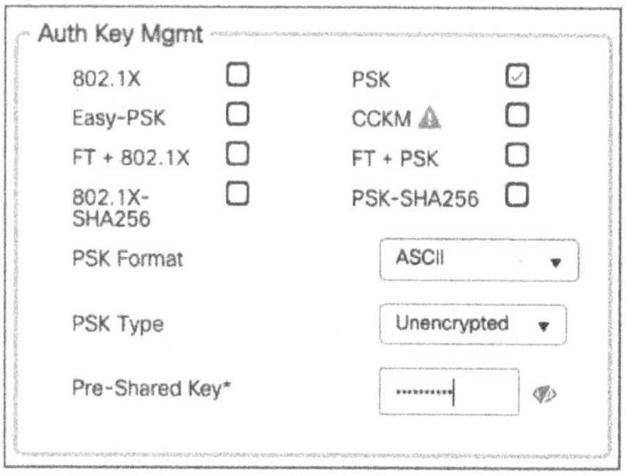

Figure 12.14 shows the Advanced tab; we don't need to change anything here, so we can click the Apply button to close the WLAN profile and go back to the previous screen.

FIGURE 12.14 Add WLAN profile—Advanced

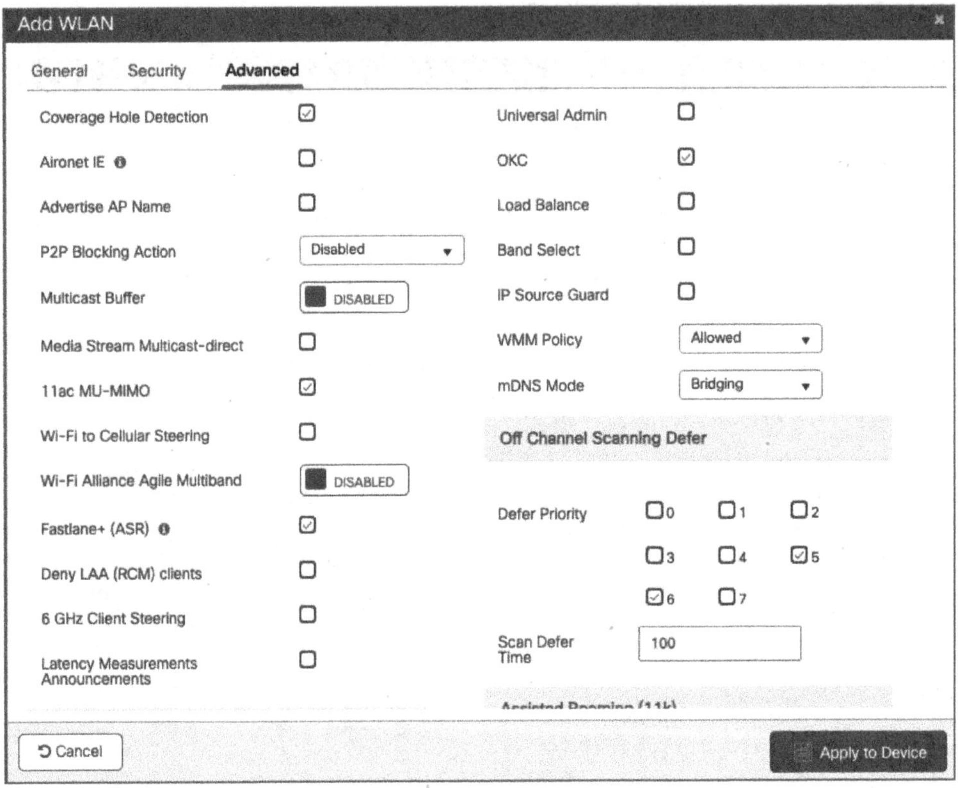

After a few seconds, the Add WLAN popup should refresh and show our new WLAN201 profile. Now, we can turn our attention to the policy profile side of things because we aren't getting too into the weeds here.

We can use the default profile that comes with the system and change the VLAN to WLAN201 because I created that when I first set up the controller at the beginning of the chapter. Figure 12.15 shows the policy configuration. To exit the popup, we can click the Add button and then move on to the last tab.

FIGURE 12.15 Add WLAN—policy

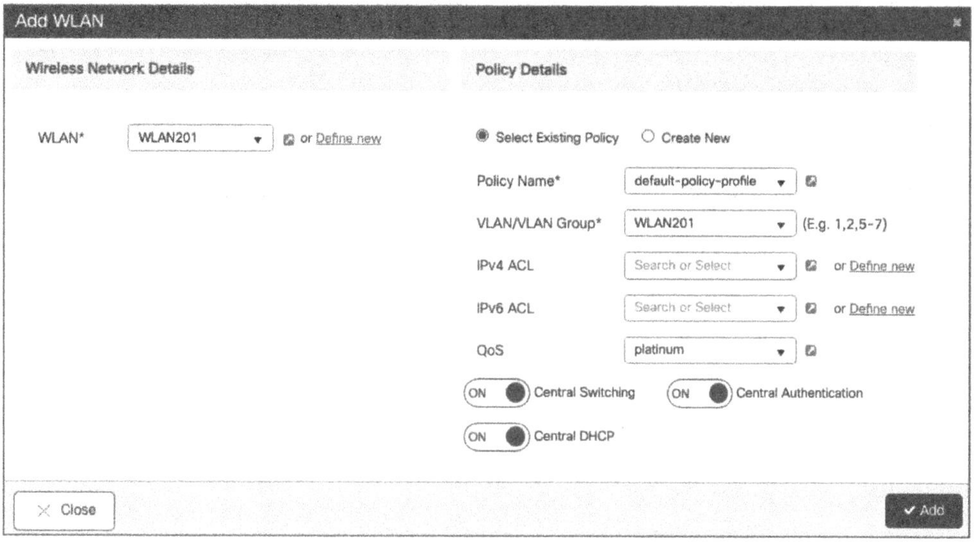

The last thing we need to do is associate the WLAN with my lab AP; I haven't gotten around to renaming it yet, but fortunately, it is the only AP on the controller, so there is no risk of getting things mixed up. I need to select the AP and click the arrow button to move it to the associated AP list. Once that is done, I can click the Apply button to push the configuration. Figure 12.16 shows the AP Provisioning tab.

FIGURE 12.16 Add WLAN—AP Provisioning

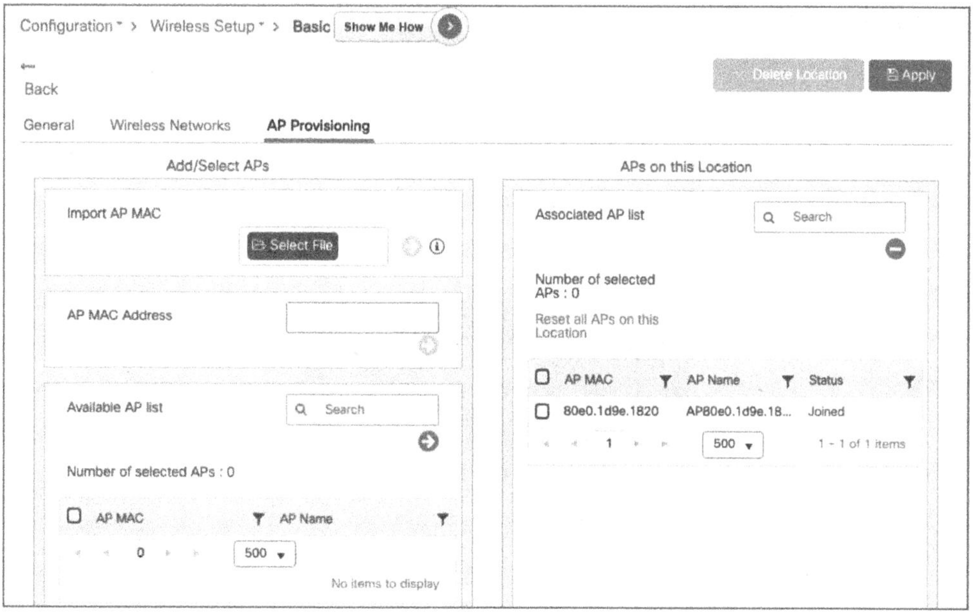

Before moving on, I'll configure the AP to match the diagram so we don't have to look at a big, scary default name. This will also show us that the AP is using those tags I discussed to apply the profiles we just made with the basic workflow. Figure 12.17 shows the AP configuration page.

FIGURE 12.17 AP configuration

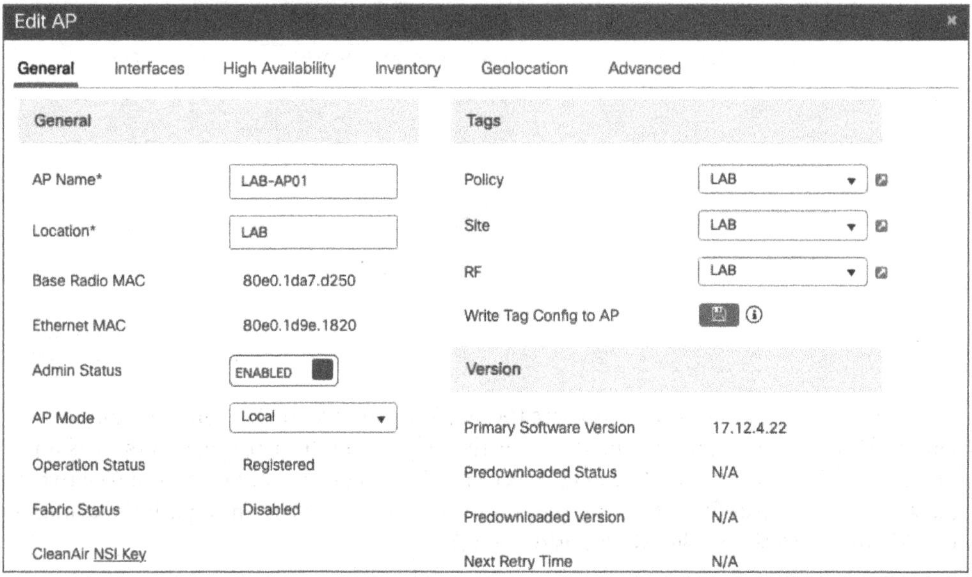

Verification

At this point, I can join our new wireless network using my Windows 11 test PC. Figure 12.18 shows the happy connection.

FIGURE 12.18 Test PC Connection

We can verify the connection on the controller just like we can with the WLC. Unfortunately, we don't get the click topology view on the 9800 because it offloads that functionality to its SDN controller, Catalyst Center. Still, the controller gives us tons of useful information if we need to troubleshoot a bad connection. Figure 12.19 shows the Client details page.

FIGURE 12.19 Client details

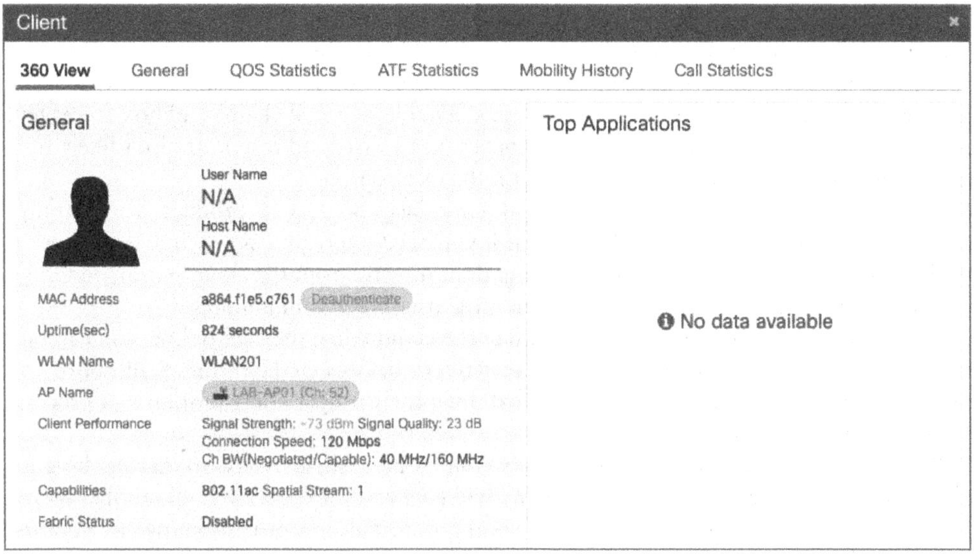

Cloud Management

We've spent the last two chapters focusing on setting up and configuring wireless controllers to build wireless networks. However, choosing a cloud-managed solution can greatly simplify the process by reducing the complexity of managing your own controller. Although this method offers a more streamlined and easier deployment, it may need some of the advanced features available with an on-premises controller.

The basic idea is that the Meraki gear will contact the Meraki cloud when it is able to get online, and then, provided you have added its serial numbers to your Meraki inventory, you are up and running.

The advantage here is that you can centrally manage your equipment from anywhere—there's even a mobile app for that, but it's pretty limited right now.

The downside to the Meraki model is predictable: because devices have to reach the Meraki cloud before you can manage anything, things get awkward fast when you're flailing around trying to resolve an outage or trying to get some pesky site online! But Meraki does equip us with basic, local management abilities that help troubleshoot connection issues.

That said, it's important to note that only some APs will work with the cloud; you'll need to use Cisco Meraki APs to take advantage of this option. Meraki, Cisco's cloud management company, offers a wide range of products, including:

- Wireless
- Switches
- Firewalls
- Cameras

Because all Meraki products are cloud-managed, they are very popular with smaller companies that don't always have highly skilled IT professionals to manage their network infrastructure, such as the typical small business. Even large retail chains and box stores find tremendous value in cloud-managed products because a fast-food restaurant isn't likely to have a dedicated IT person on site to maintain the location.

Meraki can be popular with these kinds of workplaces because its products are centrally managed by its cloud portal. This means that if you need to create a new wireless network as we did in the 9800 controller section, you can do it directly from the cloud portal, and the changes will be pushed down to the network infrastructure within minutes!

Because all your Meraki devices will contact the cloud when they get online, you can take it a step further and actually preconfigure the network devices so they work right out of the box. Once they are installed, they will download their proper configuration in a process known as zero-touch provisioning (ZTP).

The way ZTP works is that Meraki knows your cloud-managed network devices because when you buy them from Cisco, the company will give you the device's serial number so you can add it to your inventory in the Meraki cloud portal. This is a process known as *claiming* the device. Once the Meraki device gets online, it will contact the Meraki cloud, and if you have done the configuration beforehand, it will download it and start working immediately! Some companies will even just ship the equipment over to the branch office and ask the non-technical staff to plug it in for them. Figure 12.20 shows an example of adding devices to the Meraki portal.

FIGURE 12.20 Claiming Meraki devices

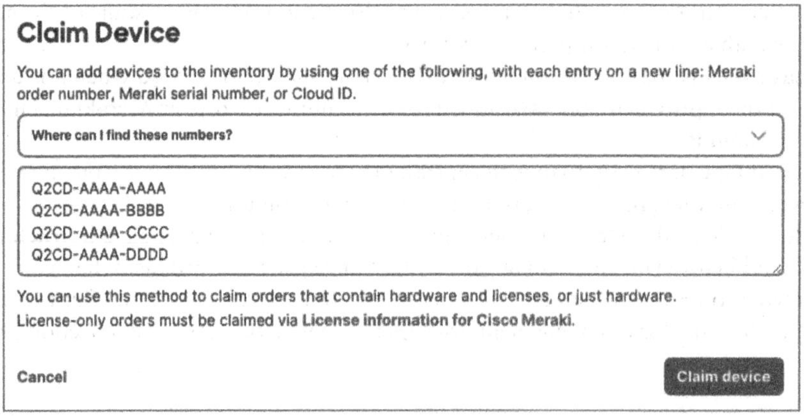

Another great benefit is that Meraki can take advantage of the fact that it knows about your entire Meraki infrastructure, so it can do useful things like dynamically drawing your network topology, as seen in Figure 12.21. It isn't the most detailed network diagram we have ever seen, but it provides a nice point of reference if you need it while troubleshooting something or even getting familiar with the setup.

FIGURE 12.21 Meraki Topology

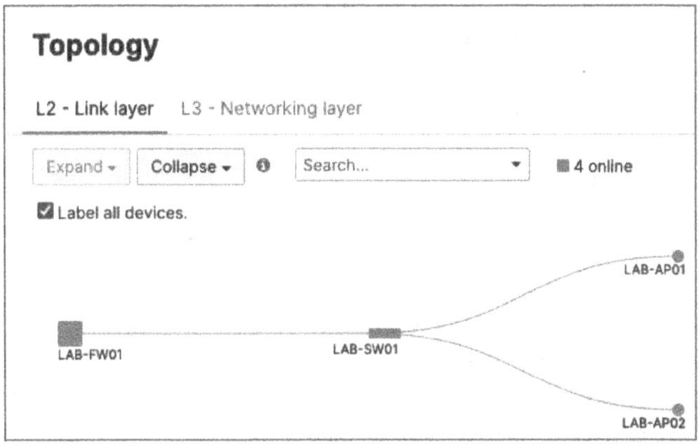

We can also use cloud management to easily upgrade firmware. We simply tell Meraki whether to stick with production-ready code or push beta code instead. Usually, you do not want to run beta firmware in your work environment, but occasionally, you will need a feature that isn't quite ready for primetime. Figure 12.22 shows the upgrade page. This is a lot nicer than the traditional method of uploading the firmware to the network device or wireless controller and then rebooting it. Instead, the Meraki devices will download the firmware from the cloud and do the upgrade whenever you schedule it.

FIGURE 12.22 Meraki upgrade

Now that we talked about some great cloud management benefits, let's take a minute to explore Meraki's products in more detail.

Wireless

Wireless products are Meraki's bread and butter, which is why I opted to include them in this chapter, although I could have just as easily decided to discuss them in the SDN chapter instead.

Meraki's wireless products are, in many cases, good enough to displace the other wireless offerings we have discussed in this book. It may sound strange that Cisco can end up competing against itself, but that is the fun reality of serving every size of customer!

Even though we have discussed wireless in three chapters of this book, we have barely touched the surface of the topic. However, it is safe to say that Meraki is a strong contender in most wireless deployment considerations.

Switches

Although I can safely say that Meraki has strong wireless offerings, I can't really say the same about its switch lineup. Its layer 2 and layer 3 switches are pretty decent, but they aim to be more suited for small and medium-sized businesses and, therefore, have a fraction of the features you would get from a regular Cisco switch. However, Meraki switches tend to be good enough for simpler environments, and they come with all the fancy cloud management benefits we discussed!

The layer 3 switches also support OSPF and BGP routing, but despite Cisco owning them for the last 12 years, they still can't run EIGRP!

Firewalls

Meraki also has a decent firewall lineup called the MX series, which offers all the modern bells and whistles, such as SD-WAN, application classification, and the ability to integrate with Cisco's other security solutions.

If you are running Meraki layer 2 switches, then you will want one of its firewalls to do routing on a stick and DHCP for your network. It is also worth noting that the Meraki firewall can only run routing protocols across site-to-site VPN tunnels and not with your LAN, which can complicate things if you run routing protocols in the rest of your network.

Cameras

You might be surprised to see cameras in this list, but using Meraki for security cameras is actually super popular. This is because cloud management removes a lot of the complexity that comes with running your own security camera solution, like storing all the video. Meraki also provides some really cool features like facial recognition and other analytics.

Configuring a Meraki Stack

By now, you should have a decent idea of what Meraki is all about and some of the benefits that cloud management offers. To drive the point home, let's configure a wireless network using all Meraki equipment. Figure 12.23 shows the lab topology; we have two Meraki APs connected to a Meraki layer 2 switch, which is connected to a Meraki firewall to provide Internet access.

FIGURE 12.23 Meraki lab topology

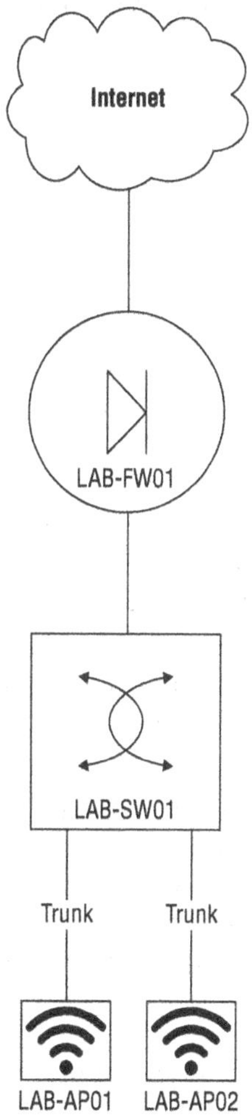

A curious thing about Meraki is that we don't need to create VLANs on the switch. Instead, it has all possible precreated VLANs, so it will simply forward traffic when needed. Because of that, I'm just going to jump straight to creating the following subnets on the firewall:

VLAN	IP address
520	10.50.20.1/24
501	WLAN501

Figure 12.24 shows the subnet configuration.

FIGURE 12.24 Meraki firewall subnet configuration

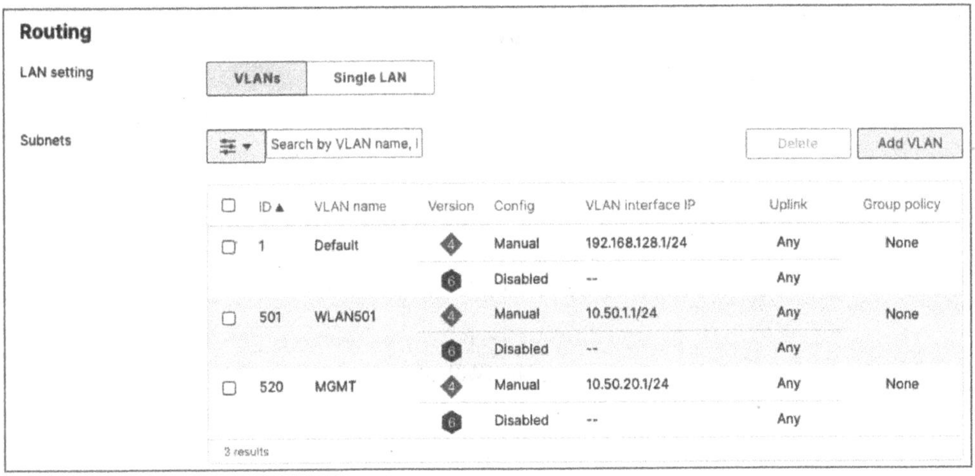

NOTE: The firewall will create VLAN 1 by default and will give it a default IP subnet as well to help get devices online so they can register to the Meraki cloud.

A Meraki firewall—I'm using an MX64 in the lab, by the way—will trunk all LAN interfaces by default when you choose to enable VLANs, so I don't need to change any interface configuration. Still, I can adjust what VLANs are allowed on the interfaces if needed in the future. Figure 12.25 shows the interface configuration summary.

The firewall will allow all outbound traffic by default, and it is also kind enough to automatically NAT the traffic for us, so we don't need to change any other firewall settings for this lab.

We actually don't need to change anything on the switch interfaces either because interfaces will be in trunk mode by default. Still, while we are here, I may as well point out that the web interface gives us a nice view of all the available interfaces and will even show helpful things like how much traffic the interface has seen and any CDP/LLDP neighbors it has. Figure 12.26 shows the interface summary page.

FIGURE 12.25 Meraki firewall interface configuration

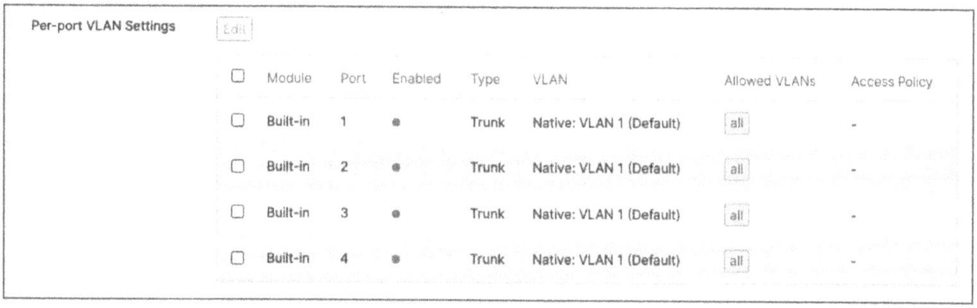

FIGURE 12.26 Meraki switch interface summary

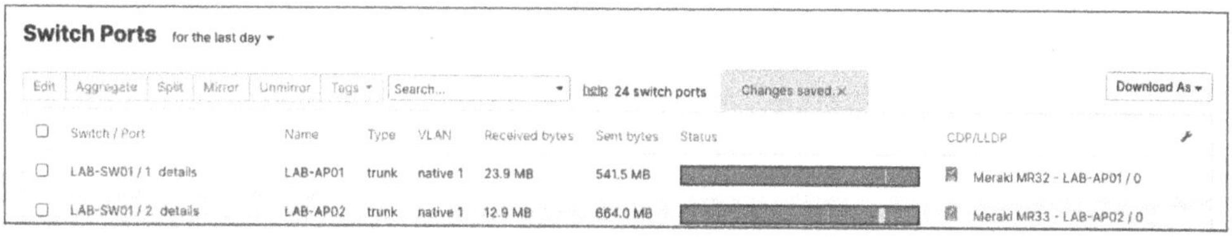

If I want to configure an interface, I click the one I want to edit and change the appropriate setting. You might notice many concepts we discussed earlier in our CCNA books, such as whether the port is running in access or trunk mode or if it is running PoE. Meraki also heavily uses tags like the 9800 controller and usually has a tag option for almost every configuration item. Figure 12.27 shows the interface configuration page.

You can also select multiple interfaces to configure them all at once, just as you can use the interface range command in IOS. This is a handy time saver; you can even select interfaces across different switches! Figure 12.28 shows the interface configuration page with a few interfaces selected.

Rather than doing my usual "change the native VLAN" trick to help the APs register, I'm going to change the VLAN ID on the AP so you can see what that looks like. I do that by going into the AP configuration page and then changing the LAN IP to use VLAN 520, as seen in Figure 12.29.

I know that went well because Figure 12.30 shows that the APs are happily online and have IPs in our VLAN520 subnet.

At this point, we can go ahead and create our WLAN501 wireless network. The first thing we need to do is set the SSID name and make sure it is enabled. Figure 12.31 shows that step.

Then, we must choose how we will authenticate to our new WLAN; because the CCNA is focused on PSK, I will choose the Password option and set my usual lab PSK. Figure 12.32 shows all the security options available to us.

Because my Meraki APs are newer than the ones I used for the WLC and 9800 labs, I'll go ahead and use WPA3 for a change, as seen in Figure 12.33.

FIGURE 12.27 Meraki switch interface configuration

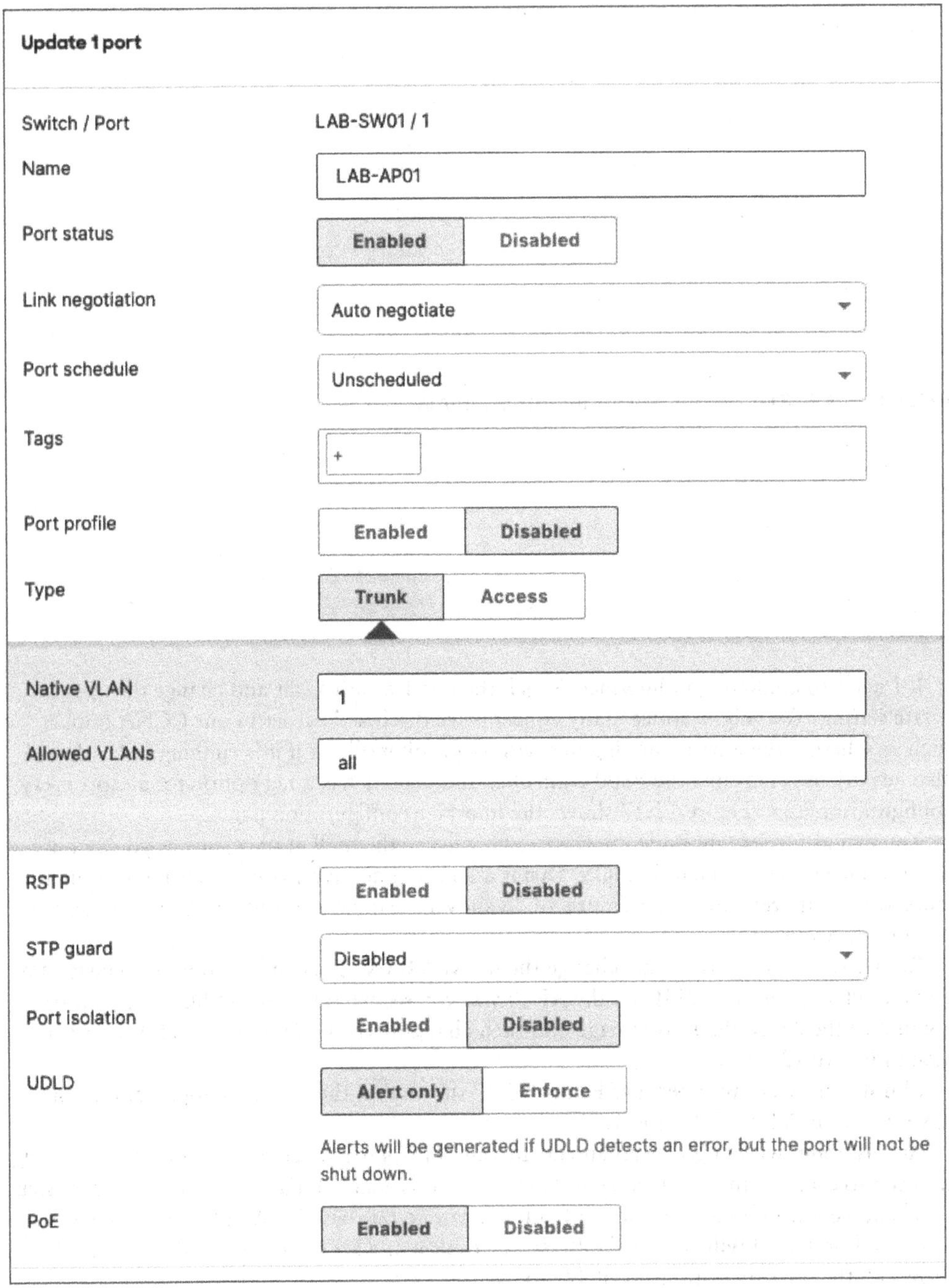

FIGURE 12.28 Meraki switch multiple interface configuration

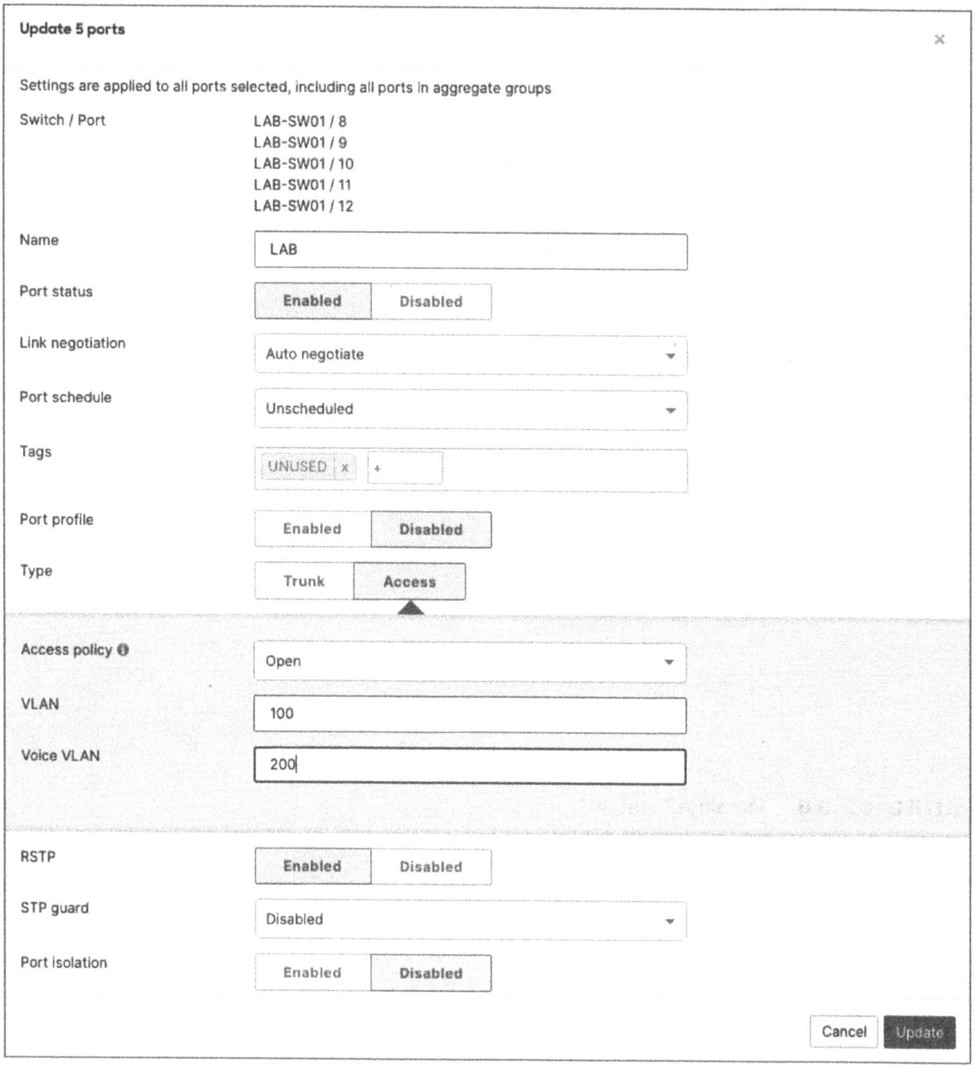

You might be wondering how Meraki handles client traffic. In the other controllers, we had the choice between tunneling traffic to the controller or using FlexConnect to switch the traffic locally. But we can't exactly do a CAPWAP tunnel to the cloud, can we? The answer is—sorta. Meraki allows you to deploy a special server called a VPN concentrator in your network, and the AP will tunnel client traffic to the concentrator instead.

But that is way outside the scope of what you need to know for the CCNA; in fact, this section might already be pushing it! So, we will locally switch the traffic onto that WLAN501 subnet I created. Figure 12.34 shows the VLAN tagging configuration; notice that we can use the tag feature to assign different APs to different VLANs.

Hopefully, you noticed that it was much more straightforward than with the other controllers; the actual configuration only took me about a minute or two in between typing up

FIGURE 12.29 Meraki wireless VLAN ID

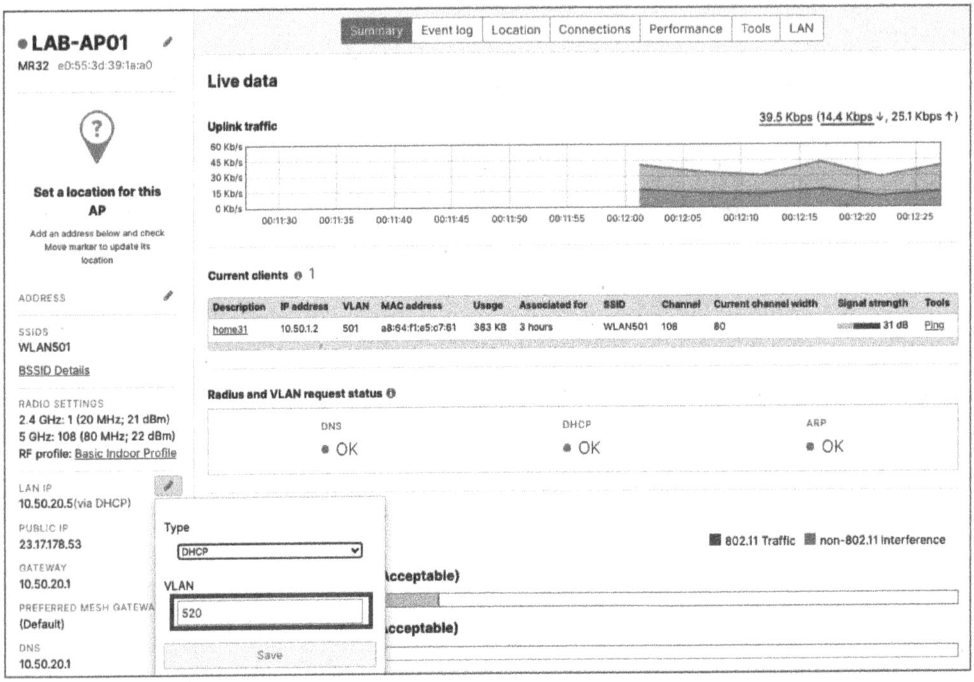

FIGURE 12.30 Meraki AP status

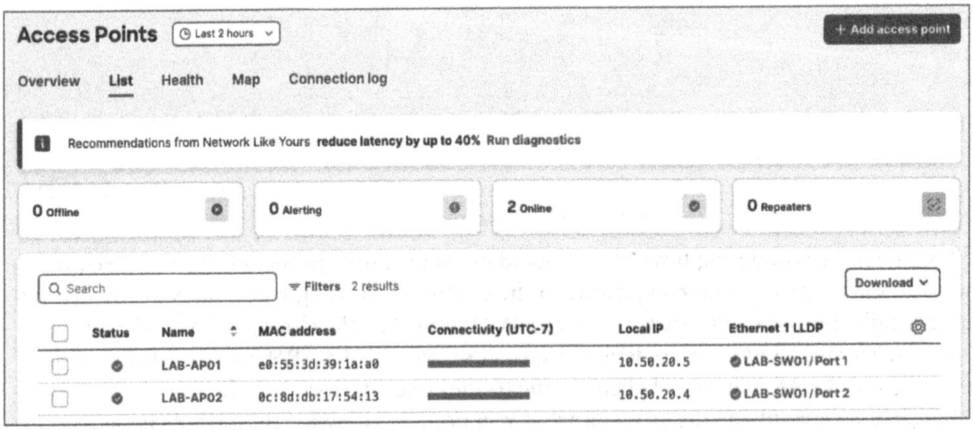

FIGURE 12.31 Meraki wireless configuration—SSID

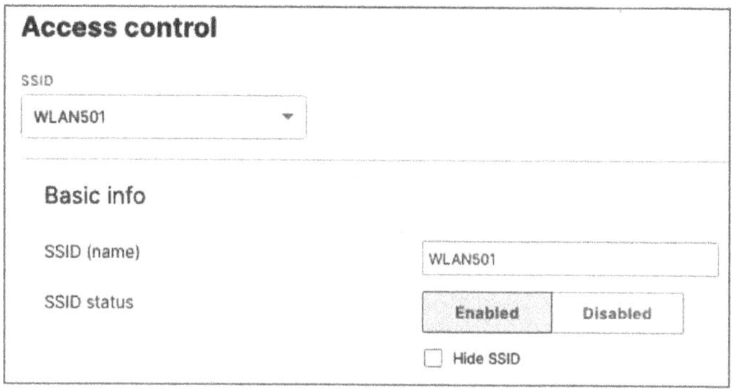

FIGURE 12.32 Meraki wireless configuration—Security

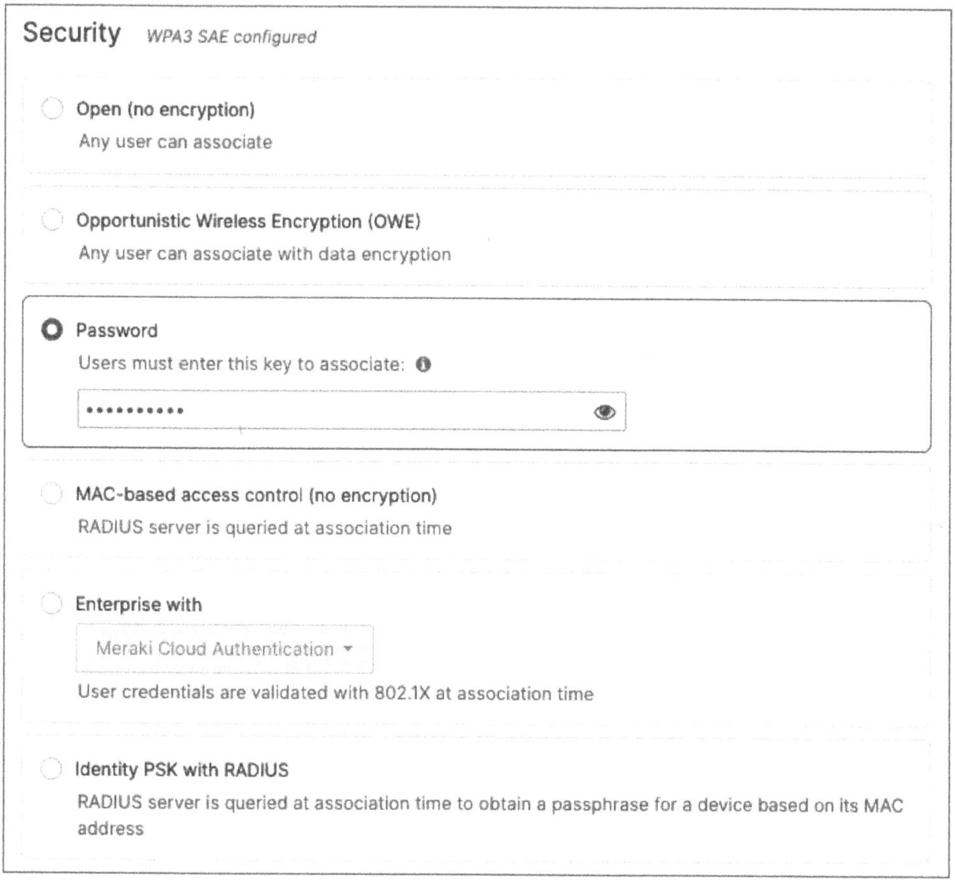

FIGURE 12.33 Meraki wireless configuration—WPA

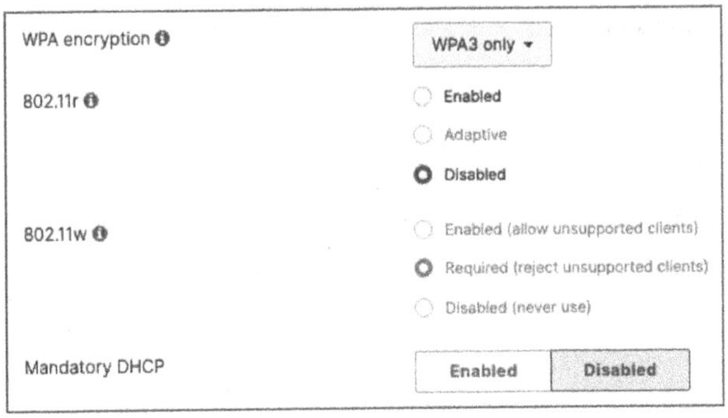

FIGURE 12.34 Meraki wireless configuration—VLAN tag

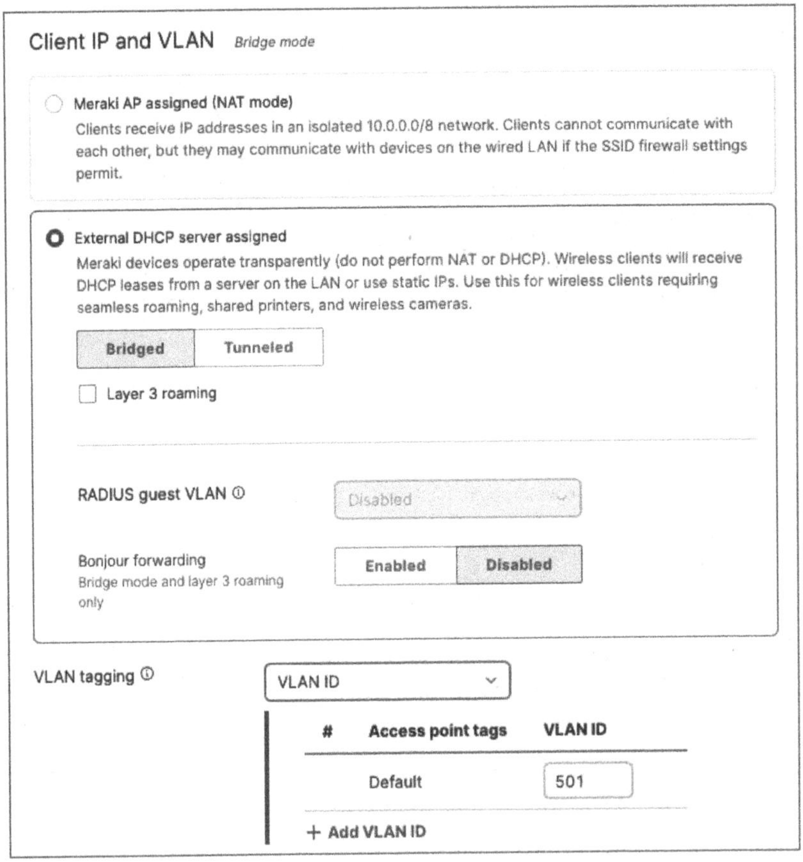

this chapter. We can verify that everything works by connecting my Windows 11 computer to the wireless network, as seen in Figure 12.35.

FIGURE 12.35 Desktop connection

Before we wrap things up, let's look at Meraki's client details for my test connection. Figure 12.36 shows a wealth of information compared to the older controllers, including a path trace feature that we will look at in the SDN chapter.

FIGURE 12.36 Meraki client details

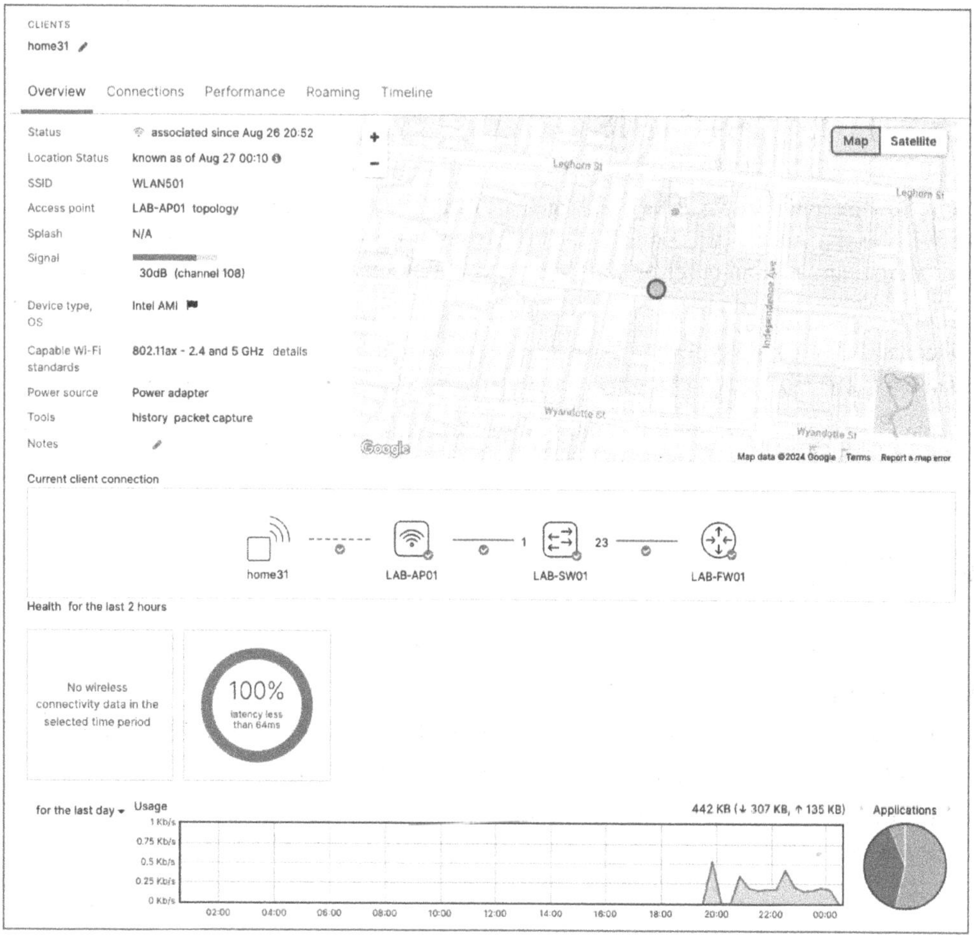

Summary

This chapter provided a concise yet comprehensive overview of how to effectively use the new Cisco 9800 wireless controllers. We started with the basics, learning how to set up the controllers, including configuring port channels and successfully joining access points (APs). Following that, we created a secure wireless network using WPA2 PSK, demonstrating the ease with which you can get a functional WLAN up and running. With the knowledge and skills covered in this chapter, you should now be well-prepared to tackle any challenges Cisco may present regarding the advanced IOS-XE wireless controllers.

In addition to mastering the Cisco 9800, we delved into the benefits of cloud management, particularly through the lens of Cisco Meraki. We explored the powerful features that Meraki offers, emphasizing how it simplifies network management by centralizing control and reducing the complexity typically associated with on-premises solutions. We then applied this knowledge by configuring a wireless network using a full Meraki stack, showcasing how seamless and efficient the deployment process can be when leveraging cloud-based tools. This hands-on experience with Meraki not only reinforced the concepts of cloud management but also highlighted its practical advantages in real-world scenarios.

Exam Essentials

Know how to configure WLANs. A large part of the 9800 configuration is creating the WLANs that clients can connect to. This has several parts, including the SSID, security method, and myriad other options we can choose to enable when creating a wireless network.

Understand cloud management. You should also be familiar with Meraki, which offers cloud-managed products, including access points, switches, firewalls, and cameras.

Be able to create WLAN physical connections. You should be comfortable creating LAGS on either the WLC or the 9800 platforms.

Written Lab

The answers to this lab can be found in Appendix A, "Answers to the Written Labs."

1. Create a VLAN on a Cisco 9800 controller using the CLI.

   Instructions: Write the commands to create VLAN 300 with the name TEST-VLAN.

2. Configure a trunk interface on a Cisco 9800 controller.

   Instructions: Write the commands to configure the interface GigabitEthernet1 as a trunk port.

3. Set up a basic user account on a Cisco 9800 controller.

   Instructions: Write the commands to create a user account with the username user1 and the password Cisco123!.

4. Enable IP routing on a Cisco 9800 controller.

   Instructions: Write the command to enable IP routing.

5. Create a port channel on a Cisco 9800 controller.

   Instructions: Write the commands to create a port channel using interfaces GigabitEthernet1 and GigabitEthernet2.

6. Create a DHCP pool on a Cisco 9800 controller.

   Instructions: Write the commands to create a DHCP pool for network 192.168.50.0/24 with a default gateway of 192.168.50.1.

7. Configure a WLAN profile with WPA2-PSK on a Cisco 9800 controller.

   Instructions: Write down the basic steps to configure a WLAN profile named Lab-WLAN with WPA2-PSK security using the passphrase LabPass123.

8. Associate an access point (AP) with a WLAN on a Cisco 9800 controller.

   Instructions: Describe the steps to associate a new AP with the Lab-WLAN WLAN profile.

9. Verify the status of a port channel on a Cisco 9800 controller.

   Instructions: Write the command to verify the status of a port channel.

10. Assign a VLAN to a policy profile on a Cisco 9800 controller.

    Instructions: Write the steps to assign VLAN 300 to the default policy profile for a WLAN.

Review Questions

NOTE The following questions are designed to test your understanding of this chapter's material. For more information on how to get additional questions, please see this book's introduction.

The answers to these questions can be found in Appendix B, "Answers to the Review Questions."

1. What is the primary difference between the Cisco 9800 controller and legacy WLCs?
   A. The 9800 controller uses AireOS
   B. The 9800 controller is based on IOS-XE
   C. The 9800 controller does not support VLANs
   D. The 9800 controller uses proprietary protocols
2. Which command would you use to create a VLAN on the Cisco 9800 controller?
   A. vlan create 200
   B. vlan 200
   C. create vlan 200
   D. new vlan 200
3. Which protocol is *not* supported for network device management access on the Cisco 9800?
   A. SSH
   B. Telnet
   C. HTTP
   D. SNMP
4. In the Cisco 9800 controller, what is the purpose of creating a port channel?
   A. To group multiple interfaces for redundancy and increased bandwidth
   B. To enable routing on a single interface
   C. To assign multiple VLANs to a single interface
   D. To configure a secure management connection
5. Which feature is used in the Cisco 9800 controller to bind multiple profiles together and associate them with APs?
   A. Tags
   B. Virtual IP
   C. Channel groups
   D. Templates

6. Which of the following is *not* a profile used in the Cisco 9800 controller?
   A. WLAN profile
   B. AP join profile
   C. QoS profile
   D. RF profile
7. What is the default IP address set as the virtual IP address in the Cisco 9800 controller?
   A. 10.0.0.1
   B. 192.0.2.1
   C. 172.31.200.1
   D. 192.168.1.1
8. Which security method is used in the basic setup of a WLAN on the Cisco 9800 controller?
   A. WPA3 Enterprise
   B. WEP
   C. WPA2 PSK
   D. 802.1X
9. What is the role of the AP join profile in the Cisco 9800 controller?
   A. To configure the SSID for the WLAN
   B. To manage AP settings such as country and failover controllers
   C. To map VLANs to WLANs
   D. To control RF settings for APs
10. Which of the following is a benefit of using a cloud-managed solution like Meraki?
    A. Complete offline management of all devices
    B. Centralized management with simplified deployment
    C. Support for EIGRP routing
    D. Ability to use any third-party access point
11. What is zero-touch provisioning (ZTP) in the context of Meraki devices?
    A. Automatic network diagram generation
    B. Preconfigured devices automatically download their configurations upon connection.
    C. Manual setup of each device in the network
    D. Automated backup of device configurations to the cloud
12. Which of the following is required to manage Cisco Meraki access points via the cloud?
    A. A local SSH connection
    B. A Meraki controller on-premises
    C. Cisco Meraki APs registered in the Meraki cloud portal
    D. Cisco AireOS firmware

13. Which of the following is *not* a product offered by Cisco Meraki?
    A. Access points
    B. Switches
    C. Firewalls
    D. Routers
14. In the Meraki setup, what happens if the device cannot reach the Meraki cloud?
    A. The device remains offline.
    B. The device automatically reboots.
    C. The device falls back to local management mode.
    D. The device requires a manual reset.
15. Which type of routing protocols are supported by Meraki layer 3 switches?
    A. OSPF and BGP
    B. EIGRP and OSPF
    C. RIP and OSPF
    D. Static routes only
16. What is the purpose of the Meraki "claiming" process?
    A. To register devices in the Meraki cloud portal before they can be managed
    B. To activate a Meraki device's warranty
    C. To manually configure Meraki devices
    D. To reset Meraki devices to factory defaults
17. What feature does Meraki offer to automatically draw network topology diagrams?
    A. Meraki Dashboard
    B. Meraki Network Map
    C. Meraki Topology
    D. Meraki Auto-Map
18. Which Meraki product can provide firewall capabilities in a Meraki-managed network?
    A. Meraki MS series
    B. Meraki MR series
    C. Meraki MX series
    D. Meraki MV series
19. Which of the following is a primary benefit of using Cisco's Meraki cloud-managed cameras?
    A. Ability to manage cameras without Internet connectivity
    B. Advanced features like facial recognition and analytics
    C. Integration with third-party cloud services
    D. High-capacity local video storage

20. What method does Meraki use to push firmware updates to devices?
    A. Direct upload via SSH
    B. Manual updates through local management
    C. Scheduled downloads from the cloud
    D. USB drive installation

Chapter 13

Virtualization, Containers, and VRFs

THE FOLLOWING CCNA EXAM TOPICS ARE COVERED IN THIS CHAPTER:

✓ **1.0 Network Fundamentals**

1.12 Explain virtualization fundamentals (server virtualization, containers, and VRFs)

In the early days of IT, we pretty much always had to buy a new server whenever we wanted to host a new application. This was very costly and often greatly delayed the project because it could take months to get solutions up and running, and as the adage goes, time is money.

Fortunately, you are reading this book in the cloud and AI era, where we have several solutions to deploy applications quickly and efficiently. In this chapter, we will first have a quick look at the types of endpoints we commonly see in a network, followed by introducing virtualization. Then we will move on to containers, the new kids on the block.

Finally, we will wrap things up by looking at virtual routing and forwarding, which is a way of partitioning our network devices to run multiple routing tables on the box.

NOTE

To find your included bonus material, as well as Todd Lammle videos, practice questions, and hands-on labs, please see `www.lammle.com/ccna`.

Virtualization Fundamentals

Before we dive into virtualization, it is useful to understand how we got here. Back in the day, things were simpler but also a lot more monotonous. For example, if you needed a new DHCP server in your network, you would have done something like this:

1. Order a new server from HP or Dell. This example is set in the dark days before Cisco joined the server market and before HP changed its name to HPE.
2. A month or two later, you and a colleague would rack the server. They tended to be pretty heavy, but you could save a lot of money on gym memberships if you racked enough of them.
3. You would make sure the server has its power and network cables connected.
4. You would "burn in" the server by powering it on and leaving it for a day to ensure that it ran properly.
5. You would typically also need to update the server's hardware firmware by booting it with a CD or DVD, which was kind of like a Frisbee with data on it that was placed into a retractable cupholder known as a CD-ROM drive.
6. Finally, you would install your Windows Server OS on it, again with a CD/DVD.

After all that, you still needed to do the actual configuration, including configuring the network, giving the server an IP address, joining it to the Active Directory domain, and, finally, setting up the DHCP server.

Those sure are a lot of steps to get a DHCP server up and running, and we could have repeated them for every server we added to the network. There were some ways to help improve the process, such as using Microsoft's System Center Configuration Manager (SCCM) to ease the OS deployment and the actual application configuration, but there was no real way to get around the time it took to physically deploy new servers.

Let's continue our trip down memory lane and consider how we would add a standard three-tier application. If you haven't heard the term before, it means we will need three servers to deploy a web-based application: a web server that the user connects to, an application server that has the actual programming logic, and a database server to store the application data. Now, your first thought may be to add one server and install all three components on it, but that isn't ideal because it would create a single point of failure, so we were forced to get three more servers ordered and racked, as seen in Figure 13.1.

FIGURE 13.1 Five servers and counting

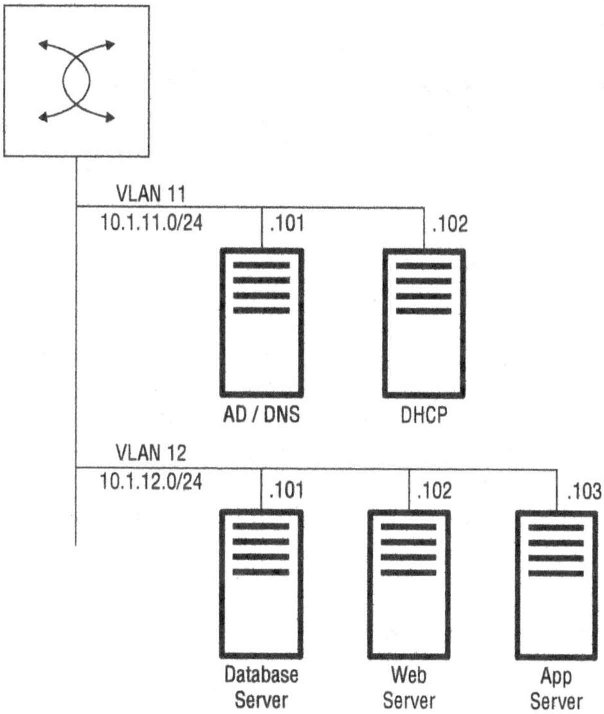

If you look closely at the diagram, you will probably realize that we didn't actually solve the single point of failure that I mentioned because we still only have one of each server. If the database server goes offline, everything does. This means we would need to double-check all the servers to make sure we have some redundancy and resiliency. As you can see, the physical method doesn't scale very well at all!

Fortunately, virtualization came along and saved us from a lot of the pain we've talked about in this chapter so far. Instead of deploying one server per application, we use a hypervisor to run many virtual computer instances called *virtual machines*. This means we can scale out our infrastructure in a much more efficient manner because we only need to add new hypervisors to get better performance and redundancy, which saves a lot of time and money.

The idea is that the hypervisor will virtualize all the hardware components a physical server would have provided, such as RAM, CPUs, network adapters, and storage, and run them in a virtual machine. Therefore, we only need to worry about installing the OS and any applications we need for our server, as seen in Figure 13.2.

FIGURE 13.2 Physical to virtual comparison

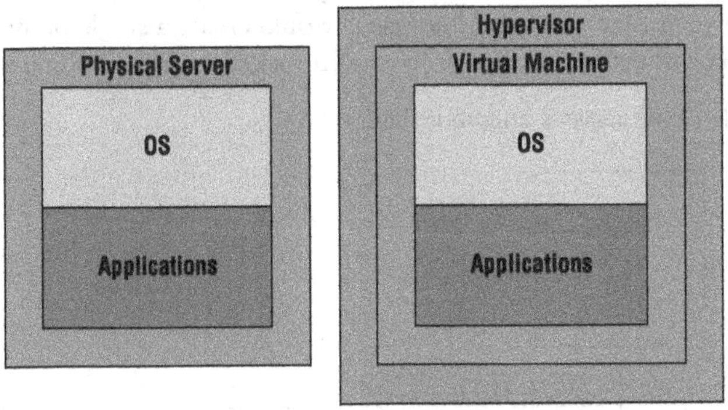

If we need to expand our three-tier solution, we simply create new virtual machines, or VMs, as the cool kids call them. As mentioned previously, this cuts out all the physical tasks, allowing us to jump straight to the OS installation and application configuration for each VM. We can even cut that down by using some of the configuration management solutions we will talk about in the last chapter. By using VMs and configuration management, we can cut the application deployment time from potentially months down to a few minutes!

Figure 13.3 shows what our new streamlined reality logically looks like. The diagram looks largely the same, except they all exist on a virtualization host, and the network switch has a trunk link to a virtual switch inside the hypervisor—something we will discuss more in just a minute.

Virtualization Components

Now that you understand the gist of what virtualization is trying to achieve, let's look at the various components that can be found in a typical virtualization solution:

- Hypervisor
- Virtual switch
- Shared storage
- Guest virtual machine
- Virtual appliance

FIGURE 13.3 Virtualized solution

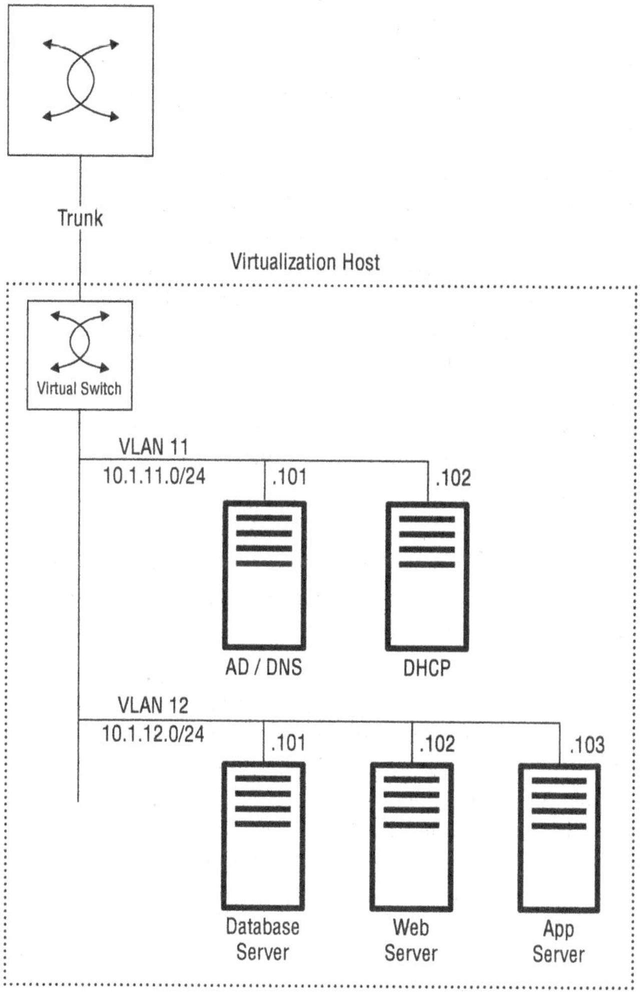

Hypervisor A hypervisor is the server that runs the actual virtualization solution. Most of the time, we refer to the hypervisor as the "host" in conversations.

Typically, the hypervisor has plenty of computational resources, like processors with many cores and large amounts of RAM, and has access to tons of storage. This is because the hypervisor must share all the resources with the various VMs it is running.

Virtual switch Just like how bare metal servers need to connect to physical switches to access the network, VMs also connect to a virtual switch—which is a software switch that lives in the hypervisor.

The virtual switch acts like a real switch and is mainly used to provide VLAN and trunking support to your virtualization solution. It also lets you use many other network features, such as QoS, CDP/LLDP, and even advanced security features like private VLANs. The biggest difference is that a virtual switch does not run STP internally.

Every virtualization vendor uses its own terms, but generally, there are two main types of virtual switches:

- **Standard:** This is usually the default "free" version of a virtual switch that comes with your hypervisor. It provides basic functionality so you can connect your VMs to the network, but it doesn't come with any bells and whistles. The biggest drawback with the standard version is that every hypervisor has an independent virtual switch. This means that if you configure VLAN11 and VLAN12 on a host's virtual switch, you need to add those VLANs on every hypervisor. So, if you have 12 hosts, you will need to manually add those VLANs on each one. Likewise, if you need to add VLAN13, you need to add it to all the hosts as well. This is very similar to adding a VLAN on all your network switches without using automation or VTP.
- **Distributed:** This option usually costs some money, but it creates a single logical switch that spans all your hypervisors and enables all the advanced network features. This makes life easier because you only need to add/remove a VLAN once, which is replicated across your virtualization infrastructure; this is like a switch stack where you configure the master switch, which applies to the full stack.

Shared storage Although you can create a VM using a host's internal storage, this approach is very limiting when you start growing your virtualization infrastructure because other hosts won't be able to access the other host's internal hard drive to access the VM files. Local storage also has other issues because if the hypervisor that is hosting a VM goes offline, it will take the VM down with it.

The better solution is to use some form of shared storage, where the hypervisors connect to a storage area network (SAN) or even a network-attached storage (NAS) through either iSCSI or Fiber Channel. This allows all hosts to access the same VM files, and that helps give us better resiliency because we can now survive a host going offline without impacting the running VMs.

NOTE Although I have been known to venture a bit deeper into topics than we need to for the CCNA, I'm not going to go much further into storage solutions because that is a vast world that would probably scare most of my readers away.

Guest virtual machine A virtualization guest, or simply "guest," is a term for a VM that runs on a hypervisor. Nowadays, a VM can practically run any modern operating system. Fun fact: I once spent an entire day trying to get Windows 3.1 running inside a VM. . . I'll never get that time back.

Virtual appliance A virtual appliance is a special kind of VM provided by a vendor. These days, nearly all vendors offer virtual appliances as an option when you buy their products. For example, Cisco has hundreds of virtual appliances that you can run in your network, but some of the most common ones that are useful to know at the CCNA level are as follows:

- Cisco 8000v: A virtual router that runs IOS-XE software.
- Cisco Secure Firewall Virtual—A virtualized version of the company's popular firewall solution.
- Cisco Unified Call Manager—A virtualized version of the company's flagship VoIP solution.

Virtualization Types

There are two types of virtualization available today: hardware virtual machines (HVMs) and paravirtualization. The main difference is whether the VM is aware that it is a VM. When you create a VM using an HVM, the OS is not aware that it is a VM, which can make it easier to maintain because you don't need to modify any OS-level configurations for it to work. The HVM can also use special hardware extensions for better performance and functionality. For example, you can actually virtualize a hypervisor in a lab and have it be able to create VMs! This is because you can present the CPU virtualization capability to the VM's CPU.

Paravirtualization VMs, on the other hand, are aware that they are VMs. They can run much faster because they can communicate directly with the hypervisor to get what they want instead of using emulated hardware, but at the cost of ease of use and functionality because you often need to install special drivers and do a bit more fine-tuning for it to function.

We also have two types of hypervisors we need to discuss.

Type 1 Virtualization

Type 1 is also known as a bare-metal hypervisor—where the entire server is dedicated to virtualization, so the hypervisor has full access to all the hardware resources on the server.

This is the most common type of virtualization that is used in the enterprise.

Here are some commonly used type 1 solutions:

- VMware ESXi
- Microsoft Hyper-V
- Xen/KVM

VMware ESXi Almost everyone has heard of VMware because it is currently the virtualization market leader; however, that may be shifting because of its recent acquisition by Broadcom.

ESXi is its fully featured hypervisor, based on a customized version of Linux. The solution is managed from either the ESXi server's web interface or VMware's central management solution called VCenter.

Broadcom recently removed the free ESXi license; however, you can still download the trial version if you want to try it out.

Microsoft Hyper-V We all know Microsoft, but you might not have heard of Hyper-V, its on-premises virtualization solution. It has two different deployment options: a dedicated OS installed on a bare metal server like ESXi, and the other is natively built into modern Windows desktop and server operating systems.

Feature-wise, Hyper-V has an answer for many of VMware's enterprise features; it just tends to be a worse answer. But its saving grace is that Microsoft tries to make Hyper-V very cost-effective by bundling it with its other solutions and licensing agreements.

Hyper-V is managed either by you installing the Hyper-V Management Tool on your desktop or by installing its central management solution, System Center Virtual Machine Manager (SCVMM).

Because Hyper-V is native to Windows, you can easily test it by installing the role on your Windows desktop if you are running at least Windows 10. There is a catch, though: because Hyper-V is a type 1 hypervisor, it will take control of your computer's hardware resources, so you will not be able to easily run type 2 hypervisors on your desktop when it is enabled.

Xen/KVM Kernel-based Virtual Machine (KVM) is a free and open-source type 1 hypervisor designed for Linux. Xen is like KVM, except it installs as a dedicated OS. Cloud providers such as AWS tend to use Xen under the hood.

KVM is hands down the hardest virtualization solution to use unless you are really strong in Linux, but it is really handy for lab environments. Because this isn't a book on Linux administration, we won't dive any further into KVM, but I just wanted to make you aware that it is out there.

Type 2 Virtualization

Type 2 is also known as desktop or hosted virtualization. It refers to virtualization solutions that run on your desktop. These solutions are mainly used by enthusiasts or developers who want a cheap and easy way to run VMs so they can study or test out a new feature they are coding.

Here are some commonly used type 2 solutions:

- VMWare Workstation
- VMware Fusion
- Oracle VirtualBox
- QEMU

VMware Workstation/Fusion VMware Workstation is a paid type 2 solution for Windows and Linux that allows you to run VMs on your desktop. VMware also has a version for Macs called VMware Fusion. It has some decent features, and Broadcom recently made the full solution free for personal use, so they aren't all bad!

There used to be a scaled-down version called VMware Workstation/Fusion Player, but it has been decommissioned because the full version is free.

It is also worth mentioning that if you are a Mac user, you may have a harder time running VMs because Apple moved to its new M processors that use an ARM64 architecture instead of the x86 that is usually used these days. The consequence is that you can easily run ARM64 VMs but not x86/x64 style ones.

Oracle VirtualBox VirtualBox is a free, open-source solution provided by Oracle. It doesn't provide as many features as VMware Workstation, but it remains a very popular option for running VMs on a desktop.

QEMU QEMU stands for "Quick Emulator" and is a popular type 2 hypervisor for network labbing software such as CML, EVE-NG, and GNS3. QEMU allows these solutions to easily run virtual appliances from Cisco and other network vendors so you can test out network topologies. You can also run it independently on Windows, Linux, and Mac, but using it directly can get pretty complex.

NOTE Some solutions can fall between the desktop shorthand for type 1 and type 2 virtualization. For example, you can install Hyper-V on a server to have it as a dedicated hypervisor, but you can also install it on Windows 11 and use it on your desktop. KVM can also be dedicated or on your desktop using QEMU.

Virtualization Features

We'll wrap up the virtualization topic by looking at some useful features that are common in virtualization solutions:

Hardware abstraction If you ever bought a new computer and found that some software or your peripherals didn't work with the hardware, you will probably appreciate this functionality. Because all the VM hardware is virtual, everything becomes nice and predictable, and you shouldn't have any surprises if you have to move a VM to a new host.

Ideally, you would build your hypervisors to use the same hardware on all the hosts, such as the same CPU families. But if you can't do that, fear not. Hypervisors have the ability to "mask" how they present their CPUs to the VMs to ensure consistency when you have inconsistent hardware in your ESXi farm!

Snapshots Snapshots are basically an "undo" button for your VM. They allow you to capture the state of the VM before you do any work on it and then revert the snapshot if something goes wrong. For example, it is a good idea to take a snapshot before you try to upgrade your VM because you can instantly roll things back if the upgrade happens to explode your application.

Backup solutions such as Veeam also utilize snapshots to create a backup copy of the VM and to restore backups faster.

You will want to delete snapshots after you no longer need them because they continuously store the VM state, which will end up wasting a lot of storage and will eventually cause problems with your VM.

Snapshots are also referred to as *checkpoints* in Hyper-V.

NOTE Snapshots aren't always a magic "get out of jail" card! If the VM makes changes to other systems, you will also have to roll back those changes if you revert a snapshot.

Clones Clones allow you to quickly create a copy of a VM. This is handy for making a "golden image" that has all the customizations you commonly need, such as applications and updates you need. Then, you can use the clone as a template for creating more VMs as needed.

Cloning can also be useful for making quick and dirty backups.

Migrations Virtual machines can be migrated between hosts to help balance the workload across your virtualization environment and keep VMs running if a hypervisor needs to be taken offline for maintenance. If shared storage is being used, then VMs can freely move across the hosts without any data loss.

Migrations come in two types:

- VM migration: Refers to moving a VM from one host to another
- Storage migration: Refers to when you need to move a VM from one storage location to another, such as from internal storage to a shared iSCSI store

Container Fundamentals

We just finished exploring how VMs are much more efficient than the old way of installing everything on physical servers, but we are still installing the OS and application on the VM, which can waste a lot of time and resources.

If we consider our three-tier application example again, as seen in Figure 13.4, we created three VMs: a web server, a database server, and an application server. If we had used the latest Red Hat Enterprise Linux (RHEL) for our VMs, we would have had to install it three times if we ignored redundancy for now. Aside from the time and effort it takes to deploy

RHEL, each VM also takes CPU, RAM, and storage to run the operating system! Beyond that, we also need to maintain the OS on each VM, so we would have to install patches and possibly do other periodic maintenance.

FIGURE 13.4 Wasted OS resources

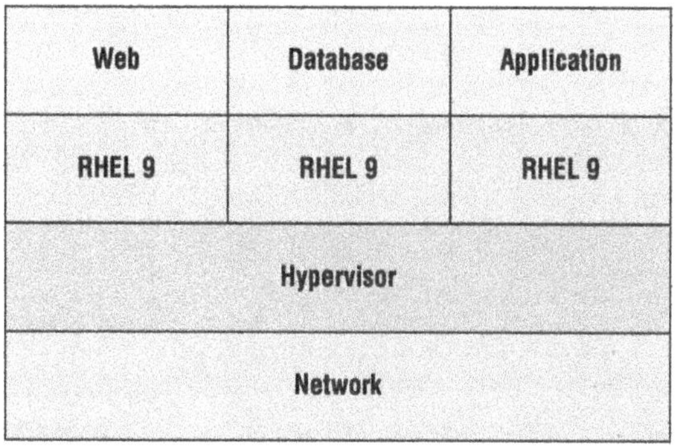

Containers solve that problem by allowing the application portion of your solution to run on a container engine such as Docker. This is an improvement because instead of creating a VM for each part of our three-tier app, we create a container for each application, and the underlying OS is shared with the containers, so we don't end up wasting any space from copying the OS over and over. Figure 13.5 shows the difference between VMs and containers for a three-tier app.

FIGURE 13.5 VM versus container

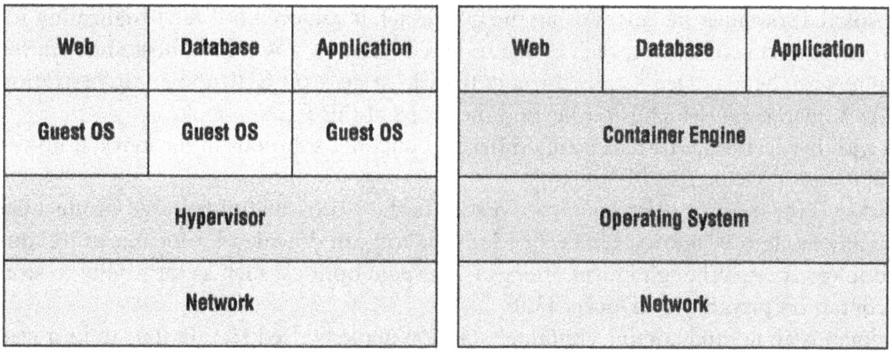

Container solutions also have a great quality-of-life feature: vendors like Docker host online repositories full of ready-to-go containers. This allows you to spin up commonly used containers almost instantly without first having to build them yourself. Figure 13.6 shows the official NGINX container in Docker's online repository called Docker Hub. The repository keeps track of all the various container versions that have been uploaded, along with instructions on how to deploy the container in your environment. However, you can also build your own containers from scratch if necessary for your project.

FIGURE 13.6 Docker Hub

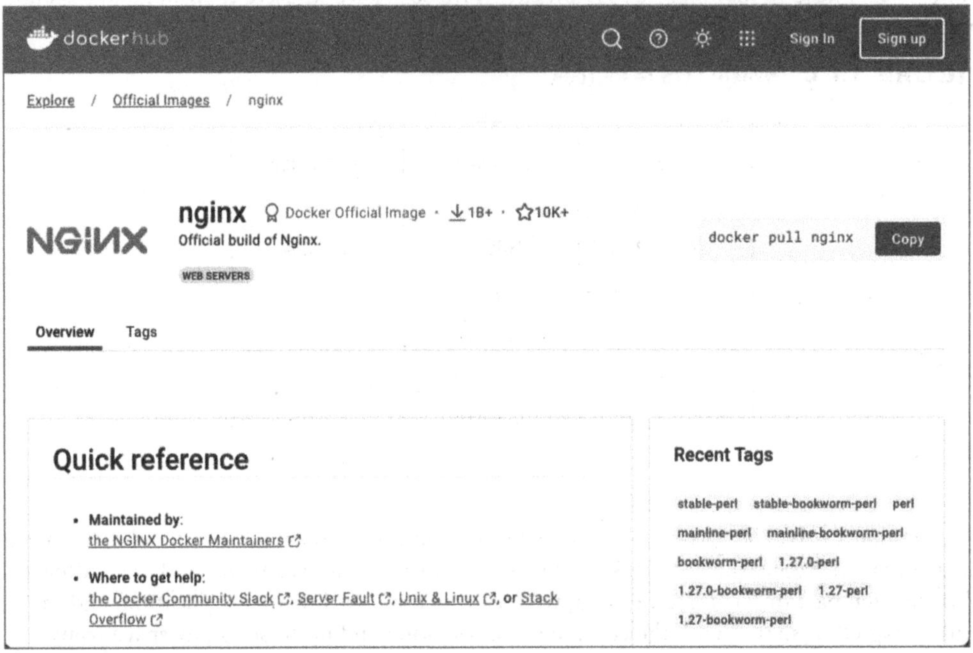

Container Engines

A container engine is essentially a container version of a hypervisor. It is responsible for creating isolated container instances using the OS kernel. It can even utilize virtualization to run cross-platform containers, such as Linux-based ones, on a Windows host and vice versa. Containers can be managed locally through the CLI, a desktop GUI, and an orchestration tool like Kubernetes—which is far beyond the scope of this CCNA book.

As with hypervisors, there are many different container solutions in the market; however, we will focus on Docker and Podman.

Docker is the most popular container vendor in the world. Its full-featured product can run on any modern Windows, Linux, or Mac OS. You can download it for free at `https://www.docker.com`, although it also offers various paid options, such as the ability to store your containers privately on Docker Hub.

Podman is an up-and-coming container solution made by Red Hat. It aims to be a leaner and faster alternative to Docker. It does this by offloading various functions, like building new container images, to another open-source product called Buildah, whereas Docker prefers to keep all the functionality inside Docker itself. It is also more secure out of the box because Docker runs its container instances under root by default, and Podman doesn't.

Podman is the new kid on the block, so it has a long way to go before it fully competes with Docker; however, Red Hat has put a lot of effort into ensuring feature parity and cross-compatibility to the point where you can use Docker CLI commands on a Podman system!

You can check out Podman at `https://podman-desktop.io`; nowadays, it is supported on all major operating systems.

For our purposes, you just need to know that containers exist and can be more efficient than VMs. But this is a pretty advanced topic, so I wouldn't recommend deep diving into it until you are ready to start studying for certifications like the DevNet Associate.

Virtual Routing and Forwarding

The last topic we'll discuss in this chapter is virtual routing and forwarding (VRF), which is a way of creating multiple independent routing tables on a network device. This relates somewhat to what we discussed with virtualization and containers because we essentially share the router or switch resources to create new instances.

VRFs have multiple uses in networking, from providing out-of-band management interfaces on devices to being the foundation for WAN technologies like MPLS VPNs. But let's focus on the management interface example so we don't get too lost in the weeds.

Figure 13.7 shows a simple topology with a single router with three interfaces. The first interface will be our management interface, the second interface will be connected to the imaginatively named Net A, and the last interface will be connected to Net B. Additionally, each interface will have its own default route, so I'll add a few static routes:

```
r01(config)#ip route 0.0.0.0 0.0.0.0 192.168.10.254
r01(config)#ip route 0.0.0.0 0.0.0.0 192.168.20.254
r01(config)#ip route 0.0.0.0 0.0.0.0 172.31.255.254
```

FIGURE 13.7 Without VRF example

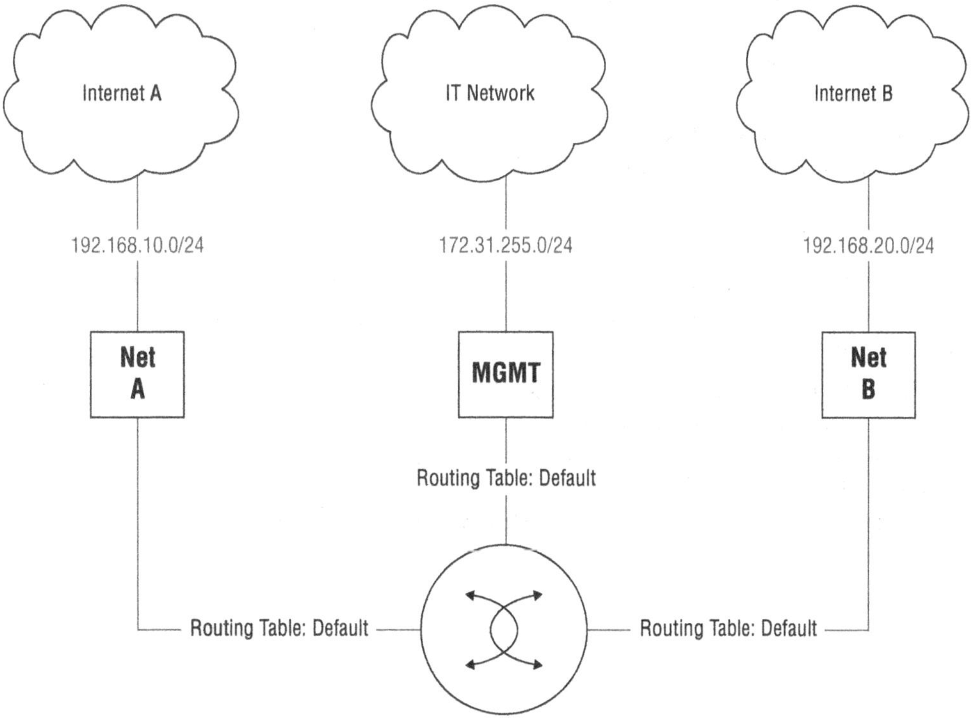

As expected, if we look at the routing table, we can see three different default routes. The router will simply use ECMP across all of them when it needs to reach a network it doesn't know about. But the problem is that the management interface route connects to the IT network and not the internet, which means the router will end up blackholing internet traffic one-third of the time!

```
r01#show ip route | begin Gateway
Gateway of last resort is 192.168.20.254 to network 0.0.0.0

S*    0.0.0.0/0 [1/0] via 192.168.20.254
                [1/0] via 192.168.10.254
                [1/0] via 172.31.255.254
      172.31.0.0/16 is variably subnetted, 2 subnets, 2 masks
C        172.31.255.0/24 is directly connected, GigabitEthernet1
L        172.31.255.1/32 is directly connected, GigabitEthernet1
      192.168.10.0/24 is variably subnetted, 2 subnets, 2 masks
C        192.168.10.0/24 is directly connected, GigabitEthernet2
L        192.168.10.1/32 is directly connected, GigabitEthernet2
      192.168.20.0/24 is variably subnetted, 2 subnets, 2 masks
C        192.168.20.0/24 is directly connected, GigabitEthernet3
L        192.168.20.1/32 is directly connected, GigabitEthernet3
r01#L        192.168.20.1/32 is directly connected, GigabitEthernet3
```

To fix this, we would either need to remove the static route for the management network and replace it with more specific static routes instead, or we could simply create a VRF to move that interface to a new routing table, as seen in Figure 13.8.

The CCNA doesn't expect you to know how to actually make a VRF, but that isn't any fun, so let's give it a try! If I wanted to create a VRF called MGMT, I would type something like this:

```
r01(config)#vrf definition MGMT
r01(config-vrf)#address-family ipv4 unicast
r01(config-vrf-af)#exit
r01(config-vrf)#exit
```

That will create a VRF named MGMT and tell the router it is running the IPv4 address-family. You can also use VRFs with IPv6 if you need to. After that is done, I need to assign it to an interface like this:

```
r01(config)#interface GigabitEthernet 1
r01(config-if)#vrf forwarding MGMT
% Interface GigabitEthernet1 IPv4 disabled and address(es) removed due to
enabling VRF MGMT
r01(config-if)#ip add 172.31.255.1 255.255.255.0
r01(config-if)#end
```

FIGURE 13.8 With VRF example

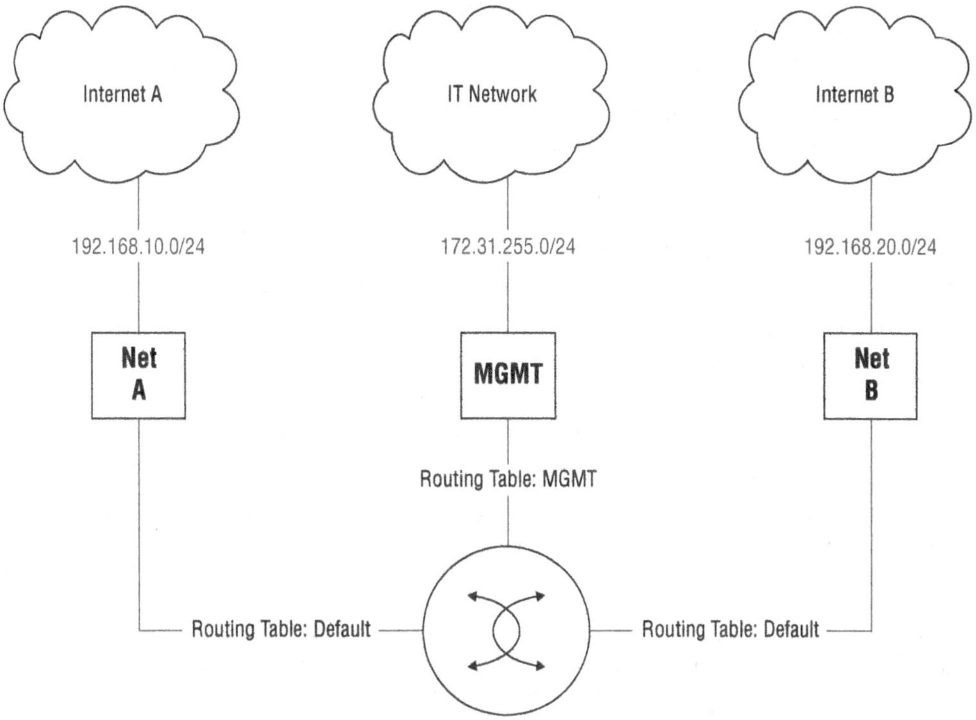

One thing to note is that the router will remove any IP address on the interface when you apply a VRF. This is because it is literally removing the interface and moving it to the new routing table instead. So, make sure you have a backup copy of the interface configuration before you do this.

We also need to create a new static route for our management interface. The old one no longer applies because the interface is no longer in the default routing table:

```
r01(config)#no ip route 0.0.0.0 0.0.0.0 172.31.255.254
r01(config)#ip route vrf MGMT 0.0.0.0 0.0.0.0 172.31.255.254
```

Now, if we check the routing table, we will only see two default routes for Net A and Net B. This is expected because we moved the management interface over to the MGMT VRF:

```
r01(config)#do sh ip route | be Gateway
Gateway of last resort is 192.168.20.254 to network 0.0.0.0

S*    0.0.0.0/0 [1/0] via 192.168.20.254
                [1/0] via 192.168.10.254
      192.168.10.0/24 is variably subnetted, 2 subnets, 2 masks
C        192.168.10.0/24 is directly connected, GigabitEthernet2
```

```
L        192.168.10.1/32 is directly connected, GigabitEthernet2
      192.168.20.0/24 is variably subnetted, 2 subnets, 2 masks
C        192.168.20.0/24 is directly connected, GigabitEthernet3
L        192.168.20.1/32 is directly connected, GigabitEthernet3
```

We can view the management route by adding the vrf keyword to our routing table command. These days, practically all features in IOS-XE are VRF-aware, which means that they fully support using VRFs. When we look at the output of the `show ip route vrf MGMT`, we can see the isolated default route:

```
r01(config)#do sh ip route vrf MGMT | be Gateway
Gateway of last resort is 172.31.255.254 to network 0.0.0.0
S*    0.0.0.0/0 [1/0] via 172.31.255.254
      172.31.0.0/16 is variably subnetted, 2 subnets, 2 masks
C        172.31.255.0/24 is directly connected, GigabitEthernet1
L        172.31.255.1/32 is directly connected, GigabitEthernet1
```

This was a very simple example, but hopefully, you can see some of the value that VRF brings to the table when it comes to isolating routes or even enabling more advanced features.

NOTE

Modern Cisco devices create a management VRF by default for the onbox management port. However, the exact name of the VRF varies between different platforms and IOS-XE versions.

Summary

This chapter provided a lot of good information on some advanced concepts! First, we looked at the exciting virtualization world, including some common components it uses and what features it supports.

Then, we looked at containers to see how they can be more efficient than virtual machines.

Finally, we wrapped up the chapter by looking at virtual routing and forwarding, complete with an example!

Exam Essentials

Understand server virtualization. Server virtualization allows you to create virtual machines (VMs) on hypervisors. VMs are much more cost-effective and efficient than deploying applications directly on physical servers.

Understand containers. Containers allow you to deploy just the application you need on top of a container engine like Docker.

Understand virtual routing and forwarding. VRFs allow you to create multiple routing tables on a network device so you can isolate interfaces.

Written Lab

The answers to this lab can be found in Appendix A, "Answers to the Written Labs."

1. Describe the main benefits of virtualization in modern network environments.
2. What is the role of a hypervisor in a virtualization environment, and what are the two main types of hypervisors?
3. Explain the difference between a standard virtual switch and a distributed virtual switch in a virtualization environment.
4. Why is shared storage important in a virtualized environment, and how does it benefit virtual machine migration?
5. Compare and contrast type 1 and type 2 hypervisors. Provide examples of each.
6. What is a snapshot in the context of virtualization, and when might it be useful to create one?
7. Define virtual routing and forwarding (VRF), and explain its purpose in a network.
8. How do containers differ from virtual machines in terms of resource efficiency, and why might they be preferred in certain scenarios?
9. List and briefly describe three popular type 2 hypervisors that can be used for desktop virtualization.
10. What is paravirtualization, and how does it differ from hardware virtualization in terms of performance and OS awareness?

Review Questions

NOTE The following questions are designed to test your understanding of this chapter's material. For more information on how to get additional questions, please see this book's introduction.

The answers to these questions can be found in Appendix B, "Answers to the Review Questions."

1. What is an example of a type 1 hypervisor?
   A. VMware ESXi
   B. Microsoft Hyper-V
   C. Xen
   D. All three
2. VMware Workstation is an example of what type of hypervisor?
   A. Type 1
   B. Type 2
   C. Type 3
   D. Type 4
   E. Type 5
   F. Type 6
3. What does the term "guest virtual machine" refer to?
   A. A VM that has limited access to resources
   B. A VM running on a hypervisor
   C. A VM that operates as a server
   D. A virtual appliance
4. Which of the following is a feature of type 2 virtualization?
   A. Runs directly on the server hardware
   B. Requires a host OS to run
   C. Does not support snapshots
   D. Is used primarily in enterprise environments
5. What type of migration involves moving a VM from one host to another?
   A. Storage migration
   B. Virtual machine migration
   C. Network migration
   D. Application migration

6. What does a "snapshot" allow you to do in a virtualized environment?
   - A. Backup the entire virtual machine
   - B. Capture and restore the VM to a previous state
   - C. Move the VM to another host
   - D. Clone the VM to create a copy
7. What is a primary feature of Docker Hub?
   - A. It hosts container images for easy deployment.
   - B. It provides network management for VMs.
   - C. It allows for the migration of VMs between hypervisors.
   - D. It is a backup solution for VMs.
8. What feature of VRF allows for isolating routes on a network device?
   - A. VLANs
   - B. Snapshots
   - C. Multiple routing tables
   - D. Hypervisor configuration
9. Which hypervisor is known for being difficult to use unless you're strong in Linux?
   - A. VMware ESXi
   - B. Microsoft Hyper-V
   - C. Xen/KVM
   - D. Docker
10. What does the term "hypervisor" refer to in virtualization?
    - A. The physical server running virtual machines
    - B. The software that creates and runs virtual machines
    - C. A type of virtual switch
    - D. A network storage solution
11. Which type of virtualization does not require the OS to be aware it is running in a virtualized environment?
    - A. Paravirtualization
    - B. Hardware virtual machine (HVM)
    - C. Containerization
    - D. Type 2 virtualization
12. What advantage does shared storage provide in a virtualized environment?
    - A. Reduced need for hypervisors
    - B. Simplified VLAN management
    - C. Lower overall costs
    - D. Easier migration of VMs between hosts

13. What is the main drawback of a standard virtual switch compared to a distributed virtual switch?
    A. Lack of VLAN support
    B. No trunking capability
    C. Manual configuration on each hypervisor
    D. Inability to connect virtual machines to the network
14. What does a virtual switch primarily provide in a virtualization environment?
    A. CPU management
    B. VLAN and trunking support
    C. Storage management
    D. Backup functionality
15. What is a primary advantage of virtualization over physical server deployment?
    A. Reduced need for power and cooling
    B. Easier physical access to servers
    C. Faster deployment of applications
    D. Improved physical security

Chapter 14

Software-Defined Networking

THE FOLLOWING CCNA EXAM TOPICS ARE COVERED IN THIS CHAPTER:

✓ **1.0 Network Fundamentals**

1.2c Spine-leaf

✓ **6.0 Automation and Programmability**

6.1 Explain how automation impacts network management

6.2 Compare traditional networks with controller-based networking

6.3 Describe controller-based, software defined architecture (overlay, underlay, and fabric)

6.3.a Separation of control plane and data plane

6.3.b Northbound and Southbound APIs

Networking itself hasn't changed much since networks were first rolled out. Of course, a modern-day Cisco router has an endless buffet of new capabilities, features, and protocols compared to older routers, but we still configure one by logging into it and making changes manually.

That said, automation has become popular enough to be included on the CCNA exam—it even has its own DevNet certification track that goes all the way up to the expert level! Even so, most companies still aren't keen on fully managing their network with a bunch of Python scripts on a shared drive. So, a better solution is to use a software-defined networking controller to centrally manage and monitor the network instead of doing everything manually.

I'm going to introduce you to software-defined networking (SDN) concepts and controller-based architecture. We'll also cover some very cool advantages a Catalyst Center-managed network offers over a traditionally managed network. This is going to be a great chapter!

NOTE: To find your included bonus material, as well as Todd Lammle videos, practice questions, and hands-on labs, please see `www.lammle.com/ccna`

Traditional Networking

To really get what SDN is, you've first got to understand how a regular router sends traffic. When a router receives a packet, it jumps through several hoops before it can send that packet out to its destination. Let's explore that process now.

Before the router can send out traffic, it must know all the available destination routes. These routes are learned via a static route or a default route, or through a routing protocol like OSPF. Because the CCNA exclusively focuses on OSPF, we've got to configure it and get the neighbors up.

Once that's done, we should have a nicely populated routing table for the router. It'll look up the proper destination route with the help of Cisco Express Forwarding, which Cisco uses to build the forwarding table these days. Exactly how CEF and the forwarding table work are out-of-scope topics for the CCNA, so I won't go into them further here.

Okay—so now that we have our route, the router will need an ARP entry for the next hop IP address before it can send the traffic. The packet's TTL will decrease by one as it passes through the router, and the IP header and Ethernet frame checksum will also be recalculated before the traffic is sent over the wire.

Routers divide these different tasks into three different planes:

- The management plane
- The control plane
- The data plane

Let's explore them now.

Management Plane

The management plane controls everything about logging in to a network device, including telnet and SSH access—not that we would ever use Telnet, right?

SNMP is also included in the management plane, which allows network monitoring systems to poll the device for information.

And HTTP and HTTPs are also part of the plane. Maybe you're thinking, "Cisco has got to have a web interface on routers!" In the IOS's early days, the web interface was, um. . .Well, it wasn't pretty. It was really just a way to run some IOS commands through a web page, and you would only turn it on if you were running an application on your router that required it, like Cisco Unified Call Manager Express. But now, with modern IOS-XE, the web interface is lovely, as shown in Figure 14.1. If the web interface looks familiar, we saw it when we worked on the Cisco 9800 controllers.

REST APIs are also considered management access, which we will discuss soon in another chapter. Ports like the console port, the AUX port, and the management port are also found here.

Control Plane

The control plane is really the brain of the router—it's where all the protocols are run and all the decisions are made. The goal of this plane is to generate all the necessary forwarding information to send the packet to its destination.

Lots of important things happen in the control plane: security functions like defining ACLs and NAT, if the packet needs to change its source, or if the destination changed. Of course, everything to do with routing protocols like OSFP, including forming adjacencies and learning the routes, occurs on this plane.

ARP is also a big part of the control plane because knowing how to reach the layer 2 address of the next hop is essential for the actual routing to occur. Other control plane protocols include STP, VTP, and MAC address tables on switches, as well as QoS and CDP/LLDP.

FIGURE 14.1 IOS-XE web interface

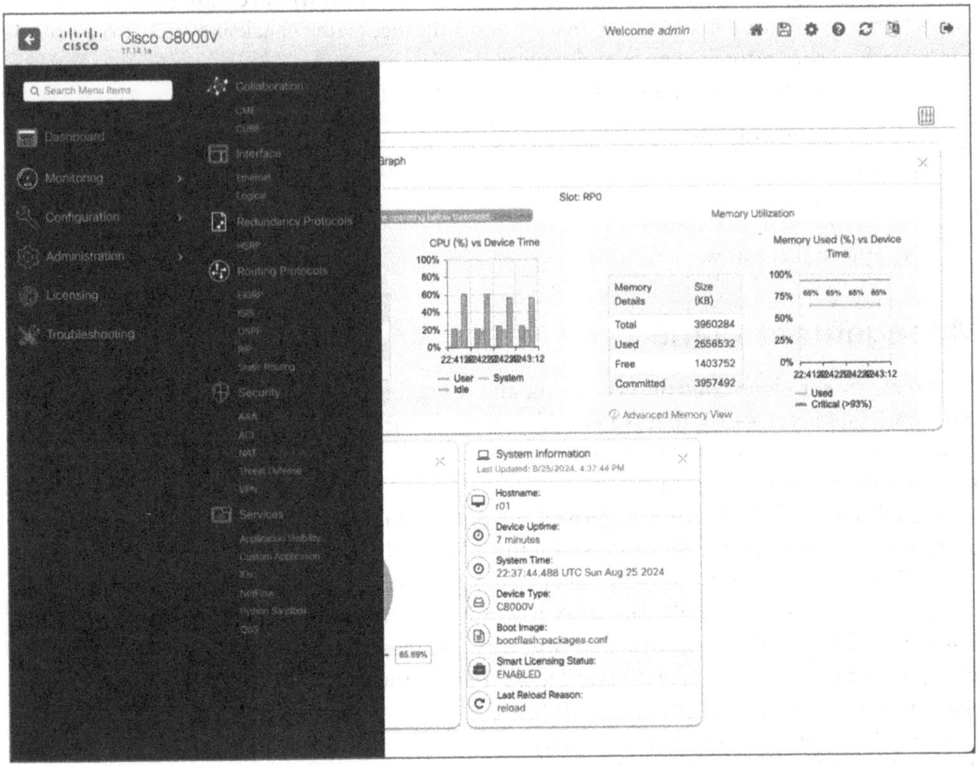

Data Plane

If the control plane is the router's brain, the data plane is its workhorse. The data plane's job is to take all the information presented from the control plane and use it to send the packet on its merry way.

Everything that happens in the data plane directly affects traffic. Activities like encapsulating and de-encapsulating traffic as it arrives at and leaves the router, adding and removing packet headers as needed, and actually dropping traffic that hits a deny statement on an ACL are all data plane tasks. Even the actual forwarding, where the packet moves from the inbound interface to the outbound interface, happens here as well.

Forwarding

Okay—now that you know what the planes are and what happens at each one, let's turn to how things work on the router. I'll start by walking through the steps R02 takes when it receives a packet from R01 that needs to be sent to R03.

First, have a look at the diagram below in Figure 14.2, which shows how the forwarding table is built from the routing table:

FIGURE 14.2 Forwarding traffic flow

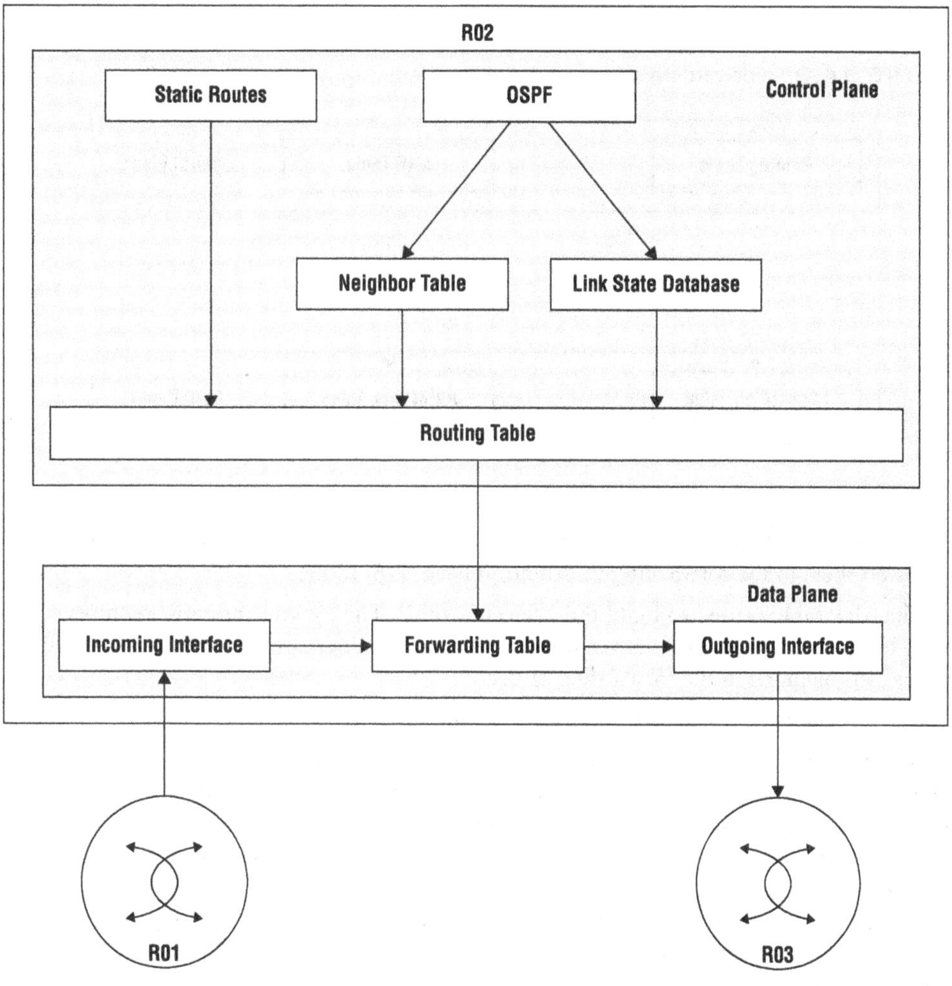

1. OSPF running on R02 will form an adjacency with R01 and R03. The control plane on R02 will then receive the routes via LSA information.
2. The link state advertisements go into the link state database (LSDB) on the three routers. The LSDB contains type 1 LSAs for each router and type 2 for the designated routers unless the OSPF network type has been changed.
3. The neighbor information is also kept track of in the neighbor table.

4. The neighbor table and LSDB are pushed to the routing table, where the best route is chosen. From here, the normal rules you're already familiar with apply, like lowest metric, lowest administrative distance, and longest match.

Now that the routing table has chosen routes, we can expand our diagram a bit to include more tables, as shown in Figure 14.3:

FIGURE 14.3 Forwarding table

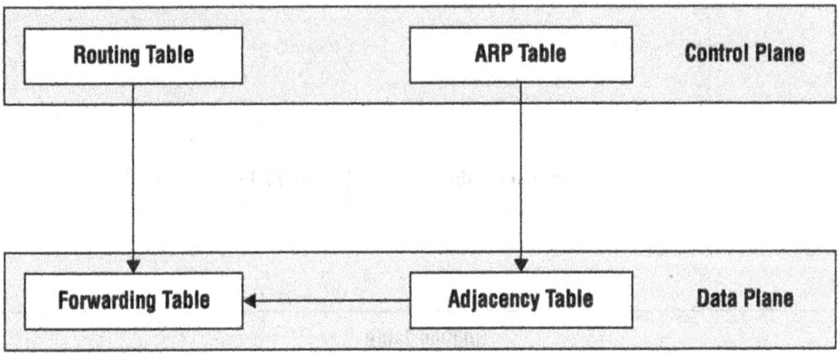

1. Cisco Express Forwarding (CEF) will take the best routes from the routing table and install them in the forwarding information base (FIB) table.
2. The ARP table is used to build the adjacency table. The forwarding table requires ARP to be resolved to the next hop before the route is considered valid. Protocols like PPP are also included in the forwarding table.
3. The information is pushed to hardware for forwarding.

The whole story about how this works is well above the CCNA level, but unpacking the information I've given you will really help when we start talking about SDN because we're going to be relocating the device's control plane onto an SDN controller.

Also, before we get into SDN, I want you to understand how much work it would be to add a new virtual machine that uses a new subnet and requires Internet access into a traditional three-tier architecture. We touched on this in the virtualization chapter, but let's focus more on the network changes this time. Check out Figure 14.4.

In general, we'd have to

1. Select a new VLAN and subnet to use—hopefully, we've got an IP address management solution!
2. Make sure the new VLAN is on all switches. VTP can be used for this.
3. We'd probably have to configure STP to ensure the new VLAN has the proper root switch.
4. We'd need to add the new VLAN to trunk allow lists.
5. The new VLAN would also need an SVI on each distributed switch, and an FHRP should also be used.

FIGURE 14.4 Full topology

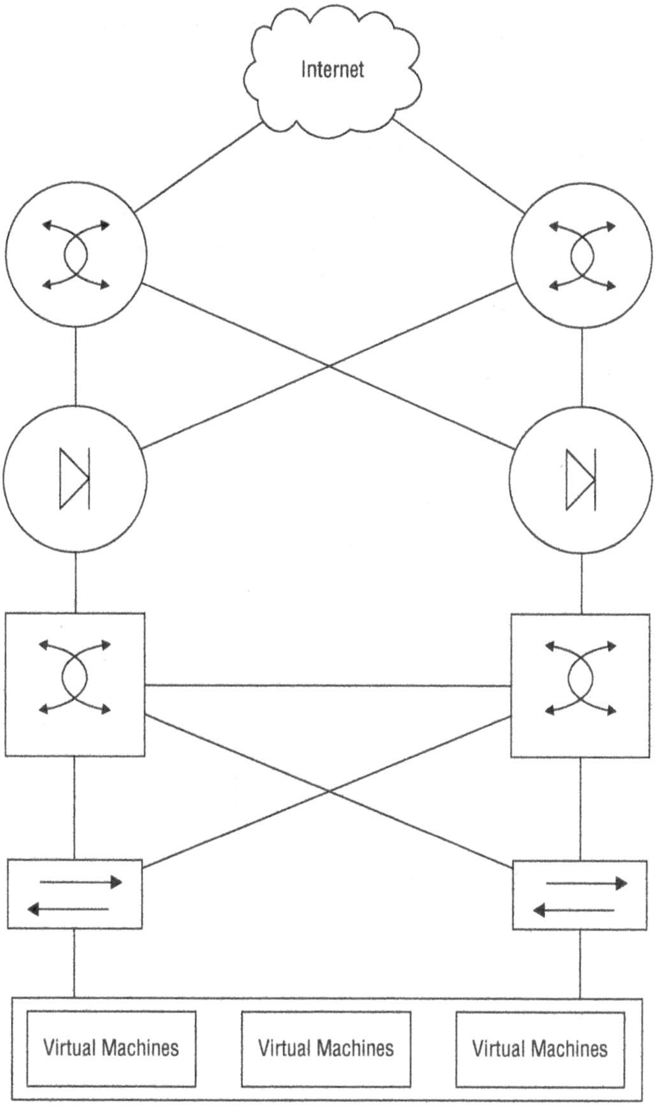

6. The new subnet would need to be added to the routing protocol.
7. Firewall rules would have to be updated to allow the new subnet through, and NAT would also need to be configured.
8. Depending on specific requirements, external routing might need to be adjusted.

Imagine receiving this request frequently as businesses are always creating new VMs. This places a significant burden on the network team, requiring extensive time to plan the changes, go through change control, and implement them. Additionally, this process introduces a lot of risk and increases the likelihood that the network won't be cleaned up after the VM is no longer needed. It's clear that adding a VM is a complex and impactful task.

Introduction to SDN

I will begin our journey into the world of SDN by introducing you to two of its important components: the northbound interface and the southbound interface. We gain access to the SDN solution via the northbound interface (NBI), which is actually similar to the management plane we just went over.

The SDN controller communicates with network-level devices through the southbound interface (SBI). Figure 14.5 gives you a picture of the architecture.

FIGURE 14.5 SDN architecture

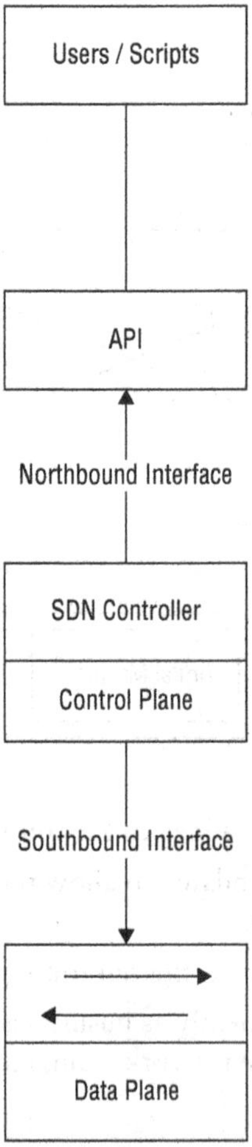

Northbound Interfaces

We access the SDN controller through the NBI. Most of the time, we do that via a GUI in Meraki or through a restful API call inside a script. The script can use whatever language we want because it will only call the restful API.

Some vital things we can do through the NBI are creating VLANs, getting a list of network devices, and polling the health of our networks. We can even automate the network to completely solve the scenario laid out at the beginning of this chapter!

Southbound Interfaces

As I said, the SBI is how the SDN controller actually talks with the network device, and there are lots of different ways it can do that, depending on your specific solution. For instance, OpenDaylight, one of the original open-source SDN controllers, uses a protocol called OpenFlow to talk to switches. On the other hand, Meraki is currently using a proprietary solution because it manages everything itself.

Here's a rundown of some common SBI protocols:

OpenFlow

This is an industry-standard API defined by the ONF (`opennetworking.org`). It configures nonproprietary, white-label switches and determines the flow path through the network. All configuration is done via NETCONF. OpenFlow first sends detailed and complex instructions to the control plane of the network elements to implement a new application policy. This is referred to as an *imperative* SDN model.

NETCONF

NETCONF (Network Configuration Protocol) is an increasingly popular standard for programmatically managing network devices. Standardized by the IETF, NETCONF offers a powerful and flexible way to install, modify, and delete device configurations across a network.

At its core, NETCONF uses remote procedure calls (RPCs) to communicate with network devices. These RPCs are encoded in XML, providing a structured and human-readable format for configuration data. The protocol typically operates over a secure SSH connection, ensuring that management operations are both safe and authenticated.

One of the key strengths of NETCONF is its ability to offer granular control over network configurations. Unlike traditional CLI-based management, which often involves sending command-line instructions one by one, NETCONF allows for more complex operations, such as atomic transactions. This means that changes can be committed as a single unit, reducing the risk of configuration errors and network downtime.

NETCONF's use of XML for data representation also makes it highly compatible with modern data interchange formats and tools, facilitating integration with other network management systems (NMSs) and automation frameworks. As a result, NETCONF is rapidly becoming the preferred protocol for network automation and orchestration in multivendor environments, enabling more efficient and scalable network management.

RESTCONF

RESTCONF is an emerging standard for network management that offers a simpler, more accessible approach compared to NETCONF. Although it shares similarities with NETCONF—such as its ability to manage network device configurations—RESTCONF differentiates itself by utilizing RESTful principles and HTTP-based communication.

RESTCONF operates over HTTPS, making it compatible with widely used web technologies and allowing it to integrate easily with modern web-based tools and applications. Instead of using XML over SSH like NETCONF, RESTCONF typically employs JSON or XML for data exchange over HTTP, which many developers find easier to work with, especially when scripting or integrating with RESTful APIs.

However, RESTCONF has some limitations compared to NETCONF. It doesn't offer the same level of advanced features, such as support for complex transactions or the ability to lock configurations during updates. Despite this, RESTCONF is appreciated for its simplicity and ease of use, particularly in environments where rapid development and integration with web services are priorities.

In summary, although RESTCONF may lack some of the advanced capabilities of NETCONF, it offers a more straightforward and accessible option for network management, particularly in scenarios where leveraging HTTP-based communication is advantageous. This makes RESTCONF a valuable tool in the growing landscape of network automation and programmability.

onePK

onePK (One Platform Kit) was Cisco's proprietary SBI designed to enable network programmability by allowing developers to inspect, modify, and manage network element configurations without requiring hardware upgrades. Introduced as part of Cisco's early efforts in SDN, onePK provided software development kits (SDKs) for Java, C, and Python, making it easier for developers to build network applications and automate network tasks.

One of the key benefits of onePK was its ability to give developers granular access to Cisco devices, enabling them to create custom network solutions and enhance network functionality without the need for significant infrastructure changes. This flexibility was particularly valuable in environments where hardware upgrades were cost-prohibitive or impractical.

However, onePK has since become a legacy solution, largely superseded by more modern and open standards like NETCONF, RESTCONF, and gNMI, which offer broader compatibility and are not tied to a single vendor. Despite this, onePK can still be found in existing network deployments, particularly in environments where organizations have invested heavily in Cisco technologies and have not yet transitioned to newer SDN frameworks.

In summary, although onePK was a significant step forward in enabling network programmability within Cisco environments, it has been overtaken by newer, more open standards. Nonetheless, understanding onePK is still valuable for working with legacy Cisco networks where it may still be in use.

OpFlex

OpFlex is a southbound API used in Cisco's Application Centric Infrastructure (ACI) to enable communication between the central controller, known as the Application Policy Infrastructure Controller (APIC), and network devices. Unlike traditional imperative SDN models, where the controller directly dictates specific configurations to network devices, OpFlex operates using a declarative SDN model.

In this model, the APIC sends high-level, abstract policies—often referred to as *summary policies*—to the network devices. These policies outline the desired state of the network without specifying the exact steps to achieve it. The network devices, which maintain some level of control plane functionality, interpret these policies and autonomously implement the necessary configurations to achieve the desired state.

This approach allows for a partially centralized control plane, where the APIC manages overall policy while distributing the enforcement and implementation tasks to the network devices. This distribution of intelligence reduces the load on the controller and enhances network scalability and resilience. OpFlex's design enables the network to continue functioning even if the central controller becomes temporarily unavailable, as the network devices can operate based on the last known policies.

By using OpFlex, Cisco ACI provides a more flexible and scalable way to manage complex networks, allowing operators to focus on defining high-level business and application policies rather than dealing with low-level configuration details on individual network devices.

SDN Solutions

There are myriad SDN controller solutions on the market today. Here's a list of the ones you might come across:

Cisco APIC-EM This was Cisco's first real attempt at an enterprise SDN controller. Its focus was configuring Cisco's IWAN solution, although it also tried to make it easier to configure QoS. These days, APIC-EM is considered a legacy, and I doubt you could find one in production; APIC-EM was succeeded by Catalyst Center.

Cisco Catalyst Center This is Cisco's main enterprise SDN controller, which we'll explore soon! It was known as DNA Center until a rebranding in late 2023.

Cisco ACI Cisco ACI is Cisco's SDN solution that offers a comprehensive framework to manage and automate data center infrastructure. ACI is designed to simplify the complexity of modern data centers by integrating hardware and software in a unified, policy-driven architecture. It provides centralized management, automation, and a programmable network infrastructure that can dynamically respond to the needs of applications.

You can learn more about ACI in Cisco's Data Center track.

Cisco SD-WAN Cisco SD-WAN is a software-defined wide area network (SD-WAN) solution that enables enterprises to securely connect their branches, data centers, and cloud environments over a mix of private and public networks. By abstracting the underlying network infrastructure, Cisco SD-WAN allows for centralized management, intelligent path selection, enhanced security, and improved application performance across the WAN.

This solution brings the benefits of SDN to the WAN. You'll learn more about SD-WAN when you tackle the CCNP Enterprise.

OpenDaylight ODL is a somewhat popular open-source OpenFlow controller. Cisco used to offer some OpenFlow support in its switches, but the company has largely moved away from supporting OpenFlow. This is because Cisco prefers its own SDN solutions due to OpenFlow limitations. Figure 14.6 shows an example of OpenDaylight.

FIGURE 14.6 OpenDaylight topology

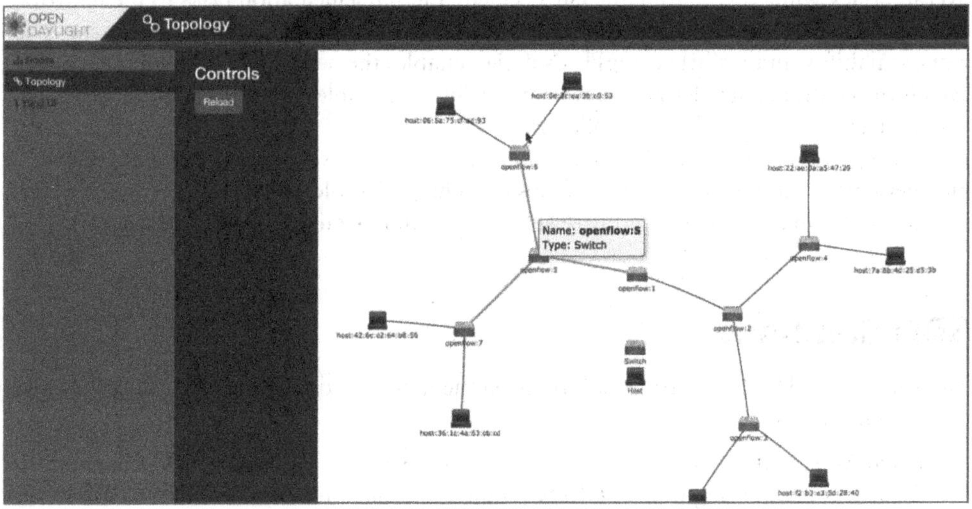

Controller-Based Architectures

SDN can actually mean lots of things, but it generally refers to separating the control plane from the data plane on a network device. Of course, this is a big help in device management because devices can be centrally managed by a controller, instead of manually.

Let's look at how things work on a plain, vanilla switch. Each device has a separate control plane, and traffic is sent through interfaces in the data plane. Figure 14.7 shows a simple switch topology. There is nothing special here yet; I am just pointing out that each switch in the topology has its own control plane and data plane.

A great example of separating the control plane without plunging too deeply down the rabbit hole is Meraki (covered in Chapter 12). We touched on it in the first book when we talked about cloud management, but it is useful for demonstrating SDN as well. Everything

FIGURE 14.7 Switch control plane

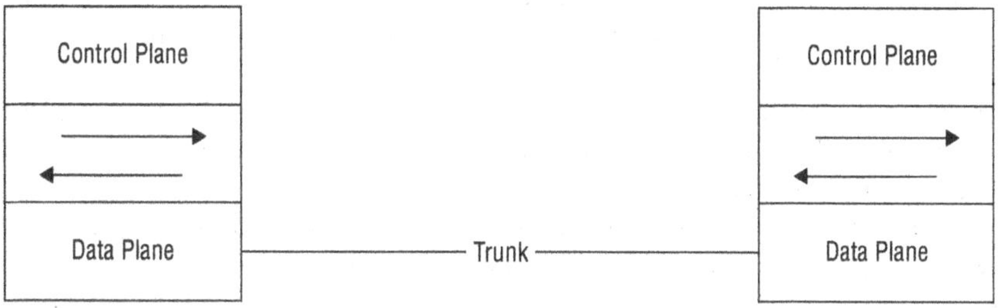

in Meraki's lineup is totally managed by the cloud, which means actual devices really only provide the data plane because they receive their control plane configurations from the cloud application. Figure 14.8 shows an SDN control plane.

FIGURE 14.8 SDN control plane

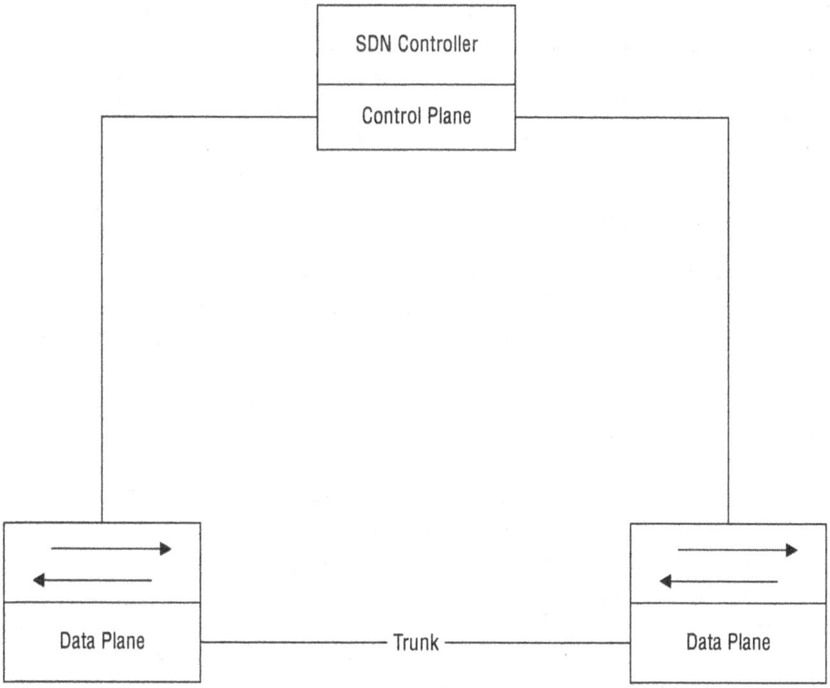

Another good central management example is brought to you by the Cisco wireless LAN controller or its new 9800 ones. The access points (APs) that join the WLC aren't too bright on their own, so they rely on the controller to push the configuration and tell them what to do.

Cisco SDN solutions like Catalyst Center/DNA Center, which we'll talk about soon, allow you to centrally manage your network device's configuration through several applications that live on the SDN controller.

This is better than traditional configuration because if you need to make changes to your network, you adjust the settings in DNA Center to be replicated to your network's relevant devices.

This is beautiful because it ensures that configuration is consistent everywhere at once, significantly reducing the risk of death by typo when making a change on 50 switches manually—nice!

Of course, there's a downside to central management. For instance, say I were to accidentally type in **switchport trunk allowed vlan 10** instead of **switchport trunk allowed vlan add 10** on a switch. I'd probably cause an outage I'd have to scramble to fix, but it wouldn't be the end of the world. On the other hand, if I made that same mistake on a template, I'm pushing to all my switches. Well, that could be apocalyptic if I didn't have any way of rolling back those changes—time to make sure the old resume is up to date for sure!

Fortunately, we can usually build out our configurations in the controller before applying them, maybe even getting someone to peer review them before sending them away.

Controllers also provide a convenient central point for monitoring and automation, as they're usually aware of a large part, if not all, of the network.

Campus Architecture

Just so you know, the only type of architecture we've covered so far is the campus architecture that's most commonly used in traditional enterprise networks. And in case you need a quick review, switches are connected to each other in a hierarchical fashion in this kind of architecture. The upside to this approach is that troubleshooting is easy because the stuff that belongs in each layer of the model is well defined, just like how the OSI model makes it easier to understand what's happening on the network and where.

All the endpoints in the network connect to the Access layer, where VLANs are assigned. Port-level features like port security or 802.1X are applied at this layer. Because Access layer switches don't have many responsibilities and generally require no layer 3 configuration aside from what's needed for managing the switch, you can usually get away with cheaper layer 2 switches and save some coin.

The Distribution layer hosts all the SVIs and provides any IP-based services the network needs, like DHCP relay. The distribution switch uses layer 2 interfaces with the Access layer switches to terminate the VLANs, plus layer 3 interfaces to connect to the core switches. It will also run a routing protocol to share routes with them.

The Core layer's only job is providing high-speed routing between the distribution switches. It doesn't offer any other services—it just makes sure packets get from one switch to another. Here's an example of a campus topology in Figure 14.9.

FIGURE 14.9 Campus fabric

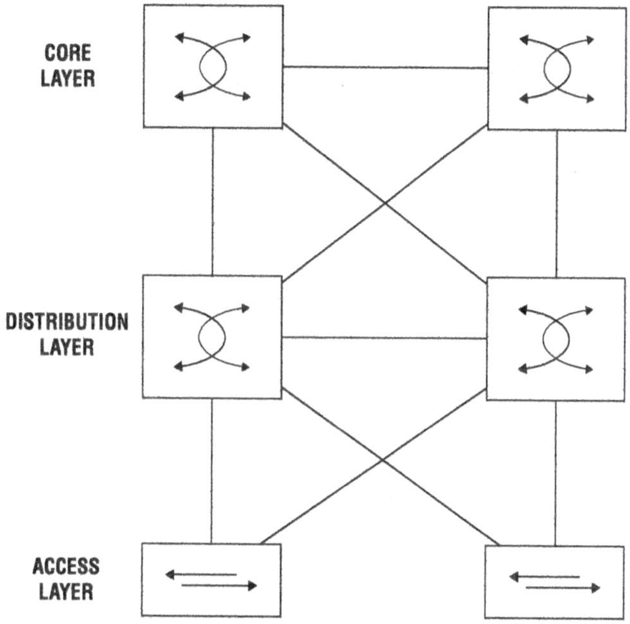

Spine/Leaf Architecture

The new and preferred architecture for controller-based networks and data centers is called CLOS, which stands for nothing other than the guy's name who thought it up. CLOS is a spine/leaf design wherein you have two types of switches: a spine and a leaf.

The leaf switch maps to the Access and Distribution layers in the Cisco three-tier model and is what you connect your devices to. Each leaf switch has a high-bandwidth uplink to each spine switch.

The spine switch is a lot like the core because its sole job is to provide super-fast transport across the leaf switches. Because leaf switches only connect to the spine switches, not other leaf switches, traffic is really predictable because all destinations in the fabric follow the same path: leaf -> spine -> leaf. Because everything is three hops away, traffic is easily load-balanced in the routing table via equal-cost load balancing (ECMP).

What's more, it's also very easy to expand the network. If you need more ports, just add a leaf switch. Need more bandwidth? Just add another spine switch. Figure 14.10 shows the CLOS topology.

FIGURE 14.10 CLOS topology

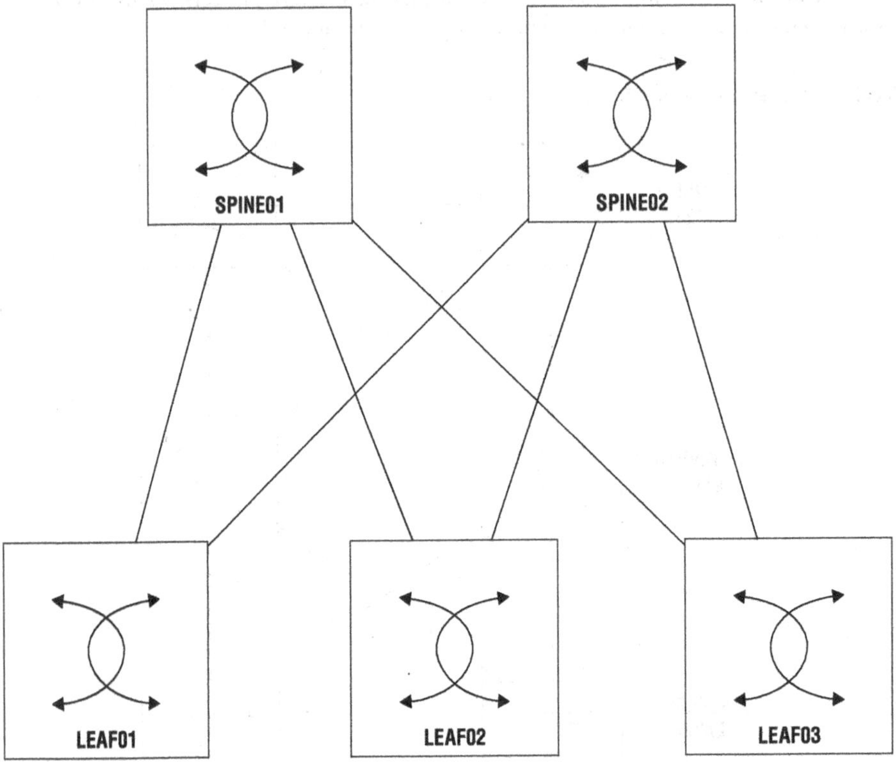

SDN Network Components

One of the benefits of SDN is that an SDN controller can abstract away the "boring stuff" so you can focus on the fun, more complex configurations.

One-way SDN achieves this is by dividing the network into two different parts. An *underlay* is a physical network that is focused on providing a lot of layer 3 connectivity throughout the network. The underlay typically uses the spine/leaf architecture we just discussed but can also use the campus architecture, depending on the solution being used. For example, DNA Center's Software Defined Access solution uses a typical campus topology because it is aimed at enterprise networks.

There is also the *overlay* component, which is where the services the SDN controller provides are tunneled over the underlay.

We'll look closer at the underlay and overlay in more detail.

Underlay

The underlay has its own components, and we'll cover each of them in this section:

- MTU
- Interface Config
- OSPF Config
- Verification

The underlay is basically the physical network that provides connectivity so that the overlay network can be built on or over it. It usually has a basic configuration, and its focus is to advertise the device's loopback IP into OSPF or IS-IS so the overlay can peer with each device, usually using BGP.

Devices in the underlay tend to be cabled in a highly redundant manner that removes single points of failure and optimizes performance. One way to implement this is via a full mesh topology, where every device is connected to every other device. Even though a full mesh network provides maximum redundancy, it can get out of hand fast because of the number of links involved as your network grows. Figure 14.11 shows an example of a standard underlay topology.

FIGURE 14.11 Underlay topology

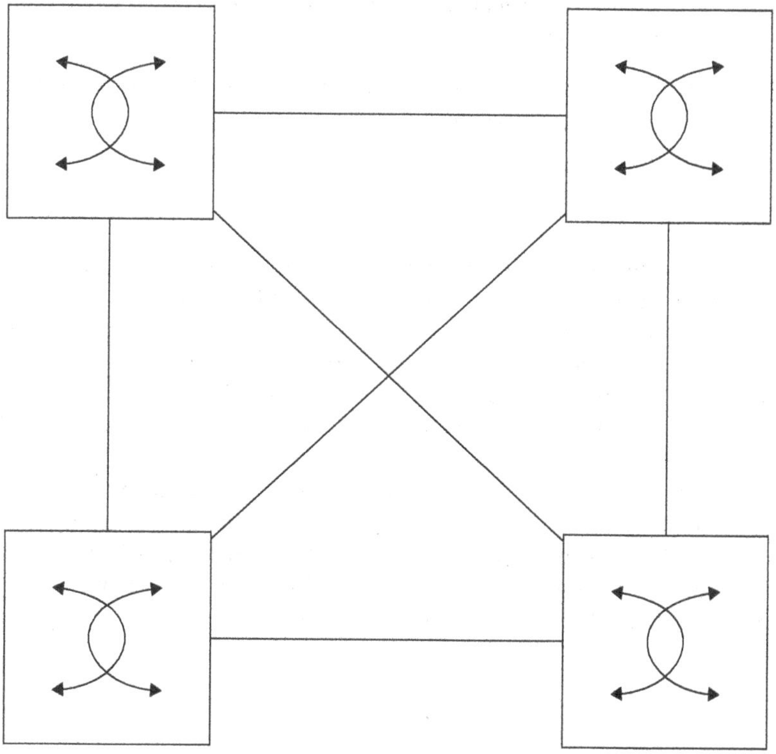

MTU

The underlay's job is to carry a lot of traffic with larger packet payloads than you'd normally see in a standard network. Because of this, raising the MTU on the underlay switches is a good idea so the larger packets don't give you any grief.

You change the MTU on most Cisco IOS or IOS-XE-based switches via the `system mtu` command. The switch must be rebooted for the change to take effect:

```
SW01(config)#system mtu ?
 <1500-9198>  MTU size in bytes

SW01(config)#system mtu 9000
Global Ethernet MTU is set to 9000 bytes.
Note: this is the Ethernet payload size, not the total
Ethernet frame size, which includes the Ethernet
header/trailer and possibly other tags, such as ISL or
802.1q tags.
SW01(config)#do reload
```

NOTE OSPF requires the MTU to match on both ends of the neighbor adjacency to work properly, so when the MTU is changed, it has to be changed on neighboring devices, too. To get around this, you can apply the `ip ospf mtu-ignore` command on neighboring interfaces to fix OSPF without changing the MTU.

Because the underlay will be running a routing protocol, `ip routing` needs to be enabled to make it act as a layer 3 switch:

```
SW01(config)#ip routing
```

Interface Config

It's a bad idea to go with running STP in an underlay topology. Its job is to block redundant links—which is a problem because it results in the underlay switch's superfast uplink interfaces that clock in between 10Gbps, 40 gbs, and even 800 gbs if we are running AI workloads—not always being used. What a waste! You can mitigate this by spending (wasting) a bunch of time adjusting the STP configuration by spreading the VLAN root across several switches, but it really won't solve the problem because each VLAN will still have blocked links.

The better way to handle this is to use only layer 3 interfaces. Doing this means STP won't run at all, so all the switch interfaces in the underlay will also run without being blocked. Plus, there won't be any loops to worry about because it's just OSPF doing the routing. As a further bonus, because the switches should all have the same number of connections, the routing table can load-balance traffic using ECMP!

With all that in mind, I will configure the interfaces connecting the switches as layer 3 interfaces and give them an IP address. To be more efficient, I'll also configure OSPF on the interfaces to use the point-to-point network type to remove the need for a designated router, like this:

```
SW01(config)#int g3/0
SW01(config-if)#no switchport
SW01(config-if)#ip address 10.1.21.1 255.255.255.0
SW01(config-if)#ip ospf network point-to-point

SW01(config-if)#int g3/1
SW01(config-if)#no switchport
SW01(config-if)#ip address 10.1.22.1 255.255.255.0
SW01(config-if)#ip ospf network point-to-point

SW01(config-if)#int g3/2
SW01(config-if)#no switchport
SW01(config-if)#ip address 10.1.31.1 255.255.255.0
SW01(config-if)#ip ospf network point-to-point

SW01(config-if)#int g3/3
SW01(config-if)#no switchport
SW01(config-if)#ip address 10.1.32.1 255.255.255.0
SW01(config-if)#ip ospf network point-to-point

SW01(config-if)#int g2/2
SW01(config-if)#no switchport
SW01(config-if)#ip address 10.1.41.1 255.255.255.0
SW01(config-if)#ip ospf network point-to-point

SW01(config-if)#int g2/3
SW01(config-if)#no switchport
SW01(config-if)#ip address 10.1.42.1 255.255.255.0
SW01(config-if)#ip ospf network point-to-point
```

Each switch in the underlay should have a loopback interface for later when we talk about the overlay:

```
SW01(config-if)#interface loopback 0
SW01(config-if)#ip add 192.168.255.1 255.255.255.255
```

OSPF Config

Next, OSPF needs to be configured. There's really nothing wrong with using another routing protocol like EIGRP here, but because the CCNA only focuses on OSPF, I'm going with that. I want all IPs on the switch to run OSPF, so I'll use the `network 0.0.0.0 0.0.0.0 area 0` shortcut to enable all interfaces:

```
SW01(config-if)#router ospf 1
SW01(config-router)#network 0.0.0.0 0.0.0.0 area 0
SW01(config-router)#exit
```

Other Underlay Config

The underlay's focus is to ensure routing is working, so there isn't much else to add to the configuration aside from a standard switch setup like configuring AAA or NTP. Some solutions require features like multicast routing, but that's above the CCNA level.

Verification

To save some typing time, I went ahead and configured the other switches in the topology, just like I showed you with SW01. At this point, we can see that all the switch interfaces have formed an OSPF adjacency:

```
SW01#show ip ospf nei

Neighbor ID      Pri   State           Dead Time   Address     Interface
192.168.255.3      0   FULL/  -        00:00:38    10.1.32.3   GigabitEthernet3/3
192.168.255.3      0   FULL/  -        00:00:37    10.1.31.3   GigabitEthernet3/2
192.168.255.2      0   FULL/  -        00:00:37    10.1.22.2   GigabitEthernet3/1
192.168.255.2      0   FULL/  -        00:00:37    10.1.21.2   GigabitEthernet3/0
192.168.255.4      0   FULL/  -        00:00:34    10.1.42.4   GigabitEthernet2/3
192.168.255.4      0   FULL/  -        00:00:34    10.1.41.4   GigabitEthernet2/2
```

When I look at the routing table, I see that SW01 has learned each switch's loopback address and is load-balancing the route across two interfaces because of ECMP:

```
SW01#show ip route ospf | b 192.168.255

         192.168.255.0/32 is subnetted, 4 subnets
O        192.168.255.2 [110/2] via 10.1.22.2, 00:11:52, GigabitEthernet3/1
        [110/2] via 10.1.21.2, 00:12:02, GigabitEthernet3/0
O        192.168.255.3 [110/2] via 10.1.32.3, 00:04:32, GigabitEthernet3/3
        [110/2] via 10.1.31.3, 00:04:42, GigabitEthernet3/2
O        192.168.255.4 [110/2] via 10.1.42.4, 00:01:40, GigabitEthernet2/3
                       [110/2] via 10.1.41.4, 00:01:40, GigabitEthernet2/2
```

Okay—we're done! The underlay is now all set and ready for the overlay configuration.

Overlay

An overlay is a "virtual network" that's tunneled over your underlay devices. This allows the SDN controller to have strict control over the traffic running through the network. The type of tunnel being used varies depending on the exact SDN solution, but generally, it uses virtual extensible LAN (VXLAN). VXLAN is a way of tunneling layer 2 traffic over layer 3. This allows you to connect VLANs across routed networks, but the details are above the CCNA level.

The overlay is where advanced configurations like security or QoS are introduced into the network. The underlay has no visibility into the tunneled networks, so it can't effectively do things like filter traffic.

Routing for the overlay is usually handled by BGP or EIGRP. Link-state protocols are a bad idea because they require all devices in an area to have the same LSAs. Plus, you can't easily improve the routing table with summaries, etc.

Dynamic multipoint virtual private network (DMVPN) is a very popular type of overlay that runs over the WAN. In this topology, each branch connects to the hub router through DMVPN using the 10.100.123.0/24 network. This allows us to run an IGP across the Internet to provide that all-important, consistent routing factor. DMVPN actually offers lots of advantages, but for now, check out Figure 14.12 for a simple example of an overlay:

Fabric

The network fabric is actually the simplest thing in this chapter to understand. It's really just a shorthand term for all the layer 3 network devices—the routers, switches, firewalls, wireless controllers, and APs involved in a solution. We can refer to the network as a *fabric* when we're talking about SDN, because the SDN controller abstracts the network details.

Put another way, a fabric is a simple, high-speed, layer 3 network. The motivation behind this trend is that IP networks scale better than layer 2 networks because we don't need to work a bunch of complex engineering magic to get around STP limitations. Also, layer 3 fabric isn't usually as risky when it comes to misconfigurations because the SDN controller dynamically builds and maintains the underlay and overlay networks for you!

FIGURE 14.12 DMVPN topology

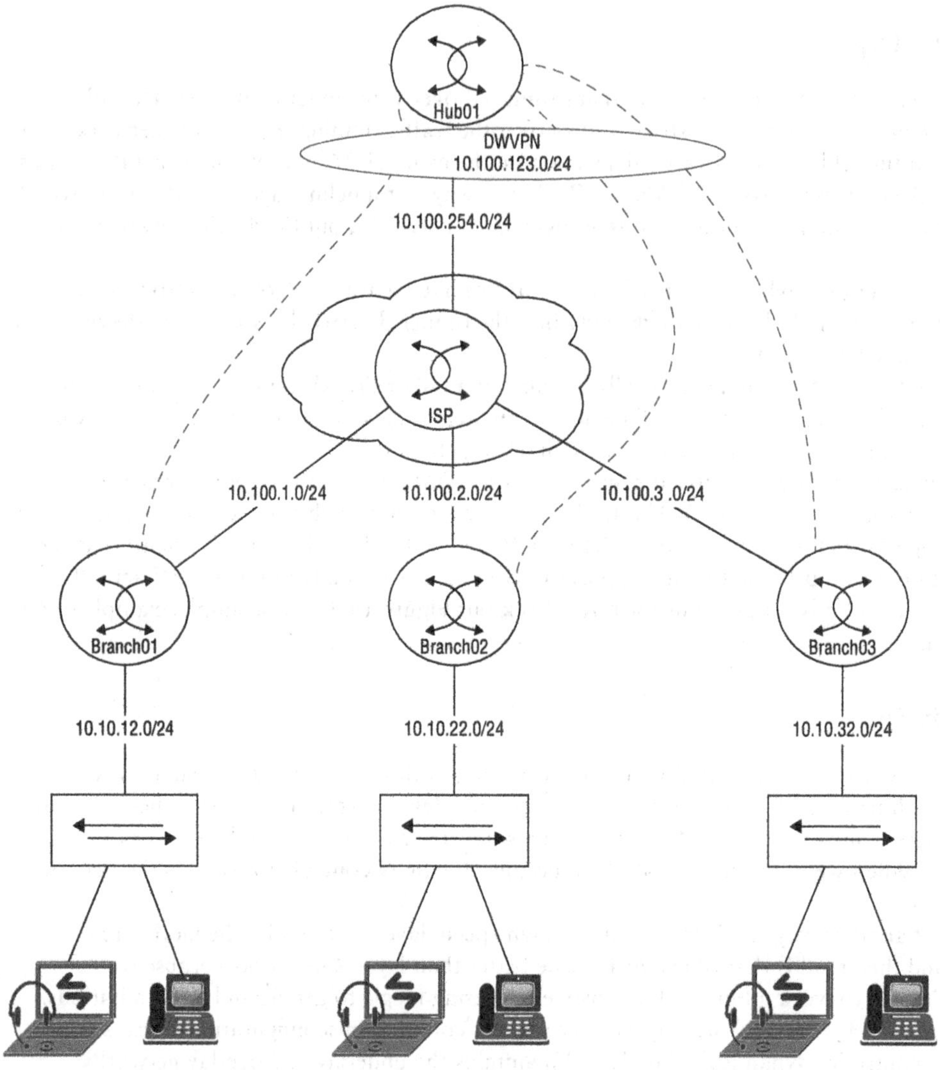

Catalyst Center Overview

The rest of this chapter will be spent reviewing some Catalyst Center features. First things first: Catalyst Center used to be called DNA Center, so you can expect to see both names being used interchangeably for a long time.

The gist is that Catalyst Center attempts to be a bit of a networking Swiss Army knife in the sense that it is an SDN controller that offers many different applications to try to make your life easier. It can do everything from simply monitoring your network to providing detailed network troubleshooting to full-on network automation. Let's dive into it!

Discovery

Before Cisco Catalyst Center can effectively manage your network, it needs to know how to access your network devices. The Discovery application streamlines this process by allowing you to automatically scan your network to identify and onboard new devices into the Catalyst Center.

To start, you provide the necessary device credentials and specify the networks or IP ranges you want to scan. Once the scan begins, the Discovery app searches for devices and attempts to establish connections using various protocols such as SSH, Telnet, NETCONF, and HTTPS, depending on the device's capabilities.

Upon successfully connecting to a device, the app gathers extensive information, including the device's configuration, routing tables, and other key details. This information is then used to integrate the device into Catalyst Center, enabling centralized management and monitoring. Figure 14.13 illustrates the Discovery app interface, highlighting its user-friendly approach to device discovery and onboarding.

FIGURE 14.13 Discovery app

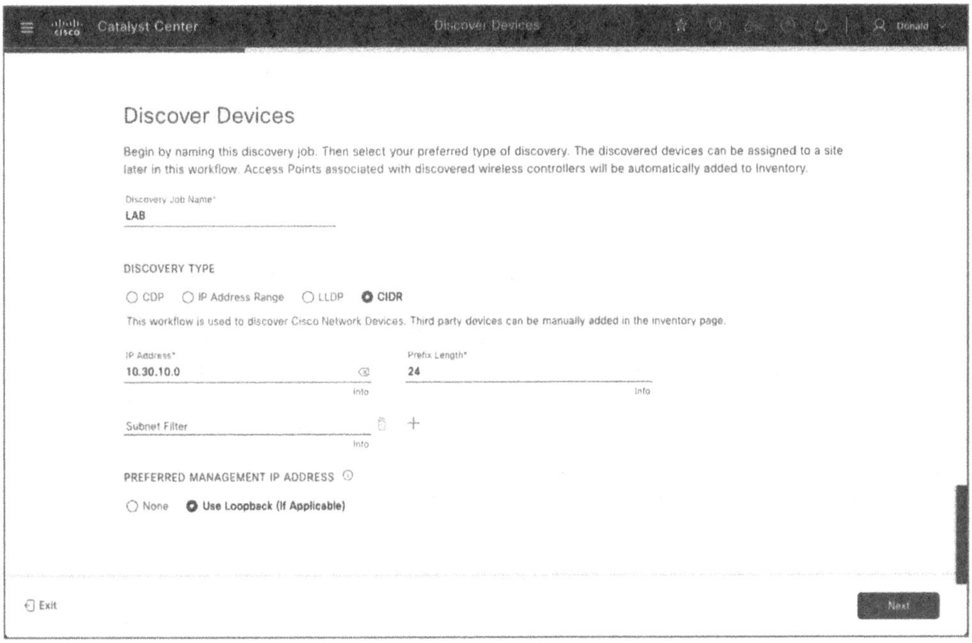

Network Hierarchy/Network Settings

One of the standout benefits that Catalyst Center offers is the ability to organize your network into structured sites and locations using the Network Hierarchy feature, as shown in Figure 14.14.

FIGURE 14.14 Network Hierarchy app

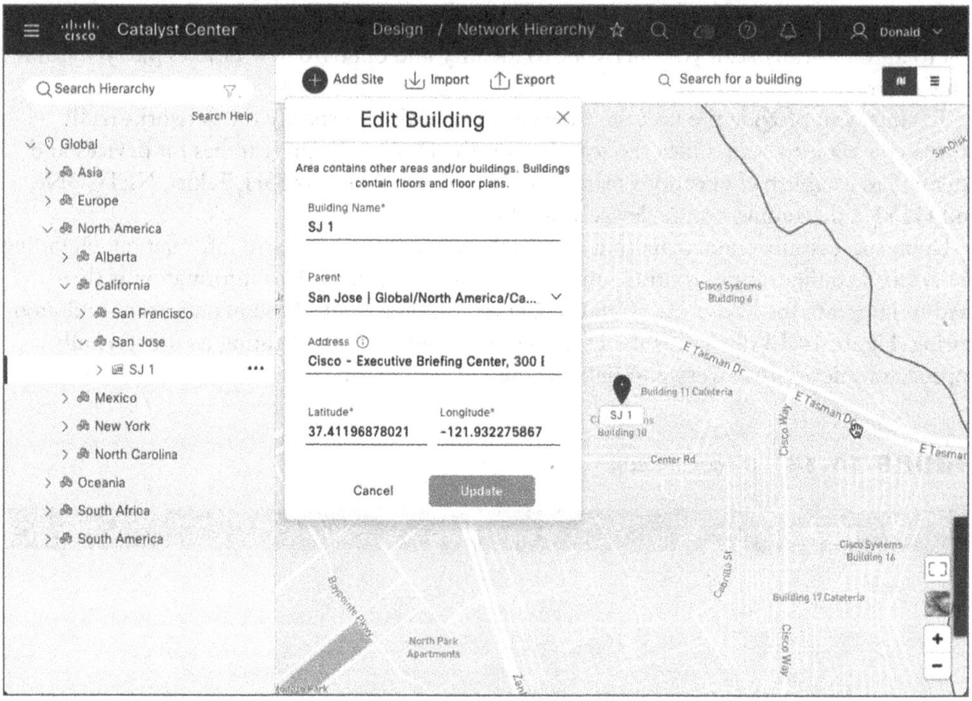

This feature not only enhances troubleshooting by providing a clear, logical view of your network's layout but also offers site-specific configurations to wireless controllers and ensures consistent settings across multiple locations. Common configurations like authentication, syslog servers, NTP servers, and even the message of the day can be automatically applied to network devices as they are onboarded into the inventory. This helps prevent issues like outdated configurations on devices after a change, such as an NTP server's IP address—updating the setting once in Catalyst Center propagates it across your network. See Figure 14.15 for an overview of how these settings are managed.

FIGURE 14.15 Network settings

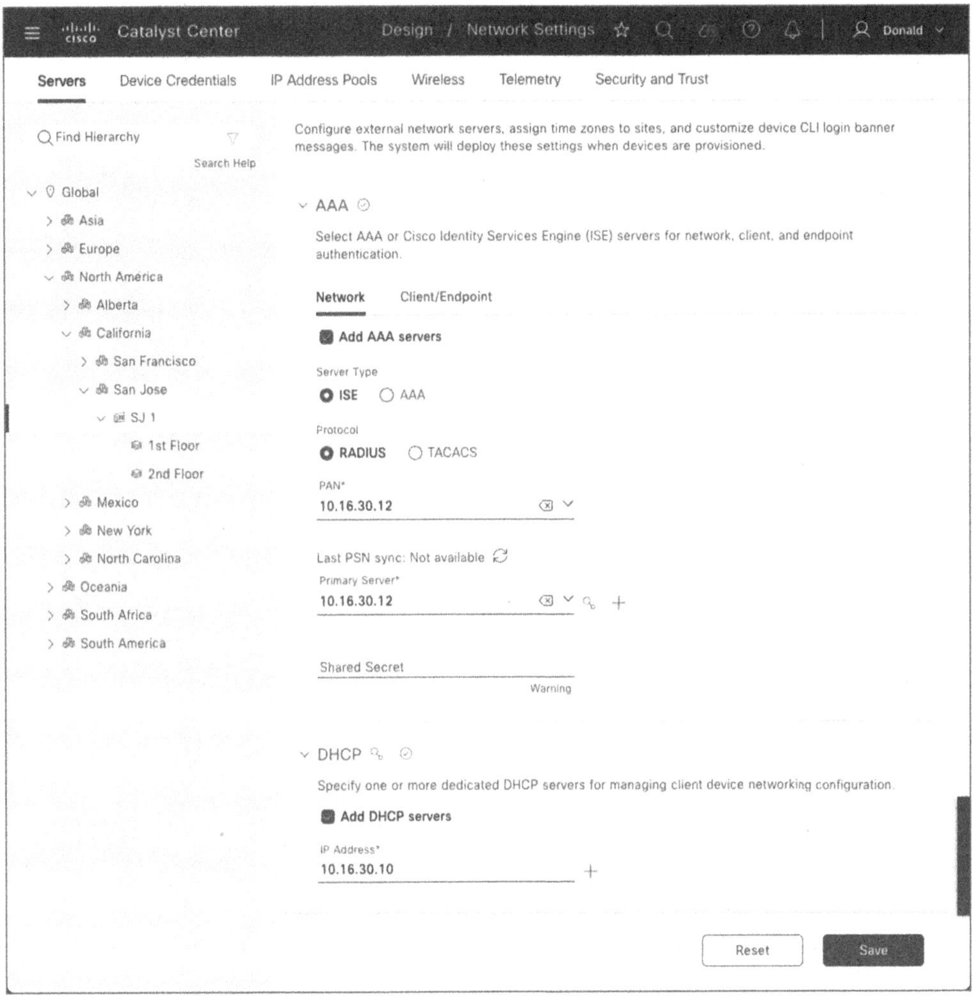

Catalyst Center can also fully manage your wireless environment. For example, when you add a new SSID, you can easily configure it using the Network Hierarchy tool, allowing you to apply wireless settings uniformly across multiple wireless LAN controllers (WLCs). This is particularly useful in large-scale deployments where configuration consistency is critical. Refer to Figure 14.16 to see how wireless settings are integrated.

Unlike traditional network configuration managers (NCM) like SolarWinds, which offer a feature called Compliance that alerts you when a device's configuration deviates from the defined standard, Catalyst Center goes a step further. It not only monitors but also actively enforces configuration consistency across your network. Additionally, although NCMs typically require you to manage each device individually and offer limited support for wireless controllers due to the need for deep vendor knowledge, Catalyst Center leverages its in-depth

FIGURE 14.16 Wireless settings

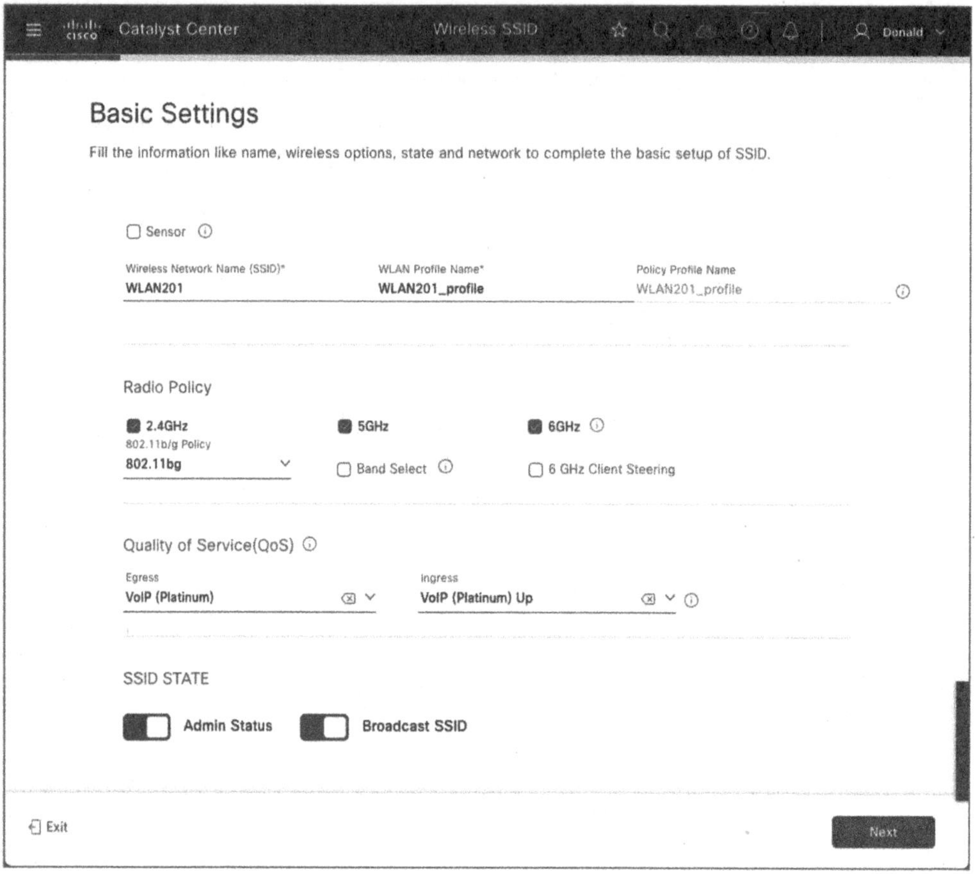

integration with Cisco devices to provide comprehensive management across both wired and wireless networks.

However, it's important to note that Catalyst Center currently lacks built-in support for device configuration backups. For now, you'll still need to rely on tools like SolarWinds and Cisco Prime Infrastructure to handle backups. That said, Catalyst Center is under rapid development, so a robust backup feature may soon be available.

Without a tool like Catalyst Center, keeping your network configuration up-to-date would be a cumbersome process, requiring frequent logins to each device to ensure that configurations remain consistent and aligned with your needs. Over time, configurations evolve due to troubleshooting or changes, making centralized management even more essential.

CLI Templates

Although the Network Settings feature in Catalyst Center is excellent for maintaining consistent configurations across your network, there are times when you need more customization and flexibility. This is where the CLI Templates feature shines. With CLI Templates, you can push complex configurations to multiple devices efficiently.

You have the option to manually enter commands line by line, applying them across your network sites. However, the real power of CLI Templates lies in Catalyst Center's integration with scripting engines like Apache Velocity and Jinja2. These engines allow you to automate the creation of configurations, making it easier to implement advanced setups, such as applying 802.1X configurations across all your access switches. By leveraging variables within these templates, you ensure that the generated configuration is tailored to the specific requirements of each device, avoiding manual errors and saving significant time.

We'll delve deeper into Jinja2 in the automation chapter, where you'll see just how powerful and versatile these templates can be. For now, Figure 14.17 provides a glimpse of what an Apache Velocity template looks like in practice.

FIGURE 14.17 Apache Velocity template

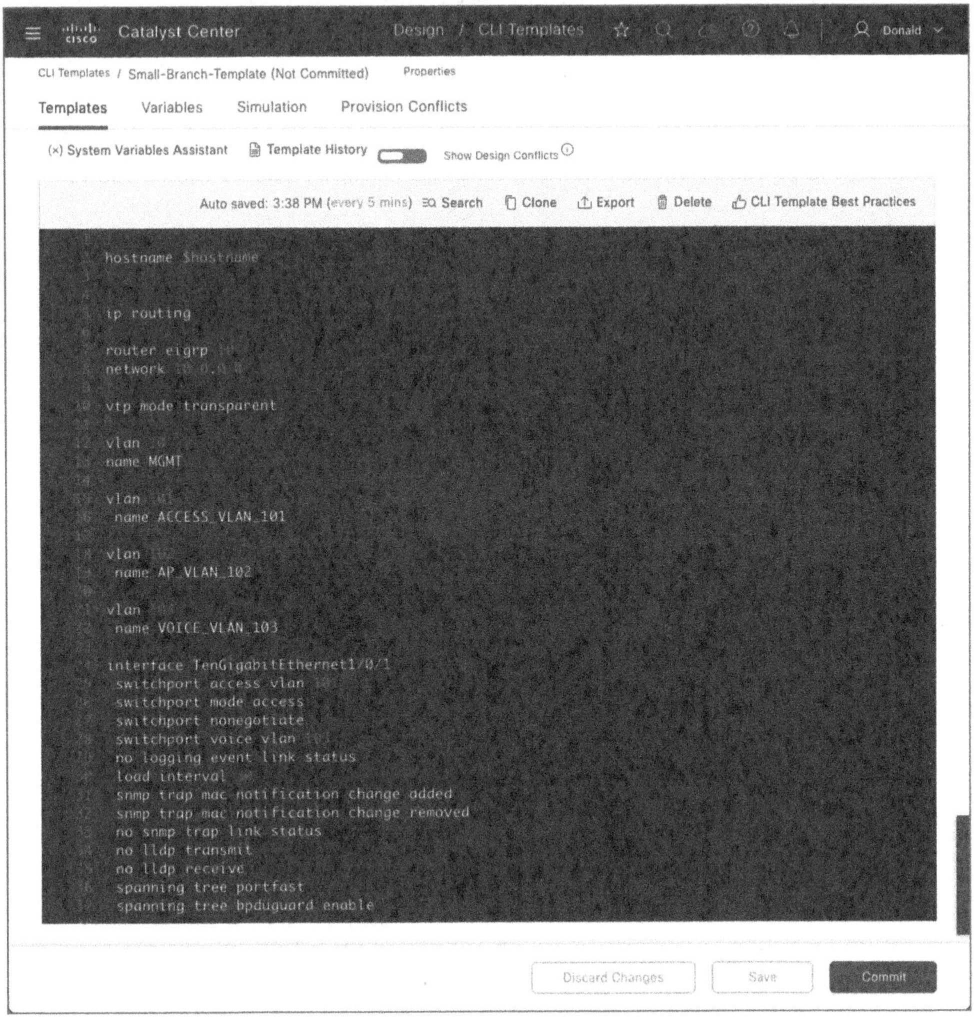

Topology

Catalyst Center's Topology feature automatically builds a dynamic layer 3 network diagram using the devices it discovers. This is a significant advantage over relying on static Visio diagrams, which often become outdated quickly. The topology is generated using information from protocols like CDP (Cisco Discovery Protocol) and LLDP (Link Layer Discovery Protocol), along with insights from MAC and ARP tables, to accurately map device connections.

If the generated map isn't entirely accurate, you can easily tweak it manually to reflect the true network layout. The Topology feature is also essential for informing other Catalyst Center functionalities, such as SD-Access, ensuring that the network is efficiently managed and visualized.

Figure 14.18 offers a snapshot of what the Topology map looks like:

FIGURE 14.18 Topology map

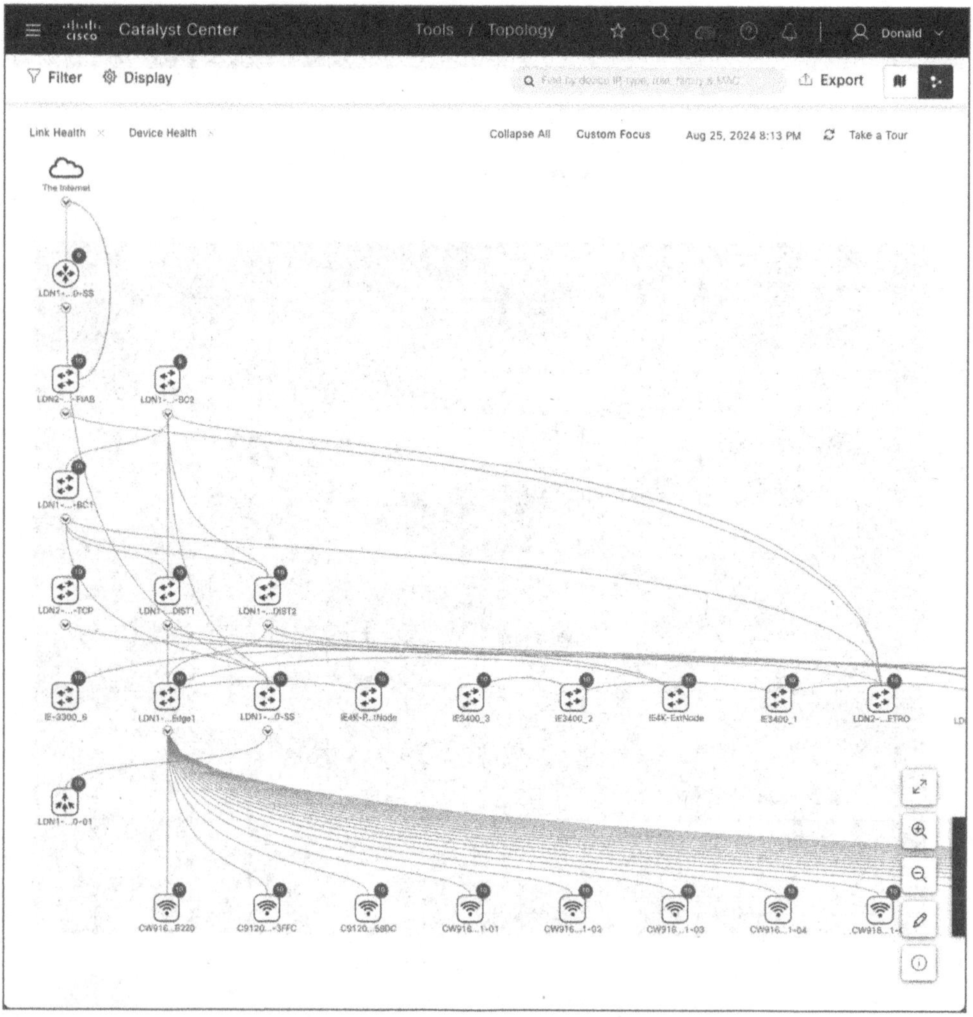

Although traditional NMSs like SolarWinds can create network maps, these are often manually constructed by the network team. Maintaining such maps in tools like Visio can be tedious, and it's rare to find anyone eager to continually update these documents!

Catalyst Center simplifies this process by dynamically creating and updating the network topology for you. Although you may need to make some manual adjustments to ensure accuracy, Catalyst Center handles most of the work, keeping your network documentation current and your troubleshooting efforts more effective.

Command Runner

One of the significant advantages of central management with Catalyst Center is the ability to efficiently manage and interact with multiple devices simultaneously. The Command Runner tool exemplifies this by allowing you to execute commands across all devices in your inventory and conveniently store the results. This feature is particularly useful for quickly verifying network-wide configurations, such as ensuring all routers recognize a new OSPF route.

A key benefit of Command Runner is the ability to export the command output as a text file, making it easy to store, share, or incorporate into documentation. However, it's important to note that Command Runner is designed for running show or diagnostic commands—configuration changes are not supported. For pushing configuration updates, you'll need to use the CLI Template feature. Figure 14.19 provides a glimpse of the Command Runner interface.

FIGURE 14.19 Command Runner

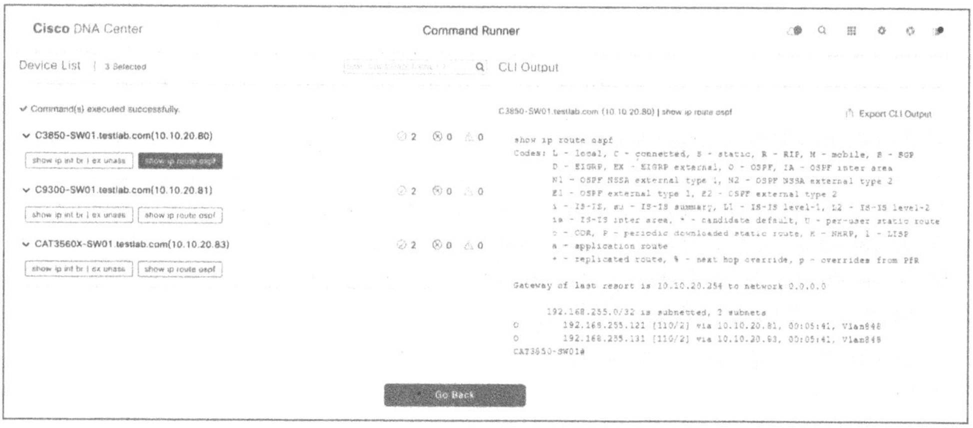

Both Catalyst Center and traditional NCMs offer similar functionalities, allowing you to run commands across multiple devices and neatly present the output. Without a centralized solution like this, you would have to manually connect to each device individually, run the commands, and then save or email the output—an inefficient and time-consuming process.

Assurance

In network management, it's all too common for the network to be blamed when issues arise, even when it's not at fault. As a network professional, you'll spend a significant portion of your time troubleshooting problems based on incomplete, outdated, or vague information. Imagine a scenario where your manager mentions in passing that they couldn't connect to the corporate wireless network a few days ago, but everything seems fine now. How would you approach troubleshooting this situation?

Traditionally, you might start by checking the ticketing system for any reported outages or asking colleagues if they recall any issues. Alternatively, you could log in to the wireless controller or Cisco ISE (if you're using it for wireless security) to hunt for relevant logs. However, finding specific logs from days ago and correlating them to the issue at hand can be a daunting task. Trying to replicate the issue on your own device would be equally challenging unless the problem recurs consistently.

This is where Catalyst Center's Assurance feature becomes a game-changer. With Assurance, you gain access to a "time machine" that stores comprehensive network information for an entire week. This includes logs, network health issues, and connection results, all easily accessible for troubleshooting. Figure 14.20 provides an overview of network health.

The Assurance feature doesn't just store data—it intelligently correlates issues and suggests probable causes, even offering troubleshooting tips and steps you can take to resolve the problem. This is invaluable because it allows you to identify and address subtle glitches that users might have become accustomed to, such as needing multiple attempts to connect to the wireless network.

Figure 14.21 illustrates the wireless troubleshooting page, where you can see details on client connectivity.

What makes Catalyst Center's Assurance feature truly unique is its ability to perform full analytics, providing you with a detailed "time capsule" snapshot of your network at any given moment. Although traditional NMSs can offer valuable insights, only Catalyst Center combines this data with advanced analytics to give you a complete picture of past network conditions.

Without a tool like Assurance, troubleshooting can feel like detective work—interviewing users, conducting endless tests, and sifting through configurations in the hope of finding something amiss. Catalyst Center's Assurance feature streamlines this process, empowering you to resolve issues efficiently and effectively.

Path Trace

In today's complex networks, the path that a user's traffic takes isn't always straightforward. Traditional tools like traceroute were once the go-to method for determining the route traffic took to reach its destination. However, traceroute has limitations: it won't show you that wireless traffic is passing through a CAPWAP tunnel, nor will it reveal if a site is connected

FIGURE 14.20 Catalyst network health

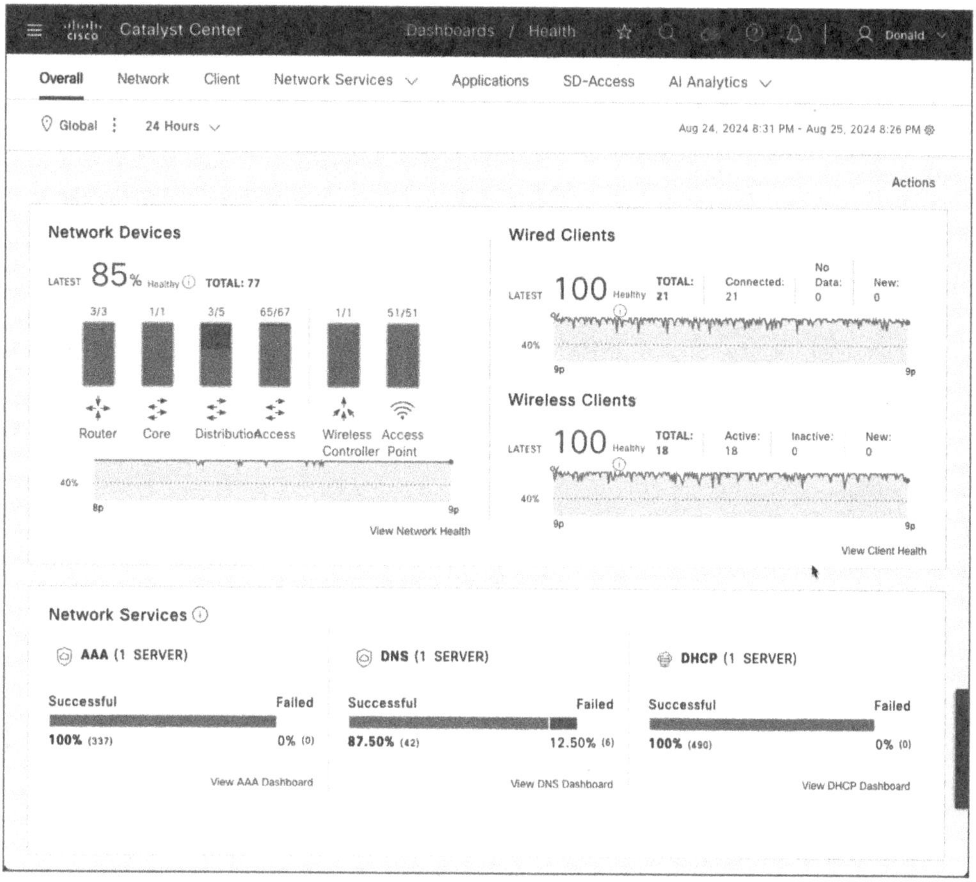

via a VPN, DMVPN, or even a VXLAN fabric. Additionally, traceroute doesn't account for the layer 2 switches that packets traverse.

Catalyst Center's Path Trace feature is a significant evolution beyond the APIC-EM Path Trace feature you might recall from previous CCNA studies. This tool leverages Catalyst Center's comprehensive awareness of all devices in your network to provide a visual representation of the actual path traffic takes from source to destination.

Path Trace goes beyond traditional tools by revealing the true paths that include tunnels and by highlighting any ACLs on network devices that could block your traffic. You can even specify which ports you want to test, offering granular insight into your network's behavior. Figure 14.22 showcases Path Trace in action.

This feature is unique to Catalyst Center (and APIC-EM, for those who still use it). Although solutions like SolarWinds offer a similar feature called NetPath, they rely on deploying agents throughout the network. In contrast, Catalyst Center uses real-time

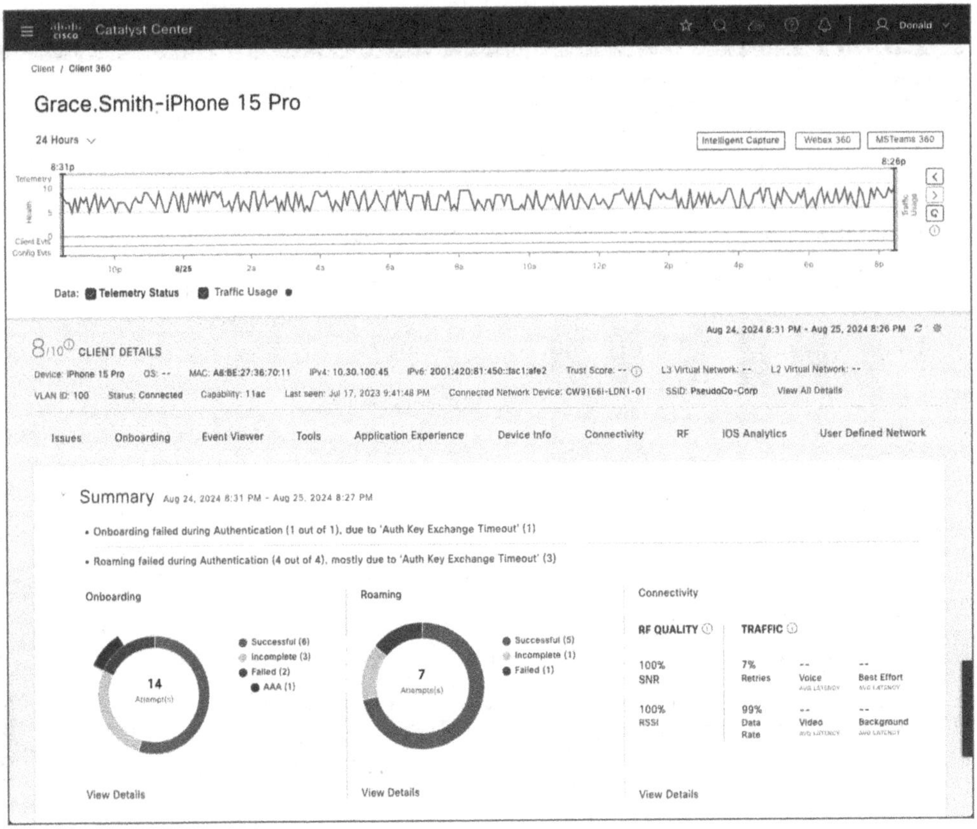

FIGURE 14.21 Catalyst wireless clients

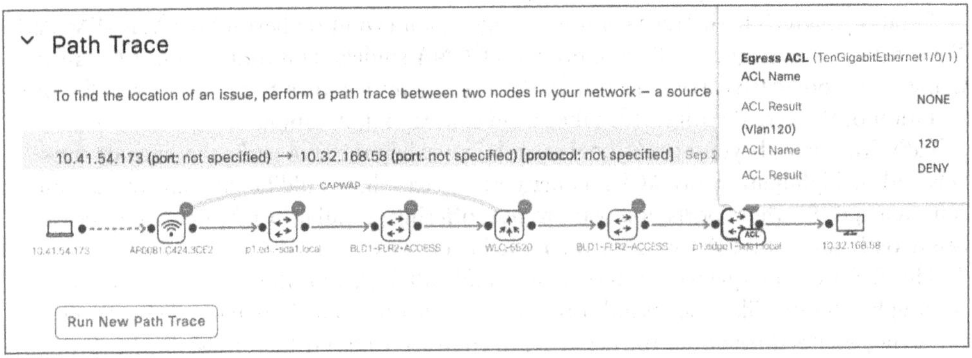

FIGURE 14.22 Catalyst Path Trace

information directly from the network devices, providing a more accurate and detailed path analysis. Additionally, Catalyst Center's Path Trace can detect issues related to ACLs, a capability that SolarWinds lacks.

What's particularly noteworthy is that the tasks Path Trace performs can't be easily replicated manually. Although tools like tcptraceroute or hping3 on Linux can offer some insights, they have limitations, especially with UDP traffic, and they don't provide the intuitive graphical display that Path Trace does. Catalyst Center's Path Trace feature simplifies what would otherwise be a complicated and time-consuming process, making it an invaluable tool for modern network troubleshooting.

EasyQoS

Implementing and maintaining quality of service (QoS) can be a complex and challenging task. Catalyst Center simplifies this process with its EasyQoS feature, a powerful successor to the EasyQoS functionality previously found in the old APIC-EM product. This tool streamlines the management of QoS policies by categorizing applications into three easy-to-manage groups:

- **Business Relevant:** Critical applications that are essential to your business operations, such as email or Active Directory
- **Business Irrelevant:** Applications that offer no business value, like BitTorrent, YouTube, and Facebook
- **Default:** Applications that don't fit into the other two categories, including essential services like DNS and database traffic

You can easily reassign applications to the categories that best fit your network's specific needs. For example, if your organization is YouTube, then YouTube would naturally be categorized as Business Relevant. The simplified QoS policy management interface is shown in Figure 14.23.

Catalyst Center automatically translates your application policy into a comprehensive QoS policy that adjusts all necessary components for you. With just a few adjustments to DSCP values and bandwidth allocations, you can ensure that a consistent QoS policy is applied across your entire network. The service provider profiles, which help manage these settings, are shown in Figure 14.24.

This EasyQoS feature is unique to Catalyst Center. Although NCMs can push QoS policies that you manually create, they don't offer the same level of ease or the ability to manage end-to-end QoS policies across your network as Catalyst Center does.

Managing QoS manually can be an incredibly complex task that requires careful planning and coordination. Every network device, including routers, switches, wireless controllers, and even firewalls, must be configured to ensure that the QoS policy is consistently applied. Catalyst Center's EasyQoS feature significantly reduces this complexity, providing a more streamlined and efficient way to manage QoS across your network.

FIGURE 14.23 Catalyst QoS policy

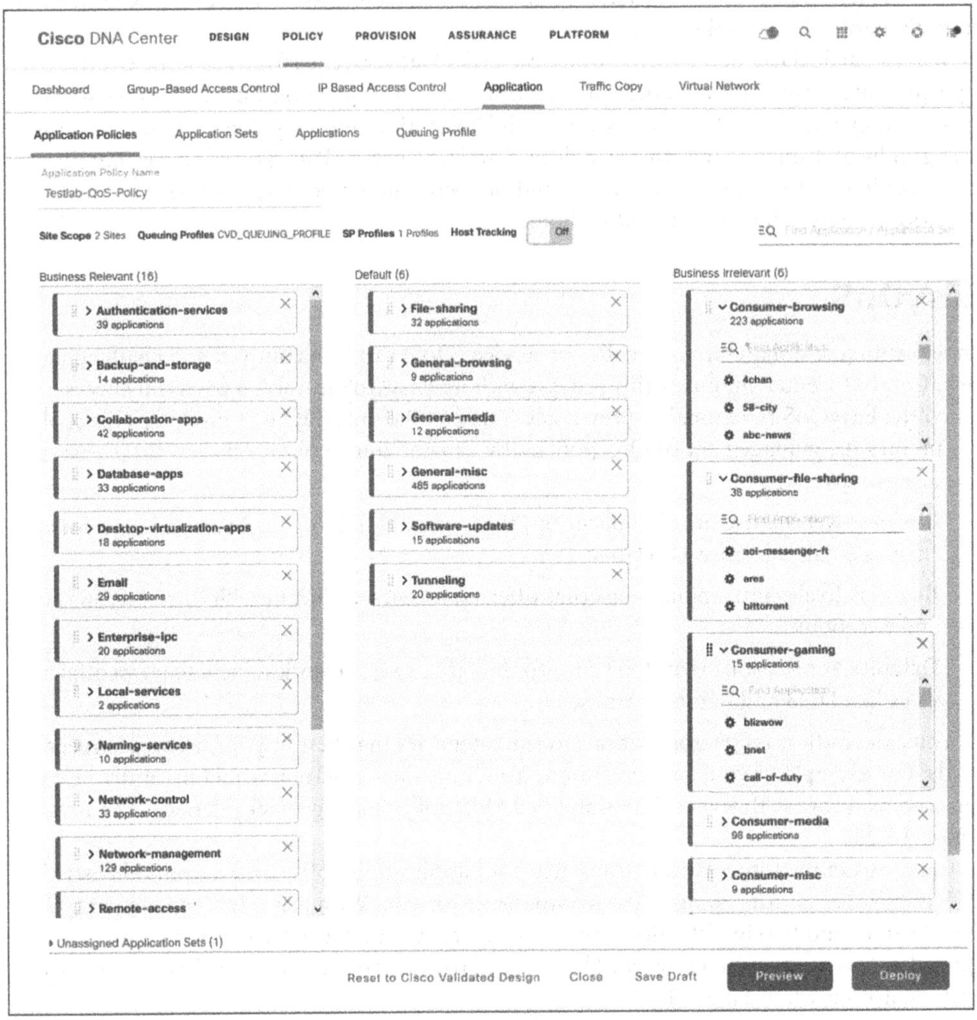

LAN Automation

Traditionally, adding a new network device to Catalyst Center required you to ensure that the device could reach the Catalyst Center server. This process involved manually setting up authentication, SSH, and SNMP so that the server could connect to the new device.

Catalyst Center's LAN Automation feature simplifies and automates this process by utilizing Cisco's plug-and-play (PNP) technology. With LAN Automation, a DHCP server is dynamically created on an upstream network device. When a new Cisco device boots up,

FIGURE 14.24 Catalyst Service provider profiles

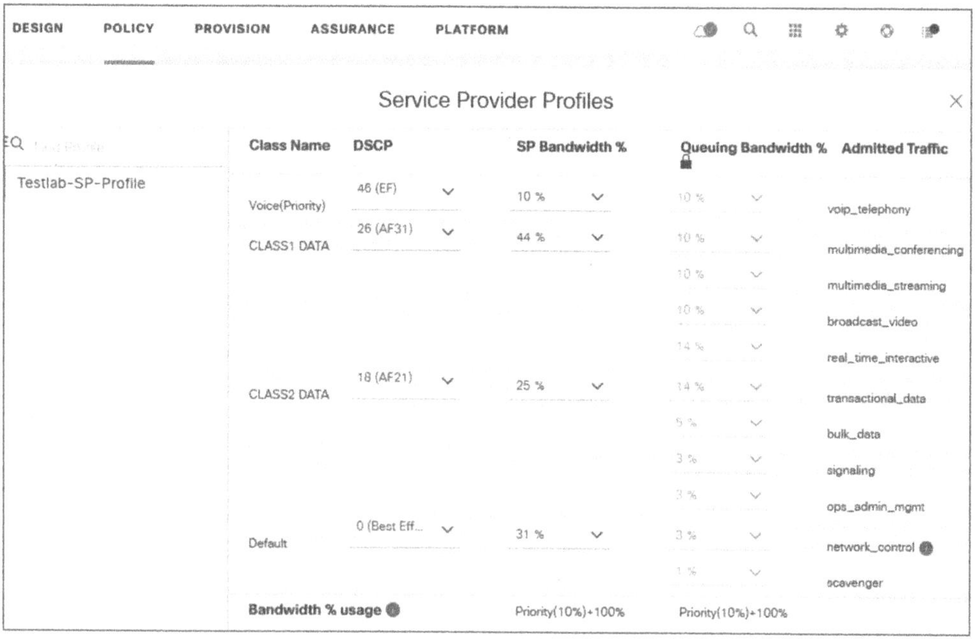

it receives an IP address and the necessary PNP server information from this DHCP server. From there, Catalyst Center automatically configures basic routing and other essential settings for the underlay network, such as multicast.

Once the setup is complete, the new device seamlessly appears in Catalyst Center under the appropriate site. The process is shown in Figure 14.25.

LAN Automation is a standout feature unique to Catalyst Center. Due to the deep integration required to make PNP work effectively, other NCMs can't match the level of automation and simplicity offered here.

Without LAN Automation, you would need to manually configure the device before shipping it to its destination, which comes with the risk of configuration errors. These errors can lead to significant delays and troubleshooting before the device is able to come online.

SD-Access

Software-Defined Access (SD-Access) is the flagship feature of Catalyst Center, revolutionizing how networks are managed by introducing intent-based networking. With SD-Access, you can simply define high-level policies, such as restricting the Marketing team from accessing IT resources, and let Catalyst Center handle the intricate details of implementation.

Under the hood, SD-Access leverages a highly sophisticated array of technologies, many of which extend beyond the scope of the CCNA. However, Catalyst Center abstracts this

FIGURE 14.25 Catalyst LAN Automation

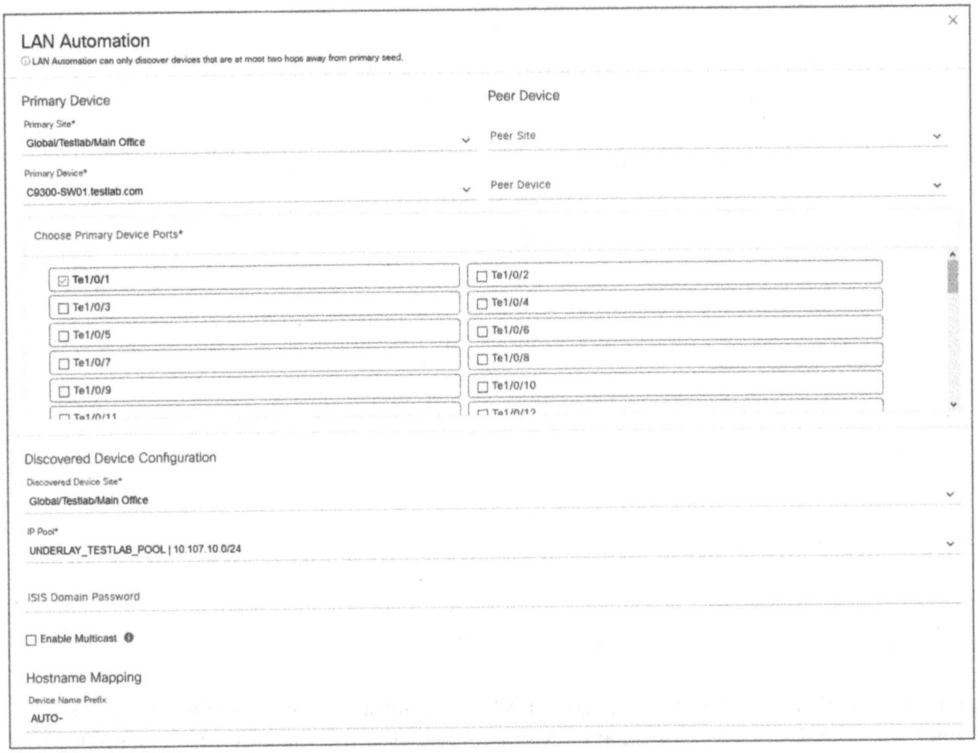

complexity, enabling even junior network administrators to manage and maintain a network that would typically demand the expertise of a much more experienced team.

Because SD-Access is a Cisco proprietary solution, it offers capabilities that no other NMS or NCM can replicate. Although it's possible to manually configure the individual components that make up SD-Access, doing so without the streamlined, user-friendly interface of Catalyst Center would be a daunting and error-prone task.

REST API

We will cover REST APIs in the next chapter, but for now, know that everything in Catalyst Center can be managed by REST. This makes it really easy to have your scripts contact Catalyst Center instead of having to individually connect to devices to get information.

A neat feature is Code Preview. DNA Center lets you test drive Restful API through the web interface to get a feel for the kind of information it will provide. The web interface can even generate Restful API code snippets for you in several languages, including Python!

Check out the Code Preview feature in Figure 14.26.

FIGURE 14.26 DNA Center Restful API

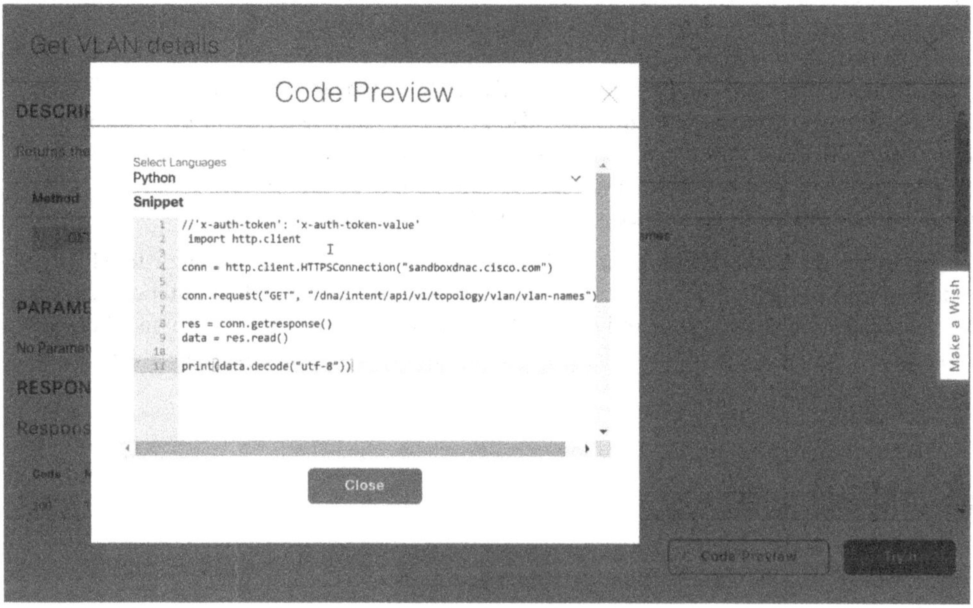

Summary

In this chapter, we talked in a bit of detail about how a router actually sends packets, because one of the goals of SDN is to separate the control plane and the data plane so that the intelligence of the network lives in the SDN controller.

You learned about several network architectures that we can see in controller-based networks before I explained what a network fabric is and what components it uses.

We closed the chapter by reviewing some common DNA Center services and how they work, comparing them with NMS/NCM solutions, and examining what would happen if you tackled the job manually.

Exam Essentials

Understand the SDN architecture. SDN solutions tunnel traffic across the underlay devices using an overlay. The underlay provides connectivity for the tunnels to be able to be formed. The overlay provides the actual services to the fabric. The fabric is simply a term for all network devices that use the SDN solution.

Understand the controller-based architecture. Rather than managing your network devices individually, you can use a controller-based solution that allows you to manage everything instead centrally. This improves efficiency because you can configure a large number of devices at once, and also reduces the risk of configuration errors because your changes aren't applied immediately and can be reviewed. It also ensures that the configuration of all your network devices is consistent. Controllers also provide a great single point to monitor or script against because they know about most or all of your network fabric. SDN controllers communicate with the network using a southbound interface toward the devices and a northbound interface to permit access to the SDN controller.

Be able to use the Catalyst Center/DNA Center. DNA Center is the successor to APIC-EM and provides SDN and controller-based features to your network. DNA Center can ensure your configuration is consistent and that QoS is working properly and set up on all devices in the network. The Assurance feature provides a unique "time machine" to view issues that happened up to a week ago.

Written Lab

The answers to this lab can be found in Appendix A, "Answers to the Written Labs."

1. What is the primary function of the control plane in a network device?
2. Explain the difference between an underlay and an overlay network in SDN.
3. What is the purpose of Catalyst Center's Assurance feature?
4. How does the Path Trace feature in Catalyst Center improve network troubleshooting compared to traditional tools like traceroute?
5. What is the role of the SDN controller in a software-defined network (SDN)?
6. Describe the purpose of the LAN Automation feature in Catalyst Center.
7. What are the three categories used by the EasyQoS feature in Catalyst Center to simplify quality of service (QoS) management?
8. What is the benefit of separating the control plane from the data plane in an SDN architecture?
9. How does Catalyst Center's Network Hierarchy feature assist in managing network configurations?
10. What is the significance of the term "fabric" in the context of SDN and Catalyst Center?

Review Questions

NOTE The following questions are designed to test your understanding of this chapter's material. For more information on how to get additional questions, please see this book's introduction.

The answers to these questions can be found in Appendix B, "Answers to the Review Questions."

1. Which plane on a router is responsible for handling routing protocols and making forwarding decisions?
   A. Management plane
   B. Control plane
   C. Data plane
   D. Access plane
2. What is the primary function of the data plane in a router?
   A. Managing SSH and Telnet access
   B. Making routing decisions
   C. Forwarding packets from one interface to another
   D. Generating routing tables
3. In a software-defined networking (SDN) environment, what is the role of the northbound interface (NBI)?
   A. It allows the SDN controller to communicate with network devices.
   B. It enables users to access the SDN controller via a GUI or API.
   C. It handles the physical connections between devices.
   D. It manages the data plane of the network.
4. Which protocol is commonly used as a southbound interface in SDN environments to communicate between the SDN controller and network devices?
   A. SNMP
   B. NETCONF
   C. HTTP
   D. SMTP
5. What advantage does Cisco Catalyst Center's Path Trace feature provide over traditional traceroute?
   A. It shows layer 2 and layer 3 paths, including tunnels.
   B. It only shows layer 3 paths.
   C. It does not require IP addresses.
   D. It is faster than traceroute.

6. Which Catalyst Center feature allows you to automate the application of quality of service (QoS) policies across your network?
   A. Network Settings
   B. Assurance
   C. EasyQoS
   D. Command Runner
7. What is the primary purpose of the Catalyst Center's Assurance feature?
   A. To automate QoS settings
   B. To provide historical network data and troubleshoot issues
   C. To create and apply CLI templates
   D. To automate device onboarding
8. Which of the following best describes an underlay network in an SDN environment?
   A. A physical network that provides the foundation for the overlay
   B. A virtual network that tunnels over the physical network
   C. A software layer that manages the SDN controller
   D. The API used to manage network devices
9. Which Catalyst Center feature is specifically used to add new devices to the network automatically?
   A. CLI Templates
   B. Command Runner
   C. LAN Automation
   D. Path Trace
10. In Catalyst Center, what does the Network Hierarchy feature allow you to do?
    A. Create dynamic layer 3 diagrams of your network
    B. Organize your network into structured sites and locations
    C. Automatically update device firmware
    D. Configure ACLs across multiple devices
11. Which of the following is a benefit of using SD-Access in Catalyst Center?
    A. Manual configuration of network devices
    B. Simplified management of intent-based networking policies
    C. Increased reliance on traditional network management tools
    D. Limited support for VLAN configurations

12. What does the term "fabric" refer to in the context of SDN and Catalyst Center?
    A. The network's physical cabling layout
    B. A shorthand term for all layer 3 devices in the network
    C. The control plane's interface with the data plane
    D. A type of QoS policy in Catalyst Center
13. How does the Catalyst Center's Command Runner feature assist network administrators?
    A. It allows for the automated configuration of new devices.
    B. It runs commands across multiple devices and stores the results.
    C. It provides a visual representation of network paths.
    D. It automatically updates device software.
14. What is the role of the SDN controller in a software-defined network?
    A. It acts as a switch that forwards data packets.
    B. It centralizes control, allowing for easier management and automation.
    C. It provides backup power to the network devices.
    D. It is responsible for managing physical cables in the network.
15. Which Catalyst Center feature can be used to manually push configurations to multiple devices using scripting engines like Apache Velocity?
    A. Command Runner
    B. Path Trace
    C. CLI Templates
    D. LAN Automation
16. What benefit does the Catalyst Center's Assurance feature offer when troubleshooting network issues?
    A. Real-time monitoring without historical data
    B. A "time machine" to access past network conditions
    C. Automatic deployment of new network devices
    D. Simplified QoS policy management
17. Which protocol is commonly used for REST APIs in Catalyst Center?
    A. SSH
    B. HTTP
    C. SMTP
    D. SNMP

18. What is the primary difference between traditional networking and software-defined networking (SDN)?
    A. SDN merges the control plane and data plane.
    B. Traditional networking separates the control plane and data plane.
    C. SDN separates the control plane from the data plane.
    D. Traditional networking allows for automation, whereas SDN does not.

19. Which Catalyst Center feature dynamically creates and updates network topology maps?
    A. Command Runner
    B. Path Trace
    C. Network Hierarchy
    D. Topology

20. Which of the following is an example of an overlay network in SDN?
    A. The physical cables connecting switches
    B. The IP routing protocol running on the underlay
    C. A VXLAN tunnel connecting different network segments
    D. The VLAN configurations on a switch

Chapter 15

Automation, Data Formats, and REST APIs

THE FOLLOWING CCNA EXAM TOPICS ARE COVERED IN THIS CHAPTER:

- ✓ **6.0 Automation and Programmability**
  - 6.1 Explain how automation impacts network management
  - 6.5 Describe characteristics of REST-based APIs (authentication types, CRUD, HTTP verbs, and data encoding)
  - 6.7 Recognize components of JSON-encoded data

When preparing for the CCNA, manually configuring everything while practicing the topics in this book is a great way to gain hands-on experience and become proficient with IOS commands. However, by the time you're nearing the exam, you might find that repeating basic configurations, like adding VLANs over and over, becomes tedious.

Additionally, you'll likely spend several hours troubleshooting unintended misconfigurations caused by typos, applying configurations to the wrong interface, or even the wrong device. Although making mistakes in a lab can be frustrating, these issues are also common in real-world scenarios. Many network outages result from simple human errors.

This is why automation is gaining traction in the workplace—it helps prevent these errors and saves time by reducing the need for repetitive tasks. In this chapter, we'll introduce the concept of automation and explore REST APIs, which are the preferred method for automating network devices today.

NOTE To find your included bonus material, as well as Todd Lammle videos, practice questions, and hands-on labs, please see `www.lammle.com/ccna`.

Automation Overview

It's a Monday morning, so of course, your boss asks you to add a new loopback interface with an IP in the 192.168.255.0/24 subnet on all your routers. It's no big deal if you have two or three routers because you can easily SSH into the devices and add the interfaces using the skills you learned from this book. But that's not the company you work at, and with your 200+ routers, it would take forever to configure all the devices individually. Plus, keeping track of which IP address to use on each router is not exactly a day at the beach, and it just gets worse if you happen to make mistakes along the way!

A whole bunch of surveys put human error in the number-one spot as the cause of network outages. Sometimes, it's because you accidentally shut down the wrong interface, sometimes, it's an old configuration lurking around that reacts rather poorly to your changes; and sometimes, you just really needed more coffee before logging in to that router!

Besides the ever-present risk when making sweeping network changes, there's the issue of your time. Getting tasked with adding 200 interfaces might be cool if it's your first time, but it grows old fast, and odds are, there's something much more interesting to spend your week on. This is a great example of when automation seriously saves the day—or week!

Network automation comes in many forms, but generally, it boils down to being able to apply tasks in a predictable way with increased odds of a positive outcome. What that means for us is that instead of tediously connecting to 200 devices, we can write a script that will apply the configuration to all of them for us.

> **NOTE** Disclaimer. . . Knowing how to automate something isn't as important as understanding what it is you're automating! This is because automation will do exactly what it's told, so if you push out a broken OSPF configuration to all your production networks, you'll have a painful night ahead of you.

Automation Components

By now you should have gained an understanding of the benefits and enjoyment that automation can offer, so let's explore how we can apply the basic concepts. Instead of attempting to teach you a full-on programming language (Python) in a few paragraphs, which is a complex topic in and of itself, I will introduce you to some common automation constructs such as

- Print statement
- Variables
- If Statements
- For Loops
- While Loops

There are hundreds of programming languages available, but Python is the preferred language for network automation. Python previously had two active versions, Python 2.x and Python 3.x. However, Python 2.x has been fully retired, so we only need to focus on Python 3.x—at least, until the possible introduction of Python 4 in the future.

Nowadays, Python 3 comes preinstalled on all Mac and Linux computers, and it is easily installed on Windows if you prefer that OS. Windows 11 also has a great feature called Windows Subsystem for Linux (WSL) that gives you access to an Ubuntu Linux shell that runs in a container. WSL makes it easier to do automation tasks from your Windows desktop.

Let's dive into these in a bit more detail and explore some examples in Python.

> **NOTE** The CCNA doesn't expect you to know any Python at all, but I'm going to show you some examples to help drive home the topics we are discussing.

Print Statement

One of the first exercises when learning any programming language is to create a "Hello World!" script. This simple program outputs the phrase "Hello World!" It might not seem very useful, but its purpose is to familiarize you with generating output and displaying it to the user.

In Python, whenever we want to produce output visible to the user, we use a print statement. In the following example, I'll enter a Python shell and create my own "Hello World!" script:

```
the-packet-thrower@macmini31 ~ % python3
Python 3.12.5 (main, Aug  6 2024, 19:08:49) [Clang 15.0.0 (clang-1500.3.9.4)]
on darwin
Type "help", "copyright", "credits" or "license" for more information.
>>> print("Hello World!")
Hello World!
```

You might think, "Well, that was underwhelming!" And you'd be right. The Python shell simply printed what I specified in the print statement. However, the print statement becomes much more valuable when your script needs to pass along more complex data.

Additionally, the print statement is extremely useful for troubleshooting more advanced scripts. It allows you to verify that your data is behaving as expected at various stages of the script.

Variables

Variables are one of the most essential concepts in automation because they allow us to store values and reuse them later in our scripts. These values can be anything from a simple string, like the "Hello World!" text from our previous example, to more complex data, such as the entire contents of a file.

Once you've created a variable, you can reference it anywhere in your code. This is incredibly useful because it means you don't have to repeat the same value multiple times throughout your script; you can simply call the variable whenever you need it.

Let's try this out by entering a Python 3 shell. I'll create a variable named "name" and assign it the value "Donald." Then, I'll use a couple of print statements to say hello and goodbye to the value stored in our variable:

```
the-packet-thrower@macmini31 ~ % python3
Python 3.12.5 (main, Aug  6 2024, 19:08:49) [Clang 15.0.0 (clang-1500.3.9.4)]
on darwin
Type "help", "copyright", "credits" or "license" for more information.
>>> name = "Donald"
>>> print(f"Hello {name}")
Hello Donald
>>> print(f"Goodbye {name}")
Goodbye Donald
```

As you can see, the script greets Donald and then says goodbye. The real advantage here is that if I wanted the script to greet someone else, like Todd, I would only need to change the value of the "name" variable to "Todd." The rest of the script remains unchanged.

If Statement

If statements are a powerful tool that allows you to introduce logic into your code. They work by using a construct known as if/then statements, which instruct the script on what to do when a certain condition is met. This concept is somewhat similar to how Cisco access control lists (ACLs) function on a router, where each line is evaluated until a match is found, and then a corresponding action is executed. For example, Figure 15.1 illustrates a simple logic flowchart where I'm deciding whether to continue writing this chapter or take a break for lunch. The key question is, "Am I hungry?" If the answer is "Yes," I'll get lunch; if the answer is "No," I'll keep Todd happy by continuing to write.

FIGURE 15.1 If/Then logic

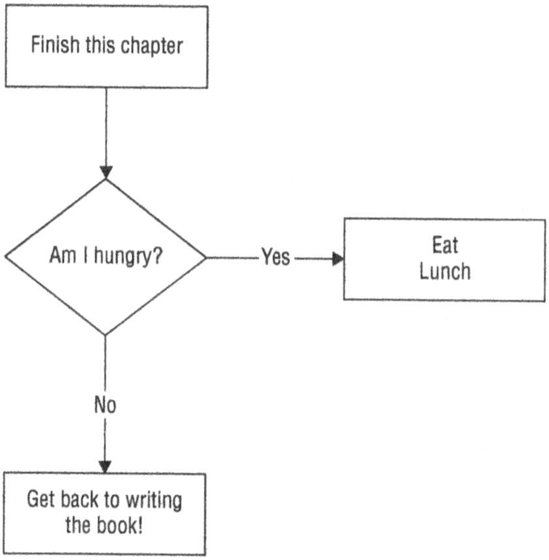

In Python, we use if statements to define logical conditions. For instance, if I asked you, "Does 2 + 2 = 4?" you'd probably say that's correct. But if I asked, "Does 2 + 2 = 87?" you'd agree that's incorrect.

Once we establish our conditions, we specify the actions the script should take if the condition is true. To demonstrate this, I'll write a Python script that checks whether 2 + 2 equals 4.

As a side note, I've been using a Python shell for these examples so far, but the shell is really only useful for basic tests. It lacks many quality-of-life features that make writing more complex scripts easier. For more advanced work, it's better to use a specialized text editor known as an integrated development environment (IDE). IDEs make your life easier by understanding the programming language you're using and helping maintain things like proper spacing, which is crucial in Python because it relies on correct indentation. They also assist with syntax, especially now that AI-powered tools are becoming more common.

I'll write this example using VS Code, a popular and free IDE. Depending on whether the math is correct, the script will print "correct" or "incorrect":

```
#!/bin/env python3
if 2 + 2 == 4:
    print("correct")
else:
    print("incorrect")
```

After creating the file, I can run it, and we'll see that the math checks out:

```
the-packet-thrower@macmini31 CCNA % python3 example.py
correct
```

But that isn't very exciting, so let's change our statement so the math is wrong:

```
#!/bin/env python3
if 2 + 2 == 249:
    print("correct")
else:
    print("incorrect")
```

Now, when I run it, we will see that the math is incorrect!

```
the-packet-thrower@macmini31 CCNA % python3 example.py
incorrect
```

We've only scratched the surface here because if statements offer a lot of possibilities. For example, you can use variables to make your code more flexible, and you can even nest if statements with elif (short for "else if") to create more complex logic. However, we don't need to dive that deep for the CCNA.

Loops

The final concept we'll cover is loops, which allow us to repeat a block of code efficiently without redundancy. Loops enable us to iterate through different data types, such as lists, number ranges, or dictionaries (which are structured collections of key-value pairs).

This might sound a bit abstract, so let's jump into a practical example. In this example, we print a name along with the loop's iteration number. In this case, we'll run the loop 10 times:

```
#!/bin/env python3
name = "Donald"
for number in range(1, 11):
    print(f"Hello {name}, this is loop iteration {number}")
```

When we run this script, it prints "Hello Donald" followed by the loop iteration number, from 1 to 10. Here's what the output looks like:

```
the-packet-thrower@macmini31 CCNA % python3 example.py
Hello Donald, this is loop iteration 1
Hello Donald, this is loop iteration 2
Hello Donald, this is loop iteration 3
Hello Donald, this is loop iteration 4
Hello Donald, this is loop iteration 5
Hello Donald, this is loop iteration 6
Hello Donald, this is loop iteration 7
Hello Donald, this is loop iteration 8
Hello Donald, this is loop iteration 9
Hello Donald, this is loop iteration 10
```

The loop iterates through the specified range, and the "number" variable keeps track of the current iteration. This example demonstrates how just a few lines of code can generate multiple outputs, saving time and effort.

Imagine that you're tasked with adding descriptions to all interfaces on a Cisco switch. Instead of configuring each interface manually, you could loop through a list of interfaces and have Python automatically apply the description commands. Whether the switch has 8 interfaces or 400, the loop handles them all efficiently without any additional work on your part.

For completeness, there are two main types of loops in Python: the for loop, which we just explored, and the while loop, which continues running as long as a specified condition remains true.

Comments

While I'm here, I should also point out that you can leave notes in your code called *comments* to explain what you are trying to achieve and generally give all kinds of useful info. It is always a good idea to leave comments as you work on a script so someone doesn't have to look through 500 lines of Python to figure out what your script will do when run.

Python has two types of comments: single-line comments that start with the pound sign (#) and multiline comments encased in three single quotes at the beginning and end. Here is a simple example that shows both methods:

```
#!/bin/env python3

'''
Author: Donald Robb
Usage: Print Hello World
'''

# Prints "Hello World!" to the screen
print("Hello World!")
```

Automation Types

There are two main types of network automation that you might encounter in your career:

- Onbox
- Offbox

Onbox

Onbox is where you run automation directly on the device itself. Modern Cisco devices can run Python directly through a feature called Guest Shell, although it isn't usually very practical because you would have to add the script you want to run on every network device, which wouldn't scale well.

However, the advantage is that it has some pretty nice integrations, such as the ability to run IOS commands directly from the Python shell, which makes automating IOS commands very easy. In this example, I will simply print out the interfaces on my router using a special guest shell package called "cli" that gives us access to the IOS side of things:

```
r01#guestshell run python3
Python 3.6.8 (default, Dec 22 2020, 19:04:08)
[GCC 8.4.1 20200928 (Red Hat 8.4.1-1)] on linux
Type "help", "copyright", "credits" or "license" for more information.
>>> from cli import *
>>> clip("show ip interface brief")
Interface              IP-Address      OK? Method Status
Protocol
GigabitEthernet1       unassigned      YES unset  administratively down down
GigabitEthernet2       unassigned      YES unset  administratively down down
GigabitEthernet3       unassigned      YES unset  administratively down down
GigabitEthernet4       unassigned      YES unset  administratively down down
GigabitEthernet5       unassigned      YES unset  administratively down down
GigabitEthernet6       unassigned      YES unset  administratively down down
GigabitEthernet7       unassigned      YES unset  administratively down down
GigabitEthernet8       unassigned      YES unset  administratively down down
GigabitEthernet9       unassigned      YES unset  administratively down down
GigabitEthernet10      unassigned      YES unset  administratively down down
GigabitEthernet11      unassigned      YES unset  administratively down down
GigabitEthernet12      unassigned      YES unset  administratively down down
VirtualPortGroup0      172.31.200.1    YES manual up                    up
```

Offbox

Offbox is by far the most common method of automation. In this method, you run your automation from an external source that connects to all the network devices the script needs to communicate with. Typically, you would put your automation server in a management VLAN so it has safe and full access to your network devices. Figure 15.2 shows how offbox reaches the network.

FIGURE 15.2 Offbox automation

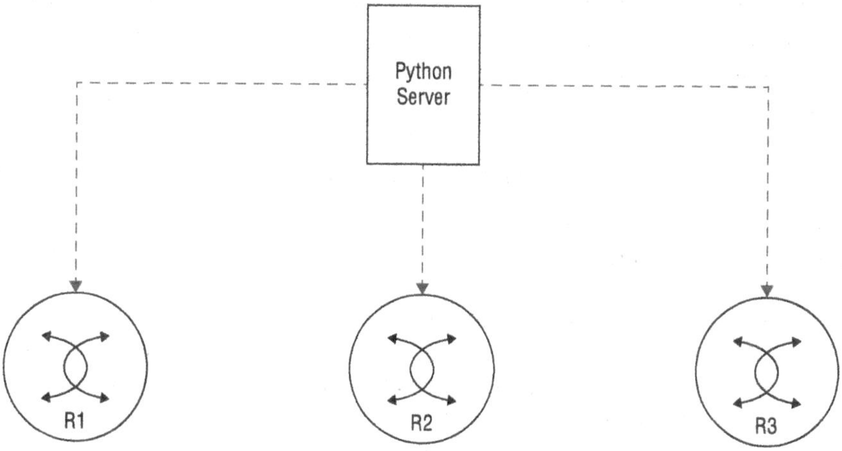

Solutions like SDN controllers and the configuration management tools we will look at later all use the offbox method of configuring the network.

Automation Methods

Finally, we need to talk about what automation methods are available to us; this is actually a really important topic because the approaches are vastly different. The simpler but more clumsy method is called *screen scraping*, and the other is utilizing APIs to get the data we need. Let's talk about both of them in more detail.

Screen Scraping

Screen scraping is a fancy term for working with the output text we receive from our script. This is fine if we want to grab some information from a device, such as the output from `show IP interface brief`. But the problems start when you need to do something more complex. Let's say I just wanted the IP address of Loopback0 in the following output:

```
r01#show ip int br
Interface              IP-Address      OK? Method Status
Protocol
GigabitEthernet1       192.168.10.1    YES manual up                    up
GigabitEthernet2       192.168.11.1    YES manual up                    up
GigabitEthernet3       192.168.12.1    YES manual up                    up
```

```
GigabitEthernet4        192.168.13.1     YES manual up                    up
GigabitEthernet5        unassigned       YES unset  administratively down down
GigabitEthernet6        unassigned       YES unset  administratively down down
GigabitEthernet7        unassigned       YES unset  administratively down down
GigabitEthernet8        unassigned       YES unset  administratively down down
GigabitEthernet9        unassigned       YES unset  administratively down down
GigabitEthernet10       unassigned       YES unset  administratively down down
GigabitEthernet11       unassigned       YES unset  administratively down down
GigabitEthernet12       unassigned       YES unset  administratively down down
Loopback0               192.168.255.1    YES manual up                    up
VirtualPortGroup0       172.31.200.1     YES manual up                    up
```

That may seem easy, but the issue is that although text output is what humans understand, computers see that interface list as a smorgasbord of letters and numbers. Because of this, I have to mix a bunch of Python techniques to make that happen.

Without getting too in the weeds here, I got the loopback address by saving the output from `show ip interface brief` to a variable. Then, I searched each line of the output for the word "Loopback0," breaking up the rest of the line so only the IP remained, and I finally stored it in a variable so I could easily print it:

```
r01#guestshell run python3
Python 3.6.8 (default, Dec 22 2020, 19:04:08)
[GCC 8.4.1 20200928 (Red Hat 8.4.1-1)] on linux
Type "help", "copyright", "credits" or "license" for more information.
>>> from cli import *
>>>
>>> output = cli("show ip int br")
>>> for line in output.splitlines():
...     if "Loopback0" in line:
...         loopback0_ip = line.split()[1]
...         break
...
>>> print(loopback0_ip)
192.168.255.1
```

The main point is that getting a simple IP address took a fair amount of effort because we are working with unstructured data, which is ordinary text that is not easily organized in a way that a computer would like.

APIs

These days, the preferred way of getting information is to interact with a device's application programming interface (API) through the northbound interface you learned about in the SDN chapter. APIs usually return output that a computer can easily work with; we call that output *structured data*.

> **NOTE** API stands for Application Programming Interface. In the context of APIs, the word Application refers to any software with a distinct function. Interface can be thought of as a contract of service between two applications. This contract defines how the two communicate with each other using requests and responses.

We are going to learn all about structured data in the upcoming data format section, but for right now APIs will usually return data in either something called JavaScript Object Notation (JSON) or another format called Extensible Markup Language (XML). This allows us to easily parse the data so we can get exactly what we are looking for.

I will jump ahead a bit to show you a practical example of why using APIs is the preferred way of doing automation. I am connecting to the same lab router we used in the screen-scraping section using a version of a REST API called restconf:

```
#!/bin/env python3

import requests, urllib3

urllib3.disable_warnings()
url = "https://10.30.10.193/restconf/data/Cisco-IOS-XE-native:native/
interface/Loopback=0/ip/address/primary/address"

headers = {
  'Content-Type': 'application/yang-data+json',
  'Accept': 'application/yang-data+json',
  'Authorization': 'Basic cmVzdGNvbmY6OHhTZXZlbj01Ng=='
}

response = requests.request("GET", url, headers=headers, verify=False).json()
print(response['Cisco-IOS-XE-native:address'])
```

The main difference is that when I run the script, I get our Loopback0 back without dealing with all that unstructured data!

```
(venv) the-packet-thrower@macmini31 CCNA % python3 example.py
192.168.255.1
```

This makes life a lot easier because all I need to do is know how to get the data out of the API by writing the correct query. Then, I can directly get the data I want, which is the IP address 192.168.255.1 from the Loopback0 interface.

You are probably thinking, "That's cool, but how do I figure out how to use a device's API?" What a great question! The answer is, unfortunately, "it depends." Most modern solutions tend to have an API reference guide that you can use to learn how to use the API; sometimes that reference guide is built into the product itself so you can easily access it, and sometimes the vendor will host the reference guides on its websites. Figure 15.3 shows Meraki's API reference website, which fully explains what the API is capable of doing and provides examples you can try.

FIGURE 15.3 Meraki API reference

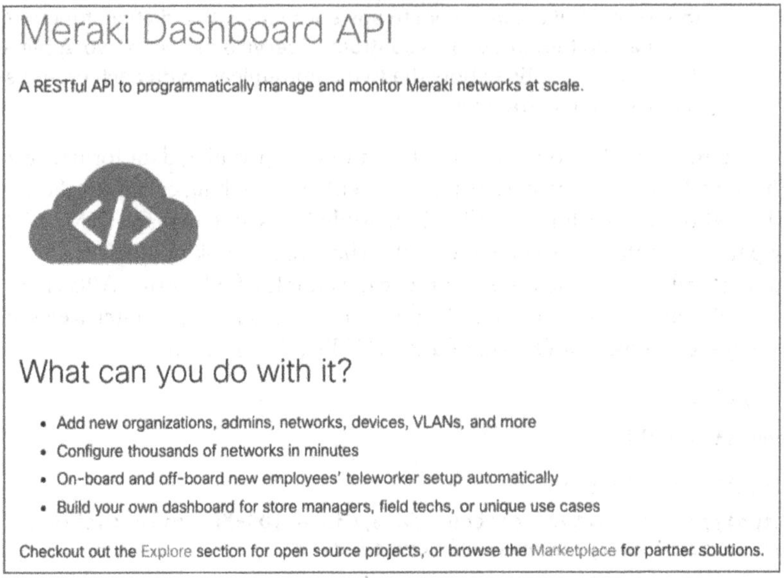

Meraki Dashboard API
A RESTful API to programmatically manage and monitor Meraki networks at scale.
What can you do with it?
• Add new organizations, admins, networks, devices, VLANs, and more
• Configure thousands of networks in minutes
• On-board and off-board new employees' teleworker setup automatically
• Build your own dashboard for store managers, field techs, or unique use cases
Checkout out the Explore section for open source projects, or browse the Marketplace for partner solutions.

The key phrase there is "what the API is capable of doing," because sometimes APIs have weird limitations. For example, the early version of IOS's REST API did not allow you to add static routes. So, if you needed that functionality, you would have to use another method, such as pushing commands directly with Python.

Nowadays, we are close to parity when it comes to what we can achieve with the CLI and what we can configure through an API on modern gear—but keep in mind that we still have a lot of older network equipment out there. Because of this, SDN controllers like Catalyst Center will prefer to use APIs to configure devices, but they can also fall back and push commands if needed.

Data Formats

Whew, that was a lot! Now that you have a good understanding of some fundamental automation concepts, we can focus on working with structured data. This is a very important topic because Cisco absolutely expects you to be able to read JSON. As a CCNA, you will probably encounter it in the real world, so it is good for you to be comfortable with it.

JSON

JavaScript Object Notation (JSON) is a widely adopted data exchange format for communicating structured information between systems. JSON's main advantage is its ability to represent data in a clear, human-readable way, making it the format of choice for many REST

APIs and software-defined solutions. Although other formats like XML and YAML are also used, JSON is particularly popular due to its simplicity.

JSON Structure and Key Rules

JSON organizes data into key/value pairs within curly braces. Here are a few important rules to keep in mind:

- **Double quotes:** Both keys and values must be enclosed in double quotes, not single quotes.
- **Boolean values:** Must be lowercase, unlike Python, where they are capitalized.
- **Key/value pairs are comma-separated:** After each new key/value pair, you must add a comma if there is another entry.
- **No trailing commas:** JSON does not allow trailing commas, unlike Python, which is more lenient in this regard.

Here's how you might represent a person's name, age, and website using JSON:

```
{
  "name" : "Todd Lammle",
  "age" : "89",
  "website" : "www.lammle.com"
}
```

For more complex data, such as a list of people, you can use arrays (denoted by square brackets):

```
{
   "Creators": [

      {
        "name" : "Donald Robb",
        "age" : "38",
        "website" : "www.the-packet-thrower.com"
      },

      {
        "name" : "Todd Lammle",
        "age" : "89",
        "website" : "www.lammle.com"
      }
   ]
}
```

Arrays are commonly used with network devices to group various attributes, such as everything under a particular interface.

JSON's simplicity and readability make it ideal for structured data exchange, especially when referencing specific data points like keys and values. This is better for computers because they need to ask for the key name in order to receive the key value. Likewise, if we need to update the configuration in that key pair, we need to update the key value for the key name.

Working with JSON

Because this is a Cisco book, let's grab some JSON from my Cisco router so we can go over how to extract data. Fortunately, modern IOS-XE can easily generate JSON from the CLI if restconf is enabled:

```
r01#show run interface GigabitEthernet 2 | format restconf-json
{
  "data": {
    "Cisco-IOS-XE-native:native": {
      "interface": {
        "GigabitEthernet": [
          {
            "name": "2",
            "description": "Connection to Internet",
            "ip": {
              "address": {
                "primary": {
                  "address": "192.168.11.1",
                  "mask": "255.255.255.0"
                }
              }
            },
            "Cisco-IOS-XE-ethernet:negotiation": {
              "auto": true
            }
          }
        ]
      }
    }
  }
}
```

Because this is an example of nested output, we need to work on the output until we get to GigabitEthernet2's IP address. To do this, we must use a concept called JSON *slicing*. In this process, we "slice" off the parts of the output we don't want until all that remains is the useful information.

The JSON we got from my router is an example of nested output; to access the IP, we will need to work on extracting the data. We can do this by starting at the outmost data structure and "extracting" each element until we get to the data we are interested in.

To demonstrate this, I've saved the JSON output to a variable on my Mac and will use a tool called `jq` to slice it. You don't need to know anything about the tool itself, but it is commonly used when working with JSON data:

```
the-packet-thrower@macmini31 CCNA % echo $output | jq '.'
{
  "data": {
    "Cisco-IOS-XE-native:native": {
      "interface": {
        "GigabitEthernet": [
          {
            "name": "2",
            "description": "Connection to Internet",
            "ip": {
              "address": {
                "primary": {
                  "address": "192.168.11.1",
                  "mask": "255.255.255.0"
                }
              }
            },
            "Cisco-IOS-XE-ethernet:negotiation": {
              "auto": true
            }
          }
        ]
      }
    }
  }
}
```

Looking at the initial output, the first outer layer I need to slice off is "data," and I can do that by adding that string to the `jq` expression, so the command would look like this:

```
the-packet-thrower@macmini31 CCNA % echo $output | jq '."data"'
{
  "Cisco-IOS-XE-native:native": {
    "interface": {
      "GigabitEthernet": [
        {
          "name": "2",
          "description": "Connection to Internet",
          "ip": {
```

```
            "address": {
              "primary": {
                "address": "192.168.11.1",
                "mask": "255.255.255.0"
              }
            }
          },
          "Cisco-IOS-XE-ethernet:negotiation": {
            "auto": true
          }
        }
      ]
    }
  }
}
```


Notice that the "data" field is gone, so I will keep doing this until we reach the end. To save some typing, these are the steps I would take:

1. Extract the "data" element:

   echo $output | jq '."data"'

2. Extract the "Cisco-IOS-XE-native:native" element:

   echo $output | jq '."data"."Cisco-IOS-XE-native:native"'

3. Continue through the hierarchy:
   - Extract "interface"
   - Extract "GigabitEthernet"
   - Specify the array index [0] because we have only one entry in the output.
   - Extract "ip," "address," "primary," and finally "address."

The full command looks like this:

```
echo $output | jq '."data"."Cisco-IOS-XE-native:native"."interface".
"GigabitEthernet"[0]."ip"."address"."primary"."address"'
```

This command will output

```
"192.168.11.1"
```

It takes some getting used to, but once you understand how to read and work with JSON, you can quickly work through the data. You might think this was a lot of work, but the beauty is that everything is structured and predictable; for example, if I also wanted the network mask, I could adjust my query to use "mask" instead of "address" like this:

```
the-packet-thrower@macmini31 CCNA % echo $output | jq '."data"."Cisco-IOS-XE-
native:native"."interface"."GigabitEthernet"[0]."ip"."address"."primary".
"mask"'
"255.255.255.0"
```

JSON is straightforward and easy to work with. As we progress through other topics, you'll see more examples and applications of JSON in real-world scenarios, such as working with a REST API.

There is another popular data format called Extensible Markup Language (XML) that you might encounter in the real world; however, it isn't in the CCNA in any form, so I'm just letting you know it exists. Generally speaking, it is more annoying than JSON because it uses more of an HTML-like structure that can be a bit more difficult to work with.

REST API

We talked about APIs earlier, but now we will focus on how to use them with Representational State Transfer (REST). REST is a resource-based API architecture, meaning that URIs (uniform resource identifiers) should represent

- Things, not actions
- Nouns, not verbs

If we break the words in *Representational State Transfer* apart, we have

- **Representational:** The resource's state is transferred between the client and the server.
- **State Transfer:** Each request contains all the information needed to complete the operation.

To be considered RESTful, an API must adhere to six key constraints:

- **Client-server:** The client always initiates requests to the server.
- **Stateless:** The server does not store any information from previous requests.
- **Cacheable:** Server responses include a version number, allowing the client to use cached data if appropriate.
- **Uniform interface:** The interaction between the client and server is standardized, divided into four aspects:
  - **Identifying the resource:** Each resource has a unique URI.
  - **Resource representation:** Data is typically returned in JSON or XML format.
  - **Self-descriptive messages:** Each message contains enough information to be processed independently.
  - **HATEOAS (hypermedia as the engine of application state):** The API should be self-discoverable, meaning you can navigate it without extensive documentation.
- **Layered system:** Additional layers like firewalls or load balancers can be added without affecting the API's operations.
- **Code on demand** (optional): The server can send executable code to the client.

Don't be scared by all those steps; they basically boil down to the API being easy to use and understand plus the actual API system being flexible and modular.

With all that out of the way, a REST API is a framework built on HTTP; all messages are simple text exchanged over an HTTP/HTTPS connection.

Understanding REST API URIs

Although it is good to understand some of the fundamentals that go into making a REST API, you are far more likely to utilize an existing API that is available on your network device or SDN controller than you are to develop one from scratch.

The way you interact with a REST API is by communicating with its URI, which is pretty much the same thing as regular URLs that you use to access websites; the difference is that although URLs are focused on providing you with a website to visit, a URI is expecting you to send it REST commands.

Let's break down a typical URI used in a REST API for Cisco Catalyst Center, as seen in Figure 15.4 (because the hosted instance is not running the current code, it still has references to DNA Center).

FIGURE 15.4 Catalyst Center URI

https://sandboxdnac.cisco.com/dna/intent/api/v1/network-device?hostnamecat_9k_2.dcloud.cisco.com

Protocol	Server / Host URL	Resource	Parameters
https://	sandboxdnac.cisco.com	/dna/intent/api/v1/network-device	?hostnamecat_9k_2.dcloud.cisco.com

Here is a description of each part of the URI:

- **Protocol:** HTTP for unencrypted or HTTPS for encrypted communication, although most RESTful APIs use HTTPS.
- **URL:** The fully qualified domain name (FQDN) of the server you're accessing; usually, it uses the default HTTPS port (443), but it can use a different port depending on the actual solution you are connecting to.
- **Resource:** The specific path to the resource you want to access through the API.
- **Parameters:** This part of the URI allows you to optionally pass parameters to filter results or do things like request another page. For example, the hostname parameter will filter results to devices with a hostname of sw1.

Now that we know what the URI looks like, it's time to discuss what actions we can take with it. RESTful architecture uses HTTP verbs to map to something called CRUD to define its common actions. CRUD stands for Create, Read, Update, and Delete, and it describes database actions, which are shown in Table 15.1.

TABLE 15.1 REST actions

HTTP verb	Typical action (CRUD)
POST	Create a new resource.
GET	Retrieve an existing resource.
PUT	Update or replace an existing resource.
PATCH	Partially update an existing resource.
DELETE	Remove a resource.

One of the great things about REST is that it uses HTTP's simple status codes to convey information. This makes it very easy to tell if your request was successful and why it failed if it wasn't. Table 15.2 shows the most common status codes; I would recommend you take a minute to learn these, because certification exams love to test people on them!

TABLE 15.2 HTTP status codes

Status code	Status message	Meaning
200	OK	The request was successful.
201	Created	New resource has been successfully created.
400	Bad Request	Request was invalid.
401	Unauthorized	There is an authentication issue: either the authentication failed, or you did not provide it.
403	Forbidden	Request was understood but you don't have permission.
404	Not Found	The requested resource could not be found. You see this when browsing the web if you go to a wrong URL.
500	Internal Server Error	The server itself had some kind of error when processing the request.
503	Service Unavailable	Server is currently unable to complete request: for example, the server is too busy to serve you, or maintenance is being done on the server.

Understanding Authentication

Some APIs are pretty benign and respond with simple things like the weather or a news report. One that I quite like is https://jsonip.com because it gives me my public IP address without fuss, as seen here:

```
the-packet-thrower@macmini31 CCNA % curl https://jsonip.com/ --silent | jq
{
  "ip": "109.174.129.234"
}
```

These kinds of APIs do not require any authentication to get information from them because they are meant to be used by the public and can't easily be abused by malicious actors.

The same cannot be said for the APIs that control your network infrastructure! These APIs have the keys to the kingdom and can cause a lot of grief if the wrong person gets into them. Because of this, all the REST APIs you will deal with for network automation will require you to authenticate before they do anything.

This is pretty much the same idea as logging on to a router; you can't see or change the configuration without a valid username and password with the proper permissions to carry out your task.

REST APIs offer many different ways to authenticate, but the most basic method is aptly called "Basic Auth," which requires you to provide a username and password when you send your request. It seems pretty straightforward forward, right? It is, but there is a catch.

Because all API communications are done through HTTP, the username and password ultimately get sent to the server as part of the URI request. But hopefully, you are following good password security and using a lot of special characters and all that best-practice stuff. The problem with that is that the API can misinterpret the special characters and cause things to break!

To get around this, we encode our username and password with a very simple algorithm that is similar to what IOS uses when you type `service password-recovery` in IOS. The encoding is called base64, and its job is to normalize the credentials so they don't cause any problems. It also has the benefit of providing some over-the-shoulder security, but I wouldn't put a lot of stock in that.

I'll show you a more efficient way of generating the base64 in a bit, but for now, let's look at some credentials I'll need to access a free DNA Center lab:

Username: devnetuser

Password: Cisco123!

The way we have to format it is `username:password` so that a colon separates them. Once we have that, we need to get the actual base64 string. The easiest way to do that on Mac and Linux is to use the `echo -n` command to pipe the content to base64 like this:

```
the-packet-thrower@macmini31 CCNA % echo -n 'devnetuser:Cisco123!' | base64
ZGV2bmV0dXNlcjpDaXNjbzEyMyE=
```

It is very important to use `-n` with the `echo` command; otherwise, a newline character will be added, breaking our encoding.

Understanding Headers

Now that we have our encoded authentication string ready to go, we need to put it in a header. A header is just some extra metadata that we include with our requests, and we can add as many headers as we need to.

There are three common headers that you should know about:

- **Authorization:** This is where we specify how we are authenticating to the API. In our case, we would type "Basic ZGV2bmV0dXNlcjpDaXNjbzEyMyE=".
- **Content-type:** This tells the API what type of content we are sending it. This will be "application/json" in most cases, but it can vary from system to system. For example, if you look at my offbox example when we were looking at Python, that used "application/yang-data+json" because that is what IOS-XE expects.
- **Accept:** This tells the API what the client is willing to accept. Normally, this will be "application/JSON" as well, but you can use it to ask the API to send you another data format like XML if you prefer, assuming the API supports it.

The content-type and accept headers are usually optional because if you don't provide them, the API will send you the system's default data format.

Working with REST

Now that we have all the pieces, we can build an API request to the DNA Center. Cisco hosts the system online for free so people can test out their automation. Feel free to follow along if you want to.

Currently, we have our encoded authenticated string and know what headers we need. So, the next step is to send a POST request to the DNA Center API so it can give us an authentication token. We then use that token in all our subsequent requests to the system. This is where those API reference pages come in handy because they explain how you can authenticate and what URIs are available to you.

Figure 15.5 shows the DNA Center's Authentication API reference page.

Let's put all the info we need in one spot:

- **URI:** https://sandboxdnac.cisco.com/dna/system/api/v1/auth/token
- **Header:** Content-Type: application/json
- **Header:** Authorization: Basic ZGV2bmV0dXNlcjpDaXNjbzEyMyE=

To try this out, I will use the `curl` command on my Mac; it is available on all systems, although Windows requires you to download it or use its PowerShell version, which I won't be getting into here. `Curl` is a handy utility that lets you interact with APIs with your command line.

FIGURE 15.5 Catalyst Center Authentication API

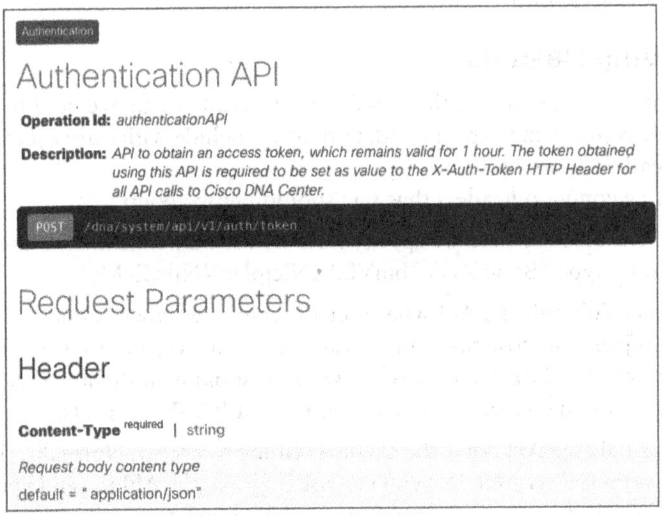

To get our token, I will send a POST request using the parameters I just listed and pass the response through `jq` so it is easier to read.

```
the-packet-thrower@macmini31 CCNA % curl --request POST
'https://sandboxdnac.cisco.com/dna/system/api/v1/auth/token' \
--header 'Content-Type: application/json' \
--header 'Authorization: Basic ZGV2bmV0dXNlcjpDaXNjbzEyMyE=' --silent | jq
{
  "Token": "eyJhbGciOiJSUzI1NiIsInR5cCI6IkpXVCJ9.eyJzdWIiOiI2Njk3NzQwYWU4ZTc5
NDc0ZjcxN2FiNWEiLCJhdXRoU291cmNlIjoiaW50ZXJuYWwiLCJ0ZW5hbnROYW1lIjoiVE5UMCIs
InJvbGVzIjpbIjY2OTZmMDFhYTA0Y2FlNjVjM2MzN2IwMiJdLCJ0ZW5hbnRJZCI6IjY2OTZmMDE4
YTA0Y2FlNjVjM2MzN2FmYiIsImV4cCI6MTcyNDkxNzc3NSwiaWF0IjoxNzI0OTE0MTc1LCJqdGki
OiI2ZTkwMmMxMC00NDFiLTQ5MTAtYjY4My04MzZhMjZkZmUyZGEiLCJ1c2VybmFtZSI6ImRldm5
ldHVzZXIifQ.N7-gPBUdgn60iH1yrgmAndhesSe1MdqGO_v3XPCfiPYBzHKv8azQwv4-wwSj5x
TEJna0-6FYxjbE6vBvRZ2YuJHqG_Sw1Z8sPXxNaojiR4eoy5rjrD7YKMbv0edEcHuxGoh8M95
fWr17YiKupmZFNh3oRuGG2Vvzk-HsXPWonoHxni_mQbDGajgQOuyeCBuNm72fiPZ-
rInXaNUGZZSGh6-mjumSdjVDFcspFS048aykx_xoLLJ1h0rUK5p-fKShMaKvz6c0NKVA0VngZ8Z-
YrRiryfI4Z0NWajMiLbzUwTx8PttwKeB1VPzEORbFNtGDUpC9XPfxwvKbq-ubuA_dw"
}
```

That long value we get back is called an *X-Auth-Token*, which is how we will authenticate going forward. Always treat your token with care because anyone who gets hold of it can do anything on the API that you are allowed to do! The token will eventually expire, though, and you will need to reauthenticate to get a new token to use with your requests.

Fortunately, we have Postman to make our life a lot easier when working with APIs. It is a desktop client available on all operating systems that helps you manage all aspects of your

API requests. It allows you to save requests so you can come to them, and it also provides robust support for variables so you can tailor your requests to support multiple systems. Figure 15.6 shows the Postman client.

FIGURE 15.6 Postman example

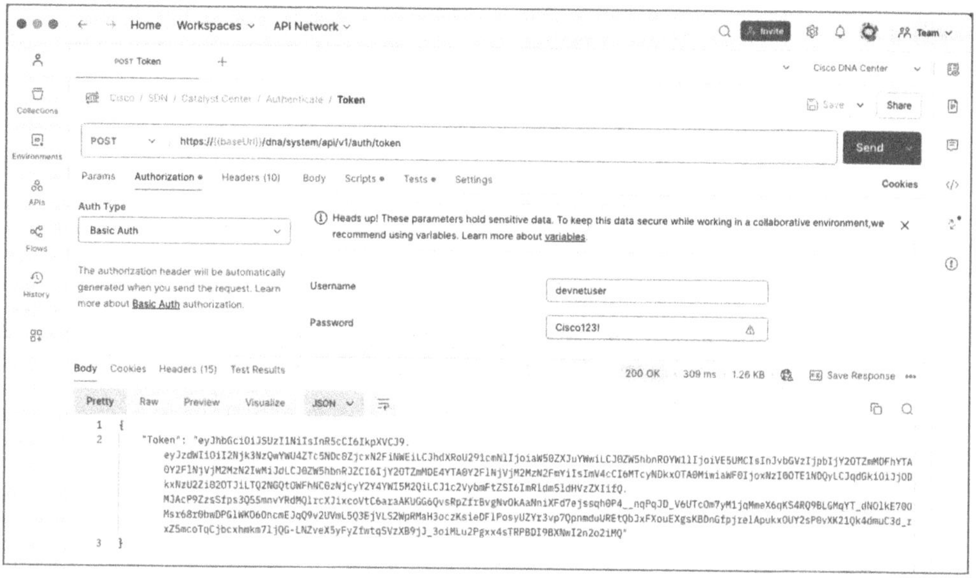

A particularly nice feature is that we can enter our username and password like we normally do, and it will handle that pesky base64 conversion for us!

Let's walk through the steps in a bit more detail. First, we need to create a new request and set the method to POST.

We need to set the URL to be

```
https://sandboxdnac.cisco.com/dna/system/api/v1/auth/token
```

In the Authorization tab of Postman, provide the following credentials:

Username: devnetuser

Password: Cisco123!

Upon sending the request, you'll receive a token in the response body. This token is your key to accessing the API and must be treated with care. We don't need to adjust any headers because the defaults work fine.

Now that we have our token, we will make a new request and query all the network devices currently registered to the DNA Center. Figure 15.7 shows the API reference for our network device query.

FIGURE 15.7 DNA Center Network Device API

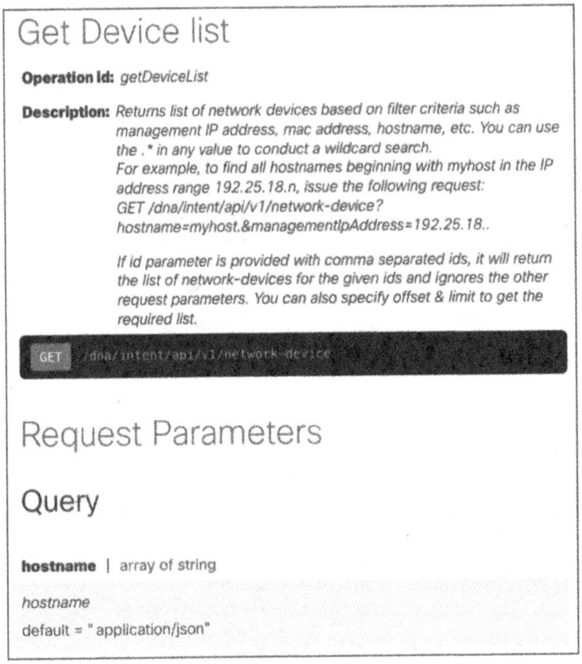

Change the request method to GET.

Set the URL to be

`https://sandboxdnac.cisco.com/dna/intent/api/v1/network-device`

Click the Headers tab, type **X-Auth-Token** under the Key field, and paste in the token we got from the previous request. While we are here, we may as well set the Content-Type and Accept headers to be **application/json** for the sake of completeness.

Once that is done, go ahead and send the request. Figure 15.8 shows my response.

FIGURE 15.8 Postman network devices

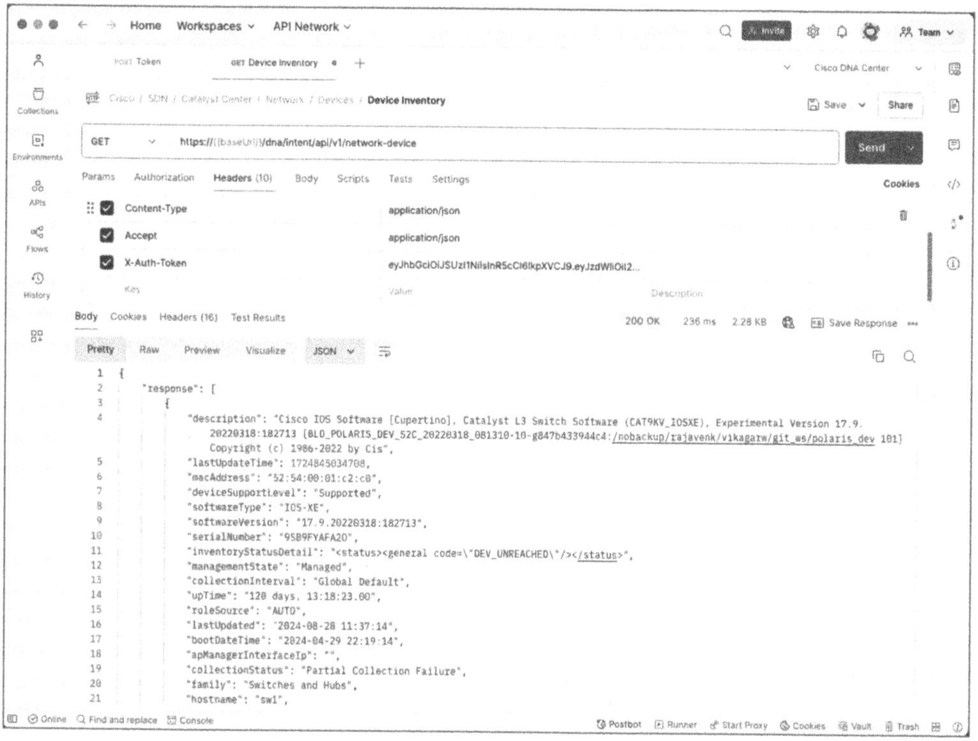

Finally, we can try out filtering our response by adding the `hostname` parameter. Click the Params tab in Postman, and then enter `hostname` as a key and the hostname of one of the results; at least at the time of writing, there is a switch called sw1, so I'll filter on that.

When I send the request, I only get sw1 returned instead of all the devices in the DNA Center. Figure 15.9 shows the filtered results.

This workflow demonstrates how REST APIs allow for efficient and secure access to application resources, making them invaluable in modern network management and development.

FIGURE 15.9 Postman filtering network devices

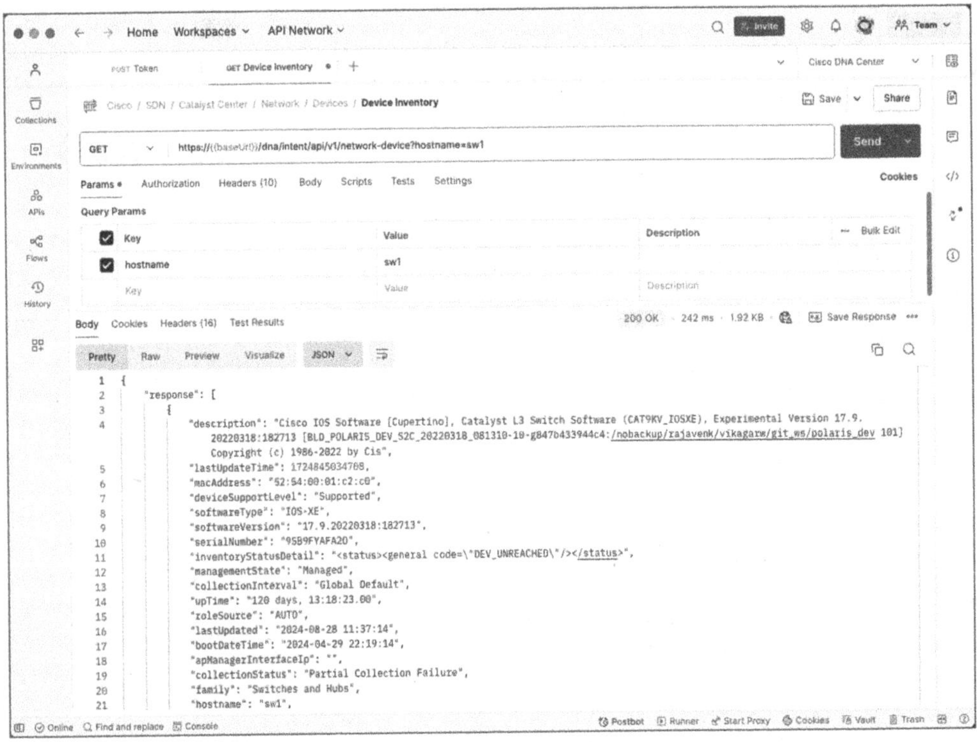

Summary

This chapter explored several key topics in network automation. We started with an introduction to essential automation concepts, including practical Python examples to illustrate how these concepts work in real-world scenarios. We then moved on to understanding JSON, explaining its structure and benefits when used in automation and APIs. Finally, we delved into REST APIs, discussing their importance in network automation, and provided a demonstration of how to interact with the API functionality of Catalyst Center.

Exam Essentials

Understand the benefits of automation. You learned how automation can help you quickly deploy mundane tasks that take a lot of time and how it also helps reduce misconfigurations.

Know how to use Restful APIs. A REST API uses common HTTP requests to GET, PUT, POST, and DELETE data from a server or device. Because HTTP is supported everywhere, it is easy to use RESTful APIs in practically all automation solutions.

Know how to use JSON. JavaScript Object Notation (JSON) is a data exchange format that presents data on a human readable format and is widely supported by most systems. Data is represented in key/value pairs, and information can also be nested as required.

Written Lab

The answers to this lab can be found in Appendix A, "Answers to the Written Labs."

1. Explain the key benefits of network automation in managing large networks.
2. Describe the difference between onbox and offbox automation. Provide an example of each.
3. What is JSON, and why is it widely used in network automation? Provide an example of a JSON object that includes a name, age, and email address.
4. Explain the purpose of REST APIs in network management and describe the six key constraints that define a RESTful API.
5. In a REST API, what is the significance of the HTTP verbs (e.g., GET, POST, PUT, DELETE), and how do they relate to CRUD operations?
6. What role do headers play in REST API requests? Name three common headers and their functions.
7. What is the difference between a 200 and a 404 HTTP status code in a REST API response? What does each indicate?
8. Describe the process of authenticating with a REST API using basic authentication. What is base64 encoding, and why is it used?
9. How can you use a loop in Python to automate the configuration of multiple network devices? Provide a basic example script.
10. What is HATEOAS in the context of REST APIs, and why is it important for API design?

Review Questions

NOTE The following questions are designed to test your understanding of this chapter's material. For more information on how to get additional questions, please see this book's introduction.

The answers to these questions can be found in Appendix B, "Answers to the Review Questions."

1. What is the primary benefit of network automation?
   A. Increases the complexity of configurations
   B. Reduces human error and saves time
   C. Requires more manual configuration
   D. Eliminates the need for network engineers
2. Which programming language is most commonly used for network automation?
   A. Java
   B. Python
   C. C++
   D. Ruby
3. Which of the following is an example of onbox automation?
   A. Running a Python script on a remote server to configure network devices
   B. Using a cloud service to manage network configurations
   C. Running a Python script directly on the network device using Guest Shell
   D. Managing network devices through a web-based interface
4. What is a key advantage of using an integrated development environment (IDE) for writing Python scripts?
   A. It allows you to write scripts without any syntax errors.
   B. It helps maintain proper spacing and syntax, which is crucial in Python.
   C. It automatically deploys scripts to network devices.
   D. It generates scripts without user input.
5. Which of the following is *not* a common type of loop in Python?
   A. For loop
   B. While loop
   C. Until loop
   D. Do-while loop

6. What does JSON stand for?
   A. JavaScript Object Notation
   B. Java Simple Object Notation
   C. JavaScript Object Namespace
   D. Java Syntax Object Notation
7. In JSON, what is used to separate keys from values?
   A. Semicolon (;)
   B. Colon (:)
   C. Equal sign (=)
   D. Comma (,)
8. Which of the following is a valid JSON key-value pair?
   A. 'name': 'John'
   B. "name": 'John'
   C. "name": "John"
   D. name: "John"
9. What is the primary purpose of JSON in networking?
   A. To execute commands on network devices
   B. To represent structured data in a human-readable format
   C. To manage network security
   D. To establish communication protocols
10. Which of the following is *not* a correct rule for JSON?
    A. Keys and values must be enclosed in double quotes.
    B. Boolean values must be lowercase.
    C. Trailing commas are allowed.
    D. JSON must be structured as key-value pairs.
11. What does REST stand for in REST API?
    A. Representational State Transfer
    B. Real-time State Transmission
    C. Resource Server Transfer
    D. Remote Service Technology
12. Which HTTP verb is used to create a new resource in a REST API?
    A. GET
    B. POST
    C. PUT
    D. DELETE

13. Which of the following is a key constraint of a RESTful API?
    A. The server must store session state.
    B. The client initiates requests to the server.
    C. Only XML data can be used.
    D. All requests must use the GET method.
14. In a REST API, what does a status code of 404 indicate?
    A. The request was successful.
    B. The resource was not found.
    C. The server encountered an error.
    D. The request was unauthorized.
15. Which of the following headers is commonly used in REST APIs for authentication?
    A. Content-Type
    B. Authorization
    C. Accept
    D. User-Agent
16. What is the purpose of the Accept header in a REST API request?
    A. To specify the content type being sent to the server
    B. To authenticate the request
    C. To specify the data format that the client expects in the response
    D. To define the HTTP method being used
17. Which of the following HTTP status codes indicates that the server is too busy or under maintenance?
    A. 200 OK
    B. 401 Unauthorized
    C. 500 Internal Server Error
    D. 503 Service Unavailable
18. Which REST API method is used to update an existing resource?
    A. GET
    B. POST
    C. PUT
    D. DELETE
19. What does the term "stateless" mean in the context of RESTful APIs?
    A. The server keeps track of client interactions.
    B. The server does not retain any client session information.
    C. The client maintains all server state information.
    D. The API uses cookies to track sessions.

20. In a REST API, which of the following best describes HATEOAS?

A. It requires clients to manage the server state.

B. It ensures that the API is self-discoverable.

C. It mandates the use of JSON data format.

D. It is a method for encrypting API requests.

Chapter 16

Configuration Management

THE FOLLOWING CCNA EXAM TOPICS ARE COVERED IN THIS CHAPTER:

✓ **6.0 Automation and Programmability**

6.6 Recognize the capabilities of configuration management mechanisms such as Ansible and Terraform

After wrapping up the last chapter, you're probably excited about the potential of automation—and who wouldn't be? Automation simplifies our lives by eliminating repetitive tasks and reducing the risk of accidental outages that could disrupt our weekends. However, the challenge often lies in creating the scripts ourselves, which can be time-consuming and may require solving complex logic to make everything function smoothly.

We also examined Catalyst Center, which ensures consistent configurations with its robust templating and automation features. But what if investing in a costly SDN controller isn't an option for your environment?

Fortunately, configuration management tools like Ansible and Terraform can fill that void. These tools not only are excellent for network management but also offer a wide range of capabilities. Ansible, for instance, can create VLANs, configure virtual machines, install and set up applications, and even integrate new systems into your monitoring and backup solutions.

The best part is that these powerful tools are surprisingly user-friendly once you get the hang of them. The real challenge is making the initial shift toward a more DevOps-focused infrastructure team, so we'll also explore what that transition looks like.

Now, let's dive in and discover the capabilities of Ansible and Terraform!

NOTE To find your included bonus material, as well as Todd Lammle videos, practice questions, and hands-on labs, please see `www.lammle.com/ccna`.

Team Silos

Before we dive into configuration management tools, it's important to understand how we arrived at this point. The reality is that if you're working in IT, you won't be dealing exclusively with IT-related tasks, especially in smaller companies with simpler infrastructures. In such environments, IT departments typically consist of one or two IT generalists who handle all things technical.

In small companies, you might not only handle IT tasks but also be the go-to person for anything that goes wrong. Figure 16.1 illustrates the career reality for an IT generalist.

FIGURE 16.1 IT generalist

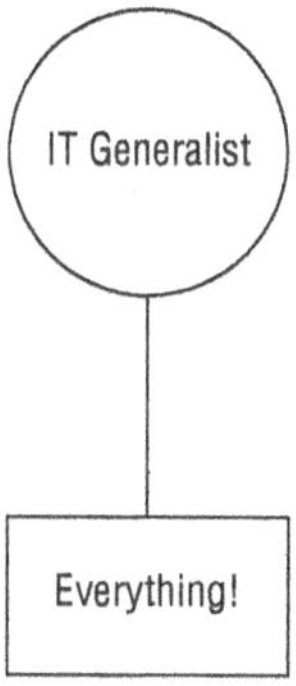

On the other hand, larger companies tend to be more structured, with clearly defined IT roles compartmentalized into different silos. These silos are specialized departments responsible for specific devices, tasks, and projects. This structure can sometimes lead to the network team being blamed for a range of issues, whether they're at fault or not. A typical network team silo is depicted in Figure 16.2.

FIGURE 16.2 Silo network team

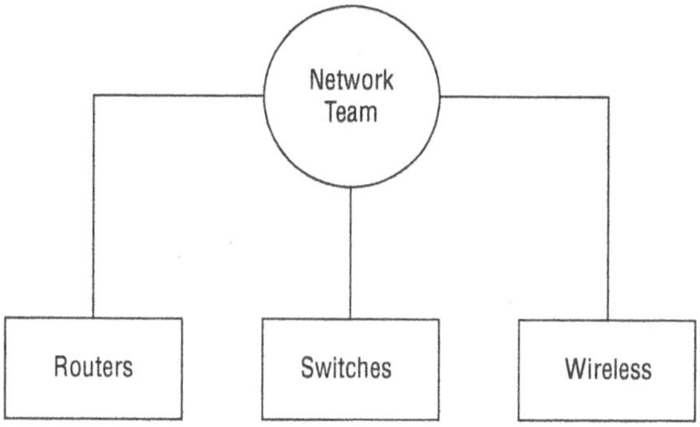

In larger organizations, the sysadmins are usually in charge of the Windows and Linux servers within the infrastructure. In some cases, there are even separate teams dedicated to managing Windows and Linux environments. Figure 16.3 shows a typical silo systems team.

FIGURE 16.3 Silo systems team

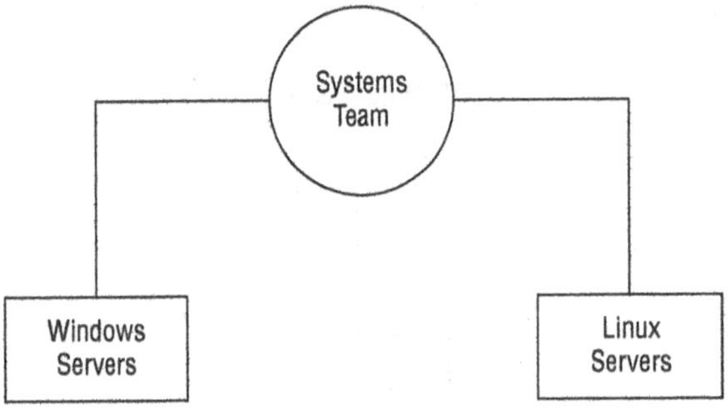

The security team typically focuses on managing the company's firewalls and may also handle tasks like creating virtual private networks (VPNs) for connectivity between companies. They might also manage remote access solutions, such as client VPNs and Citrix, and are responsible for monitoring security events and addressing vulnerabilities as they arise. Figure 16.4 represents the silo security team.

FIGURE 16.4 Silo security team

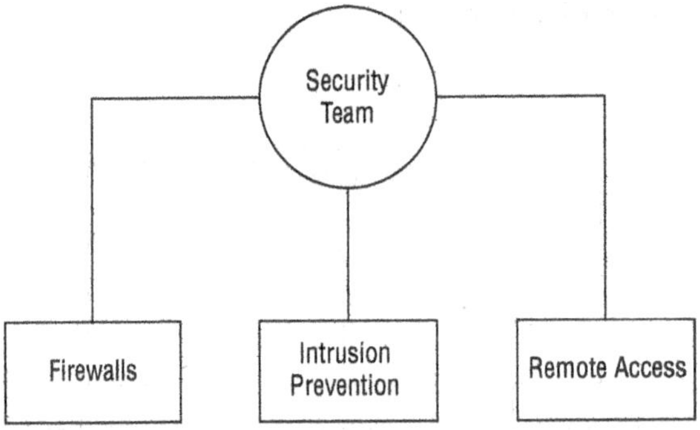

However, these neat organizational silos often blur over time because they can be too restrictive. Companies require customized solutions to meet their unique needs, leading to crossover between silos. For example, the network team might be tasked with setting up VPNs due to their advanced networking expertise.

When considering roles and services running on servers and network devices, the boundaries become even less clear. In some companies, services like DHCP, DNS, and load balancing are managed by the network team; in others, the sysadmins take charge. In some cases, these responsibilities are shared between teams. For instance, sysadmins might manage DHCP servers while the network team handles DHCP traffic on network devices like wireless controllers. Figure 16.5 illustrates how different roles might be assigned to various silos within network services.

FIGURE 16.5 Network services

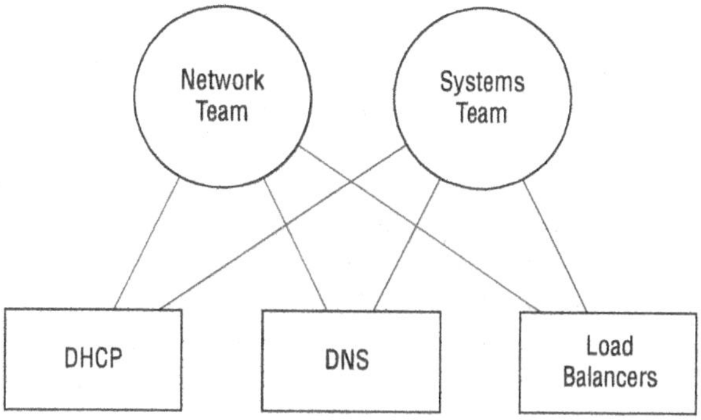

The development silo focuses on supporting software releases. The other IT teams collaborate to build the necessary infrastructure for their applications. For example, suppose a developer needs a new web server. In that case, the network team ensures that it's connected, the systems team installs the operating system and web server software, and the security team checks for compliance with security best practices. Figure 16.6 demonstrates this workflow.

FIGURE 16.6 Silo development team

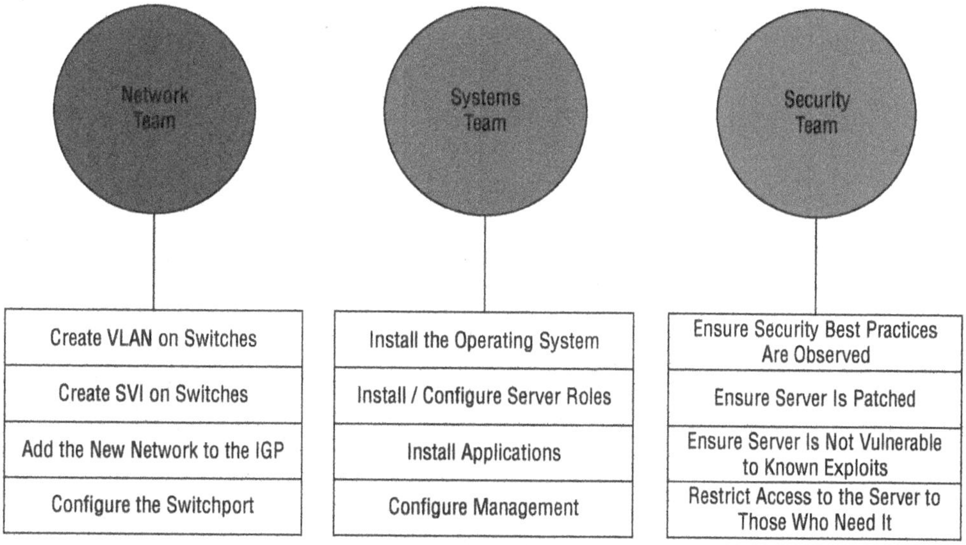

DevOps

DevOps is a widely discussed term in IT today, but it often means different things to different people. At its core, DevOps is more about a shift in corporate culture than simply automating everything. This cultural shift is one reason startups can often adopt DevOps more easily than larger, more established companies. However, many organizations are moving toward DevOps to better manage today's increasingly complex IT infrastructure and cloud implementations.

For our purposes, let's define DevOps as a way to bring teams together to address the challenges associated with working in silos. In a DevOps model, engineers focus on automating infrastructure so that resources can be quickly provisioned as needed for applications.

The most obvious benefit is that IT resources can be provisioned much faster, eliminating the weeks it might otherwise take for different IT teams to complete their tasks to bring a resource online. Additionally, DevOps simplifies change control by allowing code to be tested in various environments and provides the flexibility to roll back changes easily when necessary.

An example of DevOps responsibilities is shown in Figure 16.7.

FIGURE 16.7 DevOps team

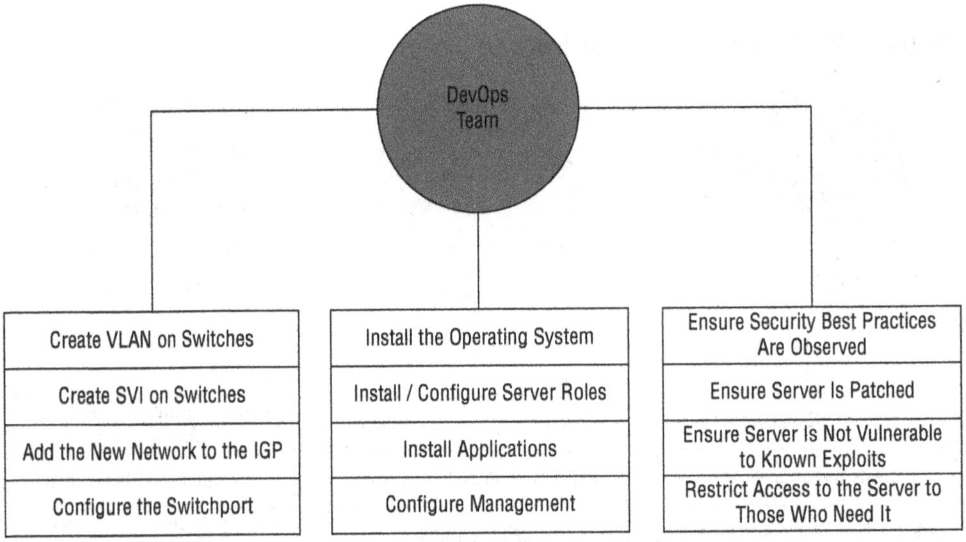

Infrastructure as Code (IaC)

Infrastructure as code (IaC) is essentially the practical implementation of DevOps principles. It's the "automate everything" aspect of DevOps, aimed at creating and managing IT infrastructure through configuration management tools. Not only does IaC speed up deployments, but it also helps prevent configuration drift—those unintended changes that creep in over time on network devices or servers.

Configuration drift is inevitable as companies grow and evolve. It occurs when a server is removed from the network but its VLAN remains on the switches, or when a firewall rule added for troubleshooting is forgotten and left in place. Over time, these small issues accumulate, leading to potential problems down the road. In such cases, IaC offers a solution by allowing us to delete and redeploy the problematic server with the correct configuration, avoiding the chaos of troubleshooting under pressure.

A key advantage of IaC is the ability to periodically destroy and re-create infrastructure, ensuring that it remains aligned with the intended configuration. This process can also automatically update and patch new virtual machines as they are spun up, further reducing drift. For environments using an agent-based configuration manager like Puppet or Chef, drift is corrected automatically, as the servers periodically check in to ensure that they remain compliant with the intended configuration.

A fundamental principle of IaC is idempotence, which means that a configuration is applied only if it results in a change. For example, if you create an Ansible playbook to install and start NTP on a server, the playbook will install NTP only if it isn't already present, and it will start the service only if it isn't already running. This behavior simplifies the configuration process and makes automation more reliable.

Here's a simple example in Ansible to install NTP on a Red Hat server:

```
- name: Install Apache on RHEL
  dnf: name=httpd state=present
```

In this case, Ansible checks whether NTP is installed and proceeds with the installation only if necessary. This contrasts with a basic bash script, where you would have to include logic to check whether NTP is already installed:

```
if ! rpm -qa | grep -qw httpd; then
sudo dnf install -y httpd
fi
```

Although this script works, it's not as clean or efficient as using a configuration management tool that follows the idempotence principle.

IaC and its idempotent behavior simplify deployments by reducing the need for complex script logic to handle different scenarios. Now that you have a solid understanding of IaC, let's explore the configuration management tools that are essential for the CCNA exam and modern network management.

YAML

Before we delve into Ansible, it's crucial to understand the data format it uses for its configuration files: YAML, which stands for "YAML Ain't Markup Language." Despite its playful and somewhat misleading name, YAML is a powerful data serialization language designed to be both human-readable and easy to write. It's becoming increasingly popular across various tools, including Ansible, due to its simplicity and flexibility in handling configuration data.

Components of YAML

YAML is composed of three fundamental components that make it intuitive and straightforward:

- **Mappings:** These are simple key-value pairs, separated by a colon (:)—for example, `name: Todd`. Mappings are used to define properties and their corresponding values, making it easy to represent structured data.
- **Lists:** These are akin to a bullet list in plain text, where each item is placed on a new line and begins with a dash (-). Lists in YAML are used to group multiple items under a single property, making it easy to manage collections of related data.
- **Scalars:** In programming terms, a scalar represents a single value, such as a string, Boolean, or number. In YAML, both keys and values in mappings, as well as items in lists, are considered scalars. Scalars form the basic building blocks of YAML, allowing it to represent simple and complex data structures effectively.

Example of YAML

Here's an example of a YAML file that illustrates these components:

```
---                     # All YAML files start with three dashes
name: Todd Lammle       # This is a mapping
books:                  # This is a list
  - CCNA
  - CCST
  - Network+
videos:                 # This is another list
  - CCNA
  - Secure Firewall
  - ISE
```

In this example, `name` is a mapping with a single value, and `books` and `videos` are lists containing multiple items. The YAML format is clean and easy to follow, making it ideal for configuration files and data interchange between systems.

Important YAML Rules

YAML's simplicity is one of its strengths, but it also comes with some strict rules that must be followed to ensure proper formatting and interpretation:

- **Whitespace:** Whitespace in YAML is significant as it defines the structure of the data. Proper indentation is essential, as it indicates the relationships between elements. For instance, the items under `books` are separate from the items under `videos` due to their indentation levels.

- **Indentation:** YAML strictly requires spaces for indentation; tabs are not allowed. This requirement ensures that the structure remains consistent and readable across different environments and tools. It's common practice to use two spaces per indentation level in YAML files.
- **Spacing in mappings:** When defining mappings, it's important to include a space between the colon and the value. For example, `name: Todd` is correct, whereas `name:Todd` could lead to errors or misinterpretation by YAML parsers.

Why YAML?

YAML's user-friendly syntax is a key factor behind its widespread adoption. Unlike other serialization formats that have a bunch of strict rules, such as JSON and XML, YAML aims to be the simplest to read and understand, which helps minimize errors during manual editing. Its intuitive structure makes it accessible, even for those with limited programming experience. However, despite its simplicity, you're almost certain to run into a spacing issue at some point—YAML's strict indentation rules can be both a blessing and a challenge.

In the realm of configuration management tools like Ansible, YAML's clear and concise syntax enables IT professionals to quickly define configurations, create playbooks, and manage IaC with minimal effort. This combination of ease of use and powerful functionality makes YAML an invaluable tool for anyone involved in modern IT automation and configuration management.

Ansible

Ansible is currently one of networking professionals' most popular configuration management tools. This Python-based solution applies configurations found in playbook files via SSH connections, making it a straightforward option for network automation.

One of Ansible's key advantages is its simplicity in setup. It doesn't require agents to be installed on target systems or a central server to operate. You can even run playbooks directly from your laptop. However, using a central location for running Ansible is generally recommended, especially because it needs SSH access to the target nodes, and your network likely has security measures that limit direct access.

Because Ansible primarily uses SSH and doesn't rely on agents, it supports nearly all major vendor systems in the networking industry. Vendors only need to provide Ansible modules, which are essentially Python scripts that instruct Ansible on what actions to perform. The IaC section briefly mentioned the yum module to illustrate how to install NTP on a Red Hat Linux system.

Playbooks in Ansible are written in YAML, a format we discussed earlier, and they contain instructions on what should be applied to the target devices.

Here's a comparison of Ansible and Ansible Tower/AWX with other solutions:

Pros:

- Easy to install and set up
- Powerful orchestration capabilities
- Widely supported by most enterprise-grade vendors
- Supports both push and pull models
- Agentless operation is faster and less complex than agent-based models
- Sequential execution order ensures predictable deployments

Cons:

- Requires root SSH access to Linux nodes
- Syntax can vary due to Ansible's scripting components
- Primarily focused on configuration management rather than resource creation, making it less suitable for provisioning tasks like Terraform is
- Troubleshooting can be more challenging than in Terraform
- Lacks native configuration rollback in case of failures

Installation

Ansible is a lightweight solution that can be easily installed on Linux or Mac systems, and it can also be installed on Windows using the WSL shell if preferred. Although you can install Ansible using your operating system's package manager, these often provide versions that are several releases behind the latest.

For the most up-to-date version, it's recommended to use pip, Python's package manager, with the command `pip install ansible`. This ensures that you're running the latest version available:

```
(venv) [the-packet-thrower@rhel01 ~]$ pip install ansible
Collecting ansible
  Downloading ansible-8.7.0-py3-none-any.whl (48.4 MB)
     |████████████████████████████████| 48.4 MB 980 kB/s
```

Once Ansible is installed, it has only two setting files you must have on your computer before you try to run a playbook—a settings file called `ansible.cfg` and an inventory file typically called `hosts`. Once those two files are in place, we can run Ansible in Ad-hoc mode or write a playbook. Let's have a closer look at those files now. In Figure 16.8, you can see a visualization of the Ansible components:

FIGURE 16.8 Ansible components

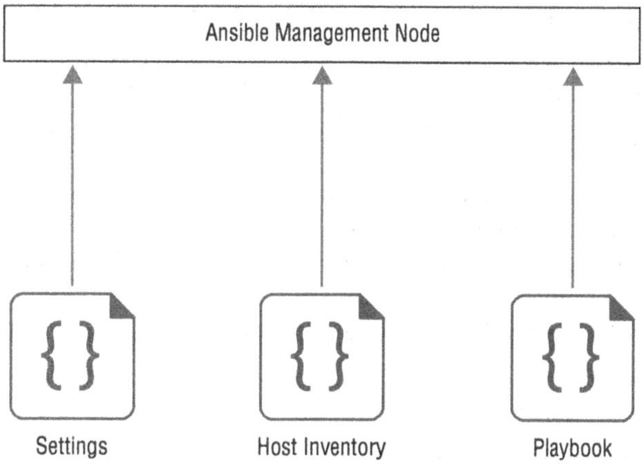

Settings

The `ansible.cfg` file is optional, as Ansible will default to its built-in settings if it can't find the configuration file. When you install Ansible via `pip`, it typically doesn't create folders or files for you.

By default, Ansible checks the `ANSIBLE_CONFIG` environment variable for a path to the configuration file. If that's not set, it looks for `ansible.cfg` in the current directory where the playbook is being run. If the file still isn't found, Ansible will search your home directory and finally `/etc/ansible/`. To keep your setup organized and easy to manage, it's a good idea to place the configuration file in the `/etc/ansible/` directory if possible; otherwise, Ansible will look in its working directory when you run Ansible.

Even though Ansible offers a wide range of settings, for simplicity, we'll create a configuration file that only disables SSH host key checking by setting `host_key_checking` to `false` under the `[defaults]` section. This makes working in a lab environment easier, as Ansible won't require saved SSH host keys for the target nodes before running the playbook. Here's how to set it up:

```
[ansible@rhel01 ~]$ sudo mkdir /etc/ansible/
[ansible@rhel01 ~]$ cat /etc/ansible/ansible.cfg
[defaults]
host_key_checking = False
```

Inventory

The inventory file in Ansible specifies which target nodes to connect to and how those connections should be made. It also allows you to group nodes for easier management. By default, Ansible looks for the hosts file in `/etc/ansible/` when attempting to access nodes. However, when running Ansible, you can specify a different location by using a command-line switch.

In the `hosts` file, you can create groups and subgroups for easier reference. For example, you could create groups for switches and routers and then combine these into a larger group for easy administration. You can define the connection variables by appending `:vars` to the group name that will use them.

Here are three built-in variables used to define how Ansible connects to Cisco devices:

- **ansible_connection:** Defines the connection method Ansible uses to connect to the nodes. Using `local` means it will SSH from the Ansible control node.
- **ansible_user:** Specifies the default username for the connection.
- **ansible_password:** Specifies the default password for the connection.

Here is an example of what an Ansible `hosts` file might look like:

```
[root@rhel01 ~]# cat /etc/ansible/hosts
[switch]
sw0[1:2].testlab.com
[router]
r0[1:2].testlab.com
[cisco:children]
switch
router
[cisco:vars]
ansible_connection=local
ansible_user=ansible
ansible_password=ansible
```

This configuration groups the switches and routers separately and then combines them into a single `cisco` group for easier management. The `:vars` section sets the connection details that will be used when Ansible connects to these devices.

Lab Setup

To set up Ansible for our lab, I'll create a playbook that configures the network topology illustrated in Figure 16.9.

I'll configure routing between R01 and R02 using Ansible, with each router connecting to VLANs 101 and 102, respectively. Both routers will have a default route pointing to the SVI. Ultimately, our playbook should enable successful pings between the two routers.

FIGURE 16.9 Ansible topology

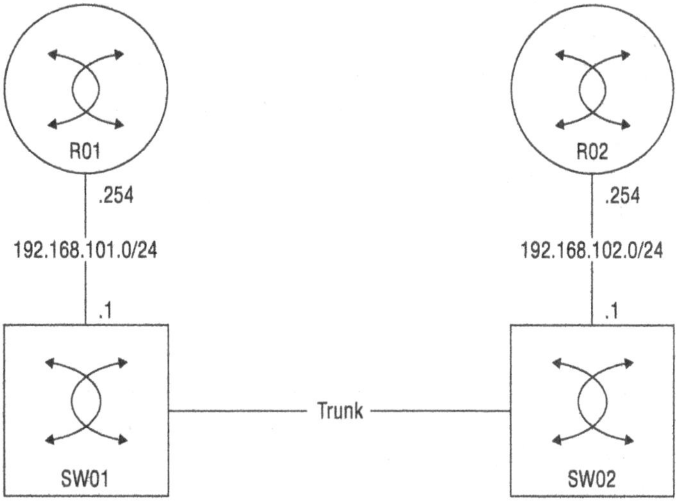

First, I'll need to enable SSH and create a user for Ansible to use on all our Cisco devices. To simplify our lab environment, I'll assign the user privilege level 15 with the following commands:

```
SW01(config)#aaa new-model
SW01(config)#aaa authentication login default local
SW01(config)#aaa authorization exec default local
SW01(config)#username ansible priv 15 secret ansible
SW01(config)#ip domain-name testlab.com
SW01(config)#crypto key generate rsa modulus 2048
```

When prompted, the name for the keys will be: `SW01.testlab.com`

```
% The key modulus size is 2048 bits
% Generating 2048 bit RSA keys, keys will be non-exportable...
[OK] (elapsed time was 2 seconds)
SW01(config)#
*Sep 23 05:29:53.728: %SSH-5-ENABLED: SSH 1.99 has been enabled

SW01(config)#line vty 0 15
SW01(config-line)#transport input ssh
SW01(config-line)#do wr
Building configuration..
```

Now that our network is set up, I'll create some host records for my Cisco devices, enabling us to use DNS names with Ansible. However, you can use IP addresses if you prefer:

```
[root@rhel01 ~]# cat /etc/hosts
127.0.0.1   localhost localhost.localdomain localhost4 localhost4.localdomain4
::1         localhost localhost.localdomain localhost6 localhost6.localdomain6
10.10.21.51     sw01.testlab.com
10.10.21.52     sw02.testlab.com
10.10.21.53     r01.testlab.com
10.10.21.54     r02.testlab.com
```

Modules

I'm currently using Ansible version 8.7.0, which comes with a whopping 8,431 modules! You can explore these modules using the `ansible-doc–l` command. Because this is a CCNA-focused discussion, I'll narrow down the list to just the IOS-specific modules and trim the output for brevity.

Typically, these modules are provided by the vendor, but you can also create your own custom modules in Python if you need more flexibility. For example, the `ios_command` module allows you to push an exec-level command to a Cisco device and capture the show output, and the `ios_config` module is used to push configuration commands.

What sets Ansible apart from a standard Python script that pushes commands is the availability of specialized modules that allow you to perform specific tasks, such as adding a banner or enabling BGP, by simply calling the appropriate module. You'll see this in action when we dive into our playbook example.

Here's an example of how to list IOS-specific modules:

```
(venv) [the-packet-thrower@rhel01 ~]$ ansible-doc -l cisco.ios
cisco.ios.ios_acl_interfaces       Resource module to configure ACL interfaces
cisco.ios.ios_acls                 Resource module to configure ACLs
cisco.ios.ios_banner               Module to configure multiline banners
cisco.ios.ios_bgp                  Module to configure BGP protocol settings
cisco.ios.ios_bgp_address_family  Resource module to configure BGP Address family
cisco.ios.ios_bgp_global           Resource module to configure BGP
cisco.ios.ios_command              Module to run commands on remote devices
cisco.ios.ios_config               Module to manage configuration sections
cisco.ios.ios_facts                Module to collect facts from remote devices
cisco.ios.ios_hostname             Resource module to configure hostname
cisco.ios.ios_interfaces           Resource module to configure interfaces
cisco.ios.ios_l2_interfaces        Resource module to configure L2 interfaces
cisco.ios.ios_l3_interfaces        Resource module to configure L3 interfaces
cisco.ios.ios_lacp                 Resource module to configure LACP
```

```
cisco.ios.ios_lacp_interfaces    Resource module to configure LACP interfaces
cisco.ios.ios_lag_interfaces     Resource module to configure LAG interfaces
cisco.ios.ios_linkagg            Module to configure link aggregation groups
cisco.ios.ios_lldp               (deprecated, removed after 2024-06-01) Manage
LLDP configuration on Cisco IOS network devices
cisco.ios.ios_lldp_global        Resource module to configure LLDP
cisco.ios.ios_lldp_interfaces    Resource module to configure LLDP interfaces
cisco.ios.ios_logging_global     Resource module to configure logging
cisco.ios.ios_ntp                (deprecated, removed after 2024-01-01)
Manages core NTP configuration
cisco.ios.ios_ntp_global         Resource module to configure NTP
cisco.ios.ios_ospf_interfaces    Resource module to configure OSPF interfaces
cisco.ios.ios_ospfv2             Resource module to configure OSPFv2
cisco.ios.ios_ospfv3             Resource module to configure OSPFv3
cisco.ios.ios_ping               Tests reachability using ping from IOS switch
cisco.ios.ios_prefix_lists       Resource module to configure prefix lists
cisco.ios.ios_route_maps         Resource module to configure route maps
cisco.ios.ios_service            Resource module to configure service
cisco.ios.ios_snmp_server        Resource module to configure snmp server
cisco.ios.ios_static_routes      Resource module to configure static routes
cisco.ios.ios_system             Module to manage the system attributes
cisco.ios.ios_user               Module to manage the aggregates of local users
cisco.ios.ios_vlans              Resource module to configure VLANs
cisco.ios.ios_vrf                Module to configure VRF definitions
```

If you want detailed information on a specific module, append the module name to the `ansible-doc` command. For instance, here's a snippet of the output from the `ansible-doc ios_vlan` command, edited for brevity:

```
EXAMPLES:
- name: Create vlan
  ios_vlan:
    vlan_id: 100
    name: test-vlan
    state: present
- name: Add interfaces to VLAN
  ios_vlan:
    vlan_id: 100
    interfaces:
      - GigabitEthernet0/0
      - GigabitEthernet0/1
```

Ad-Hoc Example

Now that you've seen Ansible in action and gotten familiar with a few modules, let's try running some ad-hoc commands without creating a playbook. Ad-hoc commands are particularly useful when troubleshooting and quickly checking if things are running smoothly.

One of the most common ad-hoc modules is `ping`, which attempts to connect to the specified group and lets you know if the connection is successful. Here's an example using the default `localhost` group where Ansible is running:

```
[ansible@rhel01 ~]$ ansible localhost -m ping
localhost | SUCCESS => {
    "changed": false,
    "ping": "pong"
}
```

Playbook Example

With everything set up, let's dive into the playbook I've put together. The final script is 144 lines long; although I could have made it more efficient, I kept it straightforward to ensure that you can follow along easily.

Because playbooks are written in YAML, each file starts with `---` at the top. I've provided descriptive names for each section so that it's clear what the playbook is doing as it runs.

The `hosts` keyword specifies which group or host in the inventory file the tasks will target. Because we're working with Cisco devices, the `gather_facts` option is set to no—this prevents Ansible from trying to gather system facts, which isn't necessary for Cisco devices. However, if you want similar functionality for IOS devices, Cisco does offer an `ios_facts` module.

In the All Switches play, I'm using a loop to create three VLANs—one for each router and one for the link between the switches. Additionally, I'm configuring the trunk port between the switches and enabling IP routing on the switches to support OSPF. Here's the playbook for that:

```
---
######## All Switches ########
- name: Configure Switches
  hosts: switch
  gather_facts: no
  tasks:
  - name: Create VLANs
    ios_vlan:
      vlan_id: "{{ item }}"
      name: "ANSIBLE-VLAN{{ item }}"
```

```
    loop:
      - 101
      - 102
      - 123
  - name: Configure Trunk Port between SW01 and SW02
    ios_l2_interface:
      name: GigabitEthernet3/0
      mode: trunk
  - name: Enable IP Routing on Switches
    ios_config:
      lines: ip routing
```

In the following `All Devices` play, I'm enabling OSPF on all devices in the `cisco` group, which includes both the router and switch groups.

NOTE Whitespace is crucial in YAML. If you're trying this on your own, be mindful of the spacing. Also, avoid using the Tab key—always use spaces for indentation.

```
######## All Devices ########
- name: Configure All Devices
  hosts: cisco
  gather_facts: no
  tasks:
  - name: Enable OSPF on All Devices
    ios_config:
      lines:
        - network 0.0.0.0 0.0.0.0 area 0
      parents: router ospf 1
```

For the remaining plays, I'm working with individual nodes because they each have unique configurations. For SW01, I'll assign VLANs to interfaces, create the SVIs with IPs, and enable them.

It's good to note that aside from the routing commands where I used the `ios_config` module, most tasks have specialized modules that make configurations cleaner. Here's the playbook for SW01:

```
######## SW01 ########
- name: Configure SW01
  hosts: sw01.testlab.com
  gather_facts: no
  tasks:
```

```
  - name: Assign SW01 VLANs
    ios_vlan:
      vlan_id: 101
      interfaces:
      - GigabitEthernet0/1
  - name: Create Vlan101 SVI
    ios_l3_interface:
      name: Vlan101
      ipv4: 192.168.101.1/24
  - name: Create Vlan123 SVI
    ios_l3_interface:
      name: Vlan123
      ipv4: 192.168.123.1/24
  - name: Enable SVIs
    ios_interface:
      name: "{{ item }}"
      enabled: True
    loop:
      - Vlan101
      - Vlan123
```

SW02's configuration is very similar to what we did with SW01. Again, there are better ways of doing this, such as using something called Jinja2 templates, but that is well beyond what you need to know for the CCNA:

```
######## SW02 ########
- name: Configure SW02
  hosts: sw02.testlab.com
  gather_facts: no
  tasks:
  - name: Assign SW02 VLANs
    ios_vlan:
      vlan_id: 102
      interfaces:
      - GigabitEthernet0/1
  - name: Create Vlan102 SVI
    ios_l3_interface:
      name: Vlan102
      ipv4: 192.168.102.1/24
  - name: Create Vlan123 SVI
    ios_l3_interface:
      name: Vlan123
      ipv4: 192.168.123.2/24
```

```
  - name: Enable SVIs
    ios_interface:
      name: "{{ item }}"
      enabled: True
    loop:
      - Vlan102
      - Vlan123
```

Next, I'll configure R01 by assigning an IP address to its interface, enabling it, and adding a default route:

```
######## R01 ########
- name: Configure R01
  hosts: r01.testlab.com
  gather_facts: no
  tasks:
  - name: Create R01 G0/1
    ios_l3_interface:
      name: Gig0/1
      ipv4: 192.168.101.254/24
  - name: Enable G0/1
    ios_interface:
      name: Gig0/1
      enabled: True
  - name: Add Default Route
    ios_static_route:
      prefix: 0.0.0.0
      mask: 0.0.0.0
      next_hop: 192.168.101.1
```

R02's configuration mirrors that of R01:

```
######## R02 ########
- name: Configure R02
  hosts: r02.testlab.com
  gather_facts: no
  tasks:
  - name: Create R02 G0/1
    ios_l3_interface:
      name: Gig0/1
      ipv4: 192.168.102.254/24
  - name: Enable G0/1
    ios_interface:
```

```
        name: Gig0/1
        enabled: True
  - name: Add Default Route
    ios_static_route:
      prefix: 0.0.0.0
      mask: 0.0.0.0
      next_hop: 192.168.102.1
```

Once the playbook is ready, I'll execute it using the `ansible-playbook` command. This process begins with Ansible performing a verification check on the playbook file to ensure that there are no syntax errors or misconfigurations that could cause issues during execution. Once the verification is complete, Ansible will proceed to execute the playbook, running each task sequentially from top to bottom.

As the playbook runs, Ansible provides real-time feedback on the progress of each play and task. This feedback includes information on whether the tasks were successfully completed, if any changes were made to the target nodes, and if any errors were encountered during the process. This step-by-step feedback is crucial for monitoring the deployment and troubleshooting any issues that may arise, allowing you to identify and address any problems in the configuration quickly:

```
[root@rhel01 ~]# ansible-playbook cisco.yml
PLAY [Configure Switches]
********************************************************************************
***************************************************************
TASK [Create VLANs]
********************************************************************************
**********************************************************************
ok: [sw01.testlab.com] => (item=101)
ok: [sw02.testlab.com] => (item=101)
ok: [sw01.testlab.com] => (item=102)
ok: [sw02.testlab.com] => (item=102)
ok: [sw02.testlab.com] => (item=123)
ok: [sw01.testlab.com] => (item=123)
TASK [Configure Trunk Port between SW01 and SW02]
********************************************************************************
***************************************
ok: [sw02.testlab.com]
ok: [sw01.testlab.com]
<Omitted for brevity>
PLAY RECAP
********************************************************************************
*******************************************************************************
r01.testlab.com            : ok=4    changed=3    unreachable=0    failed=0
skipped=0    rescued=0    ignored=0
r02.testlab.com            : ok=4    changed=3    unreachable=0    failed=0
skipped=0    rescued=0    ignored=0
```

```
sw01.testlab.com          : ok=8    changed=4    unreachable=0    failed=0
skipped=0    rescued=0    ignored=0
sw02.testlab.com          : ok=8    changed=4    unreachable=0    failed=0
skipped=0    rescued=0    ignore
```

Once the playbook completes its run, our network will be configured—similar to executing a Python script. However, the beauty of Ansible lies in its idempotency, meaning if I were to run the playbook again, no changes would be made unless something actually needed updating.

By clearly naming my plays and tasks based on their functions, I can easily identify if and where something went wrong during execution. This is crucial because although Ansible will attempt to pinpoint the error and provide a reason, its accuracy can vary. Sometimes the feedback is helpful, and other times it's less precise.

For example, if I accidentally remove the indentation on the `vlan_id` line under `Create VLANs` and rerun the playbook, Ansible correctly identifies the general area of the issue. However, the interpreter might mistakenly suggest that the problem is related to missing quotes—oops! Here's how that looks:

```
[root@rhel01 ~]# cat broke-cisco.yml
---
######## All Switches ########
- name: Configure Switches
  hosts: switch
  gather_facts: no
  tasks:
  - name: Create VLANs
    ios_vlan:
    vlan_id: "{{ item }}"
      name: "ANSIBLE-VLAN{{ item }}"
    loop:
      - 101
      - 102
      - 123
[root@rhel01 ~]# ansible-playbook broke-cisco.yml
ERROR! Syntax Error while loading YAML.
  did not find expected key
The error appears to be in '/root/broke-cisco.yml': line 11, column 7, but may
be elsewhere in the file depending on the exact syntax problem.
The offending line appears to be:
    vlan_id: "{{ item }}"
      name: "ANSIBLE-VLAN{{ item }}"
      ^ here
```

```
We could be wrong, but this one looks like it might be an issue with
missing quotes. Always quote template expression brackets when they
start a value. For instance:
    with_items:
      - {{ foo }}
Should be written as:
    with_items:
      - "{{ foo }}
```

Although it's true that no one expects you to know how to make an Ansible playbook for the CCNA, it's really good for you to see it in action anyway because the IaC concept is actually a new way of thinking for many people in this industry!

Here's a quick rundown of some key Ansible terms:

- **Inventory:** Defines the nodes that Ansible knows about and organizes them into groups for easier management. It also includes connection details and variables.
- **Playbook:** A file containing a set of instructions (plays) to be executed on target nodes.
- **Play:** A section of a playbook that applies configuration to a specific group of nodes.
- **Variables:** Custom variables you can define and use within your playbooks.
- **Templates:** Ansible supports Python's Jinja2 templates, which are particularly useful for network administration.
- **Tasks:** Actions that the playbook applies, such as installing software or configuring interfaces.
- **Handlers:** Special tasks that are only triggered by specific events, like starting a service after installation.
- **Roles:** Allow you to structure your playbooks into multiple folders, making configurations more modular and scalable.
- **Modules:** Built-in components that define how Ansible will accomplish a given task. You can also create your own modules.
- **Facts:** Global variables that contain detailed information about the target system, including its IP address and other vital stats.

Ansible Tower/AWX

Ansible offers two enterprise-focused solutions for those who need enhanced central management and security controls:

- **Ansible Tower:** A paid solution from Red Hat that adds centralized management to Ansible, enhancing security by allowing control over who can run playbooks through Role-Based Access Control (RBAC). Ansible Tower also serves as a single integration point for other tools. Red Hat provides a free version that supports up to 10 hosts if you want to try it.

- **AWX:** The upstream, open-source version of Ansible Tower, like how Fedora relates to Red Hat Enterprise Linux. It's free to use, but it comes with less stability, as frequent changes and limited testing can lead to potential issues. Additionally, support for AWX is limited.

Terraform

HashiCorp's Terraform is a powerful and widely used IaC tool, often referred to as a *provisioner*. It stands out for its ability to create and manage resources across various environments, whether deploying virtual machines, configuring networks, or building cloud infrastructure. Terraform's primary strength lies in its flexibility and cloud-agnostic approach, allowing you to define infrastructure using the HashiCorp Configuration Language (HCL). This high-level language facilitates consistent provisioning and management of resources across multiple cloud platforms like AWS, Azure, and Google Cloud as well as on-premises data centers.

Terraform is especially valuable in environments that require dynamic and scalable infrastructure. It allows you to automate your entire infrastructure lifecycle—from initial provisioning to ongoing management and eventual decommissioning. This speeds up deployment and ensures that your infrastructure remains consistent and reliable. By using Terraform, teams can apply standardized configurations across different environments, significantly reducing the risk of human error and configuration drift, which can lead to inconsistencies and potential issues.

Moreover, Terraform's state management feature ensures idempotency by tracking the current state of your infrastructure, enabling it to make precise, incremental changes and apply only the necessary updates to achieve the desired configuration. This process minimizes downtime and ensures that your infrastructure evolves in a controlled and manageable way. Overall, Terraform is an indispensable tool for organizations embracing modern DevOps practices, allowing them to maintain control over complex, multicloud environments.

Cisco recognizes the importance of Terraform in modern IT practices and has made significant investments to ensure compatibility with many of its products as part of its broader DevNet strategy. This initiative positions Cisco as a leader in automation. Consequently, Terraform has been integrated into most of Cisco's certifications, including the latest version of the CCNA, which you are preparing for with this book.

Installation

Terraform is notably more lightweight than Ansible, primarily because it operates from a single executable file, making it incredibly easy to install and manage. This streamlined approach means that Terraform doesn't require additional dependencies or complex setup procedures, which significantly simplifies its deployment and use.

Moreover, Terraform is designed to be highly versatile, supporting all major operating systems, including Linux, macOS, and native Windows environments. This lightweight, cross-platform nature of Terraform allows teams to adopt it quickly and efficiently, regardless of their existing technology stack, making it an ideal tool for modern, dynamic infrastructure management.

To install Terraform on my Mac, I need to use Brew, my preferred Mac package manager; or I could go to HashiCorp's Terraform site for up-to-date downloads:

```
the-packet-thrower@macmini31 CCNA % brew install hashicorp/tap/terraform
==> Fetching hashicorp/tap/terraform
==> Downloading https://releases.hashicorp.com/terraform/1.9.5/
terraform_1.9.5_darwin_arm64.zip
Already downloaded: /Users/the-packet-thrower/Library/Caches/Homebrew/
downloads/1efcc9b209d02554523fd176682b2c7704aee2798a40cf5a2ccd21eff7417983--
terraform_1.9.5_darwin_arm64.zip
==> Installing terraform from hashicorp/tap
🍺  /opt/homebrew/Cellar/terraform/1.9.5: 5 files, 83.8MB, built in 1 second
```

Providers

One significant difference between Ansible and Terraform is how they handle vendor support. Ansible comes with over 8,000 modules preinstalled, allowing it to immediately interact with a wide variety of devices and systems without requiring additional configuration. Terraform, on the other hand, takes a more modular approach. It doesn't include any vendor support by default, meaning there are no built-in modules when you first install it. Instead, Terraform requires you to define and configure the specific vendor support, known as *providers*, that you need.

This design choice keeps Terraform lightweight and adaptable, making it easy to tailor to the unique needs of your environment. Providers, which function as plugins, enable Terraform to interact with various cloud platforms, service providers, and infrastructure components. By selecting the appropriate providers, you can configure Terraform to manage resources across platforms like AWS, Azure, Google Cloud, and Cisco, among others. Although this approach necessitates some initial setup, it offers greater flexibility and control, allowing you to create a customized and efficient infrastructure management solution.

Because providers aren't included in the initial installation, HashiCorp hosts all of them in the Terraform Registry. The Terraform Registry contains all the necessary information, including documentation on using each provider and managing resources. In Terraform, a resource is a fundamental concept representing a single component of your infrastructure. For example, in a Cisco context, a resource might be an interface you are configuring.

Like Ansible, Terraform allows you to create your own providers if needed. The key difference is that Terraform uses the Golang programming language, and Ansible uses Python. Figure 16.10 shows the Terraform Registry page for Cisco's IOS-XE provider, which we will use in a minute.

FIGURE 16.10 Terraform providers

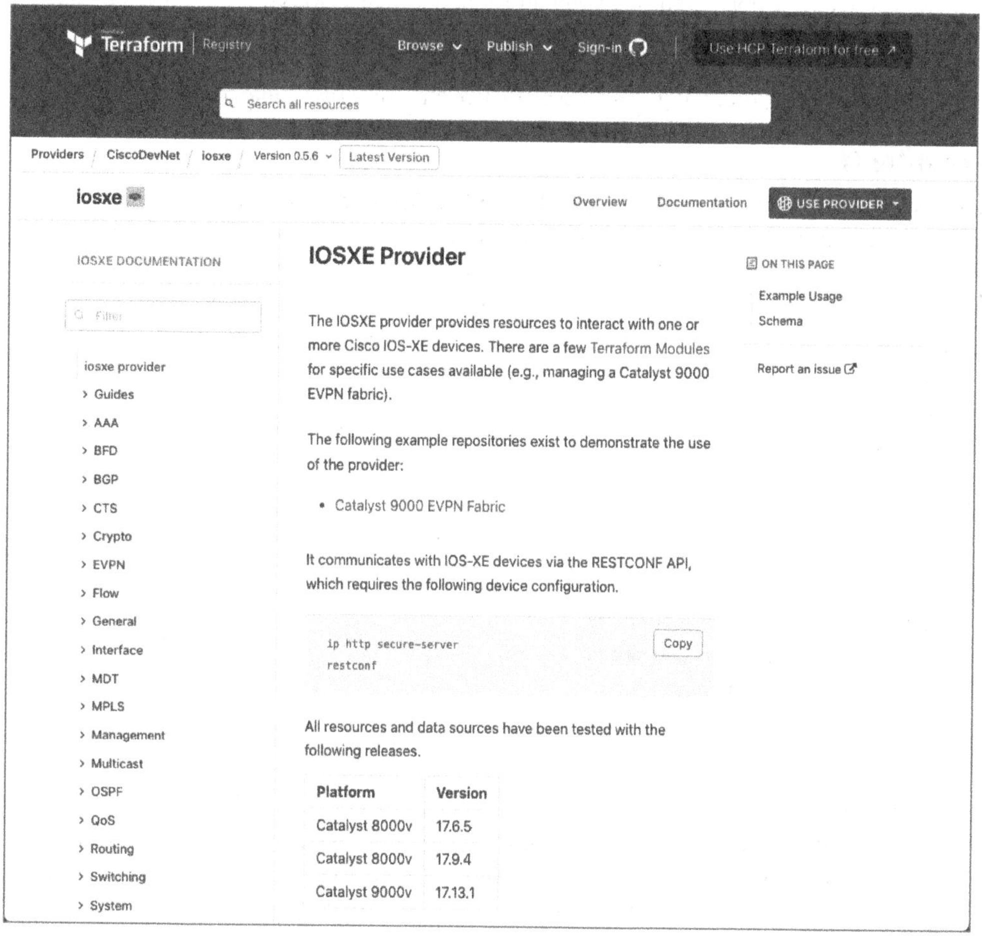

Configuration Files

Terraform is less structured than Ansible. Whereas Ansible requires you to have an inventory file and a playbook to function (with an optional settings file), Terraform allows you to place everything in a single file if you prefer. However, this approach can quickly become confusing and is generally not recommended.

Fortunately, Terraform allows you to split your configuration into as many files as needed. The application will automatically combine them in a logical order that makes sense. For instance, if you have one file that defines IP addresses for a loopback interface and another file that creates the actual interface, Terraform will intelligently create the loopback interface first and then assign the IP addresses.

The way this works is that Terraform will scan your directory for any file that has a `.tf` extension and will use it for the configuration; it will also search for another file that should store any sensitive information like passwords, typically called `terraform.tfvars`, although it looks for any file that has that extension.

With that in mind, following is the best-practice structure that I like to use.

Provider.tf

The provider information should be stored in a file called `provider.tf`. in our case, I got the `iosxe` provider information from the registry, pasted it into the file, and then added the login info that we need to log in to my lab router as variables that we will define in the next file:

```
terraform {
  required_providers {
    iosxe = {
      source = "CiscoDevNet/iosxe"
    }
  }
}
provider "iosxe" {
  username = var.router_username
  password = var.router_password
  url      = var.router_url
}
```

Variables.tf

The variables file holds all the variables you'll need for your configuration. It's good practice to set variables here because it adds flexibility, especially when updating things like login credentials. However, you shouldn't store your username and password directly in this file. Instead, those sensitive details should be placed in the `terraform.tfvars` file:

```
variable "router_url" {
  type = string
  default = "https://10.30.10.193"
}
variable "router_username" {
  type = string
}
variable "router_password" {
  type = string
}
```

Terraform.tfvars

This file is dedicated to storing your sensitive information. By isolating it in a separate file, you can better protect this data. Keeping this file out of repositories is crucial to prevent it from being accidentally shared with unauthorized individuals:

```
router_username = "admin"
router_password = "labPassword1234!"
```

Loopback.tf

Finally, we can actually configure our resources; let's do something simple like create Loopback 100 on my lab router and give it an IP address along with a description. Traditionally, you wouldn't use Terraform for this kind of task; rather, you would use it to actually create a new virtual appliance in your infrastructure; but as mentioned earlier, Cisco is working on making sure you can use Terraform for configuration management as well:

```
resource "iosxe_interface_loopback" "loopback" {
  name               = 100
  description        = "Made with Terraform!"
  ipv4_address       = "192.168.100.1"
  ipv4_address_mask  = "255.255.255.255"
}
```

Init Phase

Once we finish our files, we need to initialize the provider, which causes Terraform to download the binaries from the registry for us; once that is done, you can run your Terraform configuration as much as your heart desires:

```
the-packet-thrower@macmini31 Terraform % terraform init
Initializing the backend...
Initializing provider plugins...
- Reusing previous version of ciscodevnet/iosxe from the dependency lock file
- Installing ciscodevnet/iosxe v0.5.6...
- Installed ciscodevnet/iosxe v0.5.6 (signed by a HashiCorp partner, key ID
974C06066198C482)
Partner and community providers are signed by their developers.
```

If you'd like to know more about provider signing, you can read about it here:

```
https://www.terraform.io/docs/cli/plugins/signing.html
Terraform has been successfully initialized!
```

Planning Phase

Because Terraform is a provisioner, it can do a soft run of your proposed configuration to see exactly what Terraform would do to your infrastructure. To do this, we use the `terraform plan` command. This is known as the *planning phase* and is very useful for ensuring that your changes do not have any unintended consequences. You can even save the plan output and actually execute it later if you need to wait for a change window before you can implement it:

```
the-packet-thrower@macmini31 Terraform % terraform plan
Terraform used the selected providers to generate the following execution
plan. Resource actions are indicated with the following symbols:
  + create
Terraform will perform the following actions:
  # iosxe_interface_loopback.loopback will be created
  + resource "iosxe_interface_loopback" "loopback" {
      + description       = "Made with Terraform!"
      + id                = (known after apply)
      + ipv4_address      = "192.168.100.1"
      + ipv4_address_mask = "255.255.255.255"
      + name              = 100
    }
Plan: 1 to add, 0 to change, 0 to destroy.
_____________________________________________________________________________

Note: You didn't use the -out option to save this plan, so Terraform can't
guarantee to take exactly these actions if you run "terraform apply" now.
```

Implement Phase

Finally, we can actually implement our configuration with the `apply` command. It will automatically run the planning phase again, except this time, it will ask you if you want to approve the changes. If you do, the changes will be implemented:

```
the-packet-thrower@macmini31 Terraform % terraform apply
Terraform used the selected providers to generate the following execution
plan. Resource actions are indicated with the following symbols:
  + create
Terraform will perform the following actions:
  # iosxe_interface_loopback.loopback will be created
  + resource "iosxe_interface_loopback" "loopback" {
      + description       = "Made with Terraform!"
      + id                = (known after apply)
      + ipv4_address      = "192.168.100.1"
```

```
      + ipv4_address_mask = "255.255.255.255"
      + name              = 100
    }
Plan: 1 to add, 0 to change, 0 to destroy.
Do you want to perform these actions?
  Terraform will perform the actions described above.
  Only 'yes' will be accepted to approve.
  Enter a value: yes
iosxe_interface_loopback.loopback: Creating...
iosxe_interface_loopback.loopback: Creation complete after 0s
[id=Cisco-IOS-XE-native:native/interface/Loopback=100]
Apply complete! Resources: 1 added, 0 changed, 0 destroyed.
```

To prove that idempotency works, I'll run it again, and we can see that it is not making any changes this time:

```
the-packet-thrower@macmini31 Terraform % terraform apply
iosxe_interface_loopback.loopback: Refreshing state...
[id=Cisco-IOS-XE-native:native/interface/Loopback=100]
No changes. Your infrastructure matches the configuration.
Terraform has compared your real infrastructure against your configuration and
found no differences, so no changes are needed.
Apply complete! Resources: 0 added, 0 changed, 0 destroyed.
```

If I check our router, we can see the new Loopback interface:

```
r01#show run int l100
Building configuration...
Current configuration : 105 bytes
!
interface Loopback100
 description Made with Terraform!
 ip address 192.168.100.1 255.255.255.255
end
```

Because Terraform is a provisioner, we can undo our configuration by simply using the `terraform destroy` command:

```
the-packet-thrower@macmini31 Terraform % terraform destroy --auto-approve
iosxe_interface_loopback.loopback: Refreshing state...
[id=Cisco-IOS-XE-native:native/interface/Loopback=100]
Terraform used the selected providers to generate the following execution
plan. Resource actions are indicated with the following symbols:
  - destroy
Terraform will perform the following actions:
  # iosxe_interface_loopback.loopback will be destroyed
```

```
  - resource "iosxe_interface_loopback" "loopback" {
      - description        = "Made with Terraform!" -> null
      - id                 = "Cisco-IOS-XE-native:native/interface/
Loopback=100" -> null
      - ipv4_address       = "192.168.100.1" -> null
      - ipv4_address_mask = "255.255.255.255" -> null
      - name               = 100 -> null
    }
Plan: 0 to add, 0 to change, 1 to destroy.
iosxe_interface_loopback.loopback: Destroying...
[id=Cisco-IOS-XE-native:native/interface/Loopback=100]
iosxe_interface_loopback.loopback: Destruction complete after 1s
      Once that is done, we no longer have our Loopback100 on my router!

r01#
*Aug 31 09:11:36.900: %LINEPROTO-5-UPDOWN: Line protocol on Interface
Loopback100, changed state to down
*Aug 31 09:11:36.900: %LINK-5-CHANGED: Interface Loopback100, changed state to
administratively down
r01# show run int l100
                   ^
% Invalid input detected at '^' marker.
```

Summary

DevOps and infrastructure as code are becoming seriously popular ways to control network and server configuration. This chapter covered the basics of DevOps and IaC and demonstrated how Ansible and Terraform work, including the strengths and weaknesses of each.

Exam Essentials

Understand DevOps. To fully grasp how automation enhances network infrastructure management, it's important to consider the organization's infrastructure as a whole.

Know how to use Ansible. Ansible is a Python-based configuration management tool that pushes configuration to nodes using YAML playbooks. It's an agentless solution offering wide support for network devices because it uses SSH to reach nodes. Because there's no agent, Ansible can only push configuration to nodes.

Know how to use Terraform. Terraform is a provisioning tool that focuses on creating new resources rather than changing configuration.

Written Lab

The answers to this lab can be found in Appendix A, "Answers to the Written Labs."

1. Explain how automation in network management can reduce the risk of human error.
2. Describe the role of Ansible in network configuration management, and give an example of a task it can automate.
3. What is infrastructure as code (IaC), and how does it benefit network management?
4. How does Terraform differ from Ansible in terms of handling vendor-specific support and configurations?
5. What is idempotence, and why is it important in the context of infrastructure as code?
6. Outline the steps involved in setting up an Ansible playbook to configure a VLAN on a Cisco switch.
7. What are the main components of a YAML file used in Ansible playbooks, and how are they structured?
8. Describe the function of a "provider" in Terraform, and explain how it is used to manage resources across different platforms.
9. Why is it important to store sensitive information, like login credentials, in a separate file such as `terraform.tfvars` when using Terraform?
10. Explain the difference between the `terraform init` and `terraform apply` commands in Terraform, and describe when each should be used.

Review Questions

NOTE The following questions are designed to test your understanding of this chapter's material. For more information on how to get additional questions, please see this book's introduction.

The answers to these questions can be found in Appendix B, "Answers to the Review Questions."

1. What is a key advantage of automation in network management?
   A. It eliminates the need for human intervention entirely.
   B. It reduces the risk of accidental outages by minimizing manual tasks.
   C. It requires no initial setup and configuration.
   D. It only works with cloud-based infrastructures.
2. Which of the following tools is specifically mentioned as a solution for creating VLANs and configuring network devices?
   A. Puppet
   B. Chef
   C. Ansible
   D. Jenkins
3. What is infrastructure as code (IaC)?
   A. A type of hardware used in network infrastructure
   B. A method to create network configurations using physical components
   C. The practice of managing and provisioning computing infrastructure through machine-readable definition files
   D. A new type of coding language used exclusively for networking
4. In the context of Ansible, what is a "playbook"?
   A. A set of instructions used to automate tasks on network devices
   B. A log file that records network activity
   C. A graphical interface for network configuration
   D. A hardware component used for network security
5. What is the primary function of the Ansible `gather_facts` option?
   A. To collect detailed information about target nodes
   B. To execute all tasks without errors
   C. To automatically install necessary software on target nodes
   D. To create backup configurations of network devices
6. Which of the following is a benefit of using Terraform in network management?
   A. It operates from a single executable file, making it lightweight.
   B. It requires a central management server to function.
   C. It is only compatible with Linux systems.
   D. It lacks flexibility in resource management.

7. What is the purpose of the Ansible "inventory" file?
   - **A.** To list all available hardware components
   - **B.** To define the nodes that Ansible will manage
   - **C.** To store user credentials for network access
   - **D.** To document network performance metrics
8. What does "idempotence" refer to in the context of infrastructure as code?
   - **A.** The ability to execute multiple commands simultaneously
   - **B.** Ensuring that a configuration is only applied if it results in a change
   - **C.** The requirement to run scripts in a specific sequence
   - **D.** The need to manually verify each step of a deployment
9. Which file format does Ansible use for its playbooks?
   - **A.** JSON
   - **B.** XML
   - **C.** YAML
   - **D.** CSV
10. How does Terraform differ from Ansible in terms of module support?
    - **A.** Terraform comes with thousands of modules preinstalled.
    - **B.** Terraform requires users to define and configure specific providers.
    - **C.** Terraform uses a single, universal module for all tasks.
    - **D.** Terraform does not support external modules.
11. Which of the following is a primary component of a YAML file?
    - **A.** Mappings
    - **B.** Arrays
    - **C.** Schemas
    - **D.** JSON objects
12. What is a "provider" in Terraform?
    - **A.** A built-in module for managing network devices
    - **B.** A plugin that allows Terraform to interact with various platforms
    - **C.** A type of network hardware component
    - **D.** A file format used for storing configurations
13. What does the Ansible `ios_config` module do?
    - **A.** It manages interface configurations on Cisco IOS devices.
    - **B.** It collects performance data from network devices.
    - **C.** It pushes configuration commands to Cisco devices.
    - **D.** It automates the installation of new software.

14. In Terraform, what does the `terraform.tfvars` file typically store?
    - **A.** Network device configurations
    - **B.** Sensitive information such as usernames and passwords
    - **C.** Performance logs
    - **D.** System update scripts
15. Which command is used to initialize Terraform's provider setup?
    - **A.** terraform init
    - **B.** terraform start
    - **C.** terraform setup
    - **D.** terraform configure
16. Why is it recommended to separate sensitive information into the `terraform.tfvars` file?
    - **A.** To enhance performance by loading sensitive information separately
    - **B.** To protect sensitive data from being accidentally shared in repositories
    - **C.** To allow multiple users to edit the sensitive information simultaneously
    - **D.** To automate the encryption of sensitive data
17. What is the primary use of the `terraform plan` command?
    - **A.** To execute the Terraform configuration immediately
    - **B.** To preview the changes that Terraform will make to the infrastructure
    - **C.** To roll back previous changes made by Terraform
    - **D.** To install the necessary Terraform providers
18. Which file in Ansible defines how it connects to the target devices?
    - **A.** Hosts file
    - **B.** ansible.cfg file
    - **C.** Inventory file
    - **D.** Playbook file
19. What is a "resource" in Terraform?
    - **A.** A single component of your infrastructure, such as a network interface
    - **B.** A script that automates network configuration
    - **C.** A module that interacts with external APIs
    - **D.** A backup file of your current configuration
20. Which of the following is a benefit of using Ansible's idempotency feature?
    - **A.** It allows configurations to be applied multiple times without causing changes if they are already in place.
    - **B.** It speeds up the execution of tasks by skipping unnecessary steps.
    - **C.** It ensures that all nodes in the network are configured in parallel.
    - **D.** It automatically corrects configuration errors without manual intervention.

Appendix A

Answers to the Written Labs

Chapter 1: Enhanced Switched Technologies

1. PAgP
2. `show spanning-tree summary`
3. 802.1w
4. STP
5. BPDU Guard
6. `(config-if)#`**`spanning-tree portfast`**
7. `Switch#`**`show etherchannel port-channel`**
8. `Switch(config)#`**`spanning-tree vlan 3 root primary`**
9. `show spanning-tree`, then follow the root port that connects to the root bridge using CDP, or `show spanning-tree summary`.
10. Active and Passive

Chapter 2: Security with ACLs

1. `access-list 10 deny 172.16.0.0 0.0.255.255`

   `access-list 10 permit any`
2. `ip access-group 10 out`
3. `access-list 10 deny host 192.168.15.5`

   `access-list 10 permit any`
4. `show access-lists`
5. `IDS, IPS`
6. `access-list 110 deny tcp host`

   `172.16.10.1 host 172.16.30.5 eq 23`

   `access-list 110 permit ip any any`
7. `line vty 0 4`

   `access-class 110 in`
8. `ip access-list standard No172Net`

   `deny 172.16.0.0 0.0.255.255`

   `permit any`
9. `ip access-group No172Net out`
10. `show ip interfaces`

Chapter 3: Internet Protocol Version 6 (IPv6)

1. Unicast
2. Global unicast
3. Link-local
4. Unique local (used to be called site-local)
5. Multicast
6. Anycast
7. OSPFv3
8. ::1
9. FE80::/10
10. FC00:: /7

Chapter 4: Troubleshooting IP, IPv6, and VLANs

1. The INCMP is an incomplete message, which means a neighbor solicitation message has been sent but the neighbor message has not yet been received.
2. `switchport trunk native vlan 66`
3. Access, auto, desirable, nonegotiate, and trunk (on)
4. Verify that the default gateway is correct. Verify that name resolution settings are correct. Verify that there are no ACLs blocking traffic.
5. `ping ::1`

Chapter 5: Network Address Translation (NAT)

1. Port Address Translation (PAT), also called NAT Overload
2. `debug ip nat`
3. `show ip nat translations`

4. `clear ip nat translations *`
5. Before
6. After
7. `show ip nat statistics`
8. The `ip nat inside` and `ip nat outside` commands
9. Dynamic NAT
10. `prefix-length`

Chapter 6: IP Services

1. NetFlow
2. It sends information about MIB variables in response to requests from the NMS
3. SNMP
4. Warning (severity 4)
5. SNMPv3
6. (config)#**logging** ***ip_address***
7. Emergency, Critical, Error
8. Syslog
9. SSH
10. Notifications

Chapter 7: Security Fundamentals

1. AAA stands for authentication, authorization, and accounting.
2. Authentication, authorization, and accounting, or AAA services, which is a technology that gives us substantial control over users and what they're permitted to do inside of our networks.
3. The application requires the user to enter a PIN before it provides the second factor.
4. Man-in-the-middle
5. Physical access control

Chapter 8: First-Hop Redundancy Protocol (FHRP)

1. HSRP version 2
2. Standby
3. 0000.5E00.0101
4. `show standby`
5. GLBP

Chapter 9: Quality of Service (QoS)

1. DSCP
2. It queues excess traffic.
3. TID
4. Markings, addressing, and application signatures
5. Marking
6. Policing
7. Policing
8. CBWFQ, LLW
9. NBAR
10. Buffers and queues packets

Chapter 10: Wireless Technologies

1. 11 Mbps
2. 54 Mbps
3. 54 Mbps
4. 2.4 GHz
5. 2.4 GHz
6. 5 GHz
7. 1 Gbps
8. The values of WPA keys can change dynamically while the system is being used.
9. The IEEE 802.11i standard has been sanctioned by WPA and is called WPA version 2.
10. Three

Chapter 11: Configuring Legacy Wireless Controllers

1. Initial setup: Start by powering on the WLC and using the setup wizard to configure the system name, management IP address, and VLAN settings.

   VLAN configuration: On the connected switch, create the necessary VLANs for the management interface and any wireless networks (WLANs) you plan to create.

   WLAN creation: Go to the WLAN configuration section on the WLC, create a new WLAN, assign it an SSID, and configure the security settings (like WPA2-PSK). Finally, enable the WLAN.

2. Standalone AP: Configured individually and operates independently. It's simple but hard to manage when you have many APs.

   Lightweight AP: Managed by a central WLC, which makes it easier to configure and manage large networks. All configurations are pushed from the WLC, allowing for better scalability and management.

3. Access the AP: Connect to the AP via the console or SSH.

   Set the controller IP: Use the command `capwap ap controller ip address` *<WLC_IP_Address>* to point the AP to the WLC.

   Set the static IP: If needed, set a static IP on the AP using `capwap ap ip address` *<AP_IP_Address> <Subnet_Mask>*.

   AP registration: The AP will then attempt to register with the WLC.

4. Split MAC architecture: This divides the functions between the AP and the WLC. The AP handles real-time tasks like encryption and channel scanning, and the WLC handles tasks like authentication and management.

   Benefits: It improves performance by distributing tasks and enhances security with centralized control from the WLC.

5. CAPWAP protocol: It's a protocol that allows APs to communicate with the WLC securely.

   Importance: CAPWAP ensures that all data between APs and the WLC is encrypted and that APs can be centrally managed, making the network more secure and easier to manage.

6. VLANs in WLC: VLANs are used to segment traffic for different types of users (e.g., guest, corporate). Each WLAN is associated with a specific VLAN.

   Dynamic interfaces: These are virtual interfaces on the WLC that are tied to specific VLANs. They allow the WLC to route traffic from different WLANs to the appropriate VLANs.

7. Local mode: All traffic from the AP is tunneled back to the WLC, which handles it centrally.

   FlexConnect mode: Traffic can be locally switched at the AP, which is useful for branch offices or remote sites to reduce dependency on the WLC.

Use FlexConnect: When the AP is in a remote location, and you want to minimize traffic sent back to the WLC over a WAN link.

8. Add RADIUS server: Go to the WLC's security settings, and add the RADIUS server's IP address, shared secret, and port number.
   Assign to WLAN: Bind the RADIUS server to the WLAN you want to secure. This setup allows the RADIUS server to handle user authentication for WPA2-Enterprise.
9. Service port: Used for out-of-band management of the WLC.
   Distribution system ports: These are the main ports that connect the WLC to the network, handling wireless traffic.
   Redundancy port: Used for connecting to another WLC in a high-availability setup, ensuring that one WLC can take over if the other fails.
10. Security: HTTPS and SSH encrypt all data sent between the client and the WLC, protecting it from being intercepted by attackers.
    Risk of HTTP and Telnet: These protocols send data in plaintext, making it easy for attackers to capture sensitive information like login credentials.
    Configuration: You can enable HTTPS and SSH on the WLC through the security settings to ensure all management traffic is secure.

Chapter 12: Configuring Modern Wireless Controllers

1. Create a VLAN on a Cisco 9800 controller using the CLI.
```
C9800-WLC(config)# vlan 300
C9800-WLC(config-vlan)# name TEST-VLAN
C9800-WLC(config-vlan)# exit
```
2. Configure a trunk interface on a Cisco 9800 controller.
```
C9800-WLC(config)# interface GigabitEthernet1
C9800-WLC(config-if)# switchport mode trunk
C9800-WLC(config-if)# exit
```
3. Set up a basic user account on a Cisco 9800 controller.
```
C9800-WLC(config)# username user1 privilege 15 secret Cisco123!
```
4. Enable IP routing on a Cisco 9800 controller.
```
C9800-WLC(config)# ip routing
```
5. Create a port channel on a Cisco 9800 controller.
```
C9800-WLC(config)# interface range GigabitEthernet1-2
C9800-WLC(config-if-range)# switchport mode trunk
```

```
C9800-WLC(config-if-range)# channel-group 1 mode active
C9800-WLC(config-if-range)# exit
C9800-WLC(config)# interface Port-channel1
C9800-WLC(config-if)# description Uplink to Core-SW01
C9800-WLC(config-if)# exit
```

6. Create a DHCP pool on a Cisco 9800 controller.

```
C9800-WLC(config)# ip dhcp pool WLAN201
C9800-WLC(dhcp-config)# network 192.168.50.0 255.255.255.0
C9800-WLC(dhcp-config)# default-router 192.168.50.1
C9800-WLC(dhcp-config)# exit
```

7. Configure a WLAN profile with WPA2-PSK on a Cisco 9800 controller.

   The steps:

   1. Access the web GUI of the Cisco 9800 controller.
   2. Navigate to the WLANs section, and click Add to create a new WLAN profile.
   3. Name the profile Lab-WLAN and set the SSID to Lab-WLAN.
   4. Under Security, select WPA2-PSK and enter the passphrase LabPass123.
   5. Apply the configuration.

8. Associate an access point (AP) with a WLAN on a Cisco 9800 controller.

   The steps:

   1. Go to the AP section in the web GUI.
   2. Select the AP you want to associate with the Lab-WLAN.
   3. Assign the Lab-WLAN profile to the AP.
   4. Apply the configuration.

9. Verify the status of a port channel on a Cisco 9800 controller.

```
C9800-WLC# show etherchannel summary
```

10. Assign a VLAN to a policy profile on a Cisco 9800 controller.

   The steps:

   1. Go to the policy profile section in the web GUI.
   2. Select the default policy profile.
   3. Under the VLAN settings, assign VLAN 300 to the policy profile.
   4. Save and apply the configuration.

Chapter 13: Virtualization, Containers, and VRFs

1. Virtualization offers several key benefits, including:
   - **Cost efficiency:** Reduces the need for physical hardware, saving on costs for purchasing, maintenance, and energy consumption
   - **Resource optimization:** Allows multiple virtual machines (VMs) to run on a single physical server, maximizing the utilization of resources like CPU, RAM, and storage
   - **Scalability:** Makes it easier to scale up infrastructure by adding more virtual machines as needed without requiring additional physical servers
   - **Flexibility:** Enables quick deployment of new servers and applications, reducing the time to market for new services
   - **Resiliency and redundancy:** Enhances system uptime by enabling features like live migration and easy failover between virtual machines.
2. A hypervisor, also known as a virtual machine monitor (VMM), is the software layer that enables the creation, management, and execution of virtual machines on a physical host. It abstracts the hardware resources and allocates them to VMs. The two main types of hypervisors are
   - **Type 1 hypervisor (bare metal):** Runs directly on the physical hardware, with no underlying operating system. Examples include VMware ESXi and Microsoft Hyper-V.
   - **Type 2 hypervisor (hosted):** Runs on top of a host operating system. It's commonly used for desktop virtualization. Examples include VMware Workstation and Oracle VirtualBox.
3. **Standard virtual switch:** A basic virtual switch that operates on a single hypervisor, allowing virtual machines on that hypervisor to communicate with each other and the external network. Configuration is local to the hypervisor, so changes must be made on each hypervisor individually.

   Distributed virtual switch: A more advanced switch that spans across multiple hypervisors, creating a single logical switch. This allows for centralized management of network settings, which are consistently applied across all hypervisors. It simplifies management and reduces the chances of misconfiguration.
4. Shared storage, typically implemented using SAN (storage area network) or NAS (network-attached storage), allows multiple hypervisors to access the same storage resources. This is crucial for
   - **High availability:** Ensures that if one hypervisor fails, the VMs it was hosting can be quickly restarted on another hypervisor without data loss.
   - **VM migration:** Shared storage enables live migration of VMs between hypervisors without downtime. Because the VM's disk files are on shared storage, the VM can move to another hypervisor without needing to copy large amounts of data.

5. **Type 1 hypervisor (bare metal):** Directly runs on the hardware without a host operating system, providing better performance and more efficient resource usage. It is typically used in enterprise environments. Examples include VMware ESXi, Microsoft Hyper-V, and Xen.
   - **Type 2 hypervisor (hosted):** Runs on top of an existing operating system, making it easier to set up and use for smaller-scale or personal applications. However, it has lower performance due to the extra layer of the host OS. Examples include VMware Workstation, Oracle VirtualBox, and VMware Fusion.
6. A snapshot is a point-in-time capture of the state of a virtual machine, including its memory, disk, and configuration. Snapshots are useful for
   - **Backup:** Creating a backup before making changes to a VM, such as applying updates or installing new software
   - **Testing:** Allowing administrators to test configurations or applications and revert to the previous state if something goes wrong
   - **Quick recovery:** Providing a quick way to restore a VM to a known good state after a failure or error
7. VRF (virtual routing and forwarding) is a technology that allows multiple independent routing tables to coexist on the same router or switch. This enables the segmentation of network traffic and the creation of isolated virtual networks within the same physical infrastructure. VRF is commonly used for
   - **Security:** Isolating sensitive traffic, such as management traffic, from regular user traffic
   - **Multitenancy:** Allowing multiple customers or business units to share the same physical infrastructure while keeping their traffic separate
   - **MPLS VPNs:** Enabling the implementation of VPNs that provide secure communication between different sites over a shared infrastructure
8. Containers are more resource-efficient than virtual machines because they share the host operating system's kernel and do not require a full OS installation for each instance. This allows containers to start quickly and use less CPU, memory, and storage compared to VMs. Containers are often preferred in scenarios like these:
   - **Microservices architecture:** Containers are ideal for running microservices because they allow for lightweight, isolated environments for each service.
   - **Rapid deployment:** Containers can be deployed and scaled quickly, making them suitable for environments that require rapid changes and scalability.
   - **Consistency across environments:** Containers ensure that applications run consistently across different environments (development, testing, production) because the container includes all dependencies.

9. **VMware Workstation:** A commercial hypervisor that allows users to run multiple virtual machines on a Windows or Linux desktop. It is known for its robust features and performance.
   - **Oracle VirtualBox:** A free, open-source hypervisor that supports a wide range of operating systems. It is popular for personal use and educational purposes.
   - **VMware Fusion:** A type 2 hypervisor designed for Mac users, allowing them to run Windows, Linux, and other operating systems alongside macOS.
10. Paravirtualization is a virtualization technique where the guest operating system is aware that it is running in a virtualized environment and interacts with the hypervisor directly. This allows for better performance compared to hardware virtualization, where the guest OS is unaware of the virtualization and interacts with virtualized hardware. Paravirtualization requires modifications to the guest OS, whereas hardware virtualization does not, making paravirtualization less flexible but potentially more efficient.

Chapter 14: Software-Defined Networking

1. The control plane is responsible for making decisions about where traffic should be sent. It handles tasks like routing table management, running protocols such as OSPF, and managing ARP entries.
2. An underlay network refers to the physical infrastructure that provides basic connectivity and transport, typically using IP routing. An overlay network is a virtual network that is built on top of the underlay, providing additional services like tunneling and security, often using protocols like VXLAN.
3. The Assurance feature in Catalyst Center provides comprehensive monitoring and troubleshooting capabilities. It stores network information for up to a week, allows you to review past network health issues, and offers insights and suggestions for resolving problems.
4. Path Trace provides a visual representation of the actual path that network traffic takes, including through tunnels like CAPWAP, VPNs, or DMVPN, and reveals any ACLs that might block traffic. Unlike traceroute, it also shows the layer 2 devices involved in the path.
5. The SDN controller centrally manages and controls the network by separating the control plane from the data plane. It communicates with network devices using southbound APIs and provides an interface for network administrators to manage the network using northbound APIs.

6. LAN Automation automates the process of setting up new network devices using Cisco's plug-and-play (PNP) technology. It dynamically creates a DHCP server on an upstream device to provide IP addresses and basic configurations to new devices, simplifying their integration into the network.
7. The three categories are Business Relevant (critical applications like email), Business Irrelevant (applications with no business value like BitTorrent), and Default (applications that don't fit into the other two categories, like DNS).
8. Separating the control plane from the data plane allows for centralized management of network policies and configurations, improves scalability, reduces complexity, and enhances the ability to automate and orchestrate network functions.
9. The Network Hierarchy feature allows you to organize your network into logical sites and locations, providing consistent configuration across devices, simplifying management, and ensuring that common settings (like NTP servers or authentication configurations) are applied uniformly.
10. In SDN, the term "fabric" refers to the entirety of the network infrastructure, including all the routers, switches, firewalls, and other devices that are part of the SDN solution. The fabric is managed by the SDN controller, which abstracts the complexity of the underlying network to provide a simplified and unified management interface.

Chapter 15: Automation, Data Formats, and REST APIs

1. Network automation provides several key benefits in managing large networks, including reducing the potential for human error, saving time by automating repetitive tasks, increasing efficiency in network management, improving consistency in configurations, and enabling faster deployment of network changes. Automation also helps in scaling network operations and ensuring compliance with organizational policies.
2. Onbox automation involves running automation scripts directly on the network device itself, such as using the Cisco Guest Shell on a router. An example is running a Python script within the device to automate local configurations. Offbox automation, on the other hand, involves running automation scripts from an external server or controller that connects to and manages multiple network devices. An example is using a management server to push configurations to all devices in a network.
3. JSON (JavaScript Object Notation) is a lightweight data exchange format that is easy for humans to read and write and easy for machines to parse and generate. It is widely used in network automation because it allows structured data to be exchanged between devices and management tools, making it ideal for REST APIs. An example of a JSON object:

```
{
  "name": "John Doe",
  "age": "30",
  "email": "john.doe@example.com"
}
```

4. REST APIs provide a standardized way to interact with network devices and systems programmatically, allowing for the automation of tasks such as configuration changes, data retrieval, and system monitoring. The six key constraints that define a RESTful API are
   - **Client-server:** Separation of client and server concerns.
   - **Stateless:** Each request from the client to the server must contain all the information needed to understand and process the request.
   - **Cacheable:** Responses must be explicitly marked as cacheable or non-cacheable to improve efficiency.
   - **Uniform interface:** A standardized way of interacting with the server, including identifying resources, resource representation, self-descriptive messages, and HATEOAS.
   - **Layered system:** The ability to use multiple layers, such as load balancers and proxies, without affecting the system's behavior.
   - **Code on demand (optional):** Servers can extend client functionality by providing executable code.
5. HTTP verbs in a REST API correspond to CRUD operations, which define the fundamental operations performed on resources. The verbs and their corresponding CRUD operations are
   - GET: Read/Retrieve data (Read operation).
   - POST: Create a new resource (Create operation).
   - PUT: Update or replace an existing resource (Update operation).
   - PATCH: Partially update an existing resource (Update/Modify operation).
   - DELETE: Remove a resource (Delete operation).
6. Headers in REST API requests provide metadata and additional information about the request or the desired response format. Three common headers are
   - Authorization: Specifies the credentials for authenticating the request, such as an API token or Basic Auth string.
   - Content-Type: Indicates the media type of the request body, such as application/json.
   - Accept: Specifies the media types that the client is willing to receive in the response, such as application/json.

7. A 200 HTTP status code indicates that the request was successful, and the server returned the requested resource. In contrast, a 404 HTTP status code indicates that the server could not find the requested resource, meaning the URL is incorrect or the resource does not exist.
8. Basic authentication in a REST API involves sending a username and password as part of the request header. The credentials are formatted as username:password and then encoded in base64 to ensure they are transmitted safely and without special characters interfering with the request. The base64-encoded string is then included in the Authorization header as Authorization: Basic <encoded_string>.
9. A loop in Python can iterate over a list of network devices, sending configuration commands to each device in turn. Here's a basic example:

```
devices = ["router1", "router2", "router3"]
for device in devices:
    print(f"Connecting to {device}")
    # Placeholder for code to send configuration to the device
    print(f"Configuration applied to {device}")
```

   This script prints a message for each device in the list and could be extended to include actual configuration commands.
10. HATEOAS (Hypermedia as the Engine of Application State) is a constraint in REST API design that ensures APIs are self-discoverable. It means that clients interacting with the API can navigate and understand the available actions and resources through hypermedia links provided in the responses. This is important for API design because it makes the API easier to use and reduces the need for extensive documentation.

Chapter 16: Configuration Management

1. Automation reduces human error by minimizing the need for manual intervention in repetitive tasks. By using scripts and predefined configurations, it ensures that tasks are carried out consistently every time, reducing the chances of mistakes that can occur with manual processes. Additionally, automated processes are tested and validated, ensuring that they perform as expected.
2. Ansible is a configuration management tool that automates the deployment and management of network devices and systems. It uses playbooks written in YAML to define the tasks to be executed on target devices. An example of a task that Ansible can automate is the creation of VLANs on Cisco switches, where it can configure the VLANs consistently across multiple devices.

3. Infrastructure as code (IaC) is the practice of managing and provisioning computing infrastructure through machine-readable configuration files rather than through physical hardware configuration or interactive configuration tools. IaC benefits network management by ensuring that the infrastructure is consistently deployed across environments, reducing the chances of configuration drift and enabling version control of infrastructure changes.
4. Terraform differs from Ansible in that it does not come with built-in vendor-specific modules by default. Instead, Terraform uses "providers" that are plugins, enabling Terraform to interact with different cloud platforms, service providers, and infrastructure components. These providers must be explicitly defined and configured by the user, allowing Terraform to manage resources across various platforms like AWS, Azure, and Cisco.
5. Idempotence is a property of certain operations that means the operation can be applied multiple times without changing the result beyond the initial application. In the context of infrastructure as code, idempotence ensures that running a configuration script multiple times will not cause unintended changes to the infrastructure. This property is crucial for maintaining consistent and predictable environments.
6. a. Define the inventory file specifying the target switch.
   b. Create the Ansible playbook in YAML format.
   c. In the playbook, define the hosts (e.g., the group of Cisco switches) and disable fact-gathering if unnecessary.
   d. Use the `ios_vlan` module to define the VLAN ID and name to be created on the switch.
   e. Save and execute the playbook using the `ansible-playbook` command.
7. The main components of a YAML file used in Ansible playbooks include
   - **Mappings:** Key-value pairs separated by a colon (e.g., `name: Todd`).
   - **Lists:** Items listed with a dash (-) at the beginning of each line (e.g., `- item1`).
   - **Scalars:** Single values like strings, numbers, or Booleans. These components are structured hierarchically, with indentation defining the relationships between elements, such as tasks and their associated properties.
8. A "provider" in Terraform is a plugin that enables Terraform to interact with a specific cloud platform, service, or infrastructure component. Providers define the types of resources that can be managed and the API interactions necessary to manage those resources. For example, the AWS provider allows Terraform to manage AWS resources like EC2 instances and S3 buckets. To use a provider, it must be specified in the Terraform configuration file, and Terraform will download and install the provider when initializing the configuration.

9. Storing sensitive information in a separate file like `terraform.tfvars` is important for security reasons. This practice allows you to keep sensitive data, such as usernames and passwords, separate from the main configuration files, reducing the risk of accidentally exposing this information. Additionally, by keeping these details in a separate file, you can ensure that they are not included in version control or shared with unauthorized users.

10.
    - `terraform init`: This command initializes a Terraform working directory. It downloads the necessary provider plugins and sets up the backend configuration. It should be used when setting up a new Terraform project or when modifying provider configurations.
    - `terraform apply`: This command applies the changes required to reach the desired state of the configuration. It runs the planned configuration and makes the necessary updates to the infrastructure. It should be used after confirming that the planned changes are correct, typically after running `terraform plan`.

Appendix B

Answers to the Review Questions

Chapter 1: Enhanced Switched Technologies

1. B, D. The switch is not the root bridge for VLAN 1 or the output would tell us exactly that. We can see that the root bridge for VLAN 1 is off of interface G1/2 with a cost of 4, meaning it is directly connected. Use the command `show cdp nei` to find your root bridge at this point. Also, the switch is running RSTP (802.1d), not STP.

2. D. If you have a server or other devices connected into your switch that you're totally sure won't create a switching loop if STP is disabled, you can use something called PortFast on these ports. Using it means the port won't spend the usual 50 seconds to come up while STP is converging. Understand this doesn't completely disable STP; it just stops any port configured with PortFast from transitioning the different port states, and immediately puts the port into forwarding state.

3. A, D. It is important that you can find your root bridge, and the `show spanning-tree` command will help you do this. To quickly find out which VLANs your switch is the root bridge for, use the `show spanning-tree summary` command.

4. A. 802.1w is also called Rapid Spanning Tree Protocol. It is not enabled by default on Cisco switches, but it is a better STP to run because it has all the fixes that the Cisco extensions provide with 802.1d. Remember, Cisco runs RSTP PVST+, not just RSTP.

5. B. The Spanning Tree Protocol is used to stop switching loops in a layer 2 switched network with redundant paths.

6. C. Convergence occurs when all ports on bridges and switches have transitioned to either the forwarding or blocking states. No data is forwarded until convergence is complete. Before data can be forwarded again, all devices must be updated.

7. C, E. There are two types of EtherChannel: Cisco's PAgP and the IEEE's LACP. They are basically the same, and there is little difference in configuring them. For PAgP, use auto or desirable mode, and with LACP use passive or active. These modes decide which method you are using, and they must be configured the same on both sides of the EtherChannel bundle.

8. A, B, F. RSTP helps with convergence issues that plague traditional STP. Rapid PVST+ is based on the 802.1w standard in the same way that PVST+ is based on 802.1d. The operation of Rapid PVST+ is simply a separate instance of 802.1w for each VLAN.

9. D. BPDU Guard is used when a port is configured for PortFast, or it should be used, because if that port receives a BPDU from another switch, BPDU Guard will shut that port down to stop a loop from occurring.

10. C. To allow for the PVST+ to operate, there's a field inserted into the BPDU to accommodate the extended system ID so that PVST+ can have a root bridge configured on a per-STP instance. The extended system ID (VLAN ID) is a 12-bit field, and we can even see what this field is carrying via the `show spanning-tree` command output.

11. C. PortFast and BPDU Guard allow a port to transition to the forwarding state quickly, which is great for a switch port but not for load balancing. You can somewhat load balance with RSTP, but that is out of the scope of our objectives; and although you can use PPP to configure multilink (bundle links), this is performed on asynchronous or synchronous serial links. Cisco's EtherChannel can bundle up to eight ports between switches.

12. D. If the Spanning Tree Protocol is not running on your switches and you connect them together with redundant links, you will have broadcast storms and multiple frame copies being received by the same destination device.

13. B, C, E. All the ports on both sides of every link must be configured exactly the same or it will not work. Speed, duplex, and allowed VLANs must match.

14. D, F. There are two types of EtherChannel: Cisco's PAgP and the IEEE's LACP. They are basically the same, and there is little difference in configuring them. For PAgP, use the auto or desirable mode, and with LACP use the passive or active mode. These modes decide which method you are using, and they must be configured the same on both sides of the EtherChannel bundle.

15. D. You can't answer this question if you don't know who the root bridge is. SC has a bridge priority of 4,096, so that is the root bridge. The cost for SB was 4, with the direct link, but that link went down. If SB goes through SA to SC, the cost would be 4 + 19, or 23. If SB goes to SA to SD to SC, the cost is 4 + 4 + 4 = 12.

16. A, D. To configure EtherChannel, create the port channel from global configuration mode, and then assign the group number on each interface using the active mode to enable LACP. Although just configuring the channel-group command under your interfaces will enable the bundle, options A and D are the best Cisco objective answers.

17. A, D. You can set the priority to any value from 0 through 61,440 in increments of 4,096. Setting it to zero (0) means that the switch will always be a root as long as it has a lower MAC than another switch with its bridge ID also set to 0. You can also force a switch to be a root for a VLAN with the `spanning-tree vlan vlan primary` command.

18. A. By using per-VLAN spanning tree, the root bridge can be placed in the center of where all the resources are for a particular VLAN, which enables optimal path determination.

19. A, C, D, E. Each 802.1d port transitions through blocking, listening, learning, and finally forwarding after 50 seconds, by default. RSTP uses discarding, learning, and forwarding only.

20. A, C, D, E, F. The roles a switch port can play in STP are root, non-root, designated, non-designated, forwarding, and blocking. Discarding is used in RSTP, and disabled could be a role, but it's not listed as a possible answer.

Chapter 2: Security with ACLs

1. D. It's compared with lines of the access list only until a match is made. Once the packet matches the condition on a line of the access list, the packet is acted upon and no further comparisons take place.

2. C. The range of 192.168.160.0 to 192.168.191.0 is a block size of 32. The network address is 192.168.160.0 and the mask would be 255.255.224.0, which for an access list must be a wildcard format of 0.0.31.255. The 31 is used for a block size of 32. The wildcard is always one less than the block size.

3. C. Using a named access list just replaces the number used when applying the list to the router's interface. `ip access-group Blocksales in` is correct.

4. B. The list must specify TCP as the Transport layer protocol and use a correct wildcard mask (in this case, 0.0.0.255), and it must specify the destination port (80). It also should specify all as the set of computers allowed to have this access.

5. A. The first thing to check in a question like this is the access-list number. Right away, you can see that the second option is wrong because it is using a standard IP access-list number. The second thing to check is the protocol. If you are filtering by upper-layer protocol, then you must be using either UDP or TCP; this eliminates the fourth option. The third and last answers have the wrong syntax.

6. C. Of the available choices, only the `show ip interface` command will tell you which interfaces have access lists applied. `show access-lists` will not show you which interfaces have an access list applied.

7. D. This can be a difficult question. The rule of thumb for placing an ACL on an interface is: when filtering by source, place the list as close to the source as possible. When filtering by source/destination/ports, place the list as close to the destination host(s) as possible.

8. C. The extended access list ranges are 100–199 and 2000–2699, so the access-list number of 100 is valid. Telnet uses TCP, so the protocol TCP is valid. Now you just need to look for the source and destination address. Only the third option has the correct sequence of parameters. Option B may work, but the question specifically states "only" to network 192.168.10.0, and the wildcard in option B is too broad.

9. D. Extended IP access lists use numbers 100–199 and 2000–2699 and filter based on source and destination IP address, protocol number, and port number. The last option is correct because of the second line that specifies `permit ip any any`. (I used `0.0.0.0 255.255.255.255`, which is the same as the any option.) The third option does not have this, so it would deny access but not allow everything else.

10. D. First, you must know that a /20 is 255.255.240.0, which is a block size of 16 in the third octet. Counting by 16s, this makes our subnet 48 in the third octet, and the wildcard for the third octet would be 15 because the wildcard is always one less than the block size.

11. B. To find the wildcard (inverse) version of this mask, the zero and one bits are simply reversed as follows:

    11111111.11111111.11111111.11100000 (27 one bits, or /27)

    00000000.00000000.00000000.00011111 (wildcard/inverse mask)

12. A. First, you must know that a /19 is 255.255.224.0, which is a block size of 32 in the third octet. Counting by 32s, this makes our subnet 192 in the third octet, and the wildcard for the third octet would be 31 because the wildcard is always one less than the block size.

13. B. The scope of an access list is determined by the wildcard mask and the network address to which it is applied. For example, in this case, the starting point of the list of addresses affected by the mask is the network ID 192.111.16.32. The wildcard mask is 0.0.0.31. Adding the value of the last octet in the mask to the network address (32 + 31 = 63) tells you where the effects of the access list ends, which is 192.111.16.63. Therefore, all addresses in the range 192.111.16.32–192.111.16.63 will be denied by this list.

14. C. To place an access list on an interface, use the `ip access-group` command in interface configuration mode.

15. B. With no permit statement, the ACL will deny all traffic.

16. D. If you add an access list to an interface and you do not have at least one permit statement, then you will effectively shut down the interface because of the implicit deny any at the end of every list.

17. C. Telnet access to the router is restricted by using either a standard or extended IP access list inbound on the VTY lines of the router. The command `access-class` is used to apply the access list to the VTY lines.

18. B, E. If all or too much traffic is being allowed, your permit statements are configured too broadly, and/or the statement is too high in the ACL.

19. A. You need to use the access-class command under the VTY lines to permit traffic into the telnet/ssh lines. I'll use an extended ACL to be detailed and be able to filter by port.

20. B. To configure an extended IP access list, use the access-list numbers 100–199 or 2000–2699 in global configuration mode.

Chapter 3: Internet Protocol Version 6 (IPv6)

1. D. The modified EUI-64 format interface identifier is derived from the 48-bit link-layer (MAC) address by inserting the hexadecimal number FFFE between the upper 3 bytes (OUI field) and the lower 3 bytes (serial number) of the link-layer address.

2. D. An IPv6 address is represented as eight groups of four hexadecimal digits, each group representing 16 bits (two octets). The groups are separated by colons (:). Option A has two double colons, B doesn't have 8 fields, and option C has invalid hex characters.

3. A, B, C. This question is easier to answer if you just take out the wrong options. First, the loopback is only ::1, so that makes option D wrong. Link local is FE80::/10, not /8 and there are no broadcasts.

4. A, C, D. Several methods are used in terms of migration, including tunneling, translators, and dual-stack. Tunnels are used to carry one protocol inside another, whereas translators simply translate IPv6 packets into IPv4 packets. Dual-stack uses a combination of both native IPv4 and IPv6. With dual-stack, devices are able to run IPv4 and IPv6 together, and if IPv6 communication is possible, that is the preferred protocol. Hosts can simultaneously reach IPv4 and IPv6 content.

5. A, B. ICMPv6 router advertisements use type 134 and must be at least 64 bits in length.

6. B, E, F. Anycast addresses identify multiple interfaces, which is somewhat similar to multicast addresses; however, the big difference is that the anycast packet is only delivered to one address, the first one it finds defined in terms of routing distance. This address can also be called one-to-one-of-many, or one-to-nearest.

7. C. The loopback address with IPv4 is 127.0.0.1. With IPv6, that address is ::1.

8. B, C, E. An important feature of IPv6 is that it allows the plug-and-play option to the network devices by allowing them to configure themselves independently. It is possible to plug a node into an IPv6 network without requiring any human intervention. IPv6 does not implement traditional IP broadcasts.

9. A, D. The loopback address is ::1, link-local starts with FE80::/10, site-local addresses start with FEC0::/10, global addresses start with 2000::/3, and multicast addresses start with FF00::/8.

10. C. A router solicitation is sent out using the all-routers multicast address of FF02::2. The router can send a router advertisement to all hosts using the FF02::1 multicast address.

11. D, E. When an interface is configured with an IPv6 address, it automatically joins the all-nodes (FF02::1) and solicited-nodes (FF02::1:FFxx: xx) multicast groups. The all-nodes group is used to communicate with all interfaces on the local link, and the solicited-nodes multicast group is required for link-layer address resolution. Routers also join a third multicast group, the all-routers group (FF02::2).

12. B. An IPv6 unique local address is an IPv6 address in block FC00::/7. It is the approximate IPv6 counterpart of the IPv4 private address space defined in RFC 1918. Global Unicast address type is routable.

13. D. Packets addressed to a multicast address are delivered to all interfaces tuned into the multicast address. Sometimes, people call them "one-to-many" addresses because the FF00::/8 IPv6 address block sends packets to a group address rather than a single address.

14. B. The command `ipv6 address 2001:DB8:5:112::/64 eui-64` automatically generates an IPv6 address from a specified IPv6 prefix and MAC address of an interface using the EUI-64 method. The EUI-64 method uses the MAC address of the interface to create an interface identifier (IID) that is used to complete the IPv6 address.

15. D. The leading zeros in a group can be collapsed using ::, but this can only be done once in an IP address, which makes option A incorrect. 2002: is used with 6-to-4 tunneling, so that is incorrect for an interface. 2004:1:25A4:886F::1 is a collapsed and correct IPv6 interface address.

16. B, E, F. A new address type made specifically for IPv6 is called the anycast address. These IPv6 addresses are global and can be assigned to more than one interface, unlike an IPv6 unicast address. Anycast is designed to send a packet to the nearest interface that is part of that anycast group. The sender creates a packet and forwards it to the anycast address as the destination address, which goes to the nearest router. The nearest router or interface is found by using the metric of a routing protocol currently running on the network. However, in a LAN setting, the nearest interface is found depending on the order in which the neighbors were learned. The anycast packet in a LAN setting forwards the packet to the neighbor it learned about first.

17. A. The loopback address is ::1, link-local starts with FE80::/10, site-local addresses start with FEC0::/10, global addresses start with 2000::/3, and multicast addresses start with FF00::/8.

18. C. Stateless Address Autoconfiguration (SLAAC) is designed to be a simple, automatic approach to assigning IPv6 addresses. It is defined in RFC 4862 and is specifically used to assign only a global unicast IPv6 address, an IPv6 prefix length, and, optionally, a default router. SLAAC is a mechanism that enables each host on the network to autoconfigure a unique IPv6 address without any device keeping track of which address is assigned to which node.

19. D. In IPv6, multicast addresses send a single packet to multiple hosts simultaneously. The IPv6 address block that forwards packets to a multicast address rather than a unicast address is the FF00::/8 address block.

20. D. A global unicast address is a type of IPv6 address that is publicly routable in the same way as IPv4 public addresses. Global unicast addresses are unique, globally reachable addresses assigned to devices that need to communicate with other devices over the Internet. They are similar to IPv4 public addresses in that they can be used to reach devices on other networks, but they are structured differently and use a different address space. It's important to note that global unicast addresses are not the same as link-local addresses, which are used for communication within a single network segment or link and are not intended to be routable over the Internet. Link-local addresses are identified by the prefix FE80::/10 and are automatically generated by the device when it is connected to a network.

Chapter 4: Troubleshooting IP, IPv6, and VLANs

1. D. Positive confirmation has been received, confirming that the path to the neighbor is functioning correctly. REACH is good!

2. B. The most common cause of interface errors is a mismatched duplex mode between two ends of an Ethernet link. If they have mismatched duplex settings, you'll receive a legion of errors, which cause ugly slow performance issues, intermittent connectivity, and massive collisions—even total loss of communication!

3. D. You can verify the DTP status of an interface with the `sh dtp interface` *`interface`* command.

4. A. No DTP frames are generated from the interface. Nonegotiate can be used only if the neighbor interface is manually set as trunk or access.

5. D. The command `show ipv6 neighbors` provides the ARP cache on a router.

6. B. The state is STALE when the interface has not communicated within the neighbor-reachable time frame. The next time the neighbor communicates, the state will change back to REACH.

7. B. There is no IPv6 default gateway, which will be the link-local address of the router interface sent to the host as a router advertisement. Until this host receives the router address, the host will communicate with IPv6 only on the local subnet.

8. D. This host is using IPv4 to communicate on the network, and without an IPv6 global address, the host will be able to communicate only to remote networks with IPv4. The IPv4 address and default gateway are not configured into the same subnet.

9. B, C. The commands `show interface trunk` and `show interface` *`interface`* `switchport` will show you statistics of ports, which includes native VLAN information.

10. A. Most Cisco switches ship with a default port mode of auto, meaning they will automatically trunk if they connect to a port that is on or desirable. Remember that not all switches are shipped as mode auto, but many are, and you need to set one side to either on or desirable to trunk between switches.

Chapter 5: Network Address Translation (NAT)

1. A, C, E. NAT is not perfect and can cause some issues in some networks, but most networks work just fine. NAT can cause delays and troubleshooting problems, and some applications just won't work.

2. B, D, F. NAT is not perfect, but there are some advantages. It conserves global addresses, which allow us to add millions of hosts to the Internet without "real" IP addresses. This provides flexibility in our corporate networks. NAT can also allow you to use the same subnet more than once in the same network without overlapping networks.

3. C. The command `debug ip nat` will show you in real time the translations occurring on your router.

4. A. The command `show ip nat translations` will show you the translation table containing all the active NAT entries.

5. D. The command `clear ip nat translations *` will clear all the active NAT entries in your translation table.

6. B. The show `ip nat statistics` command displays a summary of the NAT configuration as well as counts of active translation types, hits to an existing mapping, misses (causing an attempt to create a mapping), and expired translations.

7. B. The command `ip nat pool` *name* creates the pool that hosts can use to get onto the global Internet. What makes option B correct is that the range 171.16.10.65 through 171.16.10.94 includes 30 hosts, but the mask has to match 30 hosts as well, and that mask is 255.255.255.224. Option C is wrong because there is a lowercase t in the pool name. Pool names are case sensitive.

8. A. NAT Overload applies a one-to-many relationship to internal IP addresses.

9. C. An Inside Global is the translated address from Inside Local to Inside Global. The inside global is the address the hosts use to communicate on the internet.

10. C. In order for NAT to provide translation services, you must have `ip nat inside` and `ip nat outside` configured on your router's interfaces.

11. A, B, D. The most popular use of NAT is if you want to connect to the Internet and you don't want hosts to have global (real) IP addresses, but options B and D are correct as well.

12. C. An inside global address is considered to be the IP address of the host on the private network after translation.

13. A. An inside local address is considered to be the IP address of the host on the private network before translation.

14. D. What we need to figure out for this question is only the inside global pool. Basically, we start at 1.1.128.1 and end at 1.1.135.174; our block size is 8 in the third octet, or /21. Always look for your block size and the interesting octet, and you can find your answer every time.

15. B. Once you create your pool, the command `ip nat inside source` must be used to say which inside locals are allowed to use the pool. In this question, we need to see if access-list 100 is configured correctly, if at all, so `show access-list` is the best answer.

16. A. You must configure your interfaces before NAT will provide any translations. On the inside network interfaces, you will use the command `ip nat inside`. On the outside network interfaces, you will use the command `ip nat outside`.

17. B. You must configure your interfaces before NAT will provide any translations. On the inside networks, you will use the command `ip nat inside`. On the outside network interfaces, you will use the command `ip nat outside`.

18. A. A NAT pool provides addresses dynamically to inside hosts to use as an inside global address.

19. B. Fast-switching is used on Cisco routers to create a type of route cache to quickly forward packets through a router without having to parse the routing table for every packet. As packets are processed-switched (looked up in the routing table), this information is stored in the cache for later use if needed for faster routing processing.

20. B. Once you create a pool for the inside locals to use to get out to the global Internet, you must configure the command to allow them access to the pool. The ip nat `inside source list` *`number pool-name`* `overload` command has the correct sequence for this question.

Chapter 6: IP Services

1. B. You can create and then enter the ACL into the `snmp-server` command when setting your SNMP configuration on a router.
2. A. The command `service sequence-numbers` adds a sequence number to each system message.
3. C. One of the needed steps to configure SSH on a router/switch is to generate an RSA key. To do that, it is mandatory to set the DNS domain name before generating the key.
4. F. There are eight different trap levels. If you choose level 4, levels 0 through 4 will be displayed, giving you emergency, alert, critical, and error messages as well as warning messages. Here are the levels and what they perform:

Severity Level	Explanation
Emergency (severity 0)	System is unusable.
Alert (severity 1)	Immediate action is needed.
Critical (severity 2)	Critical condition.
Error (severity 3)	Error condition.
Warning (severity 4)	Warning condition.
Notification (severity 5)	Normal but significant condition.
Informational (severity 6)	Normal information message.
Debugging (severity 5)	Debugging message.

5. B. The `show ip cache flow` command provide a summary of the NetFlow statistics, including which protocols are in use.
6. B, C, D. NetFlow, SNMP, and syslog are all different applications that provide different features for administrating your network. NetFlow is a very powerful Cisco tool that allows you to see who is doing what, understand network capacity, and even gather accounting information.

7. D. There are eight different trap levels. If you choose level 5, levels 0 through 5 will be displayed, giving you emergency, alert, critical, error, and warning messages as well as notification messages. Here are the levels and what they perform:

Severity Level	Explanation
Emergency (severity 0)	System is unusable.
Alert (severity 1)	Immediate action is needed.
Critical (severity 2)	Critical condition.
Error (severity 3)	Error condition.
Warning (severity 4)	Warning condition.
Notification (severity 5)	Normal but significant condition.
Informational (severity 6)	Normal information message.
Debugging (severity 5)	Debugging message.

8. B, D. You need to have a Cisco router to run the proprietary NetFlow application, plus you need a server to send the information to, and this is called a collector.

9. B. There are eight different trap levels. If you choose level 3, levels 0 through 3 will be displayed, giving you emergency, alert, and critical messages as well as error messages. Level 6 is Informational.

Severity Level	Explanation
Emergency (severity 0)	System is unusable.
Alert (severity 1)	Immediate action is needed.
Critical (severity 2)	Critical condition.
Error (severity 3)	Error condition.
Warning (severity 4)	Warning condition.
Notification (severity 5)	Normal but significant condition.
Informational (severity 6)	Normal information message.
Debugging (severity 5)	Debugging message.

10. C. Debugging is trap level 7. There are eight different trap levels. If you choose level 7, levels 0 through 7 will be displayed, giving you emergency, alert, critical, error, warning, notification, and informational messages as well as debugging messages. Here are the levels and what they perform:

Severity Level	Explanation
Emergency (severity 0)	System is unusable.
Alert (severity 1)	Immediate action is needed.
Critical (severity 2)	Critical condition.
Error (severity 3)	Error condition.
Warning (severity 4)	Warning condition.
Notification (severity 5)	Normal but significant condition.
Informational (severity 6)	Normal information message.
Debugging (severity 5)	Debugging message.

11. G. There are eight different trap levels. If you choose level 6, levels 0 through 6 will be displayed, giving you emergency, alert, critical, error, warning, and notification messages as well as informational messages. Here are the levels and what they perform.

Severity Level	Explanation
Emergency (severity 0)	System is unusable.
Alert (severity 1)	Immediate action is needed.
Critical (severity 2)	Critical condition.
Error (severity 3)	Error condition.
Warning (severity 4)	Warning condition.
Notification (severity 5)	Normal but significant condition.
Informational (severity 6)	Normal information message.
Debugging (severity 5)	Debugging message.

12. C. SNMPv3 uses TCP and authenticates users, plus it can use ACLs in the SNMP strings to protect the NMS station from unauthorized use.

13. C. If a notice-level messaging is sent to a syslog server, this means that a routing instance has flapped.

14. B. SNMP can be used to send BULK commands to a router, which can be used to back up multiple router configurations, for example.

15. B. If a device has an interface change state, the router sends a notice-level Notification (severity 5) message to a syslog server.

16. C. There are eight different trap levels. If you choose level 4 Warning, for example, levels 0 through 4 will be displayed, giving you emergency, alert, critical, error, and warning messages. Here are the levels and what they perform:

Severity Level	Explanation
Emergency (severity 0)	System is unusable.
Alert (severity 1)	Immediate action is needed.
Critical (severity 2)	Critical condition.
Error (severity 3)	Error condition.
Warning (severity 4)	Warning condition.
Notification (severity 5)	Normal but significant condition.
Informational (severity 6)	Normal information message.
Debugging (severity 5)	Debugging message.

17. C. A facility is a group of log messages associated with the configured severity level.

18. A. The NMS software must be loaded on the router or switch with the MIB associated with the trap.

19. C. There are eight different trap levels. If you choose level 6, for example, levels 0 through 6 will be displayed, giving you emergency, alert, critical, error, warning, and notification messages as well as informational messages. Here are the levels and what they perform.

Severity Level	Explanation
Emergency (severity 0)	System is unusable.
Alert (severity 1)	Immediate action is needed.
Critical (severity 2)	Critical condition.
Error (severity 3)	Error condition.
Warning (severity 4)	Warning condition.
Notification (severity 5)	Normal but significant condition.
Informational (severity 6)	Normal information message.
Debugging (severity 5)	Debugging message.

20. D, E. To use SSH on a Cisco Router, the IOS image must be a k9(Crypto) image, and you must configure the IP DNS domain for the router.

Chapter 7: Security Fundamentals

1. D. To enable the AAA commands on a router or switch, use the global configuration command `aaa new-model`.
2. A, C. To mitigate access layer threats, use port security, DHCP snooping, dynamic ARP inspection, and identity-based networking.
3. D. The key words in the question are "not true." DHCP snooping validates DHCP messages, builds and maintains the DHCP snooping binding database, and rate-limits DHCP traffic for trusted and untrusted sources.
4. A, D. TACACS+ uses TCP, is Cisco proprietary, offers multiprotocol support, and offers separate AAA services.
5. B. Unlike TACACS+, which separates AAA services, this is not an option when configuring RADIUS.
6. D. The correct answer is option D. Take your newly created RADIUS group and use it for authentication, and be sure to use the keyword `local` at the end.
7. B. DAI, used with DHCP snooping, tracks IP-to-MAC bindings from DHCP transactions to protect against ARP poisoning. DHCP snooping is required to build the MAC-to-IP bindings for DAI validation.
8. A, D, E. There are three roles: Client, also referred to as a supplicant, is software that runs on a client that is 802.1x compliant. Authenticator: typically, a switch that controls physical access to the network and is a proxy between the client and the authentication server. Authentication server (RADIUS): server that authenticates each client before many available services.
9. B. MFA, biometrics, and certificates are all password alternatives.
10. A. A security program that is backed by a security policy is one of the best ways to maintain a secure posture at all times. This program should cover many elements, but three are key: user awareness, training, and physical security.
11. C, E, F. There are many problems with the IP stack, especially in Microsoft products. Session replaying is a weakness that is found in TCP. Both SNMP and SMTP are listed by Cisco as inherently insecure protocols in the TCP/IP stack.
12. B. The TCP intercept feature implements software to protect TCP servers from TCP SYN-flooding attacks, which are a type of denial-of-service attack.
13. B, E, G. By using the Cisco Lock and Key along with CHAP and TACACS, you can create a more secure network and help stop unauthorized access.
14. C. Network snooping and packet sniffing are common terms for eavesdropping.

15. C. *Masquerading* or *IP spoofing* is fairly easy to stop once you understand how spoofing takes place. An IP spoofing attack occurs when an attacker outside your network pretends to be a trusted computer by using an IP address that is within the range of IP addresses for your network. The attacker wants to steal an IP address from a trusted source so it can use this to gain access to network resources.
16. A. AAA stands for authentication, authorization, and accounting.
    1. Authentication: Specifies who you are (usually via login username and password).
    2. Authorization: Specifies what actions you can do and what resources you can access.
    3. Accounting: Monitors what you do and how long you do it (can be used for billing and auditing).
17. C. This is an example of how two-factor authentication (2FA) works:
    1. The user logs in to the website or service with their username and password.
    2. The password is validated by an authentication server, and if correct, the user becomes eligible for the second factor.
    3. The authentication server sends a unique code to the user's second-factor method (such as a smartphone app).
    4. The user confirms their identity by providing additional authentication for their second-factor method.
18. C, E. It protects against keystroke logging on a compromised device or website and encourages users to create stronger passwords.
19. A. The application requires the user to enter a PIN before it provides the second factor option.
20. D. Physical access control includes a mantrap, badge reader, smart card, security guard, or door lock.

Chapter 8: First-Hop Redundancy Protocol (FHRP)

1. C. By setting a higher number than the default on a router, that router would become the active router. Setting preempt would ensure that if the active router went down, it would become the active router again when it came back up.
2. C. The idea of a first-hop redundancy protocol is to provide redundancy for a default gateway.
3. A, B. A router interface can be in many states with HSRP and established, and Idle are not an HSRP state.

4. A. Only option A has the correct sequence to enable HSRP on an interface.

5. D. A question that I used in a lot of job interviews with prospects. `Show standby` is your friend when dealing with HSRP.

6. D. There's nothing wrong with leaving the priorities at the default of 100. The first router up will be the active router.

7. C. In version 1, HSRP messages are sent to the multicast IP address 224.0.0.2 and UDP port 1985. HSRP version 2 uses the multicast IP address 224.0.0.102 and UDP port 1985.

8. B, C. If HSRP1 is configured to preempt, then it will become active because of the higher priority. If not, HSRP2 will remain the active router.

9. C. In version 1, HSRP messages are sent to the multicast IP address 224.0.0.2 and UDP port 1985. HSRP version 2 uses the multicast IP address 224.0.0.102 and UDP port 1985.

10. A, E. There's one active router and one standby router, and the two routers share a virtual IP address that is used as the default gateway for devices on the LAN.

Chapter 9: Quality of Service (QoS)

1. B. Dropping packets as they arrive is called tail drop. Selective dropping of packets during the time queues are filling up is called congestion avoidance (CA). Cisco uses weighted random early detection (WRED) as a CA scheme to monitor the buffer depth and perform early discards (drops) on random packets when the minimum defined queue threshold is exceeded.

2. B, D, E. Voice traffic is real-time traffic requiring consistent, predictable bandwidth and packet arrival times. One-way requirements include latency <150 ms, jitter <30 ms, and loss <1%. Bandwidth needs to be 30 to 128 Kbps.

3. C. A trust boundary is where packets are classified and marked. IP phones and the boundary between the ISP and enterprise network are common examples of trust boundaries.

4. A. NBAR is a layer 4–7 deep-packet inspection classifier. NBAR is more CPU intensive than marking and uses the existing markings, addresses, or ACLs.

5. C. DSCP is a set of 6-bit values used to describe the meaning of the layer 3 IPv4 ToS field. Although IP precedence is the old way to mark ToS, DSCP is the new way and is backward compatible with IP precedence.

6. D. Class of service (CoS) is a term to describe designated fields in a frame or packet header. How devices treat packets in your network depends on the field values. CoS is usually used with Ethernet frames and contains 3 bits.

7. C. When traffic exceeds the allocated rate, the policer can take one of two actions: It can either drop traffic or re-mark it to another class of service. The new class usually has a higher drop probability.

8. B. Use the police command to mark a packet with different quality of service (QoS) values based on conformance to the service-level agreement. Traffic policing allows you to control the maximum rate of traffic transmitted or received on an interface: Gold/Video, Silver/Best Effort (default), and Bronze/Background.

9. D, E. Weighted random early detection (WRED) is just a congestion avoidance mechanism. WRED drops packets selectively based on IP precedence. Edge routers assign IP precedence to packets as they enter the network.

10. A. Traffic shaping retains excess packets in a queue and then schedules the excess for later transmission over increments of time. Policers drop traffic, and shapers delay it. Shapers introduce delay and jitter, but policers do not. Policers cause significant TCP resends, but shapers do not.

11. B, C. These types of queuing methods are available: first in first out (FIFO), priority queuing (PQ), custom queuing (CQ), weighted fair queuing (WFQ), class-based weighted fair queuing (CBWFQ), and latency queuing (LLQ).

12. C. PQ guarantees strict priority in that it ensures that one type of traffic will be sent, possibly at the expense of all others. Strict PQ allows delay-sensitive data, such as voice, to be dequeued and sent before packets in other queues are dequeued.

13. D. Low-latency queuing (LLQ) is the preferred queuing policy for VoIP audio. Given the stringent delay/jitter-sensitive voice and video requirements and the need to synchronize audio and video for CUVA, priority (LLQ) queuing is also recommended for all video traffic. Note that for video, priority bandwidth is generally averaged up by 20% to account for the overhead.

14. C. IP SLA allows an IT professional to collect information about network performance in real time. Therefore, it helps determine whether the network's QoS is sufficient for IP services.

15. C. E. The two QoS tools are used to guarantee minimum bandwidth to certain traffic are CBWFQ and WFQ.

16. A, E. CBWFQ and PBR are two QoS tools that can provide congestion management.

17. D. Traffic shaping retains excess packets in a queue and reschedules these packets for later transmission when the configured maximum bandwidth has been surpassed.

18. D. Congestion management's main purpose is to provide long-term storage of buffered data.

19. D. QoS marking changes the value of the ToS field in the IPv4 packet header.

20. A. QoS traffic shaping reduces congestion in a network, uses the router's buffers, and queues packets.

Chapter 10: Wireless Technologies

1. B. WPA3 Enterprise uses GCMP-256 for encryption, WPA2 uses AES-CCMP for encryption, and WPA uses TKIP.
2. C. The IEEE 802.11b and IEEE 802.11g standards both run in the 2.4 GHz RF range.
3. D. The IEEE 802.11a standard runs in the 5 GHz RF range.
4. C. The IEEE 802.11b and IEEE 802.11g standards both run in the 2.4 GHz RF range.
5. C. The minimum parameter configured on an AP for a simple WLAN installation is the SSID, although you should set the channel and authentication method as well.
6. A. WPA3 Enterprise uses GCMP-256 for encryption, WPA2 uses AES-CCMP for encryption, and WPA uses TKIP.
7. A. The IEEE 802.11b standard provides three non-overlapping channels.
8. C. WPA3 is resistant to offline dictionary attacks where an attacker attempts to determine a network password by trying possible passwords without further network interaction.
9. D. The IEEE 802.11a standard provides a maximum data rate of up to 54 Mbps.
10. D. The IEEE 802.11g standard provides a maximum data rate of up to 54 Mbps.
11. B. The IEEE 802.11b standard provides a maximum data rate of up to 11 Mbps.
12. C. The 802.11 "open" authentication support has been replaced with Opportunistic Wireless Encryption (OWE) enhancement, which is an enhancement, not a mandatory certified setting.
13. D. Although this question is cryptic at best, the only possible answer is option D. If the SSID is not being broadcast (which we must assume in this question), the client must be configured with the correct SSID in order to associate to the AP.
14. B, E. WPA uses Temporal Key Integrity Protocol (TKIP), which includes both broadcast key rotation (dynamic keys that change) and sequencing of frames.
15. A, D. Both WEP and TKIP (WPA) use the RC4 algorithm. It is advised to use WPA2, which uses the AES encryption or WPA3 when it is available to you.
16. C. Two wireless hosts directly connected wirelessly is no different than two hosts connecting with a crossover cable. They are both ad hoc networks, but in wireless, we call this an Independent Basic Service Set (IBSS).
17. A, C. WPA, although using the same RC4 encryption that WEP uses, provides enhancements to the WEP protocol by using dynamic keys that change constantly as well as providing a pre-shared key method of authentication.

18. B. To create an extended service set (ESS), you need to overlap the wireless BSA from each AP by at least 15 percent in order not to have a gap in coverage so users do not lose their connection when roaming between APs.

19. A. Extended service set ID means you have more than one access point, they all are set to the same SSID, and all are connected together in the same VLAN or distribution system so users can roam.

20. A, B, D. The three basic parameters to configure when setting up an access point are the SSID, the RF channel, and the authentication method.

Chapter 11: Configuring Legacy Wireless Controllers

1. B. FlexConnect mode allows an AP to switch traffic locally rather than tunneling it back to the WLC. This mode is often used in remote locations where sending all traffic back to a central controller is not ideal.

2. A, C, D. The service port is used for out-of-band management, and it requires a direct connection to a switch (configured as an access port), as well as static routes on the WLC because the service port operates in a separate routing table.

3. E. The DNS record CISCO-CAPWAP-CONTROLLER allows APs to discover the WLC automatically via DNS lookup, making deployment easier.

4. D. Silver is the default QoS queue, providing best-effort service, which is typically used for normal data traffic.

5. A. The Gold queue is designed for video traffic, offering higher priority to ensure smooth video streaming.

6. C. By creating additional dynamic interfaces and using an interface group, you can distribute the load across multiple VLANs, alleviating IP address shortages.

7. B, C, E. Enabling LAG on the WLC requires a reboot, adding all distributed system interfaces to the LAG, and configuring the switch with channel-group in on mode.

8. B, C, D. Autonomous APs are configured individually, leading to challenges in maintaining consistent security policies and network-wide performance optimizations.

9. B. TACACS+ is used primarily for authenticating management users on a WLC, ensuring secure access to the controller's configuration.

10. E. TACACS+ uses TCP port 49 for both authentication and accounting, which is different from the UDP ports used by RADIUS.

11. C. Modern RADIUS servers typically use UDP port 1812 for authentication, which is the standardized port for this purpose.

12. A. Legacy RADIUS servers might use UDP port 1645 for authentication, though this has largely been replaced by port 1812 in modern implementations.

13. B. The virtual interface is used for client redirection, such as when handling web authentication or DHCP relay.

14. D. The IP address 192.0.2.1 is reserved for documentation and is commonly recommended for use as the virtual interface IP on a WLC.

15. D. Platinum QoS is reserved for voice traffic (VoIP), offering the highest priority to ensure voice quality.

16. B. Telnet is not enabled by default on the WLC due to its lack of security. SSH is enabled by default instead.

17. C. A dynamic interface on a WLC is similar to a switched virtual interface (SVI) on a switch, providing layer 3 routing capabilities for a VLAN.

18. A. The correct hex string starts with F104 (indicating one WLC) and is followed by the IP address 192.168.123.100 converted to hex (C0A87B64).

19. A. The default AP mode is local, where all traffic is tunneled back to the WLC through a CAPWAP tunnel.

20. A, C. Both local and FlexConnect modes are used to serve wireless traffic to clients, although FlexConnect can also locally switch traffic at the AP.

Chapter 12: Configuring Modern Wireless Controllers

1. B. The Cisco 9800 controller is built on the IOS-XE operating system, unlike legacy WLCs that use AireOS. This shift to IOS-XE brings enhanced capabilities and integrates better with other modern Cisco devices.

2. B. The correct command to create a VLAN on the Cisco 9800 controller is vlan 200, which is consistent with the command syntax used in IOS-based devices.

3. D. The Cisco 9800 supports protocols like SSH, Telnet, HTTP, and HTTPS for device management access. SNMP is used for monitoring rather than direct management access in this context.

4. A. A port channel groups multiple physical interfaces into a single logical interface, providing redundancy and increasing bandwidth by load-balancing traffic across multiple links.

5. A. The Cisco 9800 uses tags to bind different profiles (like WLAN, policy, and RF) together and apply them to specific APs, making network management more flexible.

6. C. Although the WLAN profile, AP join profile, and RF profile are used in the Cisco 9800 controller, the term *QoS profile* is not typically used in the context of the Cisco 9800.

7. B. The default virtual IP address in the Cisco 9800 controller is set to 192.0.2.1, which is a reserved IP address commonly used in documentation and examples.

8. C. WPA2 PSK is a widely used security method for WLANs, providing a balance between security and ease of setup. It's commonly used in basic WLAN configurations.

9. B. The AP join profile in the Cisco 9800 controller manages settings related to how APs connect to the controller, including country settings and failover controller configurations.

10. B. Cloud-managed solutions like Meraki provide centralized management, which simplifies the deployment and ongoing management of network devices, particularly for distributed environments.

11. B. ZTP allows Meraki devices to automatically download their preconfigured settings from the cloud once they are connected to the network, simplifying deployment.

12. C. To manage Meraki access points via the cloud, they must be registered in the Meraki cloud portal. This enables the cloud-based management features of Meraki.

13. D. Cisco Meraki offers a variety of cloud-managed products like access points, switches, and firewalls, but it does not provide router products.

14. C. If a Meraki device cannot reach the Meraki cloud, it can enter a local management mode that allows basic troubleshooting and management tasks to be performed.

15. A. Meraki layer 3 switches support OSPF and BGP for routing, but they do not support Cisco's proprietary EIGRP.

16. A. The claiming process registers devices in the Meraki cloud portal, allowing them to be managed remotely through the Meraki dashboard.

17. C. The Meraki Topology feature automatically generates network topology diagrams based on the devices and their connections within the Meraki ecosystem.

18. C. The Meraki MX series devices are security appliances that offer firewall capabilities and other security features, such as SD-WAN.

19. B. Meraki's cloud-managed cameras offer advanced features like facial recognition and video analytics, making them popular for security and surveillance applications.

20. C. Meraki devices download firmware updates from the cloud based on a scheduled update plan, simplifying the process of keeping devices up to date.

Chapter 13: Virtualization, Containers, and VRFs

1. D. VMware ESXi, Microsoft Hyper-V, and Xen are all type 1 hypervisors.
2. B. VMware Workstation is a type 2 hypervisor.
3. B. A guest virtual machine is a VM that is running on a hypervisor.
4. B. Type 2 virtualization requires a host OS.
5. B. Virtual machine migration refers to moving a VM from one host to another.
6. B. A snapshot allows you to capture and restore a VM's state.
7. A. Docker Hub hosts container images for easy deployment.
8. C. A VRF allows you to have multiple routing tables on a device.
9. C. Xen/KVM requires more Linux knowledge than the other solutions discussed in this chapter.
10. B. "hypervisor" refer to in virtualization software that creates and runs virtual machines.
11. B. A hardware virtual machine does not require the guest OS to have any special configuration.
12. D. Shared storage allows for easier VM migrations.
13. C. Standard switches require each hypervisor to be configured manually.
14. B. A virtual switch provides VLAN and trunking support, among many other networking features.
15. C. Virtualization allows us to deploy applications much faster than physical deployments.

Chapter 14: Software-Defined Networking

1. B. The control plane is responsible for all the decision-making processes in a router, such as handling routing protocols, making forwarding decisions, and maintaining routing tables. It processes the information required to forward packets and instructs the data plane on where to send the traffic.

2. C. The data plane, also known as the forwarding plane, is responsible for the actual movement of packets. It forwards packets from one interface to another based on the decisions made by the control plane.

3. B. The northbound interface (NBI) allows administrators and external applications to interact with the SDN controller, typically through a GUI or API. It is used for management, monitoring, and orchestration tasks.

4. B. NETCONF is a popular protocol used for communication between the SDN controller and network devices. It allows the controller to configure and manage the devices programmatically.

5. A. Path Trace provides a comprehensive view of both layer 2 and layer 3 paths, including tunnels, which traditional traceroute does not cover. This makes it more effective in troubleshooting complex network paths.

6. C. EasyQoS simplifies the management and deployment of QoS policies by automatically categorizing and applying them across the network, ensuring consistent service quality.

7. B. The Assurance feature provides a "time machine" capability, storing network data and health information for up to a week, which helps in diagnosing and troubleshooting issues that occurred in the past.

8. A. The underlay is the physical network that provides the necessary connectivity for the overlay network, which is the logical, virtualized layer built on top of the underlay.

9. C. LAN Automation automates the process of onboarding new devices into the network, using technologies like Cisco's plug-and-play (PNP) to simplify initial configuration.

10. B. The Network Hierarchy feature helps organize devices into logical groups based on sites and locations, which simplifies management and ensures consistent configurations across the network.

11. B. SD-Access allows for simplified management by enabling intent-based networking, where high-level policies are defined and automatically enforced across the network.

12. B. In SDN, the term "fabric" refers to the collective set of layer 3 devices (routers, switches, etc.) that make up the network infrastructure managed by the SDN controller.

13. B. Command Runner allows administrators to execute show or diagnostic commands across multiple devices simultaneously and stores the output for analysis, making network management more efficient.

14. B. The SDN controller centralizes the network's control plane, enabling easier management, automation, and policy enforcement across the network.

15. C. CLI Templates allow administrators to create and push custom configurations to multiple devices using scripting engines like Apache Velocity, automating complex setups.

16. B. The Assurance feature provides historical data and insights into past network conditions, allowing administrators to effectively troubleshoot issues that occurred in the past.

17. B. REST APIs in Catalyst Center typically use HTTP or HTTPS as the transport protocol for managing and interacting with network devices programmatically.

18. C. In SDN, the control plane is separated from the data plane, allowing centralized control and management of the network through an SDN controller; this is different from traditional networking, where the control and data planes are integrated within each device.

19. D. The Topology feature automatically generates and updates a visual representation of the network's layout, including devices and their connections, making it easier to manage and troubleshoot.

20. C. A VXLAN tunnel is an example of an overlay network in SDN, where logical networks are created over a physical underlay network to connect different segments.

Chapter 15: Automation, Data Formats, and REST APIs

1. B. Network automation allows repetitive tasks to be executed more consistently and efficiently by scripts, reducing the likelihood of human errors and saving time, especially when managing large networks.

2. B. Python is widely used for network automation due to its simplicity, readability, and extensive libraries that support network programming, making it an ideal choice for scripting tasks.

3. C. Onbox automation refers to running scripts directly on the network device itself. Cisco devices with Guest Shell can run Python scripts locally, which is an example of onbox automation.

4. B. IDEs provide features that assist with correct code formatting, syntax checking, and other helpful tools, which are particularly important in Python due to its reliance on indentation.

5. C. Python primarily uses for and while loops for iteration. An until loop is not a construct in Python; it's more commonly found in other languages like Bash scripting.

6. A. JSON (JavaScript Object Notation) is a lightweight data interchange format that is easy for humans to read and write, and easy for machines to parse and generate.

7. B. In JSON, each key/value pair is separated by a colon. For example, "name": "John" is a valid key/value pair in JSON.

8. C. In JSON, both the key and value must be enclosed in double quotes, making "name": "John" the correct format.

9. B. JSON is used to represent data structures in a format that is easy to read and write, making it ideal for exchanging structured data between systems.

10. C. JSON does not allow trailing commas. Each key/value pair must be followed by a comma except for the last pair in an object or array.

11. A. REST (Representational State Transfer) is an architectural style for designing networked applications, relying on stateless, client-server communication typically over HTTP.

12. B. The POST method in HTTP is used to create a new resource on the server. It submits data to the server, which often results in a change in state or side effects on the server.

13. B. In RESTful APIs, the communication is client-server based, where the client initiates the requests and the server processes and responds to these requests.

14. B. A 404 status code means that the server could not find the requested resource. This is commonly encountered when a URL is incorrect or the resource no longer exists.

15. B. The Authorization header in HTTP requests is used to provide credentials, such as a token or username/password, to authenticate the client with the server.

16. C. The Accept header tells the server what content types the client is willing to accept in the response, such as application/json or application/xml.

17. D. A 503 status code indicates that the server is temporarily unable to handle the request due to overload or maintenance. It suggests that the client can try again later.

18. C. The PUT method is used to update or replace an existing resource on the server with the data provided in the request.

19. B. "Stateless" means that each request from the client to the server must contain all the information needed to understand and process the request, without relying on stored context from previous requests.

20. B. HATEOAS (Hypermedia as the Engine of Application State) is a constraint of REST APIs that ensures the API can guide the client on how to interact with it by providing links to other related resources dynamically.

Chapter 16: Configuration Management

1. B. Automation helps reduce manual interventions, which lowers the chances of human errors that could lead to network outages. By automating repetitive tasks, you ensure consistency and reliability in network operations.

2. C. Ansible is a configuration management tool that can automate the creation of VLANs, among other tasks, making it ideal for managing network devices.

3. C. IaC allows infrastructure to be defined and managed using code, ensuring consistency and enabling automation across environments.

4. A. An Ansible playbook is a file written in YAML that contains a series of tasks to be executed on target devices, automating network management processes.

5. A. The `gather_facts` option collects details about the target nodes, such as their IP addresses, operating systems, and other critical data, which can then be used in the playbook.

6. A. Terraform is lightweight because it runs from a single binary file, simplifying installation and management across different environments.

7. B. The inventory file lists the target nodes that Ansible will interact with, grouping them for easier management and specifying connection details.

8. B. Idempotence means that running a configuration multiple times will apply changes only if something needs to be updated, preventing unnecessary modifications.

9. C. Ansible playbooks are written in YAML, a human-readable data serialization format that is easy to write and read.

10. B. Unlike Ansible, which comes with built-in modules, Terraform requires users to specify providers (plugins) to interact with different infrastructure platforms, giving it more flexibility but requiring more initial setup.

11. A. Mappings in YAML represent key-value pairs, which are used to define properties and their corresponding values, forming the basic structure of the file.

12. B. Providers are plugins in Terraform that enable it to interact with different cloud services, on-premises systems, and other infrastructure components.

13. C. The `ios_config` module in Ansible is used to send configuration commands to Cisco IOS devices, automating the setup and management of network devices.

14. B. The `terraform.tfvars` file is used to store sensitive variables like usernames and passwords, which are separated from other configuration files for security reasons.

15. A. The `terraform init` command initializes the working directory by downloading the necessary provider plugins and setting up the backend configuration.

16. B. Storing sensitive information in a separate file like `terraform.tfvars` helps keep it secure and prevent accidental exposure in version control systems or shared repositories.

17. B. The `terraform plan` command generates an execution plan, showing the changes Terraform will make without actually applying them, allowing users to review and approve changes before implementation.

18. C. The inventory file in Ansible contains the list of target devices and specifies how Ansible should connect to them, including details like IP addresses and login credentials.

19. A. In Terraform, a resource is a fundamental element that represents a single component of your infrastructure, such as a virtual machine, network interface, or storage bucket.

20. A. Idempotency ensures that when a configuration is reapplied, no unnecessary changes are made if the desired state is already achieved, making the process more efficient and predictable.

Index

A

B

C

D

E

F

G

H

I

J

K

L

M

N

O

P

Q

R

S

T

U

V

W

X-Y-Z